A HISTORY OF
BRITISH
TRADE UNIONS
SINCE 1889

A HISTORY OF BRITISH TRADE UNIONS SINCE 1889

VOLUME II · 1911–1933

BY

HUGH ARMSTRONG CLEGG

CLARENDON PRESS · OXFORD
1985

Oxford University Press, Walton Street, Oxford OX2 6DP
London New York Toronto
Delhi Bombay Calcutta Madras Karachi
Kuala Lumpur Singapore Hong Kong Tokyo
Nairobi Dar es Salaam Cape Town
Melbourne Auckland
and associated companies in
Beirut Berlin Ibadan Mexico City Nicosia

Oxford is a trade mark of Oxford University Press

Published in the United States
by Oxford University Press, New York

British Library Cataloguing in Publication Data
Clegg, Hugh Armstrong
A history of British trade unions since 1889.
Vol. 2, 1911–1933
1. Trade-unions—Great Britain—History
I. Title
331.88'0941   HD6664
ISBN 0-19-828298-2

Library of Congress Cataloging in Publication Data
Clegg, Hugh Armstrong.
A history of British trade unions since 1889.
Bibliography: v. 2, p.
Includes index.
Contents: v. 1. 1889–1910—v. 2. 1911–1933.
1. Trade-unions—Great Britain—History.
I. Fox, Alan.
II. Thompson, A. F.   III. Title.
HD6664.C3864   331.88'0941   64-5199
ISBN 0-19-828298-2

Set by Eta Services (Typesetters) Ltd.
Printed at the University Press, Oxford
by David Stanford
Printer to the University

TO

A. F. THOMPSON

Preface

This volume has been many years in the making. Volume I, which was published in 1964, went to the printer in 1963. Over the next three years, substantial collections of notes for the second volume had been accumulated in Oxford by the three authors of the first, Alan Fox, A. F. Thompson, and myself, and by two research assistants, Penelope Harmsworth and Michael Chewter. However, by the end of 1966, Penelope Harmsworth and Michael Chewter had left, Alan Fox had resigned from the project on his appointment as Lecturer in Industrial Sociology at Oxford, and I had been appointed to the Donovan Commission and to the chair of Industrial Relations at Warwick, and was about to join the Price and Incomes Board. For the time being, therefore, work on Volume II came to a standstill.

Over the next thirteen years A. F. Thompson and I were able to add a little to what had already been done, but it was not until 1979 that the task was seriously resumed. In that year, I resigned my chair to take up a Leverhulme research fellowship enabling me to devote my time to it (apart from my duties at the Standing Commission on Pay Comparability in 1979–80). At that stage A. F. Thompson decided, regretfully, that he could not spare sufficient time to enable him to continue as joint author, and I went ahead on my own.

The list of those to whom I must express my thanks for their help starts with the Leverhulme Trustees. Their original grant to Nuffield College, Oxford, in 1956, financed, among other projects, work on Volume I and the first stage of Volume II; and their grant to the University of Warwick covered my fellowship to complete Volume II. Next come Nuffield College and the University of Warwick themselves, especially their Library staffs, and, above all, the staff of the Modern Records Centre at Warwick. In addition the General Federation of Trade Unions, the General and Municipal Workers, the National Union of Mineworkers, the National Union of Railwaymen, the Transport and General Workers made their records available, and the Union of Shop Distributive and Allied Workers; as did the Engineering Employers Federation, the National Federation of Building Trade Employers, and the British Employers Confederation (now absorbed in the Confederation of British Industry).

For advice on particular points I owe thanks to my Warwick colleagues, George Bain, Alec Ford, Richard Hyman, Margaret Morgan, and Robert Price; and to Lyn Yates of Nuffield College, and

Annemarie Flanders, formerly of the Industrial Relations Research Unit at Warwick, not only for their excellent typing but also for their forbearance.

Those who contributed to the first stage of Volume II must not be forgotten. The notes left by Penelope Harmsworth and Michael Chewter have made a substantial contribution to the final text. In addition to their work at that stage, Alan Fox and A. F. Thompson have read this volume in draft and made many pertinent suggestions for alterations and additions. A. F. Thompson went a great deal further than that, drawing on his deep knowledge of the period and his editorial experience to propose thousands of detailed changes, and substantial revision of scores of passages and sections. It is for this help, as well as to commemorate over forty years of friendship and collaboration, that this volume is dedicated to him.

H. A. CLEGG

Contents

List of Tables   xiii

1. TRADE UNIONS IN 1910
   Membership   1
   Industrial Functions   6
   Political Action   11
   Finance   14
   Government   16
   Leaders and Ideas   20

2. INDUSTRIAL UNREST, 1911–14
   Causes of Unrest   24
   The Cambrian Strike, 1910–11   26
   Transport 1911   33
   Lancashire Weavers, 1911–12   41
   Coal, 1912   43
   Dundee Jute and London Docks, 1912   52
   London Cab Drivers and Midlands Metalworkers, 1913   57
   Dublin, 1913–14   60
   London Building Workers and Yorkshire Miners, 1914   64
   Causes Reviewed   71

3. COLLECTIVE BARGAINING, THE GOVERNMENT, AND UNION STRUCTURE
   The Crafts, Coal, and Cotton   75
   Other Industries and the Less-Skilled   84
   Public and Private Services   90
   The Government   97
   Trade Union Structure   105

4. ASQUITH'S WAR
   The Impact of War   118
   The Munitions of War Act, 1915   123
   Dilution   131
   Wages and Prices   141
   Conscription, Exemption, and Manpower Shortages   152

5. LLOYD GEORGE'S WAR
Lloyd George and the Unions 161
The May Strikes 168
Tensions within the Unions 174
Pay and Manpower, 1917–18 181
The Effects on the Unions 195

6. PARTY POLITICS, 1911–18
The Prewar Years 213
Unity Maintained, 1914–17 223
The Reconstruction of the Party 229
The General Election of 1918 234

7. RECONSTRUCTION AND DIRECT ACTION
Reconstruction 239
Collective Bargaining, 1919–20 252
Industrial Unrest and Its Causes 266
'Direct Action' 275
Trade Unions at a Peak of Growth 302

8. THE POSTWAR DEPRESSION
The Impact of the Depression 312
Pay Reductions 317
The Engineering Lockout 336
The Effects on the Unions 345

9. THE FIRST LABOUR GOVERNMENT
The Unions and the Labour Party, 1918–23 353
The Communists and the Left 357
The First Labour Government 363
Industrial Disputes 369
The Aftermath 377

10. THE GENERAL STRIKE
Industrial Relations, 1925 383
Red Friday 387
Autumn and Winter, 1925–6 392
Negotiations 399
The Strike 403
The Miners' Lockout 412
Inquest and Aftermath 419

11. INDUSTRIAL RELATIONS IN THE TWENTIES
Collective Bargaining under Stable Conditions   427
Industrial Relations at the Workplace   437
Inside the Unions   449
A New Philosophy   461
The Mond–Turner Talks   464

12. THE SECOND LABOUR GOVERNMENT
The Unions and the Labour Party, 1925–9   472
The Government   478
Pay Cuts and Industrial Disputes   487
Unemployment   497
The Fall of the Government   507

13. THE TURN OF THE TIDE
The National Government   512
Resisting Pay Cuts   517
Industrial Relations in the Depression   526
The Unions   534

14. TRADE UNIONS IN 1933
Growth   543
Collective Bargaining   547
Government   550
Finance   552
Political Action   553
Public Standing   557
Wages and Welfare   559
The Future   563

Statistical Appendix   567

Biographies   572

Bibliography   582

Index   595

List of Tables

1. Major strikes, 1911–14   26

2. Average money incomes of full-time wage earners by industrial groups, 1920–23   335

3. Trade union membership, 1920–23   346

4. Average money incomes of full-time wage earners by industrial groups: 1933 incomes as a percentage of 1929 incomes   525

5. Top ten industries for trade union density, 1910–33   545

6. Changes in average earnings for men and boys by industrial group, 1906–31   561

7. General indicators   568

8. Total trade union membership compared with trade union affiliated membership of the Trades Union Congress and the Labour Party   570

9. Membership of the ten largest unions in 1910, 1920, and 1933   570

10. Expenditure of registered trade unions as a proportion of income, by periods, 1911–33   571

1

Trade Unions in 1910

Membership

AT the end of 1910 there were 2.6 million trade union members in Britain, more than in any other country except Germany. Trade union density—the proportion of potential members actually in the unions—was close to one in six, a little behind Germany, and well behind Australia.[1] The strength of British unions, however, did not derive so much from their general coverage as from particular concentrations of membership. To begin with, male manual workers were much more highly unionised than either women or white collar workers. Their density figure was about 22.5 per cent, not far short of one in four, compared with about one in eighteen for women (both manual and white collar), and about one in ten for white collar workers (both men and women).[2] Domestic service, the largest employer of all, was outside the scope of trade unionism in practice if not by definition; and agriculture, where trade unionism had briefly shown considerable strength forty years earlier, now fell short of 1 per cent. At the other extreme, coalmining came an unchallenged first with a density of over 70 per cent, and accounted for more than a quarter of all British trade unionists. Cotton's density was almost 50 per cent, despite the predominance of women in its labour force. Among the public services, posts and telecommunications scored over 50 per cent, and local government and education, with nearly 33 per cent, showed that white collar workers were not necessarily poor trade union material, for this relatively high density was mainly due to the National Union of Teachers.

There was further concentration within industries, both occupational and geographical. Among manual workers density was normally higher in occupations with relatively greater skill, pay, or status, attributes which usually ran together, but not always. The mulespinners in cotton

---

References in footnotes appear in abbreviated form: full details may be found in the Bibliography.

[1] Figures of trade union density are derived from Bain and Price, or (as with figures of male manual density) from further work on their data by Margaret Morgan.

[2] In Volume I my colleagues and I hazarded a guess that in 1901 trade unionists accounted for 'about . . . one in five of adult male manual workers' and by 1910 'almost one in three' (p. 467). Bain and Price's data show that both figures were far too high.

and the faceworkers in coalmining, who were the aristocrats of their industries, came close to 100 per cent unionisation, and shipbuilding craftsmen cannot have been very far behind. Among printing craftsmen, density probably equally high in London, Manchester, and some other cities, but the overall figure for this scattered industry was far lower. Even in construction, with an overall density of no more than 16 per cent, there were places where some or all of the crafts had achieved a high level of organisation. Dock workers were well organised in the Bristol Channel and at the south end of the Liverpool docks; but in London unionism had a firm grip only among specialist groups such as stevedores and lightermen; and in Hull it had been wiped out in 1893.

Within localities and occupations there was concentration by place of work. Membership was relatively strong where the employer recognised or tolerated the union, and low or non-existent where he was hostile. This was especially true of those catered for by the general unions, whose density in relation to their potential was infinitesimal. Each strung together groups of members whose employers accepted the union in a variety of industries scattered far and wide over the country.

So far it is trade unionism in general which has been under discussion, but members were recruited to particular unions, not to trade unionism. According to the Labour Department of the Board of Trade, there were 1,269 trade unions in Britain at the end of 1910 (giving an average membership of about two thousand), far too many to be discussed separately; but ten of them accounted for 45 per cent of total membership, so that a brief description of these can serve as an introduction to the unions of that time.

The largest by far was the Miners Federation of Great Britain, with just short of 600,000 members, almost a quarter of the overall total. The district unions which constituted the federation were registered as separate unions, and were counted as such by the Labour Department. However, the federation was also a union in its own right, and, more to the point, behaved like a unified organisation in a number of important ways, quite different from such organisations as the Federation of Engineering and Shipbuilding Trades or the Printing and Kindred Trades Federation, which were manifestly alliances of independent, sovereign organisations. Since 1908 the federation had included all the major unions of mineworkers, but there were also a number of small independent unions of craftsmen—colliery enginemen, mechanics, 'safety men'—and some of the men in these grades were in national craft unions such as the Engineers. In addition a fair number of less-skilled surface workers were in the general unions.

The next largest union, with 112,000 members, was the Amalgamated Association of Weavers; and another cotton union came in seventh place: the Amalgamated Association of Card Blowing and Ring Room Operatives (45,000). The only other major cotton union was that of the Spinners, but there were also several unions of specialist workers and supervisors in weaving.

Three craft unions came into the list of ten: the Amalgamated Society of Engineers (100,000), the United Society of Boilermakers and Iron and Steel Shipbuilders (49,000), and the Amalgamated Society of Carpenters and Joiners (43,000). They held third, sixth, and eighth place respectively. The Engineers were the dominant union in the engineering group of industries. The great majority of their members were fitters and turners, but they also catered, in competition with other unions, for blacksmiths, patternmakers, toolmakers, electricians, and other craft grades. The Boilermakers held sway among the shipbuilding unions through their control of platers, riveters, and caulkers, three of the main grades in the shipyards, but they also had a fair membership in the boilershops of engineering firms. Although theirs was the largest building union, the Amalgamated Carpenters and Joiners were *primus inter pares* rather than dominant over the others. In addition, other smaller unions of carpenters and joiners competed with them, not only in construction, but also in the shipyards.

The Amalgamated Society of Railway Servants, in fourth place with 75,000 members, had to meet competition from the Associated Society of Locomotive Engineers and Firemen, the United Pointsmen's and Signalmen's Society, and the General Railway Workers Union which recruited mainly among the lower-paid grades and also in the railway workshops. There was the Railway Clerks Association as well, but the Railway Servants made no serious effort to recruit among the clerical grades. The National Union of Teachers, which came next in size with 69,000 members, was the major white collar union and also the largest public sector union. Its success in organising elementary teachers had encouraged unionisation in secondary and technical education. The Postmen's Federation (38,000), in ninth place, was the largest manual workers' union in the public sector. It confined its scope to outdoor postal staff. Sorters, clerical staff, and telephone and telegraph staff had their own unions. The National Union of Gasworkers and General Labourers (32,000) was the most widely scattered of the general unions, and had to compete with other unions in almost every grade, industry, and region in which it sought to recruit.

Three of these ten unions have been characterised as 'craft' unions. The term 'craft union' can be applied loosely to all unions in which the members, or the main group of members, are required to exercise a fair degree of skill; or, more precisely, as here, to unions organised on the basis of an apprenticeship system. The success of such a union depends on the extent to which its members can prevent workers who have not served an apprenticeship from practising their trade. Probably, given time, every craft could be picked up by an able, unskilled worker, provided the opportunity to learn was there; and few crafts were so well organised that this opportunity did not exist somewhere. A small employer or a lazy craftsman might be happy to give an unskilled assistant the opportunity to undertake any job within his capability. Many craft societies had a rule on the lines of that of the Engineers which allowed the branches to admit, regardless of apprenticeship, a man who had worked at the trade for five years and was earning the union rate. They believed that it was better to control a man who had picked up the trade outside apprenticeship than to ignore him.

This second route to craft status made little difference to a craft society so long as it remained the exception. However, neither the building nor the engineering craft societies were able to enforce apprenticeship in the Midlands and the South with the rigour with which it was applied in Scotland and the North; and union control in the furniture trades was seriously weakened almost everywhere by large numbers of entrants through unregulated learnerships of no definite duration, which came to an end when the learner found an employer to take him on as a skilled man.

An alternative method of exercising control over entry to skilled jobs was available in trades where the recognised route to skill was to learn on the job. In the days of steam the engine driver had worked first as an engine cleaner, and then on the footplate as a fireman. He became a driver, not at the end of a set period of training, but when there was a vacancy, which went to the senior fireman in the line of promotion, who might have been fully qualified ten years earlier. The cotton spinner had served as a little piecer and then as a big piecer, and the first hand melter in the steel industry in a succession of junior posts in the melting team. Men in the less-skilled jobs were not debarred from reaching the highly-paid jobs, but they had to wait their turn.

The scope of union membership varied with the method of acquiring skill. Craft societies recruited those they recognised as skilled, and some of them took in apprentices as well, but they excluded the less-skilled. Those they admitted had a right to the jobs which the societies reserved for craftsmen, and, so long as they were successful in keeping the less-skilled out of their preserve, the latter were not much of a threat to them in a dispute with their employers. By contrast the second hands in promotion-line trades presented a serious danger to the top men. Most of the former were qualified for the top jobs and eager for the day when they should succeed to them. Accordingly the latter set out to recruit those in the promotion line into their unions, though they generally contrived to keep the running of union affairs in their own hands.

The Railway Servants included a substantial group of footplate staff who followed the same practices as the Locomotive Engineers and Firemen, and many other posts within their province, such as those of signalmen and guards, were also filled by seniority from the next grade down. However, since none of these jobs had a status to equal that of the engine driver and some were relatively unskilled, the spirit of the union was less aristocratic than that of the Locomotive Engineers and Firemen.

The most prestigious and highest-paid jobs in the preparatory stages of the cotton industry, organised by the Cardroom Operatives, were those of the strippers and grinders. They were filled by seniority from the other male jobs covered by the union. Consequently the strippers and grinders formed a small élite within the union, all the more because the majority of the members were women. The women took second place to the men, and among the men the strippers and grinders had precedence.

Promotion lines were out of place in those trades where skill was acquired on the job but fully skilled workers formed the majority of the labour force. The weavers were assisted by children, many of whom went on to weaving when vacancies were available; but the great majority of adults in the weaving sheds were qualified weavers, working independently, all paid the same piece rates—men and women alike. However, their union was not egalitarian in all respects. There were some specialist types of weaving yielding higher earnings where men predominated; and though a number of women held branch offices, the men had a disproportionate share in the government of the union.

In most coalfields the colliers, or faceworkers, had worked their way through a succession of haulage jobs which finally brought them to the coalface; but, as the faceworkers outnumbered the haulage workers and some of the latter were not fit for hewing, a physically fit miner was likely to be working at the face by the time he was twenty, though he would probably work under the supervision of an experienced miner for a year or two thereafter.[3]

School-teaching could be regarded as a skilled white collar occupation. Since promotion to inspector and to head teacher or deputy was outside the control of the Teachers, they were not a 'promotion-line' union. However, they were able, by lobbying, to influence teacher training and the number of entrants to the profession, both largely determined by government finance; and they also pressed for the number of uncertified teachers to be reduced. In these respects the

[3] The Coal Mines Act 1911 required a period of two years under supervision of this kind.

concerns of the Teachers were akin to those of the craft unions. They were the third union among the top ten with a majority of women members. Like the Weavers and Cardroom Operatives, their union was run by the men; but, unlike the Weavers, women were on lower rates of pay than men.

Two unions remain—the Postmen and the Gasworkers. In contrast to the other eight, neither was built around a skilled trade or trades. Although the postman's job demanded responsibility and a minimum standard of education, it could be performed efficiently without a considerable period of learning. Like the Weavers, the Postmen set out to include every member of a given occupation, and no one outside it.

As the term 'general' union had not then come into common usage, the Gasworkers were usually described as a 'labourers' union', but by no means all their members, probably only a minority, would be classified as labourers today. The original core of the union were gas stokers whose job was relatively well-paid and prestigious, attained through promotion by seniority from yard labourer; and many of its members elsewhere would now have the status of 'semi-skilled'. Judged on the basis of skill the Gasworkers might have achieved an overall score as high as that of the Cardroom Operatives, and probably not far behind the Railway Servants. The outstanding feature distinguishing the Gas-workers from all the other nine unions was its industrial dispersion. Most of the other nine were confined to a single industry, or even to a section of an industry, like the Cardroom Operatives and the Weavers. The three craft unions all included members of their crafts who worked outside their staple industries of engineering, shipbuilding, and build-ing, but these members constituted only a small fraction of the total. By contrast, the membership of the Gasworkers was drawn from dozens of occupations and industries, none of which accounted for more than a relatively small part of the total.

By 1910 an agitation in favour of 'industrial' unionism was beginning to make itself heard. Its proponents asserted that a single union with boundaries coterminous with a single industry was a far stronger and more effective form of trade unionism than 'sectional' unions. Among the top ten only the Miners had any claim to be considered an industrial union, and perfectionists would have rejected it. Not only did a considerable number of surface workers and specialists belong to unions outside the federation, but in addition the federation consisted of local unions with considerable independence.

Industrial Functions

In industries where unions were tolerably strong, collective bargaining was, by 1910, the established way of changing rates of pay, hours of work, and some other conditions of employment—the latter varying from one industry to another. The most acceptable generalisation about methods of bargaining at that time is that agreements were made district by district, but generalisations about methods of bargaining are as dangerous as those about types of trade union. District bargaining was indeed the rule in engineering and building, where union districts dealt with local employers' associations. The same was true of printing and footwear except that the union negotiators were representatives of the local branches. However, in some industries agreements were made at two levels. Coalmining piece rates and time rates were fixed pit by pit, but general changes in these rates were settled between the coalowners and the county unions in England, and the Scottish and South Wales Miners Federations in Scotland and Wales. Moreover, the owners and county unions in Yorkshire, Lancashire, and the Midlands came together to deal with rates of pay for the whole of what was known as the Federated Area.

Negotiations for the Federated Area, which covered almost half the miners in Britain, had moved some way beyond district bargaining, and one or two industries had progressed even further, to national pay agreements. In 1909, the Shipbuilding Employers Federation and the shipbuilding unions had agreed that piece rates and time rates fixed by local negotiations should be subject to 'general fluctuations' determined nationally. In cotton weaving, payment was by the piece and the piece rates were settled by national negotiations—though, of course, the industry was confined to a single region. Elsewhere in cotton there were general increases and decreases of local piece price lists, although spinning had only two significant lists, one for the Bolton area and the other for the Oldham area.

The settlement of pay and working conditions on the railways should, perhaps, not be classed as collective bargaining because the unions were not recognised, except by the North Eastern Railway and the District Railway in London. In 1907 the other companies, under strong government pressure, had agreed to a conciliation scheme in which representatives elected by the men in each company met managerial representatives to deal with variations in pay and conditions. Within each company there were sectional conciliation boards for each department: locomotive, goods, permanent way, and so on. When a sectional board failed to agree, the issue was passed to a central company board, and an arbitrator was called on if the central board also failed to resolve it.

Teachers' salaries were settled by local education authorities, a fair number of which were prepared to deal with the unions; and some local authorities negotiated with the unions representing their manual employees. The pay of Post Office staff and other civil servants was determined by parliament, but unions were permitted to make representations to the employing departments and to give evidence to the parliamentary committees which from time to time considered their terms of employment. Finally, there were dozens of other industries and services in which local unions or local sections of national unions negotiated with district employers' associations or individual employers as opportunity offered.

Agreements settled other issues besides pay and hours. That between the Birmingham Engineering Employers and the Engineers covered overtime, nightshifts, outworkers, and payment for statutory holidays. The lists of such topics, however, were in most instances brief, and other matters not left to the discretion of the employer were regulated by 'custom'. Indeed custom had a part to play even in the settlement of wages. For instance, district engineering agreements did not settle *rates* of pay, but raised or lowered existing rates, By custom these were usually the approved union rates, but the employers had entered into no written obligation to pay union rates. This survival of earlier days was no longer of great significance, but engineering pay was also affected by customs of recent origin. A national agreement of 1898 had ordained the fixing of piecework prices 'by mutual arrangement between the employer and the workman or workmen who perform the work'. Thereafter, shop stewards in many strongly organised pieceworking shops had forbidden their members to accept a price without consulting their steward. Accordingly a custom was emerging of negotiating piece prices with shop stewards or even shop steward committees.

However, the special domain of custom was working practices, such as supervision, demarcation between jobs, manning, and promotion. It was a common custom among craftsmen to insist on taking directions only from a foreman who 'had served his time'. This practice helped to protect other craft customs, since such a foreman would have absorbed them as an apprentice and journeyman. In some coalfields miners at the face went further and refused to be supervised. Work stopped when the overman approached and was resumed when he left. Since they were pieceworkers, the way the faceworkers did their job was, they thought, their own business so long as the manager got his coal. Demarcation customs were an essential feature of craft unionism, for there was little point in insistence that only those who had qualified as craftsmen could work at the trade, without specifying the jobs which were the prerogative of the trade. In cotton spinning, and in iron and steel, both manning and promotion were determined by customs relating to the composition of working teams. In cotton weaving, custom settled the number of looms a weaver should tend.

Custom had more than one source. Demarcation rules often rested on the decisions of branch or district committees, with reference to union executives if need be. The employer might create a custom by his allocation of a job, if it went unchallenged, but, if another union claimed the job, he became the man in the middle between the contending unions. The structure of work teams in cotton spinning and in iron and steel went back to the days when the first hands were subcontractors—as some still were in iron and steel—but was now fiercely defended by the unions. Piecework bargaining by shop stewards was developed by trade unionists in the workshop.

Where unions were strong, they did not readily tolerate changes in custom without their consent, and consent was unlikely unless their members could see an advantage in it. Some employers found this attitude irksome. At a conference with the Boilermakers' representatives in 1907, the chairman of the Shipbuilding Employers said:

I don't think there is any manager who can propose the slightest alteration in work and in working conditions in the various yards without their action having to be approved by the Boilermakers' Society.[4]

His federation sought the remedy in a national disputes procedure—an arrangement whereby both parties undertook to submit unresolved disputes, first to joint district review and then, if need be, to joint national adjudication; and not to strike or lock out in the meantime. Such a procedure was included in their 1909 agreement with the unions. The engineering agreement adopted in 1898 and revised in 1907 had gone further by specifically outlawing certain types of custom, such as bans on overtime and on working with non-unionists, and gave—at least on paper—the employers 'full discretion to appoint the men they consider suitable to work all their machine tools, and to determine the conditions under which they shall be worked'.

Procedure agreements had a further advantage for employers. In industries which settled rates of pay and working hours district by district, the lead in pursuing improvements was taken by the more powerful union district committees or branches. If one of these could break through the resistance of their employers, other districts might hope to follow on behind without a strike. Under a procedure agreement, however, a district claim had to be referred to a national conference before the district committee could take action; and the union executive might take a more cautious view of the situation than a powerful district committee.

By 1910 there were national agreements in cotton weaving, cotton

4 Mortimer, p. 12.

spinning, engineering, shipbuilding, building, and the footwear industry, most of them introduced at the instance of the employers after the
unions had been reduced to submission by lengthy lockouts.

The dispute which caused the greatest loss of working days in 1910
was a shipbuilding lockout arising out of alleged breaches of procedure
by the Boilermakers, whose members struck in three different yards
over disputed piecework prices without waiting for their complaints to
be processed. They asserted that it was the employers who had broken
the agreement by altering the prices. During the three months of the
lockout, which began in September, the employers argued for the
introduction of fines for breaches of procedure and the union for a
speedier way of handling piecework disputes. By December the
depression which had brooded over the shipyards since 1908 was lifting
rapidly, and the employers, fearful of losing new orders, agreed to drop
the proposed fines. Disputes over whether a stoppage was in breach of
procedure or not were to be referred to a joint committee and thence, if
need be, to arbitration. Soon after the men returned to work there was a
round of local pay increases.

Another major conflict over breach of procedure occurred in cotton
spinning. A stripper and grinder named Howe was dismissed for
refusing to undertake a task which he did not think was part of his
customary duties. The Cardroom Operatives backed him and struck the
mill. The employers' federation announced that procedure had been
broken and posted lockout notices. The union asserted that it was the
employers who were in breach of procedure, but offered to settle if
Howe was found a job at another mill. The federation at first refused on
the grounds that they had no authority to instruct another mill to take
him on, but after the lockout had lasted a week they agreed to an exchange
of jobs between Howe and a stripper and grinder at another mill.

A stoppage at Hawarden Bridge steel mill in North Wales was
essentially an interunion dispute between the Associated Iron and Steel
Workers, who represented the subcontractors paying time rates to their
men, and the Steel Smelters whose policy was for all production workers
to be paid by the firm and to share in the piecework earnings. After more
than a year the dispute ended in December 1910 with an agreement to
abolish subcontracting.

In coalmining, which accounted for two-fifths of the year's recorded
strikes and more than half the working days lost, faceworkers in
Northumberland and Durham stopped work at the beginning of the
year in protest against the terms on which a statutory eight-hour day
was introduced into their counties. Since they already worked less than
eight hours a day they had nothing to gain from the Act, and the owners
had decided that the eight-hour day for haulage workers (in two shifts)

would entail a three-shift system at the face. Without the support of their unions the men gradually lost heart and settled on the owners' terms, but the last of them gave up only in April. South Wales, however, was the industry's storm centre with no less than four stoppages exceeding 100,000 working days. The most important of these, in the Rhondda, lasted into the following summer, and is described in the next chapter.

Overall the number of recorded stoppages in 1910 was relatively low. Since reasonably comprehensive statistics had begun to be collected in 1893, there had been a lower figure in only six years. On the other hand, the total of days lost was relatively high. Only four years had returned a higher figure. This conjunction is not unusual. Britain has experienced it in a number of years of poor trade and high unemployment when most workers have been reluctant to strike, whereas employers have been in no hurry to settle such strikes as there were, and more ready to use the lockout than at other times. 1910 had been a year of economic transition. The depression which began in 1908 continued through the winter of 1909–10, but a sharp improvement in trade and employment was visible by the summer.

Political Action

Almost from the start British trade unions had pursued their aims by political as well as industrial means, but the degree of reliance on political action varied from one union to another. The cotton unions lobbied diligently for factory legislation from early in the nineteenth century, their main object being to secure statutory limitation of working hours for women and young workers which, because of the composition and deployment of the labour force, would be bound to affect the hours worked by the men. The Factory Acts also dealt with safety, health, and welfare, and benefited other factory workers as well, but gave special advantages to cotton operatives.

Miners had three main demands of the legislature. The first was for safety regulations, formulated and extended by a series of measures from 1844 onwards; the second, conceded in 1860, was for the right of the pieceworkers to elect and pay their own checkweighmen to ensure fair treatment over their earnings; and the third was a statutory eight-hour day underground, finally achieved by the Act of 1908.[5]

Railwaymen also relied on parliament to regulate hours of work and safety. Their major achievement had been the Act of 1893 which gave the Board of Trade power to curtail 'excessive' working hours. In addition, they looked to parliament and the government to help them

---

[5] Since the statutory limit excluded one 'winding-time' average working hours 'bank to bank' were roughly eight hours and a half.

win recognition from the railway companies which, with the honourable exception of the North Eastern and District Railways, stubbornly denied the railwaymen's right to be represented through their unions. However, the settlement of 1907, engineered by Lloyd George, was a substantial step towards recognition.

The civil service and postal unions were even more dependent on lobbying than cotton operatives, miners, and railwaymen, since their pay and conditions were determined by parliament, and their rules made no provision for strikes or strike pay. The postal unions had been granted substantial facilities for presenting their members' grievances to the Post Office, but were still excluded from decisions on how they should be resolved. Like other unions organising local government employees, the Teachers dealt with local authorities over pay, but they depended on parliament and the Board of Education for pensions, for the regulation of training and certification, and for such prized concessions as the eligibility of certified teachers to be appointed inspectors.

Some unions had considerable political pull. The Miners had been represented in parliament since 1874 and there were sixteen miners in the House of Commons in 1906. In addition there were many other seats where the miners constituted a substantial part of the electorate, entitling them to an attentive hearing from the local Member (usually a Liberal) and in some instances a considerable influence within the Liberal organisation. The cotton unions, associated for political purposes in the United Textile Factory Workers Association, had to wait until 1902 for their own representative in parliament, but their ability as lobbyists was unrivalled. Moreover, with the Lancashire working class seats almost equally divided between Conservative and Liberal, they could rely on a good attendance of Lancashire Members from both parties at any meeting called to acquaint them with the operatives' views on prospective legislation. Railwaymen and postmen were more evenly spread over the country but there were a number of urban centres where their votes could not be ignored. In 1906 the postal unions claimed credit for the defeat in a Liverpool constituency of the outgoing Postmaster General, Lord Stanley.

Among legislation of concern to unions generally, the Trade Union Acts of 1871 and 1876, together with the Conspiracy and Protection of Property Act 1875 and the Trade Disputes Act 1906, established a framework of law for trade union activity which gave the unions virtually all they wanted, without exacting onerous conditions in return. The Conciliation Act 1896 confirmed the support of the state for collective bargaining. The Workmen's Compensation Acts of 1897 and 1906 provided compensation for industrial diseases and for accidents at work. Fair wages resolutions of the House of Commons in 1891 and 1909 required government contractors to pay 'fair' wages. The budget of 1908 made provision for a national system of old age pensions. In 1909 the Trade Boards Act set up minimum wage machinery in selected industries and the Labour Exchanges Act led to a network of employment exchanges. Moreover, a national health insurance scheme was in prospect, together with unemployment insurance, for a limited group of industries.

The Trades Union Congress was primarily responsible for action on issues of this kind which were regularly debated at its annual meetings. Its Parliamentary Committee led deputations to ministers, and primed parliamentary spokesmen, although the need for this diminished as more members of the committee were elected to parliament. In 1900 Congress called into being a new political organisation, the Labour Representation Committee, an alliance of unions and socialist societies (soon reduced to the Independent Labour Party and the Fabian Society) with the aim of 'establishing a distinct Labour group in Parliament'. Helped by an electoral pact with the Liberal leadership, the committee won 29 seats in the 1906 election and became the Labour Party. The adhesion of the Miners Federation in 1909 brought the total number of Labour Members to 45 and, though the party was affected by the swing to the Conservatives in 1910, it came out of the second election of that year with 42 seats. The emergence of Labour in 1906, together with the large number of radicals of one sort or another returned within the Liberal majority, was followed by a marked increase in the pace of social reform during the next few years.

Nevertheless the new party had its problems. Many trade union members continued to vote Liberal or Conservative. In many respects the party was still dependent on the Liberals, and in parliament some of the newly-affiliated miners remained Liberals in all but name, relying almost exclusively on the local Liberal organisations for their support.[6] Even among those trade union Members who were thoroughgoing advocates of independent political action, there was little enthusiasm for attempts to give the Labour Party a distinctive programme of its own or to build up an electoral organisation capable of competing with those of the traditional parties. Few of them were converts to socialism; and there was friction with the Independent Labour Party's representatives in the House and with its organisation outside, though Ramsay MacDonald of the Independent Labour Party and Arthur Henderson of the Ironfounders did their best to promote harmonious co-operation. Moreover, by ruling trade union expenditure for political purposes to be

---

[6] Three senior Miners' officials who retained their seats in 1910—Thomas Burt, Charles Fenwick and John Wilson—had openly refused to join the Labour Party.

ultra vires, the Osborne judgement of 1909 appeared to threaten the party's survival, unless the Liberals redeemed their promise to re-establish the right of trade unions to spend their funds on politics.

The Labour Party remained a federal body, with the individual unions and socialist societies sending their delegations to the annual conference and voting for representatives on the executive. With well over 95 per cent of the party's nominal membership, the unions provided an overwhelming share of the affiliation fees and of the election fund instituted in 1903. From time to time the intellectuals of the Fabian Society could offer ideas or expertise, but the major contribution of the socialists came from the Independent Labour Party, especially in terms of personnel. At all levels of the party it provided the most prominent activists, from Keir Hardie downwards, and a network of local branches which were always eager for electoral battle.

Constituency organisations were also federal. Some were local Labour Parties or Labour Representation Committees which brought together branches of affiliated unions and socialist societies. Others were Trades Councils. Both relied partly on party headquarters and partly on the unions for funds to fight parliamentary elections and to pay successful candidates. Nevertheless, some of them showed a sturdy independence, and one or two of the more effective constituency organisations also admitted sympathisers who were not members of unions or socialist societies and therefore ineligible for the Labour Party itself.

If it was to serve its purpose, this loose and diverse association needed skilled and tactful management. The diplomatic talents of the party secretary, Ramsay MacDonald, were constantly exercised in his dealings with constituency organisations, affiliated bodies, Labour Members of Parliament, and the party's Liberal allies. Before 1909, when the Miners affiliated, there was the further problem of promoting co-operation between the parliamentary party and the trade union Members outside it. This task had been capably performed by David Shackleton of the Weavers, the most influential trade unionist in the House elected in 1906. When Shackleton resigned his seat in 1910, Arthur Henderson took his place in the eyes of trade unionists, both inside and outside the party.

Finance

The Labour Department's figures for the income and expenditure of registered unions show that during the years 1901–10[7] just over a third of their income went on friendly benefits (sickness, accident, funeral, superannuation, etc.) and just over a quarter on unemployment benefit.

[7] For sources concerning trade union finance, see Statistical Appendix.

Another quarter went on administration. Only 10 per cent went on strike, lockout, and victimisation benefit, and the remainder provided a modest surplus.

In their classic analysis of British trade unions, Sidney and Beatrice Webb argued that, at least in unions of skilled workers, unemployment and friendly benefits supported industrial action by protecting trade union conditions.[8] Once such a union had established rates of pay and other terms of employment, there was constant danger of erosion. Even if the less-skilled were successfully excluded from skilled work, skilled men who were out of work might offer their services below the rate, and so might the sick and the injured, driven back to work before they had fully recovered. The prospect of the workhouse might have the same effect on older workers, conscious of their declining powers. Unemployment and friendly benefits, therefore, protected union rates and conditions.

There may be something in this interpretation; but it is possible to doubt whether it explains an expenditure on these benefits six times greater than on dispute benefit. By the end of the nineteenth century, the development of collective bargaining had lessened the need for this indirect protection by substituting the obligation of employers to honour agreements on rates and conditions. Besides, other explanations are available to account for the emphasis of trade unions on their friendly benefits.

From the point of view of the union leaders, their members' investment in insurance against unemployment and other risks was a powerful incentive for them to maintain their union contributions. It is notable that the 'new unions' of 1889, most of which initially boasted that their policy was 'no benefits but fighting benefits', soon instituted such meagre friendly benefits as their members could afford. From the point of view of the members, friendly benefits were highly desirable. Many members of skilled unions belonged to friendly societies which provided sickness and funeral benefits, but these societies did not offer unemployment benefit, or superannuation, except in so far as extended sick pay to the elderly constituted a form of superannuation. Members of unions that catered for the lower-paid were less likely to be able to afford friendly society subscriptions, so even limited union funeral and sickness benefits were welcome to them.

The special character of union finances is also relevant. Dispute benefit cannot be actuarially sound since there is no technique for predicting the size and frequency of strikes. In a major dispute a trade union might throw all its resources into the battle, suspending all friendly benefits and officials' salaries and imposing a levy on members

[8] Sidney and Beatrice Webb, *Industrial Democracy*, Part II, Chapter 1.

still at work (which, in a skilled union, might run to 20 per cent of earnings). Then, when the stoppage was over, another levy could be approved by the members to restore the union's finances.

In 1910 the average income per member of the hundred principal trade unions[9] was £1.84 a year, a little more than 3.5p a week and more than 2 per cent of the average adult male earnings of about £1.50 a week. There was wide variation between unions. The weekly income per member of the unions in the metals, engineering, and shipbuilding group was 6.7p, more than 3 per cent of the average skilled male worker's weekly earnings of around £2 a week. As might be expected, the lowest figure for income per member came from the 'miscellaneous group' which included the general unions. At 1.4p a week it was over 1 per cent of the earnings of male labourers which probably averaged about £1 to £1.25 a week in urban occupations. It is noteworthy that the income per head of the printing group, which had been a little under 5p a week in 1910, rose to 7.3p in 1911, mainly due to the heavy levies raised by the London Compositors to finance a dispute at the beginning of the year. Most adult male union members, therefore, paid between 1 and 4 per cent of their income to their unions, over half of which was returned in friendly and unemployment benefits.

Government

In 1910 the key issue in the government of the major unions was still the relationship between national headquarters and local organisations, as it had been throughout the second half of the nineteenth century, but it was now less a matter of control over finance and more a matter of control over local bargaining.

There were wide variations between unions in the structure of their local organisations. For the most part the cotton unions had only one level of local organisation—the district associations. Although some of these ran to over ten thousand members, they were not further divided into separate branches. The Railway Servants, the Postmen's Federation, and the Typographical Association also possessed a single significant level of local organisation, but for them it was the branch. The craft societies in engineering, shipbuilding, and building had for the most part two levels of local organisation, the branch and the district. Their branches were primarily administrative units, whereas the main function of the districts was to settle and to enforce the terms on which their members should accept employment. Nominally the Gasworkers used the same two levels, but whereas the craft district usually covered a single town or city and its environs, the Gasworkers' districts were regional bodies and had important administrative func-

[9] See Statistical Appendix.

tions. The constituents of the Miners Federation in England were mainly county unions of colliery branches, but in Scotland and South Wales they were themselves federations, consisting of county unions in Scotland, and in South Wales of districts, most of them roughly coterminous with one of the valleys into which the coalfield was geographically divided.

The most important aspect of relations between central and local union organisations was the control of strikes. Before the spread of collective bargaining, the management of strikes had been a matter of the wording of the rules and the insistence of the executive on carrying them out. Where a strike had not been called according to the rules, benefit was not payable, unless the executive found reason to make an exception. Now, however, there was another question of equal or greater concern: had the issue been through the procedure for handling disputes agreed with the employers? If not, it was 'unconstitutional', and the executive was morally bound to get the members back to work, whether or not benefit was being paid. Failure to do so might lead the employers to declare a general lockout.

Disputes over wage reductions in engineering during the winter of 1902–3 illustrated the issues. The proposals of the Glasgow and Newcastle employers had been modified at Central Conferences, but these compromises were rejected by local ballots of the Engineers who came out on unconstitutional strike with the support of their district committees. Strike benefit was paid until the executive instructed the local officers to stop. In Glasgow the executive also demanded a refund of benefits paid, and suspended the district committee.

The executive's difficulties were aggravated by the complications of the union constitution. Its Final Appeal Committee ordered them to pay out the strike benefit withheld from the Glasgow strikers, who were by then back at work. The constitution also figured in a dispute over a pay reduction in the North East at the beginning of 1908. On this occasion there had been no agreement at Central Conference. The leaders of the engineering unions had undertaken only to put the employers' terms to a local ballot, which rejected them. Consequently the stoppage which followed was not in breach of procedure, and benefit was authorised. Subsequently, however, intervention by Lloyd George led to an offer from the employers to maintain the existing rates of pay pending arbitration, which the union leaders recommended to their members in the North East. They turned it down and the Engineers' secretary, George Barnes, proposed to put the question to a general ballot of the whole union, but the executive would not support him. In the end the employers forced the union to act by threatening a national lockout; and meanwhile Barnes had resigned.

The 1909 shipyard procedure promised to be at least equally troublesome. In 1910 the new general secretary of the Boilermakers, John Hill, told his members in a circular to the branches that 'there is not a single case of a dispute among the many we have had this year where the procedure . . . has been carried out'.[10] When the Boilermakers were locked out in September they voted by two to one against granting authority to their executive to negotiate, and in subsequent discussions with the employers the executive was accompanied by district representatives. Even so a provisional agreement was voted down, and there was little reason to hope that the terms accepted in December would provide a final resolution of the problem.

If the building procedure of 1904 had not yet caused much dissension within the building unions, the explanation was not to be found in the superiority of its terms and their methods of union government, but rather in the ten years of recession in their industry since 1900 which had seriously weakened the unions both nationally and locally. Printing had not yet acquired a national procedure, and the likelihood of strained relations between union headquarters and branches was somewhat diminished by the independent London unions, which kept the largest and most highly-paid group of printing workers outside the scope of the national unions.

The Miners also lacked a national procedure. The employers' organisation, the national Mining Association, insisted that industrial relations was the business of the local employers' associations, and the Miners Federation had no formal status in negotiations which were handled by the constituent unions. The federation's responsibility was confined to supporting a constituent once a dispute had started. Provided a special conference approved, the federation could either impose a national levy on their behalf or call a national strike. These were powerful weapons, but in considering their use the leaders of the federation always had well to the front of their minds the preservation of the national unity of the federation, which had been achieved only two years ago with the adherence of Durham. In the 1910 negotiations over the application of the Eight Hours Act in South Wales they had to consider the likelihood that the Welshmen would appeal for support if no agreement was reached. If a special conference rejected the application, South Wales might pull out in a huff; alternatively, if support was granted and the dispute was prolonged, the other constituent unions might find that the cost of belonging to the federation was too high. They had resolved their problems over the Act; and, quite apart from a national strike, the cost of a levy to support a quarter of the federation's total membership would be enormous.

[10] Quoted in the *Economic Review*, October 1910, 'Editorial Notes'.

Consequently the leaders persuaded South Wales to settle and began to look to national bargaining as an alternative to the current arrangements, not because they had any particular desire for a national procedure, but in order to achieve national agreements on pay and conditions which would dispose of the question of one constituent seeking the support of the others; for then all would be equally affected.

This consideration helps to explain why collective bargaining in cotton, although by no means trouble-free, does not appear to have put much strain on the relationship between the unions and their district associations. Constitutionally these relationships were very similar to those within the Miners Federation, but changes in pay were negotiated nationally.

Collective bargaining had not yet had an opportunity to influence the government of the remaining four of the ten largest unions. The Railway Servants, the Teachers, and the Postmen's Federation had neither national procedures nor full recognition from their employers; and the various plant and district agreements of the Gasworkers imposed no obligation on their head office to intervene in bargaining.

At branch and district level, union business was almost universally conducted by a representative committee. National government was in the hands of an executive committee or council, whose composition varied from union to union. The 'local executive'—elected in the interest of economy from a selected district to govern the whole union—was still general among the building unions, but the nationally-representative executive continued to gain ground elsewhere. The Amalgamated Carpenters and Joiners were alone among the ten largest unions in retaining the old arrangement. Most executives, whether local or nationally-representative, consisted of members 'working at the trade', but positions on the Engineers' and Boilermakers' executives were full-time posts; and the Miners and the cotton unions allowed their constituents to send either full-time officers or 'lay' members to their national executives. Most of them sent one or more of their full-time officers. The Gasworkers provided for two representatives from each district, one of whom was to be the full-time district secretary.

The traditional device for making rules and policy was the referendum or, in unions with local executives, a nationally-representative general council, meeting annually and in emergencies. However, the Miners and the cotton unions had always relied on national delegate conferences, and this method had been gaining ground in other unions.

For some time the number of full-time officers had been increasing more rapidly than the membership. Either from their own resources or with head office assistance, more and more large branches and districts provided full-time posts for their secretaries; and more national executives were creating posts for 'organisers' in addition to their general and assistant general secretaries. These organisers might work from head office or have responsibility for a region.

At a level above the national unions came the federations. Among those which grouped unions within a single industry or a set of associated industries, the Federation of Engineering and Shipbuilding Trades and the Printing and Kindred Trades Federation were the most noteworthy. The first had not yet secured an acknowledged role in collective bargaining, but in 1910 the second was conducting an ambitious claim for a 48-hour working week throughout the printing trades. The General Labourers National Council was barely two years old; and the National Transport Workers Federation only in process of formation.

The General Federation of Trade Unions was a very different organisation. Set up by Congress in 1899, it aimed to include all unions, and its central function was strike insurance to supplement union provisions for strike benefit. In fact it covered little more than a quarter of British trade unionists, but this was enough to allow the federation to cut a figure in the trade union world. It was accepted as a third partner, along with Congress and the Labour Party, in the Joint Board which determined the bona fides of unions seeking affiliation to any one of them, handled inter-union disputes, and coordinated action on major issues. However, by 1910 the federation was in severe trouble. A series of major strikes cut its reserves from £162,210 in 1908 to £61,235 in 1911, and aroused anxiety among those members who saw their contributions spent on others' strikes. Especially indignant were those union leaders whose members were put out of work by disputes in which they were not directly involved but were denied benefit under the federal rules, as were shipwrights and labourers in the Boilermakers' lockout of 1910.

Leaders and Ideas

At the turn of the century the unions had been led by as remarkable and talented a group of men as at any time in their history: the autocratic Yorkshireman, Ben Pickard, architect of the Miners Federation; the astute James Mawdsley who made the Spinners, despite their modest numbers, the strongest union of his day; Robert Knight, whose achievement with the Boilermakers closely rivalled Mawdsley's with the Spinners; David Holmes of the Weavers, succeeded in 1906 by David Shackleton who adroitly straddled Congress and the Labour Party, and had been recognised by Liberal ministers as the spokesman for both of them; Richard Bell of the Railway Servants; and George Barnes of the Engineers. By the end of 1910 all had gone. Pickard, Mawdsley and

Holmes were dead; Knight had retired; Shackleton and Bell had accepted government posts; and Barnes was now a full-time politician.

The current generation of trade union leaders either had yet to make their mark, or never did so. Enoch Edwards of North Staffordshire, who succeeded Pickard as president of the Miners Federation, was a far less notable figure. Thomas Ashton, secretary of the federation since it was formed, was a competent administrator, but made little attempt to take the lead in policy. The new vice-president, Robert Smillie from Scotland, a committed socialist, promised greater things, but he had still to prove himself outside Scotland. With the doubtful exception of William Mullin of the Cardroom Operatives, none of the current leaders of the cotton unions cut much of a figure outside Lancashire. Bell's successor, J. E. Williams, was not his equal, though the new assistant secretary of the Railway Servants, J. H. Thomas, who had just won Bell's parliamentary seat in Derby, showed greater promise. Jenkin Jones, who followed Barnes, is justly forgotten. John Hill, the current secretary of the Boilermakers, had yet to show what he was worth.

Other unions did little to fill the gap. The veterans of the 'new unions' of 1889 were still there, among them Will Thorne of the Gasworkers and Ben Tillett of the London Dockers. Thorne was deservedly popular, but he lacked both the intellectual grasp and the personal force to lead the movement; and no one trusted Tillett, who was more concerned to maintain his reputation as an ageing *enfant terrible* than to show solid qualities of leadership. The Parliamentary Committee of Congress included several representatives of small unions who had won an established position there. These included C. W. Bowerman of the London Compositors, W. J. Davis of the Birmingham Brassworkers, and William Mosses of the Patternmakers, all limited in their vision and old-fashioned in their ways; and Gosling of the Lightermen who was more open to new ideas but no heavyweight.

The response of trade unions to the demands made upon them depended not only on the qualities of their leaders but also on the ideas that were widely held within the movement. Foremost among them was a devotion to collective bargaining—'conciliation' as it was still more commonly called—as the means to achieve trade unionism's industrial objectives. By conciliation was meant an honest and diligent attempt to resolve disputes by negotiation with employers. It did not follow that the national conciliation boards or procedures, which had been introduced in a number of industries, were universally popular. Some of them came in for a good deal of criticism, but most of the critics had no principled objection to bargaining with employers. Their objection was to the restraints put upon local bargaining by the requirement of these national agreements that employees must remain at work until all stages of the procedure had been completed.

The second widespread conviction was that, subject to their agreements, unions should be left to use their industrial power when and how they saw fit, without the intervention of the law. At the beginning of the century the *Taff Vale* case had prompted a number of leaders to think that union interests might be better served by giving express legal status to unions and their collective agreements, but the response of the rank and file, followed by the Trade Disputes Act of 1906, settled the matter in favour of keeping the law at arm's length from unions and trade disputes. Ben Tillett's continued championship of compulsory arbitration won little support among his fellow trade unionists.

Despite the traditional suspicion of the working class that the law was generally biased against them, it was now widely admitted that trade unions and their political representatives should seek a broad range of welfare measures to benefit working men and women, and their dependents. The Liberal legislation of 1906–10 had already met several trade union wishes in this respect, and the Labour Party's Right to Work Bill, which would have obliged the local authorities to provide the unemployed with either work at trade union rates or adequate maintenance, went a good deal further.

Beyond this point, however, trade union opinion on politics split several ways. Many still believed that, at least for the immediate future, progress could best be achieved through the Liberal Party. Among the majority who favoured independent political action, convinced socialists were no more than a fraction, and they were by no means united, the differences between the Independent Labour Party and the Social Democratic Party (the current title of the old Social Democratic Federation) being only the most notable division in their ranks. The rest were supporters of independent political action, with a variety of views on the choice between concentrating on gingering up the Liberals, or aiming at an ultimate Labour majority in parliament.

There were still other views, expressed by those who subsequently came to be known as 'syndicalists', though some of them would have repudiated the name. In Great Britain there were three significant groups.[11] The Socialist Labour Party, centred on the Clyde, were followers of the doctrinaire American socialist, Daniel De Leon. They allowed scope for political action—to achieve a parliamentary majority which would abolish parliament. The other two groups placed an even lower value on politics. The Plebs League had been set up at the end of 1908 by former and current students of Oxford's recently-founded

[11] For the situation in Ireland, see p. 60.

workers' college, Ruskin College, who were soon afterwards associated with a breakaway from Ruskin to establish a Central Labour College free from the influence of Oxford culture. The league's intention was to promote 'the education of the workers in the interests of the workers'.[12] They achieved rapid success in South Wales where they established a chain of classes in the valleys with the support of two full-time Miners' officials, James Winstone and George Barker. The Industrial Syndicalist Education League, launched by Tom Mann in Manchester in September 1910, owed more than the others to the influence of French syndicalism, and quickly achieved a more widespread following.

However, it was not the syndicalist attitude to politics so much as two other aspects of their doctrine that began to elicit a response from British trade unionists. The first was the view that, to be effective, trade unions must be structured on the basis of one union for each industry. The notion that there were serious defects in the patchwork architecture of British unions had a ready appeal, although the way to reconstruct it was less obvious. The Socialist Labour Party believed that it could be done only through 'dual unionism'—setting up independent organisations on industrial lines outside the existing unions. The other two groups proposed to reorganise British unions from within.

The second aspect was the syndicalists' principled rejection of conciliation. Trade unionists, they held, should extract every possible concession from the employers by using their strength wherever and whenever it suited them. A disputes procedure or any other undertaking to employers which limited their capacity to do so was merely a device to shackle them in the interests of their enemies. Collusion between union leaders, or Labour politicians, and the capitalist class was a betrayal of the working class.

[12] *Plebs*, February 1909.

2

Industrial Unrest, 1911–14

Causes of Unrest

DURING the years immediately before the First World War, Britain experienced social unrest on a scale beyond anything that had occurred since the first half of the nineteenth century. Already in 1909 and 1910 the suffragettes had organized campaigns of obstruction and violence to publicise the cause of votes for women. In the autumn of 1911 they launched a new campaign which was intensified next summer after the defeat of a bill which would have given at least some women the vote. Women chained themselves to railings, smashed windows, set fire to buildings, exploded bombs, and slashed pictures. When sent to prison they went on hunger-strike, which was countered by forcible feeding. Meanwhile Conservative politicians, facing the prospect of home rule for Ireland once the Parliament Act 1911 had limited the obstructive powers of the Lords, encouraged Ulster to resist. Volunteers were recruited and drilled. In 1914 a large consignment of arms was illegally imported. Similar preparations were made by Irish nationalists in the south. Large numbers of British officers stationed in Ireland gave notice that they would resign their commissions rather than march on Ulster. Civil war threatened.

There were also strikes on a scale not previously experienced. The annual number of stoppages recorded by the Labour Department of the Board of Trade, which had not exceeded six hundred since 1901, climbed through 872 in 1911 to a peak of 1,459 in 1913. Except in 1908 and 1910 the number of working days lost through stoppages had not risen above four million since 1901, but from 1911 to 1914 it averaged nearly eighteen million, and in 1913 reached the record figure of over forty million.

What caused this industrial unrest? It has been argued, for example by Dangerfield, that all three currents of unrest were manifestations of a common social malaise. However, even if this explanation were accepted—and evidence to prove or disprove such a hypothesis would be hard to come by—there is still need to seek for specific causes of industrial unrest. The movement for women's suffrage had been gathering strength for some years, and parliament gave the women good reason to believe they had been cheated. The progress of the Home Rule

Bill inevitably exacerbated the distrust between Protestants and Catholics in Ireland which went back to Cromwell and beyond. What material was available in industrial relations for social malaise to work on?

Perhaps the most frequently identified industrial irritant was a decline in real wages. After rising for decades, real wages ceased to grow about the turn of the century. Thereafter retail prices rose while wage rates were stationary, or even fell. Working class living standards overall were more or less static due to the migration of workers from low-paid to high-paid occupations—for example from agriculture to coalmining—but real wages fell for those who remained in the same job. The main cause was the continued fall in the rate of growth of productivity in Britain which had begun almost forty years earlier. Its effect was aggravated by the movement in the terms of trade. In the last quarter of the nineteenth century it had been in Britain's favour, thus offsetting the flagging growth of productivity. From the turn of the century it was adverse.[1]

Another irritant commonly given a share in responsibility for industrial unrest was the agitation of the syndicalist groups, which achieved considerable notoriety over those years. They insisted that the Labour Party was incapable of improving the lot of the workers, who should look to industrial action instead; and many of their members were enthusiastic strike leaders.

How can the effect of these and other factors be assessed? Studies of individual strikes could assist a judgement of their relative importance, but there is no way of analysing the four thousand-odd strikes of 1911–14. Information is lacking about the great majority of them; and, even if it were available, the task of analysis would be enormous. However, by itself a large number of strikes does not make a period of industrial unrest. The years 1936–9, and even more 1940–45, returned relatively high strike totals, but are nevertheless remembered as periods of relative industrial peace because there were few large strikes, and the annual figures for days lost were therefore low. If 1911–14 had been equally free of large strikes, the period would not have been remembered as one of outstanding industrial unrest. It was primarily a small number of large strikes which won the title. Suggested causes of unrest can therefore be tested against accounts of the major strikes, about most of which a good deal has already been written.

Fourteen strikes are listed in Table 1. Between them they account for fifty-one million of the seventy million working days lost through strikes in 1911–14. The general requirement for inclusion is a recorded loss of at least half a million working days. There are two exceptions: the

[1] Vol. I, pp. 474–5.

TABLE I

Major strikes, 1911–14[a]

Date	Strikers	Number of strikers (000s)[b]	Working days lost (000s)[b]
Sept. 1910–Aug. 1911	Coalminers (Rhondda)	13	2,985
June–Aug. 1911	Seamen and dockers (UK)	120	1,020
July–Aug. 1911	Dockers and carmen (London)	77	500
Aug. 1911	Railwaymen (UK)	145	485
Aug. 1911	Dockers and seamen (Liverpool)	48	376
Dec. 1911–Jan. 1912	Cotton weavers (NE Lancs)	160	2,954
Feb.–Apr. 1912	Coalminers (GB)	1,000	30,800
Feb.–Apr. 1912	Jute workers (Dundee)	28	726
May–Aug. 1912	Dockers and carters (London)	100	2,700
Jan.–Mar. 1913	Cab drivers (London)	11	637
Apr.–July 1913	Tube and metal workers (Midlands)	50	1,400
Aug. 1913–Feb. 1914	Transport workers (Dublin)	20	1,900
Jan.–Aug. 1914	Construction workers (London)	20	2,500
Feb.–Apr. 1914	Coalminers (Yorkshire)	150	2,654

Notes:
  [a] Details are taken from *Strikes and Lockouts in 1913*, Table XI and the *Ministry of Labour Gazette*, July 1925.
  [b] These figures are of the number of workers on strike at any time during the strike, not the daily average number of strikers.

railway strike and the Liverpool strike, both in 1911. The first was, by any criterion other than size, one of the outstanding strikes of the period. The second was part of the series of shipping, dock, and road transport strikes of that summer which altogether accounted for a loss of almost two million working days. In the following pages each of the fourteen strikes is described and analysed in turn.

The Cambrian Strike, 1910–11

On the face of things, the coal industry appeared to be floating on a rising tide of prosperity in the early years of the twentieth century. Total output continued to rise rapidly, from 225 million tons in 1900 to 287 million tons in 1913. Foreign demand for British coal had never been higher, and by 1913 one-third of total output went abroad in exports and bunker coal, providing more than 10 per cent of Britain's export earnings. However, there were also strongly adverse trends. Output per man had been falling since the early 1880s, so that the continued rise in output was sustained only by an even more rapid rise in the labour force, from three-quarters of a million in 1901 to over a million in 1911.

    The overriding reason for these trends was the exhaustion of the most favourable seams. Pits had to be sunk deeper and more remote and narrower seams had to be brought into production. This meant that the hewers had to travel further to reach the coal and to work harder if they were to extract the same tonnage, but it also increased the number of haulage workers needed underground to shift a given tonnage of coal. These trends might have been offset by the introduction of mechanical means of cutting and conveying coal which were being developed at that time. However, there were difficulties in adapting the early machines to British conditions and by 1914 only Scotland had made much progress.

In 1910 and 1911 there was also an important subsidiary cause of falling productivity—the operation of the 1908 Eight Hours Act which had reduced the working hours of faceworkers except in the North East and parts of Scotland, and those of other underground workers virtually everywhere. Since underground workers still took as long to travel to their places of work as before, the proportionate reduction in productive time was greater than in overall working time.

Over the trade cycle, demand fluctuated more widely for coal than for most other products, and this was particularly true of the major exporting coalfields, South Wales, the North East, and Scotland. Consequently coal prices were volatile, especially in the exporting areas, and falling coal prices were bound sooner rather than later to take wages with them, for labour costs accounted for just under three-quarters of total costs. The depression of 1908–9, therefore, brought reductions in South Wales and the North East. However, in the Federated Area (Yorkshire, Lancashire, and the Midlands), whose output was sold mainly on the domestic market, a new device was used to avoid a pay cut. The owners undertook to maintain existing rates provided that, when prosperity returned, the Miners would delay any claims for an advance until the owners had 'recouped' the cost of their generosity; and a similar arrangement was made in Scotland.

Almost every difficulty of the coal industy bore most heavily on South Wales. Output per head was lower there, and costs were, therefore, higher, but there was nevertheless little mechanisation. In addition, the Eight Hours Act had reduced the hours worked in South Wales more than in any other coalfield, with the possible exception of Lancashire. However, prices for steam coal, which constituted the bulk of Welsh output, were higher than those of most other types of coal. Otherwise, most Welsh pits would have shut down.

These circumstances lay behind the eagerness of the Welsh owners to strengthen their organisation. In 1908 their two most prominent leaders, Sir William Lewis and D. A. Thomas, had announced an end to the rivalry between them, and thereafter the coverage of the owners' association grew rapidly. In July 1910 a committee was set up to handle unofficial disputes, with authority to indemnify members who suffered losses through such disputes. At the time unofficial strikes were a serious problem, many of them over the use by owners of the clause in the 1909 agreement empowering them to introduce new methods of working without regard to existing customs, and others over their refusal to countenance the closed shop. In addition to these grievances, the miners were unhappy about the failure of the 1910 agreement to compensate them for their loss in earnings due to the Eight Hours Act, and the propagandists of the Plebs League were finding sympathetic audiences. The record of the South Wales conciliation board indicates the temper of both sides. Of eighty-six cases submitted to the board during 1909–10, only sixteen were settled.[2]

On 1 September 1910, D. A. Thomas's Cambrian Combine locked out the men at the Ely pit in the Rhondda valley. The dispute was over the price of getting coal in a new seam recently opened up. A trial period, during which the men had worked at a guaranteed rate of 33.75p a day, had been followed by months of wrangling. They wanted a price of 12.5p a ton whereas the company finally offered 9p, alleging that the men had been holding back during the trial period. The company suggested arbitration, but the men hesitated and the owners' association vetoed the proposal. The lockout therefore began, not just of the men affected, but of the whole pit. Other Cambrian pits were ready to work the same seam. Two of them stopped in sympathy, and more threatened to come out but waited to see what the South Wales Miners' executive would do.

The executive called a delegate conference which voted to strike all the Cambrian pits, and to ballot on whether to bring out the whole coalfield in support or to finance the Cambrian strike by a general levy. In October the ballot decided on a levy, and the Cambrian men put in their notices for 1 November. A week before the strike was due to begin, two Miners' leaders negotiated a compromise of 10.5p a ton, but this was rejected by a mass meeting of Cambrian men, and the executive failed to persuade 'the joint committee of Cambrian workmen', which included two notable Plebs Leaguers, Noah Rees and W. H. Mainwaring, to give the new price a trial.

A few days later the coalowners' association resolved to indemnify the Cambrian Company for its losses through the dispute, and bound their members to refuse employment to the Cambrian strikers. Meanwhile, another dispute over the abrogation of a custom had erupted at Aberdare where the miners' agent, C. B. Stanton, was a warm supporter of the Plebs League. When the Cambrian men came out on 1 November, the two groups co-operated in conducting their strikes as an

[2] Evans, p. 200.

exercise in class warfare, and the employers were ready to play their part.

It was the normal practice of miners to leave the safety men at work during a strike to avoid flooding the pits, which would lead to heavy costs and delays in re-opening once the dispute was settled. On the employers' side the practice of importing blacklegs in major disputes was on the wane. It had never been much of a success in well-organised trades, and there were special obstacles in the closed mining communities. These restraints were now swept aside in the Rhondda and Aberdare. A mass meeting of miners in Tonypandy, the main town in the Rhondda, voted to approach the safety men, who belonged to separate unions, to ensure general flooding. Having failed to bring them out, the strikers decided to start mass picketing on 7 November, while the owners continued to bring in safety men under heavy police protection. Mass picketing developed into rioting, and for the next two days and nights pitched battles with the police raged in Tonypandy. One striker was killed, over 500 were injured, and the damage to property was immense. Meanwhile there was widespread rioting and violence in Aberdare where the strikers were attempting to keep those men who were reluctant to join them out of the pits.

The local police found the situation beyond them and 'sent for the military'. It was an awkward predicament for a Liberal government, but—contrary to legend—Churchill, now Home Secretary, kept his head. Troops were sent under the command of General Macready, but they were not to be used until all other means had failed, and meantime contingents of police from London and elsewhere were sent ahead—at Glamorgan's expense—to reinforce the hard-pressed locals. As a result of the uninhibited methods of these imported police, the Home Office was able to announce that by 10.30 p.m. on 9 November 'reports from every part of the Rhondda Valley' were 'satisfactory'[3]

This was by no means the end of the trouble. The strikers continued to use intimidation against safety men, and there were more serious riots later in November and again in March and July 1911; but nothing to equal the disturbances of 7 and 8 November. Macready's reports showed the extent to which class conflict was a reality in the Welsh valleys. The managers, he wrote, assumed that they had 'a kind of authority over' the local police, and that they were free to indulge in any provocation 'without consideration as to how it might influence the strikers, and that the military would then be called upon to support such action. . . . The information from the managers was in practically every case so exaggerated as to be worthless.'[4]

---

[3] *Colliery Strike Disturbances in South Wales*, p. 10.
[4] Ibid., p. 48.

The two strike committees made another attempt to bring out the whole coalfield by summoning unofficial conferences of branch representatives on 21 and 29 November. These were well attended, but neither voted in favour of the proposal. The Aberdare strike was then abandoned, the executive agreeing to give financial support to those who failed to get their jobs back at once, and both sides in the Rhondda settled down to a war of attrition. The Cambrian strikers now turned their efforts to winning support from the Miners Federation of Great Britain.

There were two ways in which the federation might help. The first was with money. Most of its constituent unions required a contribution of 10p a month from their members, but the South Wales figure was only 5p, though its members were now also paying a levy of 5p a month in support of the Cambrian strikers. With about 140,000 members, the contribution and the levy together brought in £14,000 a month; but with strike pay at 50p a week, the Cambrian strikers, together with the Aberdare men who had not got their jobs back, were costing almost £7,000 a week; and there were all the other expenses of the union to be met. The reserves were rapidly draining away. At a conference on 24–26 January 1911, the national federation voted a levy to give South Wales £3,000 a week, which covered most of the deficit.

However, the militants wanted more than that. They were seeking a national strike on behalf of the Cambrian men. But the chance of shutting the whole British coal industry down to settle the cutting price of coal on a single seam was so slender that their only hope was to relate the Cambrian strike to some wider issue. The most suitable for the purpose were the questions of 'abnormal' places and a minimum wage.

Abnormal places were those parts of the coal face where geological faults or bad conditions prevented a miner making his customary earnings at current piece rates. Traditionally, discretionary allowances had been made for the shortfall in earnings where the overman or manager had assured himself that the miner was not at fault; but rising costs had made colliery managers more niggardly. Consequently the South Wales Miners had been seeking an agreement on abnormal places for several years. The opportunity to link this issue with the Cambrian strike arose in December when the strikers agreed to accept the price of 10.5p a ton 'provided that in working places where colliers cannot earn the rate of wages paid in the disputed seam before the stoppage they shall be made up to that amount', which was 33.75p a day.[5] When the Miners' conference in January debated the question of what should be done about abnormal places, several Welsh speakers tried to introduce the Cambrian dispute. William Brace, vice-president of the South

[5] Miners' executive, 4–5 January 1911.

Wales Miners Federation told the conference: 'If we can settle the abnormal place question, we can settle the dispute'. However, 'Mabon',[6] the South Wales Miners' president, assured the delegates that 'the South Wales people are not fighting now on the matter of abnormal places'; and he was right. The guarantee proposed by the Cambrian men applied to all men failing to earn 33.75p a day, whether their places were abnormal or not. In other words, the claim was for a guaranteed minimum wage on that particular seam.

The national executive also kept the two issues separate. They carried a proposal that each district should try to secure an agreed minimum for abnormal places and report back, and suggested an inquiry into the question of a minimum for daywagemen. The discussion showed that abnormal places presented problems in every district, although some districts had secured more satisfactory arrangements for dealing with them than had South Wales. However, the leading figure in the Plebs League, Noah Ablett, warned that this issue would fail to unite the federation behind the proposal for a national strike. Why should the daywagemen vote for a stoppage in a matter which concerned only the pieceworkers? 'In South Wales we have taken many ballots', he said, 'and we should have secured some results if we had had any question which united all the people. But time and again . . . we have been defeated by the votes of our own men, because only 47 per cent are colliers, and the other 53 per cent have gone against us all the time.' They should forget phrases like 'abnormal places' and 'daywagemen' in order to unite the whole mining labour force and 'use our power to get the wages for the very lowest of our men that are there to be equal to ours'.[7]

Two further attempts were made to settle the dispute. Sir George Askwith of the Board of Trade chaired a conference of the parties in Cardiff on 11 February at which the Cambrian manager gave an assurance that:

If the men throughout the seam are not satisfied with the wages which they earn, whether the place is normal or abnormal, I will take the matter in hand myself and let the Miners' Agent come down . . . Where we find the man has done a fair day's work I will pay him a fair day's wage.[8]

Despite a recommendation to accept these terms from Harvey and Ashton, representing the national federation, the Cambrian representatives found them worthless and refused to put them to their members. The South Wales executive agreed they were unacceptable, 'in view of

[6] His real name was William Abraham.
[7] Miners' conference, 24–6 January 1911.
[8] Miners' executive, 1–3 March 1911.

the absence of mutual trust and confidence between managers and workmen at these collieries'. On the same day the South Wales executive doubled the Cambrian levy to 10p a month, thus at last, together with the national levy, covering the cost of the Cambrian strike pay.[9] At the insistence of the national executive, the Cambrian men subsequently voted on the proposed terms, rejecting them by a massive majority.

In May, intervention by the national federation obtained an offer of a right of appeal to the conciliation board, and if need be to a decision of its independent chairman, to determine whether the proposed guarantee was being honoured.[10] This additional safeguard failed to impress the Cambrian committee, but the South Wales executive recommended acceptance to a delegate conference. The delegates decided against and asked for a national strike for a guaranteed minimum wage. Their request was ruled out on procedural grounds at a special conference of the national federation in the middle of June which also decided to terminate the national levy at the end of the month.

Although South Wales decided to increase their levy to 15p, there was no longer any hope of victory, and in August the Cambrian committee accepted the terms which had been offered in May. In December, Ashton wrote to ask whether the agreement was being carried out. The reply, reported to the executive on 5 March 1912, was that no instance was known of any man earning less than 33.75p a day, and 'most of the men since they resumed work had earned big wages at the tonnage rate'.

It is not easy to draw general lessons about the causation of strikes from the Cambrian dispute, which had several unique features. It must be the only occasion on which a difference over a single piece rate led to a stoppage of such magnitude. The men who had worked the seam for the trial period must have known that the price offered just before the official strike began would yield high earnings; but they and their colleagues nevertheless shut the Cambrian pits for nine months, and were supported by levies raised throughout South Wales, and for five months from the other coalfields as well. It was evident before the strike began that tempers were running high in the South Wales coalfield, and a number of special reasons, both economic and social, could be suggested for it; but they cannot account for industrial unrest elsewhere in Britain.

---

[9] Arnot, *South Wales Miners*, pp. 246–52. Whatever might be said against D. A. Thomas, who confirmed his manager's offer, it was not often that his honesty was impugned. Smillie, not a man to be easily taken in by a coalowner, said of him: 'As soon as any dispute was settled, he would move heaven and earth to see his part of the bargain should be fulfilled.' (*My Life for Labour*, p. 181.)

[10] Smillie said of the offer 'would to heaven every miner in this Federation had the same opportunity of trying it'. (Miners' conference, 13–15 June 1911.)

Transport 1911

Apart from the Cambrian dispute, the largest strikes of 1911 were in transport—shipping, docks, road haulage, and railways. At the beginning of the year the Transport Workers Federation had been formed to bring together unions of seamen, dockers, and carters. The original proposal for a body 'to control and conduct disputes in the Trades and Occupations covered'[11] proved too ambitious for the unions concerned and 'the immediate aims' of the federation were limited to 'the prevention of overlapping of membership, general recognition of the cards of each society, and the promotion of better organisation'.[12] On this modest basis it brought together the Sailors and Firemen, the two major dockers' unions—Tillett's Dock, Wharf, Riverside, and General Workers Union (the London Dockers) and Sexton's National Union of Dock Labourers (the Liverpool Dockers)—a number of small unions, and two or three larger unions with minority interests in the docks, including the Gasworkers. A vigorous recruiting campaign was launched in which Tom Mann was employed by his old friends to use his outstanding talents as an organiser, not least on behalf of the Sailors and Firemen, whose president, Havelock Wilson, was planning an attack on the shipowners.

Since the Shipping Federation had smashed his union over the years 1891–3, Wilson and the union secretary, Edmund Cathery, had kept a skeleton organisation alive. Most accounts report it as pitifully weak at this time, although the Labour Department recorded 12,000 members at the end of 1910 and Mann's efforts must have added more. Wilson knew he needed allies for an assault on the federation. In 1910 an International Committee of Seafarers' Unions, formed the previous year, had agreed to present simultaneous claims in seven European countries for a uniform wage, agreed manning scales, and union recognition. They were repulsed everywhere. Wilson asked the Board of Trade to assist in persuading the employers to set up a conciliation board. Sydney Buxton, President of the Board, agreed to help, but was rebuffed by the Shipping Federation. The international committee met again in April 1911 to decide on an international strike in June. When the day came the strike failed to materialise, and Wilson received another setback when the annual meeting of the Transport Workers Federation refused assistance. Nevertheless he went ahead, and to everyone's surprise, including his own, British seamen struck from 14 June onwards in port after port, starting with Southampton, and were soon joined by the dockers and carters whose action took their unions

[11] *Dockers' Record*, December 1910.
[12] Ibid., March 1911.

unawares. Ports which were totally unorganised, such as Hull, came out with the rest.

Wilson had chosen his time well. 1911 was a year 'when, shipowners having for some years refrained from building to any large extent owing to the impossibility of profitably employing tonnage, the increased trade caused the demand for steamers to more than equal the supply'.[13] Freight rates jumped sensationally to the highest figure since 1889. Traders competed anxiously for what shipping was available, and shipowners sought to turn their ships round as fast as possible. A meeting of Liverpool liner companies, the main group of British shipowners outside the Shipping Federation, agreed that each company should be free to make its own settlement. 'This decision proved disastrous for the shipowners, for not only was each individual settlement made by Cunard, White Star, American Dominion and other lines used as a lever to force similar concessions elsewhere, but it also generated demands in other ports.'[14]

The hitherto effective strikebreaking organisation of the Shipping Federation was virtually powerless. There were the depot ships, the organisers, the strong-arm men to protect the blacklegs, but where were the blacklegs to be found, and, if they were found, to which port should the ships be sent? Time and time again the federation had proved its ability to break a strike in a single port, but now 120,000 men were out,[15] and most ports in the kingdom were closed. The federation accepted defeat. It still refused to meet the unions, but acquiesced in the settlements reached by the local shipowners' associations.

Askwith went to Hull to deal with the situation there. He helped the owners to negotiate a settlement with the seamen, which had to be held up when it was discovered that the dockers, who were understood to be striking in sympathy, wanted a wage increase for themselves. In Liverpool, where many seamen were still on strike, now in sympathy with the claims of the dockers, a group of employers, led by Alfred Booth, persuaded the Liverpool Dockers, after a brief strike, to return to work with a promise of negotiations, which were to produce a final settlement within a month. From Hull, Askwith went to Manchester where eighteen or more unions of dockers, carters, and other transport workers were pledged to stay out until all were satisfied. After five days and nights of concurrent negotiations in the Town Hall, all of them had settled by 10 July. In Cardiff the strike built up more slowly, and it was not until 22 July that the local shipowners, through the mediation of the Lord Mayor, agreed to recognise the Sailors and Firemen, and grant a

---

[13] Kirkaldy, Appendix XVI.
[14] Bean, pp. 374–5.
[15] This is the Labour Department's figure. It must be an even rougher estimate than most.

wage increase. Even so they stayed out until the other transport workers had secured settlements.

Soon the Sailors and Firemen had written agreements 'in Manchester, on the North-East Coast, which covers from Blyth to Middlesbrough; in Cardiff, Newport, London and Leith; in the Humber ports, which cover Goole, Grimsby and Hull; and in Belfast'.[16] Besides embodying the increased rates of pay, nearly all these agreements terminated the requirement that applicants for a job at sea should produce a 'federation ticket' issued by the Shipping Federation, but few went as far as Cardiff in giving explicit recognition to the union, and providing a joint board for future negotiations, with arbitration where there was no agreement.

London was the last great port to strike. When Tillett submitted a claim to the various groups of employers on 29 June for a rate of 3.4p an hour throughout the port, they agreed to negotiate. Lord Devonport, the chairman of the Port of London Authority, brought together shipowners, short-sea traders, wharfingers, and other employers to meet the executive of the Transport Workers Federation on 10 July. The short-sea traders withdrew from the talks, and the other employers rejected the claim for a single port rate, but on 27 July agreement was reached on an increase from 2.6p to 3p an hour for employees of the Port of London Authority, the wharfingers, and the granary keepers, and the question of raising the shipowners' rate of 3p an hour to 3.4p was to go to arbitration. But when this was reported to a mass meeting next day the men would have none of it. On 29 July an unofficial strike began and spread rapidly until by 10 August nearly 80,000 London transport workers were out.

The leaders fell into line, declared the strike official and set up a strike committee, using the Transport Workers Federation to concert action. The arbitration proceedings went ahead, awarding the rate of 3.4p an hour to those working for the shipowners, but the men were instructed to stay out for the time being, for the claims of the short-sea men were outstanding and demands had now been presented on behalf of the lightermen, the bargemen, the carters, and the coal porters. Askwith intervened, and an old hero of the dockers, John Burns, assisted the Labour Department in its work of conciliation.[17] On 11 August enough had been settled for the federation to call off the strike, although a number of difficulties arose especially over the men's insistence that they should be taken on 'outside the gates' to give 'the unions every chance to enforce a card inspection'.[18] This was conceded on 18 August,

[16] *Industrial Council Inquiry*, Q. 3472.
[17] Several of the agreements carried Burns's signature.
[18] Lovell, *Stevedores and Dockers*, p. 175.

but the resumption of work was not complete for several days thereafter, and even then the short-sea claim was left for further arbitration proceedings.

Meanwhile, on 3 August, a comprehensive agreement had been reached between the Liverpool Dockers and thirty deep-sea shipowners led by Booth, along with twenty master stevedores. It set out wage scales for the port in great detail, hours of work including meal times, and provisions for overtime and nightwork. The employers undertook to allow the men to wear their union buttons at the stands where they were taken on, and not to discriminate in favour of non-unionists, although they would not pledge themselves to employ union men exclusively. The union promised not to interfere with the method of working cargo either on ship or quay.

Most important of all, a standing joint committee was set up to interpret the agreement, revise it, supplement it, and consider any question relating to the welfare of employers and employed. No change in working practices was to be introduced without reference to the committee, which was also to settle any future disputes which might arise. No stoppage was to take place until it had given its decision.

By the end of August, according to the union's report for the year, there was 'scarcely a man, either seeking work or employed at the docks, who was not a member of our organisation'. However, not all the men were satisfied with the agreement, and some sections of the dockers struck again shortly after it was signed. About the same time Liverpool employees of the Lancashire and Yorkshire Railway came out on strike when their general manager refused to consider their claim for higher wages, and some of the dockers refused to handle railway freight. Both actions broke the new agreement. Despite the appeals of their officials, the dockers did not resume normal working and on 14 August the employers imposed a general lockout throughout the port.

Tom Mann was now in Liverpool as secretary of the district committee of the Transport Workers Federation, and had been a signatory to the agreement. Making the best of a bad job, he and his colleagues declared a general transport strike throughout Liverpool in support of the railwaymen, calling out the carters and tramwaymen as well as the dockers. When the railway strike, which had spread rapidly, became official, he entered into an undertaking with the railway unions that neither the Liverpool transport workers nor the railway unions should return to work until both had settled their disputes.

In most centres the strikes were accompanied by a good deal of violence. In Hull 'fires, looting, riots had started at once' and a town councillor reported 'women with hair streaming and half nude, reeling through the streets, smashing and destroying'.[19] Casual employment made blacklegging a greater danger to strikers in the docks than in most other industries and picketing was often energetic; an attempt to sign on a crew for a strike-bound ship could easily lead to a pitched battle. The large numbers of foreign seamen in Cardiff aided the recruitment of strike-breakers who clashed with the pickets. The swashbuckling strike leader, 'Captain' Tupper, was arrested, but released on bail and subsequently found not guilty. The worst violence was at Liverpool. Fighting broke out at a monster demonstration of transport workers, led by Tom Mann, on Sunday, 13 August. Large numbers were injured and a policeman was killed. Rioting continued through the night and developed into a battle between Protestants and Catholics. Thereafter soldiers patrolled the streets, and two days later two rioters were shot dead.

The Liverpool railway strike spread to other parts of the company, including Manchester, and then to other railway companies. There was no doubt about the main cause of discontent. The 1907 conciliation scheme had been a dismal disappointment to the men. It gave the companies ample opportunities for delay, and these had been exploited. Applications for improvements had to go through the managers, and some of those submitted in the spring of 1908 had barely reached the sectional boards by the end of the year. Many of the claims went on to the central boards and thence to arbitration, and that took more time. The settlements and awards brought some marginal improvements, but no general increase in railway pay, for they were made during the depression years of 1908–9, when railway receipts were falling, and the companies' plea of inability to pay was generally accepted by the arbitrators. Where disputes arose over interpretation, some companies took the view that they alone should decide them, and it required the intervention of the Board of Trade to get them referred to the central boards. The agreements and awards were to last for a period of years, generally four, so that the railwaymen were debarred from putting in further claims during the rapid improvement in business of 1910 and 1911 which substantially increased railway profits and dividends. The origin of the Liverpool strike was the company's refusal to consider a pay claim on the ground that their agreement could not be reopened.

Well aware of these difficulties, the union leaders were nevertheless much exercised as to how to deal with them. They had accepted the conciliation scheme for a period of seven years, and they were bound by the agreements and awards which it had produced. The growing number of syndicalists in the Amalgamated Society of Railway Servants would have supported a proposal to tear up the agreement and

[19] Askwith, pp. 149–50.

call a national strike, but their leaders had no sympathy with such notions. They arranged a meeting at Liverpool on 15 August with the executives of the Associated Society of Locomotive Engineers and Firemen, the General Railway Workers Union, and the United Pointsmen and Signalmen to consider what they should do.

Such co-operation was unusual—above all between the Railway Servants and the footplate men—but these were times of crisis. The leaders could not hope to stem the unofficial strikes and decided to take them over instead. They gave the companies twenty-four hours to agree to meet them. Otherwise they would have 'no alternative but to respond to the demand now being made for a national railway stoppage'. Next day Buxton saw both sides separately. Nothing positive was achieved, but strike instructions were delayed to allow the Prime Minister, Asquith, to meet the union leaders the following morning. He emphasised the government's concern, offering a Royal Commission to investigate the working of the conciliation scheme and suggest amendments. The offer was refused, and the strike call went out.

As the strike spread, Churchill, bombarded with telegrams for help from mayors, magistrates, town clerks and chief constables, showed less restraint then in the Cambrian dispute. On 18 August two men were killed when a train was taken through Llanelly under military protection and there were disturbances in many other centres. Next day Churchill set aside the regulation forbidding the use of troops except at the specific request of the civil authorities, and troops were dispatched to strategic points.

The government was most anxious for a settlement. Lloyd George, who had bullied the companies into the conciliation scheme, was given the task of securing a further concession from them. He told the railway directors, and the union leaders, that the current international crisis over Agadir threatened war, and Britain's communications must not be endangered. The companies empowered representatives to meet the union leaders to discuss terms of settlement suggested by the Board of Trade. Agreement was reached late on 19 August. All strikers were to be reinstated, consideration of outstanding issues by the conciliation boards was to be speeded up, and both sides were to give every assistance to the Royal Commission.

Work was resumed on 21 August, except for the employees of the North Eastern Railway. Since they had already achieved recognition, they wanted some more tangible proof of victory, and were only persuaded back to work two days later. Meanwhile the announcement of the names of the Royal Commissioners[20] was accompanied by an

---

[20] Besides the chairman, Sir David Harrel, its members included Arthur Henderson and John Burnett, one-time secretary of the Amalgamated Society of Engineers.

assurance to the railway companies that the government would permit increases in maximum railway charges to cover the cost of improvements in pay and conditions,[21] showing that the companies had not forgotten their own interests in the country's hour of need. Their opposition to union recognition had always been influenced as much by their fears of the effect of rising costs and fixed charges on profit margins as by their well-known opinion that trade unionism would undermine the discipline necessary to railway operation.

The railway settlement appeared to leave the Liverpool strikers in the lurch. Later the railway unions claimed that they had received a telegram informing them that the Liverpool lockout was over and all workers were to be reinstated. In fact the tramwaymen were still out, but Askwith persuaded their employers, the Liverpool City Council, to forego the penalties they had intended to impose, and the return to work there was completed on 26 August. The dockers' agreement stood, and their union's annual report boasted that 'we have now established ourselves as part of the machinery of the Commerce of the whole port'; but Booth and his colleagues left the union officials in no doubt that firmer union discipline would be expected in the future.

The renewed negotiations on the railway conciliation boards brought some results. Average weekly earnings on the railways had fluctuated between £1.25 and £1.29 since 1904. In 1911 they rose to £1.33½ and to £1.37 in 1912.[22] This, though not generous by any standards, was something. The report of the Royal Commission, published on 18 October, gave railwaymen less satisfaction. Most of the recommendations were proposals for hastening decisions. Where the parties failed to agree, the impartial chairmen of the sectional boards were to give final decisions, thus cutting out reference to the central boards. This method of shortening the procedure was favoured by the Locomotive Engineers and Firemen, whereas the Railway Servants wanted to cut out the sectional boards. There was to be no explicit recognition of the unions, but the secretaries of the workers' side of the boards need no longer be railway employees and full-time union officials might therefore be selected.

The unions rejected the report and resolved to ballot for a strike on recognition. The companies considered that it was 'an integral part' of the agreement of 19 August that both sides 'bound themselves to accept and act upon the findings'.[23] However, the House of Commons resolved 'that . . . a meeting should take place between the representatives of the parties on whose behalf the agreement of August, 1911, was signed, to

---

[21] The promise was fulfilled in the Railway and Canal Traffic Act of 1913.
[22] *Changes in Rates of Wages in 1912*, p. xxxvi.
[23] Askwith, p. 168.

discuss the best mode of giving effect to the report of the Royal Commission'.[24] Thus chastened, the companies met the unions on 7 December with Askwith in the chair. The meeting itself was the main achievement of the unions, for the agreement which followed four days later broadly followed the Royal Commission's proposals, although there were further changes in procedure to the unions' advantage. The readiness of the unions to settle at this stage may have been influenced by the result of their ballot, due on 5 December, but never published. It was rumoured that the majority for a strike was not sufficient to encourage the leaders to call their members out again.[25]

The strikes of seamen, carters and dockers in 1911 were almost a repetition of those of the 'new unionism' of 1889. Both may be seen as series of 'organisation strikes', such as had occurred also in 1871–4, and were to be experienced in France and the United States in the 1930s. Such a series begins either with rapid recruitment into trade unions in industries where unions have hitherto been weak and unrecognised, or with spontaneous strikes leading to union recruitment. Claims for wage increases and other improvements are presented, in many instances after spontaneous strikes have begun. The employers are taken by surprise. Some concede quickly. Others resist, but they are ill-prepared, and disconcerted by the enthusiasm and determination of their employees. Most eventually yield. The new union members are confirmed in their support of their unions and further recruits flock in. Other ill-organised groups of workers are encouraged to rally to their unions, which also submit claims; and so on.

Such strikes happen only at times of prosperity when employers are under pressure to meet rising demand. But prosperity is not their sole cause. While trade union membership usually rises with economic recovery, most periods of prosperity do not bring series of organisation strikes, nor do they match the union growth of 1889–92 and 1911–13. By 1911 two more economic recoveries had gone by since 1892, and two more separated 1874 from 1889. It seems that nearly a generation had to go by before workers plucked up their courage to try again. It is also relevant that freight rates peaked in 1889 and 1911. In any event, if the outburst of 1911 was a repetition of 1871 and 1889, it cannot have been the inevitable consequence of falling real wages, since the earlier outbursts followed periods in which wages generally had kept pace with prices, or outstripped them.

[24] *Hansard*, 22 November 1911, col. 1266. This was Lloyd George's amendment to a Labour motion presented by MacDonald which 'came too near to censure for the Government's liking' (Blaxland, p. 79).

[25] On 24 November 1911 the *Labour Leader* had prophesied 'a divided and unsatisfactory vote, with many abstentions'. Thomas, however, apparently gave as his reason for not revealing the figures 'not to embitter relations with the employers further' (Bagwell, p. 304).

Unrest in the docks spread to the railways, but the railway strike was not a typical organisation strike. The railway unions already had substantial membership, and, though not officially recognised, could work through the conciliation boards set up in 1907. The main grievance of their members was the failure of these boards to yield increases even when prosperity returned in 1910–11. Railwaymen may have been embittered by the fall in real wages, but it is unlikely that they would have struck in 1911 if the companies had been willing to negotiate pay increases.

Lancashire Weavers, 1911–12

The Weavers took advantage of the improvement in the cotton trade in 1911 to launch a recruitment drive. 'Beginning in March 1911, prospective . . . union members were canvassed, mass rallies were held, and speakers were brought in.'[26] Like most other trade unionists, the Weavers were ready to use coercion against non-unionists where they could. The question therefore arose of whether the union was prepared to support members who came out on strike rather than work with non-unionists. Their delegate meeting in April discussed a proposition that such a strike should qualify for strike pay at a mill where 95 per cent or more of the workers were already union members. Next month the issue came up again and a figure of 85 per cent was substituted and agreed. The leading authority on the cotton unions notes that the Cardroom Operatives had a similar provision and suggests that the intention was 'to restrain mill sentiment against non-unionists . . . by announcing that they would not support workplace strikes on that issue' unless the required figure of membership had been reached.[27] But the decision equally bound the union to support a closed shop strike at a mill which qualified under the resolution. In November a formal request for a closed shop was submitted to the Cotton Spinners and Manufacturers Association.[28]

There is no reason to suppose that the employers were entirely unsympathetic. Probably many mill managers were prepared to exert quiet pressure on non-unionists rather than face serious industrial unrest. The employers' association told the union that they were 'prepared to . . . consider each non-unionist case separately', though they also warned that 'it would be a "mistake" for the union to pursue the issue in any other manner'.[29]

[26] White, p. 132.

[27] Turner, p. 302.

[28] Despite its name, this association had relatively few spinning firms in membership, and dealt with industrial relations issues in weaving. The major employers' organisation in spinning was the Federation of Master Cotton Spinners Associations.

[29] White, p. 134.

In December 1911 a dispute blew up in Accrington. A weaver, who had left the union complaining about the way its affairs were conducted, refused to rejoin, along with his wife who was also a weaver. The Accrington Weavers struck the mill; the employer refused to dismiss the couple; the union leaders supported the local association as they were bound to do; and the employers gave notice of a general lockout. The industry was brought to a standstill just before Christmas.

The union leaders realised at once that they had got themselves into an untenable position. If the issue could have been kept at local level there would have been opportunity to work out a deal, as many had no doubt been worked out in the past and would be in the future; but there was no possibility of the employers' association, as a whole, committing itself to the principle of the closed shop. The union, therefore, introduced the diversion of a claim for a general increase of 5 per cent on the standard piecework prices. Aside from the closed shop issue, this was not an unreasonable proposal in the current economic conditions, and a 5 per cent increase was in fact agreed by the employers in the following June. Presumably the hope of the union leaders was that the lockout could be suspended while negotiations proceeded, and, once an increase had been granted, the Accrington issue could be resolved, fudged or forgotten without renewing the lockout. The employers, however would have none of it.

Askwith came up to Lancashire to hold a series of conferences with the parties. Off and on, they lasted a fortnight, and in the end he achieved a settlement with what must be one of the most curious compromises in British industrial relations, showing the anxiety of both sides to terminate the lockout, if only a formula could be found. Work was to be resumed; there was to be no action on the non-unionist issue for six months at the end of which Askwith, if asked, was to 'submit to the parties his suggestions upon the matter, containing, if possible, a means by which both sides can maintain their principles without injury to the rights of each other'. If he failed, both sides were nevertheless bound to give another six months' notice before taking action on the non-unionist question. Needless to say, when Askwith was asked for his solution at the end of the first six months, he confessed he had none.[30]

The reception of this formula demonstrated that the pressure on the non-unionist issue came from the shopfloor. Although the great majority of weavers were back at work on 22 January, the terms had been condemned at mass meetings in many parts of Lancashire, and there were unofficial strikes and threats of unofficial strikes in several towns, including Accrington, where, it appears, the dissident weaver

[30] Askwith, pp. 190–2.

over whom the dispute had originated left the trade, and his wife joined the union.[31]

Union membership continued to grow while prosperity lasted, even faster than before. During 1911 the increase had been from 112,000 to 134,000, but at the end of 1912 membership was 179,000. In 1913 a dispute at Nelson provided further evidence that the employers' attitude to the closed shop was not bellicose so long as the issue of principle could be avoided. There was in Nelson an anti-socialist Nelson and District Weavers Protection Society, originally founded by a Catholic priest. On several occasions in 1913 Nelson weavers refused to work with members of the Protection Society, and two mills remained shut for six months. The outcome was the collapse of the society. Neither the Manufacturers Association nor the Nelson employers imposed a lockout in support of their members' right to employ whom they pleased.[32]

Like the 1911 transport strikes, the weavers' lockout followed a familiar pattern. From time to time powerful unions overreach themselves by seeking to extend their control in a manner which the employers are bound to resist, as over the issue of manning in engineering and footwear in the nineties, or over the tasks appropriate to a stripper and grinder in the cardroom dispute of 1910, all of which led to general lockouts. As a general rule, unions achieve progress by piecemeal workshop pressure, and run into trouble when an issue is posed as a matter of principle. In 1911 the Weavers paid the penalty for insisting that their employers should concede the principle of the closed shop.

Disputes of this kind are not necessarily associated with either prosperity or depression. The 1897–8 engineering lockout over managerial rights took place at a time of prosperity, and that of 1922 in a year of depression. When trade is good, trade unions are more ready to seek to extend their control; but when trade is bad, the employers are more ready to force them back. On this occasion the Weavers, encouraged by economic prosperity, were the aggressors.

Coal, 1912

After the Cambrian dispute was settled in 1911, there remained the issues of abnormal places and the minimum wage. A national Miners' conference at the end of July heard reports of varied success in district discussions over abnormal places, and decided to ask for a joint meeting with the 'coalowners of the United Kingdom'. Normally the Mining Association of Great Britain took the view that industrial relations was exclusively the business of the districts, but on this occasion a meeting

[31] White, pp. 138–40.
[32] Ibid., pp. 142, 167–8.

was arranged, if not with the association, at least with the coalowners of all districts. The upshot was that the owners recognised 'the right of workmen who are engaged in places that are abnormal to receive wages commensurate with the work performed', but felt that district circumstances varied so widely that the issue could be satisfactorily settled only by local negotiations.

The situation was considered at the Miners' annual conference at the beginning of October. The day was approaching when their members might be faced with voting for a national strike or backing down. They had to confront the problem which Ablett had already posed: why should the majority of daywagemen strike on an issue affecting only the pieceworkers? Accordingly Herbert Smith of Yorkshire moved a resolution that was intended to 'get a united vote in this Conference', and did in fact win unanimous support. It sought 'an individual District Minimum Wage for all men and boys working in the mines in the area of the Federation'. The conference agreed to pursue the claim, district by district, and to meet again on 14 November to consider the results.

District negotiations revealed two problems of interpretation. The first was whether the minimum rate was to be paid regardless of the ability and performance of the miner. William Straker of Northumberland told the conference on 14 November that he had not found it easy to deal with the employers' questions on this point, and reported that: 'we did say to them we did not seek a minimum wage for lazy men, no Association in the world would think of doing so'. However, the view of John Wilson of Durham was that 'we had to ask for a minimum wage for every man, and that the question of laziness and inefficiency belonged to the other side'. James Haslam reported that, though the Derbyshire owners had refused the minimum of 40p for faceworkers which he had asked for, he had 'no doubt whatever that we could get a minimum of [35p] but . . . we feel it is a moral certainty that the employers will not pay [35p] to a man who is worth no more than [20p]'. Enoch Edwards, the president, confirmed that the minimum was intended to apply to 'each individual going down the pit regardless of ability'.

The second problem was whether the claims which the districts had put forward were in breach of the existing conciliation board agreements. The owners in South Wales and Nottingham asserted that they were. The issue appeared to turn on whether the claim for a minimum wage could be construed as a demand for an increase in pay. In Scotland a figure of 30p a shift was recognised as the standard to be applied in abnormal places, where the faceworker had established his claim to an allowance. The Scots felt they would not be justified in asking for a minimum figure higher than that, but since 30p had been their claim, 'there is no breach of our agreement in Scotland'. Certainly, anything that could be construed as a claim for a pay increase would have been in breach of the recoupment clauses of the current agreements in Scotland and the Federated Area.

The Federated Area employers had decided that the claim was a matter for their individual districts, and one or two districts had agreed minimum rates for daywagemen, with Warwickshire also settling a rate for the faceworkers. The conference therefore agreed to continue district negotiations; to ask the employers for another national meeting; and to reconvene on 20 December. By then the employers had refused to meet them again nationally, and the district negotiations had progressed little further. Accordingly the delegates decided to ballot the members on 10–12 January 1912, and, since several districts required a two-thirds majority to sanction a district strike, to stipulate the same majority in this ballot as well.

The vote was 445,801 to 115,921 for a strike. Only the tiny ironmining district of Cleveland had a majority against, but in Durham the majority was barely two to one, and the size of the minority generally worried the leaders. Smillie found the atmosphere of the Miners' conference on 18–19 January 'too much like a funeral after all the enthusiasm we have seen'. There were also financial problems. Each district was responsible for its own strike pay, and whereas Durham was reputed to have reserves of £400,000, South Wales had been cleaned out by the Cambrian dispute; although Stanton assured the delegates that 'our people are confident, I am sure they are'. There was, however, no real alternative to giving instructions to terminate the miners' contracts, the date chosen being 28 February, while professing readiness to meet the employers meanwhile, both in the districts and nationally.

The next business, taken at a further conference on 1 February, was to settle the details of the claim. Some districts had proposed minimum rates which would give increases to most of their members. It was decided that this was unacceptable, and the executive therefore scaled down many of the figures. In the end the rates sought for faceworkers ranged from 37.5p a day in Nottinghamshire and Yorkshire (and for some grades in Derbyshire and South Wales) through 35p for Lancashire, 30.5p for Durham and 30p for Scotland, to 24.5p for Bristol and Somerset. Other rates were to be settled by the districts, but no man working underground, except in Bristol, Somerset and the Forest of Dean, was to receive less than 25p and no boy less than 10p. It was held that to insist on these rates in those three districts would lead to heavy unemployment there.

Another national meeting with the employers brought no change in the situation. The government now took a hand. Asquith and other ministers held a series of meetings with the parties. On 27 February they proposed district negotiations, each attended by a government representative who was to settle any outstanding points. A comfortable majority of the owners—the Federated Area and Durham—were ready to agree. Other districts prevaricated. The only outright rejection came from South Wales. The Miners, however, insisted that the 25p and 10p must be settled nationally. The strike was on.

The Welsh militants boasted that they had won over the English and Scottish miners to their policy; but the causes of the strike were more complex than that. South Wales was by no means alone in asking for action on abnormal places and a national minimum wage. When South Wales carried their resolution on abnormal places at the Miners' annual conference in 1910, Bristol proposed an 'individual minimum daywage' for every pieceworker, and the Midlands Federation asked for 'a standard or minimum rate of wages for each grade in employment in or about mines'. All three resolutions were passed unanimously. In July 1911 it was Yorkshire and Lancashire, not South Wales, that sought but failed to get a majority for a ballot vote on a national strike on abnormal places. The successful resolution on the 'individual District Minimum Wage for all men and boys working in the mines', passed at the October conference, was put forward by Herbert Smith on behalf of the business committee. Speakers from Scotland and Northumberland showed themselves as keen for action on the issue as the men from South Wales. The claim for the minimum wage was generally popular without the need for prompting from them.

Why should the proposal have won such widespread support at this particular time? Tom Greenall of Lancashire told the conference that the 'unrest in the different mining districts' was due to 'so many people going home at the end of the week with very little wages'. With rapid economic recovery, which was already far advanced by the end of 1910, the trend in wages during 1911 was upwards in every industry included in the Labour Department's figures, except pig-iron manufacture, ironmining, and coalmining. No less than 370,000 miners suffered pay cuts that year, and only 13,000 secured increases.[33] Coming on top of the cuts in wages in many districts in 1909 and the effect of falling productivity on piecework earnings, this prompted miners to look for a new way to improve their earnings. A general wage increase was debarred in the Federated Area and Scotland by their recoupment clauses, and the level of coal prices gave it little chance elsewhere; but a minimum wage, they thought, was a different matter. It might not yield an increase to everyone, but falling earnings had brought many more miners within the scope of a reasonable minimum wage than would have

[33] *Changes in Rates of Wages in 1911*, p. 9.

been the case three years earlier; and even high-earning pieceworkers were liable to experience a bad week or two from time to time when they would be able to claim the minimum rate. It was the economic position of the industry, rather than agitation from South Wales, that put the steam behind the demand for a minimum wage.

The Welshmen did indeed launch an agitation. At the Miners' conference in June 1911, delegates from Durham, Northumberland and North Staffordshire complained that Welsh 'missionaries were touring the coalfields seeking funds and urging a national strike for a minimum wage'. In Derbyshire they were 'well received by the men but not by the leaders'.[34] However, there is no evidence that these 'missionaries' succeeded in stirring up any substantial unofficial movement sympathetic to their syndicalist views.

The one significant unofficial movement outside South Wales was in Durham. John Wilson, the Durham miners' leader, was the most outspoken opponent of the strike, and a number of his colleagues agreed with him. In August 1911, representatives of fifty-four miners' lodges passed resolutions 'in effect calling for a minimum wage . . . supported by a national strike if necessary'.[35] Mass meetings were held, the leaders were attacked, circulars were issued, one of them urging a vote for a strike.[36] They objected to their leaders 'making speeches against the minimum wage while they are, at the behest of the men, in the middle of negotiations with the employers with the object of having the principle established'.[37] After the strike was over the 'Durham Forward Movement' was formed to follow up the minimum wage campaign by 'bringing up to date . . . the Miners' Association along constitutional lines'.[38] There is, however, no evidence of contact with South Wales, and the most prominent speaker at the meetings of the movement was Tom Richardson, Member of Parliament for Whitehaven and an active member of the Independent Labour Party, much closer to Smillie and Herbert Smith than to the Plebs Leaguers.

By now a new generation of leaders were taking over from the Lib–Labs who had directed the Miners Federation through its first two decades. The Lib–Labs were still in control in Durham, Derbyshire, Nottingham and the smaller districts in the Midlands, and Enoch Edwards was still national president, but Smillie, the Scottish president,

[34] J. E. Williams, p. 404. In Derbyshire and Nottingham there was a special reason for supporting a minimum wage. The subcontracting or 'butty' system was still widely in use there, and some of the men employed by butties 'believed that the adoption of a minimum wage would bring an end to the contract system' (Ibid., p. 411).

[35] *Durham Chronicle*, 8 September 1911.

[36] Ibid., 15, 29 September, 6 October, 29 December 1911, 5 January 1912.

[37] Ibid., 19 January 1912.

[38] Ibid., 10 May 1912.

who had been on the executive since 1898 and vice-president since 1908, was to succeed him later in 1912. Yorkshire's president, Smith, came on the executive in 1908. Although Ashton, who had been national secretary of the federation from the start, was still Lancashire's secretary, the most influential leaders of the Lancashire Miners were now Greenall and Stephen Walsh, Member of Parliament for Ince. Northumberland's representative on the executive was William Straker, soon to succeed Burt as Northumberland's secretary. Most of them members of the Independent Labour Party, these men were committed to achieving rapid progress in improving the miners' lot including safety at work, pithead baths, housing, reduced working hours, and, of course, higher and more regular pay. They were naturally disposed to favour a minimum wage which would benefit the lower-paid.

In September 1911 they were reinforced by a change in the South Wales representation on the executive. Barker, Hartshorn and Stanton were elected to replace Brace, vice-president of the South Wales Miners Federation and soon to be its president, Richards, the secretary, and Onions, the treasurer.

Had coal prices responded normally to the rapid upturn in the economy during 1910 and 1911, Smillie and his colleagues would have been busy negotiating pay increases. As it was they could not ignore the unrest in the coalfields over falling earnings, and sought to direct it to achieve some major improvement in the lot of the miner, if need be with the threat of a national strike behind it. Above all, however, they treasured the unity of the federation. The improvement which they sought must have the united support of the miners.

Accordingly they joined with the older leaders in isolating South Wales over the Cambrian issue. There was enough sympathy for the Cambrian strikers in the other coalfields to carry a proposal for a national levy, which had the advantage of binding South Wales closer to the federation, but a ballot for a national stoppage in support of a claim relating to a single seam would have torn the federation apart. Thereafter they decided that, unless the owners throughout the country gave way on the minimum wage, unity could be preserved only by a national strike. The issue was not ideal, for the minimum wage would bring little or no direct benefit to the majority of miners,[39] and that consideration may explain the relatively disappointing figures of the strike ballot; but it was the best issue available, and they had to take the risk.

[39] Union leaders in Derbyshire estimated that 75 per cent of the faceworkers there were earning more than the 40p a shift which they originally put forward as their minimum (J. E. Williams, p. 414).

Once the strike began, the government showed more interest in a solution that the parties, who were prepared to settle down to a trial of strength. From 12 to 15 March representatives of both sides met under Asquith's chairmanship, but then the government abandoned hope of a settlement and decided, unwillingly, to enforce its own terms by statute.[40] Their bill, introduced on 19 March, provided for district boards to settle statutory district minima for underground miners, but not for surfaceworkers. Each board was to have a neutral chairman, selected if necessary by the government, with power to determine issues on which the parties could not agree.

The Miners' executive decided to continue the strike until the bill became law, and demanded that the overall minimum rates of 25p and 10p be included in the bill, with higher district minima for the faceworkers. Lloyd George and some of his radical colleagues argued their case in the cabinet, fearing that, without the figures, the bill would not be enough to get the miners back; but Asquith was adamant. If parliament were to fix miners' rates of pay, elections in the mining constituencies might become contests of competing bids from rival candidates. A number of the government's radical followers voted for the Labour amendment to include the figures in the bill, but the Conservatives and the Irish supported the government. The bill became law on 29 March.[41]

Preparations had already been made for a ballot of the Miners, their conference on 25–27 March having resolved that 'it does not advise but leaves the ballot paper as agreed to decide for itself'. The results were out on 3 April, and showed 201,013 for resuming work and 244,011 against. Durham, Lancashire and Yorkshire were for continuing the strike, by majorities of two to one or more, but South Wales had voted two to one for a return. This was a startling reverse for the militants. At the conference on 20 March, Barker had asked the federation 'to repudiate altogether any responsibility for this Bill' which was a 'carefully thought out plan on the part of the Government to split, to undermine the foundations of this Federation'. The South Wales vote was prompted by the lack of funds, which forced South Wales strikers to exhaust their savings and their credit, and even turn to the Poor Law to support their families. The Plebs Leaguers bore a large share of the blame for the empty treasury, not only by their exploitation of the

[40] Asquith told the House that it was 'with great and unaffected reluctance' that he asked for leave to introduce the bill (*Hansard*, 19 March 1912, col. 1723).

[41] The Labour Party voted with the government for the second reading which passed by 348 votes to 225, against the opposition of the Conservatives. When their amendments were defeated in the committee, the Miners instructed the party to vote against the third reading, which was carried by 213 to 48.

Cambrian dispute, but also by their opposition to increased contributions.[42]

The vote led to rifts in the cherished unity of the federation. With so many miners in favour of resumption, a continuation of the strike would have invited disaster, but there was no constitutional basis for calling it off. The executive proposed that the decision to require a two-thirds vote for calling a strike should also apply to continuing a strike. Smillie put this to a special conference on 6 April 'for the sake of the continuance of the strength of this great Federation, especially for the rank and file of the people', and carried the day. The recovery of the old leaders in South Wales was confirmed by the vote of the Welsh delegation for the resolution, and Smillie's former allies, Lancashire and Yorkshire, were alone in their opposition. Greenall had the pleasure of delivering a slashing attack on the Welshmen for the apostasy. Hall of Yorkshire accused certain leaders of infringing the conference resolution by advising the men to vote for a return, and Smillie frankly admitted that he had been among them.

Smillie's attitude deserves examination. According to Lloyd George, Smillie was 'the evil genius of the men', and 'the breakdown of the negotiations was in large part due to the fanatical obstinacy of Smillie'.[43] Smillie could be obstinate. In 1909 he had opposed the Scottish recoupment agreement, and refused to sign it. He 'felt that the concessions claimed [by the employers] would be found to work against the best interests of the miners in the future' and 'it would be better to fight'.[44] However, once the agreement was made he 'went back by the side of the Executive and put it before the men'.[45] During the 1912 negotiations, his concern with unity led him to insist on putting the figures in the bill, fearing that, without them, the stronger districts would stay out and the weaker go back. However, when arguing at the conference on 6 April for the retrospective application of the two-thirds requirement to the ballot on a return to work, he maintained that unity now required a return to work without any assurance on the figures. 'There are many districts who would not be able to hold on for half the time necessary until the figures were put in' by the district boards, and 'our position would be considerably weakened ... if it occurred that section after section returned to work' while the boards were coming to their decisions. Smillie's undeserved reputation as a militant was due to

---

[42] When the national federation, having decided to give financial support to the Cambrian strikers, encouraged South Wales to raise its subscription rates to provide for the future, Ablett repulsed the suggestion, saying that it was the unions with the largest reserves that were 'breaking up most quickly' (Miners' conference, 24–6 January 1911). This reflected the syndicalist view that the wish to protect union reserves sapped militancy. Without reserves, they thought, there was nothing to lose.

[43] Wrigley, p. 69.   [44] Smillie, p. 194.   [45] Miners' conference, 29 March 1910.

his habit of making up his own mind and, once he had done so, paying little attention to what others had to say.

In the event, a national coal stoppage had proved a good deal less damaging than had been feared. A million workers had been on strike for more than a month, but they had not brought the owners, the government or the country to their knees. 'There was, of course, much loss, distress, and inconvenience—to an acute degree in some four or five districts; but matters were never desperate, and the vast mass of the population . . . pursued their daily tasks exactly as usual.' Unemployment rose from 2.8 per cent at the end of February to 11.3 per cent at the end of March, and fell back to 3.6 per cent a month later. Production of iron and steel, bricks and glass, and especially pottery, was sharply reduced, but employment in textiles, building, and shipbuilding was hardly affected. The railways continued to run, although cuts in services 'caused great public inconvenience', and the volume of exports, apart from coal itself, rose in both March and April.[46] The long notice of the stoppage had permitted the owners to accumulate large stocks of coal which they sold at inflated prices after the strike had begun. The strike had cost '11 per cent of a year's working time in the . . . industry, but owing to increased activity both before and after the dispute, . . . the total output in 1912 was only about 4 per cent less than in 1911.'[47]

The machinery of the Act was soon set in motion and the decisions of the boards[48] began to appear within a few weeks. They caused a good deal of initial dissatisfaction, voiced at length at Miners' conferences in May and August, especially over the failure of some boards to grant overall minimum rates of 25p and 10p. Asquith had given them reason to believe they would get at least this.[49] In fact, although Lancashire and Yorkshire achieved 25p, most districts, including South Wales and Scotland, got 24p, and in Somerset the figure was 20p. For colliers the minima ranged from 35p in Warwickshire to 24p in Somerset. Subsequently, however, as a result of 'enquiries of the miners' agents', H. S. Jevons found that 'it is generally admitted that the Act has been a great advantage to the workmen, now that they are beginning to understand how to make their claims'.[50] South Wales was probably the greatest beneficiary, for in February 1912 nearly 22,000 faceworkers and over 30,000 other workers had been earning less than the minimum rates now established. 'Perhaps the day-wage workers of North Staffordshire gained as much', and almost everywhere there were some material gains,

[46] *Economic Journal*, 'Current Topics', June 1912.
[47] *Strikes and Lockouts in 1912*, p. ii.
[48] In most areas the two sides of the existing conciliation boards—with the addition of an independent chairman—became Joint Boards under the Act.
[49] *Hansard*, 22 March 1912, col. 2242, and 26 March, col. 234.
[50] Jevons, p. 565.

as well as the assurance to faceworkers that they would not suffer disastrously from working in abnormal places.[51]

Acceptance of the Act was made easier by the rise in coal prices, which began with the shortage of coal induced by the strike and continued thereafter, leading to general wage increases in practically every district in 1912 and again in 1913. In the Federated Area one increase of 5 per cent in October 1912 was followed by two more in 1913, reaching the prescribed maximum of 65 per cent over standard. The increase in the coalmining wages bill over those two years was greater than the combined total for all other industries included in the Labour Department's returns.

The Miners shared a common grievance with the railway unions. Both found themselves debarred from negotiating pay increases in a period of rising prosperity, the former by their recoupment clauses and stagnant or falling coal prices, the latter by their conciliation board arrangements. Both had special reasons for seeking wage increases, the Miners because of falling earnings due to declining productivity and the Eight Hours Act, the railway unions because of the failure of their conciliation boards to yield any substantial pay increases since they had been set up. The rise in the cost of living was not the primary cause of either strike.

Dundee Jute and London Docks, 1912

The wave of organisation strikes continued into 1912, though there was nothing on the scale of the 1911 transport strikes. The largest was in Dundee. There were already two specialist unions in the jute industry there, and the Mill and Factory Operatives catered for the general run of production workers, most of them women. However, the latter union had no strike benefit and was run by a Unitarian minister, the Rev. Henry Williamson, whose authoritarian methods and opposition to strikes made him widely suspect in the Labour movement. In 1906 the Jute and Flax Workers Union was established to win the factory workers to more orthodox trade union methods, and John Sime, who had previously worked as a foreman, became its secretary in 1909. He showed both imagination and determination in his struggle to win recognition from the employers. Needing allies and financial backing, he formed a joint committee with the other three unions which submitted a claim for a wage increase in January 1912; and he sought to persuade the General Federation of Trade Unions, to which his union alone of the

---

[51] Rowe, *Wages in the Coal Industry*, pp. 106–9. In most districts the owners were protected by a clause under which men who failed to perform a fair day's work forfeited their right to the minimum, and 'many of the colliery managers do not consider that they have lost much through being obliged to make up the wages of piece-workers' (Jevons, p. 565).

four was affiliated, to bend its rules to allow payment of federation strike benefit to his members, although his funds did not amount to the minimum required by the federation's rules. He succeeded in 'the delicate task of assuring the Federation of its [his union's] restraint while coercing the joint committee into adopting a tough line'.[52] The employers rejected the claim and the joint committee waited to see what the workers, most of them non-unionists, would do, resolving to support them if they struck. The strike began on the same day as the national miners' stoppage. Before long, Williamson's union was in trouble and ceased to play an effective part in the dispute. The other three unions carried on, surprising the employers by their tenacity, and on 14 April an agreement was signed, granting a small wage increase and embodying a promise from the employers to try 'to establish average wage rates . . . between one firm and another'.[53] thus giving the lower-paid workers the prospect of a further increase. The two sides also undertook to establish a standing joint committee for future negotiations; but the talks to devise a constitution for the committee broke down because 'the employers were pressing the unions to adopt a measure of control over their members much more stringent than the Association was capable of exerting over its constituent firms'.[54] Nevertheless Sime and his union had by now achieved a status in Dundee such that the employers could no longer refuse to deal with him when he wanted them to do so. By the end of the year his membership exceeded eight thousand.

However, 1912 brought losses as well as gains. The victories of the seamen and dockers in 1889 had been followed by employees' counter-attacks which had come close to destroying trade unionism in the ports. In May 1912 it appeared that the cycle might be repeated. The London employers brought their port to a standstill again, less than nine months after the Devonport agreement. Although the unions subsequently claimed that 'it was generally understood by our side that there should be a conciliation board . . . to deal with these various little crotchets that crop up',[55] no provision had been made for revision or interpretation of the agreement, except by reference to arbitration. This proved disastrous, for at no other port was joint machinery for settling disputes so badly needed as in London, with its workforce split into many sections and organised by a number of unions. The employers remembered that the 1911 strike had been in breach of the Devonport agreement, signed before it began, and regarded that strike and almost every subsequent move of the Transport Workers Federation and the unions as proof that they could not be trusted. They had some excuse

[52] Walker, p. 180.   [53] Ibid., p. 182.
[54] Ibid., p. 310.   [55] *Industrial Council Inquiry*, Q. 438.

for this attitude. Tillett admitted that 'there exists to-day a tendency to "down tools" at what they [the men] deem justifiable provocation. While we admire this spirit of revolt, it is not always actuated by wisdom.'[56]

The unions complained that the employers were not honouring their commitments. The Stevedores took a wharfinger, who was also a shipowner, to arbitration to make him follow the recent award for the deep-sea trade, and then complained that the other wharfingers would not fall in with the decision. There was also trouble over the observance of the carters' agreement. The bargeowners refused to pay retrospective increases due under their agreement, and some of them even disregarded the new rates.

In May 1912 the tugmen—the only group in the port not covered by an agreement—tried to open negotiations with their employers, who refused to meet them, even when the Board of Trade intervened. This might easily have led to a strike of their union, the Lightermen, if an issue of union membership had not brought them out on 19 May. The dockers and stevedores streamed after them, and on 23 May the national executive of the Transport Workers Federation called out all transport workers on the Thames and the Medway—100,000 in all.

In the absence of the Prime Minister, a group of ministers led by Lloyd George had already talked to the parties, and even before the federation's decision they announced that Sir Edward Clarke would conduct an inquiry. His report, promptly presented on 27 May, drew attention to the 'breach in some cases, and neglect to make use in others', of the clause in the 1911 agreement for reference of differences to the Board of Trade, and suggested that they should now take advantage of it. The question of enforcing agreements on employers who were not members of their associations could 'only be dealt with by legislation'.

The ministers tried to arrange a conference with both sides, but the employers refused. They put to the employers the unions' proposals for a joint board in which the federation was to be 'recognised as the representative of the men's side', and for the reinstatement of the strikers. The employers refused to guarantee reinstatement and 'under any circumstances' to 'consent to the recognition of the Union or Transport Workers' Federation ticket, or to any discussion for such recognition'.[57] Ignoring the employers' clear determination to fight to the finish, the ministers produced a set of proposals based on appeal

---

[56] *Dockers Record*, February 1912.

[57] For good measure they also rejected as 'impracticable' the ministers' suggestion that all their associations should come together in a single federation (*Strikes and Lockouts in 1912*, pp. xxxv–xxxvi).

panels with power to impose penalties for breach of agreement. On 10 June the employers turned them down.

The annual conference of the Transport Workers Federation, which had no authority to instruct its affiliates to strike, had decided to 'recommend' a national sympathetic strike unless the employers accepted the proposal for a joint board. When the executive heard that it had been rejected they wired all ports: 'employers point-blank refuse to accept proposal for a settlement. National Executive recommend general stoppage at once.' In the provinces, however, the federation was a very different organisation from London. In London it brought together twelve unions catering for dockers, carters, seamen, and many specialist groups. Outside London some two-thirds of the federation's members were in two unions, the Sailors and Firemen, and the Liverpool Dockers.

Both unions had powerful reasons for keeping the peace. Their leaders knew that their recent gains in membership owed much to their agreements with the employers. Sexton took the view that 'our one grave danger was to know how to use the new power we had gained by the enormous addition to our ranks'.[58] His Liverpool agreement had already been imperilled by Tom Mann's strike of the previous August, and in Leith his officers had signed an agreement which ruled that 'no strike shall in any case take place . . . on account of the action of any employer not a member' of the local employers' association.[59] His executive rejected the federation's recommendation.

The Sailors and Firemen's executive had already considered the prospect of a national strike at an emergency meeting on 7 June. Havelock Wilson was absent in America, and the lead was taken by 'Father' Hopkins, who, like 'Captain' Tupper, was a friend of Wilson's brought on to the executive to give it greater strength. A third non-seafaring member, Tom Mann, was in gaol.[60] The union was already paying out £1,000 a week to its London members and there was no prospect that they would be able to meet the cost of a national strike. In addition, all their provincial agreements would be imperilled. They resolved to inform the Transport Workers Federation that the calling of a national strike 'would be detrimental to all concerned', but that if the call was made the Sailors and Firemen would hold a ballot before striking. The ballot was held, giving a majority of 3,678 to 2,137 against a national strike.[61]

---

[58] National Union of Dock Labourers, *Annual Report*, 1912.
[59] *Industrial Council Inquiry*, Q. 7338.
[60] He had been sentenced, along with Guy Bowman, for inciting troops to mutiny by publishing an appeal not to allow themselves to be used against strikers.
[61] *The Times*, 18 June 1912.

Without the support of the two major unions there could be no national strike. Only Manchester and the ports controlled by the London Dockers—the Bristol Channel ports, Plymouth and Southampton—showed any inclination to respond, and in a few days it was all over. The strikers in London now had little prospect of success.[62] Ships could be diverted to other ports; there was not the threat to London's food supplies which had put pressure on the employers the previous August; and the strike had been incomplete from the start, due mainly to the Carmen's poor response. At the beginning of June the Port of London Authority announced that 5,000 men were at work and a month later the figure was 13,000.[63] The unions continued a desperate search for outside help. From the Parliamentary Committee of the Trades Union Congress they secured a sympathetic resolution and a collection of £1,161, of which £500 came from the Liverpool Dockers.[64] On 1 July the House of Commons accepted James O'Grady's resolution recommending a meeting of the two sides, but the moment was far less favourable than in the railway dispute of 1911, and the employers would not budge. On 22 July Wilson, back from America, set off with Tom Mann, now released from gaol, to investigate the possibility of promoting sympathetic strikes and raising funds. He had no need to go beyond Hull to find the task hopeless and advise his executive to send their London members back to work.[65] Askwith persuaded Devonport to meet Harry Gosling, the Lightermen's secretary, and Harry Orbell, an official of the London Dockers, both members of the Port of London Authority as well as the Transport Workers Federation executive. He gave them assurances on maintaining existing agreements, which were repeated in a letter to the press on 18 July. By 23 July 19,000 men were back and on 27 July the strike committee ordered a resumption of work. The men drifted back during the next few days, and the employers insisted on taking them on inside the dock gates, making it impossible for union officials to prevent non-members seeking employment. The London unions suffered considerably. The Stevedores' membership was almost halved, and the London Dockers lost 15,000 members; but the losses were confined to London.

---

[62] In frustration at the impasse, Ben Tillett had publicly prayed God to strike Lord Devonport dead. Questioned in the House, Reginald McKenna, who had replaced Churchill as Home Secretary, said that this was not 'a definite threat', and he proposed to take no action (*Hansard*, 24 June 1912, cols. 33–5).

[63] *Strikes and Lockouts in 1912*, pp. xxxviii–xxxix.

[64] Trades Union Congress, 1912, pp. 86–8.

[65] A mass meeting at Hull voted unanimously for 'a national strike if necessary, after ports consulted and conference called to decide'. (*Daily Herald*, 25 July 1912.)

London Cab Drivers and Midlands Metalworkers, 1913

In 1912 an arbitration award obliged London cab drivers to pay for their petrol, which was at that time costing their employers $3\frac{1}{2}$p a gallon. At the end of the year the price was suddenly increased by no less than 60 per cent to $5\frac{1}{2}$p. The employers gave notice that they meant to pass on the new price in full. The men replied that the arbitrators could not possibly have intended such a cut in their earnings, which they estimated to be about £1.50 a week including tips. A strike began in January 1913.

The drivers had recently changed the name of their union to the London and Provincial Licensed Vehicle Workers, in the hope of attracting London busmen into membership, but so far their success had been slight, and they had to finance the strike from their own resources. However, about a third of London's taxis were still running, either because their owners had agreed not to insist on the new charge, or because they were owner-driven. Effective picketing ensured that their drivers bought a 'ticket' from the union each day before taking their vehicles out. Initially the charge was 5p a day, rising to 10p by the end of the stoppage. Extra earnings due to the shortage of taxis helped to cover the cost of the tickets, and as the vehicles were worked on shifts, the scheme—according to the *Daily Herald* of 15 March—brought in £2,000 a week. Strike pay, initially 75p a week, was still $67\frac{1}{2}$p at the end of the strike, and the union also distributed weekly food parcels to the five thousand strikers. Those who suffered serious hardship were the six thousand garage hands put out of work by the strike. They had no union. By the beginning of March the owners were making approaches to the union. Individual companies began to make settlements. On 20 March the employers' federation capitulated, agreeing to revert to $3\frac{1}{2}$p a gallon, to reinstate the strikers, and to dismiss strike-breakers.

The drivers were probably right in their belief that the arbitrators would have fixed a maximum charge for petrol if they had envisaged a sharp increase in its price. It was unreasonable to expect the men to sustain a heavy loss of earnings at a time of general prosperity. A parallel can be drawn with the railway strike. In both instances the employers insisted on adhering to the terms of earlier settlements, despite changed circumstances. Although the final settlement showed that the cab owners were under no economic necessity to pass on the full amount, before the strike they had rejected a union offer, subsequently withdrawn, to share the increase in costs equally.

As in 1889–91, so in 1911–13 strikes of seamen and dockers had been followed by a general upsurge among unorganised or badly organised workers in a wide range of other industries. Members poured into the

'new unions of 1889' once more, or rather into those which had
survived, notably the Gasworkers and the National Amalgamated
Union of Labour, but this time an even newer union shared their gains—
the Workers Union, founded in 1898.

Circumstances were even more favourable than in 1889. A continued
high level of economic activity sustained the boom through several
years, and potential membership had grown considerably since 1889.
From the start these three unions had sought to recruit in such new and
expanding industries as chemicals and food manufacture in which the
traditional distinction between craftsmen and labourers had little
relevance. The bulk of the labour force were production workers, often
with some degree of skill but lacking craft training. In addition there
were older industries in which the traditional craft structure was
beginning to break down and pre-eminent among them, both for its size
and the speed of change, was engineering. Mechanisation and standardisation were replacing craftsmen by assemblers and automatic machine
operators, whom the craft unions refused to admit.

In those engineering centres where the Amalgamated Society of
Engineers was strong, less-skilled workers were organised mainly by the
Gasworkers and the National Amalgamated Union of Labour. In the
Midlands, however, the craftsmen themselves were ill-organised, the
National Amalgamated Union had no foothold, and the Gasworkers
were weak. Yet the Midlands was the home of the most rapidly
expanding sections of engineering, for it was there that new cycle and
motor car manufacturers had established themselves, the latter finding
'in the local brass, screw, nut and bolt, paint, pressed steel, tube, iron-
foundry, leather, spring and plating trades . . . a multitude of independent producers who could adapt themselves to the manufacture of motor
parts'.[66] The local officer of the Workers Union, John Beard, had been
organising less-skilled engineering workers in Birmingham since 1904.
During 1911 and 1912 he established a foothold in the Black Country,
built up his organising staff to five, including a woman, Julia Varley, and
developed a campaign for a minimum wage of £1.15, protesting that 'no
increases of wages had been granted during the preceding eighteen
years.

Since most employers refused to 'recognise the Workers' Union and
the demands they were putting forward',[67] conflict was inevitable.
From November 1912 to April 1913 a series of strikes and settlements
had won the £1.15 minimum in 'most of the principal firms in
Birmingham, Smethwick, and West Bromwich'.[68] Then

[66] G. C. Allen, p. 176.
[67] Leask and Bellars, p. 8.
[68] Hyman, p. 52.

Throughout the latter part of May and the whole of June the dispute spread through West Bromwich, Wolverhampton, various parts of Birmingham, and other towns in the district, involving tube works, railway carriage and waggon works, metal rolling works, boiler and bridge works, nut and bolt works and other works in allied trades,[69]

until 50,000 workers were out, a number of them craftsmen put out of work by the action of the less-skilled. Although it is a flight of fancy to ascribe the origin of the stoppage to a strike of 'some girls at Dudley' who 'lit the torch which fired the Midlands',[70] women joined the strike in large numbers, adding their demand for a 60p minimum to the men's claim for £1.15.

The union's reserves were small and most of the strikers, as non-unionists or new recruits, were not eligible for strike benefit. Local collections were arranged, barrel organs toured the streets, marchers went as far afield as Manchester and London, and a national appeal was organised. There was a good deal of public sympathy shown in gifts of food from 'local trades people', and an appeal by the mayor of Smethwick to landlords to 'show tolerance towards their tenants who were in arrears with the rent'.[71] The spirits of the strikers were also raised by the new groups of workers who continued to come out throughout its duration, and by the individual settlements with which firm after firm bought peace.

The employers formed a Midland Employers' Federation, at first to combat the union rather than to treat with it, for 'in some sections there was a strong objection to recognition of the Workers' Union, no account being taken of the fact that the Workers' Union had been organising until it had become a very powerful body'.[72] But by the middle of June they were ready to meet the union and to make an offer of £1.05. When this was rejected, Askwith, whose department had been acting with great circumspection, decided the time was ripe for his intervention and a settlement was reached on 7 July. It granted a minimum of 60p for women, and, for men, £1.15 in Birmingham, Oldbury, and Smethwick, and elsewhere £1.10, to be brought up to £1.15 in six months; and it established a procedure for dealing with future disputes. 'It created quite a new spirit in the Midlands', declared Askwith, concluding that the strike had 'perhaps been 'a blessing in disguise, because it provided methods of dealing with difficulties which proved of service during the war'.[73] The Workers Union, which had 5,000 members in 1910 and

---

[69] *Strikes and Lockouts in 1913*, p. xxiii.
[70] Askwith, p. 252, followed by Phelps Brown, p. 331. 'Just as years ago the London match-girls had started the London dock strike', wrote Askwith, with unusual licence.
[71] Leask and Bellars, p. 11.
[72] Askwith, p. 253.
[73] Ibid., p. 256.

23,000 at the end of 1912, claimed 91,000 in December 1913. Within a year it had risen from obscurity to a place among the country's half dozen major unions.

Dublin, 1913–14

In sharp contrast to the period of the 'new unionism', the counter-attack of the London port employers in 1912 did not lead to a general offensive against the unions in other British ports. Instead the new arrangements for collective bargaining were maintained and consolidated. Only in Dublin was London's example followed.

Up to 1913 events there had taken much the same course as in Great Britain, the main beneficiary being the Irish Transport and General Workers Union, set up in 1908 as the result of a breakaway from the Liverpool Dockers. Its leader, James Larkin, who had up to then been one of Sexton's organisers, was a flamboyant orator and charismatic leader, whose main achievement was 'to raise the whole of industrial trade union activity to a higher level of significance, to involve not merely the professional trade unionists but the great mass of the people'.[74] He was widely regarded as a syndicalist, and in 1909 he was joined by James Connolly,[75] one of the outstanding theorists of industrial unionism, who was to become his second-in-command. Nevertheless Larkin was no orthodox syndicalist. Not only did he win a seat on the Dublin Council in 1912, along with four other Labour candidates,[76] but he was also prepared to propose a comprehensive system of wages boards for Ireland, with power to arbitrate, as an alternative to industrial conflict. Moreover, his union was no industrial union. It had spread from docks and road transport to factories, breweries, building sites, and even to agriculture.

However, in the circumstances of Dublin at that time, with its slums, its 'poverty, low wages, and bad conditions . . . mingled with . . . the prejudices of politics and religion . . . amongst both employers and employed',[77] Larkin unquestionably believed in the use of militant methods. 'Especially in 1913', the union initiated a 'large number of sectional strikes. . . . Many of these . . . were of a sympathetic character, aiming at the complete dislocation of the trade or firms involved in disputes by the refusal of other firms to handle their goods.'[78] Larkin

[34] McCarthy, p. 21.

[75] Connolly had just returned after several years in America working for the Socialist Labour Party, the Detroit Industrialist Workers of the World, and finally the less sectarian Socialist Party of America.

[76] After a few weeks on the Council, he was ruled ineligible as a convicted felon, having been sentenced to prison for his part in a strike in Cork in 1909 where strong-arm methods were liberally used.

[77] Askwith, p. 259.   [78] *Strikes and Lockouts in 1913*, p. xxv.

was willing to sign agreements with employers, but he showed little compunction about breaking them afterwards. The employers also accused him of using widespread intimidation in recruiting members and maintaining strikes, an accusation easily supported by quotations from the union's highly popular newspaper, *The Irish Worker and People's Advocate*, which Larkin edited.[79]

In August 1913 W. M. Murphy, a Dublin employer with diverse interests and a reputation as a hard man but fair, decided to be done with Larkin. He dismissed from the dispatch department of his paper, the *Independent*, all those who would not repudiate the Irish Transport and General Workers Union—about half the staff—and then warned the Dublin tramwaymen, among whom the union was agitating for improved conditions, that anyone using intimidation to recruit to the union would be dismissed. On 23 August the dockers organised a boycott of the *Independent*'s distributors. The port employers called Larkin's attention to an agreement which he had signed on 2 June undertaking not to strike until after a dispute had been through the agreed procedure. For a day or two Larkin havered, and then told the employers he could not restrain his members. On 26 August the tramwaymen were called out, but enough stayed at work to maintain a restricted service.

The union's attempt to picket the trams got out of hand, and from 30 August to 1 September Dublin was the scene of continuous riots and fighting. Two men were killed and hundreds arrested. Larkin was arrested on a charge of incitement to violence, released on bail, arrested on a second charge, and subsequently released again. More and more employers supported Murphy, and on 3 September four hundred, in a variety of industries, pledged themselves to cease employing members of the union. Others subsequently joined them.

On 1 September the annual meeting of the Trades Union Congress at Manchester dealt with the Dublin issue as a matter of urgency,[80] and decided to send a delegation to Dublin 'to address meetings in favour of free speech, the right of organisation and free meeting; and to inquire into the allegations of police brutality'. Advised from the Castle that

[79] The issue of 19 August 1911 stated that 'when a man deserts from our side in time of war (for a strike is a war between capital and labour) he . . . forfeits his life to us. If England is justified in shooting those who desert to the enemy, we are also justified in killing a scab. If it is wrong to take a scab's life, it is right for British soldiers to desert to the enemy in war-time. You can't have it both ways.' (Wright, p. 58.) Larkin afterwards disclaimed foreknowledge of the article and argued only for meeting 'violence with violence in self-defence' (issue of 7 October 1911, quoted Ibid.).

[80] Tillett described 'this Liberal government as a bloody Government . . . which has scotched our liberties. . . . It is clear that the man who has the pluck to strike must have in mind the right to have firearms and to use them (Cheers). War has been declared on the workers.' (Trades Union Congress, 1913, pp. 70–72.)

they were taking their lives in their hands, the delegates nevertheless held their public meetings in favour of freedom of speech and freedom of combination. They reported that the employers 'are determined to crush out Trade Unionism in Dublin' with the support of the 'Castle Authorities', who were 'using military authority and armed force to assist the employers in coercing Trade Unionists into abject subjection'.[81]

Much depended on what material assistance the English unions might decide to give, since Larkin's union, forced to support the majority of its members, was soon in financial difficulty. Crossing to England to whip up a campaign, he was met with the news that the National Union of Railwaymen (as the Amalgamated Society of Railway Servants had now become) had ordered back to work the 7,000 men who had refused to handle 'tainted goods'.[82] Only the most sanguine militant could have hoped that, when the Parliamentary Committee met on 23 September, they would impose any kind of strike or boycott in support of the Dublin workers. They had no constitutional power to do anything of the kind, and almost to a man they were moderate leaders such as Larkin constantly abused in his speeches and the columns of the *Irish Worker*.[83] In the circumstances, their decision was prompt and bold, reflecting the widespread sympathy with the Irish union among their own members, as well as general hostility to the attitude of the Irish employers among all classes in Britain. They decided to raise a fund, pledging £5,000 to begin with, and to send food-ships to Dublin.

The government also took a hand by appointing a 'court of inquiry' whose members were Askwith, Sir Thomas Ratcliffe Ellis and J. R. Clynes. They opened their hearings at Dublin Castle on 29 September and reported on 14 October, finding fault with both sides, and recommending them to establish an agreed conciliation scheme. On the same day the employers reiterated their refusal to deal with the union unless it was 'reorganised on proper lines ... with new officials who have met with the approval of the British Joint Labour Board'.[84]

The stoppage continued. Larkin was brought to trial on 27 October and sentenced to seven months, but so great was the outcry that he was

---

[81] Ibid., 1915, pp. 111, 114.

[82] Even the militants on the executive could not deny that the principle of 'tainted goods' would involve their members in bearing the brunt of almost every strike. All they could do was to urge the Parliamentary Committee to call a national conference on the matter (Railwaymen's executive, 15–25 September 1913).

[83] 'Our whole trade union movement is absolutely rotten.' he said at Manchester on 14 September. 'If we were the men we think we are the employing class would be wiped out within the hour' (Wright, p. 172). As for the Labour Party in the House, on 10 October he likened its members to 'mummies in a museum' (Ibid., p. 215).

[84] Wright, Appendix II.

released on 13 November.[85] Meanwhile the Parliamentary Committee became more closely involved in the dispute, for on 25 October James Seddon of the Shop Assistants, who was representing them in Dublin, wired that the position there was 'desperate' and money was needed for strike pay. Two days later he arrived to plead the case in person.[86] Up to this point the committee had insisted that their fund, which was mounting apace, was for food alone. They had refused a request for a loan from the Dublin Trades Council which had taken over formal responsibility for the dispute. Now they sent Seddon back with Gosling and Bowerman and authority to disburse £2,000; and from the beginning of November the committee made a weekly payment to Dublin. In the first week it worked out at 13p each for the 13,656 strikers,[87] and by January it had risen to over 20p a head.

This was not a large sum, but it must be remembered that the committee was spending more than twice that much on food, so that its total expenditure per striker was about 50p a week (the accepted rate of strike pay in many British unions) at a time when £1 was a good wage for an unskilled man in Dublin; and large sums were coming into Dublin from other sources. A further scheme to alleviate distress was to send strikers' children to English homes for the duration of the dispute; but it ran up against the opposition of the Catholic church.

At its meeting on 18 and 19 November, the Parliamentary Committee considered the 'many letters' they had received asking for a conference to consider a 'down tools policy' in support of the Dublin strikers, along with a personal appeal from Larkin and representatives of the Dublin Trades Council. When questioned about his refusal to meet with the employers and about his attitude to agreements, Larkin replied: 'We never break agreements. We are too honourable. The other side never carry them out.' Nevertheless the committee called a conference of affiliated unions for 9 December, at which the attitude of the British unions was made abundantly clear. Larkin was shouted down. With six dissentients, the conference condemned 'the unfair attacks made by men inside the Trade Union movement upon British Trade Union officials'. The main resolution, passed unanimously, was for a resumption of negotiations. A proposal from the Gasworkers for a boycott by the transport unions of 'blackleg cargo' to and from Dublin firms in dispute, and a monthly levy on British trade unions to support it, was

[85] 'The Government.' he said, 'made a mistake in sending me to prison, and they made a greater mistake in letting me out' (Ibid., p. 234).

[86] At the meeting on 18 November he justified his action by predicting that if no money had been sent, the strike would have collapsed, and its failure would have been attributed to the committee.

[87] About 1,800 of them came from unions other than the Irish Transport and General Workers—the United Labourers, the Bricklayers, and the Plasterers.

lost by a majority of eleven to one.[88] Accordingly the delegates set off once more for Dublin, where they almost succeeded in their efforts to negotiate a return to work, but the talks broke down on reinstatement.[89]

Relations with Larkin worsened. Up to the end of the year the Sailors and Firemen had been providing strike pay for their members employed by the Dublin Steam Ship Company, who had struck in sympathy. Now they decided that, as they had no dispute with the company, the men should go back to work. Larkin told them to stay out and added their number to the weekly claim for cash from the Parliamentary Committee, who indignantly refused to pay the additional sum. Finally, at the beginning of February, the strikers whose jobs were still open to them resumed work, signing an assurance 'to handle all goods and obey all orders', and in some instances also renouncing the Irish Transport and General Workers Union. From the middle of January lack of funds forced the Parliamentary Committee to stop their weekly subventions to Dublin, although they continued to send food. At the end of February they resumed payments for those without work and continued them into April. By then they had raised nearly £94,000.

London Building Workers and Yorkshire Miners, 1914

During 1911 and 1912 the building industry, which has an economic rhythm of its own, more leisurely than that of the economy as a whole, was slowly emerging from a decade of depression and unemployment, and of relative industrial peace. By 1913 a strong demand for building labour was having a marked effect on industrial relations, especially in London, where there were major strikes of painters and plasterers, and a large number of smaller stoppages, almost all of them in breach of the agreed conciliation procedures.

The industry's methods of collective bargaining were also distinctive. In each district there was a set of rules for each trade. These rules dealt with pay and hours of work, overtime and apprenticeship, but also with restrictions on the materials which the craftsmen would be prepared to handle. Perhaps the most notorious of these restrictions were the 'worked-stone' or 'dressed-stone' rules of the Stonemasons. The volume of masons' work on a building site could be greatly reduced by bringing in stone which had already been cut by machine at the quarry, and the masons sought to limit the practice. If they could not prohibit worked stone, they might insist that it was worked within the district, and therefore under local control. Alternatively, they might insist that those who worked the machines must be paid the mason's rate, for their union

---

[88] Trades Union Congress, 1915, pp. 121–2.

[89] Immediate reinstatement was agreed to be impossible, but the unions wanted fuller assurances than the employers were prepared to give.

was attempting, with some success, to organise the men who cut the stone at the quarries. Other crafts had comparable rules, such as the carpenters' rules concerning fixing joinery made outside the district.

The rules were periodically revised by negotiation through the conciliation machinery. Failure to agree locally led to reference to one of the regional conciliation boards, from which appeal lay to the national board. Contrary to normal practice, cross-voting was allowed on these boards so that a dispute might be settled in the employers' favour by a representative of one of the unions voting against his colleagues. It also happened on occasion that one or more of the representatives of the National Federation of Building Trade Employers, which supplied the employers' side of the boards, voted against the other employers and for the union proposal. The national conciliation scheme did not extent to London which had its own separate board.

There was a good deal of debate in the unions about the advantages of conciliation. Most of the officials were in favour, but a good many branches disagreed, feeling, as the Hull branch of the Stonemasons put it to their executive in July 1911, that 'the time has arrived when we should put ourselves on our old footing, and be able to enforce our rules and resist infringements promptly'. In September 1913 the Derby branch proposed that the union should withdraw from the conciliation scheme but a ballot went in favour of staying in by 660 to 229. The Operative Bricklayers, however, had voted two months earlier to withdraw by 2,204 votes to 1,183, and subsequently gave the required six months' notice to the employers. There were rumblings in the other unions.

The issue which caused most trouble, because it affected all the unions, was non-unionism, or the 'no-disability rule' as it was called in the building trade, for rules which required trade unionists to work with non-unionists were rules which laid down that non-unionists should suffer no disability because they were outside the union. All the unions accepted the right of their members to refuse to work with non-unionists—a particularly important aid to union strength in a casual industry in which union organisation had to be established from scratch on each new building site. As Griffith Jones, one of the Stonemasons' organisers, put it:

In my opinion, the question of working with a non-union man does not come within the purview of the conciliation rules; in fact, it is a principle that does not admit of conciliation. We cannot conciliate on fundamental principles. . . . Times there are when we are compelled to work with non-union men, but it is because we have not the power to force them into our ranks.[90]

[90] Operative Stone Masons Society, *Journal*, 5 March 1913.

Jones, it should be noted, was a firm supporter of conciliation, attacks on which he attributed to the syndicalists, 'whose chief pastime is to misrepresent and discredit every union official who does not happen to accept Syndicalism'.[91]

It is also relevant that the national conciliation agreement included no rule on non-unionism. The employers argued that the rule permitting any subject to be brought up by either party entitled them to raise the question, and in May 1912 the Leeds joiners were censured by the National Conciliation Board for striking against non-unionists. However, Jones argued this was due to a bricklayer who had voted with the employers, and could not be held to settle the principle.

London, by contrast, had a no-disability rule which forbade the unions to support strikes against non-unionists, and the Plasterers, who had their own conciliation machinery, had agreed a rule allowing them to object to 'a defaulter to his society' or to a man 'who has made himself specially objectionable',[92] but, if the employer did not accept their objections, the dispute had to be submitted to the conciliation board before a strike could be called. Nevertheless London building trade unionists did not regard themselves as bound by these rules. Following a general increase in pay in 1912,

it became a question of paramount importance now as to what steps should be taken to bring into line all those non-members who were participating in the improved rate but not paying to support it. As a result there gradually developed a policy through the LBIF [the London Building Industries Federation—the joint body of the London building unions] for taking joint action to bring about the desired result. Periodical ticket inspections were held on the jobs, with the result that where non-unionists were working several strikes occurred, and on the introduction of blacklegs the other Trade Unions left the job. . . . [The London Master Builders] quite failed to see that friction was being caused owing to the new spirit prevailing among Trade Unionists generally, and how irritating to the operatives was the disability rule, and by its removal alone could peace be assured.[93]

Out of at least forty-eight strikes in London between May 1913 and January 1914, no less than 'seventeen strikes affecting twenty firms [were] against sub-contracted non-union labour'.[94] On 23 December 1913 the London Master Builders met the London unions to ask them to discipline union members who struck in breach of the conciliation procedure and to deposit financial guarantees against such strikes. The

[91] Ibid., 8 January 1913.

[92] Operative Bricklayers Society, *Trade Circular and General Reporter*, May 1914.

[93] Operative Stone Masons Society, *Report and Financial Statement of the Central Dispute Committee*, 1914.

[94] Price, p. 258.

Bricklayers' representatives refused and left, followed by those of the Plasterers and Cranedrivers. The other unions prevaricated.

On 7 January 1914 the London employers announced that they were withdrawing from the conciliation agreement. Henceforth they would offer each worker an individual contract—to be enforced by a penalty of £1—binding him to work peaceably with non-unionists. They claimed that they had 'no desire to permanently adopt the principle of individual guarantee; it was only adopted whilst a collective guarantee was withheld'.[95] The unions instructed their members not to sign, and the employers issued lockout notices which became effective on 24 January. Meanwhile the London Building Industries Federation called a meeting of London branch delegates which approved counter-proposals: the no-disability and conciliation rules were to be abolished; the federation was to be the only bargaining agent in London; all overtime was to cease; and card stewards were to be recognised on the sites.

On 28 January the National Federation of Building Trade Employers resolved that unless the unions could assure them that agreements would be 'backed by sufficient disciplinary power and [they] will use such power to secure their observance, it would be better to cancel such agreements'; but they did not take up the London scheme for individual contracts. For their part the national unions refused to back the demands of the London Building Industries Federation, but authorised strike pay. The rate in the craft unions was 75p. With their funds exhausted by their 1913 strike in London, the Plasterers had to order a 10p a week levy at the beginning of February, followed by the Operative Bricklayers with 5p. The Amalgamated Carpenters and Joiners could afford to wait until the beginning of April and settle for a rate of 1.25p, which was doubled in May.

As early as 16 January *The Builder* had commented:

The issues are regarded as vital ones by both parties, so the struggle may be long and the result dubious. Whichever way it turns out, however, a *modus vivendi* must be found between the parties in the end, and, if then, why not now and save a demoralising struggle which may spread far beyond the London area?

These sentiments probably represented a widespread opinion. Early in February Bowerman, secretary of Congress, tried his hand at conciliation, but found that the London employers would have nothing to do with the London Building Industries Federation. In any event, the parties in London were much too far apart to give an outside conciliator any effective starting-point at this stage. In March the two sides of the National Conciliation Board decided that it was time to intervene, and

[95] Ibid., p. 259.

over the next few weeks they worked out a compromise, along with representatives of the London employers and unions. Terms were agreed on 17 April: the individual contracts were to be forgotten, and a revised version of the 'objectionable workmen' clause in the Plasterers' rules was to be extended to the other trades. In return there were to be no card inspections on site without the employer's permission; the unions were to guarantee the enforcement of the new rules 'in every respect', and, if necessary, to use their disciplinary powers 'to the utmost extent'. Henceforth London was to be included in the national conciliation scheme.[96]

The strikers rejected these terms by 23,481 votes to 2,021; but the Stonemasons voted for acceptance by 460 to 449. The negotiators were now left with little room for manoeuvre. All they could do was to refurbish the proposals with minor concessions, and submit them to further ballots, which they did in May and again in June. On the first occasion they were rejected by 21,077 to 5,724 (with several small unions joining the Stonemasons in giving approval) and in June by 14,081 to 4,565 (the Stonemasons voting 866–107 in favour).

On 23 June the executive of the National Federation of Building Trade Employers resolved to ballot their members on a proposal for a national lockout if the London dispute was not settled. On 24 June a meeting of London district committees of the unions decided that they should make individual approaches to the London employers, provided no union went back to work until all had settled. On 4 July the London Stonemasons signed an agreement, and started work two days later. Several minor unions followed their example, but the other main craft unions introduced various sectional claims which hindered agreement; and when they did reach settlements, their members rejected them. On 24 July the Operative Bricklayers voted against their latest terms by 1,853 to 825. On 28 July the national employers decided to inform the unions of the result of their ballot which had endorsed the proposal for a lockout by 7,319 votes to 1,739; and to fix the date for 15 August. At last the national union executives acted with resolution. New terms were agreed including reinstatement as soon as practicable, and when the London district committees of the Operative Bricklayers and the Amalgamated Carpenters and Joiners proposed a further ballot, their executives settled over their heads.

Why did the strikers hold out for so long against any compromise? The London Master Builders employed a minority of London building workers. The Labour Department's estimate of the number of building workers locked out was 20,000, less than a fifth of the total number of construction workes in the London area. The unions therefore had

[96] Higenbottam, pp. 186–8.

many members at work on whom the district committees imposed heavy additional levies (the Stonemasons levied 5p a day, and the Operative Bricklayers 2.5p). This gave them substantial sums with which to augment national strike pay, support non-unionists who refused to work on the employers' terms, and assist the hard-pressed labourers' unions. In addition, because of the current demand for building labour, many of those locked out found jobs, either in London or outside, thus reducing the cost of strike pay and adding to the number of those paying the levies.

The one exception was the Stonemasons. Stone was used mainly on large buildings in central London, for which the contracts were held by the big firms which belonged to the London Master Builders Association. Few of the smaller builders had any use for a mason. Consequently the majority of the union's London members were locked out, and the numbers actually rose during the dispute. Their London strike committee contrasted the situation with that of the other unions:

One large society who are voting almost unanimously against a settlement has scarcely a member on the [strike] roll; another has, according to their own figure, about 75 per cent at work for non-associated firms.[97]

In March the London unions decided on measures to step up pressure on the employers, including the withdrawal of labour from firms working on subcontract for members of the London Master Builders Association. This decision also affected the Stonemasons more than other unions. Many of the subcontractors concerned worked the quarries which delivered stone to London, and their union recruited the men who cut the stone. The decision was approved by the union executive, a local executive chosen from the Manchester district which included several syndicalists, but the London district appealed to the General Council which represented the whole country. The General Council voted by post. Six opposed the extension of the dispute to subcontractors, one abstained, and one (another syndicalist) gave it his approval. Thereafter the quarrel between London and the executive continued. Early in June the General Council took over the conduct of the union, and the executive resigned in protest.

There were syndicalists in the other building unions, notably in the London district of the Operative Bricklayers. The most prominent was George Hicks, formerly chairman of the executive, who was appointed a temporary national organiser in 1912, and confirmed in the post by ballot at the end of 1913; but his official duties limited his participation in the dispute. More active were J. V. Wills, a Labour Councillor and prominent member of the Plebs League, and Harry Adams, the London

[97] Operative Stone Masons Society, *Journal*, 24 June 1914.

district secretary. However, it seems unlikely that they had a major influence on the successive rejections of proposed terms of settlement. Among the major building unions, the Amalgamated Carpenters and Joiners were probably the least affected by syndicalist ideas, yet their London members gave larger majorities against the terms than those of some of the other unions, and their London district committee held out until the end. The executive had to take over the management of the London district in order to get the agreement signed. The main influences at work were devotion to craft control and local independence, coupled with the absence of those financial pressures for a settlement which normally operate during a prolonged strike.

Devotion to craft control and local autonomy also help to explain the long delay before the national executives intervened decisively to close down the dispute, but some of the unions had another reason for their indecision. In July 1914 the Plasterers' *Monthly Report* noted that several districts had asked for a ballot on a proposal to include provincial representatives on what had been up to then a local London executive, and commented: 'It is quite clear in the present dispute—also the one last year in London—that the EC are either ruled or influenced by their London district committee.' The Operative Bricklayers also had a London executive.

In its origin this stoppage had much in common with the Weavers' lockout of 1911–12. In both disputes the employers felt that the unions were asserting a right to intervene in their business which must be repudiated by a lockout. However, whereas the Weavers' leaders were able to retreat quickly once they realised their mistake, the national leaders of most of the building unions could not persuade their London members to approve any of the successive modifications of the original terms which they were able to obtain from the employers. Continued levies and favourable economic circumstances allowed the stoppage to drag on for seven months, until the union executives finally plucked up the courage to close it down.

By that time the third great coalmining strike of the period had come and gone. The Minimum Wage Act said nothing about adjusting the minimum rates in step with general wage changes in the various coalfields. Some minimum wage boards arranged for automatic adjustment, and others left it to the union to apply to them for an increase in the minimum in step with any increase which might be granted by the relevant conciliation board. Among the latter districts were South Yorkshire and West Yorkshire (each district in the Federated Area having its own minimum wage board). However, the conciliation board for the Federated area decided that the increases in standard rates which they awarded, amounting to 15 per cent by April 1913, should, for those workers who would have been earning less that their minimum rates but for the Act, be added to those minimum rates, and not to their (lower) standard rates.

Early in 1914, Sir Edward Clarke, chairman of the South Yorkshire board, awarded increases in the minimum rates, that for colliers being from 34p to 36p. The miners claimed that the 15 per cent should now be added to the new rates, but the most that Sir Edward would say was that it appeared to him that this should be so in view of the conciliation board's decision. However, influenced by a downturn in prices, the owners asserted that they were under no obligation to pay more than the bare statutory minimum. The union leaders tried to persuade their members to stay at work until the conciliation board had a chance to give its verdict, but the men felt they had been cheated, and a strike which started in Rotherham spread throughout the district and lasted for five weeks, many of the pits in the West Yorkshire district stopping in sympathy. Eventually the conciliation board and the minimum wage board between them proposed that the percentages should be added to the new, higher rate except where a colliery could be proved to the minimum wage board to be unprofitable at that rate. These terms were accepted by the men. 'There ensued a most unusual eagerness on the part of many colliery managements to disclose the entire details of their working costs to the workmen's representatives.'[98] In asserting their legal right to pay no more than the statutory minimum, and thereby denying to many miners the wage increases to which they believed they were entitled, the Yorkshire owners had acted in much the same spirit as the railway companies in 1911 and the London cab owners in 1913.

Causes Reviewed

Five of the fourteen major strikes of 1911–14—the three waterfront strikes of 1911, the jute strike of 1912 and the Midlands strike of 1913—were the result of resistance by employers to claims for wage increases and union recognition which accompanied an upsurge of union recruitment among ill-organised workers. Two more major stoppages—the London dock strike of 1912 and the Dublin lockout of 1913–14—were further consequences of the same series of events. They arose from counter-attacks by employers aimed to push the unions back from the positions they had occupied as a result of the upsurge.

This wave of strikes also affected other industries beyond those directly involved. The railway strike began unofficially in Liverpool where railway trade unionists were in close contact with the resurgent unions of seamen, dockers and carters, and it spread in much the same way as the waterfront strikes had spread during the two previous

[98] Jevons, p. 597.

months. Although the railway unions were relatively well-established, they had not achieved direct recognition from the railway companies, and their leaders were desperately anxious to get it. When these leaders took over the strike, they made recognition its primary aim, just as it had been a major aim of Sexton, Tillett and Havelock on the waterfront.

The extraordinary series of victories won by the transport strikes of 1911 was bound to encourage many other unions to believe that the time was now ripe to advance beyond the defensive positions which most of them had occupied for some years past; and the spread of rapid union growth from the waterfront and general unions to established unions was a further boost to confidence. The Weavers and London building workers might not have pressed the closed shop in such an open and militant fashion unless their expectations had been raised in this way.

However, there was little reason for the Miners to be overconfident. Their membership was almost stationary through 1911 and 1912. The economic trends in their industry were unaccountably gloomy. The South Wales Miners were indeed in an aggressive mood in 1910, especially those in the Rhondda and Aberdare, but this mood did not survive the Cambrian dispute. The national leaders handled the minimum wage issue with impressive caution, giving ample time for repeated negotiations with the owners before taking a leisurely ballot and giving notice of a strike. It is the behaviour of the owners which needs to be explained.

In 1910 the South Wales owners were as militant as their employees, and thereafter more so. The claim for a minimum wage was not a revolutionary, nor necessarily a very costly, demand, but the owners rejected it. The adverse trends in productivity and coal prices which depressed miners' earnings and gave rise to the demand for the minimum wage also eroded profit margins, putting pressure on the owners to resist the claim; and in addition general wage claims were ruled out in the Federated Area and Scotland until the owners had recouped the cost of forgoing wage cuts in the depression. Similarly the railway companies were inhibited from entertaining wage demands in 1911, both by their existing settlements which still had some years to run, and by statutory limitation of the rates they could charge. The London cab employers were faced with a staggering jump in the price of petrol and insisted that their drivers must honour the terms of an arbitration award by meeting the increased charge. In 1914 the Yorkshire coalowners departed from their previous practice in interpreting minimum wage awards, and insisted on a narrow reading of their obligations under the Act, because they faced a fall in coal prices.

Thus nearly all the major strikes in 1911–14 can be largely accounted for by two factors: firstly, the boom in union organisation which was a repetition of 1871–3 and 1889–90; and, secondly, the adverse cost position of a few groups of employers, notably the coalowners and the railway companies, which, in conjunction with the terms of their current wage agreements, impelled them to reject what might otherwise have been considered not unreasonable demands.

What of the other suggested causes of industrial unrest set out at the beginning of the chapter? It would be idle to deny that the fall in real wages since 1900 must have had a considerable influence on the attitude of wage-earners. However, the series of 'organisation' strikes in 1871–3 and 1889–90 had not followed periods of falling real wages. It is therefore reasonable to conclude that it was the recurrence in 1911 of circumstances similar to those of 1871 and 1889 which prompted another series. In most of the remaining strikes it was the attitude of the employers which was crucial, and they were influenced by costs, not retail prices.

In four of the stoppages—the Cambrian strike, the general transport strike in Liverpool, and the lockouts in Dublin and the London building trade—a significant part was played by syndicalists, or men like Larkin, who sympathised with syndicalist aims and practised their methods. The Liverpool strike, however, was a desperate attempt to cover up a potentially disastrous unofficial stoppage on the Liverpool docks, and was terminated as soon as was decently possible. The other three stoppages affected relatively small groups of workers and might not have made such a mark for themselves if they had not been so prolonged. All three could have been settled much earlier on terms as good as were available at the end, or better. In South Wales the only rational purpose for continuing was to provoke a national coal strike; in Dublin it was to provoke a boycott of Irish goods in Britain, which could have led to a general transport stoppage throughout the country; and in the London building lockout the strikers, apart from the Stonemasons, were under no pressure to settle. The Cambrian, Dublin and London strikers were financed by bodies which did not control them, and which were slow to cut off their subventions even when it became clear that the strikers could not win: the rest of South Wales and the Miners Federation in the Cambrian dispute; the Trades Union Congress in Dublin; and the provincial building trade unionists in London.

There was little to connect industrial unrest with suffragette agitation or the drift towards civil war in Ireland. Although most trade union leaders were supporters of votes for women, the suffragette movement was predominantly middle class, whereas trade unionism was predominantly working class. The only occasion when British union leaders, most of them Home Rulers, were seriously confronted with Irish problems was at the time of the Dublin lockout. They were then ready to give generous financial support, but throughout they refused any form of sympathetic industrial action.

It is, of course, impossible to deny that there was a spirit of industrial unrest abroad in those years. It can be glimpsed through the record of events—in the spontaneity of the 1911 transport and 1913 Midlands strikes; in the response to Tom Mann's recruiting campaign on the waterfront; in the proliferation of syndicalist and industrial unionist groups and journals; in the emergence of factions of enthusiasts for industrial action in the Independent Labour Party, the British Socialist Party, and even among the Fabians.

This spirit is best illustrated by a new newspaper which first appeared on 15 April 1912, announcing that it was 'run by Labour men in Labour's own interest', promising the unions that it would be 'a persistent and fearless advocate of their principles', and telling 'Socialists and Industrial Unionists' that its columns were available 'for the open expression of their views'. This was the *Daily Herald*. The title had been used by the strike committee which ran the London printing dispute in 1911. Their news-sheet appeared from January to April that year, and left behind aspirations for a permanent Labour daily and a committee which included Tillett and later George Lansbury, who subsequently became editor of the new newspaper. In stark contrast to the staid *Daily Citizen*, started at much the same time as the official organ of the Labour movement, the *Herald* provided expression and focus for the mood of rebellion and the boundless enthusiasm of young left-wing intellectuals and active trade unionists. Charles Lapworth, who preceded Lansbury as editor, saw to it that the paper supported every strike. From its columns G. D. H. Cole and William Mellor expounded their 'Greater Unionism', which might be described as a sophisticated syndicalism. Desperately short of money itself, the *Herald* nevertheless organised its own fund to support the London dockers, and gave its unwavering backing to the workers locked out in Dublin and in the London building dispute. A *Herald* League of supporters throughout the country helped to spread its enthusiasms and to collect money for the paper and for strikers. But all this was not a *cause* of unrest. Rather it was one of its manifestations.

3

Collective Bargaining, the Government, and Union Structure

The Crafts, Coal, and Cotton

EVEN in a period of outstanding industrial unrest, an examination of strikes presents a very limited aspect of trade unionism; and an examination confined to major strikes is even more restricted. A stoppage not included in the list of major strikes, the London printing dispute at the beginning of 1911, provided a classic example of traditional craft union methods; and the way the same issue was handled in the provinces showed how these methods were being modified by collective bargaining.

A claim for a uniform forty-eight hour working week submitted by the Printing and Kindred Trades Federation two years earlier had been discussed with the employers at several conferences, and the time was near when the unions must act or draw back. Already chafing at the delay, the London unions, led by the Compositors, had formed their strike committee, and held a rally at the Albert Hall on 31 December 1910. The provincial unions met separately on 8 January in a more apprehensive mood. He 'admired the courage of the Londoners', said Templeton of the Scottish Typographical Association, 'but they must look after the interests of their own unions'.[1] There were some cities, such as Manchester and Liverpool, where their branches rivalled the strength of the London Compositors, but there were also many smaller centres where they were relatively weak. Two days later the federation put a compromise proposal for a fifty-hour week to the employers, who countered with an offer of fifty-two hours. On 13 January this was rejected by the federation, but it was also decided, against the opposition of the Londoners, not to tender notices. The door would thus be open for further negotiation.

The London unions now went ahead on their own, revising their claim to fifty hours with a guarantee of no further changes for five years. By 4 February, when the notices ran out, 350 London firms, including most of the large offices, had agreed to these terms. The London

[1] The minutes of this meeting are included in the Typographical Association's *Executive Minutes* for 1911.

newspapers were not affected since, some years earlier, they had formed their own association, the Newspaper Proprietors Association, with the intention of keeping out of disputes in the general trade; nor was the Stationery Office. The Compositors therefore began the stoppage with only 1,613 of their 12,000 members on strike pay, although there were also 874 on unemployment benefit.

Impressive resources were assembled to meet the needs of the strikers. At the beginning of the year the Compositors' funds stood just short of £65,000. Throughout the year weekly levies were imposed on members at work, at the rate of 25p a week during the dispute, with those working at newspaper offices paying an extra 25p a week for the first five weeks, and 15p a week for the next six weeks. The Printing and Kindred Trades Federation decided that the London unions were entitled to federation strike benefit and the General Federation of Trade Unions also paid out. The Compositors' total income for 1910 had been almost £45,000; for 1911 it was over £117,000.

Although the employers' association refused to surrender, the number of strikers continued to fall, and in July, when over five hundred firms had agreed to their terms, the unions decided that each of them should wind up the dispute separately, so long as no agreement was signed for more than fifty hours a week. By the end of the year the Compositors estimated that six hundred members were still out of work due to the dispute, most of them now on unemployment benefit. On 29 October 1912 the government announced their acceptance of the fifty-hour week as the standard under the fair wages resolution. At the end of 1912 the Compositors still had no agreement with the employers' association, 'although', reported the executive, 'our transactions with union employers, including those who are members of the Association, are of the most friendly character.' However, in 1914 a dispute over bank holiday pay led to a renewal of relationships with the association, and an agreement. Individual firms which had been struck off the union's 'fair list' in 1911 were being reinstated as late as 1918.

Meanwhile Herbert Skinner, secretary of the Typographical Association, had arranged a further meeting at the beginning of March with the British Federation of Master Printers and the associations representing the provincial newspapers. They agreed on a working week of fifty-one hours, to be reached in stages. Those working fifty-two hours or less were to shift to fifty-one; the rest should be brought down by one hour with further reductions at annual intervals until the fifty-one-hour week became the universal standard.

Concurrently with these discussions the Typographical Association had been negotiating over their working practices. In contrast to most other craft societies, the Typographers drew up national rules, not district rules, on such matters as apprenticeship, the jobs reserved for craftsmen, limits on the amount of work to be performed in a day, transfers between jobs, and overtime; and tried to get employers to apply them across the country. The 1908 quinquennial conference had revised the rules, and added another which asserted their right to represent provincial machine managers. The employers protested. Protracted negotiations followed, in which the employers insisted on an increase in the ratio of apprentices to craftsmen, and the inclusion of a procedure for settling disputes (a 'committee of reference') which had been one of their objectives for some time. Agreement was reached in May 1911, and subsequently ratified by the union members.

Nevertheless the delegates to the next conference of the Typographical Association in 1913 were not satisfied with the agreement. They altered several rules, and resolved that agreements should in future be put to a ballot before they were finalised. Negotiations were begun the following summer, but adjourned on the outbreak of war.

A similar series of events had occurred in Scotland where the parties were the Scottish Typographical Association and the Scottish branch of the Master Printers Federation. In 1913 the union attempted to impose on the employers a set of rules drawn up by their conference in 1911. The employers forced them to negotiate by threatening a lockout, and an agreement was reached in 1914.

Although successive conferences of the Typographical Association adopted belligerent postures over their rules, the approach of their officials to enforcing them on individual firms was conciliatory. The executive minutes for those years show that the union secretary and organisers spent much of their time visiting firms to persuade their managers to pay district rates, to comply with the new agreement on hours of work, and to discuss ways in which they could conform with the rules on the exclusion of female compositors, the employment of non-unionists, the limit on the number of apprentices and the payment for, and limitation of, overtime. The union officials were particularly helpful in suggesting means whereby non-union firms could gain union recognition. In May 1912, for example, an employer in Ulverston was told that if he 'promised not to take any more females and allow their number to gradually dwindle away, the Executive Council would accept the men as members'. The sanction of withdrawing union members from an offending firm was employed only with great reluctance. The executive was more willing to grant victimisation pay to an individual who had given up his job at such a firm, but even then they insisted that he substantiate his claim that he had left because the rules were being broken.

The issues which the Typographical Association sought to regulate nationally in printing were subject to district regulation in engineering. By 1910 a number of the Engineers' district committees were settling them by agreement with the local employers' associations. Others still relied on unilateral action, but as one of the organisers remarked of Coventry in 1910:[2]

As in the case of many other districts the so-called 'district rules' have been largely an expression of pious aspirations, some of them meeting with fairly general support, others having little relation to actual workshop practice.

Over the next four years many more district agreements were concluded, constituting a substantial extension of collective bargaining in the engineering industry.

For the most part these negotiations appear to have been amicable. Controversy centred on two issues regulated by national agreement: the manning of machines governed by the 1898 agreement, as revised in 1907, and the premium bonus system of payment by results—the main characteristic of which was that earnings rose proportionately less as output increased—governed by a separate memorandum drawn up in 1902. The other engineering unions also objected to the premium bonus system, for the employers sought to introduce it wherever they could, regardless of whether the union concerned had signed the memorandum or not. Some unions objected because they were opposed to all forms of payment by result, and others because they preferred straight piecework.

For two years the unions which were affected had been trying to agree on a joint programme of action to abolish premium bonus, but in 1911 they decided to leave the matter to a more opportune occasion. Thus 'the question of joint action to procure the abolition of a system which had been universally condemned, especially by those who did not work it, came to an untimely, painless, and inglorious end';[3] but discontent continued, at least among the Engineers.

The manning of machines was not a general issue, for most of the smaller skilled societies were less affected by mechanisation than were the Engineers. The agreement gave employers 'full discretion to appoint the men they consider suitable to work all their machine tools', and the 1907 revision included a recommendation from their federation to do what they could for those who might be displaced. Despite their acceptance of managerial prerogative in the agreement, the Engineers were now beginning to challenge individual cases through the procedure, and beyond. Early in 1911 a Blackburn case was settled in the employer's favour at a central conference between the federation and the union. The men continued to resist, and local discussions ran on with

[2] *Monthly Report*, January 1910.   [3] Mosses, p. 214.

the federation's approval until August 1912, when the men struck. Subsequently, they rejected a compromise worked out between the federation and the Engineers' executive. The other engineering unions at Blackburn threatened to close the firm down unless it withdrew the men who had been employed to replace the strikers. Even then the federation did not retaliate, and in December further concessions at last brought an agreement. In their report for 1913, the emergency committee of the federation advised that

it was most desirable that nothing should be done which would increase the existing tension, and instructed that every firm should be requested to exercise the greatest care in connection with this question.

This conciliatory approach by the federation did not deter the 1912 delegate conference of the Engineers from instructing the executive to hold ballots on withdrawal from the premium bonus memorandum and the 1907 agreement, nor the members from voting in favour by majorities of five to one in each case. After these results were announced in December 1913, the Engineers and other signatory unions gave notice to terminate. The consequences would have been their withdrawal from the conciliation procedure which was part of the 1907 agreement, had not the federation persuaded the union executives to sign a new agreement in April 1914 dealing only with procedure, leaving out the sections on non-unionists, piecework, overtime, and manning included in 1898 and 1907. The first stage of procedure was still a deputation of workmen meeting with their employer, but they could now be accompanied by a full-time union officer, and if so a representative of the local employers' association was to be present as well. The professionals on both sides must have welcomed this opportunity to influence their members' conduct of disputes while still under discussion in the plant.

Two other issues which came to the front in 1914 were the forty-eight-hour working week and the closed shop. During the discussions on procedure, the federation had indicated to the unions that they might be willing to listen to a claim for a forty-eight-hour week. At first they asked for an assurance that there would be no loss of output, which the unions could not give, but, by the end of July, the employers were nevertheless prepared to discuss a more modest reduction in the working week. Then the war brought negotiations to a halt. A few weeks before, however, the district committee of the Federation of Shipbuilding and Engineering Trades on Merseyside persuaded the local shiprepairing employers to grant a forty-seven-hour working week.

Once the 1907 agreement had lapsed there was nothing to prevent the unions from raising the non-unionist question, and the Engineers'

Glasgow district brought it before a central conference in July 1914 as a local issue. The federation replied that 'it was open to the society to take what action they pleased, but it was also open to the Federation to take what action it considered necessary to assist any firm or district that was attacked'.[4] The union executive and organisers met to consider what was to be done. They decided that it would be 'inimical to the best interests of the society to take drastic action on the non-union question at the present juncture'.[5]

Even after the revisions which they had secured in 1910, the Boilermakers remained unhappy with the shipbuilding procedure agreement, primarily because it prohibited rapid action by them to enforce their claims in piecework disputes. The union held a ballot early in 1912, in which the members decided to do without a national procedure. Notice was therefore given to the employers. John Hill, the secretary, commented that 'no more wanton attack will ever be made upon our Society without an agreement than was made on us eighteen months ago under an agreement'.[6] The executive went back to the employers, against Hill's advice, with a proposal for a revised procedure that would leave local disputes to be determined in the districts. The union members voted for it, but the employers rejected it, and for many years thereafter the Boilermakers remained outside the shipbuilding procedure. When the other shipyard unions agreed to a procedure for dealing with demarcation disputes in 1912, the Boilermakers rejected it, too, because it provided for an employer to take the chair with power to decide issues on which the unions could not agree.

Two other topics of controversy were apprenticeship and discharge notes. To meet a current labour shortage in 1911 the employers wanted to amend their agreement with the Boilermakers to permit adult apprentices. The union submitted alternative proposals, including the introduction of indentured apprenticeships to give the apprentices security of employment until they had served their time. No agreement was reached, and next year the union introduced its own scheme of registration for apprentices, and an apprentices' section within the union to give them protection. Discharge notes, on which a record of conduct was entered, had been introduced by local employers' associations in order, they said, to reduce absenteeism, which ran at a high level among boilermakers, who were able to make up their earnings on piecework. In 1912 the union gave instructions that no member should accept or tender such notes, and the practice was discontinued.

These controversies, along with the termination of procedure, did not mean that open warfare had broken out in the shipyards. The union

---

[4] Wigham, p. 84   [5] *Monthly Journal and Report*, October 1914.
[6] Mortimer, p. 39.

continued to negotiate nationally with the employers on general issues, and to join with the local employers' associations in attempting to resolve local disputes without stoppages of work.

Perhaps the most celebrated procedure of all was the Brooklands agreement of 1893 for cotton spinning. It also came under attack in this period, over the issue of 'bad spinning'. Poor material hindered the operative from reaching his normal level of earnings by increasing the number of breakages. Compensation was usually demanded and, unless it was granted quickly, the men were likely to stop work. As with piecework disputes in the shipyards, or abnormal places in coalmining, the evidence was liable to disappear unless action was taken promptly. The Brooklands agreement provided a leisurely procedure which the union had come to believe was unsuitable for dealing with 'bad spinning'. They proposed a number of amendments in 1912 which the employers rejected. Next the union launched official strikes at a number of Oldham mills against alleged 'bad spinning', and in January 1913 gave notice of withdrawal from the procedure which was allowed to run out. The strikes continued through the spring and summer. In October a one-clause procedure was agreed, forbidding strikes on 'bad spinning' complaints until 'representatives of the two organisations (local and central) have jointly enquired into the dispute'.

By the end of the year the Cardroom Operatives had also withdrawn from the Brooklands agreement, so that the new agreement for 'bad spinning' disputes was now the only industry-wide procedure in spinning. The weavers' equivalent of these disputes was the 'bad materials' dispute, which had a similar effect on their earnings, and caused a number of strikes, but these strikes appeared to be settled more readily than 'bad spinning' disputes. They did not lead to an attack on the current procedure agreement for the weaving industry, which had been drawn up in 1909.

Procedure agreements were under attack in the building industry as well. The Operative Bricklayers withdrew from the national procedure and the London building workers repudiated their separate London agreement. Some or all of the unions in four great industries—building, cotton spinning, engineering, and shipbuilding—had withdrawn, at least temporarily, from the joint rules for handling disputes which they had agreed with their employers. Nevertheless, the principle of collective bargaining was not under attack—except by syndicalists. The unions continued to negotiate locally and nationally with the employers as issues arose. Moreover, the engineering unions signed a new agreement without delay, followed by the cotton spinning unions in 1915, and even the Boilermakers were willing to do so, provided the agreement was on their terms.

Although the syndicalists in the Miners Federation, like their colleagues elsewhere, attacked the principle of conciliation, no district miners' union showed an inclination to abandon its conciliation board; and, in contrast to the Boilermakers and the Spinners, who wanted to decentralise their procedures, the Miners Federation aimed at greater centralisation. In 1910 their annual conference had voted, with only three dissentients, for a Scottish resolution seeking 'one Conciliation Board to deal with miners' wages throughout Great Britain' with 'a uniform standard and agreement for all districts'. This remained their objective throughout the period, and they arranged that district agreements should terminate together in 1915 so that the field should be clear.

Despite widespread unrest elsewhere, building, cotton, engineering, shipbuilding, and printing all managed to avoid major stoppages over the central issue of pay. This is the more remarkable in that the Spinners and the Cardroom Operatives received no increase at all, being bound by a five-year standstill agreement signed in 1910, and the majority of district engineering agreements on pay between 1909 and the war were arranged to last for a period of years. The North-East coast, for example, was committed to five years in return for a wage increase granted in 1910, and Manchester to three years by an agreement in 1912.

The reason why this situation did not lead to widespread revolt among cotton and engineering workers was that their earnings were rising without general pay increases. Average earnings of cotton operatives increased by 15.5 per cent from 1910 to 1913.[7] Besides the 5 per cent advance agreed for the weavers in 1912, this growth was due to the change from periods of short-time working to full-time working, and the opportunity to increase piecework earnings by raising output without risk of reverting to short-time working. No reliable records exist for the growth of earnings in the engineering industry, but there are two grounds for supposing that they were rising faster than could be explained by the advance in district rates. The first is the rapid spread of payment by results in the engineering industry since 1898; and the second is the growth of overtime working. Little overtime was worked in cotton because of the restrictions placed on overtime for women and young persons by the Factory Act and the adamant opposition of the unions; but these restraints did not apply in engineering. In January 1914 the Engineers' Liverpool organiser commented in their journal on 'our readiness to work unlimited overtime in order to augment the wage rate'; and in the North east overtime was 'of a character unprecedented'. Activists made efforts to arrest the growth of overtime, but, according to

[7] White, p. 24, table 8.

the Manchester organiser in March, it continued to provide a 'monetary solatium' and to sap 'the vitality and thinking capacity of those thus engaged'.

The growth of earnings in engineering was associated with a new form of collective bargaining—workshop bargaining between managers and shop stewards. The practice of appointing shop stewards went back a long way in some of the Engineers' districts, and had been recognised in the union's rules since 1892. At that time their main responsibility had been the observance of union rules and customs in the workshops, and the reporting of infringements to their district committees for action to be taken. However, the terms imposed by the employers in 1898 had the unintentional effect of widening their functions. The agreement banned many of the union's rules and customs, including those on apprenticeship, the closed shop, the manning of machines, and overtime. The district committees were, therefore, debarred from overt attempts to enforce them, and it was left largely to the shop stewards to secure their observance where they could, without calling for official assistance. Even more important was the clause empowering employers to introduce piecework and to settle piece rates by 'mutual arrangement between the employer and the workman or workmen who perform the work'. The intention had been to keep the union out of piecework negotiations, so long as earnings exceeded the time rates. In practice, shop stewards in many plants tried to ensure that no member accepted a rate which would not yield considerably more than that. Committees were formed 'for the purpose, among others, of considering all prices before any man was allowed to accept them'. Chief stewards or 'conveners' were elected. Some of the committees were recognised by employers.

In a few cases . . . the secretary of the Committee was accorded special facilities for negotiation with the rate-fixers employed by the firm, with, in at least one case in Glasgow, an office of his own in the works and full access to all departments for the purpose of dealing with workshop grievances.[8]

Most other unions in engineering, both craft and general,[9] had their shop stewards, though few of them were so involved in piecework as the Engineers. In other industries where piecework was common but production methods, unlike those in engineering, were standardised, it was, for the most part, governed by district or even national piece-price

---

[8] Cole, *Workshop Organisation*, p. 15.

[9] The National Amalgamated Union of Labour had appointed shop stewards 'from the start'. In the Gasworkers and the Workers Union the job was often done by collecting stewards, appointed to bring in the contributions. (Clegg, *General Union in a Changing Society*, pp. 28–9, 85; Hyman, p. 117.)

lists negotiated by full-time officials or district committees, as in cotton and shipbuilding—although the shipbuilding unions had their shop stewards. District pay agreements in coalmining made general adjustments up or down to piece rates and time rates settled in the pits; but since the practice was for each colliery to have its own union branch, these rates were negotiated by the branch officials with appeal to their full-time officials. In engineering such an appeal was debarred by the 'mutuality' clause.

The appointment of shop stewards was also common in printing (where they were called 'fathers of the chapel') and in building. Both, however, were timeworking industries and the responsibility of their workplace representatives was, as that of the Engineers' stewards had once been, to watch over the observance of union rules and customs, with, in building, the additional task, so essential in a casual industry, of building up union organisation on new sites.

Other Industries and the Less-Skilled

Together with transport (where many of the developments of collective bargaining during this period have been described in the previous chapter), coal, cotton, and the craft trades in building, engineering, printing, and shipbuilding provided over two-thirds of Britain's trade unionists at the beginning of 1911, something like three-quarters of the recorded strikes and lockouts during 1911–14, and more than 90 per cent of the working days lost in them. They also represented well over 90 per cent of the workers covered by district and national collective agreements. But they accounted for only about a third of British employees.

There were, nevertheless, a few unions in other industries which were as well organised as any in the country. One was the Lace Makers Society, by 1911 'so strong in Nottingham that a threader who was expelled the union was given notice' by his employer.[10] Its contributions, and the range of its benefits, exceeded those of most other craft unions. Another was the group of eight unions in the North Staffordshire silk industry, six of them sharing the personable and popular William Broomfield as secretary. In the summer of 1913 they struck successfully against an attempt by their employers to cut some of their piece rates because of high earnings. The tinplate industry in South Wales had been enjoying a period of prosperity since the turn of the century, during which the control of the conciliation board had extended to the wages and conditions of all tinplate workers, and its decisions were accepted without question through the trade.

The main concern of several relatively powerful unions was to bring

[10] Cuthbert, p. 63.

the poorly-organised sections of their industries within their control, both to improve pay and conditions in those sections, and to protect their existing members from undercutting. There were three main hosiery unions centred on Leicester, Nottingham, and Ilkeston. The Leicester union launched a campaign to organise the workers in the small towns and villages around the city, many of whom were employed by Leicester firms, but at rates below those paid in the city. Their task was made more difficult by the lack of an effective employers' association in hosiery, so that they had to deal with each employer individually. Nevertheless, 'by June, 1914, the Union's membership in the villages had risen to almost 1,400, out of a total membership of just under 3,500', and wages in the villages had been substantially increased. The Nottingham union left it to the Ilkeston union to organise hosiery workers in the environs of their city, and this task was also successfully accomplished, wages being forced up 'to the levels obtaining in Nottingham'.[11]

The Boot and Shoe Operatives, whose membership was mainly concentrated in the same part of the country, negotiated with a powerful employers' federation with which they had agreed a fifty-two-and-a-half-hour working week in their 1909 settlement. However, they still needed to make sure that the agreement was applied by federated employers, and to extend it to non-federated firms. Wage rates, moreover, were negotiated with the local employers' associations, and in dealing with them the union was seeking to win acceptance for its target minimum wage of £1.50 a week for men. By 1913 both objectives 'had been generally achieved in such well-organised centres as Leicester, Northampton, Edinburgh, Glasgow, Leeds and elsewhere'.[12]

In 1913 a lockout of furniture workers by the High Wycombe employers enabled the Furniture Trades Association, through Askwith's intervention, to obtain its first agreement in that important but previously unorganised centre of their industry; and in 1911 the last great bastion of non-unionism in the iron and steel industry fell, when a strike of three thousand workers at Dowlais in South Wales forced the company to concede union recognition and a wage increase. Meanwhile, in the sheet steel section of the industry, the underhands, who had previously been employed on a subcontracting basis by members of the Associated Iron and Steel Workers, 'took advantage' of the Hawarden Bridge settlement to extend 'the three essentials for which the Steel Smelters' Union had fought at Hawarden Bridge . . . throughout the trade'.[13] These were: the end of subcontracting; the extension of piecework to the underhands to allow them to share in the rewards of rising output; and direct representation in dealings with management

[11] Gurnham, pp. 61–2.   [12] Fox, p. 343.   [13] Pugh, p. 165.

and on the conciliation board for the sheet trade. In addition, the union substituted its control of the promotion system for selection by the subcontractors; and the union's authority over promotion came to be unquestioned throughout all sections of the industry.

The finishing section of the woollen and worsted industry was efficiently organised by the Amalgamated Society of Dyers, Bleachers and Finishers, based on Bradford, and the National Society of Dyers and Finishers, based on Huddersfield, both with a long record of amicable dealings with the employers; although, early in 1913, the Bradford union struck for a wage increase. After six weeks they returned with a 10 per cent increase in time rates, pending the introduction of group piecework. In the manufacturing sections of the industry there were some small sectional societies, and the General Union of Textile Workers which, though recognised by the Huddersfield employers, was still pitifully weak at the beginning of the period. By 1913, however, they had secured a series of agreements with five employers' associations, between them covering most of the industry. Thereafter, union membership grew rapidly.

The largest union in the clothing industry was the Amalgamated Society of Tailors and Tailoresses which organised the handicraft workers, and had negotiated 'logs' of piecework prices in most large towns. They faced competition from a separate London society which called an unsuccessful six-week strike in 1912.[14] In the expanding factory section of the trade the Clothiers Operatives had made little headway by 1910, but they were able to take advantage of the establishment of a Trade Board under the 1909 Act. At first, the employers insisted that they would deal with union claims only through the machinery of the Trade Board; but they were forced to withdraw. In February 1913, a threat of a strike in Leeds, where the union now had five thousand members, secured permanent conciliation machinery, and an advance in pay above the Trade Board rates.

Success prompted some unions to raise their sights. In 1912 the Boot and Shoe Operatives decided to ask for a national minimum instead of district minima, and put the figure for men at £1.75 a week. Tough negotiations ultimately led to a settlement in May 1914 conceding, among other things, an increase in minimum rates for all male workers; national minimum rates for certain groups of both men and women; the removal of the 'managerial rights' clause of the original agreement of 1895; and an acknowledgement by the employers of the desirability of workers joining the union. The steel unions aimed to substitute eight-hour shifts for twelve-hour shifts, and made progress, particularly in

---

[14] Dobbs (p. 138) alleged that 'the leading figures in this disastrous dispute was Mr. Tom Mann'.

Wales. By the outbreak of war there were few Welsh mills in any branch of the industry still working twelve-hour shifts.

In most of these industries there is little evidence to suggest that this was a period of particularly bitter conflict. On the contrary, several unions enjoyed considerable support from their employers in achieving their objectives. The steel unions made a practice of fostering good relations with employers, and a representative of the South Wales Siemens Steel Association told the Industrial Council in 1913 that the Smelters' Union was well-organised and efficient, with 'very good discipline'. He continued:

Personally, we welcome such a union . . . Any strong, well organised union is of assistance to us in managing our business. I should like to see the unions actually increase in power, provided they increase in their responsibilities.[15]

In tinplate an older generation of autocratic employers and intransigent trade union leaders had been replaced by a 'new generation of employers and workers [who] were much more conciliatory and eager for orderly industrial relations'.[16] During the negotiations in the footwear industry over the winter of 1913–14, the more moderate employers 'became alarmed at the rapid hardening of attitudes on both sides, and began to make their influence felt on Federation policy'.[17]

Some unions admitted all grades of manual worker of both sexes, although success in recruiting women varied considerably. The Clothiers Operatives had more women members than men, and so, by 1914, had the Leicester hosiery union. The other hosiery unions and the textile finishing unions included few women, and the Boot and Shoe Operatives lost a number of theirs, who were led out by a militant suffragette to form a rival union for women alone. Others, like the Lace Makers, supported auxiliary unions which organised men and women outside the ranks of the skilled males. The steel unions, however, were in an exclusively male industry, and most of them ignored labourers and other ancillary workers, so that collective bargaining remained 'the exclusive preserve of the skilled and semi-skilled process workers' up to the war. The others 'had so far failed to secure any significant measure of recognition from the employers, despite the growth of trade union organisation amongst their ranks'.[18]

These labourers and ancillary workers were organised by the general unions, particularly the National Amalgamated Union of Labour. The general unions also catered for surfaceworkers in coalmining, and had secured recognition from several county coalowners' associations,

[15] *Industrial Council Inquiry*, Qs. 5702, 5726. [16] Minchinton, p. 136.
[17] Fox, p. 347. [18] Wilkinson, p. 114.

though the Miners were now in competition with them, sometimes forcefully. They also recruited less-skilled workers in the major craft industries, except for printing where the job was done by the Warehousemen and the Operative Printers and Assistants. In the building industry there were a number of local unions for builders' labourers and at least three unions which recruited more widely—the United Builders Labourers, the United Order of General Labourers, and the Navvies. Nevertheless there was room for the general unions, and the ballots conducted during the 1914 lockout in London indicated that the Gasworkers had more members involved than any other union, except the Amalgamated Carpenters and Joiners. In 1909 the National Conciliation Board had ruled that, where the craft unions and the employers were willing, the labourers could be represented on local conciliation boards and, subject to certain conditions, could refer unsettled disputes to the regional and national boards.

The most important extension in the coverage of collective bargaining in the engineering industry during these years was the 1913 agreement between the Workers Union and the Midland Employers Federation, but there were others. Early that year a short strike called by the Workers Union in Coventry had gained a minimum of £1.32½p a week for the less-skilled men, substantially higher than in all other districts except London, and an invitation from the Coventry engineering employers' association to sign the procedure agreement, 'its first such "recognition" agreement with a local member of the [Engineering] Employers' Federation'.[19] In the North East local employers' associations in both engineering and shipbuilding had for some time accepted the Gasworkers and the National Amalgamated Union of Labour as spokesmen for the less-skilled workers. After 1910 the rapid growth of the membership of the Gasworkers in Lancashire, and of both unions in Scotland, led to the concession of recognition in these areas.

However, the most important contribution made by the general unions to the extension of collective bargaining was in industries where there had previously been no other unions, or none of much consequence. Most of these extensions were in chemicals, food and drink manufacture—chocolate, edible fats, breweries, soft drinks, for example—and building materials—quarries, cement, glass, bricks, asphalt, and timber yards. At this time there were few employers' associations in these trades, so most of the agreements were with individual firms, and were not included in the Labour Department's list of collective agreements. However, they constituted the starting point from which district and national agreements developed during and after the war.

[19] Hyman, p. 61.

Two further ventures of the Workers Union deserve special mention. In 1911 they began to recruit among Cornish clayminers, and in 1913 called a general strike of the industry. Refusing to negotiate, the employers brought in blacklegs. There were violent incidents, and police were fetched in from Glamorgan. The brutality of their methods showed that they had not forgotten the skills practised in Tonypandy in 1910. They attracted the attention of the national press, and the condemnation of the Trades Union Congress. The strikers were forced back to work on the employers' terms, but they remained loyal to the union and, the following year, firm after firm granted recognition and pay increases.

The second venture was in agriculture. Beginning in Herefordshire in 1912, the union began to recruit in other Midlands counties, East Anglia and Yorkshire. By 1914 their agricultural membership ran into some thousands, and, although most farmers ignored their claims, strikes in Herefordshire, Gloucestershire, and Wiltshire brought concessions. However, the major union in the field was the Eastern Counties Agricultural Labourers, who now changed their name to the National Agricultural and Rural Workers. At the beginning of the period the Liberal philanthropists who had founded the union still retained a dominant position on the executive; but they were removed from office early in 1911. Many strikers failed to get their jobs back after a bitter eight weeks' strike for an increase of 5p a week in the Norfolk village of St. Faiths was terminated. The decision to close the strike was inevitable, but the members made scapegoats of the executive and voted on a militant majority with the socialist Walter Smith, of the Boot and Shoe Operatives, replacing the Liberal Member of Parliament, George Nicholls, as president.

The union began organising outside East Anglia, especially in Lancashire where, as in most highly industrialised counties, agricultural wages were considerably above those in East Anglia. With the help of the local railwaymen, who threatened to refuse to handle agricultural produce, a strike at Ormskirk in 1913 won recognition, a weekly half-day holiday, and wage advances varying from 5p to 15p a week on top of 'the existing wage of round about' £1 a week;[20] whereas the St. Faiths strikers had been seeking a rate of 65p. This provoked a good deal of jealousy in East Anglia, which was not mollified by the rapid increase in Lancashire membership to exceed that of the rest of the union put together. R. B. Walker, the new secretary, summoned the 1914 conference n the basis of 1912 membership in order to block proposals for constitutional changes from Lancashire, and many of the Lancashire branches broke away to form a splinter organisation.[21] However, the

[20] Groves, p. 141.   [21] Newby, p. 214.

parent union won successes in Northamptonshire and elsewhere in 1914, and the concession of 80p a week with a weekly half-day by the king's agent at Sandringham led to a new slogan in Norfolk—'The King's pay and the King's conditions'.

Public and Private Services

There were two unions of some strength in retail distribution: the Amalgamated Union of Co-operative Employees which catered for employees in the factories of the Co-operative Wholesale Society as well as in the retail societies; and the National Amalgamated Union of Shop Assistants, which confined recruitment to the retail trade but made no exception for co-operative employees.

Previously, both unions had dealt with individual employers and co-operative societies, but now they began to develop larger ideas. At their 1912 conference the Co-operative Employees were told by their president that 'the day was coming when the Union would have to take district action, and make their requests to all societies in a district at one time',[22] and next year the Shop Assistants reported that 'the whole of the Glasgow [Co-operative] societies have formed themselves into a joint committee to meet the Union officials for the purpose of dealing with the wages question'.[23]

Both unions guided local settlements by means of target minimum wages. The Shop Assistants set up a committee in 1907 which drew up proposals trade by trade, and in 1911 inaugurated a campaign to achieve them. For drapery, the target for men was £1.20 at 21 rising to £1.60 at 28; and for women £1 to £1.30. The branches and districts were empowered to make the best settlements they could get, subject to ratification by the committee. Their journal reported that 1913 had been 'a glorious year' for the minimum wage campaign.[24] The Co-operative Employees' national target for men was £1.20, which by December 1914 was observed by 274 co-operative societies. District councils drew up their own scales above the minimum which they pressed on local societies. In 1913 the Co-operative Wholesale Society agreed to a minimum wage for women and girls in its factories. By the end of 1914, ninety-two societies had accepted the closed shop.[25]

In both unions 'the persuasive policy was abandoned and an aggressive policy taken up'.[26] The Shop Assistants paid strike pay in only one dispute in 1913 because elsewhere concessions were made

---

[22] *The Co-operative Employee*, October 1912.
[23] *The Shop Assistant*, 13 December 1913.
[24] Ibid., 27 December 1913.
[25] William Richardson, p. 71.
[26] *The Co-operative Employee*, January 1911.

'before the time limit expired'.[27] The Co-operative Employees, who had been debating the merits of a strike fund for some years, took the plunge in 1912. There were strikes over victimisation, as well as pay and hours of work; and the Shop Assistants faced two problems which did not concern the Co-operative Employees—living-in and the 'radius agreement', under which an assistant bound himself not to take another job in the same trade within a given distance of his present employment. Their union's campaigns to end both of these practices led to further disputes.

The unions also achieved some success over the statutory regulation of working hours. After several false starts in the preceding years, the government introduced a Shops Bill in 1911 which included a sixty-hour working week, weekly half-day closing, early closing in the evening by local agreement, and severe limits on Sunday trading. After savage attacks led by Horatio Bottomley and Frederick Banbury, who said that the bill put the Home Secretary 'in the position of a dictator',[28] the government settled for half-day closing, the promotion of early closing by local arrangement, and the appointment of local authority inspectors.

A number of 'trading' services were provided by local authorities in some areas, and by private undertakings elsewhere. They included tramways and the supply of water, gas, and electricity. Considerable headway was made in these and in the 'non-trading' local authority services during these years by the Amalgamated Association of Tramway and Vehicle Workers, the Municipal Employees Association, and the general unions. None of them had a monopoly of any one service. The Tramwaymen dealt with most major tramway undertakings, but a few recognised the Municipal Employees; the Gasworkers took the lead in gas and electricity undertakings, but there were several other unions in the field, including the Electrical Trades Union. In non-trading departments the general unions competed with the Municipal Employees.

In both trading and non-trading services the unions dealt with individual undertakings, whether public or private. At this time, local authorities looked upon themselves as 'sovereign' employers, whose decisions on pay and conditions of work could not be restricted by negotiations conducted on their behalf by an employers' association. The only conciliation board was confined to a single undertaking—the London County Council Tramways Department. The normal procedure was for union representatives to seek an interview with the chief officer of the appropriate department which could lead on to a meeting with his committee; but in some instances the council as a whole took a

[27] *The Shop Assistant*, 27 December 1913.
[28] *Hansard*, 31 March 1911, col. 1706.

hand. The most important dispute of these years was the strike of Leeds Corporation workers in 1913 led by the Gasworkers and subsequently joined by the Tramwaymen. Their claim for a 10p increase all round brought an offer from the council of increases, grade by grade, to bring them up to the level of neighbouring towns, but this was rejected. The dispute was enlivened by blacklegging by students from Leeds University, encouraged by their vice-chancellor. In the end the men were obliged to go back on the committee's terms.

White collar employees of local authorities were just beginning to feel their way to collective action. In 1905 a number of their local 'guilds', hitherto mainly concerned with social functions and friendly benefits, came together in the National Association of Local Government Officers. Their objectives included a national pension scheme for local government officers, and the raising of the status of their members by promoting professional examinations. Although their secretary, Levi Hill, asserted that 'anything savouring of trade unionism is nausea to the local government officer and his Association',[29] their chairman, Hubert Blain, helped to organise the electoral defeat of members of the East Ham Council, after it had announced proposals to dismiss a number of officers and to cut salaries. In 1910, memorials and deputations from local guilds persuaded Newcastle Corporation to withdraw an extension of working hours, and the Congleton Rural District Council to retract resolutions obliging officers to send in their resignations with any requests they made for advances in salary.

The National Union of Teachers already negotiated salary scales with many of the education authorities established under the Act of 1902, but others, especially in rural areas, refused to deal with the union and even insisted on fixing salaries on an individual basis. The result was wide variations in pay, with 31 per cent of male certificated head teachers receiving over £200 a year in 1912–13 and 4 per cent less than £100. There were similar inequalities in other grades, and most uncertificated teachers were especially ill-paid.[30] At the beginning of 1913 the union launched a campaign aimed at securing the adoption of the minimum scale of salaries, which its conference had just approved. The moment was opportune, due to a shortage of teachers. The old pupil–teacher system of training was being replaced by bursaries to encourage continued attendance at secondary school, followed by a training-college course. These bursaries were too meagre to enable many working-class children to stay at school, so the number of entrants to the profession had fallen off sharply.[31] The climax of the campaign came in January 1914, when the majority of Herefordshire teachers resigned, closing

[29] Spoor, p. 47.   [30] Thompson, Appendix VI.
[31] Tropp, p. 186.

sixty-five schools. Harried by parents and the Board of Education, the education committee capitulated within a month, granting recognition and salary scales which embodied substantial advances in pay.

There were other organisations of teachers. Associations of head-masters, headmistresses, assistant masters, and assistant mistresses, with their main strength in the grammar schools, came together to form the 'joint four' to represent them 'nationally on matters of common concern to all secondary teachers.[32] There was also the Association of Teachers in Technical Institutions; and the National Union of Women Teachers which had broken away from the National Union of Teachers in 1909 over the issue of equal pay for men and women. In 1913 all the teachers' associations joined in making representations to the Board of Education on the need for the grants to education authorities to provide for increased staffing and salaries.

The civil service unions faced a different problem from that of unions elsewhere in the public sector. One of the main concerns of the latter was to bring a degree of standardisation into the settlements on pay and conditions they made with those individual authorities which recognised them. In the civil service, by contrast, pay and conditions were already rigorously standardised by central regulation, and the objective of the unions was to gain some control over the process of regulation, which was in the hands of the Treasury and the individual departments, from time to time guided by the reports of parliamentary committees. The unions were restricted to making representations to the departments and giving evidence to the committees.

The Post Office was by far the most highly unionised department. Besides the Postmen's Federation, there were unions of postal clerks and postal telegraph clerks, the Fawcett Association for London sorters, the Engineering and Stores Association, and the Sub-Postmasters Federation. Outside the Post Office, the Amalgamated Society of Telephone Employees was primarily concerned with negotiations over the terms of the transfer of the assets of the National Telephone Company to the Post Office, due to take place at the end of 1911.

Post Office employees had been bitterly disappointed by the report of the Hobhouse Committee in 1908, but the only remedy available to their unions was to seek another inquiry. Pledges were sought from candidates at the 1910 general elections; and the 1911 conference of the Postmen's Federation, which instructed the executive to continue its pressure for an inquiry, gave it 'no choice in the matter of preparing the wages claim. It must be based on the cost of living.'[33] In September the National Joint Committee of Postal and Telegraph Associations demanded immediate action. Herbert Samuel, the Postmaster General,

---

[32] Gosden, p. 14.   [33] *Postman's Gazette*, 1 July 1911.

promised the union deputation to put their case to the cabinet, who at first tried to fob them off with a suggestion of a select committee in 1913, and then capitulated to further pressure for immediate action.

The composition of the new committee, which held its first meeting in May 1912, appeared to favour the unions.[34] so the report, which appeared in 1913, came as a shock. There were substantial increases for London postmen, and the maximum rates of most grades were raised, but, to the 'great indignation' of the unions, the increases did not match 'the admitted rise in the cost of living since the last revision,'[35] and many of the lower paid got nothing. The unions rejected the report. The Postal Clerks had already declared 'its inalienable right to withdraw the labour of its members should it think fit',[36] and a special conference of the Postmen's Federation voted by 549 votes to 175 for a 'strike policy'. They were somewhat placated when the government modified the committee's proposals for worsening conditions (for instance the abolition of meal reliefs) and granted small advances to the lower paid; and decided to concentrate on parliamentary pressure (which meant still another committee) before resorting to 'drastic action'.

Their decision was rewarded on 10 June 1914, when a Conservative Member, Sir Gilbert Parker, proposed that a committee consisting of a Post Office official, a staff representative, and an impartial chairman should review the Holt Report. With the votes of their Radical supporters by no means certain, the government were relieved to accept Ramsay Macdonald's motion for a committee of five so as to include a Treasury official along with a second staff representative. The inclusion in the new committee of two staff representatives, one of them the secretary of the Postmen's Federation, G. H. Stuart, was a considerable step towards the acceptance of collective bargaining. The report came after the outbreak of war.

In 1910 Haldane and Buxton had accepted that the fair wages resolution as amended in 1909 was to be applied to government industrial employees as well as the employees of government contractors.[37] Their wages and hours had therefore to be 'not less favourable than those commonly recognised by employers and trade societies', or, in their absence, than those prevalent 'amongst good employers'. Thereafter the Engineers and other unions concerned were able to use this concession to raise wages in a number of War Office and Admiralty establishments. In 1913 the Admiralty agreed to receive and

---

[34] Holt, the chairman, was a Liverpool shipowner with a good record as an employer, and the members included Tyson Wilson, a Labour Member of Parliament and an old champion of the Post Office employees.

[35] *Postman's Gazette*, 6 September 1913.

[36] Ibid., 19 April 1913.

[37] *Hansard*, 9 March 1910, cols. 1321, 1339.

meet the expenses of deputations elected from among their workers in 'matters concerning large classes of men'.[38]

The 'non-industrial' civil service unions, including the Assistant Clerks, the Tax Clerks, the Employment Department Clerks, and the Boy Clerks, had not progressed as far as the Post Office unions towards collective bargaining. However, their aspirations received considerable encouragement from the proceedings of the Royal Commission on the Civil Service appointed in 1912, with Lord MacDonnell as chairman and Philip Snowden among its members. On behalf of the Labour Party, Snowden, a former civil servant, had strongly advocated the setting up of a Royal Commission.

One of the grievances of the service was the staffing of the labour exchanges. It had been the original aim of the founders of the labour exchange system, notably William Beveridge, to create 'an entirely new breed of civil servants, who would bridge the gulf between Whitehall and the shop floor' and preference was given 'to men with business rather than bureaucratic experience'.[39] This smacked of 'jobbery' to the established civil servants, some of whom may have hoped for senior posts in the administration of the labour exchanges, and feared that they might be passed over again when the National Insurance administration was appointed. Further ammunition was provided in 1911 with the publication of a Board of Education circular of the previous year making unfavourable comparisons between the board's school inspectors, recruited from Oxford and Cambridge graduates, and the local authorities' inspectors, recruited from elementary teachers, who were characterised as, 'as a rule, uncultured and imperfectly educated'.[40] The National Union of Teachers now joined in the agitation for a Royal Commission and before the end of the year Asquith gave his consent.

The commission encouraged the associations by taking 'oral evidence from the more important of the general Service associations at an early stage in [their] proceedings'.[41] The report, published in April 1914, dealt principally with selection, recommending that open competition should be retained but be adapted more closely to the educational system as it was then developing. This adaptation would have to replace the existing grades—many of them 'apparently arbitrary'[42]—by a new

[38] Shepherd, p. 33.
[39] Harris, *Unemployment and Politics*, p. 352. According to Halévy (p. 447) during 1913 'labour statistics proved' that, during the previous six years, '117 active union workers' had been appointed to the Board of Trade, 124 to the National Insurance Departments, 48 to the Home Office, and 85 to other branches of the civil service.
[40] Tropp, Appendix A.
[41] *Fourth Report*, p. 2. The evidence of the Boy Clerks' secretary, W. J. Brown, who at 18 had succeeded in recruiting nearly the whole of his grade, was 'remarkable for its clarity, directness and understanding of the issues involved' (Humphreys, p. 71).
[42] Shepherd, p. 71.

grading system, whose salary scales would inevitably bring greater increases for some of the existing classes than for others. The reception in the service was, therefore, mixed, but by no means universally unfavourable. The report praised the work of the associations and approved their recognition by heads of departments 'in the sense of receiving from them directly representations on matters affecting their interests', but proposed there should be another inquiry into whether recognition should be 'carried further'.[43] None of the recommendations had been carried out by the outbreak of war.

An account of the work of the civil service unions which dealt only with lobbying and the work of select committees and Royal Commissions would be misleading. The Post Office unions had frequent dealings with their departments over many other issues such as the employment of auxiliary workers, boys and girls, and casual labour, over the general rules for the allocation of duties, and about instructions to be given in the 1911 railway strike so that 'postmen would not be called upon to act as strike-breakers'.[44] A deputation from the Postmen's Federation saw Samuel in October 1911 to ask for representation on relevant departmental committees, and for an extension of local office recognition in order to deal with duties and hours of work—'hardly any revision of duties is satisfactory to the staff unless the local people are consulted in its framing'.[45] The Holt Report gave its approval to both these methods of consulting the opinions of the staff, saying of local consultation on duties, accommodation and equipment that it was 'a course which appears to be frequently taken'.[46] Among industrial civil servants, a strike at Woolwich Arsenal in 1914 led to the recognition of shop stewards there.

Comparison may be made with the railways, where the unions still did not see themselves as 'recognised' by the railway companies—in contrast with the Post Office unions whose members believed that they had achieved official recognition, because they were allowed to make formal representations to senior officials and the Postmaster General himself. In dealing with local issues, however, the railway unions had quite as much scope as the Post Office unions, if not more. Hundreds of railwaymen, most of them elected as union candidates, served on the conciliation boards whose business went far beyond the settlement of wages and hours of work. The executive of what was now the National Union of Railwaymen were informed, at their meeting of 2–8 March 1914, that the boards on the Great Western Railway had reclassified a number of signal boxes; dealt with a signalman's claim for travelling expenses when sent to a remote box; settled an application for the pay of

[43] *Fourth Report*, pp. 98–9.   [44] *Postman's Gazette*, 26 August 1911.
[45] Ibid., 21 October 1911.   [46] Ibid., 23 August 1913.

a higher grade when working temporarily at a job within that grade; interpreted the overtime rules in relation to goods guards and brakesmen; and dealt with dozens of other detailed matters of a similar kind. On 15 January a deputation from three of the London and North Western boards had gone to Euston to discuss the working of the 'control system' with the result that a circular was issued on the relief of brakesmen and enginemen in order to avoid protracted duties, and on the payment of brakesmen when trains were delayed.

Discipline was a particularly important issue both in the Post Office and the railways. The skills acquired by their employees were of little use to them if they were dismissed (for the likelihood of a dismissed railwayman being employed by another railway company was remote); and the hierarchical pay scales made demotion a severe punishment. The Holt Committee recommended that the Post Office unions should be allowed to represent their members in disciplinary cases, and, although this facility was denied to the railway unions, they nevertheless intervened in several instances. Among them were the demotion of Driver Knox of the North Eastern Railway in December 1912 for alleged drunkenness, which led to a strike and a Home Office inquiry that rejected the evidence against Knox; and the case of Guard Richardson, of the Midland Railway, who was dismissed in January 1913 for refusing to obey oral instructions which were in conflict with the written rules. This led to a successful demand for reinstatement from a joint meeting of the executives of all the railway unions. The company also undertook to revise their regulations to prevent a similar incident in the future.

The Government

In his report to the annual conference of the Railway Servants in 1910, their secretary, J. E. Williams, noted that:

The Board of Trade has undoubtedly become one of the most active and greatest benefactors to the community of all State Departments.

Quickly and almost unnoticed remarkable progress has been made in the past few years in the establishment of arbitration and conciliation boards, joint committees, and other machinery for averting strikes and lock-outs and settling disputes in wages and hours of work.

This activity by the Board's Labour Department continued throughout the next few years. Askwith, its chief, or one of the former trade union officials who were now his henchmen, D. C. Cummings and Isaac Mitchell, were either on stage or in the wings in almost every significant industrial dispute of the period, exercising their influence on the negotiations. Their philosophy was not in doubt. They believed that industrial relations issues should be handled jointly by employers and workers. To deal with them effectively, the parties needed to be organised into trade unions and employers' associations, and to set up joint machinery through which disputes could be settled and agreements made and interpreted.

The intervention of the Labour Department therefore had two objects: to settle the issues currently in dispute; and to establish or improve permanent arrangements for the conduct of industrial relations. In this they had enjoyed the support and active assistance of successive presidents of the Board of Trade, beginning with Lloyd George's successful intervention in the railway dispute of 1907 which led to the setting up of conciliation boards. His successors, Churchill and now Buxton, had tried to follow his example, and other Liberal ministers, including Burns, Grey, Masterman and Samuel, tried their hands at mediation at one time or another. In the London dock strike of 1912, according to Askwith's account, 'first one [minister] and then another had informal interviews with the representatives of the parties'. When the prime minister, who had been abroad, learned from Askwith what had been happening, he gave 'strict orders that Ministers, even the President of the Board of Trade, . . . were to leave industrial disputes alone', an edict which was apparently respected up to the war.[47]

Increasing industrial unrest led to doubts as to whether the conciliatory methods of the Labour Department, which had no authority to take stronger measures, were sufficient to deal with current industrial relations problems. In April 1912 a cabinet committee was set up to examine the question, with Lloyd George in the chair. The cabinet was divided. Asquith, though not entirely a non-interventionist, was certainly a minimalist, in the sense that he disliked intervention, wanted to limit it to the minimum required to deal with the issue in hand, and was adamantly opposed to some forms of intervention, such as fixing rates of pay by Act of Parliament. Lloyd George, however, along with some of his Radical colleagues, appreciated the political appeal of strong measures in troubled times. It was Lloyd George's committee that made proposals for settling the 1912 London dock strike. Smarting from the rebuffs of the employers, Lloyd George told the Commons that 'the Government have come to the conclusion that it will be necessary to deal with this problem. It is not merely this dispute; there are disputes constantly cropping up.' The dock dispute raised 'the general issue, which constantly arises, of agreements being entered into, and of charges being made on both sides that the agreements are not enforced'. He continued:

47 Askwith, pp. 222, 230.

All we can do is to employ the machinery of conciliation and persuasion, and I am sure that the public has come to the conclusion that that is inadequate. Labour disputes are becoming more and more serious. They are becoming more and more a challenge to our commercial prosperity. . . . The Executive must be armed with more formidable powers than those with which they are entrusted at present.[48]

Taking up a suggestion from Sir Charles Macara, chairman of the Master Cotton Spinners, the government had in October 1911 set up an Industrial Council of thirteen trade unionists and thirteen employers under the chairmanship of Askwith, who was appointed Chief Industrial Commissioner, with the rank of permanent secretary. They were entrusted with the task of

considering and enquiring into matters referred to them affecting trade disputes and especially of taking suitable action in regard to any dispute referred to them affecting the principal trades of the country;

but they were given no powers beyond those already available to the Labour Department. It must, therefore, be presumed that the government believed that the recommendations of such a body would have greater authority than those of the Labour Department. However, more than one trade union leader had to make it clear that he did not represent his union and Will Thorne, the current chairman of the Parliamentary Committee, refused to serve, telling his colleagues on 13 September that 'he thought such a scheme would tend to limit the power of the worker to strike'. They were 'divided in their opinions', and decided to see how the council turned out.

Whether because, as Askwith thought, 'Committees are singularly inapt bodies for these purposes',[49] or because they were not given sufficient opportunity, the council did not make a name for themselves as conciliators. In 1912 the Miners would not allow their minimum wage dispute to be referred to the council, insisting on dealing direct with the government. Asquith, however, found a use for the council when he asked them to consider 'the best way of securing the due fulfilment of industrial agreements'; and whether statutory enforcement of agreements was desirable. After interviewing many witnesses, they reported in June 1913. Their main finding was that 'where agreements are the outcome of properly organised machinery for dealing with disputes, they are, with very few exceptions, loyally observed by both sides',[50] and the main need was therefore to improve the machinery for collective bargaining. However, they conceded that observance might be facilitated by making agreements 'applicable to the whole of the trade or

---

[48] *Hansard*, 23 July 1912, cols. 1116-7.   [49] Askwith, p. 182.
[50] *Report*, p. 4.

district concerned', provided that the parties to the agreement asked for this to be done, that they represented 'a substantial body of those in the trade or district', and that an inquiry by the Board of Trade found in favour.[51]

This was hardly the kind of extension of executive power which Lloyd George had in mind the previous July, and he fobbed off a question asking him when he would be able 'to formulate legislative proposals with a view to definite action'.[52] Nevertheless in January 1914 Buxton proposed that the cabinet should go ahead with legislation on the lines of the report and on 7 April the Parliamentary Committee was informed through Burns that legislation was intended; but nothing came of it.

Two Acts of Parliament concerning industrial relations which had been passed in 1909 were still taking effect in 1911. The direct impact of the first, the Labour Exchanges Act, was less than expected. There was no compulsion on workers to register, or on employers to notify vacancies. In many instances the craft unions continued to provide the best means of finding jobs for their members and supplying craftsmen to employers; most other workers found their jobs through informal contacts. Nevertheless the average number of vacancies filled rose from 903 a day in the first five months of 1910 to 3,092 in the first six months of 1914.[53] Trade union fears were allayed by allowing applicants to reject jobs at less than union rates, and by refusing to supply labour to employers in search of workers to replace strikers. The importance of the exchanges was enhanced by Part II of the National Insurance Act 1911 which introduced unemployment insurance for selected trades, to be administered through the exchanges.

The second was the Trade Boards Act. During 1910 Trade Boards were set up in chainmaking, lace finishing, paper box manufacture, and tailoring; and in 1913 five new boards were added in cotton and linen embroidery, hollow-ware, tin box manufacture, shirtmaking, and sugar confectionery, but none of these had minimum wages in force by the outbreak of war. In 1914 R. H. Tawney brought out his study of the work of the chainmaking board, followed by a study of the tailoring board the following year. He reported substantial increases in earnings in chainmaking. In 1911, before the statutory rates came into force, the median figure of earnings in his sample of journeymen had been between 65p and 70p a week; by 1913 it was between £1 and £1.05, and the increase in piece rates for male outworkers ranged from 15 per cent to 50 per cent.[54] Increases in pay in tailoring had been more modest, but

[51] Ibid., p. 16.   [52] *Hansard*, 11 August 1913, col. 2053.
[53] Gilbert, *National Insurance*, p. 263.
[54] Tawney, *Minimum Rates in the Chain-Making Industry*, p. 81.

'about one-third of the women and one-fifth of the men have received an increase in their earnings'.[55]

The effect on trade union organisation was also marked. Men in the chainmaking factories already had a strong union, but the women and the men in the outshops were able to use the board to build up their organisations. The two craft unions in tailoring reported substantial recruiting among women because they were now able to afford union contributions, and the membership of both the Amalgamated Jewish Tailors and the Clothiers Operatives rose fourfold between 1910 and 1913. The chainmaking trade had progressed further towards collective bargaining than tailoring because many of the decisions of its board were made by agreement between the two sides without calling on the independent members to vote, whereas in tailoring, where the master tailors were generally prepared to pay more than the factory employers, the latter insisted on voting by sides and the independents therefore settled the important issues. Tawney's conclusion was that the effect of the minimum rates on employment was marginal. Thus the first modern experiment in minimum wage legislation in Britain seemed to show that it could combat sweating, increase organisation and promote collective bargaining without serious adverse economic consequences; but it was too early to make a final judgment, for the Act had so far been applied only to a tiny minority of low-paid workers in a period of unusual prosperity.

The impact on industrial relations and trade unions of both labour exchanges and Trade Boards was outweighed by the National Insurance Act of 1911, which established two systems of insurance for employees engaged in manual labour. Part II of the Act provided for unemployment insurance for a selected group of industries which, roughly speaking, covered construction, engineering and shipbuilding. For equal contributions from employer and employee of just over 1p a week, and a rather smaller sum from the government, a benefit of 35p a week was payable to an unemployed worker for a period of up to fifteen weeks in the year. The scheme was managed by the labour exchanges, except that, with certain provisos, trade unions were allowed to administer it on behalf of their members, but repayment was at three-quarters of benefit paid, so they had to pay out almost 47p before they could receive the full 35p. In addition any trade union, whether in an insured trade or not, was entitled to reimbursement of a sixth of any unemployed benefit paid out, up to 60p per person per week. Relatively few unions outside the insured trades had taken advantage of this second scheme before the outbreak of war.

[55] Tawney, *Minimum Rates in the Tailoring Industry*, p. 95. Nevertheless, the workers at Hebden Bridge 'never before believed that it was possible they could get so much money' (p. 96).

Part I provided a free medical service for the employee (but not his family), a sickness benefit, a disability benefit, a maternity benefit, and a sanatorium benefit for tuberculosis patients. As with unemployment insurance, the contributions for these benefits were split between employer, employee and the government, but with the employee making the largest contribution. The benefits were administered by 'approved societies', which might be insurance companies, or friendly societies, or approved societies established by trade unions; but trade unionists, many of whom were already members of friendly societies, were not obliged to join the unions' approved societies. Most of them did not do so.

Under Part II of the Act the Unemployment Fund made periodic payments to each recognised union in the insured trades of the total amount which the labour exchanges would have paid its unemployed members if they had not been receiving benefit through the union, so long as this payment did not exceed three-quarters of the benefit paid out by the union. The collection of contributions was handled by the state; but the unions had to maintain records of payment in the form required by the Unemployment Fund, make periodic returns, and ensure that they did not pay benefit except under the conditions specified in the Act.

The administration of their approved societies to the requirements of the Insurance Commissioners was an even more testing task for the unions. The Parliamentary Committee recommended to Congress in 1911 that the individual unions should come together 'into as few groups as possible' to constitute approved societies which would administer the benefits and deal with the Commissioners.[56] The General Federation of Trade Unions set up its own approved society, which was open to all its affiliated unions, and a number of smaller unions took advantage of it; but otherwise almost every union, which had the five thousand members required to qualify, decided to have its own approved society. Each hoped to use their own society to recruit new union members, who might not come their way under a group scheme. Moreover, in a group scheme the reimbursement of administrative costs would go to the group administrators, whereas the approved society of an individual union could pay additional salaries to the union general secretary and other full-time officers for supervising its work; or create new full-time posts to which junior officers could be promoted; and branch officers would be entitled to commission if they acted as the society's local agents.

During 1912 there were loud complaints from the unions about the heavy load of administration and secretarial work involved in setting up

[56] Trades Union Congress, 1911, p. 71.

approved societies; and some were involved in special problems. The Railway Servants employed victimised railwaymen on a temporary basis to handle the additional load. During 1912, when the system was in working order, their job came to an end and they were dismissed. They campaigned for reinstatement, and a member of the permanent staff was dismissed for writing to the *Daily Herald* on their behalf. The annual conference, to which he appealed, was told that he had 'joined the temporary staff in taking an office a few doors away from the Head Office, and where the whole of the arrangements for picketing are conducted'; and had given several interviews to the press. Nevertheless he was reinstated, although the temporary clerks lost their appeal. These events were said to have 'led to the breaking down of the health of the General Secretary', J. E. Williams.[57]

The Act also played a part in a battle for power among the Engineers. Their 1912 delegate conference had raised the number of divisional organisers to twelve and converted the district secretaryships in London, Glasgow, Manchester, and Newcastle into full-time posts. Henceforth there were to be seven executive council members instead of eight, and a new post of 'independent' chairman was to be created. The holder was to be chosen in a ballot of the whole membership, so that the status of his office would rival that of the secretary.

The conference ruled that these changes required the election of a new executive. The existing executive appealed to the members against this and other decisions of the conference. The delegates were recalled. Insisting that they alone were entitled to make the rules, they appointed a provisional executive to take over. The old executive barricaded themselves in the head office, but were driven out by the provisional executive after a pitched battle. The conflict was submitted to the courts, which upheld the provisional executive.

When an elected executive took office under the new rules, they were faced with another conflict. The assistant secretary, Robert Young, defeated Jenkin Jones, the incumbent, in an election for the general secretaryship. In the campaign Young made much of Jones's alleged inefficiency. Jones successfully sued for libel. The new executive dismissed Young. However, the last word lay with the union's Final Appeal Court. They reinstated Young and paid salaries to the members of the old executive for their unexpired periods of office.

The authors of the schemes for labour exchanges and national insurance had envisaged that they would help to tackle the problem of casual labour. In practice the exchanges had no immediate effect in this respect; but the Insurance Act included inducements to employers to decasualise. Schemes for the administration of insurance by the

[57] Alcock, p. 419.

exchanges along with the payment of wages on a weekly basis were started in the ports of Glasgow and Manchester, but the Glasgow dockers refused to wait until the end of the week for their money, and the Manchester scheme was terminated by a strike in 1913. In London Tillett rejected similar proposals, describing them as 'an attempt to bring the Labour Exchange methods into being in the docks';[58] but Sexton in Liverpool was prepared to co-operate. The employers were to engage only registered dockers; to aid the rapid deployment of labour, the 'stands', at which dockers were taken on, were to be linked by telephone to six 'clearing houses'; and the clearing houses were to deal with the payment of wages and the deduction of insurance contributions.

The dockers mistrusted the scheme. Some, especially those who could rely on high piecework or overtime earnings, found a casual life to their taste. The men failed to register even when it was agreed that the union should issue the cards. 'Mischief-makers . . . tried to convince them that their own officials were in the pay of the bosses and backing them in an effort to have the workers numbered and registered like cattle.'[59] They struck in July 1912, when the scheme was due to come into operation, and the Birkenhead men stayed out until the middle of August. Thereafter, the scheme came into operation, and in 1913 it was closed to all except the sons of dockers and men who could prove that they had previously worked as dockers.

The clearing house committees of union representatives and employers became negotiating bodies settling 'disputes as to wages, broaching of cargo, the time of commencing pay', transfers, and the imposition of fines.[60] Sexton judged the scheme 'of enormous advantage to the members' and asserted that 'the branches of our union practically control it . . . through the Area Committees'.[61] But there were still problems. It was difficult to limit the supply of 'tallies' to registered dockers; and a high rate of absenteeism caused severe labour shortages at times of peak demand. Richard Williams, divisional officer for the exchanges in the North West, concluded that permanent employment was the only answer, although it 'stinks in the nostrils of the dockers'.[62]

One other consequence of national insurance has been grossly exaggerated. The Webbs alleged that the Act, 'which practically compelled every wage-earner to join an "Approved Society" of some kind, led to a dramatic expansion of Trade Union membership';[63] and Postgate attributed the failures of the syndicalists to 'the great number

---

[58] *Dockers Record*, June 1911.   [59] Sexton, p. 226.   [60] Richard Williams, p. 12.
[61] National Union of Dock Labourers, *Annual Report*, 1912.
[62] Richard Williams, pp. 130–32.
[63] Sidney and Beatrice Webb, *History*, p. 498.

of "insurance members" who had joined the unions as a result of Lloyd George's Act'.[64]

The Act demonstrably led to some recruitment to the unions. In his report to the Railway Servants' conference in 1912, J. E. Williams affirmed that 'thousands of non-unionist railwaymen have made this society their approved society, and simultaneously with their declaration a Trade Union membership form has been received'. The Shop Assistants launched a recruiting campaign around their approved society in March 1912, instructing the organisers to give it priority over all other duties. In August they claimed to have increased their membership from 23,000 to 60,000 as a result. However, they added that this was 'the largest increase made by any Trade Union in connection with the Insurance Act',[65] and there is little evidence that there was a marked overall effect. It must be supposed that trade union approved societies were more attractive to existing trade union members than to non-unionists, not only because of the loyalty of the former to their unions but also because the latter would have to start paying union dues in addition to their insurance contributions. However, although there were over three million trade unionists at the beginning of 1912, the trade union approved societies had less than 1.5 million members by October 1912, after the scheme had been in operation for three months. Finally, the increase of 8 per cent in total trade union membership in 1912 was well below the figures of 20 per cent for 1911 and 21 per cent for 1913. The Act could therefore not have been a major influence on union growth in the period as a whole.

Trade Union Structure

Periods of rapid trade union growth are associated with enthusiasm for amalgamation between unions. Rapid growth breeds competition between unions in which the larger seek amalgamation as a means of pushing ahead, and the smaller as the best way to get into the race. It was so in the years immediately after the First World War, and again in the period of growth which began in 1968. Before the First World War, enthusiasm for mergers was fomented by the syndicalists who, after the coal and dock strikes of 1912 were over, turned their attention to the reconstruction of the trade union movement as the essential preliminary to achieving their long-term goals.

A Provisional Committee for the Amalgamation of Existing Unions, set up in 1910, does not appear to have been inspired by syndicalism. However, it had its greatest success among the building unions where the lead was soon taken by the syndicalists of the Operative Bricklayers Society. In August 1911 Hicks and Adams persuaded their union to

[64] Postgate, p. 143.   [65] *The Shop Assistant*, 24 August 1912.

establish a consolidation committee to negotiate with the other building unions. Amalgamation committees were also set up in other industries, and in November 1912 the Syndicalist Education League took a hand by calling a conference of the committees in building, engineering and shipbuilding, printing, and transport. By February 1913 a federation of amalgamation committees had been formed with another bricklayer, J. V. Wills, as secretary, and the *Industrial Syndicalist* contained an 'Amalgamation News Page'.[66]

Meanwhile the Plebs Leaguers had set up an Unofficial Reform Committee in South Wales which was responsible for the classic statement of British syndicalism, the *Miners' Next Step*. They kept in touch with the amalgamation committees elsewhere, but since the South Wales Miners Federation already approximated fairly closely to an industrial union, they saw their task as the accomplishment of its internal reconstruction to make it a more effective instrument to fight the owners and take over the industry.

The amalgamationists had their successes. A large number of schemes were floated. Most of the major unions outside coal and cotton were involved. Favourable resolutions were carried at the Trades Union Congress in 1910 and 1911, the second committing the Parliamentary Committee to offer active assistance; and over the next two years the committee did its best to comply. By way of actual amalgamations, however, there was little to show.

The one achievement was the merger of the Railway Servants, the General Railway Workers, and the United Pointsmen and Signalmen, in which the assistance of the Parliamentary Committee was not required and the influence of the syndicalists was probably of little importance, although their supporters in the railway unions gave it enthusiastic backing. The Railway Servants had been founded as a union for all railwaymen. They had always sought to bring the wanderers back into the fold, especially the Locomotive Engineers and Firemen; and united action between the four unions in the 1911 strike presented them with an opportunity to try again. The Locomotive Engineers and Firemen, who had no intention of being taken over by the Railway Servants, proposed federation, but that was not enough for the three remaining unions who therefore went ahead with an amalgamation which could not now constitute an industrial union, and amounted to the absorption of two minor organisations by the Railway Servants. What justified the considerable attention given to the new union was its rate of growth, from

[66] During the autumn of 1913 a controversy between Mann and Bowman split the Industrial Syndicalist Education League. Bowman retained the *Industrial Syndicalist*, and printed bitter attacks on Mann, who joined with the amalgamationists to form yet another organisation—the Industrial Democracy League.

156,000 for the three constituents at the end of 1912 to 268,000 a year later. Many of the new members came from the railway workshops.

The General Railway Workers' membership in the railway work-shops had reached 10,000 by 1912. They refused to proceed with the amalgamation unless the new union was open to all employees of the railway companies, including shopmen. The Railway Servants were compelled to agree or abandon the merger. When the amalgamation was completed the National Union of Railwaymen began an active and successful campaign to organise shopmen of all grades, despite the inevitability of conflict with the craft unions.

Another merger which was set in train during these years, but not consummated until 1915, showed even more clearly how remote were the principles of industrial unionism from the realities of British trade union structure. Prior to the takeover by the Post Office of the National Telephone Company and almost all the municipal telephone exchanges in 1911, their staffs had been organised by the Amalgamated Society of Telephone Employees which entered the civil service ten thousand strong. Samuel refused recognition on the grounds that the existing Post Office unions adequately represented telephone staff, and recommended a transfer of membership. The Telephone Employees countered with a proposal for an amalgamation of all the Post Office unions, but this was unacceptable to the existing unions and to the Post Office which 'rejected it, advancing the standard Civil Service objection to an association whose membership would transect the lines of the grades'.[67] By 1915 the Telephone Employees felt they had done all they could to secure fair treatment for their members from the Post Office and agreed to a merger which split them up between the Engineering and Stores Association and three unions organising telephone operators, clerical workers and inspectors.

Otherwise all was failure. In 1912 the Parliamentary Committee sent out ballot papers to twenty-one building unions for them to distribute to their members. The Painters and nine small unions decided not to comply. Parsonage, the Painters' secretary, argued that it was no use voting on the principle of one union for the building trades without seeing the detailed proposals. The remaining eleven unions voted by almost three to one in favour of a single building union, but less than 40 per cent of their members recorded a vote, and among the Bricklayers, Plumbers, and Stonemasons the figure was considerably lower. Conse-quently there was little prospect of a detailed scheme receiving the two-thirds majority of the membership of each union required by law.

Nevertheless, a scheme for a Building Workers Union was drafted. At this stage the Amalgamated Carpenters and Joiners withdrew, because

[67] Bealey, p. 113.

the 'stipulation that only persons employed in the building industry of the United Kingdom could be eligible for membership . . . meant us relinquishing our shipyard members and also our members in the overseas districts'.[68] Another vote was taken by the remaining unions in 1913. This time the scheme won only a narrow majority, and the numbers voting were far below the minimum figures required by law; it was therefore dropped. During the final stages of the London building strike, Wills and a few other syndicalists decided to go ahead on their own. The Building Workers Industrial Union was set up at a meeting in Birmingham in August 1914 as a tiny splinter organisation.

None of the other amalgamation committees succeeded in getting serious discussion on their proposals. In 1911 the Federation of Engineering and Shipbuilding Trades promoted a plan for a common strike fund. When it was put to a ballot of the constituent unions, the Engineers rejected it. According to their *Monthly Report* of November 1911, the vote showed that the members considered the objectives of the proposal 'would be better met by amalgamation'. Such an amalgamation would have been a takeover of the smaller craft unions by the Engineers. There was no enthusiasm for this alternative among the smaller unions, and without the Engineers the proposal for closer federation was dropped.

Among the steel unions the champion of amalgamation was the autocratic John Hodge of the Steel Smelters, who were as ready to take over the small unions in their industry as the Engineers were to incorporate the smaller engineering unions. In 1912 he secured the assistance of the Joint Board in bringing the other unions together to discuss his proposals. Most of them would go no further than a federation, from which he held aloof, but he was able to persuade the Enginemen and Cranemen into a merger.

The efforts of the Parliamentary Committee to promote an amalgamation between the two shop assistants' unions ran into trouble over the Co-operative Employees' members in the Co-operative Wholesale Society's factories. A joint committee tried to resolve the problem, but the Co-operative Employees drew back when they found they had become the junior partner in the scheme because of the members who poured into the Shop Assistants' union through their approved society. They now saw amalgamation as 'absorption and extinction by another body which depends for its boasted superior strength on a horde of persons . . . who are not trade unionists at all, but simply joined as assured persons'.[69]

This was not the end of the story, for there were other unions with grievances against the Co-operative Employees. The Parliamentary

[68] Higenbottam, p. 124.   [69] *The Co-operative Employee*, July 1913.

Committee was charged to conduct an inquiry into their 'bona fides' as a trade union by the Boot and Shoe Operatives, the Bakers, the Tailors, and the National Amalgamated Union of Labour, all of whom had members in Co-operative Wholesale Society factories. There was a precedent for their complaints. In 1906 the Trades Union Congress had resolved that 'any method of organisation which seeks to divide workmen employed by public authorities or private employers from their fellows in the same occupation employed by private firms is detrimental to the best interests of Trade Unionism', and, after the decision had been confirmed by the Joint Board in 1908, the Municipal Employees Association disaffiliated from both Congress and the Labour Party rather than accept the alternative of handing over their members to other unions. The Co-operative Employees accepted the Parliamentary Committee's finding in 1912 that they should not recruit 'workers in the skilled trades', but after further pressure from the competing unions, now including the Shop Assistants, the Parliamentary Committee ruled in 1914 that all existing members eligible to join other unions must be transferred; and in 1915 the Co-operative Employees withdrew their affiliation, announcing that all co-operative employees were once more eligible for membership.

A similar problem arose when the Transport Workers Federation debated amalgamation at their 1913 conference. They had to face the problem of what to do with the affiliated general unions such as the London Dockers, the Gasworkers, and the National Amalgamated Union of Labour. The Liverpool Dockers, who wanted to dismember the general unions by confining amalgamation to transport workers alone, was opposed by Thorne and a Bristol organiser of the London Dockers called Ernest Bevin, who argued that case for one big union of the less-skilled. Talks on this proposal were opened with the General Labourers National Council.

Such a scheme was anathema to the syndicalists. They had little room for general unions. Their ally, G. D. H. Cole, suggested the function of a general union was to serve as 'a sort of Trade Union clearing-house'. It should 'organise those classes of workers who are engaged in scattered or unorganised trades, till a separate Union becomes possible'.[70] By contrast, the General Labourers National Council believed that an amalgamation of its constituent unions would create an 'irresistible' organisation of four hundred thousand members, which would avoid 'much wasted labour, overlapping, and make it possible to thoroughly organise the . . lesser skilled workmen throughout the country';[71] and

---

[70] Cole, *The World of Labour*, pp. 239–40.
[71] National Amalgamated Union of Labour, Conference of Executive and Officials, 27–8 March 1914.

they were prepared to include the Transport Workers Federation. But the difficulties were formidable. The proposals were whittled down to cover strike benefit and industrial matters only, in order to meet the demands of the individual unions for autonomy in other respects. The dockers who had already 'suffered by reason of the Transport Federation Ticket affording access to [their] jobs . . . looked askance upon any suggestion calculated to aggravate this state of affairs'.[72] When the scheme languished, Tillett came forward with a proposal for a merger between his union and the Gasworkers which the latter were disposed to consider favourably. However, the outbreak of war postponed detailed discussion.

The greatest achievement of the Unofficial Reform Committee in South Wales was to persuade the annual conference of the South Wales Miners in June 1912 to set up a committee of twelve members, six from the executive and six elected by the conference, to prepare a scheme of reform. Their proposals, which Brace outlined to a further conference in July, were 'simple and radical'.[73] The districts with their own elected agents were to go. Henceforth the agents, drastically reduced in number, were to be subject to election every three years and to work directly under the control of an executive consisting of lay members only, which would in turn be responsible to a delegate conference meeting quarterly. Contributions were to be doubled to 10p a month. The scheme was a frontal attack on the agents, whose influence was sufficient to persuade the conference to vote by a small majority to retain the districts, although another small majority refused to reject the scheme entirely, and referred it back. Since the abolition of the districts was central to the scheme, that issue was submitted, on its own, to a coalfield ballot which supported abolition by a majority of ten thousand in a vote of 85,000. Rather hesitantly the executive told the drafting committee to continue their work. A full scheme was put to another ballot, after a further conference had made 'numerous amendments'.[74] The result, reported in February 1913, was almost two to one against the proposals, and the South Wales Miners continued under their old constitution. 'By the summer of 1914 the Unofficial Reform Committee had largely disbanded.'[75]

Why did the syndicalist plans for structural reform come to nothing? The primary reason was that their proposals were drawn up to conform to the principle of industrial unionism, and not to deal with the practicalities of current trade union organisation. In order to preserve

---

[72] National Transport Workers Federation, *Annual Report*, 1914.
[73] Francis and Smith, p. 17.
[74] Arnot, *South Wales Miners*, p. 324.
[75] Morgan, p. 171.

the purity of the principle, the Building Workers Union was designed to divorce substantial sections of the largest building union, the Amalgamated Carpenters and Joiners, from their fellow craftsmen, and to have a similar effect on several other unions, especially the Bricklayers and the Plumbers. In other words, they were asking craftsmen to cut themselves off from their brothers in their own craft, in order to achieve unity with the members of other crafts and labourers with whom they did not feel the same bond.

In addition, syndicalism taught hostility to officialdom; and it is extremely difficult to carry through a trade union amalgamation or reorganisation against the opposition of the officials. With the law as it stood at that time, it was impossible. Despite the general popularity of the railway union merger among the Railway Servants, a special session of their executive learned in April 1912 that their ballot had not achieved the required vote of two-thirds of the members, because many branches had not returned any votes at all. They decided to keep the ballot open until the end of May 'to give branches and individuals an opportunity to express their opinion'; but who, other than the officials, was going to travel round the country to see that the opportunity was taken? In South Wales the reformers chose to launch a frontal attack on the most powerful group in the union, the agents, by proposing to abolish their fiefs, the districts, to dismiss many of them and to subject the remainder to periodic election and central control.

The syndicalists were not alone in suffering a loss of reputation through failure to reconstruct the trade union movement. The Parliamentary Committee had also invested a good deal of their time and authority in promoting amalgamations which came to nothing. They could have done with some successes in this aspect of their work to offset the diminution of their political role. They still set off on their annual round of deputations to ministers to acquaint them with the wishes of Congress, and promoted a number of private members' bills. They were still useful to government departments in the drafting of the details of legislation, especially the National Insurance Bill, and the bulky amending bill, made necessary by the experience of the first few months of the Act's operation. But, after the departure of Shackleton, they no longer had much part in the design of political strategy. It was Ramsay MacDonald and Arthur Henderson who negotiated with ministers over the main issues involved in payment of Members of Parliament, national insurance, and the restoration of the right of trade unions to undertake political action. It was they who could deliver votes in the House of Commons, and their abilities clearly surpassed those of the successive chairmen of the Parliamentary Committee and of C. W. Bowerman, who succeeded Steadman as secretary of Congress in 1911.

The growth in the authority of the Parliamentary Labour Party might have been expected to induce the Parliamentary Committee to concentrate their attention on their industrial functions, especially at a time of rising industrial unrest. Certainly they tried to keep in touch with the major strikes; but the Dublin strike in 1913 was the only one in which they played a major part. In that dispute they undertook responsibility for feeding and later for paying the strikers; they sent deputations to Dublin and held public meetings there; and they interceded with the Castle and negotiated with the employers. However, in three other major disputes it was the Labour Party which took the limelight. In the rail dispute of 1911 the companies were finally forced to negotiate by a resolution of the House of Commons prompted by the Labour Party; and next year the party used the same device in the London dock strike, this time without success. In the interval, they served as the spokesmen for the Miners in the passage of the Minimum Wage Bill. It seemed that growing government intervention in industrial relations was enabling MacDonald and Henderson to outclass the Parliamentary Committee on what should have been their own ground.

During 1912 the Parliamentary Committee arranged a series of demonstrations on an old issue which was coming to the forefront again in several industries—the eight-hour day—and at the beginning of 1913 they set about organising a ballot of affiliated unions. The ballot paper caused problems. On 2 January they agreed to ask whether their constituents favoured the eight-hour day 'with rigid restriction of overtime', and believed it should be attained by negotiation. Two weeks later they added another question asking whether, if negotiations failed, the committee should support unions which fixed a date 'after which none of their members will work more than eight hours in any one day'. After another two weeks this question was amended to ask the unions whether they would give support through the Parliamentary Committee in such circumstances; and the unions were also asked whether they were in favour of a general eight-hour bill. In September Congress was informed that of the 2.2 million affiliated members, 204,000 had been given the opportunity to vote by their unions; in unions with 780,000 members the executives had replied on their behalf; and no replies had been received from the remaining unions which accounted for 55 per cent of the total. Congress thereupon voted for an eight-hour working day by legislation and nothing more was heard of the matter.

These were disappointing years for the Parliamentary Committee; but it should not be concluded that Congress was on the point of disintegrating. It was still valued at least as a publicity platform—which was all that its founders had claimed for it nearly a half-century earlier. Membership of the Parliamentary Committee was still a mark of distinction to be coveted. The committee was still a major organ of the labour movement.[76]

Only one important union disaffiliated from Congress in the years 1911–14, the Amalgamated Carpenters and Joiners. Their secretary, Francis Chandler, wrote to the committee to tell them that 'secession had been persistently engineered by a small section' who had now achieved a slender majority in a ballot;[77] and the union's executive roundly condemned the decision.

Writing in the *Daily Herald* of 5 May 1914, Cole and Mellor saw in the General Federation of Trade Unions

the germ of the future central controlling force of the Trade Union movement. Its scope must be widened; every union must pay . . . to the general fund, and there should be in addition the power to raise compulsory levies. . . . In this remodelled General Federation the Trade Union Congress and the Parliamentary Committee should be absorbed.

In fact, however, the General Federation was in no state to compete with Congress. Industrial unrest continued to eat into its reserves. By 1912 they were down to £35,000. Its chairman told a special meeting of the council in January 1912 that the federation

had just enough by pawning all its resources to pay the Weavers three weeks' benefit. The probability of a crisis like the present one has frequently been placed before the General Council, which has just as frequently postponed consideration of the problem.

At its annual meeting in July, the council restored the original level of contributions, which had been cut to two-thirds during the years of industrial peace, and reduced the maximum period of benefit. However, the demand on the funds outstripped the increase in income, so that the reserves dropped to £16,000 in 1913. Moreover, the increase in contributions had an effect on membership. Four affiliates withdrew, including two of the largest, the Gasworkers and the Liverpool Dockers.

Potentially even more damaging was an attack on the federation in 1913 by the Miners, who were not affiliated. A dispute between the Cumberland Miners and the National Amalgamated Union of Labour over membership among colliery surfaceworkers led to the dismissal of some members of the National Amalgamated Union who refused to join the Miners, and a strike in which the Miners were alleged to have done the work of men on strike. The National Amalgamated Union appealed

[76] Ross M. Martin, pp. 130–31.
[77] Parliamentary Committee, 24 April 1911.

to the General Federation, which decided to investigate the dispute; but the Miners challenged their authority to do so. The case was submitted to the Joint Board whose authority was also challenged by the Miners because of the presence of the General Federation. The Miners then took their case to Congress in September. Congress refused to support them, but the incident drew attention to the weakness of the General Federation's position on the Joint Board. Less than a quarter of total trade union membership was affiliated to it, and the great majority of its constituent unions were also affiliated to both the Trades Union Congress and the Labour Party. There was very little for the Joint Board to do that could not have been done as well without the General Federation. Apart from adjudicating in inter-union disputes, the board's major functions were to co-ordinate the actions of the Labour movement over issues such as national insurance and the Osborne judgment, and to call general conferences to take decisions about them. These activities would have suffered little from the absence of the General Federation.

It was in these circumstances that a number of trade unionists began to see the possibility of a more powerful co-ordinator of trade union industrial action in the proposal for a 'triple alliance' of the Miners, the Transport Workers, and the Railwaymen, which was discussed by these three organisations over the winter of 1913–14. The alliance appears to have been first mooted by Hartshorn in an interview published in the *Labour Leader* on 13 October 1911, when he looked forward to a 'working alliance' between miners, railwaymen and seamen. His idea was taken up again on several occasions during the next two years, and in October 1913 Frank Hodges, a Ruskin rebel recently elected miners' agent for Garw at the age of twenty-four, was chosen to move a resolution for South Wales at the Miners' conference instructing the executive 'to approach the Executive Committees of other big Trade Unions with a view to co-operative action and support of each others' demands'. The Railwaymen and the Transport Workers were approached. The leaders of all three organisations gave virtually unanimous approval. Rules were drafted during the early months of 1914 and provisionally accepted by the three executives in June. However, the Miners intended to take their final decision at their annual conference in October, and before that the outbreak of war had postponed the whole scheme.

Although Hodges was at that time something of a syndicalist, the alliance cannot be explained as a syndicalist victory over moderate union leaders. For one thing, the syndicalists had no power to force Smillie or Thomas or Sexton or Havelock Wilson into a course of action that they did not want to follow. That had been amply demonstrated during the previous three years, and the influence of the syndicalists was now on the decline. For another, the leaders did not resist the proposal. They welcomed it so long as the constitution of the alliance was framed on their terms.

The three organisations had special reasons for wishing to concert industrial action. The last three years had shown that railwaymen, dockers and seamen were laid off in large numbers by a national coal strike, and that transport strikes shut down the pits as soon as the limits of stockpiling had been reached. If they were going to strike, there was a lot to be said for doing so at the same time, and for co-ordinating the timing of their agreements to allow this to be done.

Then there was the problem of sympathetic strikes. The Railwaymen's executive was plagued with demands to pull other people's chestnuts out of the fire. Even the militants within the union were tired of these importunings.[78] The other transport unions were also liable to be called upon. Robert Williams told the 1913 conference of the Transport Workers Federation that 'every official agreed with sympathetic action on the part of other unions when his own was in trouble, just as he repudiated it when his own members were called upon to assist other unions'. The Railwaymen's executive more than once asked the Parliamentary Committee to deal with the matter, for example by calling a national conference to decide on requests for assistance from other unions 'in a businesslike manner' (25 September 1913). Accordingly, 'the NUR leadership supported the new venture in the hope that sympathetic and local strikes might be reduced to the minimum.[79]

The leaders of all three unions appreciated that the alliance could equip them with an awesome bargaining strength which by mere 'threat of massive strike measures would be enough to force the government to intervene in disputes, more or less as a protagonist of labour—as it had done in the railway and transport strikes of 1911 and (more reluctantly) in the mining dispute of 1912'.[80] The leaders could therefore see the alliance as likely to 'do more than anything else ever instituted to prevent strikes as we know them', as Burton of Northumberland told the Miners when he supported Hodges's resolution.

The draft constitution of the alliance provided weighty safeguards against hasty use of the combined power of the three organisations. Each

[78] In December 1911, on the motion of two militants, Edwards and Cramp, the executive of the Railway Servants rejected a request from their Acton and Ealing branch to be allowed to refuse to work troop trains intended to take troops to the scene of a strike, regretting that 'the division of Trade Unionists into so many unions' rendered it 'impossible for us at this time to give the authority desired'.

[79] Bagwell, p. 307.

[80] Phillips, 'The Triple Alliance in 1914', p. 65.

of them was entitled 'to take action on their own behalf'. Joint action required a decision of the executive 'of the organisation primarily concerned', submission to the joint body 'for consideration', confirmation from 'the members of the three organisations . . . by such methods as the constitution of each organisation provides', and a conference of the three organisations 'to consider and decide the question of taking action'. The Railwaymen's executive had authority to call a national strike; the Miners' rules now required a two-thirds majority in a ballot; and in 1913 the conference of the Transport Workers Federation had approved a new rule empowering their executive to

control and conduct disputes in the trades and occupations covered by the Federation when requested by the Executives of the affiliated unions interested, and after consultation with the Executives of all the affiliated unions likely to be affected.

Since a number of the affiliated unions required ballots to sanction a strike, calling a strike of the Triple Alliance in accordance with its rules could be a clumsy, prolonged and uncertain undertaking. There were safeguards enough to justify the verdict of the Railwaymen's president, Bellamy, in his address to their annual conference in 1914: the alliance 'is neither revolutionary nor Syndicalistic. It is a force which is not intended to be used indiscriminately or frivolously.' It 'is a solidifying movement for mutual co-operation in times of emergency'.

Dangerfield was therefore indulging his imagination when he wrote: 'At the slightest excuse, the Triple Alliance was prepared to go into action', and asserted that its leaders in July 1914, 'balancing so precariously upon the edge of their precipice', at the foot of which 'lay a General Strike . . . began to totter, to sway forward'.[81] For this there would have to have been an issue to put to the alliance (not yet officially in being). There was none such in evidence in the Transport Workers Federation. A failure of the negotiations on a new railway agreement might have provided the occasion for a request for assistance at the end of the year, but so far they appeared to be proceeding smoothly, with the companies fully prepared to meet and discuss with the unions. The one trouble-spot was the Scottish coalfield, where the faceworkers' minimum now stood at 35p a day, after two reductions awarded by the chairman of the conciliation board due to falling prices; and the owners were asking for another reduction. Towards the end of July the Miners Federation agreed to hold a ballot on a general stoppage if the Scottish

[81] Dangerfield, pp. 328, 398–400. In support, Dangerfield (p. 330) quoted from a speech by Askwith in November 1913: 'Within a comparatively short time there may be movements in this country coming to a head of which recent events have been a small foreshadowing.' (Askwith, p. 349.)

owners pressed their claim. However, before the ballot was held, the Scottish negotiations would have had to reach a final impasse—and in fact the owners waived their claim as soon as war broke out. Before the federation could strike the ballot would have to have returned a two-thirds majority for a strike in support of Scotland; and there never had been nor would be an occasion on which the national federation struck in support of a district.

Even then, once the ballot was declared, the government would inevitably have intervened, and its intervention would have had to fail before the alliance came into action. The Miners had not followed the consultative procedure laid down in the alliance's rules before they decided on their ballot; and nothing had yet been done to co-ordinate the agreements of the three partners, so that the railwaymen and many transport workers would have been obliged to break their agreements if they came out in support. If they had nevertheless consented to proceed at the request of the Miners, the Transport Workers Federation would have been constitutionally obliged to consult their constituents, some of whom were bound by their rules to conduct ballots.

4

Asquith's War

The Impact of War

DURING the last days of July 1914 and the first days of August, many British trade union leaders and some of their followers had been taking part in meetings and demonstrations which proclaimed their opposition to war. On 4 August Britain declared war on Germany; the unions now had to respond to this *fait accompli*, and decide what advice to give their members. The Joint Board had called a conference of a wide range of labour organisations for 5 August, which had been intended to set up a National Labour Peace Emergency Committee to co-ordinate opposition to Britain's involvement in war. Instead it founded the War Emergency Workers National Committee, representing virtually every section of the Labour movement, to assist workers to cope with the expected economic consequences of war. Next day the Labour Party executive reaffirmed its opposition 'to the policy which has produced the war', but advised that the immediate task of 'Labour and Socialist organisations' was to 'concentrate their energies . . . upon the task of carrying out the resolutions' of the conference held on 5 August. The Parliamentary Committee met on 12 August and decided to postpone the meeting of Congress due in September, but no advice was given to its constituent unions on industrial relations in wartime until 24 August when a meeting of the executives of the three bodies affiliated to the Joint Board asked 'that an immediate effort be made to terminate all existing trade disputes', and advised that 'whenever new points of difficulty arise during the war period, a serious attempt should be made by all concerned to reach an amicable settlement before resorting to a strike or lock-out'.[1]

The request for existing disputes to be terminated was hardly necessary. Almost all had been, including the London building lockout and the Scottish Miners' pay dispute. The appeal for a serious attempt to settle disputes before a stoppage was one that most trade unionists would have been willing to endorse at any time, peace or war, but was nevertheless generally regarded as inaugurating an 'industrial truce'. Some employers interpreted it to mean that there should be no stoppages for the duration of the war, and even no wage increases. It was

[1] Trades Union Congress, 1915, p. 185.

a flattering compliment to the three executives to suppose that they had the authority to issue such an edict.

On 3 September the Parliamentary Committee brought out a considered statement on the war in a *Manifesto to the Trade Unionists of the Country*. Upon the outcome 'rests the preservation and maintenance of free and unfettered democratic government'. The action of the Parliamentary Labour Party in giving support to the government's recruitment campaign was fully endorsed; and the manifesto added that if voluntary recruitment failed to yield the numbers required 'the demand for a national system of compulsory service . . . may prove to be so persistent and strong as to become irresistible'.[2] The contrast with their attitude at the beginning of August does not condemn them as hypocrites. The concern of union leaders for the preservation of peace was genuine and strong, as they were to show more than once after the war; but they had not previously had cause to consider what they should do once a major war had started.

One immediate economic effect of the war was a sharp reduction in exports. Cotton textiles and some of the exporting coalfields were particularly badly hit. Uncertainty also affected domestic industries and services, such as building, printing, and the retail trade. Foreseeing this and also the difficulties of families in which the breadwinner volunteered for the forces, the government had on 4 August appointed a committee for the relief of distress arising out of the war. Two days later a start was made on setting up local committees, and the Prince of Wales launched a national relief fund.

At the end of August the percentage unemployed in trade unions providing unemployment benefit was 7.1, compared with 2.8 a month earlier; but by that time many industries were beginning to recover from the initial impact, and many workers had volunteered for the forces. Thereafter unemployment continued to fall until the end of the year, when it was below the July figure, but several industries, including cotton, printing, and furniture, suffered heavier unemployment and took longer to recover.

Both government and employers showed themselves sympathetic. Already on 19 August the Engineering Employers Federation had agreed to recommend to local engineering associations that they should confer with union representatives on means of reducing unemployment as much as possible. On 11 September the War Office advised contractors to take on extra workers or sublet contracts rather than work overtime. And on 2 October, following a plea from the Joint Board, the government announced a scheme under which unions 'suffering from abnormal unemployment' and prepared to impose a special levy to meet

[2] Ibid., p. 212.

it could qualify for an emergency grant increasing with the amount of the levy. By the end of March 1915 over £76,000 had been paid out, more than £64,000 of it to the cotton unions.

A second economic effect of the war was rising prices. Food prices rose by no less than 10 per cent during August, and the increase was up to 18 per cent by the end of the year, when the general cost of living index was given as 10–15 per cent above July. The War Emergency Committee took the matter up along with its demand for an increase in pensions and dependants' allowances for the armed forces. A series of local conferences was held on the latter issue in November 1914, and local protest meetings on food prices were arranged early in 1915.

Not all current wage claims were abandoned when war broke out. In August the London shiprepair employers rejected a general claim, but in October they agreed to pay an 'abnormal rate' on Admiralty work for the duration of the war only. General increases were awarded to engineering workers in London and Birmingham by Central Conference, and in Leicester by local agreement. Within a fortnight of the outbreak of war the Sailors and Firemen had persuaded the Admiralty to pay an additional £1 a month on requisitioned merchant vessels, promising in return to ensure a prompt and adequate supply of men. In November several groups of iron and steel workers secured pay advances under their sliding-scale agreements. On the other hand falling coal prices brought a reduction for Durham miners in the same month; and for shop assistants the war brought 'dismissals, cutting down wages, curtailing food allowances in living-in houses'. In October their union instructed them to resist all wage reductions unless accompanied by a corresponding cut in working hours, and wlecomed the wartime tendency to earlier closing.[3]

Early in 1915 came the first acknowledgement from the government that the increase in the cost of living since July justified an advance in wages, at least in industries essential to the war effort. At the outbreak of war they had assumed control of the railways for the duration, appointing a Railway Executive Committee of railway managers to run them on their behalf. In February, having been assured that the government would meet three-quarters of the cost of the increase, the committee bypassed the company conciliation boards with a national agreement for an increase of 15p to all railwaymen paid less than £1.50 a week, and of 10p to those paid more.

Four days after the railway settlement the first serious strike of the war began in Glasgow. Just before the war the engineering unions on the Clyde decided to submit a claim for an advance of 45p a week when their current three-year agreement on pay ran out in January 1915. An offer

[3] *The Shop Assistant*, 29 August, 24 October 1914.

of just over 11p was rejected and referred to Central Conference, due to meet on 12 February 1915. They raised the figure to 17p which was submitted to a ballot. Before it could be held the news spread abroad that Weirs was paying 45p above the current rate to American engineering workers who had been brought over to help meet the growing labour shortage on the Clyde. The firm alleged that the additional rate was a lodging allowance, but this did not satisfy their employees, who struck on 16 February, followed by workers at other local factories, until nearly 10,000 were out. The strike was organised by a committee of shop stewards from the factories affected who gave themselves the title of Central Labour Withholding Committee, which they considered less provocative than 'strike committee'. The ballot rejected the 17p by an overwhelming majority, and an impasse was reached.

Since many of the strikers were engaged on the manufacture of urgently needed munitions, the government had to intervene. They referred the dispute to the Committee on Production which had been appointed on 4 February to discover

the best steps to be taken to ensure that the productive power of the employees in engineering and shipbuilding establishments working for Government purposes shall be made fully available so as to meet the need of the nation in the present emergency.

The chairman, Askwith, informed the parties that work must be resumed on 1 March, after which his committee would arbitrate. The Engineers' executive visited Glasgow to persuade their members to accept these terms, but failed to convince a mass meeting of shop stewards. However, sensing that their grip was weakening, the Labour Withholding Committee issued their own instructions for a return to work, naming the day as 4 March. The award was for $22\frac{1}{2}$p a week on time rates and 10 per cent on piece rates. A few days before a national claim for shipbuilding workers had been settled by a similar award. These increases, however, were war bonuses for the duration only.

Shortages of skilled workers in engineering and shipbuilding had begun to make themselves felt during the previous autumn. In November 1914 the shipbuilding employers had discussed the matter with the unions, which considered local discussions would be more useful; but they were not, and in December there were further national joint meetings in shipbuilding and in engineering as well. The engineering employers asked for freedom from craft restrictions on the employment of women and less-skilled men; freedom from limitations on the manning of machines; and the removal of demarcation and over-time restrictions. The union leaders doubted whether their members were ready to make such concessions, and suggested as alternatives the placing of contracts with firms not engaged on war work, the transfer of skilled men from private work to munitions, travel and subsistence allowances to encourage mobility, recruitment in the dominions, and the return of skilled men from the services. The employers found these suggestions inadequate.

In mid-January Askwith was asked to inquire into all the manpower issues in dispute in the two industries. His view, given in a memorandum of 28 January 1915, was that the ideal solution would be to persuade the parties to reach satisfactory agreements; but, since success in this could not be guaranteed, the government might have to propose, and even enforce, a solution of their own. A few days later he was appointed chairman of the Committee on Production which was to explore the first alternative. His colleagues were Sir Francis Hopwood of the Admiralty and Sir George Gibb of the War Office.

Their first report dealt with the problems caused by heavy absenteeism among boilermakers in the shipyards, proposing an agreement for making up 'broken squads' so that work could proceed. The next report was in two parts. The second of them proposed that there should be no strikes or lockouts on government work during the war, and unresolved disputes should be referred to an 'impartial tribunal'. The government immediately empowered the committee to 'deal with any cases arising under the above recommendation',[4] and the Clyde arbitration followed. The first part of the report, which was held up until the outcome on the Clyde was known, dealt with the production of shells and fuses, proposing that, in order to induce workers to abandon limitations on output, the employers should give an undertaking that there should be no reduction in piece rates unless the method of production was altered; and that there should be 'an extension of the practice of employing female labour on this work, under suitable and proper conditions'.[5]

These reports were soon followed by a shipyard agreement on broken squads and an engineering agreement on shells and fuses. The third report, issued on 8 March, dealt with far wider issues: the general questions of relaxation of demarcation between crafts, and the use of women and less-skilled men on craft jobs in both shipbuilding and engineering. The committee recommended relaxation of existing practices under both headings, with suitable guarantees against loss of earnings and for the restoration of the original practices after the war. At this stage the government decided to intervene directly, by calling a

---

[4] Askwith, p. 370.

[5] The two parts of the second report of the Committee on Production are reproduced in Cole, *Trade Unionism and Munitions* (pp. 62–4), where they are described as the second and third reports of the committee.

conference of the principal unions concerned with the production and distribution of munitions, along with representatives of the Parliamentary Committee and the General Federation of Trade Unions. The conference, which began on 17 March, was chaired by Lloyd George, and held 'in the gloomy boardroom of the Treasury, with the gilt throne of Queen Anne at one end of the room'. He had invited Balfour, who

was surprised to find the workmen's representatives talked so well. . . . He saw these stalwart artisans leaning against and sitting on the steps of the throne of the dead queen, and on equal terms negotiating with the Government of the day upon a question vitally affecting the conduct of a great war. . . . [He] was bewildered by this sudden revelation of a new power.[6]

The Munitions of War Act, 1915

The armaments manufacturers had succeeded in steering debate about the inadequate supply of munitions onto the shortcomings of skilled workers and their unions. It was of course true that skilled labour was in short supply and relaxation of craft practices would help to meet the deficiency; but that was far from being the whole story. The armaments firms had accepted contracts well beyond their capacity and that of their subcontractors to fulfil, even if they had had all the labour they wanted. In the longer term the needs of the forces were met by building national factories. The most promising immediate remedy was to let contracts to engineering firms still engaged on private work, but this avenue was blocked by the organisation and attitudes of the War Office.

The military departments were responsible for estimates of requirements, for prescribing quality, for the allocation of contracts, and for administering the Ordnance Factories. . . . The Contracts Department did not administer the contract when made, they had no first hand knowledge of the reliability of performance by different firms. Neither were they authorised to facilitate the placing of contracts or extension of supply where this involved any departure from specification or substitution for materials difficult to procure. Their ignorance of future . . . requirements made it impossible to plan for increase in capacity, the demand for which was not formally registered.[7]

The War Office was extremely reluctant to move outside the established armaments firms, and left it to them to select their own subcontractors.

These defects were evident to the various individuals and committees appointed by the government to help resolve the problems. There were proposals for reorganisation in the War Office, blocked by Kitchener,

[6] Lloyd George, p. 177.
[7] *History of the Ministry of Munitions*, Vol. I, Part I, p. 69.

who had been appointed Secretary of State for War; and in their fourth report, never published, the Committee on Production proposed that:

the Government should assume control of the principal armament and ship-building firms. They pointed out that the general Labour unrest of the previous few weeks was accompanied by a widespread belief among workpeople that abnormal profits were being made, particularly on Government contracts. . . . An Executive Committee, on the lines of the Railway Executive Committee should be established (a) to search for new sources of supply, and (b) to exercise continuous and responsible supervision with representatives of the firms concerned. . . . The existence of a central executive with wide authority over the sources of supply would make possible the control over the output of the various works, the supervision and co-ordination of sub-contractors' work according to relative urgency, and some regard to efficient and co-ordinated utilisation of labour on private and Government work.[8]

The cabinet approved the recommendations of this report, and negotiations with the armament firms were opened by Runciman, the President of the Board of Trade. The firms 'barred any interference with their direction and management'.[9] The talks were, therefore, restricted to methods of limiting excess profits. Eventually it was agreed that profits should be related to output, and that after deducting the usual allowances, and a further special allowance to cover depreciation due to war work, the final net profit should not exceed that shown in the previous two years' balance sheets by more than 20 per cent.

Lloyd George therefore misled the Treasury conference when he told them in his opening statement on 17 March that the government intended 'to assume control of . . . the great works which are now being used for the production of munitions of war',[10] but his assurance that profits would be limited was well-founded. He went on to ask the unions to accept the Committee on Production's proposals for a ban on stoppages; compulsory arbitration; and the suspension of restrictive practices.

The conference lasted three days during which a draft memorandum was drawn up by a committee chaired by Henderson, with Mosses as secretary, and approved by the conference with two dissentients. The representatives affirmed that 'during the war period the relaxation of the present trade practices is imperative'. They recommended each union 'to take into favourable consideration such changes in working conditions or trade customs as may be necessary with a view to accelerating the output of war munitions or equipment'; and accepted

[8] Ibid., Vol. I, Part II, p. 69.
[9] Ibid., p. 72.
[10] Trades Union Congress, 1915, p. 220.

the proposals on banning stoppages and on arbitration.[11] However, the Miners' representatives withdrew, and the Engineers' representatives had been instructed not to commit themselves before reporting back. After they had done so, the whole executive came to the Treasury on 25 March, along with representatives from the districts, to secure more specific undertakings on limiting relaxation to war work only, on an eventual reversion to prewar practices, and on profit limitation.

The agreement required ratification by the unions before it could take effect. At the end of May the shipbuilding employers reported that most of the unions had taken no steps to secure ratification, and the Shipwrights had proposed additional items for the employers to accept before they would do so. The Engineers conducted a ballot which gave the agreement a majority of more than four to one, but, by the time the result was out, the unions were back at the Treasury discussing proposals for a Munitions Bill, which was to impose the terms of the agreement. The Treasury Agreement was no more than a stage on the road to compulsion, as Lloyd George had probably intended. He was convinced of the need for compulsion. In a speech in Manchester early in June, which caused a considerable stir, he said (according to the paraphrase of the *History of the Ministry of Munitions*):[12]

The State as an organised democracy had a right to the service of its citizens. Every man and woman was bound to render the services that the State required of them, and which in the opinion of the State they could best render. In time of war it was every citizen's duty either to work or to fight.

Meanwhile, Kitchener had appointed an Armaments Output Committee on 31 March 'to provide such additional labour as may be required'. Its searches in London produced the meagre total of 142 mechanics. However, the provinces showed better results. Armaments Committees, including representatives of the main government departments along with equal numbers of employers and trade unionists, were set up in Newcastle and Glasgow. By approaching workers as well as employers, the Newcastle committee secured promises of release for 1,661 men and then enrolled 5,730 more in a King's Squad of Armaments Workers by 30 June, when 1,680 of them had already been placed. Glasgow's scheme was less effective, but 540 men had been placed by 15 July. The committees also settled a number of disputes, and asked for wider powers. However, an alternative scheme of local organisation had already been adopted for Local Munitions Committees which included union representatives, but operated through boards of management

[11] Cole, *Trade Unionism and Munitions*, pp. 72–3.
[12] Vol. II, Part I, p. 9.

consisting only of employers. This trend to centralisation and managerial control was encouraged by yet another committee, the Munitions of War Committee, chaired by Lloyd George and including ministers, senior civil servants, and industrialists, which ranked higher than the Armaments Output Committee. It rapidly built up a national organisation with departments and sections for dealing with various aspects of munitions supply.

Lloyd George was also the central figure in an extraordinary agitation over the effect of drunkenness on munitions output, which sought to blame production shortages on 'bad time-keeping' due to excessive drinking. The king proposed, and observed for the duration, total 'abstinence' in the royal household, but the public response convinced Lloyd George that he had made a mistake. He dropped his advocacy of the nationalisation of the liquor trade, and settled for restrictions on opening times.

Hard on the heels of this agitation came the revelation of the shortage of shells on the Western Front, vigorously publicised by the press as the 'shells scandal'. The Conservatives, who regarded themselves as the country's natural leaders in times of war, and favoured more forceful methods to deal with manpower problems, had so far been restrained by their leader, Bonar Law. However, on 13 May Conservative backbenchers put down a critical motion which (followed by the resignation of the first sea lord, Fisher, over the Dardanelles campaign) led to the resignation of the Liberal government and the formation of a coalition. Henderson joined the cabinet as government labour adviser with the nominal appointment of President of the Board of Education and two other Labour members accepted junior posts; but the balance of cabinet opinion was heavily weighted in favour of compulsion by the inclusion of nine Conservatives. Lloyd George was to take over a new department which was formally established as the Ministry of Munitions on 9 June. Preparations for a wide extension of its powers were put in hand at once.

The committee of trade unionists which drafted the Treasury Agreement had accepted Lloyd George's invitation to become the National Advisory Committee on War Output. Its members were naturally aware of the course events had taken, and on 9 June they summoned another conference of trade union representatives which agreed that 'all the resources of labour should be brought into play' but 'without having resort to any form of compulsion, even as a temporary expedient'.[13] The committee then submitted a scheme, based on the Newcastle Armaments Committee's experiment, for the enlistment of skilled men who would volunteer for a period of six months to work

---

[13] *History of the Ministry of Munitions*, Vol. I, Part IV, p. 32.

wherever they were sent, subject to satisfactory terms of employment. The scheme was accepted by the conference, and the committee were also empowered 'to accept such extension of the proposals . . . as may be necessary to provide a full supply of the necessary munitions required for a speedy termination of the war'.[14] On 16 June the conference was recalled to hear Lloyd George present the details of what was now called the War Munitions Volunteers Scheme, along with the other provisions of the Munitions Bill, and went on to endorse a general prohibition of strikes and lockouts. Lloyd George could therefore present the bill as an agreed measure, and it became law on 2 July 1915.

Part I of the Munitions of War Act, as it was named, made a strike or lockout on munitions work an offence; permitted the extension of this provision to other stoppages by royal proclamation; and enabled the government to refer disputes to binding arbitration. Part II created a special class of 'controlled establishments' in which profits were limited, and rules, practices, or customs which tended to restrict production or employment were suspended for the period of the war. Inducement to comply with such rules became an offence, and the determination of which rules were restrictive was a matter for the Board of Trade. Section 6 sanctioned the War Munitions Volunteers Scheme, and the imposition of penalties on defaulters. Section 7 forbade the employment of munitions workers without 'Leaving Certificates' from their former employers, unless six weeks had elapsed since they left their munitions jobs. Those guilty of offences under the Act were to appear before munitions tribunals empowered to impose fines, each chaired by a lawyer sitting with an employer and a trade unionist.

The provision for extension of the ban on stoppages by royal proclamation was due to the failure of Lloyd George and Henderson to persuade the Miners and the cotton unions to agree to their specific inclusion in the Act. The attempt had been made because at that time disputes in both industries appeared to be threatening major strikes.

Since 1913 cotton spinning had lacked a disputes procedure other than the one-clause agreement relating to bad spinning. After the outbreak of war Askwith persuaded the parties to extend this agreement to cover all disputes. However, in the spring of 1915 both sides of the industry were in a belligerent mood. The Cardroom Operatives claimed a 10 per cent war bonus; several mills were struck; the employers threatened a lockout; the Spinners, who would have been put out of work by a lockout, submitted a claim of their own, and an altercation ensued as to whether it was the Spinners or the employers who were in breach of their five-year agreement due to expire in July. The unions refused to be included in the Munitions Act, but agreed to a voluntary

[14] Ibid., p. 34.

reference to the Committee on Production which awarded a war bonus of 5 per cent on standard.[15]

The coal dispute was more complex. In March the Miners had put forward a claim for a national advance of 20 per cent on earnings. As usual the Mining Association replied that it was not competent to deal with wages, and recommended an approach to the owners' associations in the districts. Instead the Miners appealed to the Prime Minister, and it was ultimately agreed that he should settle their claim. He recommended reference back to the districts with instructions to disregard the maximum percentage figures in their current agreements, which would, in most instances, have precluded any advance at all. The amounts granted varied from district to district, but their weighted average came to almost 12 per cent, a more generous increase than any other industry had so far received.

At the same time negotiations were proceeding on claims submitted in all districts on 1 April in pursuance of the Miners' 1914 conference decision to terminate district agreements, so as to make progress towards a uniform standard of pay. The owners argued that the existing agreements should be allowed to run on for the duration of the war, but eventually all the districts except South Wales either revised the old standards in conformity with the resolution, or agreed to defer the matter. The South Wales Miners were determined on a new agreement, but the owners refused.

Because of the effect of the war on the demand for both steam and bituminous coal, prices in South Wales had risen faster than those of other coalfields, whereas the miners' wages had already reached the maximum prescribed by the 1910 agreement. They therefore proposed that, along with several other concessions, the maximum should be raised, and the terms of the new agreement should apply only to members of the South Wales Miners Federation. This proposal was particularly directed to force the members of the small unions of craftsmen and other surfaceworkers into the federation.

There seemed little prospect of a peaceful outcome if the Welshmen were left to themselves, and Lloyd George made a determined effort to have the industry brought within the terms of the Munitions Act with the agreement of the Miners. Armed with a resolution of the trade union conference of 16 June asking for the prohibition on stoppages to 'apply

---

[15] Wage agreements in cotton and coal made percentage adjustments to 'standard' piece rates and time rates. Consequently an increase of 5 per cent 'on standard' was a pay increase of 5 per cent only when wages stood at standard prior to the increase. If wages were already twice the standard, an increase of 5 per cent on standard added only $2\frac{1}{2}$ per cent to pay. As piece rates in cotton spinning stood at 5 per cent above standard in July 1914, the war bonus of 5 per cent increased pay by a fraction less than 5 per cent.

to all work and all trades during the present crisis',[16] he saw the Miners' leaders on 24, 25, and 26 June, but the most that they would offer was a guarantee that, if the South Wales dispute was settled, they would enter into arrangements with the owners in each district whereby unsettled disputes would be referred to the chairmen of the conciliation boards, with full power to resolve them.

Last minute negotiations with Runciman, president of the Board of Trade, and other ministers persuaded the South Wales Miners' executive to propose working for a fortnight on daily notice after their existing notices ran out on 1 July. This recommendation won a slender majority from a delegate conference, but, when the delegates learned on 12 July that the terms proposed by Runciman did not meet several of their demands, including the limitation of the benefits of the agreement to union members, they voted by two to one to strike for their original demands. Next day the national executive appealed to them to stay at work and the government proclaimed the dispute under the new Act, both to no avail. On 15 July the whole coalfield was at a standstill. 'Government transports and hundreds of other vessels were held up in port for lack of cargo and bunker coal. . . . The number of unemployed workmen rapidly approached half a million.'[17]

With 20,000 miners on strike it was, of course, useless to attempt proceedings under the Act. Lloyd George joined in the negotiations in his now accustomed role of a conciliator who could persuade recalcitrant employers that they must make further concessions in the national interest. The new terms granted the Miners almost everything they had asked for, including the withdrawal of the proclamation which had become 'a most dangerous factor, since the men greatly resented the coercion involved thereby'.[18] These terms were accepted, but their interpretation almost caused another strike at the end of September. The question was whether the clause granting an extra shift's pay for five afternoon or night shifts applied to craftsmen or not. If it did not, the clause limiting the benefits of the agreement to members of the federation gave no leverage over the craftsmen's unions. At first Runciman decided against the Miners, but the threat of a further strike caused him to persuade the employers to sign a supplementary agreement which conceded the point, and the main craftsmen's union, six thousand strong, joined the South Wales Miners Federation.

The federation promptly took advantage of the increase in the permitted maximum to submit a further pay claim, and on 14 September the chairman of their conciliation board, Lord St Aldwyn, awarded an increase of just over 11 per cent on current rates, making 23

---

[16] *History of the Ministry of Munitions*, Vol. I, Part IV, p. 36.
[17] Carter, p. 453.   [18] Ibid., p. 454.

per cent since the outbreak of war. The South Wales Miners were now enjoying their share of the exceptional profits being earned in their coalfield; and, equally important for some of them, they had extracted revenge for their humiliation in the Cambrian dispute.

Loudly hostile, the press detected syndicalist influence and even German sabotage among the miners. The latter charge was nonsense, and the syndicalists had not yet recovered their strength in South Wales. What the strike showed was the continued strength of class feeling on both sides of the Welsh coalmining industry. Because the new Act had been put to its first test in these circumstances, suggestions that it was a failure were premature. As the Home Secretary, Sir John Simon, had said in the Second Reading debate on 28 June:[19]

> It would be a very foolish and short-sighted proposal if we simply imagined that by legislating that there is to be no stoppage of work the whole problem will be solved. You can only secure that there will be no stoppage of work in a munitions factory if you will take the trouble to find out what are the fair conditions on which employers . . . and workpeople . . . will require to be satisfied that that object is to be secured.

Askwith was vituperative in his condemnation of Lloyd George's part in the dispute. 'The example', he wrote, 'was set to strike first and apply to Mr. Lloyd George, whatever Ministers, officials, employers, or union leaders might say, with a view to the allowance of all claims as the reward of violence or pressure'.[20] But Askwith did not say what he would have done. The strike had to be brought to an end quickly, and the only alternative to conceding virtually all the men's demands was for the government to take over the coalfield, as was done at the end of 1916; but, even then, substantial concessions would have had to be made to the Miners.

The first experiences of the Act in the munitions factories were also unhappy. In relation to Leaving Certificates there was 'no authority to prevent managers and foremen from misusing the new powers conferred on them in a thoughtless and arbitrary fashion, or to penalise them for such misuse'.[21] The tribunals were initially reluctant to override an employer's refusal to grant a Leaving Certificate even where it could be shown that the worker concerned was underpaid. Employers were entitled to lay off workers without pay in the knowledge that they could not accept another job and must therefore keep themselves available; and some employers did so. The tribunals also had power to enforce works rules. Most employers posted the model rules drawn up by the

---

[19] *Hansard*, col. 1540.
[20] Askwith, p. 395.
[21] *History of the Ministry of Munitions*, Vol. IV, Part II, p. 17.

Ministry, but others adopted the rules prepared by the Engineering Employers Federation; still others drew up their own rules, some of which 'are and should be keenly resented by the employees', and 'conflict with the usual working conditions of the "Districts"'.[22] The main objections were to those sections of the federation rules and some individual codes which imposed fines for loss of time or bad work.

Penalties exacted by the tribunals caused resentment all the more because they appeared so one-sided. Up to 27 November 1915 the tribunals had convicted 2,012 out of 3,074 workers brought before them for breach of works rules, and 407 out of 589 accused of striking in contravention of the Act. Fines imposed on workers totalled £2,236.42½. Of eighty employers accused of taking on munitions workers without a Leaving Certificate, fifty-five were fined a total of £289.72½, and one other offence by an employer led to a fine of £1.[23]

Serious trouble threatened on the Clyde in October 1915. At the end of August shipwrights at Fairfield struck for the reinstatement of two of their fellows whose Leaving Certificates had been endorsed with the reason for their dismissal—'not attending to work'. To the men this appeared to be the reintroduction of the discharge note which they had stamped out just before the war. The Ministry prosecuted and on 3 September a tribunal fined seventeen strikers £10 each. The union persuaded the men to go back and agreed to pay the fines. However, three men refused to accept payment on their behalf, and went to gaol on 6 October. An agitation began for their release and the repeal or drastic amendment of the Act. Lord Balfour of Burleigh and Lynden Macassey were commissioned to investigate the unrest on the Clyde, but union officials would not give evidence unless the three men were released. On 23 October a meeting of representatives of the Clyde shipbuilding and engineering unions wired to Lloyd George a demand for the remission of the remainder of the sentences and 'an answer within three days'. On the 26th Lloyd George suggested to a deputation from the Clyde that the outstanding fines should be paid whether the prisoners wanted it or not. The hint was taken; the men were released; and the Commissioners were allowed to proceed with their investigation.

Dilution

Apart from the ban on strikes, the main purpose of the Munitions Act had been to increase the effective supply of skilled manpower for munitions work by the relaxation of trade practices. The Act was first used in this connection to deal with another strike at Fairfield at the end

---

[22] Amalgamated Society of Engineers, *Monthly Journal and Report,* October 1915.
[23] *History of the Ministry of Munitions*, Vol. IV, Part II, p. 13.

of July, this time of coppersmiths who objected to the transfer of some of their work to plumbers. However, the greatest gains were not expected from the relaxation of demarcation between crafts, but from the substitution of less-skilled workers for craftsmen to permit the latter to concentrate on jobs requiring a high degree of skill. In August, on government instructions, Lang and Sons on the Clyde set about introducing women workers into the manufacture of lathes for making shells. With the support of their district committee, the Engineers' shop stewards refused to co-operate. It was the union's intention, according to the Scottish member of the executive, 'to oppose strenuously the introduction of female labour into the workshops where engineering and toolmaking was carried on apart from the production of shells and fuses'. At Woolwich Arsenal the district committee vetoed 'the introduction of semi-skilled men on work now done by fully qualified mechanics, as it is not proved there is the shortage claimed'. Accordingly the Ministry decided to await 'further negotiations with the Trade Unions . . . lest a serious strike might cause bitter and widespread resentment, which would effectually prevent the men from doing their best in the all-important months that lay ahead'.[24]

Negotiations were needed because the Act had left a number of issues unsettled. Most important was the question of the rates to be paid to the dilutees. This was not only the concern of the unions which organised the dilutees, but also of the craft unions, whose members were ceding their jobs, or part of them, to the dilutees. In addition, the process of dilution within the workshop involved considerable reorganisation of jobs and transfer between jobs, and there was so far nothing laid down as to how these alterations were to be carried out, and the part which union workshop representatives were to play.

Yet another committee was established in the middle of September to deal with these issues. It was the Central Munitions Labour Supply Committee. Henderson was in the chair and there were several representatives of the Ministry of Munitions, including William Beveridge, who had been transferred from the Board of Trade; Brownlie and three other craft union leaders, along with Duncan of the Workers Union and Mary Macarthur of the Women Workers Federation; and Allan Smith to represent the employers. They prepared a series of proposals which, when approved by the Minister, were issued as 'L' circulars. Circular L2 first laid down a national rate for women employed on munitions work customarily done by men, and then dealt with the payment of women 'employed on work customarily done by fully skilled tradesmen'. Such women were to receive the craft time rates. Women paid by results were to receive the same piecework prices

[24] Ibid., Vol. IV, Part I, pp. 36–7.

or bonus rates as the men they were replacing. Circular L3 dealt with semi-skilled and unskilled men 'employed on work identical with that customarily undertaken by skilled labour'. They were to be paid the craftsman's time rate, piecework price or bonus as the case might be. Circulars L5 and L6 recommended detailed arrangements for the introduction of dilution, including discussions with representatives of the workers in the shop concerned.

The committee met the Engineers' executive on 27 October and secured their agreement to the circulars, on condition that it was 'to be incumbent on . . . employers that they must observe the rates and conditions of labour as governed by Circulars L2 and L3'.[25] Subsequently the other unions also gave their approval. By now, however, the unions had accumulated a mass of complaints about the working of other sections of the Munitions Act. These can be illustrated from divisional reports in the Engineers' journal for December 1915. Liverpool was experiencing 'so much discontent and unrest caused by its administration that the temper of Labour has been thoroughly aroused'; Manchester complained of 'the inequalities and injustices brought about by . . . the obnoxious Munitions of War Act'; Birmingham told of 'a constant succession of individual cases arising from the working of the Munitions Act'; and Brownlie reported that 'both District Committees and branches have been urging your EC to demand a drastic reconstruction of the whole Act'. These and other complaints were discussed at a conference on 30 November where Lloyd George met representatives of fifty-five trade unions and a number of amendments to the Act were agreed; but the Engineers were not satisfied. They drew up a list of further amendments including the statutory enforcement of L2 and L3.

The obstruction of the unions was not the only obstacle to dilution. Most employers were reluctant to introduce it. If they substituted unskilled labour for skilled, their craftsmen might be transferred elsewhere. They feared that 'some of the new methods would result in a permanent diminution of output, if there was any output at all'; and that women workers would need 'special accommodation and wages beyond what they could earn'.[26] They were also afraid of industrial unrest. Lloyd George told the House of Commons that:[27]

Unless the employer begins by putting on the lathes unskilled men and women we cannot enforce that Act of Parliament. . . . He is not going to do so because of the trouble which a few firms have had.

Even on the Clyde, where the North West Engineering Employers, led

[25] Ibid., p. 68.   [26] Ibid., pp. 91–2.
[27] *Hansard*, 20 December 1915, col. 121.

by William Weir and his half-brother John Richmond, had for months been demanding drastic action and severely criticising their national federation for failing to give a firm lead, the employers were waiting for the government to 'enforce different conditions under the sanction of law'.[28]

A further excuse for delay was that there were other things to be done to improve the supply of munitions which might yield quicker results at the cost of less disturbance than dilution was causing. The first and most rewarding was the extension of government contracts to more engineering firms. Now that the obstruction of the War Office could be overridden, there was a rapid increase in the number of 'controlled' establishments. The consequent expansion of the labour force engaged on munitions greatly reduced the scope for the transfer of skilled labour from private work to munitions work through the War Munitions Volunteers Scheme, but the scheme nevertheless proved useful.

The eventual result was that we had a mobile corps of some 38,000, and it is no exaggeration to say that without them the munitions programme could not have been carried out. By their aid many national factories were started in the first instance, and they were used in the early days of many aero-engine shops, for special parts of the augmented gun programme, for tanks, and in kindred ways.[29]

By the end of the year a number of national factories were under construction. Finally, a scheme for the bulk release of skilled munitions workers from the armed forces stationed in the United Kingdom was launched in September 1915. Just over 40,000 of those who offered themselves were passed as suitable, and about half of them were ultimately placed, although the placements, which began in October, were slower than had been hoped.[30]

When these various measures had been put in hand, and the Engineers had given conditional support to dilution on 27 October, the Ministry returned to the question of the employment of women on lathes at Lang's factory. On 29 October Brownlie, and the Scottish member of the Engineers' executive, Gorman, persuaded their Paisley district committee and Lang's shop stewards to give their consent. At first all went well, and a number of women were transferred to the lathes over the next six weeks, but on 15 December the shop stewards told the firm that any more transfers would lead to a strike. The objection was that the women were not paid the full craft rate. The firm's view was that

---

[28] Wigham, p. 90. Weir's proposals included 'to hold wages steady and to abrogate union rights and the rights of employers' associations as well for the duration of the war'. (Reader, p. 40.)

[29] Addison, *Politics from Within*, Vol. I, p. 178.

[30] *History of the Ministry of Munitions*, Vol. IV, Part I, p. 30.

the craft rate was not justified since the women were not employed to do a full craft job; but there was no such qualification in circular L2.

Lloyd George decided that he must visit the Clyde over Christmas. Besides the official plans for his visit, a special reception was organised by the Clyde Workers Committee. This committee was descended from the Labour Withholding Committee, which ran the strike of the previous March. The members had come together again on a more permanent basis in October to voice their opposition to the Munitions Act. Although it included many conveners and stewards from the munitions factories, the committee was not, properly speaking, a shop stewards' organisation, for 'probably . . . outside a few major arms firms the delegates represented minority militant groups rather than es-tablished workshop organisation',[31] and members also came from the mines, the railways and co-operative societies. John Maclean, the militant socialist schoolmaster, came to the meetings, as did Peter Petroff, a Russian emigré. The committee's manifesto, *To All Clyde Workers*, condemned support for the Munitions Act as 'An Act of Treachery to the Working Class'. Their aims were 'ever-increasing control over workshop conditions' and organisation of 'the workers on a class basis and to maintain the Class Struggle, until the overthrow of the Wages System'.

Lloyd George planned to visit the main Glasgow factories to talk to shop stewards on 24 December. The committee instructed its members to refuse to see him. David Kirkwood, convener at Parkhead, could not resist the opportunity for an exchange with the Minister, but Lloyd George had to abandon his other visits. Then, after the Allied Trades had refused to come to the conference which had been postponed at the last moment from Christmas Eve to Christmas Day, the committee got hold of the tickets from the Engineers' district secretary, and packed the meeting. Lloyd George was heckled noisily and the meeting broke up in disorder after John Muir, convener at Barr and Stroud, was prevented from presenting the committee's case on dilution.

Meanwhile the Engineers' executive continued to press for the inclusion of their proposals in the bill currently being prepared to amend the Munitions Act, and summoned a national conference of divisional organisers and district representatives to ensure that their policy was endorsed by a fully representative body. The bill already gave the Minister power to make regulations concerning the pay of women munitions workers, but this was not enough for the conference. They sent a deputation to meet Asquith and Lloyd George to insist on the enforcement of L3 as well. Ministers and union leaders agreed that the business would already have been settled but for the fresh demands

[31] Hinton, p. 120.

repeatedly made by the members, because they did not like dilution. In the end the deputation gave an assurance, which was endorsed by the conference, that the enforcement of L3 was their final demand; and the relevant amendment went through.

Four weeks later the Munitions of War (Amendment) Act received royal assent. In addition to the enforcement of the two circulars, Leaving Certificates were not to be refused to workers dismissed or kept idle for two days or more without wages, and discharged workers must be given a week's notice or a week's wages. The penalty of imprisonment for non-payment of fines was abolished.

Meanwhile members of the Engineers' executive toured the country explaining the contents of the bill, and pointing out that further opposition to dilution on war work would not have official support from the union. The government decided to proceed by sending out dilution commissioners to oversee the introduction of dilution on the spot, a method which had been suggested by Weir, recently appointed director of munitions in Scotland. Lynden Macassey, Sir Thomas Munro and Isaac Mitchell were appointed as commissioners for the Clyde. They decided to proceed factory by factory, drawing up schemes suited to the circumstances as they found them. They made it a condition of each scheme that a shop committee be formed to discuss and settle any difficulties which might arise in its application.

The Clyde Workers Committee had experienced some difficulty in working out their policy on dilution. Although William Gallacher, the chairman, was a member of the British Socialist Party, and Kirkwood had recently transferred from the Socialist Labour Party to the Independent Labour Party, the majority of the leaders belonged to the Socialist Labour Party, whose narrow sectarianism had been modified by the war sufficiently to allow participation in a popular industrial movement which did not conform with the party's narrow industrial unionism; but industrial unionists they remained, committed to the belief that the destruction of craft sectionalism was a necessary preliminary to achieving socialism. They could not therefore oppose dilution as such. Instead they proposed that the government take over the factories, 'and organised labour should be vested with the right to take part directly and equally with the present managers in the management and administration in every department of industry'.[32]

While resolving their dilemma, this policy gave little guidance on how they should respond to the dilution commissioners. After some hesitation, the committee told the shop stewards in each factory to refer all approaches from the commissioners to the committee, so that a common approach could be adopted. With a few days, however, their

[32] Ibid., p. 131.

front had been broken by Kirkwood and his colleagues at Parkhead. They negotiated an agreement with the commissioners, who thereafter proceeded from factory to factory as they had planned. Initially the only sign of unrest was another strike at Lang's over the interpretation of L2 in which the Engineers' executive once more supported the men, who went back to work on the promise of further negotiations. However, the authorities displayed their uneasiness. The Independent Labour Party's Scottish newspaper, *Forward*, had been suppressed under defence regulations for printing what seems to have been an accurate account of Lloyd George's Christmas Day meeting. At the beginning of February, Maclean and two colleagues were arrested on charges of sedition, and Gallacher, Muir and Walter Bell for an article entitled 'Should the Workers Arm?' in the Clyde Workers Committee newspaper, the *Worker*,[33] of which Muir was editor and Bell manager. Many workers struck when they heard the news, but returned to work when the three shop stewards were released on bail.

At the end of February the Parkhead management denied Kirkwood his customary access to all departments to carry out his job as convener. After a pause of two weeks in which the firm did not give way, a strike began on 17 March. Several other factories followed, but Kirkwood's defection in January had upset his colleagues on the Clyde Workers Committee, who did not support the strike. This split among the leading stewards gave the government an opportunity to settle with the committee. On 25 March five stewards, including Kirkwood and Arthur MacManus, were arrested and deported from Glasgow. Others followed a few days later. Initially the news of the deportations brought other factories out, but on 30 March thirty men from three factories were fined £5 each, and the strikers began to go back to work.

To justify their actions, the government fabricated a plot aimed at 'holding up the production of the most important munitions of war in the Clyde district, with the object . . . of compelling the Government to repeal the Military Service Act and the Munitions of War Act'.[34] The documents leave no doubt that the senior officials at the Ministry of Munitions, including Beveridge, Macassey and Weir, had been seeking an opportunity to suppress the Clyde Workers Committee.[35] Macassey had already proposed that 'the leaders of the agitation should be dispatched "to some official post remote from Clydeside"' to avoid the martyrdom of prison.[36] The government's work was completed when

[33] The conclusion of the article, that the 'worker's labour power is . . . his strongest weapon', does not seem particularly seditious. The publication of the *Worker* had been financed from the expenses paid to those attending Lloyd George's Christmas Day meeting.

[34] Christopher Addison, *Hansard*, 28 March 1916, cols. 564–5.

[35] Hinton, pp. 143–4.

[36] Harris, *Beveridge*, p. 220.

Bell was sentenced to three months in prison, Gallacher and Muir to a year each, and Maclean to three years.

The question of payment for women dilutees on skilled work had been left unsettled when the Lang strikers returned to work on 7 February. They and their union executive maintained that L2 required the payment of the full craft rate to a woman performing any part of a skilled man's job, and these terms were eventually granted to them as a special concession; but the Clyde Dilution Commissioners introduced a different principle into their other factory dilution agreements. Reduced payment was allowed for a probationary period, and thereafter there was to be a deduction from the craft rate to pay for supervising and setting-up. The objective was to make the total cost of the operation much the same as when only skilled men were employed. The only other dilution commission to be appointed was for the Tyne, where a provisional agreement at Armstrong Whitworth's works at Elswick had already granted the full craft rate without deductions. The Tyne commissioners avoided trouble by adopting these terms elsewhere. Eventually, in February 1917, after reference to the special arbitration tribunal on women's pay, a statutory order settled the matter by establishing a probationary period of three months and, thereafter, a deduction of up to 10 per cent from the skilled rate.

Up to that time, and probably afterwards, most employers outside the Clyde area were deterred from employing women on skilled work. In the North East no more than five of 150 munitions firms employing women did so.[37] In the North West, according to the Ministry's reply on 14 June 1916 to complaints from the Engineers and the Federation of Women Workers, their

investigating officers found *no clear cases* in which a woman was doing the work customarily done by a fully skilled tradesman. In one or two cases, where they appeared to be doing so, the firm was able to show that they had simplified the operation by an adjustment of the machine or that the nature of the work had otherwise been modified. The majority of questions at issue affect the machine tool trade, and are cases where women and girls are replacing boys, youths, and apprentices of various ages.[38]

In Sheffield there was less scope for dilution than on the Clyde, 'because the very heavy nature of much of the work involved made it unsuitable for female labour'.[39] In Coventry and Birmingham the weakness of the Engineers had already, before the war, led to a wide extension of the practice of upgrading men without craft qualifications on to machines which would elsewhere have been claimed by the Engineers. Only on

[37] *History of the Ministry of Munitions*, Vol. V, Part II, p. 38.
[38] Cole, *Trade Unionism and Munitions*, p. 111.
[39] Hinton, p. 165.

the Clyde, where the commissioners claimed that they had released 7,500 skilled men and apprentices in their first six months, replacing them with ten thousand other workers, mostly women,[40] was there evidence of substantial progress in the employment of women on skilled work.

It therefore seems that, apart from the Clyde, the Engineers had been largely successful in their efforts to keep women off what was recognised as skilled men's work. Nevertheless by the summer of 1916 the shortage of skilled men was less acute. Despite the great expansion of war production, the unsatisfied demand for fitters, toolfitters, turners and metal machinists fell from 18,358 on 14 January 1916 to 11,924 on 28 July;[41] and shortage of skilled munitions workers was never again to be a major issue during the war. What is the explanation of this paradox?

The answer can be supplied by a closer examination of the demand for, and the supply of, dilutees. Demand varied widely from industry to industry. There was, for example, no need for dilution of skill in steel production, where the promotion system ensured that qualified men were available to fill vacant top jobs. Shortages of labour merely hastened promotion. The result was a demand for labourers which was often met by employing women, two of whom might replace one labourer because the work was heavy. This was a form of dilution, but not dilution of skill. That was generally confined to the craft trades.

Within the craft trades the scope for dilution varied inversely with the degree of flexibility required of the craftsmen. Where they were called on to undertake a wide range of tasks, the inflexibility of dilutees, trained for one or two tasks only, rendered them almost useless. Consequently there was little dilution in such specialist engineering departments as the boiler shop and the drawing office; and also in the toolroom and the maintenance section which fell within the domain of the Engineers. It seems that relatively few dilutees were introduced into the foundries. 'No serious attempt was made to dilute patternmakers', for two reasons. One was the high degree of skill demanded of them so that the only substitutes who could have been introduced were skilled joiners; and the second was that 'there was no occasion to do so' because there were enough patternmakers to do the work.[42]

There was also little dilution in the shipyards, but not because a high degree of skill was required of all shipbuilding craftsmen. Riveting and caulking did not need anything like the full period of apprenticeship to achieve proficiency.[43] Slow progress was due to the obstruction of the Admiralty, who did not relish the thought of His Majesty's ships being

[40] Ibid., p. 146.
[41] *History of the Ministry of Munitions*, Vol. IV, Part IV, p. 21.
[42] Mosses, p. 257.   [43] More, pp. 137–8.

built by dilutees. They insisted on handling the matter through their own independent labour department because they 'could not allow any interference with the labour at their disposal. ... Nor could the Admiralty accept the standards of the Ministry' of Munitions.[44]

Demand for dilution was also affected by the requirements of the services which were mainly for standard products in vast quantities— ideally suited for further exploitation of the new engineering techniques which had been introduced over the past thirty years. Metal parts could be made on automatic machines, to which, according to the Engineering Employers Federation, the craft unions laid no claim,[45] and assembled without need for the skills of the fitter. The outstanding example was the manufacture of ammunition. Many national factories were designed for this manner of production from the start, and employed mainly female labour. Skilled men were needed for toolmaking, toolsetting, and maintenance, but, as these jobs required a high degree of skill, there was no question of diluting them. Dilution was therefore irrelevant to much munitions work.

The demand for dilutees came mainly from factories engaged in munitions work which did not lend itself to mass-production techniques, but where some repetitive tasks could be singled out, as in the manufacture of heavy guns and machine tools. The jobs involved were mainly those that had been in dispute between the Engineers and their employers for many years, involving the use of 'semi-automatic machines' over which 'the employers are frequently in difficulty in maintaining their rights'.[46] However, where these jobs were diluted, they did not all have to be filled by women. There was an alternative source of supply in the 'handymen' and semi-skilled workers whose numbers had been growing rapidly before the war, and in the labourers and boys who would be only too willing to undertake work at a higher rate of pay, which might also exempt them from conscription. Women could then take on the jobs which they vacated.

One of the main objectives of the Munitions Act had been to hasten dilution by providing statutory sanctions to enforce it upon skilled men and their unions. However, six months passed between the passage of the Act and the first serious attempt to apply dilution. During this time negotiations between the government and the unions, which began with the Treasury Conference, were continued and led up to substantial revisions of the Act. Even then the government decided that they must start a new round of negotiations, on this occasion with the representatives of the skilled men in the plants. As much might have been achieved

[44] *History of the Ministry of Munitions*, Vol. IV, Part IV, pp. 94–5.
[45] Engineering Employers Federation, *Emergency Committee Report*, 1913.
[46] Ibid.

as quickly, without legislation, by opening negotiations with the unions immediately after the Treasury Agreement on the detailed issues which were eventually settled by the L circulars and plant negotiations. Perhaps the existence of statutory sanctions against workers and unions assisted the government negotiators. On the other hand the use of the Act to enforce works rules and punish strikers aroused widespread indignation, which cannot have helped them.

Acceptance of dilution by the unions was, however, facilitated by the limitation on profits in controlled establishments in the original Act, and by the enforcement of the L circulars on employers in the amending Act. If coercion of employers was essential to achieve dilution, then it is probably true that, in the climate of 1915–16, the clauses needed to achieve this objective were best wrapped up in a measure which apparently dealt with trade union obstruction; but there is no evidence that the government were aware that they had adopted such a devious stratagem.

Wages and Prices

By the end of the first year of the war the cost-of-living index had risen by 25 per cent, with food prices up by 32 per cent. Seamen were the only major group of employees to have received general pay increases that fully compensated for rising prices. At the beginning of 1915 the Admiralty had offered an increase of £2 a month if the 'Unions would agree to the crews of transports coming within the Naval Discipline Act',[47] but their members would have none of it. However, after Havelock Wilson had informed their union executive on 23 June 1915 that wages 'were being forced up all round', Tom Mann, still a member of the executive, said that the time was 'opportune for the Executive to step in and endeavour to secure uniformity in the various ports'. A committee was set up to deal with the Admiralty and other employers, and in July agreement was reached on a second advance of £1 a month, 'making £2 a month since the outbreak of war, both on transports and commercial vessels'[48]—an increase of 30–40 per cent on prewar wages.

Settlements for dockers had brought them an average increase in basic rates of 11 per cent. Increases for iron and steel workers varied according to their sliding scale agreements, and some of them probably came close to the rise in retail prices. The advances for coalminers in the major districts varied from 7 per cent in Durham to $15\frac{1}{2}$ per cent in the Federated District, and 18 per cent in Scotland. The awards of the Committee on Production to engineering and shipbuilding workers had raised the wages of craftsmen by a little over 10 per cent and of labourers by about 16 per cent. The railwaymen's increase of 15p for those

[47] Fayle, p. 94.   [48] Ibid., p. 111.

earning less than £1.50 a week brought 15 per cent to the lowest paid railwaymen. Employees in the wool industry had averaged about 15 per cent; and most clothing, footwear, and agricultural workers had also received increases through local settlements.

On the other hand the spinning section of the cotton industry had obtained an increase of just under 5 per cent, and the weaving section nothing. Few building and printing workers had received advances, though high rates of pay for those employed on the construction of munitions factories were reported in the Operative Bricklayers' *Trade Circular and General Reporter* as early as January 1915. The Co-operative Employees reported advances in 114 societies in May 1915, and the Shop Assistants recorded many increases through the summer, but most white collar employees had probably had no wartime increases so far. After telling the postal unions that 'the rise in the cost of living is not by itself a sufficient reason at the present time for increasing the wages of their employees',[49] the government allowed their claim to go to arbitration, and on 8 July modest bonuses were awarded to postal employees earning up to £3 a week. The Civil Service Federation had already lodged a claim on behalf of the other departments, and they now asked for the award to be applied to them. The claim was referred to the Comittee on Retrenchment, recently set up to review expenditure in government departments.

The major influence at work was of course the state of the labour market. Relatively large increases were granted to seamen, dockers, railwaymen, miners, munitions workers, and those making clothing and equipment for the forces, because the demand for their services had risen while their numbers had been depleted by recruitment to the forces; whereas little or nothing had been conceded to cotton, building, and printing employees, among whom unemployment had continued into 1915 despite recruitment to the forces. However, there were also other influences. The anxiety of the government to avoid stoppages in essential industries and services had been strikingly demonstrated in South Wales, and other relatively generous settlements had followed strikes, or threats of strike. In addition, the awards of the Committee on Production had brought an unusual degree of standardisation into the round of increases in the engineering industry. The unions in districts where they had been offered less than the going rate, or had already settled for less in the early months of the war, were able to appeal to the committee and were brought into line.

Piecemeal adjustments continued through the autumn of 1915. The South Wales miners received their second wartime increase in September, and the railway workers followed in October. In June the

[49] Quoted in Cole, *Labour in War-Time*, p. 159.

Railwaymen's annual conference had been sharply critical of the previous settlement, threatening to curtail the executive's authority to settle claims. Branches began to pass resolutions in favour of strike action for another increase. On 5 September a speech by Thomas drew attention to the unrest by condemning a 'cleverly engineered movement' which was backing a 'demand . . . that unless the Executive Committee did a certain thing at a certain time the law would be taken into the men's own hands'.[50] Whether or not as a result of this warning, the government allowed the companies to reach agreement with the unions for increases of 15p for those who had received 10p in February 1915, and 10p for those who had then received 15p, making 25p all round since the outbreak of war. In return, the Railwaymen and the Locomotive Engineers and Firemen undertook to present no more claims until after the war.

Meanwhile the first round of increases was under way in building and printing. At the end of July 1915 the building employers informed a meeting of their National Conciliation Board that, although in their opinion the circumstances of the industry did not warrant a war bonus, they would allow local associations to hear claims at their discretion; and, if no agreement could be reached locally 'the usual conciliation arrangements' were 'to come into operation'. This decision led to a series of local increases. In August the London Society of Compositors voted by four to three in favour of a strike for higher wages. Thereupon, the employers opened negotiations which led to an increase of 5 per cent, to be followed by another 2.5 per cent in April 1916, and also at last recorded their formal acceptance of the 50-hour working week. In September 1915, in some instances after issuing strike notices, the Typographical Association secured local advances in the South East, which spread north and west to cover the whole of England and Wales. They were almost all for 5 or 7.5 per cent.

The engineering employers and the Committee on Production rejected claims which might have led to a second round of increases for male engineering workers, but there were substantial increases for women. In most parts of the country there had previously been no agreement on women's rates. The major exception was the settlement between the Midland Employers Federation and the Workers Union after the 1913 strike. In November 1915 their rate under this agreement was raised to 80p a week at 21 years of age, and a similar agreement was signed in Manchester. Meanwhile the L circulars had been promulgated. Besides dealing with the payment of women on work customarily done by skilled craftsmen, L2 prescribed a minimum rate of £1 at the age of 18 for women employed on work customarily performed

<hr>

[50] Cole and Arnot, pp. 55–6.

by unskilled or semi-skilled men. This brought substantial increases to some women munitions workers, although many more had to wait until the amending Act set up the special tribunal on women's pay. This tribunal took over the regulation of women's pay in all controlled establishments, and

was very active indeed. It arbitrated, and fixed wages and conditions, in many hundreds of cases . . . laying down both rates for women on the less skilled types of work, and special higher rates for women on semi-skilled work, and even sometimes according women the rate of the skilled men whose work they had undertaken.[51]

In June 1916 the tribunal recommended a uniform minimum rate for women employed on women's work in controlled establishments of 90p for timeworkers and for a 48-hour week and 80p for pieceworkers, thus completing their coverage of women's pay in controlled establishments. The employers criticised this recommendation, which was embodied in an order, because of the effect they feared it would have on the pay of women who were employed on private work.

Soon after taking office the coalition government decided that war expenditure must be brought under closer control. The first two war budgets presented by Lloyd George, in November 1914 and May 1915, had done little to curb inflation. Their proposals for tax increases were remarkably modest, and almost the whole of the additional expenditure was met by borrowing. This meant that the war was to be financed through increased prices, which would, of course, fall most heavily upon the working class.

The coalition government adopted a more prudent policy of pruning expenditure and increasing taxation. On 29 June 1915 the Prime Minister and Bonar Law inaugurated an economy campaign at the Guildhall. On 20 July the Retrenchment Committee was appointed. In November Lloyd George's successor as Chancellor, Reginald McKenna, introduced the third wartime budget with substantial increases in the rates of existing direct and indirect taxes and an excess profits duty. Finally, on 1 December a conference of trade unionists heard speeches on the national financial situation from Asquith, McKenna and Runciman. They

urged two things—that, apart from bonuses to meet increased expenses, there should be no wage increases, and that those who are earning much higher wages than usual should invest as much as possible in the war loan. Though the resolution which was passed did no more than commend to the rank and file for favourable consideration the appeals made by the Premier and his colleagues, as

---

[51] Cole, *Trade Unionism and Munitions*, p. 104.

the delegates had no mandate for anything further, it was too much for a few of them. But the general sense of the conference was with Mr. Asquith.[52]

The Committee on Production had already asked for guidance on the implications of the policy for their awards. The answer came close to a prescription for a general pay freeze—'any further advance of wages (other than advances following automatically from existing agreements) should be strictly confined to the adjustment of local conditions, where such improvements are proved to be necessary'.[53] The letter was not published, but the National Advisory Committee were informed and circulated copies to the unions. In a hearing before the Committee on Production concerning Bristol transport workers, Askwith confirmed that the committee was bound by the government statement. Bevin, who was presenting the case, registered a protest and walked out.

The protest spread to other unions, and on 29 February 1916 Asquith received a deputation of union and Labour Party leaders to tell them that the Committee on Production had misunderstood their instructions. The government 'had no wish to limit the wages of any class of low-paid wage-earners or of those who had not received adequate advances to recompense them for the rise in the cost of living',[54] and he proposed to see Askwith and his colleagues to put the matter right. However, he gave a rather different version of the government's view to the House of Commons on 7 March when he reported that he had seen the members of the Committee on Production who now understood 'that in the matter of the low-paid earners their discretion is not fettered by the communication from the Government. This applies also to the case of local adjustments.'[55]

In practice the committee's awards followed the version given to the House of Commons. The great majority of district engineering claims were now referred to Central Conference, and thence to arbitration. Between January and March 1916 only a few 'local adjustments' of 5p a week were awarded. In April the committee relaxed to the extent of allowing advances of 5p in the majority of cases submitted to them, but this sum was far short of what was needed to compensate for the rise in prices since the previous pay increase.

[52] *Yorkshire Factory Times*, 9 December 1915. 'How long will the Labour movement tolerate such "leaders"?' asked the *Labour Leader* of the same date.

[53] Clay, p. 33. According to Beveridge, the Ministry of Munitions had to ask ministers what had been decided (there being no cabinet minutes in those days), and got three answers: '(1) that the Arbitration Tribunal was to hold wages; (2) that the Arbitration Tribunal was not to hold wages; (3) that the Cabinet had reached no decision at all. We chose the answer which seemed to us most desirable in the national interest—the first of the three', and drafted instructions accordingly. (*Power and Influence*, pp. 133–4.)

[54] Trades Union Congress, 1916, p. 88.

[55] *Hansard*, 7 March 1916, col. 1369.

The curb on wages directly affected only the engineering and shipbuilding industries, where the employers, most of them now running controlled establishments, feared that increases would not be allowed as approved costs unless they had the sanction of the Committee on Production. Elsewhere unions could achieve better results by direct approaches to their employers. No one could grudge the cotton weavers their first wartime wage increase of 5 per cent. Their union had repeatedly submitted and resubmitted a claim since March 1915, and the employers had as often turned them down, the final rejection coming in October. On 15 October the *Cotton Factory Times* hinted at 'extreme action' by the Weavers, and a few weeks later the employers finally agreed to a 5 per cent war bonus, to be paid from January. Other laggards were doing better. Towards the end of 1915 competition between government departments for building labour, particularly to attract workers to the massive munitions complex under construction at Gretna, prompted the Ministry of Munitions to set up an inter-departmental committee 'to consider and make recommendations with regard to the rates of wages and other questions . . . with regard to the supply of building labour for government purposes'.[56] In January 1916 the committee was considering what could be done to prevent contractors paying 'exorbitant rates'.

The envy of engineering and shipbuilding workers, however, was more likely to be directed at the seamen and railwaymen, who had already received their second substantial wartime increases. The South Wales coal trimmers had agreed to work on Saturday afternoon at overtime rates which Gosling described to the conference of the Transport Workers Federation in 1916 as 'fabulous' and Robert Williams said had been 'obtained only by reason of the men's exceptionally strong organisation in the district'. The sliding scales of the iron and steel industry continued to bring wage increases to the men on tonnage rates, and additional war bonuses already negotiated for the lower-paid timeworkers in the industry were extended to workers in South Wales earning less than £2.75 a week in March 1916. At the end of 1915 'a proposal was discussed in the Ministry of Munitions to limit the movement of the sliding scales to 50 per cent above pre-war levels, but this was rejected as impracticable'.[57] All the major coalmining districts but South Wales received two further general pay increases in the first half of 1916, at the end of which the Scottish rates were 36 per cent over the prewar level, and those in the Federated Area were up by 27.5 per cent.

To fuel the discontent in the munitions factories, the cost of living

[56] *History of the Ministry of Munitions*, Vol. V, Part I, pp. 206–7.
[57] Carr and Taplin, p. 315.

index, which had stood nearly steady at 35 per cent above the prewar figures from the end of November 1915 to the beginning of April 1916, began to rise rapidly again in that month, and reached 45 per cent above prewar in June. In these circumstances the unions had to act. An official general shipbuilding and engineering strike against the law was unthinkable, and they chose instead a campaign for price controls, and enlisted the aid of the whole Labour movement.

The campaign against rising food prices launched by the War Emergency Workers National Committee early in 1915 had come to an end when the first round of wartime wage increases had gathered momentum. The government had subsequently taken powers to control the price of coal and rents. The high level of coalmining profits had led the Coalmining Organisation Committee, on which both owners and men were represented, to propose statutory limitation of domestic coal prices, and in July 1915 a Price of Coal (Limitation) Act fixed maximum pit-top prices initially at 20p a ton above the average of the twelve months before the war. In November 1915 a number of tenants in Glasgow received summonses for refusing to pay rent increases demanded by their landlords. On the day the cases were to be heard, workers from several factories and shipyards on the Clyde struck, and demonstrated outside the Sheriff's court. The government promised legislation, and a Rent and Mortgage Bill was rushed through to restrict the rents of houses with an annual rental of up to £35 in London, £30 in Scotland, and £26 elsewhere.

Encouraged by these precedents, the Engineers' executive approached the Engineering Employers Federation in April 1916 to ask them to join in representations to the government. On 5 May the emergency committee of the federation agreed that the government should take steps 'to reduce the present undue inflation of prices and to regulate prices and supplies for the future' but decided that representations should be simultaneous rather than joint. The Parliamentary Committee took up the issue, and visited the Board of Trade on 22 June. In Runciman's absence, they received a lecture from Lewis Harcourt, his parliamentary secretary, on 'the vicious circle of, first, an increase in wages, then an increase in prices, again leading to demands for further increases in wages'.[58]

On 30 June a special Trades Union Congress passed a series of resolutions, including a demand for higher pensions, another for the control of prices and stocks of food and fuel, and a third for the 'conscription of riches'. A deputation to Asquith on 19 July obtained only an assurance that action would be taken to raise the earnings

[58] Trades Union Congress, 1916, p. 93.

allowance for pensioners, who were still receiving the prewar 25p a week, but by this time the agitation had had an effect on wages. From the beginning the Engineers had insisted that wages must rise unless prices were controlled, and this demand had been taken up by the special Congress. Already 'in the middle of June', Askwith had written a memorandum to the cabinet to say that 'unless there was grave reason to the contrary, which would have to be published, the Committee intended to meet the situation by further increases, which were bound to be general'.[59] The committee's decision had been hastened by an agreement a few days earlier, signed by the Coventry engineering employers, 'for a $12\frac{1}{2}$ per cent increase in the wages of day workers which was approved by the Ministry of Munitions in spite of representations by the [Engineering Employers] Federation that it would seriously prejudice the position of employers elsewhere'.[60] Starting with Glasgow, the Committee on Production began a round of wage increases of 15p a week (or 10p for those who had already received 5p that year), limited, as at Coventry, to timeworkers. This left the increase in the skilled engineer's time rate still well below half what was needed to compensate him for the wartime increase in prices, and far behind the advances of seamen, miners and steel workers; and the *rates* of engineering pieceworkers were still only 10 per cent up on prewar figures.

These relatively small increases in engineering and shipbuilding pay might have been expected to provoke more unrest than they did. However, the earnings of many engineering workers had risen considerably faster than their wage rates. Figures for the movement and levels of wartime earnings are sparse, but the wages section of the Ministry of Munitions conducted a census of the pay of skilled engineering and shipbuilding workers on the Clyde in June 1916. Wage rates were then just over 10 per cent above July 1914. Average earnings for fitters were 43.5 per cent up, for drillers 37.3 per cent up, and for turners 34.6 per cent up. Timeworking trades did not do so well. Shipwrights' earnings had risen by 20.7 per cent, those of joiners by 17.6 per cent, and those of painters by only 2.0 per cent.[61] High wartime earnings were also reported from many other industries. The secretary of the Boot and Shoe Operatives, for example, admitted that by December 1915 'there were many men in his union earning £6 and £7 a week'.[62]

[59] Askwith, p. 410.
[60] Wigham, p. 88. An agitation for the expulsion of the Coventry Association from the federation did not succeed.
[61] *History of the Ministry of Munitions*, Vol. IV, Part IV, p. 128.
[62] Fox, p. 385.

A general impression of the effect of war conditions on earnings is given by Bowley:

In dealing with time wages and resulting earnings we ought to take account of not only the nominal rates for a normal week, but also the disappearance of broken time and the prevalence of overtime and nightwork. With piecerates the question is much more complex. . . . There is no doubt that earnings increased more rapidly than rates from two distinct causes. The first was the acuteness in demand which induced extra effort for patriotic reasons, while the fear that this effort would lead to cutting of prices was temporarily removed. . . . The second was due to circumstances which increased earnings without calling for greater effort; machinery was improved, the orders were so large and urgent that waiting for material became rare, and the same processes had to be followed with such endless repetition that machines did not have to be readjusted, and also the processes became easy from continued practice. . . .

The general effect of the increased demand for and diminished supply of labour was so to raise earnings as to produce the appearance, at any rate, of greater prosperity among the working-classes. Those who continued at their former work got more pay; many were promoted in the scale of work; women and girls' wages approximated more nearly to men's, and in some cases they undertook men's work at men's rate of pay. Nearly every able-bodied or partially able-bodied person was able to get work and to get it continuously. At the same time multitudes of families received government allowances on account of their absent men folk. Even if rates of wages increased less rapidly than prices, the household earnings often increased more rapidly.[63]

Thus many munitions workers may have been cushioned against rising prices by increased earnings, and other additions to household income. However, these additions to income were not evenly distributed. As the latest increases awarded by the Committee on Production indicated, it was widely supposed that the earnings of pieceworkers had run ahead of those of timeworkers, and these and other additions to family incomes were just as likely to accrue to those already on high earnings as to those on low earnings.

In the autumn of 1916 several pay increases were conceded under the threat of strikes in essential industries. The woodworking craftsmen engaged in aircraft manufacturing were paid the district rates of their various trades. They submitted claims for a common hourly rate, which was to be that of the highest paid craft. Such a claim from Glasgow was rejected twice by the Committee on Production, and twice from London, the second occasion being in July 1916. On 16 September nearly all the London men applied individually for their Leaving Certificates and stopped work. Faced by this new variant of the strike,

[63] Bowley, *Prices and Wages*, pp. 89–90.

Henderson persuaded the National Aircraft Committee, which had been formed by the unions concerned during August, to keep the men at work on the promise of a 'definite settlement'. On 19 September they accepted a graduated increase of 20p a week for those on the lowest rate, declining to 10p for those on the highest rate, which was at least a step towards a common rate.

During the summer of 1916 the Railwaymen's executive had come under pressure, both from the branches and from unofficial 'vigilance committees' of local militants to submit a new claim. In July a claim was put in, despite the undertaking that the 1915 settlement was to be the last during the war. At a special conference in August the rules were changed to divest the executive of the final authority to settle claims, and a substantial minority voted for handing in strike notices there and then. The companies temporised, and the South Wales district of the union, having been refused permission to go ahead on its own, nevertheless handed in strike notices in September, quite unconstitutionally. Four days before the stoppage was due, the companies offered a further increase of 15p a week. By this time a special conference was in session, 'to which', according to the executive minutes for 4–9 December, 'the negotiating Sub-Committee reported direct' which 'had the effect of eliminating the EC from the negotiations'. The offer was rejected. The district committee suspended their notices for a week. The government entered directly into the negotiations and offered 25p, which was accepted. The wages of the lowest-paid railwaymen had now caught up with wartime price increases.

In South Wales the coalowners asked for a wage reduction in December 1915, on the ground that coal prices had fallen below the peak figure for the year. Lord St. Aldwyn, the chairman of the conciliation board, awarded a 5 per cent cut on standard, and resigned shortly afterwards. His successor, Lord Muir Mackenzie, refused a claim from the Miners for the restoration of the cut in February 1916. The owners had asked for a further cut due to rising costs, which was also rejected. In May the Miners claimed an advance of 15 per cent on standard, and the owners a cut of $7\frac{1}{2}$ per cent. Before the conciliation board could meet, Muir Mackenzie wrote to the parties setting out his view of a proper basis of settlement. Seeing this as prejudgement of the issue, the Miners forced him to resign. The government decided to give the Miners their 15 per cent, which brought them to 32 per cent over prewar rates. The owners protested, but paid up when the government increased their maximum prices *pro rata*. In August the next chairman, Lord Justice Pickford, rejected claims for a $12\frac{1}{2}$ per cent advance and a 15 per cent cut. In November the claims were for a 15 per cent advance with joint audit of colliery books, and a 10 per cent cut. The Miners refused to allow their claim to be settled by Lord Pickford, submitting it to the government instead, and informing them that, 'failing an immediate settlement, a general stoppage of the coalfield was inevitable'.[64] On 29 November the government issued an order taking control of the coalfield under the powers conferred on them by the Defence of the Realm Act, and a few days later the 15 per cent on standard was granted in full, bringing South Wales wages to 46 per cent above those of July 1914.

The munitions workers were not pacified for very long with their 15p for timeworkers only. On this occasion their minds turned to an alteration in the procedure for handling wage claims. Already in the spring the four general unions, the Workers Union, the Gasworkers (who had now changed their title to the National Union of General Workers), the National Amalgamated Union of Labour, and the London Dockers, had begun canvassing a proposal for a national advance in pay for all semi-skilled and unskilled male munitions workers, without bothering with references to local conferences. In the summer they submitted a claim on these lines to the Ministry of Munitions, which said it had no power to deal with it; so they sent it to the Board of Trade, and added a further claim for a national advance in pay for all women workers in controlled establishments. The skilled unions began to fall in line. In the October issue of the Engineers' journal one of their London organisers said that it was time for 'a national demand for increased wages on one common basis', and in the same month a meeting of their executive and organisers decided to refer all claims rejected by local conferences direct to the Committee on Production, ignoring Central Conference.

The autumn of 1916 brought many white collar workers their first increase in salaries. The report of the Retrenchment Committee had found against a general bonus for civil servants, but in September, with the cost of living index now 50 per cent over July 1914, the Treasury relented sufficiently to grant a bonus of 20p a week for those earning up to £2 and 15p for those earning between £2 and £3. As the rates were a little higher than the Post Office bonus of the year before, postal employees were allowed the difference. Since they had been agitating for a further substantial increase, the *Postman's Gazette* of 30 September not unnaturally described the concession as a 'fraud'. A further piece of Treasury meanness was to give departments 'discretion to withhold or reduce the bonus for temporary employees or Women Clerks'.[65] Earlier in the year the Treasury had tried to apply another recommendation of the Retrenchment Committee, for an extension of the seven-hour

[64] Cole, *Labour in the Coal-Mining Industry*, p. 47.
[65] Humphreys, p. 82.

working day of civil servants to eight hours with an extra payment of less than the overtime rates which civil servants were currently receiving. This brought an immediate outcry. A petition was sent to the Privy Council, and the Central Hall was booked for a mass meeting. The proposal was withdrawn.

In July the executive of the National Union of Teachers took up the salaries campaign which they had suspended at the outbreak of war, and during the following months pursued it with vigour. Education authorities who refused increases were threatened with strikes. In October the executive published new scales, and in December they requested the Board of Education to adopt them, and to increase grants to cover them.

Conscription, Exemption, and Manpower Shortages

It had been realised in the early months of the war that one means of conserving the supply of skilled munitions workers was to protect them against pressure to join the forces. Writing of 'essential and pivotal men' in 'the Territorials or the Kitchener Armies', Lloyd George commented that by May 1915 'many of these workers had fallen in futile battles, owing largely to lack of guns and ammunition they could have helped to provide'.[66] The government had agreed to the issue of badges by the Admiralty and the War Office to workers they did not wish to lose, signifying that they were employed on essential war work. The Munitions Act transferred control of badging on War Office contracts to the Ministry of Munitions, but the Admiralty insisted that they must retain control of all those who were working for them, including dockers and the crews of vessels which they had chartered or registered. The Ministry of Munitions recognised that 'even unskilled labour was very scarce in some districts' and, where the case was made, issued badges 'to experienced fitters' and erectors' labourers, to storekeepers, to fettlers and cupola men. . . . This problem was most pressing in blast furnaces, in steel works and rolling mills, in tube works and in foundries.'[67] Accordingly, there was no standard system of badging; a great deal depended on the employer 'making a case'; many workers who might not have appeared to be irreplaceable received badges, and, as it turned out in 1916, a good many skilled men lacked them.

In July 1915 the agitation for conscription led to the National Registration Act, known as the 'Derby Scheme', whereby men were encouraged to 'attest' their willingness to serve. They could then be called up as needed, but as volunteers, and conscription would be avoided. Given the fairly haphazard manner in which badges had been

[66] Lloyd George, pp. 91–2.
[67] *History of the Ministry of Munitions*, Vol. IV, Part III, p. 23.

issued, it was now considered that a more reliable system of protection for essential workers was needed. Lists of 'starred' occupations were therefore drawn up, with tribunals to handle appeals from those who attested, but believed they were in essential jobs.

The Labour movement gave the Derby Scheme enthusiastic support. Although Thorne had long been a champion of the Social Democratic proposal for a citizens' army in which all should be obliged to serve, and Tillett was soon to produce, at the Transport Workers Federation's 1916 conference, the memorable argument that 'in a strike they were conscriptionists; they were more than conscriptionists, they were coercionists, and God help the conscientious objectors!', the vast majority of trade unionists were horrified at the prospect of conscription. In September 1915 the Trades Union Congress unanimously and 'emphatically' protested, 'amid loud and repeated cheering and the waving of handkerchiefs', against attempts 'to foist on this country conscription, which . . . will divide the nation at a time when absolute unanimity is essential'.[68]

The Labour Party claimed that the Derby Scheme had been a success; but it was a success only for the advocates of conscription. The results were announced on 4 January 1916. Over 2.8 million out of an estimated five million men of military age had offered themselves; over 0.2 million had enlisted for immediate service, and, after excluding the medically unfit and those exempted because of their jobs, over 0.8 million of the remainder would be available for service. However, it was estimated that over a million unmarried men had not offered themselves, and Asquith had promised that no married men who attested would be called up until all fit unmarried men, not in starred occupations, had gone. Without this pledge, the results might have been considered enough to go on with. With it, Asquith and his Liberal colleagues were forced to concede compulsion for single men; and a bill to render them liable for military service was introduced next day.

The Labour movement was in a turmoil. Resolutions of protest came from all over the country and from every kind of organisation. The three national organisations summoned a conference on 6 January 1916, which voted by 1,998,000 votes to 783,000 'to use every means in its power to oppose' conscription, and recommended 'the Labour Party in Parliament to oppose the measure in all its stages'. This resolution committed the Labour ministers to resign, but on Asquith's solemn assurance 'that there would be no extension of compulsion to married men, that the Bill was to operate during the war only', and 'that amendments would be introduced obviating any possibility of industrial compulsion', the Parliamentary Labour Party agreed to the withdrawal

[68] Trades Union Congress, 1915, pp. 79, 91.

of the Labour ministers' resignations pending the party conference at the end of the month. The issue was debated on 27 January, the day on which the bill became law. The delegates condemned it by nearly five to one, but then by a marginal majority refused to agitate for its repeal. Next day Labour's continued participation in the coalition was endorsed by an overwhelming majority.[69]

There was no immediate need for conscription to step up the intake to the armed forces. 'The army', as A. J. P. Taylor says, 'had more men than it could equip'.[70] However, compulsory military service was an essential step towards making fully effective use of the nation's manpower.[71] Had the criteria for exemption and the machinery for applying it been well-designed, the first Military Service Act would have made it possible, ultimately, to place every single man where his services were most needed. As it was, their inefficiency cut enlistment to half the figure which had been achieved by voluntary recruitment, and an agitation began for the extension of conscription to married men.

A bill was presented on 26 April, and on the same day Asquith, Bonar Law and Kitchener met the leaders of the Labour movement, including representatives of the Engineers, the Miners, the Railwaymen, and the Transport Workers Federation, to present their case for breaking Asquith's pledge that there should be no extension of conscription. Next day, the Parliamentary Committee decided to advise the unions to support the bill. They rejected an amendment asking for a special Congress because 'the delegates at such a Congress could not give a proper decision, as it would be impossible to divulge all the facts that had been given . . . the previous day'. The bill also had the support of the Labour Party and the General Federation.

Meanwhile a number of agreements had been made with trade unions outside munitions to release men for the forces, or for other essential work, by substituting women. Among the industries concerned were clothing, cotton, footwear, pottery, printing, rail and road transport, textile finishing, and wool. The printing agreement was of limited value, because the London Compositors refused to be a party to it,[72] and the Typographical Association, although accepting other economies in the use of manpower, refused to allow women or unskilled men on skilled work.[73] Most of the agreements specified the type of work women were

---

[69] Labour Party, 1916, pp. 5–7, 117–25.   [70] Taylor, p. 53.

[71] 'The ideal', wrote Lloyd George, 'would have been for the whole population to be conscripted at the very outbreak of the War, and every man posted forthwith in accordance with a wisely thought-out plan to the job where he would be of most service to our war effort' (p. 803).

[72] They maintained, however, that they had no objection to women who were paid the full craft rate, and in 1916 had no less than eight female members! (Howe and Waite, p. 306.)

[73] 'Many employers, however, did introduce females and "diluted labour", though strikes often resulted, and the Monotype Corporation established schools to train women operators. Nevertheless the T.A.'s stand was generally successful.' (Musson, p. 368.)

to be permitted to undertake, and guaranteed that the men would get their jobs back after the war. Provisions on payment were more varied. In July 1915 the Railwaymen's executive told the government that the companies' proposal to pay women substitutes less than the current minimum rates for men was a violation of their conciliation agreement, which would be cancelled unless the companies gave way. The companies gave way, but a year later the Committee on Production found that they were entitled to supplement the basic rate with a female war bonus lower than the male bonus. The Amalgamated Tramwaymen and the Licensed Vehicle Workers insisted on the male rate when female conductors were introduced into road passenger transport.[74] Other agreements provided for a lower rate to allow for additional supervision and extra costs, and there were also some which left decisions on payment for local settlement.

Three vital industries besides munitions experienced special manpower difficulties in 1915—shipping, docks, and coalmining. The number of available seamen had been reduced by the internment of enemy aliens serving on British ships, and their replacement was hindered by the bitter hostility of the men and their unions to increasing the number of Asiatic seamen on British ships. In July 1915 seamen and dockers in Hull struck when a company paid off its white crews and engaged 'coloured' men. A further complication was that, although the Admiralty engaged men to serve on transports for the period of the war, their contracts were terminated by the loss of their vessel. Thus torpedoed crews were free to sign on with private vessels, and many did so because labour shortage and war profits had pushed wages well above Admiralty rates. Consequently, in July 1916 the Admiralty introduced an additional payment of 50p a month for ratings willing to sign new contracts giving the Admiralty the right to transfer them from one ship to another.[75] When the new contract proved insufficiently attractive, those who would not sign were refused discharges, so that they were subject to much the same compulsion as those who had signed, without the extra pay.

The first remedy for labour shortage in the docks was the negotiation of agreements permitting weekend work. When a dispute over the rates to be paid for it led to an unofficial ban on weekend work at Liverpool, early in 1915, Sexton's union agreed to the raising of a Liverpool Dockers Battalion, organised as a military unit, to provide a mobile force of dockers. Volunteers were to be paid-up union members, and were

[74] When 'a few towns' introduced women tram drivers, the Amalgamated Tramwaymen instructed their members to 'strenuously oppose' this innovation (*Annual Report*, 1916).

[75] The Admiralty's first suggestion was to extend the Naval Discipline Act 'to practically all seamen' but a series of discussions with the Board of Trade and the Transport Workers Federation dissuaded them. (Transport Workers Federation executive report, 1916.)

guaranteed both civilian and military pay. Suggestions that the scheme should be extended to other ports were vehemently and successfully opposed by all the other dockers' unions. However, in November 1915, a National Port and Transit Executive Committee was set up to plan the use of dock labour and expedite the turn-round of ships. The unions' demand for representation on the committee led to the appointment of Gosling, and local committees with union representatives were set up to assist its work. The committee were granted powers to raise a Transport Workers Battalion from servicemen experienced in dock and transport work. Its units—initially three, of one thousand each—were to be under military discipline, with army pay and rations, and the union rate as well while working in the docks. Even so the Transport Workers Federation refused to sanction the scheme, and their protests redoubled in November 1916 when there were rumours that the battalion was to be increased to ten thousand men.

By June 1916, 285,000 miners had volunteered for the services, but new recruits to the pits had kept the total reduction in manpower down to 153,000. Output fell from 287 million tons in 1913 to 253 million in 1915, and over the same period exports fell from $73\frac{1}{2}$ million tons to $43\frac{1}{2}$ million. Addressing a conference of miners and owners in October 1916, Asquith said that the level of exports was dangerously low in view of the need to supply the allies and to maintain trade with neutrals to pay for necessary imports. Eleven thousand ex-miners serving in the home forces had been released to work in the pits, but no more reserves were available. He therefore proposed that output should be increased by reducing absenteeism from the current rate of 10 per cent down to 5 per cent. Joint pit committees had been set up in many collieries 'to watch and deal with absenteeism', but he hoped they would be established universally to keep records and to bring 'moral pressure to bear on those who are not doing their duty'. Smillie, on behalf of the Miners, proposed a resolution, which was carried, pledging the conference 'to do everything in its power by co-operation between employers and workmen to secure' an increase in output.[76] On 6 December the Miners approved a proposal that local joint committees be empowered to impose fines.

Compulsory military service had brought a running battle between the War Office and the Ministry of Munitions over exemptions, exacerbated by the disappointing numbers enlisted. The first Military Service Act had attempted to fulfil Asquith's pledge that compulsory military service would not lead to industrial conscription, by providing a right of appeal to a man dismissed without a Leaving Certificate. He was also allowed eight weeks' grace—long enough to allow him to find

[76] *Coal Output and the War.*

another protected job after the end of the six-week period of waiting imposed by the Leaving Certificate. These provisions added considerably to the difficulties of the recruiting officers. To weed out men with badges whose job did not fully warrant exemption, the list of starred occupations was curtailed, and the Ministry attempted to produce a register of all exempted persons, withdrawing badges when their possession was not justified and otherwise issuing certificates; but the process of inspection and withdrawing badges was long and tiresome. There were many genuinely marginal cases; and different departments applied different criteria. A cabinet committee, chaired by Walter Long, was set up to adjudicate between the War Office and the Ministry; but the battle continued.

In June 1916 Kitchener was drowned on his way to Russia, and Lloyd George succeeded him at the War Office. The new Minister of Munitions, Edwin Montagu, proved ineffective, and Christopher Addison, who continued as parliamentary secretary, was competent but pompous and unimaginative. Following the customary wartime expedient for dealing with a tiresome problem by setting up a new authority to handle it, Long's committee proposed a Manpower Distribution Board, which was appointed in September 'to determine all questions arising between Government Departments relating to the allocation or economic utilisation of man-power', with Austen Chamberlain as chairman. For all his talents, Chamberlain's ignorance of the issues made the choice less than inspired. Two Labour Members of Parliament, Barnes and Walsh, were included in the membership.

The board set about devising bold schemes which would sweep away rather than resolve the current controversies. Over the next two months they set out their proposals in a series of reports. They recommended that the issue of badges should be drastically curtailed, and later discontinued; that exemption should be withdrawn from all men under twenty-six years old, although only a third of less-skilled men in any establishment should be called up, and no skilled men; that substitutes should be found from any source available; and that additional skilled men for munitions should be found by introducing dilution on private work, despite the pledge given to the unions at the time of the Treasury Agreement.

Skilled men were to be protected from conscription by cards issued by their unions, and their exemption was to be withdrawn only after an investigation of each case. This device was forced on them by an agitation organised by the Engineers, who on 27 September presented Montagu with a list of six hundred of their members who, they alleged, had been called up in breach of the government's pledges. Next day Asquith saw a deputation including other craft unions and promised that no skilled man would be called up for general service. Henderson, who had been appointed Paymaster General to allow him to devote himself to his job as government labour adviser, gave his support to a suggestion that this could be done by exempting all men whose skill could be authenticated by their union or by apprenticeship papers.

Nevertheless, when the complete proposals appeared, Henderson predicted that they would 'precipitate a most formidable industrial outbreak'.[77] The Ministry of Munitions criticised them severely. On 8 November the Engineers started negotiations on them. Next day they brought a telegram from their Sheffield district threatening a strike unless one of their members called Hargreaves, who had been called up, was returned to civilian life within seven days. This move had been initiated by their Sheffield district committee who then 'passed the control into the hands of the shop stewards' committee'.[78] On 16 November the strike began and 'a fleet of motor cycles with their cyclist shop stewards ready to be dispatched to the engineering centres' set off to spread the stoppage.[79] The Ministry sent a telegram promising Hargreaves's release, but the strike continued until he arrived in person on the 18th with an excort of stewards.

In the spring of 1916 the district committee had decided 'to ensure that in every department there shall be fully accredited representatives of the men, empowered to take action on their behalf and recognised as part and parcel of the Union's machinery'.[80] Their efforts achieved a good deal of success and in the autumn a local Engineering Shop Stewards Committee was formed to link the stewards in the various factories, with J. T. Murphy as its secretary. The transfer of responsibility for the conduct of the strike was facilitated by the overlapping membership of the district and shop steward committees. It was only after the strike that a Sheffield Workers Committee was inaugurated to link up with shop stewards in the other unions.

Although the Sheffield strikers had no support from the Engineers' leaders, their action had come at the right moment to strengthen the union's hand in its negotiations with the government. A conference of full-time officers and district representatives had been summoned for 16 November to discuss the problems of exemption, and next day sent a deputation to meet the relevant ministers and to agree a 'trade card scheme'. All skilled men who had been 'either journeymen or apprentices prior to August 15, 1915' should, if they were on war work or enrolled as War Munitions Volunteers, receive a card of exemption

[77] *History of the Ministry of Munitions*, Vol. VI, Part I, p. 34.
[78] Murphy, *Preparing for Power*, p. 128.
[79] Ibid., p. 130. The *History of the Ministry of Munitions* confirms this account and quotes a report that in another day 'probably 100,000 would be out' (Vol. VI, Part I, p. 37).
[80] Hinton, p. 168.

from military service 'issued through the trade unions'. The government had hoped to make it a condition that all recipients of cards should be War Munitions Volunteers, but the Engineers would not have it. They also rejected a proposal that they should be responsible for supplying artificers to the forces, undertaking only to help to find them. Addison commented in his diary that it was 'the first fruit of Chamberlain's doctrinaire methods'.[81]

Although the agreement had been signed by the Engineers alone, the use of the plural 'unions' throughout the text indicated that other unions were expected to add their authorisation; and they queued up to do so. At a meeting on 23 November, which voiced complaints at the special treatment accorded to the Engineers, the scheme was extended to the Boilermakers, Shipwrights, Sheet Metal Workers, Ironfounders, Scottish Moulders, and the Steel Smelters. On the other hand, the applications of the woodworking unions were rejected, despite their considerable membership in aircraft manufacture. The meeting 'showed that the application of the scheme proceeded on no well-defined principle, and that those who were denied its privileges would resent their exclusion bitterly'.[82]

The proposal for supplying substitutes for munitions workers who were called up also ran into difficulties. Early next year the War Office reported that they had found seventy thousand substitutes partly from men of a low medical category serving in the home forces and partly from men exempted from military service, but over half of them were 'unfit for work of any kind' and many of the remainder were not available because their medical category had been raised. In anticipation of these difficulties, a proposal had been made for recruiting 'coloured' substitutes in Africa and Asia, and was put to some of the unions. At a conference of building unions convened by the government on 21 November the representatives of the Amalgamated Carpenters and Joiners were 'much surprised' to receive from Henderson and Montagu 'a memorandum recommending the introduction of black labour' to meet a shortage of manpower on government construction work.[83] Scandalised protests poured in from the Labour Party executive, the Parliamentary Committee, the Triple Alliance and individual unions; and the proposal came to nothing.

Some years later Addison wrote of the proposal for dilution on private work that:

Those of us at Munitions who knew what the difficulties had been, even where the work was obviously war-work and in 'controlled' establishments, were

[81] Addison, *Four and a Half Years*, p. 263.
[82] *History of the Ministry of Munitions*, Vol. VI, Part I, p. 41.
[83] Higenbottam, p. 196.

frankly aghast at the vista of troubles the project opened out in thousands of factories and shops that no one wished to control and in many of which the labour employed steadily decreased as the sphere of war-work extended.[84]

However, at the time it seemed that it might have an easier run than the rest of the Manpower Board's projects. On 22 November it gained majority approval at a conference of representatives of the engineering and shipbuilding unions, although the Engineers refused to attend, and, on 18 December, rejected the proposal.

Meanwhile Asquith's coalition had fallen. The prime cause was the failure of the Somme offensive, launched in July 1916, to achieve any of its objectives, at an enormous cost in casualties. In addition, the navy had failed to destroy the German fleet at the battle of Jutland, and merchant ships were being sunk at an increasing rate by German submarines. The cabinet appeared to have lost their grip on the conduct of the war. The press denounced their incompetence. Lloyd George proposed a council of three to run the war, with himself in the chair. The Conservative backbenchers demonstrated their discontent in the House of Commons. Bonar Law took the hint. Addison canvassed the Liberal Members and found substantial support for Lloyd George. Asquith resigned, and, after further manoeuvring, Lloyd George formed a new coalition.

Production failures had figured prominently among the charges laid against Asquith's administration. In his diary for 12 December, Addison, who had just taken over as Minister of Munitions, wrote:

Supplies of aeroplanes are utterly inadequate—the types are far too numerous and complex and, at the moment, there are no places of big scale manufacture available. . . . An immense transport manufacturing programme also is not far ahead, and this, with the new tank programme, will require an immense amount of material. The demands for increased home-food production . . . have compelled us to become responsible for the provision of agricultural machinery. . . . Before long also the delays over shipbuilding will have to be dealt with and the two greatest difficulties all the time will be how we are to scrape together the material for these things and how to find the men to make them.[85]

The unpopularity of the Manpower Board's schemes for finding the men to make them and to meet the needs of the forces provided further ammunition for Asquith's critics. Very shortly after Lloyd George took over, the board was wound up.

[84] Addison, *Politics From Within*, Vol. II, p. 117.
[85] Addison, *Four and a Half Years*, pp. 282–3.

5

Lloyd George's War

Lloyd George and the Unions

IN the course of putting together his government, Lloyd George met the Parliamentary Labour Party and the Labour Party executive at noon on 7 December 1916 at the War Office. He needed their support. At this stage he had been promised the backing of about half the Liberal Members of Parliament, but Bonar Law had not so far succeeded in swinging the Conservatives behind him. The news that he had the votes of the thirty-five Labour Members would help in these negotiations. In addition, a coalition of the Conservative Party and half the Liberal Party threatened to make him a prisoner of the Conservatives. By including Labour, he would give himself more room for manoeuvre. Furthermore, Lloyd George's commitment to 'the relentless prosecution of the war' entailed action on the home front as much as on the military fronts. He had to increase still further the production of munitions, while finding more men for the forces, and he had to extricate his government from the muddled manpower policies left by Asquith's administration. To achieve these things he must have the support of the unions; and the inclusion of Labour in his coalition would be a major step towards winning union support.

Many of those he met at noon that day where not predisposed in his favour. The previous day the Parliamentary Committee of Congress had resolved:

That we express our profound regret that certain statesmen of the country, led and influenced by a Press campaign have, in the hour of the nation's crisis, entirely failed to observe the loyalty and self-sacrifice they have repeatedly urged upon the workers during the War.

On 7 December the leaders of the Labour movement should have been on the platform of a national conference which they had called in London to demand action on food prices. In the circumstances, the platform was almost empty, and the Parliamentary Party and the Labour Party executive met on their own to discuss the political crisis. Henderson brought a message from Lloyd George that, in return for Labour support, he was prepared to offer more places in the new government than in the old, and to carry out a number of reforms which the Labour movement had been demanding. They decided to see Lloyd George in a body.

Impressions of the meeting differ. According to Beatrice Webb, Sidney found Lloyd George 'at his worst—evasive in his statement of policy and cynical in his offer of places in the Government'. In reply to questions he gave 'non-committal answers. All he definitely promised was a Ministry of Labour and a Food Controller—whilst he clearly intimated compulsory mobilisation of labour.'[1] Where or not this last item was 'clearly intimated', it does not appear to have been picked up by others present, and at least two other promises seem to have been made—government control of the mines and of shipping. Henderson, who told his colleagues that 'they ought to concern themselves more with what they are going to give than with what they were likely to get', nevertheless believed that adequate commitments had been obtained, 'especially where that policy might affect the social and economic well being of the masses of those whom the Party represented'.[2] Congress had demanded a Ministry of Labour before the war, and again in 1915 and 1916; and control over food supplies and prices, which might be expected to follow from the appointment of a Food Controller, had been at the top of the list of measures sought by the movement since the early months of the war. Nevertheless Henderson had a difficult meeting with his colleagues after they had left Lloyd George, but in the end participation in the new coalition was approved by eighteen votes to twelve, the Miners abstaining as they were without instructions.

Given Lloyd George's reputation for slippery dealing, the most important question was not what he promised, but what he would deliver, and in this respect those who voted to join the government were richly rewarded. Within the week, Beatrice Webb's view was changing. The new government, with Henderson as a member of the five-man war cabinet, Hodge as Minister of Labour (after Thomas had refused the post) and Barnes as Minister for Pensions, was 'a brilliant improvisation'; and she now expected it to be 'boldly and even brutally interventionist—it will break all conventions and even control inconvenient vested interests'.[3]

The chief disappointment was the Ministry of Labour. Hodge was not a success. He did not handle his civil servants tactfully, and his choice of Shackleton as his permanent secretary was not well received. The authority of his officials was trammelled by the insistence of the Ministry of Munitions and other departments on continuing to handle industrial relations in the industries for which they were responsible,

---

[1] *Beatrice Webb's Diaries*, Vol. I, pp. 72–3.
[2] Labour Party, 1917, p. 87.
[3] *Beatrice Webb's Diaries*, Vol. I, p. 74.

and by the war cabinet's decision to transfer the functions of the discredited Manpower Board to a Department of National Service instead of the Ministry of Labour.

At first the Miners' executive viewed the prospect of government control over their whole industry 'with the utmost concern', but at a meeting with Lloyd George on 21 December they were assured that the idea that government control was to be introduced because 'they wanted a more complete hold over the miners never entered anybody's head'.[4] Coal prices were already controlled, and there was little that the Coal Controller, Sir Guy Calthrop, who was appointed in February 1917, could do to arrest the continued decline in coal output, which was due to loss of manpower, and the curtailment of development work on new seams. Instead demand was cut to match supply, through coal rationing and economies in consumption. Britain had long been notoriously wasteful in its use of its greatest natural asset, and there was little difficulty in finding more efficient ways of burning coal.

From the Miners' point of view the overriding gain was a system of national wage settlement, for which their federation had been agitating since before the war. The standard response of the owners to this proposal had been that variation in circumstances from one district to another made district settlements essential; a national decision on pay could not suit all the districts. Given the very different market conditions for different types of coal their argument had considerable force in normal circumstances. Now, however, the Coal Controller was empowered to retain 15 per cent of the earnings of the colliery companies, after their guaranteed profits had been met, to constitute a pool from which any shortfall in profits elsewhere could be made good.[5] With profits guaranteed in this way, the owners' argument had lost its validity for so long as control continued.

By the summer of 1917 many miners had not received a wage increase for nearly a year, and with both prices and wages elsewhere rising fast, the Miners' conference in July applied for a 25 per cent increase on current earnings which would have brought them, on the average, to about 70 per cent over prewar earnings. The Controller decided that 15 per cent was the appropriate figure, but the cabinet insisted on a flat-rate increase in line with other industries; and an offer of 5p a day was made. In September agreement was reached on 7.5p, which gave an advance of about 25 per cent to surfaceworkers, but less to those working underground.

The Shipping Controller, Sir Joseph Maclay, faced two major problems. At the beginning of 1917 the Germans launched an all-out

---

[4] Miners' executive, 21 December 1916.
[5] Another 5 per cent was retained by the companies, and the rest went to the Inland Revenue.

submarine campaign against allied shipping, which increased British monthly losses up to 545,000 tons in April—almost half a year's output of the shipyards. By this time the top rates for British seamen on private ships had reached £10 a month, 70 per cent above prewar rates, whereas 50 per cent above prewar rates was paid on ships chartered by the Admiralty, which therefore had difficulty in engaging new crews. The union had obtained allowances at Admiralty scales for the dependants of seamen who were killed, interned or made prisoners of war, but contracts ceased when a ship went down; some companies paid a month's wage to torpedoed men, others nothing. In these circumstances, further inroads into the supply of labour were made, following the entry of the United States into the war, by Congressional legislation, which encouraged foreign sailors in American ports to desert to American ships at more than double British wages.

The adoption of convoys cut shipping losses dramatically, but the labour shortage remained. In August 1917 Maclay prevailed upon the Shipping Federation to forgo their long-standing objection to direct dealing with the unions, and a joint committee was set up to examine what could be done. In October the crews of three Liverpool liners went on unofficial strike, refusing to sail for less than £12 a month. The union could not get the men back to work, and in the end Maclay met the unofficial leaders and promised a minimum rate of £11 a month, pending a general settlement. Next month a National Maritime Board was formed to negotiate pay and conditions, with six representatives of the owners and four trade union panels, each of six trade unionists who represented respectively deck officers, engineers, seamen and firemen, and cooks and stewards. The chairman was Sir Leo Chiozza Money, parliamentary secretary to the Ministry of Shipping.

The board began by discussing the supply of labour. The union proposed that they should provide the crews. The owners demurred, but finally accepted Havelock Wilson's next suggestion—joint supply through district joint boards with agents in all the major ports. Henceforth no one would be able to obtain a job as a seaman without the consent of the unions. Next standard rates were fixed at £11.50 a month for able seamen and £12 a month for firemen—roughly double prewar rates. The unions had secured full recognition from their old enemies, the Shipping Federation, national machinery for negotiating pay and conditions, national rates of pay, and what amounted to a closed shop. In addition the harsh discipline which applied on board ship had been modified by an agreed procedure to deal with grievances once a ship had returned to port, and the national board was authorised to settle disputes that could not be resolved by the district boards.

There had been no expectation of control of the cotton industry when

Lloyd George announced his programme, but the entry of the United States into the war led to a further reduction in imports of raw cotton, and reduced Britain's need for foreign exchange. Cotton exports were henceforth regarded as inessential. In June 1917 the Board of Trade appointed a Cotton Control Board to deal with the threatened unemployment in Lancashire.

The board, consisting of four union officers, four employers and four independents under the chairmanship of a fifth employer, A. H. Dixon, differed from most of the other new government agencies in being largely self-governing. Its main tasks were to pay unemployment benefit, and to raise a levy to cover their cost. The Bolton area was little affected because the Egyptian cotton spun there was in ample supply. In the other spinning centres, which relied on American cotton, and in weaving, a rota system was arranged whereby workers were laid off in turn, usually every fourth or fifth week, and drew benefits through their unions of £1.25 a week for men and 75p a week for women. The employers were able to keep their mills open and enjoy large profits from current famine prices. Union officers could use the payment of benefits as a means of recruiting non-unionists. As for the operatives, the great majority affected were women;

and their periods of 'playing off' yielded as a rule a full equivalent for the reduction of earning-power in the services which it set them free to render in the home, whether their own or their parents'. Above all the whole character of their existence was rendered infinitely more congenial. The weary monotony of factory life was pleasantly broken. . . . The rota week became a cherished institution.[6]

Soon after the board was established, Dixon was asked to arbitrate on a wage claim submitted by all sections of the industry. He awarded 15 per cent on standard, making an overall increase in pay of 33 per cent since 1914.

The diminished importance of export earnings also affected the wool trade, and a Board of Control—with union and employer representatives—was set up to control civilian production in the wool and worsted industries. However, exports accounted for a much smaller proportion of wool than of cotton output, and there was no need to introduce an unemployment scheme in Yorkshire. Short-time sufficed. The working week was cut from 55 to 45 hours for most branches of the industry in May 1917, but already in August Ben Turner told the half-yearly meeting of the General Union of Textile Workers of his 'strong hopes that they might go on to 50 hours a week, or possibly even full time'.[7] The board did not have any part in the negotiation of wages. The

[6] Henderson, p. 33.   [7] *Yorkshire Factory Times*, 9 August 1917.

major development in this respect began in May 1917, with the
submission by the National Association of Unions in the Textile Trades
of an application to nine separate employers' associations for a uniform
increase in the war bonus. The claims were sent on to the Committee on
Production which made a single award covering all of them, giving an
overall advance since 1914 of about 50 per cent on time rates. Almost
200,000 operatives were affected. The award was the first fully national
pay settlement in the wool industry.

The government's achievements in relation to the supply of food were
unimpressive through most of 1917. After Smillie had refused the post
of Food Controller, Lloyd George turned to the scourge of the London
dockers, Lord Devonport, who had made his name and his fortune in
the grocery trade. It was one of the Prime Minister's worst appointments. Devonport set up committees, exhorted the public, and
recommended a voluntary scale of rations which 'bore no relation to the
facts of life of three-quarters of the population'.[8] In July he resigned,
and the coalowner D. A. Thomas, now Lord Rhondda, took on 'with
unconcealed reluctance a thankless task'.[9] Clynes was appointed
parliamentary secretary. The one substantial achievement in 1917 was
the Corn Production Act, which guaranteed corn prices as an incentive
to farmers to increase production. This arrangement would have been
unacceptable without a corresponding guarantee of farmworkers' wages,
so the bill included provision for an Agricultural Wages Board together
with a clause specifying that the initial minimum should be £1.25 a
week. This was not enough for the Agricultural Labourers, and they
persuaded the Parliamentary Labour Party to move a list of amendments, including maximum working hours, the payment of wages in
cash, and a minimum wage of £1.50. However, some Labour Members,
including, of course, the ministers, voted for the original £1.25, which
was carried.

Nevertheless, the Act was an important step forward for the union.
According to Bowley, the £1.25 minimum was above the level of
earnings at the beginning of 1917 'in the whole of England south of
Lincolnshire (except Middlesex) and in the great part of Wales' but 'the
North of England was not affected'.[10] In addition the unions now had
statutory machinery for revising the national minimum rate, and
statutory District Wage Committees, in most instances covering a
county, to recommend district minimum rates—which could exceed the
national rate—for ratification by the national board. Like the Trade
Boards, both the national board and the county committees consisted of
equal numbers of union and employer representatives, together with

[8] Beveridge, *British Food Control*, pp. 34–5.   [9] Ibid., p. 50.
[10] Bowley, *Prices and Wages*, pp. 170–1.

independent members. 'For the first time in history the farmworker' had 'been invited to state his case through his accredited representatives'.[11]

In the munitions industry the new government had to deal with union demands for a national advance in wages, and for reform of the machinery of wage settlement. The second of these issues had been taken up by the Parliamentary Committee, who met Hodge on 18 January 1917 to press, among other things, for the inclusion of trade unionists in the membership of the Committee on Production. The committee themselves were in favour of a new procedure in order to deal with their heavy and rising case-load. As a result, both trade union officers and employers' representatives were added to the membership, and the committee henceforth handled cases in panels, each panel normally consisting of an independent chairman, an employer, and a trade unionist. The Engineering Employers Federation was persuaded to enter into an agreement with the engineering unions under which, for the duration of the war, the committee was to hear representations in February, June, and October each year, and award 'what general alteration in wages, if any, is warranted by the abnormal conditions then existing and due to the war'. The awards were to apply from 1 April, 1 August, and 1 December. The agreement covered all federated firms, and awards were to be enforceable under the Munitions Act. The Engineers insisted that they should be enforced on non-federated firms as well.

On 1 March the committee announced its first award under the new procedure. Any district which had so far received a war advance of less than 35p a week was to be brought up to that figure, and an additional 25p was granted to all adult males including pieceworkers. Piece rates were not altered. With this award the total increase in time rates since July 1914 amounted to about one-third for skilled workers and a half for the unskilled. Subsequent awards indicated that the committee's criteria for wage increases had altered along with its composition. At the time of the April increase, the cost of living index stood at 70–75 per cent above July 1914. By December the index had risen to 85 per cent over prewar, but the committee's award which applied from the first day of that month brought the skilled rate up to almost three-quarters above July 1914, and the unskilled rate to more than double. Advances for women continued to be settled by their special tribunal—even for women doing skilled jobs. The Ministry insisted that, while employers were obliged to pay these women the skilled man's *rate*, the bonuses fixed by the four-monthly reviews were not part of the rate, and they should receive the separate and lower increases awarded by the women's tribunal.

[11] Selley, p. 163.

The shipbuilding industry also adopted four-monthly reviews by the Committee on Production, and the same increases were awarded. They were followed by the third major munitions industry, chemicals, where the workers were represented by the general unions, and collective bargaining before the war, where it existed, had been carried on with individual firms. By July 1917 there had been formed a Wages Committee of Chemical Manufacturers, later to become the Chemical and Allied Employers Association, and the Committee on Production awarded a general pay increase for the whole industry, followed by four-monthly reviews. The Committee on Production rejected claims for increased rates for overtime and weekend work, but these were subsequently settled by a negotiated agreement. Thus national collective bargaining was introduced into the chemicals industry; and other industries followed on behind.

Two major industries, cotton and shipbuilding, with roughly a million employees, had adopted national pay bargaining before the war. Within a few months of the outbreak of war they had been joined by the railways, and the total number of employees affected rose to well over a million and a half. In 1917 engineering, coalmining, chemicals, shipping, and wool were added to the list, accounting for another three million workers on 1911 census figures, and considerably more if allowance is made for the expansion of munitions industries during the war. If the statutory system of pay regulation introduced into agriculture is counted as collective bargaining, almost another million workers are added to the total. Including agriculture, therefore, by the end of 1917 national collective bargaining had been adopted in industries accounting for at least a third of the employed labour force, a larger share of the manual labour force, and well over half of total trade union membership.

The effect of these developments is evident in the general wage index. During the first two and a half years of war, real wage rates had fallen by about 30 per cent. In the first year of Lloyd George's administration wage rates began to catch up with prices and the shortfall was reduced to about 15 per cent. However, despite these substantial benefits to trade unions and their members, Lloyd George's policies did not put an end to industrial unrest. On the contrary, the number of strikes in 1917 was the highest annual total for the war so far, and in May there occurred an engineering strike—or a series of related strikes—which was the largest and most notable of the whole war.

The May Strikes

There were signs of unrest in March. In November 1916 the engineering unions on the Tyne, which had been in the forefront of engineering pay increases since 1914, claimed a further 30p a week, but reference to the Committee on Production was delayed by the negotiations over the national wage advance. On 19 March 12,000 skilled men came out. The General Workers and the National Amalgamated Union of Labour protested, but brought their members out as well. After a week a separate hearing before the Committee on Production gave the Tyne 10p a week for timeworkers and a proportionate advance to pieceworkers, in addition to the general increase.

A similar issue arose on Merseyside. Although it was the only district to receive advances totalling 50p a week since the outbreak of war, the unions submitted a further claim in the autumn of 1916, which, unlike the Tyne's submission, was sent directly to the Committee on Production. The hearing was on 10 January, but no award was announced, presumably in the hope that the men would be satisfied with the national award in March. They were not. The Committee on Production forestalled a strike by announcing a special award of 20p a week, making Merseyside the highest paid district in the country. Even so the award was accepted by only a narrow margin. The Engineers' organiser commented: 'Never in the history of the trade has there been such feeling exhibited as there was on this issue. We were living near to the crater of a social and industrial volcano.'[12]

Later in the same month there was a strike of 8,000 skilled men at Barrow over allegations of rate-cutting. It was of course understood that piece rates and bonus times on munitions work were not to be cut 'as a consequence of the increase in output due to the suspension of restrictions'; but this did not prevent the alteration of rates, or the retiming of jobs, when new methods or machinery were introduced. The men came out on 21 March, protesting against the cutting of time allowances on flimsy pretexts of changes in the job. The union executive came to Barrow as a body. Having failed to persuade the men to return to work, they issued a condemnation of the strike as 'a menace to the national interests' and 'a violation of the rules of the society'.[13] At the beginning of April the men at last went back after their attempts to bring out other centres in sympathy had failed.

Two other issues were threatening to cause unrest throughout the engineering industry: the trade card scheme and the proposal to extend dilution to private work. The new government had little difficulty in deciding that trade cards must go. Their dilemma was to extricate themselves from the agreement between the previous government and the skilled unions without provoking a major strike.

While they were wrestling with this problem, the general unions

---

[12] *Monthly Journal and Report*, March 1917.   [13] Ibid., April 1917.

showed their mounting strength by launching an effective campaign against the trade card system. By now they, and especially the Workers Union, had many thousands of members doing skilled work on munitions. The trade card system excluded these men. They were liable to conscription whereas craft union members doing the same job were protected. Thorne raised the issue in the House, and was told by Kellaway, the parliamentary secretary to the Ministry of Munitions, that 'the Department have been in communication with the War Office as to the steps to be taken to extend some consideration to the same class of men who belong to other trade unions or are non-unionists'.[14] The general unions kept up their pressure, and, on 2 February, Neville Chamberlain, who had been appointed Director-General of National Service in December, assured a deputation that 'a case had been made out for the lesser skilled unions which was unanswerable. He had promised to give the case consideration and reply in a few days.'[15] At the same time

it was evident that the [trade card] scheme was unnecessarily limiting the field of recruiting for the Army, inasmuch as it was protecting many semi-skilled machinemen, whose work could be done by women after a short training, and others, for example, sheet metal workers, who were not required as artificers, and of whom there was no marked shortage for munitions work.[16]

Chamberlain recommended that the needs of the services should be met by a 'clean cut'—withdrawing exemption from all men aged 18–21 regardless of occupation and union membership. This proposal held a good deal of attraction, but the Admiralty and the Ministry of Munitions objected that the loss of skilled men would seriously retard the output of munitions, and in the end the cabinet approved it, subject to exemption for men in the most-needed occupations. Consequently during February and March the relevant departments at last worked out a comprehensive Schedule of Protected Occupations. The administrative machinery for applying the schedule was to include Labour Enlistment Complaints Committees and Sub-Committees throughout the country, each of the latter consisting of the Ministry's area dilution officer and a carefully chosen trade union representative, who became a full-time officer of the Ministry. This arrangement was to prove more economic and quick than the previous centralised system, and trade union participation led to readier acceptance of its decisions.

On 3 April the unions which had been authorised to issue trade cards gave the government's proposals an unfriendly reception. Next day it

[14] *Hansard*, 21 December 1916, cols. 1631–2.
[15] National Amalgamated Union of Labour executive, 9 February 1917.
[16] *History of the Ministry of Munitions*, Vol. VI, Part I, pp. 76–7.

was the turn of the unions excluded from the trade card scheme. Clynes, speaking on behalf of the general unions, voiced their 'deep sense of resentment' at the way they had been treated, but added that the new proposals seemed 'on the first examination' to be 'eminently fair'.[17] In subsequent discussions the skilled unions continued to insist that no skilled man should be called up while fit dilutees remained in the workshops, and this was also the position of the Engineers although, as usual, they insisted on separate discussions. The scheme was to have been introduced on 1 May, but at the end of April the government postponed it for a week to allow further discussions.

Meanwhile the Ministry of Munitions was going ahead with the proposal for dilution on private work. The Engineers' executive now insisted that all the safeguards concerning the payment of dilutees and the restoration of prewar practices should be extended to cover private dilution, without promising acceptance if that were done. On 27 April the Ministry introduced a bill to enforce dilution on private work with these safeguards, but there was no discussion with the Engineers 'lest they should force the issue by taking a ballot of their members, which would almost certainly result in an adverse vote'.[18]

By this time a storm was brewing in Lancashire. In February the firm of Tweedale and Smalley near Rochdale dismissed a number of skilled members of the United Machine Workers for refusing to instruct women in the operation of grinding machines for the manufacture of textile machinery. Having waited a month for redress, their colleagues struck on 20 March. At the beginning of April the Ministry decided to prosecute the firm. The case had not yet been heard when a mass meeting at Rochdale decided to bring out the whole district on strike, unless action had been taken by 3 May. Meanwhile the Joint Engineering Shop Stewards Committee in Manchester had conducted a workshop ballot on a strike in sympathy with the dismissed men. The vote was for a strike, and the committee called the men out on 29 April, adding a demand for the retention of the trade card scheme a few days later.

On 2 May the government resumed negotiations with the Engineers over the schedule of protected occupations. Three days later agreement was reached on a formula which gave the Engineers everything they had asked:

Before any skilled man or apprentice who is not covered, owing to age, by the Schedule of Protected Occupations is taken for military service, all male diluted labour liable and fit for general military service in the occupation in the munitions area in which he is employed shall first be withdrawn.

[17] Ibid., pp. 97–8.   [18] Ibid., p. 54.

The government had failed to persuade the Engineers to accept 'the establishment in which he is employed' instead of 'the area', and they had to agree to the rider that 'no munitions area shall be singled out to be dealt with specially'.[19] With these provisos it became extremely difficult to call up any skilled men or apprentices.

By this time 60,000 men were on strike in Lancashire. On Sunday, 6 May, executive members and other officials of the Engineers addressed meetings all over the country to win support for their agreement; but the value of the government's guarantees was not as readily appreciable as the fact that the trade card scheme had been terminated, and unrest was increased by the censorship of all news of the strike. During the next few days Sheffield, Rotherham, Derby, Coventry, Crayford, Erith, and Woolwich had joined the strike. Several smaller centres followed them. London electricians came out on 16 May.

On 12 May a conference of representatives from the local strike committees met at Derby, and reconvened at Walworth in London on the 15th, where they elected ten of their number as a deputation to the Ministry of Munitions. Since the government refused to deal directly with unofficial strikers, the Engineers' executive, who saw the Walworth conference as an 'unofficial and unauthorised conference of ASE members, and representatives from two or three other organisations',[20] begin discussions with the deputation, who denied any hostility to the union or its executive and asked the executive to help them to get a hearing for their grievances.

At this point the government arrested seven strike leaders under defence regulations. The executive agreed to introduce the Walworth deputation to Addison on condition that the delegates put the matter entirely in their hands. On the 19th Addison heard the deputation's objections to the withdrawal of trade cards and to dilution on private work, and their complaints against the goverment's broken pledges. They had only struck, said one of their spokesmen, William McLaine of Manchester, to strengthen the hands of their leaders. They had come to London to end the dispute, an objective which the arrests had made more difficult to attain.[21] When the deputation had left, Addison agreed with the executive that, provided the unofficial leaders called off the strike and accepted the authority of the executive, there would be no more arrests, and those already arrested, now numbering eight, would be released pending trial.[22] The strike was called off.

---

[19] Ibid., pp. 106–9.
[20] *Monthly Journal and Report*, June 1917.
[21] *History of the Ministry of Munitions*, Vol. VI, Part 1, pp. 116–17.
[22] They included Arthur MacManus, formerly of Glasgow, now of Liverpool; George Peet, of Manchester; Tom Dingley, of Coventry; and W. F. Watson of London.

The immediate result was confusion. On 8 May a Munitions Tribunal fined Tweedale and Smalley £35 with twenty guineas costs. Action against the firm had been the main objective of the Rochdale strikers, and they returned to work a few days later, followed by other Lancashire centres, including Manchester. Elsewhere, however, the strike was still spreading. Liverpool, Leeds, and Barrow came out, and there were more stoppages when the news of the arrests was heard. A further return to work began in some centres on 21 May; others resolved to stay out until the fate of the arrested men was settled. On the 23rd the Attorney-General asked leave at Bow Street to withdraw the charges on the ground that they had signed an undertaking to abide by the decision of the Walworth conference to call off the strike, and the resumption of work became general. The official estimate was that 1.5 million working days had been lost.

It is not easy to be sure what it had all been about. The strikers were concerned over the withdrawal of the trade card scheme. They wanted to be sure that skilled men would not be called up. If the central issue in the dilution struggle was the craftsman's belief in his inalienable right to his job, never mind what happened to anyone else, the struggle over exemption centred on his discovery of a new right, the inalienable right of a craftsman to his life, whoever else might be sent to the front to risk being killed. But although the implications of the new agreement between the government and the Engineers' executive might not be immediately obvious, it surely did not take more than three weeks for the craftsmen to appreciate that it gave them substantially what they wanted. Otherwise, once Tweedale and Smalley had been fined, the only remaining purpose could be to emphasise their opposition to dilution on private work. Accordingly there began a search for explanations of the 'labour unrest'.

On 12 June Lloyd George set up a commission of inquiry. Three commissioners—a chairman, an employer and a labour representative— were to investigate the causes of unrest in each of the eight munitions divisions, and report. Their reports were then collated and summarised by Barnes. From the start of the inquiry to publication took only six weeks. According to Barnes, three 'universal causes of unrest' were noted. 'All the Commissioners put in the forefront . . . the fact that the cost of living had increased disproportionately to the advance in wages, and that the distribution of food supplies is unequal'. Secondly there were the Munitions of War Acts, and the commissioners picked out Leaving Certificates as 'the leading cause of dissatisfaction under this heading'. Thirdly came the proposal to withdraw the trade card scheme. Among 'acute, but not universal causes' were mentioned housing, liquor restrictions, and industrial fatigue. Many of the specific causes had 'their root' in a 'want of confidence' showing itself 'in the feeling that there had been inequality of sacrifice, that the Government had broken solemn pledges, that the Trade Union officials are no longer to be relied upon, and that there is a woeful uncertainty as to the industrial future'.[23] The reports did not attribute the strikes to the work of disloyal agitators.

Insofar as the commissioners' findings bore on the Munitions Acts, Addison took them into account in the amending bill which was already being discussed. He proposed so many amendments concerning Leaving Certificates that the employers preferred to have them abolished. Addison agreed, and put the proposal to the Engineers as a concession to win their assent to dilution on private work. The executive were willing to recommend acceptance, but insisted on holding a ballot whose result was a foregone conclusion: five to one against.

At this point Churchill took over as Minister of Munitions from Addison, who became Minister for Reconstruction. Lloyd George had for some time been looking for a way to bring Churchill back into the government. Addison had been given the extremely difficult task of extricating the new administration from the confusion of manpower policies left by the Manpower Board, and had received a bad press over the May strikes, while Lloyd George took all the credit for the settlement. Churchill quickly came to a decision to drop dilution on private work. Given that over 80 per cent of engineering manpower was now engaged on government work, it could not have tapped large reserves of skilled men; and resistance in the private workshops might have been even stronger than in the munitions factories, because of the more direct consequences of dilution on private work for the postwar employment prospects of skilled men. The last of the proposals of the Manpower Board was therefore abandoned.

Tensions within the Unions

Commenting on the reports of the Commission on Industrial Unrest, John Hill said in his presidential address to Congress in September 1917:

Perhaps the most important finding is that 'Trade Union officials are distrusted'. As leaders we were appointed to lay down the hammer or the trowel, and stand on the ramparts to warn our members of the danger, and in their opinion we had either fallen asleep at our posts, or we have sold their birthright for a mess of pottage.[24]

Earlier that year Gosling had made more specific complaints at the 1917

---

[23] *Summary of the Reports*, pp. 6–7.
[24] Trades Union Congress, 1917, p. 55.

conference of the Transport Workers Federation. He said that the government had gone too far with appointments of trade unionists to committees and other posts, which had

led to a feeling of disaffection and suspicion. Moreover the principle of selection without consultation is certainly mischievous. . . . The very essence of Labour representation is that Labour leaders should be allowed to remain in their Trade Union positions, so that while their services can be made use of in every possible way, they will still be in close touch with and responsible to those whom they represent.

Union leaders can therefore be quoted in support of the notion that trade union officials had now become 'agents of the state', and lost touch with their members who had as a consequence turned to militant shop stewards to take the place of the leaders who had deserted them.[25] However, such a view is grossly misleading.

The Engineers were at the centre of most of the main controversies over wartime industrial relations policy. From 1915 onwards, their executive followed the practice of summoning a conference of full-time officials and district representatives whenever they were in critical negotiations with the government. These conferences were called not merely for consultation, but also to approve the agreements which emerged from the negotiations. It is also relevant that the Engineers' districts were relatively compact units, covering a single city or town and its environs, and that the district committee representatives were men working at the bench. In these circumstances the notion that the executive was 'out of touch' is simply fantastic. Nor were its members 'agents of the state'. On the contrary they appeared at times to carry their dogged opposition to the government's proposals to extreme lengths. They insisted on statutory enforcement of Circular L3, concerning the payment of the skilled rate to unskilled and semi-skilled men transferred to skilled work, although they could quote no instance where that was not already being done. They stood out for even more advantageous terms for women transferred to skilled work than the Clyde shop stewards were willing to settle for. Their members could not have faulted their determination to protect skilled men from conscription, and it was the executive who insisted that the members should settle the fate of the proposal for dilution on private work.

The one issue on which the executive diverged sharply from the more militant of their members was unofficial strikes. They opposed them, and strove to get unofficial strikers back to work, though on several occasions they pressed the government to make concessions to strikers to make it easier for that to be done. In this respect the executive were

[25] See, for example, Miliband, pp. 53–4.

working with the government, but they had their own very good reasons for doing so, besides the risk of arrest for incitement to strike, which open advocacy of stoppages might have brought. Their bargaining power in dealing with the government depended on their authority within the union. The May strikes were a serious challenge to their authority, not merely because they had not authorised the strikes, but also because the strikers were repudiating what the executive believed were the highly satisfactory terms which they had just agreed with the government.

The leaders of the general unions might seem more susceptible to the charge of losing touch with their members. Beard and Duncan, the president and secretary of the Workers Union, who had once 'stood well to the left', now 'adopted an uncompromising right-wing stance'. Beard joined his local Volunteer Force, and took up 'the habit of attending meetings in uniform'. Both of them supported conscription, and welcomed the Munitions Act 'almost unreservedly'. Beard urged a conciliatory attitude to employers, and denounced unofficial shop stewards' movements.[26] The change in Thorne's attitude was, if anything, even sharper. He had been a champion of militant action and left-wing causes right up to the war. Now he acquired the uniform of a lieutenant-colonel in the West Ham Volunteers, and a fur coat as a gift from F. E. Smith, later Lord Birkenhead. Together with his attitude to the war and conscription, these adornments led to his repudiation as their candidate for the next election by a conference of trade union branches and socialist societies in his constituency of South West Ham.

Nevertheless there was no serious challenge to these leaders within their own unions. After all, 'the Munitions Act and the associated changes in workshop practices were in many ways advantageous to the lower-skilled membership of the Workers' Union',[27] and of the General Workers, the National Amalgamated Union of Labour, and the London Dockers. Some of these wartime advantages came without asking, including flat-rate pay increases, and skilled rates for those put on to skilled work; but the leaders of the general unions initiated the campaign for national wage settlements in engineering and chemicals; they denounced the trade card scheme from the start; and they complained bitterly that the May strikes had put tens of thousands of their members out of work in a cause which was diametrically opposed to their own interests. There is no reason to suppose that on these issues the leaders of the general unions were out of touch with their members, nor that more than a small minority of their members disapproved of 'patriotic' attitudes to the war.

[26] Hyman, p. 82.
[27] Ibid., pp. 82–3.

The national leaders of the Miners were protected from the risk of losing touch with their members because the national officers and executive members were all office-holders in the districts; and, even more, by the practice of holding a national conference or a ballot whenever an issue of importance arose. It is true that they co-operated with the government and the coalowners in the Coal Mining Organisation Committee, and over issues such as absenteeism, but the subject on which the miners felt most strongly was pay. It had been the main issue in the South Wales strike of 1915, which the national leaders refused to condemn. District negotiations kept the miners' pay increases substantially ahead of the national average up to the end of 1916, and, when the national leaders took over responsibility for pay under government control, they took care to see that this position was maintained.

One major union in which the leadership appeared reluctant to respond to the wishes of the members was the National Union of Railwaymen. In most areas the union's branches had formed semi-official district councils to co-ordinate their activities and discuss union affairs, but without the formal sanction of the rule-book. In wartime local vigilance committees were also set up to act as wholly unofficial pressure groups. In June 1916 the Liverpool Vigilance Committee was fined for issuing an unauthorised circular to the branches demanding a special meeting of the executive to call a strike. Two months later the union's conference expressed its discontent with the executive's conduct of wage negotiations by terminating their authority to finalise settlements. District councils began to vie with vigilance committees in putting pressure on the executive. It was the South Wales District Council that hastened the wage increase of September 1916 by threatening a strike. In August 1917 a conference of fifty-five representatives of district councils and vigilance committees was held in London. In November the Liverpool District Council organised a 'go-slow' to goad the executive on in further pay negotiations.

One cause of tension between the executive and the districts was the wartime innovation of national bargaining over pay. Before the war collective bargaining had been conducted within each company by sectional councils, each consisting of elected representatives of related grades of employees, with a full-time union officer to act as secretary. The union thus had within its ranks several hundred elected local leaders accustomed to give a considerable number of working days each year to preparing and conducting negotiations and settling pay claims. National pay bargaining did not put an end to the work of sectional councils, for there were many other issues to settle besides pay, but it cut back their authority severely. It was therefore not surprising that these men, and their constituents, felt that they still had a right to exert an influence on pay bargaining.

Similar pressures were at work in engineering after the introduction of the system of four-monthly reviews in 1917. Up to that time pay claims had been the business of union district committees. In many districts the smaller unions submitted joint claims through 'Allied Trades Committees'. Before the war the Engineers' district committees had customarily negotiated their own settlements and the local Allied Trades Committees had normally had no option but to accept similar terms; but the special circumstances of the war tended to bring greater co-operation. More and more claims were put forward jointly, and the Engineers' districts began to affiliate to the Allied Trades Committees.

Like the Railwaymen's sectional councils these committees began to look for other functions after national wage bargaining was instituted, and turned their minds to influencing national pay negotiations. On 1 and 2 September 1917 seventy-three delegates attended a national conference of Engineering and Allied Trades Committees in Leeds. They passed several resolutions, including one in favour of a 50 per cent reduction in the price of necessities. They also appointed an emergency committee, consisting of 'the presidents and secretaries of the Allied Trades Committees in large centres'. A few weeks later this committee issued a statement saying that they had experienced great difficulty in preventing unconstitutional protests against the last award of the Committee on Production, and their members were 'expectantly' awaiting the next award. They claimed to be 'responsible officials, deeply concerned that the guidance of our members should not pass out of our hands and the hands of our executives', and it was for that reason that they felt it their duty to warn 'the authorities'.[28]

Wartime tensions were not confined to the relationship between local and national committees. Equally important was the tension between workplace representatives and official bodies outside the factory, whether at district or national level, due to the emergence of new issues which had to be settled at the place of work, and the accession of bargaining power to workplace representatives.

There had been tensions even before the war when workplace organisations had fomented strikes, or failed to comply with some item agreed between their union and the employers' association, and the management called the union in, to bring their members to order; but indiscipline of this kind was endemic even in trade unions with the most rudimentary workplace organisation, and it had long been one of the

---

[28] *Yorkshire Factory Times*, 25 October 1917. The signatories came from Barrow, Coventry, Derby, Leeds, Leicester, Lincoln, Luton, and Sheffield.

duties of district committees and union officers to deal with it. New and more difficult strains developed in wartime where workplace organisations banded together to form local or national bodies outside the control of their unions, and especially where these bodies sought to influence decisions on district or national issues, or, still worse, to settle matters themselves.

Even so, local groups of workplace organisations did not necessarily compete with the district committees and their officers. In Sheffield the Engineers' district committee had itself brought the shop stewards in the factories together in an Engineering Shop Stewards Committee, and had co-operated closely with their creation in the conduct of the Hargreaves strike. Coventry went further. After the May strikes the Coventry Engineering Joint Committee—the local Allied Trades Committee—drew up their own rules for the election of shop stewards, chief stewards, and works committees, regardless of the unions to which they belonged, with provision for each factory to report to the joint committee, and for the joint committee to call meetings of all chief stewards in the district. In other districts, such as Barrow, Tyne, and Woolwich, the engineering industry was dominated by one single large munitions factory with its own powerful workplace organisation, so that there was little 'need to link up the rank and file in different factories outside the official machinery of the unions'.[29]

By contrast, in Manchester the Joint Shop Stewards Committee was formed by the stewards themselves and regarded by the Engineers' district secretary as aimed to 'overthrow the recognised leaders and place the executive power in the hands of shop stewards'.[30] Moreover, co-operation between district committees and shop stewards' organisations had to be kept within the scope of the district committees' authority if it was not to cause tension between the districts and the national union. In the May strikes the Engineers' district committee in Sheffield were involved in calling the men out. They were suspended by the executive, and subsequently elected by a mass meeting to serve as a strike committee.

In November 1916 MacManus had made the first attempt to establish a national organisation of 'workers committees'—which may be taken to mean shop steward bodies, such as the Clyde Workers Committee, covering a number of factories and unions, and independent of official union control. Few committees were represented, and the meeting did little more than elect a provisional committee to arrange a second conference. This met at Manchester on 5–6 May 1917, when the May strikes were already well under way. It 'was not a very representative

[29] Hinton, p. 179.
[30] Ibid., p. 200.

gathering';[31] it 'made no attempt to assume direction of the strike';[32] and it did little or nothing to establish a permanent organisation.

Many of the local strike leaders were already in touch with each other through another unofficial body which had established a national organisation before the war—the Engineering and Shipbuilding Amalgamation Committee. W. F. Watson was the leading figure in this body as well as in the London Workers Committee. In March 1917 he had called a conference in Birmingham, which decided to give the national leaders of the engineering and shipbuilding unions one last chance to amalgamate into a single industrial union, failing which the rank and file would go ahead on their own.

However, the informal links between the local leaders were insufficient to spread the May strikes to all major engineering centres. Tyneside and Clydeside remained at work throughout. After the deportations, the Clyde Workers Committee had fallen into the hands of the more doctrinaire members of the Socialist Labour Party, who were concerned with education in De Leonite principles of industrial unionism, to the exclusion of industrial action. Gallacher, who had set about wresting control from them after his release from prison, was sent south by a meeting of shop stewards on 13 May to make contact with the strikers. In London he formed the impression that 'they hadn't their hearts in the strike. . . . In Birmingham and Manchester this feeling became still more pronounced; only in Coventry and Sheffield was any spirit shown.'[33]

The first successful national conference of workers' committees was held in Manchester on 18 and 19 August, with MacManus in the chair. The Shop Stewards and Workers Committee Movement was established as a permanent body, with a National Administrative Council, of which MacManus was president, Peet secretary, and Murphy assistant secretary. The delegates, however, were so nervous of 'leadership' in any form that the council was denied 'executive authority'. In effect, this meant that it could not call a strike, but had to refer each issue back to the workshops for decision.

Twenty-three committees were represented at the conference. Among these, the Sheffield and Manchester committees had already shown considerable strength, although the union officials had launched 'a campaign of persecution against the unofficial leaders' in Manchester which 'appears to have succeeded in crushing the unofficial Committee by the winter of 1917'.[34] The Clyde committee was still recovering from the effect of government repression in 1916. Watson's London Workers Committee was 'largely a propagandist body without direct contact with

---

[31] Murphy, *Preparing for Power*, p. 136.   [32] Hinton, p. 202.
[33] Gallacher, pp. 145–7.   [34] Hinton, p. 214.

the London engineering workshops';[35] although the West London Workers Committee, formed by the syndicalist, Jack Tanner, probably had more industrial strength. The Coventry Workers Committee, in competition with the semi-official organisation of the Coventry Engineering Joint Committee, 'never succeeded in capturing the leadership of any significant proportion of engineering workers'.[36] The national movement was therefore largely a propagandist organisation. 'Outside Glasgow, Sheffield and, for a short period, Manchester, fully-fledged Workers' Committees representative of workshop organisation and capable of leading mass strike action in defiance of the trade union officials were never to emerge.'[37]

Nevertheless, the movement had at least sufficient vitality to take over Watson's Amalgamation Committee. Attempts to persuade the existing unions to merge having failed, Watson conducted a 'workshop ballot'. Only 37,000 engineering and shipbuilding workers—less than 5 per cent of the membership of skilled engineering and shipbuilding unions—were persuaded to vote. They gave an overwhelming majority for setting up an Engineering and Shipbuilding Industrial Union. Watson then summoned a conference at Newcastle on 13 and 14 October 1917, which at first gave him authority to set up the new union. However, the workers committees were there in some strength, and Peet carried a proposal that, since 'the cause of Industrial Unionism cannot be furthered by creating further divisions', a vote should be taken on 'fusion with the Shop Stewards' and Workers' Committees, with a view to concentrating our activities at the point of production'.[38] This proposal reflected the theory of the movement later expounded by Murphy in a pamphlet, *The Workers' Committee*, published by the Sheffield Workers Committee in 1918, and accepted by the movement as the standard exposition of its aims and doctrine. By organising all the workers in the factories, regardless of skill and union membership, Murphy believed, the workers committees could supersede existing unions without the need for amalgamations, or for 'dual unionism' as advocated by the De Leonites. The proposal was approved by the conference and carried through by the National Administrative Council early in 1918—this being apparently an administrative and not an executive decision.

Pay and Manpower 1917–18

When Churchill took over from Addison as Minister of Munitions in July 1917 he inherited a commitment to abolish Leaving Certificates, and the third Munitions Act in August provided that this should be

[35] Pribićević, p. 96.
[36] Hinton, p. 215.
[37] Ibid., p. 242.
[38] *Fusion of Forces*.

done by ministerial order when possible 'consistently with the national interests'. He explained the delay by the need for prior action to improve the earnings of skilled timeworkers. Otherwise the removal of the limitation on mobility of munitions workers provided by the certificates 'might lead to a serious migration from the higher ranks of labour into the less highly-skilled, though more highly-paid, forms of labour'.[39] Once the prospect of higher pay had been offered to the skilled men, something had to be done quickly. There was a flurry of committees and consultations, and various proposals were canvassed. The final decision was for a $12\frac{1}{2}$ per cent bonus on earnings for certain categories of fully-skilled timeworkers in the engineering and foundry trades; and the necessary order was published on 14 October, the day before Leaving Certificates were abolished.

The problem of skilled timeworkers had been a cause of concern throughout the year. One of the early decisions of the Lloyd George government to improve the utilisation of manpower was to extend payment by results in order to increase the output of munitions, and Hodge, as Minister of Labour, undertook the task with enthusiasm. However, his experience of nationally-agreed tonnage rates in the steel industry was far removed from the practice of the engineering industry, in which numerous variations in methods and machinery meant that piece rates and bonus times had to be set for each job, in each place of work. His ignorance and his arrogance hindered his conduct of the negotiations. At the beginning of 1917 he proposed to a conference of unions affiliated to the Federation of Engineering and Shipbuilding Trades that there should be a joint inquiry into the extension of payment by results in shipbuilding, in order to discover the best method and adopt it. They turned him down. Next month Lloyd George himself tried his hand, and persuaded the federation to accept the principle of payment by results, though they refused to bind their constituents. The Ministry of Labour prepared detailed proposals and held local meetings to explain them. The Shipwrights accepted a general agreement on payment by results and the Woodcutting Machinists agreed to its use for the war period only; but the other timeworking trades would not have it. The May strikes then persuaded the government that it was inopportune to apply further pressure. Hodge's handling of these negotiations helps to account for his transfer to the Ministry of Pensions later in the year. He was succeeded by another Labour Member, G. H. Roberts.

The opposition of the timeworking craftsmen themselves was by no means universal. Although the national woodworking unions refused to countenance payment by results generally in aircraft manufacture, it

[39] *Hansard*, 15 August 1917, col. 1305.

was the common practice in Coventry. When employers introduced it, the patternmakers 'succumbed to the new order without anything more than the merest show of resistance'.[40]

Where payment by results was resisted, skilled timeworkers, nevertheless, looked with envy at the earnings of pieceworkers. The Scottish Ironmoulders had a special grievance since their rules forbade both piecework and overtime, and during the summer of 1917 an unofficial campaign for a 75p increase in weekly rates won support among their members. According to one of its leaders, they formed

an emergency committee of representation from each branch in Glasgow. Then extended the Committee throughout Scotland by throwing up an emergency committee in every town and linking them up through an emergency EC. We took a ballot vote . . . and the ballot decided to down tools.[41]

The strike began on 14 September with 6,000 men involved, and ended three weeks later after the leaders had visited London to convince Churchill of the justice of their case. Although he promised no concessions, their strike persuaded the departmental committee then considering a bonus for skilled timeworkers to extend their proposals to include the foundries.

Some categories of skilled munitions workers were excluded from the $12\frac{1}{2}$ per cent bonus, and their unions were soon bombarding the Ministry with complaints. Moreover, less-skilled munitions timeworkers had exactly the same grievance in relation to the earnings of pieceworkers as the skilled timeworkers had. The Federation of General Workers summoned a conference at York on 9 November, which decided that all engineering timeworkers must receive a bonus.

Strikes had already taken place in the Manchester district, and it was urged that a meeting should take place with the Ministry of Munitions, and if the concession was not granted that a national strike be declared.

A final decision was postponed until the Ministry's reply was received, and, when the federation's representatives came on 21 November, the Ministry agreed to extend the increase to all skilled, semi-skilled, and unskilled timeworkers in engineering and shipbuilding not covered by the original order.

This was by no means the end of the trouble. Many engineers were employed on maintenance work in other industries, and they demanded their $12\frac{1}{2}$ per cent. In December the Engineers' Glasgow organiser wrote in their journal that 'the $12\frac{1}{2}$ per cent delirium is still raging. . . . These belligerents will have the society officials as daft as themselves

[40] Mosses, p. 275.   [41] Quoted by Gallacher, pp. 182–3.

before long.' The railway workshops began an agitation. 'Representatives of the Electrical Union came', wrote Askwith, 'telling me that they would never be able to hold their workpeople in the electrical power stations.'[42] Before the end of January 1918 all timeworkers in iron and steel, electricity supply, electrical contracting, brass foundries, constructional engineering and several other industries had been brought within the scope of the order; and still more claims poured in.

Pieceworkers were now becoming restive. Although there were high earnings on piecework—an aircraft firm wrote to the Ministry in December 1917, reporting that sixty of their skilled men were earning over £10 a week, and one fitter had earned £22.28 in the previous week[43]—and *average* piecework earnings were relatively high, there were also many pieceworkers whose earnings were relatively low. Low piecework earnings were common in Lancashire whose textile machinery manufacturers were traditionally parsimonious; and in December the Engineers' organiser in Glasgow reported that those workers on payment by results, who were not guaranteed so much as $12\frac{1}{2}$ per cent over the time rate, were especially incensed. On the advice of the Committee on Production, therefore, the war cabinet granted a $7\frac{1}{2}$ per cent bonus for pieceworkers. By now the original purpose of the bonus had been quite lost, but there was no mass transfer of skilled munitions workers to other jobs. Skilled men of military age may have been deterred from seeking higher earnings on less-skilled jobs by the consideration that their skilled jobs gave them exemption from conscription.

Throughout the winter the bonus continued to be a major cause of unrest. No less than six of the 'principal disputes' reported in the *Labour Gazette* for February 1918 were over demands for its extension. Two more followed in the March issue, three in the April issue, and one in May. Every dispute was settled by an extension of the bonus, or by an agreement to negotiate on it. It was not granted to the aircraft industry as a whole until March, when it was also applied to tramwaymen and gasworkers. Thereafter, it spread through the building, printing, furniture, and footwear industries, and even to local authority employees. Bonus awards were still being issued after the armistice. The bonus added very substantially to the load of cases before the Committee on Production.

In October 1917 Churchill agreed that woodworkers in the aircraft industry should receive uniform local rates, based on the rate of the highest-paid woodworking craft in the area, with a maximum working week of 53 hours. In return he tried to insist that the unions must accept

42 Askwith, p. 431.
43 *History of the Ministry of Munitions*, Vol. V, Part I, p. 108.

payment by results, but all they would concede was to allow it where it had been 'mutually agreed'. The engineering employers were therefore effectively blocked from any extension of payment by results, and obliged to pay rates which in many districts were higher than those in the engineering agreements, in some instances for a shorter working week. They refused to apply the agreement, and in February 1918 Churchill was driven to enforce it by order.

On 23 March 1917, following the Tyne and Barrow strikes, the Management Committee of the Engineering Employers Federation had drawn attention 'to the lack of any centralised control of labour questions by the Government and the overlapping and conflicting jurisdiction of the Admiralty, the Ministry of Munitions and the Ministry of Labour'. Askwith took up the matter and submitted a memorandum to Lloyd George in April. Nothing more was done until after the Coal Controller's award to the Miners in September. The cabinet then appointed a committee which reported that the case for a single authority was 'incontestable', though the Coal Controller had told them that there was 'the strongest possible opposition' on the part of both coalowners and Miners to 'any interference by the Ministry of Labour'.[44]

Subsequently a co-ordinating committee was appointed by the cabinet, but it could not cope with the consequences of the $12\frac{1}{2}$ per cent bonus. Claims poured in, and the committee had no power to deal with them, so they were passed to the Ministry of Labour for reference to the Committee on Production. In January 1918 the cabinet transferred the responsibility for co-ordination back to the Ministry of Labour. 'It cannot be said that complete co-ordination was secured.'[45]

Askwith's verdict is expressed more harshly:

My view is that in labour matters the Government had no policy, never gave signs of having a policy, and could not be induced to have a policy. . . . The Departments never followed any policy in labour matters except a policy of disintegration; . . . and went their own way in a manner which cost or lost hundreds of millions of money, precious time, and urgently needed supplies.[46]

However, even if a single authority had been given power to settle all disputes and to authorise all wage increases with which the government was concerned, individual unions would still have demanded special treatment for their own pay claims.

Many unions signed up for the four-monthly awards introduced for engineering, which gave the engineering and shipbuilding workers three increases totalling 65p a week in 1917 with the $12\frac{1}{2}$ and $7\frac{1}{2}$ percentages in

[44] Ibid., p. 222.   [45] Ibid., p. 225.   [46] Askwith, p. 443.

addition, but others insisted on individual treatment. The railway unions obtained two increases, one of 25p, and the other of 30p; the Miners secured one increase of 45p for a full week, and claimed another 45p in June 1918. The Coal Controller was empowered to offer 15p. The reaction of the Miners' leaders was so emphatic that the cabinet went up to the full 45p the very next day, the only proviso being that the pit committees, which 'had fallen into abeyance' or were 'being only half-heartedly worked', should be reinvigorated.[47] A co-ordinating authority could not have refused them without risking a national stoppage when coal output was falling to a dangerously low level, due not only to the call-up of more miners, but also to the influenza epidemic which cost nearly three million tons in July alone.

Even without co-ordination, the wide disparities in pay which had emerged in the early years of the war were now diminishing. By July 1918 railwaymen's, dockers', and miners' rates of pay had risen on the average about 90 per cent above prewar rates, with engineering workers not far behind. Bricklayers, compositors, and cotton operatives were all at 55 to 60 per cent over prewar rates, and for bricklayers' labourers the increase had been 85 per cent. Even Trade Board rates, some of which had been stationary for the first three years of the war, were moving up rapidly. A co-ordinated policy might well have been directed to achieve the same result.

Salaried workers were less fortunate, although the civil service received better treatment than most. Continued agitation by their associations led to the appointment of a Conciliation and Arbitration Board for Government Employees in January 1917, limited to dealing with salaries of less than £500 a year. The board encouraged the development of collective bargaining by insisting that a serious attempt be made to achieve a settlement by negotiation before a claim was referred to them. Even so, the total increases for the various clerical grades over the whole of the war years were only 'from 10 to 65 per cent over pre-war scales'.[48]

Teachers were no better treated. In April 1917 the Board of Education secured powers to prescribe minimum salaries to education authorities; but the rates prescribed were little above the National Union of Teachers' prewar minimum scale. The best that the President of the Board, H. A. L. Fisher, could do was to appoint a committee to inquire into the principles that should determine salary scales in teaching. Between 1914 and 1918 the average salary increase for male certificated teachers (including head teachers) was 23 per cent, from £147 to £180. The latter figure was well below the average earnings of

47 Redmayne, p. 189.
48 Humphreys, p. 87.

engineering craftsmen, and had been attained only after 'militant action
. . . in thirty-two areas', and an unofficial strike in the Rhondda.[49]

With the loss of many of their active members, the local branches of
the National Association of Local Government Officers went into a
decline, and some even ceased to function. It was not until 1917 that the
leaders started a revival by means of a reorganisation which introduced
an annual conference, cut the executive down to a manageable size,
created a post of organising secretary, and related subscriptions to the
level of salary. The secretary was able to report to the first conference,
held in May 1918, that membership and funds were rising again. The
conference referred a proposal for a national salary scale to the
executive, but passed a resolution in favour of blacklisting local
authorities which treated their officers unjustly, or 'inflicted unnecessary
hardships upon them'.[50]

Private employers were, if anything, meaner to their white-collar
employees than public authorities. 'By the beginning of 1918 the highest
bonus paid in any bank was 20 per cent, no bonus being paid at all by
Barclays until October 1918. Insurance companies followed a similar
pattern.'[51]

Both wage-earners and salaried workers benefited from the introduction of rationing. In the autumn of 1917 food queues appeared, and
grew longer. The Ministry was struggling to devise a viable scheme of
rationing, and issued sugar ration cards which were to come into use
at the end of the year. Local food committees, including Labour
representatives, had been appointed by local authorities in the summer,
and in December some of them set up their own schemes for several
other goods, based on the sugar ration cards. A meat shortage developed
and a meat ration scheme for London, introduced in February 1918,
'had an immediate and almost unqualified success'.[52] It was extended to
other areas. Queues diminished rapidly. Finally a national scheme was
brought in for a range of commodities.

Rationing was not used to restrict overall consumption. It supported
the schemes of government bulk purchase and price controls introduced
in 1917 by ensuring that goods were available at controlled prices; and
enabled wages to rise faster than prices through 1918. In July Lord
Rhondda died, and Clynes, 'that most painstaking and able Trade
Union official', as the *Yorkshire Factory Times* called him on 5 July
1917, was promoted to Food Controller. He proved to be the most
successful of Labour's wartime ministers after Henderson.

Shop stewards were in the news again at the end of November 1917,
when the Coventry Engineering Joint Committee called out some fifty

[49] Tropp, p. 87.   [50] Spoor, p. 65.
[51] Humphreys, p. 87.   [52] Beveridge, *British Food Control*, p. 205.

thousand munitions workers in Coventry in order to secure their formal recognition by the engineering employers. The committee had been pressing the local engineering employers to accept the rules governing shop stewards which they had drawn up earlier in the year, but the employers took the view that the recognition of stewards was a national issue. On 20 November the workers at a Coventry firm struck over the refusal of the manager to deal with a deputation of the men when he found it was led by a shop steward. A local conference failed to resolve the problem, the employers pointing out that a national conference had been fixed for 14 December. Fearing that the national employers' federation would have little sympathy for the special arrangements they had made in Coventry, the committee called their members out on 26 November. Four days later talks were held between the committee, the Coventry engineering employers, and government representatives, with Barnes in the chair.

There was no doubt that the government supported recognition. Circular L6 and the dilution commissioners had adopted it; the report of the Whitley Committee on works committees had been accepted; on 6 November Kellaway had told the House that workshop committees might 'do more than any other piece of industrial machinery to get rid of industrial grievances and industrial unrest'.[53] His enthusiasm surpassed that of the trade union leaders who, 'while in theory supporting works committees, showed great anxiety that their functions should be restricted to purely domestic matters', and that nothing should be done to 'encourage them to undermine the authority of the trade union executives'.[54] Barnes gave the Coventry union leaders to understand that the government would use their influence with the Engineering Employers Federation in favour of recognition, and work was resumed on 4 December. On 20 December a national agreement was signed, providing for the appointment of shop stewards, subject to the control of the unions, to deal with managers over grievances on which individual workers had failed to obtain satisfaction, and to form deputations to management on collective matters, in either case passing on to union officials those issues which they failed to resolve. However, the unions fell out over a further clause requiring stewards in other respects to 'conform to the same working conditions as their fellow workmen'. The Engineers wanted special protection for shop stewards. They were outvoted by the other unions, but refused to accept the majority decision, and withdrew from the talks, thus robbing the agreement of much of its significance. The National Shop Stewards and Workers Committee Movement played little part in these events. They

---

[53] *Hansard*, 6 November 1917, col. 2091.
[54] *History of the Ministry of Munitions*, Vol. VI, Part II, p. 33.

met in conference in Manchester on 5 and 6 December, congratulated the Coventry strikers, and undertook to try to organise a national strike if recognition was not conceded.[55]

The next crisis which the movement had to face was over the government's demand for more men for the forces at the beginning of 1918. Auckland Geddes had taken over as Minister of National Service with wider powers than his predecessor Neville Chamberlain. Even so, he still had to negotiate for the release of men with the responsible departments, who had in turn to deal with their own unions. The chief troublemakers in 1917 were the Miners. In June they reluctantly agreed to a 'comb-out' of men who had entered the industry since the outbreak of war. When this failed to achieve the numbers anticipated, Geddes proposed to withdraw exemptions from miners under twenty-five years old. In August 27,000 Yorkshire miners struck in protest, and on 7 September a national conference insisted that all wartime recruits to the industry must go first. There were sporadic strikes in South Wales, and in November the South Wales Miners threatened to stop the coalfield. General Smuts was sent by his colleagues in the war cabinet to pacify the Welsh miners, which he claimed that he had accomplished by getting them to sing 'Land of our Fathers'.[56] The government accepted the Miners' terms.

The disastrous losses in France during the autumn convinced the government that they could no longer allow their manpower policy to be determined by the production departments and the unions. Some reduction in output, and even strikes, would have to be faced if that was the price of sending more men to the front. They therefore approved a pruning of the Schedule of Protected Occupations and a 'clean cut', with no proviso that dilutees must go before skilled men. Geddes put the case for withdrawing occupational exemptions to the munitions unions on 3 January 1918. The Engineers withdrew after hearing him, protesting that the scheme was a departure from their agreement with the government, and demanding separate talks. They also disaffiliated from the Federation of Engineering and Shipbuilding Trades, a move sanctioned by a four to one ballot vote. The government went ahead resolutely. There were no separate talks with the Engineers; details were settled with the other unions; and the bill giving the necessary powers became law on 6 February.

On 5 and 6 January a conference of the shop stewards' movement in Manchester recommended that national action should be taken against the government's manpower proposals. The workers were to be consulted as to the form this action should take. At first there seemed to be widespread enthusiasm for a strike. A conference of Allied Trades

[55] *Solidarity*, January 1918.   [56] Lloyd George, pp. 814–15.

Committees 'absolutely' rejected the proposals. The Clyde district committee of the Federation of Engineering and Shipbuilding Trades advised their members to down tools unless the proposals were withdrawn, and many similar resolutions were passed elsewhere by other local bodies and mass meetings. However, when the National Administrative Council of the movement met on 25 January to learn the outcome of their consultations, they found that London had not held a ballot, the Engineers on the Clyde were almost equally divided for and against a strike, and workshop meetings in Manchester and Sheffield had opposed a strike against the war. Perhaps in order to avoid appearing as the champions of craft privilege,[57] the council resolved that 'they were not the body to deal with technical grievances arising out of the cancellation of occupational exemptions, but that such grievances should be dealt with by union executives'.[58] Even given the strict limitation placed on the council's authority by its constitution, this was a striking abnegation of responsibility.

The Engineers' executive had also begun to retreat from their exposed position. On 22 January a conference of officials and district representatives decided on a ballot, cleverly worded to give a choice for or against resisting the manpower proposals 'until the Government had conferred with the union representatives and arrived at an agreement'. Inevitably the result was a massive majority for prior consultation. The Prime Minister consented to receive a deputation on 28 February, and the executive, worried by 'the statements made in the Press and elsewhere, that the society was indifferent to the views and claims of other Trade Unions',[59] decided that their demand for separate negotiations had been met. They now put the government's proposals to another ballot. While it was in progress the outcome was determined by the German offensive, opened on 21 March, which also disposed of the decision of an unofficial conference of representatives of the Engineers' district committees on the same day, but before they heard of the offensive, to call a strike on 6 April unless the government agreed that all dilutees should go before skilled men were called up. Meanwhile the Miners' leaders were considering what action they should take, following a ballot which narrowly rejected Geddes' demand for another 50,000 miners at once, with a further 50,000 to be held in reserve. On 22 March their conference advised against resistance.

The cancellation of exemptions now proceeded without a hitch, but very few of those who were called up saw active service. They were still in training at the time of the armistice.

---

[57] This explanation is put forward by Hinton (pp. 262–3).
[58] *History of the Ministry of Munitions*, Vol. VI, Part II, p. 44.
[59] *Monthly Journal and Report*, March 1918.

In place of Leaving Certificates, the Ministry of Munitions introduced two new devices to control the movement of labour. Rejecting the opinion of their trade union advisers, they embarked on a general extension of the War Munitions Volunteers Scheme, thus rendering those whose skills were not fully used, or who were surplus to requirement, liable to transfer. Those who refused to enrol would be liable to be called up, or, if over age or unfit, to dismissal. Secondly, poaching skilled workers was to be discouraged by 'embargoes' on the employment of skilled men, either immediately, or after a given quota had been reached. These embargoes were expected to be acceptable because they placed restrictions on firms, and not on individual workers. However, when embargoes were placed on three Coventry firms on 1 July, one of them announced that the firm should in future make 'every effort . . ., wherever it is necessary to employ men, to make use only of semi- or unskilled men'.[60] The skilled men took this to mean that their jobs would be given to less-skilled men, and on 23 July ten thousand of them struck in Coventry; next day they were joined by twelve thousand men in Birmingham, and many Manchester workers handed in their notices. Two days later Lloyd George issued one of the sternest warnings of the war, stating that men still on strike on the 29th would be liable to military service. The strike collapsed.

Before the Coventry men came out, the National Administrative Council of the shop stewards' movement had wired the Coventry Engineering Joint Committee asking them to suspend notices pending a conference of the movement summoned to Sheffield on 24 July. Instead, the Coventry committee struck, and called a conference of Allied Trade Committees in Leeds for 25 July, which recommended a national strike;[61] but when the delegates reassembled on 29 July the men in Birmingham and Coventry were back at work. 'The bankruptcy of the shop stewards' movement became quite clear in the course of the Embargo strike.'[62]

The movement's ineffectiveness was due to a clash of aims between leaders and led. The leaders sought an all-embracing movement in which all workers would be equal. The craftsmen in the workshops wanted to protect their jobs against dilutees, and to ensure that all eligible less-skilled men should be called up before they had to go themselves. Moreover, because the Engineers were the only major union extensively affected by dilution, the movement was overwhelmingly a

[60] *History of the Ministry of Munitions*, Vol. VI, Part II, p. 64.

[61] There is some confusion over whether shop stewards' representatives were present at this conference. Murphy's account in *Solidarity* (September 1918) says they were not; but McLaine's version in the *Call* (8 August 1918), which is more coherent, says they were allowed to attend 'with a watching brief only'.

[62] Hinton, p. 268.

sectional movement of Engineers.[63] The leaders also wanted to develop the workers' committees into an alternative to the existing unions. During the war the Socialist Labour Party relaxed its rule against acceptance of trade union office, allowing Tom Bell to become a member of the Scottish Ironmoulders' executive, but Murphy warned that 'to think that by the *capturing* of official positions we can change the nature of organisations is to think wrongly'.[64] By contrast, most of the Engineers who joined in the May strikes, or other unofficial disputes during the war, had no quarrel with the structure of their union. They wanted to push its leaders into offering even stronger resistance to government interference with their privileges.

For these reasons the Allied Trade Committees were a more congenial channel of rank and file discontent than the workers' committees. They, too, tried to bring the members of the engineering unions together; but since they used the official district committees of the unions for this purpose, they were more effective. The committees were dominated by craft unions, so they had no difficulty in advocating the protection of craft privilege; and they had no objection to holding union office, or to existing union structure. The most effective organ of local discontent was the Coventry Engineering Joint Committee, which overshadowed the feeble Coventry Workers Committee. During 1918 the Liverpool Workers Committee met local unions to discuss a wider scheme for a somewhat similar organisation, including both district representatives and shop stewards, but giving the shop stewards a greater say than in Coventry. The scheme was 'for Local Engineering Councils composed of two delegates from each society and an equal number of representatives drawn from the shop, who must be shop stewards'. They put the proposal to a conference of the movement in Birmingham on 7 and 8 September, with the support of one of the Coventry delegates, but it was rejected by forty votes to nine.[65] By this time, however, the movement was showing more interest in politics than in industrial action.

The aversion of the Shop Stewards' and Workers Committee Movement to existing trade union organisation was not shared by other unofficial movements. The Railwaymen's Vigilance Committees were avowedly pressure groups within their union. Among the Miners the only important unofficial movement during the war was in Scotland, which had been the first coalfield to throw up a socialist leadership, but

---

[63] Gallacher was a member of the Scottish Brassfounders, Tom Bell of the Scottish Ironmoulders, and Tom Dingley of the Workers Union; but they were exceptions.

[64] *Solidarity*, September 1918. 'We don't want the Trade Unions any more than the capitalist system, then why capture either?' (Ibid., June 1918.)

[65] *Workers Dreadnought*, 21 September 1918, which gives Watson's account of the conference.

these leaders were now ageing, and several of them had followed the pro-war lead of Hyndman. With Smillie's attention concentrated on national affairs there began to emerge the clique of right-wing leaders who dominated the Scottish Miners after the war. 'For a considerable time', reported the *Call* on 6 September 1917, 'there has existed in the ranks of the Lanarkshire Miners' Union widespread dissatisfaction with undemocratic methods used in the conduct of the Union's affairs.' A Reform Committee was set up to agitate for a revision of the constitution, and another was established in Fife. John McLean's lieutenant, James Macdougall, was brought in to organise the movement, and during 1918 David Gilmour, secretary of the Lanarkshire Miners, was forced to resign on the ground that he was trying to run his union office in harness with a government post.

In other mining districts there was little need for an unofficial movement. In South Wales a hard core of militants maintained the Rhondda and Pontypridd Socialist Society (commonly called the South Wales Socialist Society), but the members of the prewar Reform Committee were now well represented on the executive, in delegate conferences and among the agents. Elsewhere the militants imitated them in the pursuit of influence through office. In Northumberland and Durham, Ebby Edwards and Will Lawther competed in union elections while energetically building up local branches of the Plebs League. In Derbyshire, Harry Hicken's 'heart was set on a career as a trade union leader'.[66] Another graduate of the Central Labour College, Herbert Booth, built up something of an unofficial movement among daywage colliers in Nottingham, but in 1918 he left for the post of full-time agent in the Forest of Dean.

The London busmen did not need an unofficial movement after December 1916 when their Vigilance Committee took control of their union's delegate meeting and elected a new executive. Next year they repudiated their agreement with the London General Omnibus Company that the company should not 'be affected by any dispute with companies with whom they (the LGOC) have no direct concern'.[67] Ten thousand London busmen came out in an official strike in wartime to assert their right to call sympathetic strikes. The company refused 'further to acknowledge the union or deal with its officials';[68] but the Transport Workers Federation intervened to patch up the quarrel.

It seems that these differences towards the use of official trade union machinery prevented the formation of a national body to link the shop stewards' movement and the other unofficial movements together.

[66] J. E. Williams, p. 584.
[67] *Licensed Vehicle Trade Record*, 16 May 1917.
[68] Transport Workers Federation, *Annual Report*, 1917.

Murphy says that the National Administrative Council met unofficial leaders of the Miners and Railwaymen in March 1918 to discuss such a venture, but the Miners and Railwaymen insisted that they could 'change the structure and the leadership of their unions through the ordinary machinery of the unions'.[69]

The decline of the shop stewards' movement in 1918 did not diminish industrial unrest. From 730 in 1917 the number of strikes rose to 1,165, a figure exceeded before only in 1913. The aircraft industry was particularly agitated, and unrest spread to industries previously unaffected. On 9 September the executive of the General Workers heard that there was likely to be 'serious trouble' in the gas industry in London over the 'non-union question. . . . Disputes had suddenly broken out, and it was feared that unless a settlement could be speedily arrived at the strike would spread all over London.' In August the Spinners called a national official strike. Because of further cuts in cotton imports, the Cotton Control Board had announced in May that they must terminate the system of 'playing off' in rotation, and discharge a proportion of the operatives instead. This put all Lancashire in a turmoil, and a 'Spinners' shop steward movement', which had emerged the previous July to protest against their executive's 'mismanagement and incompetence',[70] now revived 'to rouse to action the latent mind' of their union.[71] The operation of the new scheme was postponed until August, when it was finally approved by a narrow margin at a meeting of the cotton unions' federal body, the United Textile Factory Workers Association. Even so, the Spinners' executive voted for a strike, but the force of their complaint was weakened by the news of an increase in cotton imports, and on the second day of the stoppage they agreed to Lloyd George's offer of an inquiry. An injunction had been obtained under Defence Regulations to prevent the payment of strike benefit.

In August 1917 the Locomotive Engineers and Firemen gave notice of an official strike for an eight-hour working day. Much of the history of industrial relations on the railways has to be seen in terms of the competition between their union and that of the Railwaymen, and this dispute was no exception. Up to that point the footplatemen had had to follow on behind the Railwaymen, accepting the war advances won by the larger union which, being flat-rate increases, narrowed their differential. In April 1917 Thomas and his colleagues had added to the grievances of the footplatemen by bringing a libel action against John Bromley, their secretary, and winning it. Now the footplatemen were able to retaliate. The government proclaimed the strike under the

[69] Murphy, *Preparing for Power*, pp. 155–7.
[70] *Cotton Factory Times*, 6 July 1917.
[71] Ibid., 14 June 1918.

Munitions Act, but three days later Albert Stanley, President of the Board of Trade, gave a solemn pledge, on the government's behalf, that the question would be settled within a month of the end of the war, while the railways were still under government control, and that the case for a shorter working week would then receive a sympathetic hearing. Henceforth, the Railwaymen would be beholden to the Locomotive Engineers and Firemen for winning the eight-hour working day, for it could not be granted to some railwaymen and not to others.

In September 1918 there was an unofficial show of unity between the members of the two unions, when locomotivemen in both unions struck in South Wales—protesting at the acceptance of a further wage advance of 25p a week which the Railwaymen's executive had at first rejected, and then accepted by a vote of thirteen to eleven after an interview with the war cabinet. Addressing a stormy meeting at Cardiff on 24 September, Thomas urged the men to go back and threatened to resign if they did not do so. Two days later his resignation was handed in. The men went back to work. Resolutions urging Thomas to reconsider were passed by 840 branches. He relented, and resumed office. Within a few weeks a further advance of 15p had been agreed.

The most startling instance of unrest was an official strike of the London police. An unrecognised National Union of Police and Prison Officers, formed in 1913, called London policemen out on 30 August. The immediate issue was the dismissal of a prominent member of the union, but, besides his reinstatement, the union demanded recognition and a pay increase. Policemen's pay had fallen far behind the rise in the cost of living, which was by now almost double the prewar figure. Up to that time the prewar minimum pensionable pay had been increased by only 40 per cent, to £2.10, so that a new recruit received less than an engineering labourer. 'By midday on Friday, 30 August, with very few exceptions the entire Metropolitan Police Force, numbering 12,000 men, and nearly all the City of London Police Force had withdrawn from duty.'[72] Next day Lloyd George himself met the union executive to negotiate a settlement. Pay was raised by a further 65p a week, pensions and allowances were increased, and the Desborough Committee was appointed to make a further review of police remuneration. The dismissed man was reinstated. Lloyd George told the leaders that he could not formally recognise a police union in wartime, but negotiations with the Prime Minister appeared to be a giant step towards recognition.

The Effects on the Unions

One outcome of the industrial relations policies of Lloyd George's government was a resumption of trade union growth at a rate

[72] V. L. Allen, pp. 135–6.

comparable with 1910–13. Growth had continued after the outbreak of war, but at a relatively modest pace. Total membership rose by 12 per cent between 1913 and 1916. In 1917 alone the increase was 18 per cent, and in 1918 it was 19 per cent.

The most convincing theory of union growth is the mathematical model designed by Bain and Elsheikh which gives a highly satisfactory fit to British data throughout the years 1893–1970. It relies primarily on three variables: changes in prices, in money wages, and in unemployment. Unemployment was low throughout the war except for the first few weeks, and prices and money wages rose almost continuously. The changes in all three variables therefore favoured growth. However, Bain and Elsheikh distinguish three ways in which the movement of prices and wages affects the propensity of workers to join unions. There is the 'threat effect' of rising prices on living standards, the 'prosperity effect' on the ability and willingness of employers to concede wage increases, and the 'credit effect' on workers of the wage advances secured by trade unions.[73] With wage rates lagging behind prices up to the end of 1916, the threat effect should have been powerful, but the credit effect weak; and the prosperity effect was restrained initially by the widespread sentiment among employers, to some extent shared by trade unionists, that wages should not be influenced by the special conditions of wartime, and subsequently by pressure for wage restraint. Under Lloyd George this restraint was relaxed; the prosperity effect was allowed to operate; and the credit effect began to work. The credit effect was reinforced by the rapid extension of national pay bargaining, which brought more workers within the scope of collective bargaining, especially in industries where collective bargaining had previously been weak, and advertised the part played by the unions in securing higher wages.

Growth was uneven. Another variable included in the Bain and Elsheikh model is the proportion of workers already unionised—or 'union density'. One reason for this is to capture the 'saturation effect'. The scope for growth is limited in an industry already highly unionised. For this reason the growth of the Miners was slow—no more than 20 per cent throughout the war. The Sailors and Firemen did not add to their numbers at all. With a high density and a declining labour force, the total number of cotton trade unionists declined a little. Among major unions the Engineers benefited considerably from the war. By 1918 they were 90 per cent up on 1913. Overall, the four major general unions increased threefold, ending the war with almost a million members between them; and the Workers Union outpaced the others with a fourfold increase. The pace of growth was faster among women

[73] Bain and Elsheikh, pp. 62–5.

than among men, with an overall wartime increase not far short of threefold, from which the general unions were the chief beneficiaries. Between them the Workers Union and the General Workers (at that time the Gasworkers) had less than 10,000 women members in 1913; in 1918 they claimed 140,000. By comparison the performance of the Federation of Women Workers was modest, from 12,000 to 40,000. However, the most spectacular figures of overall growth were returned by the Agricultural Labourers with almost a tenfold increase, and by the Warehousemen and General Workers whose growth was almost thirteenfold.

The renewal of rapid union growth brought a revival of schemes for union reorganisation and amalgamation set aside in 1914. Further stimulants to reconstruction were the inauguration of national pay bargaining in industry after industry, and some acrimonious inter-union disputes.

In 1914 the craft unions had attempted to settle their battle over skilled workers in the railway shops by asking the Joint Board to apply the 1906 ruling, under which the Municipal Employees had been excluded and the Co-operative Employees already stood condemned, to the Railwaymen as well. The board steered away from a decision to expel Congress's second largest affiliate, which might have led on to the expulsion of the largest—the Miners Federation. The matter therefore came before Congress in 1915, when the craft unions won a small majority for a resolution clarifying the 1906 ruling by condemning 'any method of organisation which seeks to divide workmen from their fellows in the same occupation'. All the arguments were deployed. The Railwaymen, so the craft societies asserted, were not only in breach of the 1906 principle; they were poaching craft society members; their craft members were accepting rates below those sanctioned by the craft societies; and they would be unable to find jobs outside the railway workshops. Their complaints were supported by Bromley of the Locomotive Engineers and Firemen who said that the Railwaymen and Miners had joined in threatening that his union would be crushed out of existence.[74]

For the Railwaymen, Bellamy denied poaching; his union had organised the unorganised, and now had between fifty and sixty thousand shopmen in membership; the major craft union concerned, the Engineers, was not even affiliated to Congress; the Railwaymen were willing to work with the craft unions, but not to recognise all the craft pretensions. He was supported by the Miners. There were also differences over methods of negotiation. The craftsmen wanted district rates; the Railwaymen wanted national negotiations, which they had

[74] Trades Union Congress, 1915, pp. 339–52.

now got on a wartime basis. Competing claims were submitted, and the credit for every advance in pay was disputed.

The Parliamentary Committee attempted to wear the disputants down. After a protracted series of meetings they reported to Congress in 1918 that, as

the points in dispute had been . . . almost narrowed down to the one issue of providing a satisfactory and acceptable form of transfer of membership your Committee came to the conclusion that for the time being, at any rate, the matter might be left as it was.[75]

However, the controversy over industrial unionism could not be shelved so easily.

In most coalfields the Miners were pursuing a merciless campaign against the independent unions of craftsmen and surfaceworkers. After their strike in 1915, the South Wales Miners had, with Askwith's help, secured a formal closed shop agreement for the period of the war. On 1 June of the same year the executive of the National Amalgamated Union of Labour complained that the affiliates of the Miners Federation in the Federated Area had sent 'a personal letter to every member of . . . unions having members on the pit top requesting them to leave their present union and join the miners not later than June 2nd. . . . Nothing short of resolute action could prevent the miners Germanising the pits of Yorkshire and Derbyshire.' The Enginemen's Federation and the newly-formed Surface Workers Federation took their case to Congress, and in 1918 succeeded in getting the Parliamentary Committee's report referred back, in order to persuade the committee to convene a meeting between themselves and the Miners.[76] At the same Congress, Arthur Pugh carried a proposal for a committee to fix boundaries between industries, make 'suggestions for the unification of forces in each industry', and provide for transfers and uniform standards of contributions and benefits;[77] but the proposal secured only a meagre majority and nothing was done.

In 1916 a quarrel between the Co-operative Employees and the other unions organising co-operative society staff broke out in Plymouth. Having been refused arbitration over a wage claim, the Co-operative Employees struck. The Shop Assistants, the Bakers, the Tailors, and the Clerks advised their members to stay at work. Eventually an award of the Joint Committee of Trade Unionists and Co-operators led to increases in pay, but excluded the Co-operative Employees from the settlement. Their members were given three months to join a union eligible for affiliation to Congress. The Co-operative Employees ignored this ultimatum with the support of the London Dockers who had struck

[75] Ibid., 1918, p. 69.   [76] Ibid., pp. 144–51.   [77] Ibid., p. 213.

with them in 'a bond of comradeship . . . between the lorryman and the shopworker'.[78]

In 1918 the Co-operative Employees felt, as one of their critics put it, 'strong enough not only to defy the Trades Union Congress, but to fight the Trade Union movement'.[79] They brought three hundred printing workers out on strike for a pay increase at the Co-operative Wholesale Society's printing works in Manchester, but the directors, who had made a separate agreement with the printing unions, gave notice that all workers must 'identify themselves with the Trade Unions applicable to their respective crafts'.[80] The Co-operative Employees then struck nearby co-operative undertakings until seven thousand workers were out, and in some areas the London Dockers blacked the products of the works concerned. Congress, which was in session, condemned the strike, and the government proclaimed it under the Munitions Act. On 1 October a special arbitration court found against the Co-operative Employees, but the Wholesale Society did not henceforth try to force their members into other unions, and the Co-operative Employees set about securing re-admittance to Congress by means of an amalgamation with the Warehousemen and General Workers, who were affiliated.

Following the Midlands strike of 1913 the Workers Union ran into trouble with the Engineers. Given the widespread disregard for apprenticeship in Birmingham and Coventry, and the relative weakness of the Engineers there, the rapid expansion of the Workers Union had swept in machinists and other relatively skilled workers, who might have been considered eligible to join the Engineers. The Engineers protested. Early in 1915 discussions between the two unions led to a draft agreement on recruiting and transfer of members. The Workers Union undertook to recruit no more skilled men eligible to join the Engineers. Their existing skilled members would be allowed, but not obliged, to transfer. However, in May 1915 the Engineers rejected these proposals, reverting to a policy of non-cooperation with the Workers Union, and 'seceded from joint negotiating bodies which included the Workers' Union, taking the other craft societies with them'.[81]

The Engineers were neverthelss willing to come to terms with other unions organising less-skilled workers from whom they had less to fear. In June 1915 they recognised the National Federation of Women Workers as the appropriate body for women workers in engineering.

The Women Workers Federation was an offshoot of the Women's Trade Union League, a federation of unions interested in the organisation of women workers. Before 1906 the league had promoted

[78] *The Co-operative Employee*, October 1916.
[79] Trades Union Congress, 1918, p. 181.
[80] Ibid., 1919, p. 156.   [81] Hyman, pp. 118–19.

several trade unions for women only, all of them small. In that year these unions were brought together in the Women Workers Federation, a union 'open to all women belonging to unorganised trades or not admitted to their appropriate trade union'.[82] They already had members in the metal trades, for example a branch in chainmaking, but the Workers Union had as good a claim, or better, to be recognised as the appropriate union for women engineering workers, and the agreement with the Engineers was part of the Engineers' campaign against the Workers Union.

In fact the agreement was of less value to the Women Workers Federation than might have been expected. The general unions had more success in recruiting women munitions workers than the federation, who found that they had to work closely with the general unions. In July 1916 they came to an agreement with the General Workers on exchange of cards and spheres of influence, in which the latter recognised them as the appropriate union for 'clearly recognised women's industries' where workers were not already organised, but that, of course, did not include munitions. Two months later the Engineers signed an agreement with the General Workers on similar lines to their draft agreement with the Workers Union. Eight other craft unions subsequently put their names to it. Finally, in 1917 the Engineers rescinded the rule passed by their 1912 delegate conference which permitted unskilled workers to be admitted to membership, but had been ignored by the branches.

Elsewhere there had been amalgamations between craft societies and unions of less-skilled workers which had assisted the organisation of women. In 1914 a tiny union of vellum and parchment workers had joined with the Paper Mill Workers and the Printers Warehousemen and Cutters to form the National Union of Printing and Paper Workers which made the first effective efforts to recruit women workers in paper and printing, and grew from an initial eighteen thousand to nearly fifty thousand in 1918, more than half of them women. In 1915 the Clothiers Operatives absorbed several smaller unions, including the London craft society. As a consequence the new union, the United Garment Workers, set about organising craftsmen wherever it could. The Amalgamated Society of Tailors and Tailoresses regarded this as a 'gross act of trespass', and began to recruit factory workers, after years of fruitless debate as to whether to do so.[83] Between 1915 and 1918 the Garment Workers' membership rose from 20,000 to 65,000, 84 per cent of them women, and that of the Amalgamated Tailors from 12,000 to 27,000, two-thirds of them women.

The leaders of some of the iron and steel unions succeeded in

[82] Soldon, p. 57.   [83] Dobbs, pp. 127–8.

circumventing the requirement of the Trade Union Act 1876 that an amalgamation must be approved by two-thirds of the members of each union concerned. In January 1916 all the unions of any importance in the industry, except the general unions, agreed to make another attempt at amalgamation, and a sub-committee devised an ingenious scheme whereby all of them were to join a new federation, the Iron and Steel Trades Confederation, which would settle policy and conduct negotiations; and all new recruits were to join a new union, the British Iron, Steel, and Kindred Trades Association, to which members of the existing unions were encouraged to transfer. Not all the unions could be persuaded to join, so the federation came into being in 1917 with 53,000 members, of whom the Smelters contributed over 39,000. Hodge, now Minister of Labour, became president and the secretary was Arthur Pugh, formerly Hodge's assistant.

In the same year Hodge introduced a bill to alter the law on trade union amalgamation. It was another of Lloyd George's concessions to attract trade union support, and the intention was to allow amalgamations to be sanctioned by simple majority vote. This, however, was too much for the House of Commons, and an amendment required that the votes of at least 50 per cent of the members entitled to vote should be cast, and the votes in favour should exceed those cast against by at least 20 per cent. In their report to Congress in 1917 the Parliamentary Committee called this 'distinctly begrudging',[84] but nevertheless the Trade Union Amalgamation Act 1917 was a considerable advance on the 1876 Act.

The Workers Union had been making approaches for a merger to the union whose industrial coverage most nearly matched its own, the National Amalgamated Union of Labour. Detailed proposals were ready at the end of 1917, but they did not take advantage of the new Act because of difficulties over friendly and unemployment benefits concerning which the Workers Union had always made a great virtue of their relatively generous provision. Accordingly they proposed that the individual unions remain in business to administer these benefits and recruit members, and that a National Amalgamated Workers Union be set up to provide dispute benefit and pay the salaries of all full-time officers under the control of a central executive consisting of the two general secretaries and five other members from each union. It was open to other unions to join, and the Workers Union hoped to attract the other general unions. However, the first application was from the Municipal Employees who thought to regain thereby the status of a *bona fide* union in the eyes of Congress and the Labour Party. The Workers Union may originally have had the same motive for promoting the scheme. In 1900

[84] Trades Union Congress, 1917, p. 93.

they had left Congress on grounds of economy. On 24 May 1916 an application for re-admission was rejected by the Parliamentary Committee 'owing to the Workers' Union encroaching on the membership of other unions'. However, a year later the committee agreed to re-admit them.

The scheme turned out to be far less effective than the arrangement made by the iron and steel unions. Each union continued to negotiate with employers separately. At their meetings on 5 and 6 November 1918 the executive of the National Amalgamated Union of Labour complained of the 'aggressive tactics' of the Workers Union in poaching their members, and of a breach by the Workers Union of an understanding that the joint executive should, apart from the three general secretaries, be a lay body. Nevertheless, the National Amalgamated Workers Union was formally established on 1 January 1919.

Many other proposals for amalgamation were canvassed, not only because of the new Act, but also because of rapid development of industry-wide collective bargaining which led many small unions to suppose that they would cease to count on their own, and major unions to believe that they must find a more effective way of working together with unions in the same industry. But none of them was consummated until after the end of the war.

Federation could be accomplished more easily and quickly than amalgamation, and the law placed no limitations upon it. The Amalgamated Carpenters and Joiners had already shown their preference for federation to the schemes of amalgamation into one building union which had absorbed so much effort to no effect just before the war. In 1916 they suggested to the other building unions that the National Associated Building Trades Council which had been formed the year before, with very limited functions and powers, should be converted into 'a real federation for mutual assistance'.[85] Agreement was reached during the following year, and early in 1918 the National Federation of Building Trades Operatives came into existence. It was given authority to sanction disputes, with resources to pay a federal dispute benefit of 25p a week. 'Composite' branches were established in places where the individual trades had not enough members to set up branches of their own, and the 'federation executive' and regional councils took over the conduct of common negotiations with the employers.

The Federation of General Workers arose directly out of the development of industry-wide bargaining. Under the new national engineering procedure for pay negotiations, the general unions had an

[85] Higenbottam, p. 126.

equal right to state their case along with the craft unions,[86] and J. N. Bell, who was secretary of the General Labourers National Council as well as of the National Amalgamated Union of Labour, argued that they should convert the council into a federation to enable them to take advantage of this and similar opportunities which were opening up in other industries. The other unions agreed, and in July 1917 the new federation held its inaugural conference with Clynes in the chair. As secretary they appointed James O'Grady, a Member of Parliament and formerly a union officer in the furniture industry.

The driving spirit in the move to national agreements was Bevin, who represented the London Dockers on the federation executive. At its meeting on 27 September he proposed a regular procedure for dealing with 'wage movements'. Once a request from an individual union for a 'national policy' in a given industry was endorsed by the other unions concerned, representative conferences were to draft claims and supervise negotiations. Over the winter the procedure was set in motion in cement, cocoa and chocolate manufacture, flour milling, gas supply, paint and related industries, and rubber manufacture. In every case an agreement or an award of the Committee on Production was eventually obtained. In March 1918 Bevin persuaded the executive to support his proposal for a 'Statistical Department' to assist negotiations.

Even more closely under Bevin's influence, the conference of the Transport Workers Federation had, in June 1917, established a similar procedure for promoting and negotiating pay claims. In August a conference of seventeen unions in road haulage decided to submit a claim. Some of the employers were persuaded to agree to personal arbitration by Askwith in February 1918, when he awarded that advances since the outbreak of the war should be made up to a minimum of £1 a week. In June the Committee on Production increased the amount to £1.25 and extended the coverage of their award to those local employers' associations which had refused to come before Askwith in February.

In January 1918 the two main unions of road passenger transport workers, the Amalgamated Tramwaymen and the Licensed Vehicle Workers, both now affiliated to the federation, submitted a national claim through its machinery. The employers were slow in responding, and on 26 February the two unions gave seven days' notice of a strike. The government persuaded the employers to accept arbitration, and the Committee on Production awarded an inclusive war wage advance of £1 a week.

[86] Claims were presented by the Engineers, the Ironfounders, the Federation of Engineering and Shipbuilding Trades, and the General Labourers National Council (subsequently the Federation of General Workers).

Meanwhile the federation had run into trouble with its old antagonist, Lord Devonport, who had returned from the Ministry of Food to his job with the Port of London Authority. When a conference of dockers in January 1918 agreed on a national claim, Askwith undertook to ask Devonport to convene a national conference of port employers to consider it. He refused, but other port employers agreed to arbitration. The Committee on Production issued a national award which gave substantial increases to most dockers. The Port of London Authority declined to be party to the proceedings, so the government forced them into line with a proclamation under the Munitions Act.

The shift towards national bargaining received further encouragement from the reports of one of the sub-committees of the government's Reconstruction Committee. This sub-committee, chaired by the Speaker of the House of Commons, J. H. Whitley, and including employers and trade union leaders, was charged with making 'suggestions for securing a permanent improvement in the relations between employers and workmen'. Their reports, the first of which was signed in March 1917 but not published until the end of June, won fame as the Whitley reports. Echoing the Royal Commission on Labour in 1894, the Whitley Committee in their first (interim) report concluded that 'an essential condition of securing a permanent improvement in the relations between employers and employed is that there should be adequate organisation on the part of both employers and workpeople'; but they went beyond the Royal Commission in advocating some form of industry-wide regulation of industrial relations in every industry. 'Where they do not already exist', well-organised trades should be invited to set up 'Joint Standing Industrial Councils' to deal with issues affecting a whole industry.[87] In industries 'having no adequate organisation of employers and employed, Trade Boards should be continued or established' to provide statutory regulation and to assist in developing organisation on both sides with a view to the supersession of the boards by voluntary arrangements.[88]

In addition the committee wished to see the system of industrial relations include three features which had not been present before the war. At the workplace, works committees should be set up; nationally, there should be a permanent court of arbitration, with disputes submitted only by agreement between the parties, and no power to issue legally binding awards; and the business of the new bodies should not be confined to wages and conditions of employment. National councils, and the district councils which they were expected to set up, should provide for 'regular consideration of matters affecting the progress and well-being of the trade' in order to achieve 'the better utilisation of the

[87] *Interim Report*, pp. 3, 6.   [88] *Second Report*, p. 6.

practical knowledge and experience of the workpeople' and 'co-operation in carrying new ideas into effect'.[89] The works councils should not interfere with 'questions, such as rates of wages and hours of work, which should be settled by District or National agreement' but should concentrate on 'questions closely affecting daily life and comfort in, and the success of, the business, and affecting . . . efficiency of working, which are peculiar to the individual workshop and factory'.[90]

The first report had been made available to the Commissioners on Industrial Unrest who warmly recommended its adoption; but the government decided that they must first consult the principal employers' associations and trade unions. The Parliamentary Committee gave a cautious provisional approval subject to Congress in September, where Bevin suggested it should be referred to a special sub-committee, which finally accepted the report in October, subject to two qualifications. The government must not interfere 'where well-established means exist for negotiation' and works committees must leave 'the working rules of the trade' in the hands of 'the responsible and experienced officials of the unions'.[91]

By this time sufficient replies had accumulated for the war cabinet to give its approval, and the Ministries of Reconstruction and Labour, both anxious to promote the formation of councils, began to get in touch with likely industries. Most of the unions with long-established collective bargaining arrangements took the view that the Whitley reports had 'little to offer that was not already in existence',[92] and the annual conference of the Railwaymen in 1918 declared that 'the scheme . . . does not sufficiently safeguard the interests of Labour'.

However, the response from the general unions was very different. Will Sherwood of the General Workers told Congress in 1917 that they had 'the greatest trouble to compel employers to give our class the recognition to which we are entitled'.[93] At the beginning of 1918 the Federation of General Workers welcomed the suggestion from the Ministry of Reconstruction that meetings should be called with a view to setting councils up in the industries in which their affiliated unions had substantial membership. During the following months talks about establishing councils were set on foot in cement, chemicals, chocolate manufacture, flour milling, fertilisers, rubber manufacture, sugar refining, and other industries. The Transport Workers Federation had made an even earlier start. Already in December 1917 they were

---

[89] *Interim Report*, pp. 3, 5.
[90] *Supplementary Report on Works Committees*, pp. 2–3.
[91] Trades Union Congress, 1918, pp. 88–93.
[92] Pugh, p. 292.
[93] Trades Union Congress, 1917, p. 234.

discussing with the Ministry of Labour the prospects for councils in docks, road passenger transport, road haulage, and other industries.

There were also industries with a longer tradition of collective bargaining in which the employers as well as the unions saw advantage in extending joint action to 'the progress and well-being of the trade'. At the beginning of 1917 the two sides of the pottery industry, who had formed an alliance to stabilise prices and wages in 1899, were discussing another attempt. The Whitley proposals provided a convenient device for their purpose, and by January 1918 they had established the country's first Joint Industrial Council. Early in 1918 the boot and shoe employers proposed a conference on the Whitley report, one of their concerns being that 'only through Union control could the production of shoddy, low-quality goods at cut-throat prices be checked'.[94] A council was established the following year. Another council was formed in the Welsh tinplate and sheet steel trade in which the employers' association had for years relied on the unions to prevent undercutting by forcing non-federated employers to observe the agreement. In April 1917 the printing employers had placed before the unions proposals for 'trade betterment', which meant joining forces to maintain wages and prices. Subsequent conferences took note of the Whitley reports and early in 1919 a council was set up, with co-operation in the maintenance of 'fair' wages and prices written into its constitution.

In building it was the unions which took the initiative, by approaching the employers early in 1917 with a proposal for an 'industrial parliament' intended 'to promote the continuous and progressive improvement of the industry, to realise its organic unity as a great national service, and to advance the well-being and status of all connected with it'. In particular they hoped that it would yield wage rates 'designed to maintain *real wages* as nearly as possible on a level throughout the country' with 'advances . . . on a national basis', and deal with unemployment, casual employment, and technical training.[95] In fact, when a council was set up in May 1918, wages were not included in its terms of reference, and it concerned itself with safety and training, and with plans to provide pensions and unemployment benefits which would cover time lost through bad weather.

The first Whitley report was distributed only to private industries. The Reconstruction Committee suggested that it should also be brought to the notice of government departments and municipal authorities. The response from the civil service and postal unions was enthusiastic. They saw it as a means of substituting genuine collective bargaining for the prewar system of memorialising ministers and submitting evidence to committees. At first the cabinet prevaricated over the meaning of the

[94] Fox, p. 403.   [95] Higenbottam, p. 214.

word 'industry', but in July 1918 Bonar Law announced in the Commons that the government accepted the Whitley reports 'in principle' as applying 'with any necessary adaptations to Government establishments where the conditions are sufficiently analogous to those existing in outside industries'.[96] In October 1918 a departmental committee recommended that the Whitley proposals should apply with little variation to government industrial establishments, but administrative, clerical, and Post Office employees were still waiting to learn their fate at the end of the war.

These developments in collective bargaining had two important effects on industrial relations. Firstly they promoted union growth; and in this they were helped by the insistence of the dilution commissioners and dilution officers on dealing with trade union representatives in the workplace, and by the trade card scheme, which must have been a potent inducement to join a union while it lasted. The general attitude of the Ministry of Munitions on support for trade unionism is illustrated by a quotation from Addison's diary of 21 June 1916[97] concerning

a firm down in Essex, who dismissed some of their men because they were trade unionists and against whom we supported the Workers' Union in taking action. I am glad to say that, on Appeal, our view that the firm's action was 'in restraint of output' was supported. . . . The head of the firm refused to take back some of the men. . . . I told Crittall that he could tell the man and his partners, that if they did not play the game, we should step in and take over the whole place, if necessary.

The second effect was a centralisation of power within the unions. Several features of wartime industrial relations had led to decentralisation of trade union authority, among them plant-by-plant negotiations on dilution; the spread of piecework; and the shortage of labour, especially of skilled men. These centrifugal influences probably predominated during the first two-and-a-half years of the war; but not thereafter. In most major unions it was now the union executive and the national leaders who were 'delivering the goods' to trade union members. The change was evident in their behaviour. Before the war the executive of the Workers Union had limited functions and met infrequently. Industrial matters were handled at the branch or plant, and occasionally at district level. During the war, however, 'the extension of formal recognition by employers' made it necessary 'to specify clearly who had the right to negotiate, and to undertake that members would observe agreements made on their behalf. The rule

[96] *Hansard*, 4 July 1918, col. 1850.
[97] Addison, *Four and a Half Years*, p. 225.

book of 1919 bore the imprint of this new situation', by making explicit that the conduct of 'trade movements' and the control of strikes were the business of the executive. The union gained recognition on 'some fifty Joint Industrial Councils and similar bodies' and executive members sat on these along with full-time officers. By 1920, head office staff numbered a hundred, including an 'Arbitration Department, created during the war, [which] supervised all details of the union's industrial work at national level'.[98]

Changes in the distribution of power within individual unions were matched by similar shifts within the trade union movement as a whole. During the first half of the war authority was dispersed. At the centre the War Emergency Workers National Committee took its place alongside the Parliamentary Committee, Labour Party executive, and the management committee of the General Federation. The balance of power between the Parliamentary Committee and the Labour Party was altered. Although the War Emergency Committee helped to formulate common policies on a number of issues, it was the party which 'emerged as the principal source of such wartime coordination as the labour movement achieved',[99] due partly to the entry of Labour ministers into the government, which put them in a position to mediate between government and unions which the Parliamentary Committee could not rival, and partly to the unique position of Henderson. He was still president of the Ironfounders, and in that capacity was one of the leading union negotiators in the early months of the war. He attended the Treasury Conference in 1915, was elected chairman of the union side, and subsequently became chairman of the National Advisory Committee on War Output. As a member of the coalition cabinet, he chaired the Central Munitions Labour Supply Committee. For most of the war he was leader as well as secretary of the Labour Party, and chairman of the Joint Board. Such plurality of offices has never been equalled in the British Labour movement.

The invitations to the Treasury Conference and the membership of the National Advisory Committee indicated that the government did not perceive any of the existing national bodies as an effective co-ordinator of the unions. Representatives of the Parliamentary Committee and the General Federation were summoned to the Treasury on equal terms with those of thirty individual unions and three trade union federations. As secretary of Congress, Bowerman became a member of the National Advisory Committee, but under Henderson's chairmanship, and with Mosses as secretary.

In fact, the Parliamentary Committee could not have served as a satisfactory agency for selecting the trade union side of the conference.

[98] Hyman, pp. 113–15.   [99] Ross M. Martin, p. 149.

Most of the unions affiliated to Congress had no direct interest in the business of the Treasury Conference. Moreover, the Engineers were not affiliated to Congress, nor were the Workers Union and the Amalgamated Carpenters and Joiners.

However, the most striking feature of the organisation of relations between wartime governments and the unions was not the development of new channels of communication with the unions collectively. It was the opening up of channels of communication between the government and individual unions or groups of unions from a single industry. From the Treasury Conference onwards, the Engineers insisted on negotiating direct with the government. Even before that the Miners had taken their pay claim direct to Asquith, and later they dealt with the government through the Coal Controller. The Sailors and Firemen did business first with the Board of Trade and then with the Ministry of Shipping; the dockers' unions had their Port and Transit Committee; the Cotton Control Board and the Wool Board of Control served the needs of the unions in their industries. These developments reflected the sectional interests of the unions. Dilution was peculiarly a problem for the skilled men organised by the Engineers. There was no sense in using the Parliamentary Committee as a channel for dealing with the Miners on coal production and absenteeism in the pits; or with the Sailors and Firemen over the supply of crews to requisitioned ships; or with the textile unions over the regulation of unemployment in Lancashire and short-time in Yorkshire. But even on more general issues, such as the release of more men for the army, each union or group of unions (such as the general unions) believed that they could do best for their members on their own.

Throughout the war, however, Congress and the Parliamentary Committee retained their positions as the most representative trade union bodies in Britain. At the beginning of 1916 their affiliated membership stood at 2.85 million, well short of total trade union membership at 4.34 million, but comfortably ahead of the Labour Party's trade union affiliations of 2.17 million, and far ahead of the General Federation with 0.73 million. The seniority of Congress was acknowledged by Lloyd George in 1915 when he came to tell the delegates that the war was an 'engineers' war', and to make his plea for the removal of all restrictions on war production. In January 1916, when Asquith sought Labour's support for the first Military Service Bill from the Parliamentary Party and the Labour Party executive, the Parliamentary Committee 'expressed surprise' that they had not been invited. When a decision was required on the extension of conscription to married men the government made sure of having a fully representative gathering by summoning the executives of the Miners, Railwaymen,

Engineers, and Transport Workers, as well as the three national committees, but the final decision to support the bill was taken by the Parliamentary Committee with the agreement of the party executive.

In some respects the position of Congress was strengthened during the second half of the war. Henderson resigned from the war cabinet in August 1917, and subsequently from the party leadership. His successor in the war cabinet, Barnes, no longer carried much weight with the unions. The General Federation had ceased to be a competitor for the position of industrial representative of the Labour movement, having been excluded from the Joint Board in 1915, the year in which its largest remaining affiliate, the Engineers, withdrew. At the time the Engineers were outside Congress as well, but they reaffiliated in 1918, as did the Workers Union. The General Federation retained their right to represent Britain at international trade union conferences, but the Parliamentary Committee now insisted on joint representation.

The Joint Board was subsequently reconstituted without the federation, but met rarely. Instead, the Parliamentary Committee and the Labour Party executive co-ordinated their activities by means of joint monthly meetings. From these emerged proposals that the two bodies should acquire a building to house both of them, with the possibility of some joint services; and in 1918 a property was acquired in Eccleston Square. Meanwhile the Parliamentary Committee decided to appoint an assistant secretary, and an additional clerk to allow their existing clerk 'to concentrate on data preparation'. Early in 1918 they appointed Fred Bramley, an official of the Furniture Trades Association and a member of the Parliamentary Committee, to the first of these posts. He was a more forceful and enterprising man than his chief. In addition he was more in touch with majority opinion in the unions than Bowerman, who was still a Lib–Lab at heart. This expansion in staff did not mean that the Parliamentary Committee had abandoned their financial caution. Shortly after Bramley took up his post they agreed that, as the cost of a new typewriter would be 'prohibitive', they should accept his offer to sell his own machine to them for £10, provided that he could buy it back if he should want to.

Although the War Emergency Workers National Committee had won acknowledgement as a 'fourth national committee', and was a useful body for securing widely representative opinions, it did not present a serious challenge either to Congress or the Labour Party and was expected to disband after the war. On the other hand, the Triple Alliance, its constitution finally approved in December 1915, had begun to intervene with the government on issues of general interest to the Labour movement, such as the proposal to import 'coloured' labour; and its authority to co-ordinate industrial action by the three allies,

necessarily kept in the background during the war, was a potent threat
for the future.

By the autumn of 1918 the attention of trade unionists and their
leaders was shifting from current grievances to postwar prospects. The
unions had, of course, been involved in drawing up the Labour Party's
programme for reconstruction after the war, but there were also many
issues which the unions regarded as within their own jurisdiction, and
on these they were busy framing their own sectional programmes to be
implemented, for the most part, by collective bargaining.

In September 1918 Congress had voiced the fears of trade unionists
that peace might bring heavy unemployment. They could not see how
jobs could be found for the four million members of the armed forces,
who might be expected to come on to the labour market, in addition to a
similar number of munitions workers who would have to be transferred
to peacetime production. One means of increasing the demand for
labour which lay within the province of collective bargaining was a
reduction of the working week. But how big a cut was needed? At the
same meeting of Congress the hardy annual in favour of forty-eight
hours was almost defeated by an amendment to substitute forty-four. In
moving it, Hill quoted Lord Leverhulme's opinion that 'a six-hour day
is going to be better from a capitalist's point of view, because the man
will do more and better work than now'.[100] If that were true, even a
reduction to forty-four hours might not be enough. In Scotland a
meeting of trade union officials in March 1918 had declared themselves
in favour of a forty-hour week, and next month the annual meeting of
the Scottish Trades Union Congress voted for thirty hours. The
Miners, who already had their statutory eight-hour day, wanted it cut to
six.

Whatever the size of the cuts they demanded, the claims for
reductions in the working week which the unions were preparing were,
almost all of them, claims for a national adjustment throughout the
industry concerned, for the unions which had achieved temporary
national bargaining on pay during the war, through government
intervention or compulsory arbitration, now wished to keep it on a
permanent basis and extend it to conditions of work; and many of those
which still bargained locally were hoping to achieve national agreements. Most unions were also preparing national pay claims, and many
of them wished to substitute standard national rates of pay for their
current national or regional wartime bonuses on top of prewar local
rates.

Although the unions were anxious to be rid of conscription and
controls over civilian labour, they did not seek immediate termination of

[100] Trades Union Congress, 1918, p. 192.

wartime powers to apply compulsion to employers. Before the war the railway companies and the Shipping Federation had refused to recognise trade unions, and the railway and shipping unions would have to be given firm assurances that the wartime recognition was to be made permanent before they would agree to decontrol. The Locomotive Engineers and Firemen had been promised that their claim for a forty-eight hour working week would be favourably considered before the government relinquished control to the railway companies. The craft unions in the munitions industries were certain to insist that the government should fulfil its pledge to restore prewar practices.

Some unions would be unable to achieve all their postwar objectives without a permanent alteration in the structure of management and ownership in their industries, and that they could not realistically expect to achieve without government intervention. National standard wages featured in the Railwaymen's programme despite Thomas's warning that it was an unrealistic demand. 'Some companies would be able to afford it but others would not.'[101] In those circumstances, government intervention to reorganise the industry would be an essential preliminary to standard wages. The Railwaymen also wanted 'equal representation both national and local for this union upon the management of all railways in the United Kingdom'.[102] There was little likelihood that they could achieve this except through legislation.

The Miners were currently redrafting their 1913 Nationalisation of Mines and Minerals Bill to provide for joint control and administration. Nationalisation had become an urgent industrial issue for them. Their 1918 conference had accepted a South Wales resolution 'that the machinery for dealing with the general wage rate should be centralised in the National Federation'. This was taken to involve the dissolution of the Federated Area conciliation board. The issue was discussed at a conference of Federated Area representatives on 23 August which decided that the board, soon due for renewal, should be allowed to lapse. George Spencer of Nottingham pointed out that national wage regulation made sense only if 'after the war, when we return to normal conditions, we have secured permanently control or nationalisation of the mines'.[103] All the leaders accepted that national wage regulation depended on the retention of the profits pool; and, since a voluntary pooling of profits could not be expected from the owners, government control must continue on a permanent footing, which meant nationalisation.

---

[101] Bagwell, p. 371.   [102] Ibid., p. 370.   [103] Griffin, pp. 28–9.

6

Party Politics, 1911–18

The Prewar Years

THE four years before the First World War have often been presented as a period of irresolution, dissension, and decline within the Labour Party. Certainly the party experienced difficulties. After the general elections of 1910, the Liberal government needed Labour's votes in the House of Commons. If the Irish abstained, the Labour Party had the choice of bringing the government down or keeping it in office. As there were a number of measures which they hoped the Liberals would put through, the party was 'tied' to the Liberals. Moreover, the Labour Party was unable to make much headway with legislative proposals of their own, being hampered by a run of bad luck in the annual ballot for facilities for private members' bills. By the autumn of 1914 the party had lost six of the forty-two seats won in December 1910 through by-elections and the defection of sitting Members to the Liberals. There had been dissension in the party, both in parliament and in the country, over several issues, including syndicalism and strikes, national insurance, and votes for women, leading to flagrant breaches of discipline over the last two issues. The parliamentary party was also criticised for its record of attendance at the House. Beatrice Webb's verdict in April 1914 was that

The cold truth is that Labour Members have utterly failed to impress the House of Commons and the constituencies as a live force, and have lost confidence in themselves and each other.[1]

A few weeks earlier she had put the blame for this state of affairs primarily on the trade union Members. The socialists, she wrote,

are by their adhesion to the present Parliamentary Party bolstering up a fraud—pretending, to the outside world, that these respectable but reactionary Trade Union officials are the leaders of the Social Revolution.[2]

However, there were successes as well. In February 1911 Barnes was succeeded as chairman of the parliamentary party by Ramsay MacDonald. MacDonald in his turn handed over the secretaryship to Henderson. Thereby both men got the jobs they wanted, and for which

[1] *Beatrice Webb's Diaries*, Vol. I, p. 23.   [2] Ibid., p. 19.

they knew they were fitted. Although relations between them were often strained, they made 'one of the most effective partnerships in British Labour history'.[3] MacDonald had an imposing presence, and could be a very effective orator, more by the impression he gave than by the logic of his argument. Especially in his dealings with the Liberals, he had proved himself a capable negotiator, and he possessed other qualities which helped him to hold the two wings of the party together. He had by now supplanted Keir Hardie as the outstanding leader of the Independent Labour Party, but his organic, evolutionary socialism was highly flexible. It did not dictate a doctrinaire stand on any of the issues of the day, on which his pragmatic approach made it easy for him to come to an understanding with the trade union members of the parliamentary party. He was therefore able to develop the office of chairman into an acknowledged party leadership, assisted by the arrangement made shortly after his election that he should be party treasurer, with a seat on the party executive. Beatrice Webb despised him, but had to admit his achievements. The 1914 party conference, she wrote, was 'a personal triumph' for him. 'So long as he chooses to remain leader of the Labour Party he will do so. In his old-fashioned Radicalism—in his friendliness with Lloyd George—he represents the views and aspirations of the bulk of Trade Unionists.'[4]

Arthur Henderson was a trade union official and Methodist teetotaller who began his political career as a Liberal. He therefore already represented—and understood—three important strands within the Labour movement before he joined the Fabians in 1912. 'The unequalled authority he came to possess in the Labour movement was perhaps less a result of his ability to lead it in the direction he wanted, than of his sensitivity to its wishes'[5]—far exceeding MacDonald's. Neverthelss he knew MacDonald was the man to lead the party, and, despite their differences, his loyalty to MacDonald was not in doubt. If his opinions on many issues were Lib–Lab rather than socialist, he was fully convinced of the need for an independent Labour Party—more so than MacDonald—and, once he took command of the party's head office, he turned his outstanding gifts as an organiser to transforming the party into an effective electoral machine.

The overriding reason for the dependence of the party on the Liberals was the electoral understanding which had been responsible for the breakthrough of 1906, and the maintenance of Labour's position in the two general elections of 1910. The Labour Party could not be both effective and independent until they could dispense with this alliance without serious damage to their parliamentary strength; and to win

[3] Marquand, p. 129.
[4] *Beatrice Webb's Diaries*, Vol. I, p. 17.   [5] McKibbin, p. 4.

anything like forty seats against Liberal and Conservative opposition they needed better organisation in the constituencies, where up to now they had depended mainly on the Trades Councils. Among the local bodies affiliated to the party in 1910 had been 92 Trades Councils; 59 local Labour Parties, Labour Representation Committees, or other bodies including delegates from the local branches of both the unions and the socialist societies; and three local Labour Associations which recruited individual supporters. Trades Councils generally made poor constituency agencies, because they had other concerns besides politics, and because they did not harness the energies of non-union sympathisers. Consequently the improvement of organisation involved persuading the union branches and Trades Councils to allow local Labour parties to be formed.

In most mining constituencies, however, there was no local Labour organisation at all. The Miners' district unions had won most of their seats by means of electoral alliances with the local Liberal Associations which allowed the Miners' candidate a clear run, and employed their resources to make sure that he did win. Despite the affiliation of the Miners to the Labour Party, these arrangements were continued in 1910 when most of the Miners' Members of Parliament and their district unions had seen no reason to develop independent constituency organisations of their own. However, the understanding with the Liberal Party was at its most vulnerable in such constituencies, because the local Liberals did not regard them as Labour seats. They had allowed the sitting Members, most of whom had originally been chosen as Liberals and whose Lib–Lab views were well-known, to continue despite the change in their formal allegiance, but there was no reason why they should continue these arrangements for a new Miners' nominee, standing unequivocally as a Labour candidate.

In the summer of 1912 Enoch Edwards died, and the North Staffordshire Miners, who had previously paid the Liberal Association at Hanley £200 a year towards constituency expenses, nominated their president, Sam Finney, as Labour candidate. The Liberals put up their own candidate, 'far more radical' than Finney, and won the seat. The Miners 'abruptly cut [their] financial ties with the local Liberal Party and resolved to set up a separate Labour organisation in Hanley'.[6]

The Miners' Member for Chesterfield, James Haslam, died next year. The Derbyshire Miners nominated one of their agents, Barnet Kenyon, to take his place. Perhaps with the example of Hanley in mind, Kenyon insisted on ingratiating himself with the local Liberals to such an extent that the Labour Party refused to endorse him, and persuaded the Miners Federation to do the same. He therefore ran and won as a

[6] Gregory, pp. 172–3.

'Progressive and Labour' candidate. Derbyshire threatened to withdraw from the federation unless Kenyon was endorsed and his election expenses paid. For a time he was granted the Labour whip, but, with Smillie as president in place of Edwards, the Miners' executive stood firm. Early in 1914 Derbyshire capitulated and Kenyon resigned the whip.

When the death of W. E. Harvey in April 1914 created a vacancy in North-East Derbyshire, the Derbyshire Miners chose James Martin, their president, to run as a straight Labour candidate although up to that time he had been a vice-president of a local Liberal Association, and made no secret of his Liberal sympathies. The Liberals nominated their own candidate, and the seat went to the Conservatives. The breach between the Derbyshire Miners and the Liberals had been 'a long time coming . . . ; but when it did it was acrimonious, noisy, and final'.[7]

Soon after the outbreak of war the Labour whip was withdrawn from two other Miners' Members of Parliaments: J. G. Hancock of the Nottinghamshire Miners, who held Mid Derbyshire by grace of the Derbyshire Miners and the local Liberals, and William Johnson of the Warwickshire Miners, whose constituency was Nuneaton. Their offence was persistent flouting of the Labour Party constitution. Hancock had originally been elected at a by-election in 1909 when he had 'brought off a remarkable trick: he had been officially adopted by both the Liberal and Labour Parties'. By more remarkable manoeuvring he had avoided having to make a final choice between them for five years.[8]

In Scotland and Lancashire the Miners did not rely on the Liberals, but in South Wales, Yorkshire, Northumberland and Durham they were only a little less dependent on them than in the Midlands, so there were several other seats at risk. In the long run, however, the loss of highly vulnerable seats was of less importance than the changes in organisation and commitment, which were soon to make the mining constituencies the safest Labour seats in the country. Smillie told a Miners' conference in June 1914 that, if an election were to be held in the next eighteen months, lack of funds would prevent the federation from giving financial support to more then twenty-one candidates, including their eleven sitting Members; but the districts were free to finance further candidatures from their own resources. 'Altogether it seems likely that twenty-seven miners would have stood under the auspices of the Labour Party at the next general election, and in at least seven further mining seats there would have been Labour candidates who were not miners.'[9] Most, if not all of them, would have been backed by constituency Labour organisations.

Elsewhere gradual if patchy progress had been made towards setting

⁷ Ibid., p. 167.   ⁸ Ibid., pp. 149, 153–5.   ⁹ Ibid., p. 50.

up effective local organisation. Henderson, usually accompanied by Arthur Peters, the national agent, made extensive tours of the constituencies, 'teaching them organisational techniques, broadcasting Westminster political gossip, and generally encouraging local efforts'.[10] Between February 1910 and January 1914, the number of Trades Councils affiliated to the party fell by seven to 85, probably as a result of the Osborne judgment, whereas the number of local Labour Parties, Labour Representation Committees and similar bodies rose by eight to 67, and the number of Labour Associations doubled to six. However, the major success was the establishment in 1913 of a central Labour Party in London, where Labour held only two seats. The central party was expected to take on the responsibility of building up the constituency parties. A similar central party had been formed in Glasgow in 1912; and by the beginning of the war the Scottish unions had been persuaded, by the promise of generous representation, to accept a proposal for a Scottish Advisory Council, although the council had not yet held its inaugural meeting.

The overriding concern of the parliamentary party at the beginning of 1911 was to secure legislation to nullify the effects of the Osborne judgment. The government had already announced their intentions before the election. They proposed to introduce salaries for Members of Parliament, and to allow unions to finance political activities, provided that the money came from a special fund authorised by a ballot of the members and raised by a separate 'political levy'; and that individual members were entitled to refuse to contribute to the fund by 'contracting out'.

At their conference in February 1911 the Labour Party made a gesture by dropping from their constitution the requirement, known as the 'pledge'—which had been one of the main issues in the Osborne judgment—that: 'Candidates and members must . . . agree to abide by the decisions of the Parliamentary Party in carrying out the aims of this constitution' and substituting an obligation 'to accept the responsibilities established by Parliamentary practice'.[11] This, however, was not enough to deflect the government.

Churchill introduced a bill in May 1911 which was denounced by both unions and party. Their main argument against it was one of principle, that decisions about spending money for political objectives ought to be made in the same way as any other decision, according to the rules of the union; and that it was unjust to pick out trade unions for special limitations on the way they spent their money. The *Labour Leader* went further, saying that 'a Bill making Trade Union levies a voluntary affair would be merely a mockery. The Premier might just as

---

[10] McKibbin, p. 22.   [11] Labour Party, 1911, p. 78.

well propose to bring in a measure establishing voluntary taxation.'[12] A special conference called by the Joint Board on 20–21 June unanimously rejected the bill.

Meanwhile provision had been made in the budget for the payment from August 1911 of an annual parliamentary salary of £400—five times the average earnings of male manual workers—which greatly eased the pressure on the finances of the Labour Party. Churchill's bill was dropped; and nothing more was done until the summer of 1912, when the government, seeing no need to modify their original proposals, introduced them again. Labour amendments were blocked in committee, and the party was faced with accepting the bill as it stood, or continuing to operate under the Osborne judgment. Another Joint Board conference met on 3 January 1913, and decided to accept the bill as an 'instalment of justice'.[13] It went through its remaining stages without trouble.

The financial consequences of these two measures taken together were highly favourable to the party.[14] The Osborne judgment had taken effect slowly, as injunctions were given union by union. Many unions responded to injunctions by raising voluntary funds which allowed them to pay at least something to the party. The central funds were strong enough to pay Members whose union salaries had been cut off by injuctions, as well as making loans to several unions in the general election of December 1910. By 1911 the payment of parliamentary salaries had become by far the heaviest burden on party funds. Payment by the state therefore enabled the party to last out until the Trade Union Act 1913 came into force; and, by freeing the party from the need to pay any parliamentary salaries—even to Members who were not sponsored by trade unions—reduced its expenditure below what it had been before

[12] *Labour Leader*, 3 February 1911.

[13] Ibid., 9 January 1913.

[14] Nevertheless, the advantages of the 'political levy' were not so great as A. J. P. Taylor suggests in his *English History 1914–1945*. On page 114 he writes:

The political fund could not be used for anything else. In the old days a union felt generous when it had subscribed £100 to the Labour party. Now it thought nothing of handing over £5,000, if the money were lying idle in the political fund. . . . The income of the Labour party multiplied by ten overnight.

The Act reduced the proportion of trade unionists affiliated to the party through contracting-out. Between 1909, before the Osborne judgment had taken effect, and 1915, when the Act was in operation, trade union membership rose by 90 per cent but trade union affiliation to the party increased by only 40 per cent. Over that period subscriptions from affiliated organisations actually fell from £15,058 to £11,322. This was partly due to the halving of the rate of subscription in 1912, but had the proportion of trade unionists affiliated to the party remained the same as in 1909, income from subscriptions would have been little less than in 1909 despite the reduced rate.

It may be that the existence of separate political funds enabled unions to be more generous in their contributions to election funds after the war than they had been before it, but the effect of the Act on the regular income of the party was decidedly, if not disastrously, adverse.

the Osborne judgment. By 1913 the growth in trade union membership had made certain that, even with contracting-out, the income from a given rate of subscription would be considerably larger than before. Although the rate was halved by the 1912 party conference, Henderson was able to introduce a grant of 25 per cent towards the salaries of full-time local party agents, and to appoint two national organisers, thus furthering his endeavours to guide and strengthen local organisation, which had also been hit by the Osborne judgment.[15]

For parliament as a whole, and for the country, the two major legislative proposals of 1911 were the Parliament Bill and the National Insurance Bill. The first, enabling the Commons to override the Lords' veto by passing a bill in three successive sessions, with a minimum delay of two years, and virtually removing the veto in respect of money bills, proceeded through its stormy sessions without demanding much more of the Labour Members than their attendance and their votes. National insurance, however, divided them. The issue was considered at the Joint Board conference in June 1911. An amendment to the Joint Board's recommendations opposed a contributory scheme as 'detrimental to the organisation of workmen for the purpose of protecting their wages and conditions'. The bill's defenders did not trouble to argue the merits of the scheme. Their case was that parliament would not accept a non-contributory scheme, and Lloyd George's proposals were substantially better than nothing. The amendment was lost by only 135 votes to 179 on a show of hands, but a card vote against it of 284,000 to 1,164,000 (the Miners abstaining) showed where the trade union majority stood.

Essentially the controversy was between those socialists who favoured a non-contributory scheme on principle and the majority of union representatives who considered that the benefits which Lloyd George's scheme offered were worth paying for. A few trade unionists sympathised with the argument advanced by Hilaire Belloc and his friends that the whole scheme should be rejected on the grounds that it involved subjecting workers to registration and regimentation. Tillett wrote in the *Dockers' Record* of March 1911:

The interference with wages, the power to utilise the Labour Exchanges, the Doctors, the Health Committees, the Commissioners, Assessors, Courts of Referees would make the life of the average workman a burden to him.

However, Tillett was always ready to fly a kite, and the objection of many dockers to the scheme was that it might, as many of its advocates hoped, be used to terminate casual employment on the waterfront.

---

[15] 'In many places it has been impossible to form local Labour Parties, owing to fear of injunctions, and in some cases Unions have been compelled to withdraw their local . . . affiliations' (*Labour Leader*, 7 November 1912).

Elsewhere there was no sign of opposition to the scheme's bureaucratic procedures when it came into effect. Previously, most workers had avoided the labour exchanges because they believed that when they needed new jobs they could find them for themselves. Once entitlement to benefit under national insurance depended on registration with the exchanges it became clear that they had no objection in principle to using them.

Some members of the parliamentary party continued to use their votes to uphold the non-contributory principle. Meanwhile the bill had run into trouble with the friendly societies, the doctors, and upper-class housewives who objected to 'licking stamps' for their servants' insurance cards; and the government were forced into an autumn session for the second year in succession in order to get it through. The government had too much trouble on their hands to tolerate tiresome insubordination among their allies. Their chief whip, the Master of Elibank, remonstrated with MacDonald, who was personally strongly in favour of the scheme, and considered 'the contributory principle . . . was a positive advantage'.[16] MacDonald passed on the message to his colleagues, but three intransigent socialists, Jowett, Lansbury and Snowden, and two trade unionists, O'Grady and Thorne, opposed the third reading.

Dissension arose also over the issue of votes for women, although there was little controversy within the party over the principle. Their ultimate objective was universal suffrage, although in the meantime most of them were very willing to accept the enfranchisement of every adult male as a stage on the road. They were also ready to support a Conciliation Bill, produced by an all-party committee, to give women the vote on a property qualification, but only because a bill to give some women the vote, even women who would probably vote Conservative, was better than nothing. When this proposal was finally defeated in 1912—to the fury of the suffragettes—they welcomed the prospect of a government bill for adult male suffrage along with a promise from Asquith to accept any amendment to include votes for women which had the support of a majority in the Commons. The Speaker, however, ruled all such amendments out of order; and nothing had been achieved by the outbreak of war, despite the campaign of violence organised by the suffragettes.

The trouble arose over tactics. In the autumn of 1912 Lansbury circulated a proposal that the party should vote against every government measure until Asquith introduced a bill giving women the vote. He was censured and told to conform to party policy in future—the first test of the new rule on the conduct of Members and candidates. Instead

[16] Marquand, p. 138.

Lansbury, who in Beatrice Webb's eyes had 'become a raging revivalist preacher of general upheaval',[17] resigned his seat for Bow and Bromley to fight a by-election on the issue of votes for women. Since he refused to give assurances concerning his future conduct, he could not be endorsed as a Labour candidate, and party speakers were told not to support him. Nevertheless Hardie, O'Grady, Snowden and Thorne pledged themselves to assist him in his campaign in November 1912 which led up to his defeat by a relatively small margin. This insubordination was too much for the executive, who reported the rebels to their organisations, and won the support of the party conference in January 1913 for a proposal that, when a complaint was made concerning a 'violation of the constitution in the country', or 'conduct . . . in the House . . . contrary to the principles and policy of the Party', or persistent opposition to 'the collective decisions of the Party', and a satisfactory explanation was not given, a joint meeting of the executive and the parliamentary party should be empowered to withdraw the whip.[18]

The reforming zeal of the Liberal government evaporated after the passage of the Parliament Act and the National Insurance Act, and during the last twelve months before the war parliament was more and more occupied with their increasingly desperate flounderings over Ulster.

Unfortunately the hands of the Labour Party have largely been tied. . . . The Home Rule Bill has stood, like an insurmountable wall, in the way. . . . There are not a few constituencies where the Irish vote turns the scale, and that vote will always be cast for the Liberal candidate . . . until the Irish nation has gained self-government.[19]

If the Labour Party's own legislative proposals came nowhere near winning parliamentary majorities, this was not only because of the pressure of government business and bad luck in the ballots for private members' bills. The two to which they gave priority were their Right to Work Bill, and their motion for a statutory minimum wage of £1.50 a week. Both were frankly propagandist. The first sought to put an obligation on the government to force local authorities to provide the unemployed with work at trade union rates, or adequate maintenance. It played its part in pushing the Liberals first towards labour exchanges and then into unemployment insurance, as well as the gesture of the Development Commission set up in 1910 to promote public works; but thereafter lost its significance. On the other hand, there was, despite the Coal Mines Minimum Wage Act, no possibility that a government

---

[17] *Beatrice Webb's Diaries*, Vol. I, p. 7.   [18] Labour Party, 1913, p. 82.
[19] *Labour Leader*, 23 October 1913.

headed by Asquith would legislate for a *national* minimum wage, and, in addition, the figure chosen by the party, roughly equivalent to current adult male average earnings, could hardly have been intended as a serious proposition. A more realistic proposal was an amendment to the government's Railway Bill which allowed the companies to recoup the cost of higher wages. The amendment sought to impose a weekly minimum wage of £1.05 on the railways, and won the support of nearly fifty Liberal votes on 11 February 1913.

There were, however, other ways in which the parliamentary party could serve the unions. From Tonypandy onwards, Hardie pursued a personal campaign against police and military violence in strikes. It was the party's resolution in the Commons that forced the railway companies to meet the unions in 1911. The party handled the Miners' case during the passage of the Coal Mines Minimum Wage Act with some success, and did what little they could to help the unions in the London dock strike of 1912. In 1913 and 1914 they made some amends for their indiscipline over the passage of the National Insurance Act by their detailed committee work on the subsequent amending bills.

The parliamentary party therefore hardly deserved the charge of ineffectiveness often made against them during those turbulent prewar years. Their misfortune was to be caught up in bitter quarrels among their supporters over insurance and votes for women, in which there was no possibility of satisfying everyone. A third controversial issue was syndicalism and strikes. However, despite Crooks's private member's bill to ban strikes and lockouts until there had been an opportunity for conciliation to bring about a peaceful settlement—which was unanimously disowned by Congress in 1911—this debate was conducted almost entirely outside parliament.

Syndicalists argued that the social revolution could be achieved only by a general strike, whereas Snowden propounded the view that strikes could not even 'be effective as a general policy for raising the condition of labour'.[20] There was considerable enthusiasm for syndicalist ideas at the founding conference of the British Socialist Party in 1911, which brought together the Social Democratic Party, a dissident section of the Independent Labour Party and other socialist groups; but the traditionally lukewarm view of the Social Democrats towards industrial action was still upheld by Hyndman and most of the other leaders, and the conference refused by a substantial majority 'to declare identity with the industrial revolt'.[21] Thereafter the debate continued at all levels in the new party up to the outbreak of war and beyond, along with a controversy over rearmament.

Their established leaders were conscious of the danger of German

[20] Snowden, Vol. I, p. 237.   [21] Kendall, pp. 42–3.

militarism, and advocated rearmament to keep it at bay. They were opposed by the 'internationalists' who managed to secure a majority without deposing the 'old guard'. Elsewhere in the British Labour movement and in other European socialist parties, there was at least formal acceptance of the official policy of the Second International, laid down in 1907, that it was the duty of the workers and their representatives to prevent a threatened war 'by means of co-ordinated action', and, if war broke out, 'to work for its speedy termination' and to use the opportunity 'to arouse the population and to hasten the overthrow of capitalist rule'.[22]

At the outbreak of war the Labour Party had little reason to be ashamed of its record during the previous four years. In the circumstances, their parliamentary achievements had not been discreditable. Their organisation had been considerably strengthened. Despite the loss of six seats the party's popular vote in by-elections was rising, and in local elections 'from 1908 onwards Labour made an unbroken series of gains'.[23] Moreover, with the successful, if uncomfortable, absorption of the Miners and the fading of the old Lib–Lab faction in parliament, the party emerged as the undisputed political voice of organised Labour— partly at the expense of the Parliamentary Committee.

The Trade Union Act 1913 offered an opportunity for union members to give their verdict on the party's record, for there could be no doubt in anyone's mind that a vote to establish a political fund was a vote for continued support for the Labour Party. Among the major unions the Miners recorded a 65 per cent poll, the Railwaymen 50 per cent, the Weavers 88 per cent, the Engineers 21 per cent, the Gasworkers 29 per cent, and the Amalgamated Carpenters and Joiners 36 per cent. As union ballots go, the participation rates of the Miners and Railwaymen are impressive, and that of the Weavers is almost incredible. Nearly all the results were in favour of political funds, the majorities in these unions being: Miners, 57 per cent; Railwaymen, 75 per cent; Weavers, 56 per cent; Engineers, 62 per cent;[24] Gasworkers, 87 per cent; and Carpenters and Joiners, 53 per cent. Although the size of the minorities shows that working-class Liberalism—and Conservatism—were by no means dead, these results were very far from being votes of no confidence in the Labour Party.

Unity Maintained, 1914–17

The most important achievement of the Labour Party during the first three years of the war was to avoid a destructive split between those who

---

[22] Ibid., p. 50.   [23] McKibbin, pp. 84–5.
[24] This was a vote on the principle. A few months later the Engineers defeated a proposal for a political levy of 5p a year; and it was not until 1916 that they were able to establish a political fund.

gave their full support to the war effort and those who refused to do so. French and German socialists split along this divide and so did many smaller European socialist parties. The Labour Party, an alliance between overwhelmingly pro-war unions and an anti-war Independent Labour Party, might have seemed especially vulnerable, but they held together.

When MacDonald followed Grey's famous speech in the House of Commons on 3 August 1914, the line he took—that Britain should remain neutral—had been agreed at a meeting of the parliamentary party; but two days later the party decided to vote the war credits sought by the government, and MacDonald felt compelled to resign as chairman. Henderson took his place. By the end of the month the party had agreed to an electoral truce, and to join the other parties in a recruitment campaign. All the trade union Members were by this time giving their support to the war. Clynes, who was nominally sponsored by the Independent Labour Party, although for all practical purposes a trade union Member, went with them, as did James Parker. Hardie, Jowett, and Richardson followed MacDonald, and Snowden, who was abroad, joined them on his return in February 1915.

Although they refused to give full support to the war effort, these men were far from being outright pacifists. MacDonald, who excused himself from participation in the recruiting campaign, nevertheless held that 'it was unthinkable that Germany should win',[25] and did nothing to impede the campaign. Smillie told the annual conference of the Miners in 1915 that he was a 'bitter opponent of militarism and war'. Nevertheless, he said,

I do not think there is a likelihood of peace being secured so long as the Germans and Austrians are on French and Belgian soil. I feel even as a pacifist that it would be too much to expect our country in view of the sacrifices in blood and in treasure to lower itself, unless it is beaten down to the ground, . . . to even negotiate peace terms so long as the enemy is not on their own soil, but on the soil of France and Flanders.

Within a few days of the outbreak of war MacDonald met with Norman Angell, E. D. Morel, Arthur Ponsonby, Charles Trevelyan and others to form a committee, subsequently the Union of Democratic Control, to voice their view that the war had originated in 'secret diplomacy', and that such entanglements must be avoided in future. They also favoured a negotiated peace in contrast to unconditional surrender, but they accepted that the circumstances in which it would be possible to negotiate were at that time remote.

However, these views were not incompatible with full support for the

---

[25] *Labour Leader*, 27 August 1914.

war effort. Henderson joined the Union of Democratic Control before the end of 1914 and, although he resigned from its council when he entered the government, he continued to express his sympathy with its objectives. As party leader, Henderson always saw himself as a caretaker for MacDonald. He helped MacDonald to retain his post as party treasurer—the more easily because MacDonald's views on the war were so near to his own. For his part MacDonald helped Henderson by expressing these views so as to give the least possible offence. On the whole, the 'patriots' and the critics of the war were able to work together reasonably well on the party executive, and in the parliamentary party. In the country, the party nominated a critic of the war, W. C. Anderson of the Independent Labour Party, to the Sheffield seat vacated by the death of William Pointer in 1915; and when, in the same year, Stanton, who had shifted from syndicalism to extreme patriotism, stood for Merthyr after Hardie's death against Winstone, the Miners' candidate and a critic of the war, the party gave Winstone firm support. Stanton nevertheless won the seat.

Co-operation between the two groups was also assisted by changes in the relationship between government and the Labour movement, brought about by the war. The work of the parliamentary party was reduced as a consequence of the new channels opened up for the unions to deal directly with government departments and members of the cabinet, especially after Henderson entered the government in May 1915 as 'the voice of Labour'. Even where legislation was involved, the details were generally settled 'out of doors' rather than through debates and committees in the House of Commons. Thus the opportunities for friction were much reduced. Furthermore, on matters which could not be handled in this way, such as war profits, food prices, rent control, rationing, pensions, wages, and pay and allowances for the armed forces, the members of both groups usually took the same line. On issues of this kind the handful of Independent Labour Party Members led by Snowden—for MacDonald left this job to him—who constituted themselves, along with a few leftwing Liberals, the main parliamentary inquisitors of the government, more often than not spoke for the whole Labour movement.

Co-operation between the factions was further facilitated by their participation in the work of the War Emergency Workers National Committee. With the Labour Party's assistant secretary, J. S. Middleton, as secretary, and Henderson in the chair until he joined the government, the committe became the regular means of discussing and deciding the Labour movement's attitude to the social problems arising from the war. One reason for its success was its resolve from the start to 'preclude all debate about the merits of British participation in the struggle'. A second was that 'the sane patriots and the discreet opponents of the War were able to establish a harmonious working majority', thus isolating the 'super-patriots', while the 'revolutionary defeatists' were 'barely represented on the Committee at all'.[26]

Even over major issues relating directly to the conduct of the war, the critics were by no means always isolated. A majority of the parliamentary party shared their doubts about accepting Asquith's invitation to join his coalition. It was only when they met jointly with the executive, who had voted in favour, that a majority could be found for going in. A majority of the party at all levels opposed conscription up to the point at which the first Military Service Act was passed in January 1916.

Nevertheless, there was friction and increasing polarisation. At the end of 1914 a group of young Independent Labour Party members led by Fenner Brockway and Clifford Allen founded the No-Conscription Fellowship. On the other side, Victor Fisher, a journalist and businessman who had been a member of several radical and socialist organisations, founded the Socialist National Defence Committee in April 1915 to counteract propaganda for 'peace at any price' in the Labour movement. As well as Hyndman and other 'patriots' in the British Socialist Party, a number of trade union leaders gave their backing, including Duncan, Hodge, G. H. Roberts, Seddon, Tillett, and, of course, Stanton, who had been supported by Fisher in his election campaign. The committee was launched as a national movement in July. Hodge became president, and several of the others vice-presidents. Early in 1916 it became the British Workers National League. Contact was established with Lord Milner who arranged for substantial subsidies from the newspaper magnate, Astor. There were discussions with officials of the Conservative Party over an electoral arrangement, which materialised in 1918 when the league became the National Democratic and Labour Party.

Meanwhile Hyndman and his friends retained control of the British Socialist Party's paper, *Justice*, so their opponents founded the *Call*. At the conference held in April 1916 it became evident that the Hyndman faction was outnumbered, and they marched out; but they did not lack support outside the party. Violence at meetings became common, either to eject hecklers from patriotic meetings, or to break up meetings of the Independent Labour Party, the Union of Democratic Control, and the No-Conscription Fellowship.

The Military Service Acts created a new issue. They provided for conscientious objectors, who established their *bona fides*, to be granted exemption by the military service tribunals. The majority of the 16,500

[26] Harrison, pp. 216, 224, 225.

applicants were religious objectors—Quakers and Christadelphians—
but there were also political objectors, the great majority of them from
the No-Conscription Fellowship. Many of those rejected by the
tribunals, or offered alternative service, decided to resist and 'experienced a painful confrontation with the civil or military authorities, often
involving incarceration', but in the end most of them 'accepted
improved offers of alternative service'.[27]

In March 1917 the first Russian revolution, which brought their
democratic parties to power, evoked an enthusiastic response from the
British Labour movement generally. After it became clear that the
provisional Russian government, in addition to preparing for a new
military offensive, also wanted to initiate discussions on war aims and
the terms on which peace might be secured, the United Socialist
Council, formed in 1916 by the Independent Labour Party and the
British Socialist Party, sent out invitations to a 'convention' to be held in
Leeds on 3 June, and attracted more than a thousand delegates from
socialist and trade union organisations. Extravagant oratory from
MacDonald and Snowden was enthusiastically received; and resolutions
were passed congratulating the Russians on their revolution and their
foreign policy, and, more surprisingly, proposing that Workers and
Soldiers Councils should be established throughout Britain. The
outcome disappointed the hopes of the convention. Some local
conferences were held, but they established no lasting organisation, and
a national council met only once, in October.

Nevertheless, the convention was followed by a good deal of
recrimination in the unions. At the annual conference of the Transport
Workers Federation a few days later, its secretary, Robert Williams, the
most notable trade union supporter of the convention, had to apologise
for his unauthorised use of the name of the federation, after a debate in
which Sexton described the meeting at Leeds as 'the most bogus, the
most dishonest, and the most corrupt conference ever conceived'; and,
at the Sailors' and Firemen's executive on 23 June, Tom Mann, still a
member, had to defend his conduct at Leeds where he had represented
the Mersey district of the federation.

The war cabinet also took notice of the convention. They decided to
set up a National War Aims Committee to counteract 'pacifist'
propaganda; and authorised the Home Office to investigate. This task
was given to an assistant commissioner at Scotland Yard, Basil
Thomson, who had been in charge of the labour intelligence service of
the Ministry of Munitions. He

was too loyal a subordinate to tell his superiors a plain truth they did not want

[27] Ceadel, pp. 40–1.

to hear. . . . For the benefit of the War Cabinet, he filled his accounts with carefully-phrased allusions to non-existent connections between British dissenters and the enemy.[28]

Henceforth, during the war and in the immediate postwar years, successive cabinets continued to receive from Thomson exaggerated reports of the importance of pacifist, socialist, shop steward, and other 'disloyal' organisations.

The cabinet's worries were augmented by the proposal of socialist parties in several neutral countries to call a conference in Stockholm to which all socialist parties would be invited, including those of belligerent countries on both sides, in order to draw up peace terms which the belligerent governments would be urged to accept. In May Henderson went to talk to the Russians,[29] and came to appreciate the difficulties of the provisional government, and their urgent need for support. He decided that the Stockholm conference could help them. On 24 July he returned to Britain with the intention of persuading the party executive to reverse its decision not to send delegates. On 10 August he put his case to a special party conference which voted by a large majority for sending delegates, but added a rider that no representatives of the other British bodies affiliated to the socialist international, including the Independent Labour Party and the British Socialist Party, should be allowed to go. An attempt to change this decision on 21 August almost succeeded in reversing the vote for attending the conference, and reaffirmed the ban on the socialist bodies by an overwhelming majority. The patriots had taken their revenge for the Leeds conference.

That was the end of Stockholm, and the worst point in relations between the unions and the socialists. Thereafter, an improvement began which was mainly due to Henderson. The war cabinet, who saw no advantage in the Stockholm conference once the Russian offensive had ended in disaster, had apparently expected him to speak against it at the party conference on 10 August. They forced him to resign and chose another Labour minister, George Barnes, to replace him in the war cabinet. Shortly afterwards Henderson also resigned the party leadership. Apparently to the surprise of Lloyd George, the Labour Members chose a Scottish Miners' leader, William Adamson, to replace him,

[28] Schwartz, p. 184.
[29] The government agreed that MacDonald should also go, after he had assured them that 'he regarded a separate peace with absolute horror, as it would mean the destruction of everything he cared for in Europe, and he would do his utmost to prevent the Russians from taking any such step' (Marquand, pp. 213–14); but, on instructions from Havelock Wilson, the crew of his ship refused to sail.

rather than Barnes. Thereafter Henderson, who had remained secretary of the Labour Party, devoted himself to its reconstruction.

The Reconstruction of the Party

Henderson's first concern was to take up and complete his prewar task of making the Labour Party into an effective electoral machine. This was to be achieved by setting up constituency (or 'divisional') parties, and giving formal recognition to individual party membership. In addition to organisations affiliated nationally and locally, the party was henceforth to include 'men and women who are individual members of a Local Labour Party', and seats on the party executive were to be reserved for representatives of the divisional parties. Where local Labour Parties existed alongside Trades Councils, every effort was to be made to amalgamate the two, and the councils were not normally to be allowed to affiliate to the party except through the divisional parties.

To win the support of the unions for these proposals, Henderson proposed to incorporate a change in rule adopted by a bare majority at the 1917 conference which provided that all members of the executive were to be elected by conference as a whole, and therefore effectively by the unions. Indeed, he strengthened the unions' grip even further at the expense of the socialist societies. Five seats were to go to the divisional parties, four were to be reserved for women, and eleven were to represent the affiliated organisations, both trade union and socialist. The unions would therefore be enabled, if they chose, to exclude socialist representatives.

Henderson worked fast. His outline was presented to the executive before the end of September, when a sub-committee was appointed to help with detailed drafting including MacDonald, Webb and Egerton Wake, a national organiser, along with three trade unionists and Wardle, a Labour minister. The draft was in circulation by the middle of October, giving Henderson time to drum up support in the country before it came to the party conference on 23 January 1918. There a narrow majority referred the proposals back, but only for the purpose of introducing amendments to make sure of trade union support. The number of executive seats allotted to affiliated organisations was raised from eleven to thirteen; and the parliamentary party, which might be expected to include a majority of trade unionists, was to share with the executive the responsibility for drafting election programmes, to which candidates were to 'give prominence' in their election campaigns. Thus altered, the constitution won a comfortable majority from the re-convened conference on 26 February 1918. There was no argument over a doubling of affiliation fees. These had not been altered since 1913, and prices had almost doubled since then. The real increase in party income came from the growth of union membership.[30]

The Independent Labour Party protested against the changes in the composition of the executive, but there was nothing they could do about it, short of disaffiliation. The unions could hardly have asked for more unless they were prepared to expel the socialist societies altogether. Wiser union leaders appreciated the need for strong constituency organisation, and the contribution to meeting it which could be made by encouraging and recognising individual membership. Wise or not, national trade union leaders had no reason to defend the Trades Councils. They had no direct control over the councils, which were usually more militant in their attitudes than the national leaders.[31]

There were, however, still some trade union leaders who wished to exclude socialist societies from the Labour Party. Sexton had flown a kite at the end of the 1916 Trades Union Congress by proposing that trade unions should henceforth take political action only through Congress:

In the country we have the Fabian Society, the Women's Organisation, the ILP, the LRC, the BSP and the UDC. Every one of these bodies are of mushroom growth, but after the manner of the fungus specie, they are fastening themselves on the Labour movement and sucking its life's blood away.[32]

By the end of 1917 J. B. Williams was proposing that a Trade Union Labour Party be set up, and he was not without support. Along with Sexton and Davis he was a member of the Parliamentary Committee. Their seats on the committee depended on support from major unions, for their own unions were relatively small; but they were nevertheless re-elected in 1918, when their colleague in this venture, Havelock Wilson, also gained a place on the committee. Even so, the proposal was easily defeated. On 9 April 1918 a joint meeting of the Parliamentary Committee and the party executive condemned the move as 'calculated

---

[30] In the immediate prewar years the Labour Party's income from affiliation fees was severely affected by the Osborne judgment, but by 1915 the 1913 Act was fully in operation, and comparisons with later years are therefore valid. Between 1915 and 1920 the party's income from this source rose more than fourfold, from £11,322 to £48,776, but when price increases are taken into account, the real rise was about 120 per cent. However, membership also had more than doubled over those years. It was only with a further increase in the fee to three times the prewar rate, which took effect in 1921, when prices were falling again, that real income per head rose substantially above the 1915 level.

[31] In 1917 W. J. Davis had brought his union out of the Birmingham Trades Council on the grounds that the council had been using union contributions for pacifist propaganda. Many Trades Councils had sent delegates to the Leeds convention, and had taken part in organising the subsequent local conferences. The Sheffield Trades and Labour Council had congratulated Russia on the Bolshevik revolution in December 1917, with only one dissentient.

[32] Trades Union Congress, 1916, p. 387.

to disrupt a movement built up by years of sacrifice', and asked Williams and his supporters to desist. When Davis asked Congress to support the formation of a Trade Union Labour Party in September, he lost by about seven votes to one.

The Trade Union Labour Party suffered from the same weakness as the British Workers League, a weakness noted by the *Yorkshire Factory Times* in its issue of 11 May 1916, when it said of the league that: 'It has not the backing of any single Trades Union. It has not the backing of any single representative Labour man, with authority to speak for his union.' Other trade union leaders who sympathised with Davis, Sexton, Williams and Wilson had enough influence with their union delegations to Congress to get them to vote these men on to the Parliamentary Committee, but few of them could persuade their members or their delegations to Congress to vote for the organisations which they were promoting.

The British Workers League was now moving towards an alliance with the Conservatives. In December 1917 the Miners complained that the league was proposing to run candidates for parliament, and the Labour Party executive decided to discipline its supporters. A number of Labour Members, including Hodge, were forced to resign their positions in the league. An associated venture, in the autumn of 1916, was the foundation, in conjunction with the leaders of the recently-established Federation of British Industries, of the National Alliance of Employers and Employed to promote harmony in industry, particularly with postwar reconstruction in mind. Appleton, Brownlie, Davis, Havelock Wilson and Tillett were among its trade union sponsors, but most major trade unions regarded it with considerable suspicion. The *Yorkshire Factory Times*[33] remarked of the alliance's conference in May 1917 that the trade union representatives were 'largely a gathering of the Executive Council of the General Federation of Trade Unions'; and it was a further weakness of the sponsors of these various moves that most of them were associated with this declining organisation.

The only concession to the socialists in the new constitution was contained in the revised statement of objectives. The section which became known as Clause Four gave the party a clear doctrinal commitment for the first time by binding it

to secure for the producers by hand or by brain the full fruits of their industry, and the most equitable distribution thereof that may be possible, upon the basis of the common ownership of the means of production and the best obtainable system of popular administration and control of each industry and service.

[33] 31 May 1917.

Although a spokesman of the Liverpool Dockers told Congress in September that the 'clause in the constitution dealing with the production, distribution, and exchange of everything must come out or we must leave the party',[34] this section aroused little controversy.

What can account for this easy conversion of the trade unions to socialism? The main reason was a widespread belief that the war had proved that the country's resources could be more efficiently used by means of control and planning. Under wartime controls, living standards had been maintained at a reasonable level while about half the nation's productive capacity had been devoted to the manufacture of armaments and other materials of war, and millions of men had been away in the armed forces.

A partiality for national control of economic resources can be seen in the work of the many bodies established by the government to make plans for postwar reconstruction. The original Reconstruction Committee appointed by Asquith in March 1916 had been a group of ministers who set up sub-committees to report on particular topics. By the end of the year a number of reports had accumulated on agriculture, demobilisation, and economic policy, but no decisions had been taken. Lloyd George transferred the task to a committee of intellectuals and specialists, including Beatrice Webb, Rowntree, and J. H. Thomas, chaired first by Montagu and then by Addison. By the autumn of 1918 plans for military demobilisation had been completed, and supplemented by plans for the demobilisation of war workers, and the disposal of war materials. There were also plans for the rationalisation of transport; aid for new industries; a massive housebuilding programme; and the abolition of the Poor Law and the creation of a Ministry of Health.

The planners envisaged that there would be continuing need for the close contact between individual industries and the government which had developed during the war, and welcomed the Whitley reports, whose proposed Joint Industrial Councils seemed to provide representative bodies appropriate to fulfil this function after the war. It was for this reason that the Ministries of both Reconstruction and Labour set about promoting councils with such zest during 1918.

Labour's postwar planning also began in March 1916, when a joint sub-committee of the four national committees was appointed. A number of memoranda were published, providing the basis of a 'reconstruction manifesto', *Labour and the New Social Order*, a draft of which, written by Sidney Webb, was circulated along with Henderson's proposals for a new constitution; but not considered in detail until the conference in June 1918, when twenty-six policy resolutions based upon the manifesto were passed.

[34] Trades Union Congress, 1918, p. 261.

There was a substantial measure of agreement with government proposals already announced, or shortly to be made known, on maintaining wages, providing for demobilised servicemen and munitions workers, restoring trade union practices, and on a range of social and economic reforms including the abolition of the Poor Law, an ambitious public housebuilding programme, and the rationalisation of transport and electricity supply. The main distinctive features of Labour's programme were adult suffrage for both men and women; self-determination for Ireland and regional assemblies for England, Scotland and Wales; further educational reform beyond Fisher's 1918 Act; nationalisation of coalmining and life insurance; and a capital levy.

These were domestic policies. The party's foreign policy was based on the work of a joint committee which Henderson had persuaded the party executive and the Parliamentary Committee to set up in October 1917. Their memorandum on war aims was approved at a joint conference at the end of December. It proposed a League of Free Nations; no annexations; frontiers redrawn on the basis of self-determination; no indemnities; the end of secret diplomacy; the principle of the 'open door' for international trade; and Labour or Socialist representation on delegations to the peace conference. The policy of the Union of Democratic Control had become the policy of the Labour Party.

Even in foreign policy, however, the party was not so far from the coalition government as might have been expected. War weariness was at its height in the winter of 1917–18 with the continued heavy loss of life in France, the goverment's demand for more men for the forces, and the rapid growth of queues for food. On 29 November 1917 Lansdowne's famous letter in the *Daily Telegraph* had proposed peace negotiations, and in the Brest–Litovsk negotiations with the Bolsheviks, the central powers had offered self-determination, open diplomacy, and no indemnities. On 5 January 1918 Lloyd George chose a conference of trade union delegates on manpower as the appropriate forum for a statement of British war aims which covered much of the same ground as the Labour memorandum. However, he was overshadowed by President Wilson in America, who presented his Fourteen Points, also on similar lines, to a joint session of the two Houses of Congress three days later.

Nevertheless, the considerable common ground in policy statements did not check the growing enthusiasm of the Labour Party for independent action. They distrusted Lloyd George, fearing that he would exploit war-weary yearnings for a better world. They did not believe that the Conservative majority in the coalition would allow the more radical proposals of the reconstructionists to be carried out.

Asquith's rump was hardly worth bothering about. Labour, bereft of the Liberal alliance, must look after its own interests. In January 1918 the party conference had decided to remain in the coalition by a majority of five to two; but in June the delegates voted by two to one to terminate what was left of the electoral truce, and Smillie expressed a new mood of confidence when he said that 'the country were as sick of the political truce as they were of the Government, and the Labour Movement was not so strong as it would be and ought to be if the Labour men were outside the Government'.[35] In August the party executive narrowly avoided a decision in favour of an election before the end of the war. On 7 November they decided to recommend to another party conference, to be held on 14 November, that Labour should withdraw from the coalition; whereas the majority of the parliamentarians argued that, by leaving the coalition, Labour would lose the chance of influencing reconstruction and the peace settlement. The conference voted five to two for leaving when parliament was dissolved, although a minority supported Clynes in wanting Labour to remain until the peace treaty was signed. On the same day it was announced that parliament was to be dissolved on 25 November, with an election on 14 December.

On 19 November the Parliamentary Committee authorised the endorsement of candidates fulfilling the conditions laid down in the standing orders of Congress, and the drafting of an election manifesto. There is no evidence that any candidates were endorsed, but the manifesto was written and published. In most respects it corresponded fairly closely to the party's proposals, but it opened with the assertion that the election should have been delayed until 'the Peace Conference had met and determined the issues involved in the final settlement, and the people should then have been consulted upon the . . . reconstruction proposals',[36] thus indicating sympathy with the position which most of the parliamentary party had taken up.

The General Election of 1918

With the help of Bonar Law, Lloyd George persuaded the Conservatives to continue the coalition. Conservative and Liberal Members of Parliament who had served the government loyally were endorsed by the issue of 'coupons', as were new candidates who could be expected to do so. The remaining Liberals, led by Asquith, resisted Lloyd George's blandishments, but the election found them unprepared, with their constituency organisation in disarray. By contrast the Conservative machine was in good order and was used to support coalition Liberals as well as the party's own candidates.

[35] Labour Party, June 1918, p. 33.
[36] Trades Union Congress, 1919, p. 91.

Henderson's reorganisation of the Labour Party was already making big changes. In January 1918 there were 157 Trades Councils among the 258 local bodies affiliated to the party. By June 1919 they were down to 49, out of a total of nearly 450. However, many of the new divisional parties had only just been formed when the dissolution was announced, and there was inevitably much hurried work in the constituencies. It was, therefore, a considerable achievement to bring 363 candidates to the poll, no less than 140 of whom were sponsored by their local Labour Parties. Fifty more were sponsored by the Independent Labour Party, and four by the British Socialist Party whose application to affiliate had recently been accepted. There were also six candidates standing for University seats.[37]

This left 163 Labour candidates sponsored by trade unions, including two from the Teachers who were not affiliated to the party. In addition a number of prominent trade unionists were sponsored by divisional parties, including J. R. Leslie of the Shop Assistants, Peter Tevenan of the Municipal Employees and Walter Citrine of the Electricians; and David Kirkwood was sponsored by the Dumbarton Burghs party, but included in the Engineers' list of sponsored candidates during the course of the campaign.

Several trade union Members of Parliament had been under attack in their constituencies for their outspoken patriotism, including Barnes, Duncan, Hodge, Roberts, and Thorne. Duncan was defeated in a local ballot conducted in his constituency, but subsequently gave sufficient assurances to retain the nomination. Similarly, Hodge managed to save himself by undertaking to resign from the government. Thorne was rejected by South West Ham, but was able to persuade the neighbouring consituency of Plaistow to adopt him instead. Barnes and Roberts decided to throw in their lot with the coalition, as did two other Labour ministers, Parker and Wardle. All four were rewarded with the coupon. The other four ex-ministers, Brace, Clynes, Hodge, and Walsh, fought the election as Labour candidates.

An officially-sponsored candidate of the General Workers, Jack Jones, whose views on the war had been much the same as Thorne's, stood for another of the West Ham constituencies, Silvertown. The local party refused to endorse him, although they were unable to find a candidate to run against him. He therefore stood as an 'Independent Labour' candidate. At least two of the twenty-eight candidates put forward by the National Democratic and Labour Party were sponsored by their trade unions: Eldred Hallas of the Birmingham Gasworkers and John Ward of the Navvies. Havelock Wilson stood as an independent with the support of his union. There were also several independent

[37] These figures are taken from the Labour Party's *Annual Report*, 1919, Appendix VI.

candidates of the extreme left, including four put forward by the Clyde Workers Committee.

The largest group among the trade union candidates was, as usual, from the Miners who sponsored fifty-one. For the first time, second place went to the Engineers, with eighteen candidates including Kirkwood. Next came cotton, with ten candidates sponsored by the United Textile Factory Workers Association; the General Workers with eight, including Jones; the Railwaymen and the Railway Clerks with six apiece; and the Boilermakers with five.

One of the reconstruction measures already put through was the Representation of the People Act, 1918. For men, adult suffrage replaced household suffrage; and for the first time women were allowed to vote, provided that they were over thirty and either they or their husbands were qualified, as householders, to vote in local elections. So far as the Labour Party was concerned, the effects of these two changes tended to cancel each other out. Under male household suffrage before the war about two-thirds of adult males overall had the vote, but only 50 to 55 per cent of the working class, so that Labour could expect to gain dramatically from the change to adult male suffrage,[38] as it did from the drastic reduction of plural voting. On the other hand many electoral studies have found that women tend to vote for rightwing parties more than men do, and that the proportion of leftwing voters tends to diminish with age. These two factors, together with the class bias of the women's household qualification, make it virtually certain that the party drew disproportionately few votes from women. Another novel element in this 'khaki' election was the large number of servicemen entitled to vote. Although special arrangements were made, and the count was delayed for a fortnight to allow time for postal votes from the Continent to come in, only one serviceman in four cast his vote, suggesting 'that a large number of men never received either the addresses of the candidates or the ballot papers'.[39]

As Henderson feared, the result was a triumph for Lloyd George. A large part was played in the campaign by notions of German war guilt, and how the Germans should be made to expiate it. Against his better judgment, Lloyd George was driven to demand that Germany should

---

[38] Volume I (pp. 269–70) estimated the prewar proportion of adult males with the vote at 60 per cent. This figure has been shown to be too low by Matthew, McKibbin and Kay whose calculations indicate that the correct figure is probably rather more than 65 per cent. However, the estimate in Volume I of 50–55 per cent of working class adult males with the vote at that time still seems to be valid. The class bias in the prewar franchise must therefore have been greater than suggested in Volume I. No estimates exist for whatever class bias may have remained among males in 1918, but since by 1921 'the English adult male enfranchisement level was 94.9 per cent' (Matthew et al., p. 731), it cannot by then have amounted to much.

[39] Labour Party, 1919, p. 29.

pay the full cost of the war, and the Kaiser be brought to trial.[40] For their part Labour candidates who were not associated with the Independent Labour Party or the Union of Democratic Control drew as little attention as possible to Labour's declared views on peacemaking, but they could hardly disown them. However, the campaign centred on the record and personality of Lloyd George, the man who had 'won the war' and was now promising 'a land fit for heroes to live in'.

The low proportion of servicemen voting, and probably also the apparent failure of the newly-enfranchised women to take anything like full advantage of their rights, help to account for an extremely low poll. In Ireland a new party, Sinn Fein, swept the board with 73 seats to 7 held by the traditional Nationalists; and set up their own parliament in Dublin. This reduced the effective size of the House of Commons to 634. With a little less than half the popular vote, the coalition, including the National Democratic and Labour Party, took 478 seats. Within the coalition were 335 Conservatives, who therefore had an overall majority even without the forty-eight other successful Unionists who for one reason or another had not received the coupon. The Asquithian Liberals won only 28 seats, and none of their leaders was returned. The Labour Party, with almost a quarter of the votes cast and 57 seats, claimed to be the official opposition, although privy councillors from other groups successfully established their right to share the opposition front bench. Immediately after the election three Members who had been elected as independent candidates—Jack Jones, Josiah Wedgwood and the solitary Co-operative candidate—applied for the Labour whip, bringing the total to sixty. Shortly afterwards Eldred Hallas was also admitted, making sixty-one.[41]

No less than fifty of the Labour Members were sponsored by trade unions. Exactly half of these were Miners, five from the General Workers, four from cotton, and two each from the London Dockers and the Steel Smelters, who retained a separate affiliation to the party after their merger with other steel unions. Twelve more unions, including the Engineers and the Railwaymen, supplied one each. However, despite these gains, the new parliamentary party was as short of leaders as the Asquithian Liberals. Hardie was dead, and both MacDonald and Snowden had been defeated. Only three candidates sponsored by the Independent Labour Party had been returned—William Graham, Neil McLean and Ben Spoor.[42] More serious still, Henderson, who had

[40] Barnes was said to be the first politician to assert that he should be hanged.

[41] Here and elsewhere in this volume figures of election results are drawn from Butler and Freeman, *British Political Facts, 1900–1960*, except where other evidence indicates the need for corrections.

[42] These results reveal the extent to which association with pacifism was an electoral handicap in 1918, for none of these three had been a prominent critic of the war.

moved from Barnard Castle to East Ham South, was another casualty. Four of the wartime Labour ministers were included in the new government, with Barnes in the 'inner' cabinet. Clynes was unquestionably the most capable and experienced Labour parliamentarian who survived, but the colourless Adamson was re-elected as leader.

The immediate future clearly lay with Lloyd George and the Conservatives, but Labour could afford to be cautiously optimistic. The party's representation at Westminster was now two-thirds higher than in 1914, and nineteen seats had been won in direct competition with Liberal candidates. Moreover, in seventy-nine other constituencies Labour had come second, in all cases ahead of the Liberal. Electorally, if not yet ideologically, Lib–Labism was dead. Should Lloyd George fail to satisfy the aspirations for a better world he had so capably exploited, Labour might hope to be the principal beneficiary of that failure.

There was of course always the possibility of a Liberal revival, and in 1918 many people assumed this would one day occur. But the split between Asquith and Lloyd George had wrought havoc with the Liberal Party machine, whereas the Labour Party, as reorganised by Henderson, promised to be capable of extracting further gains from the Representation of the People Act, whose full effects had still to be realised—especially given the extremely low poll in 1918, and the high proportion of trade unionists there must have been among the newly-enfranchised.

7

Reconstruction and Direct Action

Reconstruction

THE coalition government had been well aware that they would be faced by grave and complex labour problems as soon as the war was over; and they had been making preparations to handle them. Committees had been sitting to examine them; reports had been written; plans had been made; and, on some issues, decisions had been taken before the armistice. The Whitley proposals were already being put into effect.

The most pressing problem was demobilisation of the armed forces and munitions workers. Their numbers had been built up over four years. They were now expected to fall to near peacetime establishment within a few months. It had already been decided that members of the forces would receive a month's leave and a bounty varying with rank and service, and that a 'donation' benefit—a non-contributory unemployment benefit—would be payable for a period thereafter. Even allowing for inflation the rates of benefit—£1.45 for a man, £1.25 for a woman, with 30p for the first child and 15p for other children—were far more generous than the prewar 35p a week unemployment insurance benefit. They were intended to provide maintenance, not merely a contribution to assist the thrifty. A similar benefit had been recommended for munitions workers, but no decision had been taken before the armistice. It was then agreed that the donation benefit should be extended to all health insurance contributors, so that, 'broadly speaking, all civil workers were counted as war workers and were eligible for out-of-work donation'.[1] The only difference between civilians and the forces was that benefit was initially made available to the former for six months, in which applicants were entitled to thirteen weekly payments, and the latter were entitled to twenty-six payments over the course of a year.

Other preoccupations were that heavy unemployment might present employers with an opportunity to cut wages; that both employers and unions had made it clear that they did not want compulsory arbitration and the ban on strikes and lockouts to continue; and that the government had promised that prewar practices would be restored. Churchill had argued strongly in cabinet that this pledge should not be kept on the grounds that restoration would severely hamper industrial

[1] Pigou, p. 29.

efficiency, but he was overruled. On 13 November the principal unions, whether signatories of the Treasury Agreement or not, were called together to hear from the Prime Minister that a draft bill on restoration was ready, along with a bill to prevent wage reductions. A joint committee was appointed to consider them. Restoration was a complicated issue which would take time, but almost immediate approval was given to the Wages (Temporary Regulation) Bill which became law on 21 November. Wage rates in force on 11 November were to be maintained for six months unless altered by agreement or by arbitration. The right to strike and lockout was restored as it had stood before the war, and compulsory arbitration was terminated, except as a means of determining disagreements about the rates guaranteed by the Act, with the Committee on Production replaced by an Interim Court of Arbitration.

So far there was no serious difference of opinion on what should be done. Controversy arose over the best means of ensuring that jobs would be made available for the millions of men and women who would come on to the labour market. On the one hand the trade unions, the Labour Party and a good many of the planners were in favour of keeping the national factories in government hands; arranging a gradual transition to production for commercial sale; and retaining controls over materials and prices as a means of guiding the transition to a peacetime economy. On the other hand, the cabinet and a majority in the relevant committees believed that private enterprise must provide the great majority of the new jobs, and such measures would prevent it from achieving its full potential. Controls had proved their worth in wartime when the nation's energies had been directed towards a single overriding goal, but they could not handle a situation in which the aim must be to meet the needs of individual consumers both at home and abroad. On Armistice Day the Ministry of Munitions instructed contracting firms to release all workers who wanted to leave, and to cut production by stopping overtime and piecework. Controls, including those over iron and steel, were terminated as soon as sufficient supplies were available, and a large number had gone by the end of the year. Nearly all the remainder were withdrawn in the early months of 1919. With few exceptions the national factories were returned to their prewar owners or put up for sale.

The demobilisation plans provided that men from the forces should be released according to the importance of their jobs and their industries in the process of reconversion; but demobilisation did not start for a month after the armistice, and even then it was slow. Eric Geddes took charge just before Christmas, and greatly accelerated release within the existing industrial priorities, but too late to allay unrest among servicemen.

Units rioted at Folkstone and Dover. When Churchill took over the War Office in January, many units were close to mutiny. Some were already refusing to obey orders. He switched from industrial priority to release by length of service, and increased service pay. Even so the situation was not immediately brought under control. Riots and mutinies continued for several weeks, in the navy as well as the army; but with accelerated demobilisation the difficulties diminished. Despite some protests and demonstrations from munitions workers, civilian demobilisation proceeded more smoothly.

It is impossible to give figures for the numbers of unemployed in this period. The index compiled from trade union returns, usually a fair guide, was almost entirely confined to skilled workers, and took no account of women and little of servicemen. It rose from 0.4 per cent at the end of October 1918 to a peak of 2.8 per cent in February 1919. The numbers of those receiving donation benefit reached a peak in April 1919 when the figures were 619,000 men (380,000 of them ex-servicemen) and 474,000 women. However, these latter figures give an exaggerated impression of the volume of unemployment. Probably a considerable proportion of the women, and some of the men, had no intention of taking up paid employment after their entitlement to donation benefit had run out. Civilian entitlement to benefit was extended for a second period of six months, and servicemen's entitlement to two years in all. October 1919 was therefore the last month in which benefit was paid to civilian workers. There were then 135,000 of them, 101,000 men and 34,000 women, in all less than 1 per cent of the employed population; and 344,000 ex-servicemen and women. By this time, therefore, the transition had been largely accomplished, and the government's gamble that the jobs could be provided by private enterprise had so far paid off. Well over three million ex-servicemen had been demobilised—although some of them were still on post-demobilisation leave.

Meanwhile the Wages (Temporary Regulation) Act had been continued for a second period of six months. The drafting of a bill on the restoration of prewar practices ran into both procedural and substantive difficulties. Firstly, the Engineers would not serve on the committee appointed at the conference held on 13 November 1918. They demanded that the restoration of engineering practices should be discussed by the engineering unions alone. Secondly, many of the early changes had not been properly recorded, if at all. The Engineers had set up a special department for the purpose early in 1916, and the Ministry of Munitions had improved their recording system later the same year, but the backlog had not been wholly made up. In addition there were problems about enforcement. Consequently the Restoration of Pre-War

Practices Act was not passed until August 1919. Even then its provisions were to be enforced only for twelve months and by a maximum fine of £25 a day as long as the offence was not rectified. Nevertheless there was remarkably little trouble in its application, and a great deal appears to have been accomplished before the Act was passed.

At first difficulties were reported in several engineering centres, including Birmingham, Leicester and London, mostly over the retention of dilutees while craftsmen were unemployed, but as early as February 1919 the Engineers' Halifax organiser reported in their journal that many employers were causing no difficulty over dilutees 'because they themselves have readily dispensed with them as bad-paying units', and this seems to have been the common experience. There were a few strikes over the issue, but nearly all the disputes which arose were successfully settled by local or central conferences. The general unions made a number of complaints, but in June 1919 the executive committee of their federation decided not to oppose the bill, but 'to seek a Conference with the skilled unions with a view to persuading them not to operate the Act harshly against our members'.

This outcome is the more surprising because the management committee of the Engineering Employers Federation had in April 1918 received a report from a sub-committee dealing with postwar problems which told them that the 'only course' was to negotiate a new agreement which would 'absolve either party from their obligations'. Why, then, was there so little trouble? The answer is that the extent of the problem had been greatly exaggerated. The Engineers had successfully resisted the extension of dilution to private work; and there had been relatively little dilution even on munitions in the more skilled engineering departments and in marine engineering and shipbuilding generally. In addition, 'most of the forms of dilution introduced during the War . . . were not suited for direct and immediate application to the forms of normal production to which employers reverted when their contracts for munitions came to an end.'[2] The problem was further eased by the readiness of many women to give up paid employment, and the strong demand for labour in other industries.

However, the transition from wartime to peacetime employment was no more than a preliminary to the long-term task of reconstruction, which was not to restore Britain as it had been before the war, but to build a better Britain. The plans of the reconstructionists to that end touched on almost every corner of the social and economic life of the country, but those affecting three major areas were of particular importance to the unions: the social services; the continuing regulation

[2] Cole, *Trade Unionism and Munitions*, p. 196.

of certain industries; and proposals for improving the conduct of industrial relations.

The Education Act of 1918 had only an indirect effect on the unions other than those of the teachers, but it went a considerable distance towards meeting the aspirations of the unions and the Labour Party by giving 'strong encouragement and greater power' to the local education authorities to 'develop a comprehensive system of education from the nursery school to the evening class'.[3] It increased the central government grant to 50 per cent or more of expenditure; made education to the age of fourteen universal, and empowered the authorities either to raise it by a further year or to provide day continuation schools for one day a week for two years.

The coverage of unemployment insurance had been extended in 1916 by an Act which roughly doubled the number of contributors to almost four million, and would have covered more but for its unpopularity with some groups of workers. All munitions workers were included, but with provision for the exemption of trades to whom its application could be shown to be unnecessary. Because its requirement of six waiting days before qualifying for benefit meant that it was of little value to trades which dealt with decreased demand for their products by short-time working, cotton and wool, among other industries, insisted on being exempted. Workers in certain other industries were included without provision for exemption, but when both employers and workers in footwear, which was one of the industries concerned, refused to pay contributions, their industry had to be excluded by retrospective legislation. This fiasco was one of the reasons why a general scheme was not ready at the end of the war. However, donation benefit was almost universal, with the promise of a permanent general scheme to follow. The promise was redeemed by the Unemployment Insurance Act of 1920 whose provisions came into force in November of that year. Agriculture, domestic service, and most of the public sector were excluded. As before, contributions were levied on worker, employer, and the state, with the rates nearly double those of 1911. Benefits were slightly more than doubled, at 75p a week for men and 60p for women. There was no allowance for children. These rates emphasised that, unlike the donation scheme, the Act was not intended to provide full maintenance. With the experience of 1916 in mind the draftsmen reduced the waiting period to three days and allowed broken spells of unemployment to be treated as a continuous period.

For trade unionists the new rates were minima. As under the 1911 Act, trade unions were permitted to administer the scheme for their

[3] Pollard, p. 265.

members, provided they paid an additional minimum benefit of their own. Because the 1920 scheme had a far wider coverage, this facility attracted not only the skilled unions which had long provided unemployment benefit, but many others besides. Among the general unions, the Workers Union, which already offered an unemployment benefit to its members, was now joined by the General Workers, the London Dockers, and the National Amalgamated Union of Labour. In response to the prevailing sentiment in favour of industrial self-government the Act also provided for industries which devised a satisfactory scheme of their own to contract out of the statutory arrangements; and unions and employers in several industries began to discuss what they might be able to do in this respect.

The unions wanted higher benefits, but otherwise they were well satisfied by the Act except for an amendment, moved on behalf of the friendly societies, to permit them to administer it on the same terms as the unions. The argument was that this merely balanced the right of the unions to administer health insurance through their approved societies. The Conservative backbenchers took considerable pleasure in allowing the clause to go through, and the unions rose to the bait. The Parliamentary Committee protested, and a special meeting of Congress recommended that affiliated unions 'refuse to have anything to do with the Act, unless the objectionable clause is removed'.[4] But this was too fatuous a decision for anyone to take seriously. In the event no friendly society took advantage of the provision.

Housing had been one of the early concerns of the reconstructionists. A committee chaired by Seebohm Rowntree had predicted a postwar shortage of 300,000 working class houses. Working class tenants could not be expected to pay the full rents which would be required to cover current building costs of houses of a reasonable standard. They proposed therefore that houses should be provided either by the government or by local authorities, and subsidised, with provision for control of building materials and compulsory purchase of land. The need for action by the state was generally accepted, all the more so because estimates of the housing shortage increased, and it was made more acute by the decision in 1919 to continue rent control on houses built up to that date. However, three damaging alterations were made to the original plans. Firstly, it was decided that, instead of paying all 'abnormal' costs, the government should meet all costs over the proceeds of a given rate, thus providing no incentive to efficiency for the local authorities which were to be responsible for building the houses. Secondly, the carefully-designed plans for control of building materials were scrapped along with other material controls. Thirdly, the

---

[4] Trades Union Congress, 1920, p. 117.

proposals for compulsory purchase of land were severely weakened. The local authorities were therefore required to build houses to meet working class needs, at a time when the building labour force had been severely depleted by the war, and stocks of most materials were in short supply, in competition with a huge backlog of demand for construction of almost every kind, with the help of an unlimited subsidy.

The Housing and Town Planning Act of 1919, nevertheless, laid down principles which have applied to the provision of public housing ever since, and which were to play a substantial part in meeting the shortage of housing during the interwar period. It became an obligation on local authorities to survey and meet their housing needs; the obligation was general, and not confined to slum clearance which had been the main objective of local authority building before the war; and the authorities were obliged to take account of the need for town planning. However, nothing was done to remedy the defects of the current scheme. Addison did his best to hustle things along, first as President of the Local Government Board and then as the first Minister of Health. Progress was slow, and there were severe shortages of materials and labour. Towards the end of 1920 he turned his attention towards persuading the building unions into a dilution scheme to meet the labour shortage.

The industries chiefly affected by proposals for continuing regulation were agriculture, transport, electricity supply, and coal. A Royal Commission, including several trade unionists, was appointed in 1919 to consider the future of agriculture, and charged to produce an interim report on cereal prices as soon as possible. Twelve members wanted price guarantees to continue, with a period of four years' notice to give farmers time to adjust if and when the guarantees were to be terminated; eleven members thought guarantees were unnecessary, since they did not expect prices to fall; and one member signed his own report. The government decided to adopt the recommendations of the first report, at least for the time being, and the Agriculture Act of 1920 retained both the price guarantees and the system of agricultural wages boards on which the farmworkers' trade unions depended so heavily.

In 1918 a Select Committee on Transport reported that 'the organisation of the transport agencies of the country—and particularly of the railways—cannot be allowed to return to its pre-war position'; and that unification of the railway companies was needed; but left open the question whether unification should be achieved by amalgamation or nationalisation.[5] Another reconstruction committee recommended central control of electricity generation. The government proposed to deal with both issues in the Ways and Communications Bill which was

[5] Pratt, p. 1118.

introduced in February 1919 to create a new government department to take over all existing government powers in relation to transport and the supply of electricity. The government also tested the water with a clause empowering the Minister to acquire by order the whole or part of any transport undertaking. This was widely interpreted as a device to authorise the Minister to nationalise the railways, and the response in the House of Commons was emphatically hostile. The clause was withdrawn by Eric Geddes, 'in view of the fact that there is undoubtedly a strong feeling in the House against that procedure'.[6] Before it became law as the Ministry of Transport Act, the bill also lost the clauses dealing with electricity.

However, another clause, empowering the Minister to take over the wartime powers of control over the railways for two years pending 'the consideration and formulation of the policy to be pursued', was allowed to stand. Proposals were published in June 1920. The companies were to be compulsorily amalgamated. At that stage seven new companies were envisaged, and their boards were to include a minority of representatives of the employees. Subsequently the number of companies was reduced to four and the unions rejected the offer of representation on the boards. The Railwaymen's executive explained in their annual report for 1921 that if they 'had accepted minority representation on private boards of directors we would undoubtedly have prejudiced the Labour Party in its policy of nationalisation'. They were more concerned to make sure that the Railway Act 1921, which sanctioned the amalgamations, should also give statutory authority to the machinery for national negotiations which they had negotiated in 1919 with representatives of the companies, and that the functions of this machinery should 'embrace all questions arising out of the men's employment, including questions of discipline and management'. Amalgamation also meant that the economic prospects of the companies were sufficiently similar to allow them to take over the responsibility for paying the standard rates of pay, which the unions had by this time negotiated with the government.

Provision for the future of coalmining raised greater problems. Early in 1919 the matter was referred to a Commission of Inquiry, chaired by Mr Justice Sankey, which was even more divided in its recommendations than the Royal Commission on Agriculture. There were four final reports, one signed by six members, another by five, and two from individual members, one of them the chairman. His report and the one signed by six members both advocated forms of nationalisation, which had been strongly pressed on the commission by the Miners Federation. However, given the reaction of the Conservative majority in the House

[6] *Hansard*, 17 March 1919, col. 1781.

of Commons when they suspected that the Ways and Communications Bill might provide a cover for railway nationalisation, there was no chance that a bill to nationalise the coal mines would pass even if the government chose to introduce it. On the other hand, the government could not hand the mines back to the owners at this stage. The Miners would not have it, and the owners did not want it. Sir Robert Redmayne, the chief inspector of mines, summarised the owners' views as they might have put them to the government:

We have, at your request, worked the mines without looking too far ahead, so as to give you as much coal as possible during the war period. You have granted advance upon advance to the workmen—wages which, except at the present high price of export coal, we could not afford to pay, and some collieries (which owing to their geographical position have no export trade) cannot in fact pay. We say when you hand over the collieries to us, see to it that conditions are on all fours with those existing prior to control.[7]

The government therefore produced a scheme in August 1919 which had much in common with their subsequent proposals for the railways. The colliery companies were to be amalgamated into district groups on whose boards the Miners were to be represented. The Miners Federation rejected this scheme with contempt, and continued to campaign for nationalisation; and the owners were equally hostile. In June 1920, therefore, the government introduced a Ministry of Mines Bill which established the mines department of the Board of Trade on a permanent footing and continued the wartime coal control, due to expire at the end of August, for another year. Part II provided for a system of joint pit and district committees and joint area boards which were to handle negotiations and also make recommendations on issues such as safety, health, welfare, and output. There was also to be a joint national board, but it was made clear that wages were to be adjusted area by area. The bill was passed in August, but by that time the annual conference of the Miners Federation had resolved not to operate it. The future of the coalmining industry was therefore still unresolved at the end of 1920.

The steps taken for the improvement of industrial relations consisted of further applications of the Whitley recommendations. The Industrial Courts Act of 1919 replaced the Interim Court of Arbitration by a permanent Industrial Court. Access to the court was only by agreement between the parties, and its awards carried no legal sanction. The Minister of Labour might also appoint Courts of Inquiry to investigate the circumstances and causes of an industrial dispute without the consent of the parties and with power to compel witnesses to attend and

[7] Redmayne, pp. 212–13.

give evidence under oath. Their reports were to be presented to parliament. Since the Minister of Labour was already empowered under the 1896 Act to inquire into disputes and to provide conciliation and arbitration services, these new provisions were intended primarily to emphasise the importance of those functions; and thus to ensure that public opinion and the public interest were brought to bear more fully in industrial disputes.

More important was the continued progress in establishing Joint Industrial Councils. Twenty had been formed by the end of 1918. A further thirty-two followed in 1919 including cement; electrical cable-making; electrical contracting; electricity supply; flour milling; gas supply; heating, ventilating, and domestic engineering; quarrying; road haulage; tramways; water supply; and wool. Next year the pace fell off; sixteen councils were set up, mainly in small industries but also including one for the port transport industry. In addition a number of Interim Industrial Reconstruction Committees were established in industries where it was considered that circumstances were favourable for rapid development towards a Joint Industrial Council, but the trade unions and employers' associations were not yet strong enough to support it. Twelve of these interim bodies ultimately became full councils.

The Joint Industrial Councils included several in national and local government. In March 1919 the Heath Committee issued their recommendations on the application of the Whitley reports to the non-industrial civil service. They proposed a national council for the whole service, together with individual councils for each department, which should concern themselves with 'utilising the ideas and experience of the staff', and also with education, training, office machinery, and organisation. On salaries and conditions of employment, however, they were to be concerned only with 'consideration of general principles', since 'the State is the ultimate employer' and 'Heads of Departments . . . have not the freedom of decision in regard to wages and conditions enjoyed by the private employer'.[8] On 8 April ministers and senior officials met union representatives to discuss the report. The unions moved the rejection of the whole report except a paragraph proposing a National Provisional Joint Committee to draw up a detailed scheme; and the resolution was accepted by Austen Chamberlain as Chancellor of the Exchequer. On 28 May the committee reported in favour of substituting 'determination' of general principles for 'consideration'; decisions were to 'be arrived at by agreement of the two sides', and 'reported to the Cabinet, and thereupon shall become operative'.[9] The national council was not to act as a court of appeal on issues which the departments could

---

[8] *Report*, pp. 2, 6.   [9] *Report*, pp. 4, 5.

not settle, but to deal with issues affecting more than one department. Departmental questions, including the pay of departmental classes, such as the majority of postal and Inland Revenue employees, were to be settled by the departmental councils. Appeal was to the Civil Service Arbitration Board. There were also to be local joint councils to deal with local issues within each department. Most of the rest of the year was taken up with forming the eighty departmental councils required to cover all sections of the service.

The prewar objections of the local authorities to any collective regulation of wages and conditions going beyond the boundaries of a single authority had been eroded by the need for frequent wage adjustments during the war, and no constitutional objection was made by the authorities to joining with private undertakings in gas, electricity, and water supply, and in the tramways, to establish Joint Industrial Councils to conduct national wage negotiations. Local authority non trading services were a different matter. During the war a number of authorities in Lancashire and Cheshire had instituted common negotiations with the unions covering the manual employees in these services, and in 1919 their example served as a pattern for setting up 'provincial' joint councils, in which the authorities in England and Wales came together, region by region, to negotiate with the unions. The national council, on which the local authority associations formed the employers' side, was concerned only with the settlement of disputes which the provincial councils could not resolve. Even this appeared to some authorities as too great a degree of centralisation, and in 1921 the national council was reconstituted to include elected representatives of the employers' sides of the provincial councils.

The National Association of Local Government Officers were more ambitious than the unions representing manual local authority employees. After months of negotiation they persuaded the employers' associations to establish a Joint Industrial Council for Local Authorities Administrative Technical and Clerical Staffs in February 1920. The employers wanted to leave the settlement of salaries to provincial agreement for the time being, but the union insisted on national salary scales. At first they asked for the scales recently agreed for the civil service, but later settled for lower scales which were nevertheless 'far better than most local government officers were getting'.[10] These scales were circulated to local authorities in the 'confident hope' that they would adopt them; but most of them did not. Then the associations began to withdraw from the national council, first the Urban District and the Rural District Associations in October, then the County Councils Association in November, and finally the Association of

[10] Spoor, p. 84.

Municipal Corporations in January 1921; by April the union acknowledged that the national council had ceased to exist. A national council in
Scotland had already fallen by the wayside.

All was not lost, however; five provincial councils had been
established in England and Wales. Two of them also disappeared, one in
the West Midlands and the other in Northumberland and Durham, but
three survived: those in Lancashire and Cheshire, the West Riding, and
the City of London. They continued to settle salary scales and
conditions of employment, and a number of authorities in other parts of
the country negotiated individually with union officers.

The teachers' unions had more success. After negotiations with the
Association of Education Committees and the unions, the Minister of
Education, Fisher, set up standing joint committees of representatives
of the two sides, which differed from most Joint Industrial Councils in
having an independent chairman, Lord Burnham, who gave his name to
the new bodies. Since the Minister already had power to prescribe
national minimum scales for teachers, there could be no objections on
the grounds of interference with the sovereignty of individual education
authorities, and the Burnham Committees were asked to draw up new
minimum scales as quickly as possible.

For industries in which voluntary organisation was insufficient to
support a Joint Industrial Council, or even an Interim Industrial
Reconstruction Committee, the Whitley Committee had recommended
the establishment of Trade Boards; and the Trade Boards Act 1918 had
made provision for this to be done by changing the criterion for setting
up a board. It was no longer to be 'exceptionally low' wages. Instead, the
Minister of Labour was empowered to set up a board where 'no
adequate machinery exists for the effective regulation of wages
throughout the trade', although he was also to have regard 'to the rate of
wages prevailing in the trade, or in any part of the trade'. Even with the
considerable growth of organisation on both sides of industry during the
war, there were many industries which came within the scope of this
new criterion, but progress was slow. The Ministry had to carry out
extensive inquiries not only into the state of organisation but also into
levels of pay. However, ten boards were set up in the second half of 1919
and twenty-three more in 1920, making the total coverage about three
million employees, most of them women, and 300,000 employers.
Among the more important industries covered by the new boards were
boot and shoe repairing, jute and flax manufacture, laundries, milk
distribution, tobacco manufacture, and several further branches of the
clothing trade in addition to tailoring.

The distributive trades also fitted the new criterion admirably, and in
March 1919 the Ministry convened a conference to discuss the institution

of a board in the grocery trade. A further conference of unions and employers' associations in May proposed that there should be a single board for all branches of distribution with provision for any trade which established adequate voluntary machinery to be excluded; but they were unable to convince the Ministry. In November plans were announced for separate boards in each section of distribution, perhaps thirty or forty of them in all. The *Shop Assistant* of 22 November asserted that this would create 'friction, annoyance and disappointment' since it would not provide one 'rock bottom price for labour'. In July 1920 two Grocery and Provisions Boards were at last established. During the autumn proposals for minimum rates of pay were submitted to the Minister, but he delayed giving his approval until the end of the year and beyond.

The remaining aspect of reconstruction which closely affected trade unions was overall economic policy. In this respect the proposals of the reconstructionists had been piecemeal. They had made plans for individual industries, plans for the social services, plans for industrial relations, plans for releasing materials controls, plans for finance, and plans for overseas trade; but no overall plan. The initial approach of the government was expansionist. Industry was encouraged to absorb demobilised soldiers and munitions workers as rapidly as possible; meanwhile those without jobs were given a generous unemployment benefit; and a number of ambitious reconstruction schemes were endorsed and financed. The pound, which had been pegged at 4.76 dollars during the war with the help of loans from the American government, was allowed to float, and naturally drifted downwards. Bank rate was maintained at 5 per cent. The rapid resumption of trade and the release of stocks brought a fall in prices through the first half of 1919; but they resumed their upward trend in the autumn.

By November the cabinet were scared. Government indebtedness was unprecedented and still rising. There was a substantial adverse balance of payments. The pound had fallen to four dollars. They decided that the time for retrenchment had come. Bank rate was raised to 6 per cent and a search was made for economies in government expenditure. In April 1920 bank rate was raised to 7 per cent and further economies were sought. By the autumn there were plenty of signs that the boom was over. The trade union unemployment index, which had stood at 0.9 per cent in April, rose to 2.2 per cent in September, and 6 per cent in December. The cost of living index peaked in November, but wholesale prices had already been falling for some months.

It is unlikely that either the earlier policy of expansion or the subsequent retrenchment had much influence on the economic downturn. This was primarily due to a world economic crisis from which the government had no means of isolating Britain. What is more important for the history of British trade unions over these two years is that for most of the time the high level of demand permitted the government to pursue policies in relation to industrial relations generally, to the affairs of individual industries, and to social welfare which were, on balance, highly favourable to the unions.

Collective Bargaining, 1919–20

The reform and extension of the machinery of industrial relations were primarily due to the government reconstructionists. For the most part they had the support of the trade unions, and in many instances their enthusiastic co-operation. But reform could not have been carried through in the face of determined resistance from employers; and in fact many employers agreed with the reconstructionists in envisaging a greatly increased role for trade unions and collective bargaining in the postwar world. In 1916 a new national organisation of employers, the Federation of British Industries, had been formed, absorbing the old Employers Parliamentary Committee. In July 1916 the federation had brought out a pamphlet on *Reconstruction* for private circulation. Noting that 'Trade and Labour are vitally and inextricably inter-dependent', its authors insisted that employers must not give 'the impression . . . that there is the slightest intention of organising Capital to the detriment of Labour'. To plan the transition to peacetime production they envisaged a network of joint committees for trades and districts, subordinate to a central joint committee. The work of these committees could lead on to 'the joint discussion of the controversial points connected with wages, Trade Union restrictions, and the like' so that 'a basis of negotiation . . . will have been reached'.

The federation was also mainly responsible for founding the National Alliance of Employers and Employed. On 11 December 1916 *The Times* reported a meeting of the alliance, with the federation's leading figures on the platform, which proposed that the government should set up a Central Statutory Board to oversee postwar industrial reconstruction. One-third of its members were to represent employers, one-third the unions, and the rest were to come from the relevant government departments.

Not all employers accepted the federation's lead. Its membership consisted mainly of individual firms and of associations concerned with commercial matters. The big employers' organisations remained aloof. Allan Smith of the Engineering Employers insisted that his organisation 'could not join any body which embraced a Commercial as well as a Labour policy'.[11] In its first annual report in November 1917 the

[11] Federation of British Industries, *Organisation Sub-Committee Minutes*, 5 December 1916.

federation, therefore, drew back, asserting that 'it has always been the declared policy of the Federation not to interfere with the work of the existing Trade Associations established for the purpose of negotiating direct labour questions'. An Employers Advisory Council was formed to embrace the Federation of British Industries and the major employers' organisations outside it 'for the purpose of consultation and discussion', but it soon fell into disuse.

However, it does not follow that the members of the independent employers' organisations rejected the approach to industrial relations advocated by the Federation of British Industries. The attitudes of employers in industries with established bargaining procedures were revealed in their approach to the postwar demands of the unions for improvements in pay and conditions. In a number of instances they were ready to make substantial concessions. On 25 April 1918 the management committee of the Engineering Employers Federation received a sub-committee report on postwar problems. They were told that engineering had no need for Joint Industrial Councils on the Whitley model, since central and local conferences already fulfilled the functions proposed for those bodies. However, despite the refusal of the federation to countenance works committees in their recent negotiations over the recognition of shop stewards, the report now suggested that such committees might be acceptable—with limited functions. National negotiations on wages should be maintained, and the wartime system of periodic references to arbitration continued. 'Overtime, nightshift, Sunday, Holiday and other allowances should as far as possible be standardised on a national basis.' A reduction of the working week would 'have to be faced' but forty-eight hours on a one-break basis should be the 'maximum concession'.

On this last issue the Federation of Engineering and Shipbuilding Trades had put in a claim for a forty-four hour week in June 1918. Since the Shipbuilding Employers Federation were faced with a similar claim, both groups of employers entered into negotiations jointly before the armistice. Pleading that they could not get their members to accept a forty-eight hour week as a sufficient concession, the unions pushed the employers down to forty-seven, on a one-break system, and promised in return to do their best to maintain output. The agreement was to operate from 1 January 1919. Hard on the heels of the engineering and shipbuilding workers came the railway unions. On the day after the armistice was signed, Bromley, the secretary of the Locomotive Engineers and Firemen, reminded the president of the Board of Trade of the government's promise to give sympathetic consideration to shortening the working week when the war was over. Stanley tried to postpone the matter until after the election, but the unions would have none of it, and an agreement to introduce an eight-hour working day on 1 February 1919 was signed with the Locomotive Engineers on 2 December, and with the Railwaymen a few days later.

From these beginnings it was inevitable that reductions in the working week should spread throughout the great majority of industries and services. In some industries there were special problems, for example where shiftwork was widespread. Negotiations covering all sections of the iron and steel industry began shortly after the engineering and shipbuilding settlement. The principle of an eight-hour working day was agreed, leaving each section of the industry to work out the details and report to a central committee. Since, for most of the industry outside Wales, the reduction was from a twelve-hour shift to an eight-hour shift, the issues of maintaining pay and production were of special importance. In most other industries where the reduction was from between fifty and fifty-six hours a week to forty-eight or forty-seven, the weekly time rate of wages was maintained and employers hoped that output per hour would increase to offset at least part of the cost of the change. In steel the proportion of pay and output at stake was far larger. The employers would have to bring in a third shift to maintain continuous production over six days in the week. It was, therefore, agreed in the heavy steel section that existing wages should be maintained only for the lower-paid and mostly timeworking employees; for the rest a reduction was to apply to tonnage rates starting at gross earnings of £4.87$\frac{1}{2}$ a week and rising to one-third at £11.50 and above. Pugh commented that:

The clear implication was that output would increase under the eight-hour shift. . . . That is precisely what happened once the works adjusted themselves to new conditions, and to the mutual advantage of workmen and employers.[12]

For most steelworkers the working week was now less than forty-eight hours because of the continued operation of the 'customary restrictions' on weekend work.

The adverse reaction of their members to their forty-seven-hour working week agreement drove the engineering and shipbuilding unions back to their employers in the summer of 1919 with a claim for forty-four hours. Allan Smith told them 'no data you can get at this moment will justify the demand that you have made. You have not allowed yourselves to prove the value of the 47-hour week.' In September it was agreed that a joint committee should 'investigate the economic relation of production to hours of work' in 'shipbuilding and engineering . . . in this and other countries'.[13] The investigations dragged on through the following year and were, in the end, abandoned.

Other industries achieved more. The dockers had established Saturday as a half-day in most ports before the war, and when their employers conceded the eight-hour working day, it therefore gave them a forty-four-hour week. The building unions, some of whose members were already working a forty-eight-hour week by local agreement, put in their claim for a national forty-four-hour working week at the beginning of 1919, and refused to consider any offers from the employers which fell short of that figure. The negotiations dragged on until September when, at a meeting of the National Conciliation Board, a resolution in favour of forty-four hours to start on 1 May 1920 secured a majority of two votes as a consequence of cross-voting by employers' representatives, despite a ballot conducted by the National Federation of Building Trade Employers in which the vote had been 6,204–378 against the concession. There had already been a good deal of concern among the employers about recent experience of the practice of cross-voting, and in June 1920 the national board was replaced by a National Wages and Conditions Council for the Building Industry, which was to observe the normal procedure of arriving at settlements by agreement between the two sides. Meanwhile the employers first attempted to delay the introduction of the forty-four-hour working week, then to secure an increase to $46\frac{1}{2}$ hours in summer, and finally persuaded the unions to agree that, on housebuilding only, an extra hour could be worked each day from Monday to Friday at plain time rates, provided that no workers should be penalised for not working the extra hour.

The engineering unions agreed that their four-monthly pay reviews should continue after the war, and the shipbuilding industry fell into line. The Committee on Production's role as arbitrator was played first by the Interim Arbitration Court and then by the Industrial Court. In December 1918 the Committee on Production gave its final award of 25p a week. Thereafter claims for further increases were rejected until a year later when the Interim Board gave another 25p, followed by a further 30p in March 1920, to be paid in two parts of 15p each, the first at once, and the second in May.

Disappointed by the rejection of their claims in March and July 1919, the unions turned to district claims. Many were submitted to local engineering employers' associations, which rejected them all. At central conference the employers' federation insisted that they must be adjourned pending the next national award. In the shipyards the

---

[13] Amalgamated Engineering Union, *Monthly Journal and Report*, August, September 1920.

Boilermakers were more fortunate. They submitted claims for improvement in district and yard piecework rates, and in many instances improvements were secured.

The Boilermakers were forced to pay attention to the grievances of the platers' helpers, most of whom were organised by the National Amalgamated Union of Labour. Each plater worked with several helpers who still received their pay, usually at a time rate, from the plater's gross piecework earnings. During the war the helpers had complained loudly that they had been expected to play their part in increasing output without any share in the consequent higher earnings, and in 1919 they claimed, first a substantially increased time rate, and then a share of the platers' gross earnings. The Boilermakers replied that they favoured the claim in principle, but insisted that the increase should come from the employers. The dispute was next referred to the Industrial Court which awarded an increase in the helpers' time rate. The Shipbuilding Employers Federation thereupon fell out with the Boilermakers over which of them should meet the bill, and it was only after several strikes of helpers, both unofficial and official, and two more arbitration awards, that it was finally settled that the platers would have to pay.

By the summer of 1920 the system of four-monthly reviews was coming in for a good deal of criticism from the skilled unions. They considered the increases insufficient, and they were becoming more and more dissatisfied with flat-rate awards. At a conference of the Engineers' officials and executive members in May 1920, there was 'a consensus of opinion' that national wage settlements were to be preferred to district negotiations 'inasmuch as national applications were less costly in time and money, economised energy, and the full weight of the society was brought into being on behalf of less efficient organised areas'.[14] They therefore decided to put in one more national claim under the existing procedure, and to approach the employers to discuss a new procedure for negotiating national wage settlements thereafter. The other skilled unions fell into line, and the general unions acquiesced reluctantly, for they had been well content with the results of the four-monthly reviews. The final four-monthly claim was rejected by the Industrial Court and then resubmitted to the engineering and shipbuilding employers along with the proposal for a new method of pay settlement. On 17 November the employers met the unions to consider a permanent system of national pay settlement. Allan Smith believed that 'a scientific basis must be established upon which wages may be regulated in future'. As the basis for future negotiations he proposed regular surveys of trade

[14] Amalgamated Society of Engineers, *Monthly Journal and Report*, June 1920.

and profit prospects, which should be analysed by independent accountants. The claim for an increase was rejected.[15]

Although the dockers had won a national wage increase through arbitration in the last year of the war, and the various groups of dock employers had conceded a working week of forty-four hours since then, there was no firm prospect of continued national negotiations in their industry, for there was no national organisation of employers with which the Transport Workers Federation could deal. They nevertheless submitted a claim for a national minimum rate of 80p a day in October 1919, to which the several employers' groups replied suggesting that the Minister of Labour should be asked to set up an inquiry under the new Act. Bevin persuaded his colleagues to agree, and the Minister appointed a court consisting of three transport union representatives (Gosling, Tillett and Williams), three port employers and three independent members, one of whom, Lord Shaw, was chairman. Bevin presented the dockers' case. The hearings, which took twenty days during February and March 1920, were held in public. Fifty-three witnesses were heard, no less than thirty-seven of them being employers.

The employers made the double mistake of choosing a distinguished lawyer, Lynden Macassey, to present their case, and allowing him to rest much of it on the testimony of A. L. Bowley, the statistician. It is now generally accepted that either of these forms of assistance can be disastrous for the employers' case. Legal precision and an eagerness to establish fine points compare unfavourably with the human touch and practical experience of the competent trade union official, and the averages of the statistician wilt when confronted with a succession of well-presented instances, even if not entirely typical. Nevertheless, Bevin's eleven-hour opening speech contained a good many figures. Some of them rested on shaky foundations, such as those supporting the claim that dockers' wages had fallen behind the cost of living during the war, and that employers could meet the claim without raising charges; and his budget of £6 a week presented as a moderate estimate of the cost of maintaining a family of five was an aspiration for the future rather than the experience of more than a fraction of manual workers in the docks and in most other industries; although many dockers earned more than that in good weeks. On the other hand, the wartime profits of the shipowners, and the evils of casual labour, were two subjects on which he could safely expand. In his famous peroration he told the court that, if his claim was rejected,

You must go to the Prime Minister, you must go to the Minister of Education and tell him to close our schools, tell him that industry can only be run on the

[15] Amalgamated Engineering Union, *Monthly Journal and Report*, December 1920.

pure fodder or animal basis, teach us nothing, let us learn nothing, because to create aspirations in our minds, to create the love of the beautiful and then at the same time to deny us the wherewithal to obtain it, is a false policy.[16]

Bevin continued to dominate the inquiry by his interrogation of witnesses, in which he showed an impressive knowledge, or at least skilful briefing, about conditions in port after port. Then, changing tactics, he produced in court the exact amount of bacon, fish, and bread which Bowley said could sustain a working man.

The court spent three weeks considering its findings. The independent and trade union members concurred in a majority report which agreed with Bevin that 'the time had gone past for assessing the value of human labour at the poverty line' and recommended the 80p minimum. They acknowledged that there were restrictive practices in the docks, but accepted Bevin's view that it was 'a question of creating confidence' and that the 80p minimum would help to do that. They proposed that a Joint Industrial Council be established, and that the system of casual labour 'must, if possible, be torn up by the roots', although they left the method of providing permanent employment to the council, when established. One employer signed the report with the reservation that he was not in favour of the 80p minimum, and the other two signed a minority report which rejected it.[17] However, after another three weeks the employers' organisations announced their acceptance. The minimum came into force in May, while local negotiations dealt with consequential adjustments in differentials and piece rates. A National Association of Port Employers was formed to provide the employers' side of the new Joint Industrial Council.

Two other important recruits to the ranks of national pay bargainers were printing and building and in both instances the pressure for change came mainly from the employers, who were anxious to put an end to leapfrogging local claims. During the war the provincial printing unions had developed a group system of pay settlement, under which a number of adjacent branches submitted a joint claim to their employers. In 1918 there were two rounds of wage increases, both led by the Typographical Association's branches in Manchester and Liverpool. The Federation of Master Printers tried to resist, and, on the second occasion, their Manchester association replied to a strike threat from the local branch with notices of dismissal; but both times the newspaper proprietors conceded the advance and the federation had to do the same. After the second round the executive of the Typographical Association agreed to

[16] *Minutes of Evidence*, p. 44.
[17] *Report*, pp. vii–viii.

discuss a system of national pay adjustments, despite a decision by their last delegate conference against it; and the other provincial unions followed them. However, although the forty-eight hour working week agreement for the printing industry was handled through the Printing and Kindred Trades Federation in January 1919, the Typographical Association insisted on negotiating their own pay agreement. A special procedure was therefore devised whereby the unions could negotiate either jointly or separately, and agreements were concluded in April 1919 covering all the crafts in England and Wales outside London. Towns were grouped into six grades and, for the major crafts, the rates varied from £3 in grade six to £3.75 in grade one. In order to conciliate the Manchester and Liverpool branches of the Typographical Association they were allowed to negotiate a further local increase before the national scales were settled. However, when they found that this increase was to be absorbed in the rate of £3.75 for grade one under the new agreement, they protested vigorously, saying that they should have received at least £4.

Towards the end of the war, wage increases in the building industry had come to be settled by the regional conciliation boards, and the practice of regional settlement continued after the war. In May 1920 the employers' federation decided to approach the unions to discuss a national arrangement, 'provisional or otherwise', in order to cope with the fierce wage competition due to the current extreme shortage of building labour. They were particularly concerned at a decision of the Liverpool employers' association, in September 1919, to break away from the Lancashire and Cheshire agreement, in order to concede a further wage increase. About the same time the Master Plumbers had agreed a wage rate above those under the building trade agreement; and more recently the London association had come under strong pressure due to a substantial wage increase in the furniture trade. When the employers' federation gave notice to withdraw from the National Conciliation Board in June, they stated as their reason that 'wages have reached their utmost limit in present circumstances'.

The new Wages and Conditions Council set about negotiating a grading system on much the same lines as that of the printing industry, except that all the crafts in the same town or district were paid the same rate, and the agreement, signed by the union federation on behalf of all its members, covered London as well as the provinces. It also provided for wages to be adjusted in accordance with changes in the cost of living index, but, since both sides accepted that building wages had been too low before the war, the scale was such that if the cost of living fell to the July 1914 level, wage rates would on the average be 30 per cent higher than at that time.

Area grading systems were also adopted by many of the Joint Industrial Councils, including tramways, gas, water, and electricity supply. In January 1920 the Industrial Court awarded an increase of 25p a week to the largest gas undertakings only, with 20p or 15p to the others according to their annual output of gas; and in August wage rates were standardised by output and region.

Whereas many employers were even more anxious than the unions to regulate wages nationally, others demurred, and even refused where they thought the unions too weak to insist on it. Having failed to exclude the settlement of wages and conditions of employment from the functions of the National Joint Industrial Council for Commercial Road Transport, the road haulage employers refused to consider a claim for a national minimum rate of £4.35 which was submitted in June 1920. The Transport Workers Federation consulted the nine unions with members in the industry on the question of a strike. Two failed to answer, four wanted a strike, one did not, and two asked for a ballot on the issue. At this stage the Scottish employers left the national council, and their colleagues in England and Wales followed them in October. The federation recommended the unions to issue strike notices, but in most instances they did not do so. Instead they proceeded to make the best terms they could with the local employers' associations. Only in Yorkshire was there a strike—of ten thousand men for nearly a month. The council in the rubber industry suffered a similar fate. In October 1920 the General Workers' executive reported it 'defunct due to the refusal of the employers to deal with our last national wages application'.

As a result of these and other negotiations, real wages, which were still about 10 per cent down on 1914 at the end of the war, had moved a little ahead of the 1914 figure by the end of 1920. The postwar recovery in salaries was more dramatic, for salaries had more ground to make up. Some advances had been secured in the non-industrial civil service early in 1919, but thereafter further increases had to await the outcome of a thorough reorganisation of the service instituted by the National Whitley Council. A special committee reported early in 1920 in favour of four general classes: administrative, executive, clerical, and female writing assistants. Similar changes were instituted among the departmental classes by the departmental councils, including those of the Post Office. New, and very substantially higher, pay scales were announced, and a cost of living sliding scale brought further increases by the end of the year.

The delay had encouraged the development of a militant spirit within the unions. Both the Post Office Engineering Union and the newly-amalgamated Union of Post Office Workers had voted in favour of a strike 'policy' and followed these decisions up by instituting strike funds. However, they suspended payment to the funds once the new rates of pay were announced.

The Burnham Committee announced pay increases for teachers in November 1919. The new minimum rates for men were £160, rising to £300, giving an average salary almost double that of prewar. Women teachers, with a scale from £150 to £240, improved their relative position even more. After a further year of negotiation, the committee agreed on standard scales for four different grades of schools, to be introduced by stages over the years 1921 to 1923. They 'meant extra remuneration to elementary teachers of 159 per cent above the pre-war average'.[18] In addition their union rejected a proposed cost-of-living sliding scale at exactly the right moment, just before prices began to fall.

No figures exist for the changes in local government salaries. Towards the end of the war some local branches of the National Association of Local Government Officers had begun to submit claims to arbitration for war bonus on the same scale as civil servants. They were successful, and their example was followed elsewhere 'to such effect that, by the end of 1921 the [executive] could claim with pride that . . . more than 300 local authorities were paying the civil service bonus'.[19] The National Poor Law Officers Association did even better. They had begun their pressure on Boards of Guardians to pay the civil service bonus at the beginning of 1918. In 1919 they met with the Poor Law Unions Association to set up a Conciliation Council, and agitated through it for the universal application of the civil service bonus. When this was refused in February 1920 their representatives withdrew, but in July the council was reconvened to hear that the employers were now willing to recommend that all boards should pay the latest bonus.

There were also substantial increases in the salaries of white collar workers in private employment, but for the most part they owed little to the activities of the unions. In its issue of January 1919, the journal of the National Union of Clerks (which added 'and Administrative Workers' to its title in 1920) carried a 'list of agreements and arbitration awards registered in the last quarter of 1919' which 'occupied two pages of very small type; and similar lists were appearing each quarter'.[20] Most of them, however, applied to individual firms. There were also one or two district agreements, for example with coalowners' associations, but no national agreements were signed for clerical, still less administrative, employees in private industry, except for the railways, where the Railway Clerks Association was recognised early in 1919. A Guild of Insurance Officials negotiated with one or two insurance companies, and the Bank Officers Guild had recruited nearly half the staffs of English banks by the end of 1920. A strike of Irish bank officers secured

[18] Tropp, p. 212.   [19] Spoor, p. 94.   [20] Hughes, p. 57.

recognition and a very substantial salary increase in 1918, and there was an unsuccessful strike in Scotland. In England a judicious mixture of prevarication, unilateral salary concessions, and encouragement for internal associations kept the guild at bay.

In retail distribution the Shop Assistants secured pay increases from a large number of individual firms, and some district associations, by means of agreements and awards. In 1919 the divisional committees of the Co-operative Employees submitted claims for their new target rates of pay. They were now negotiating with district Hours and Wages Boards set up by the co-operative societies during the war under the auspices of the Co-operative Union, although some societies refused to affiliate, and continued to negotiate on their own. In May 1920 the union's president claimed that in the Northern district they had 'almost succeeded' in securing general observance of their current target of £3.75 for men, and that it had been accepted 'over the greater part of Scotland'.[21] This figure was 168 per cent above the minimum of £1.40 which the union adopted in 1913. By the end of 1920, the forty-eight hour working week was general 'in retail societies . . ., with 44 hours in Northern Societies and many productive works'.[22]

Only two of the Trade Boards established before the war had granted an increase in pay by July 1916, and chainmaking still had not done so by July 1917. Even at the end of the war their rates for men were mostly less than 50 per cent over 1914 rates. However, by July 1920 their weekly rates ranged between 210 and 260 per cent over prewar, and in addition they had granted reductions in the working week.

Wages and hours were by no means the only subject of negotiations. In 1919 the Engineers signed the 1917 agreement on shop stewards in the engineering industry, after it had been amended to provide for the election by shop stewards of works committees in place of deputations of shop stewards under the earlier agreement. In September 1920 they negotiated a national overtime and nightshift agreement, which standardised payments and conditions for these forms of work, and deprecated systematic overtime. Where overtime was necessary, it was to be limited to thirty hours a month, apart from emergencies. In December a double-dayshift and three-shift agreement was added.

The several printing unions continued to deal separately with their own 'rules'. In March 1920 the Typographical Association signed a new agreement on rules covering, among other things, overtime, the right of the union to represent readers and machinemen, and the detailed regulation of manning and extra payments on machines. However, as had happened often before, no settlement could be reached on

---

[21] *The Co-operative Employee*, May 1920.
[22] William Richardson, p. 87.

apprentices, for the union persisted in their obsessive fear of 'flooding' the market. Having standardised wages, the new National Wages and Conditions Council in building proceeded to deal with overtime, night gangs, travelling allowances, extra payments, and other items, and a comprehensive agreement was signed in 1922.

Before the war holidays with pay, other than bank holidays, had been almost exclusively a white collar preserve, but early in 1919 the railway unions won the right to an annual week's paid holiday, and a good many other semi-public services, such as the tramways, followed suit. Among manufacturing industries printing led the way, when an agreement for a week's annual holiday was negotiated by the Printing and Kindred Trades Federation in 1919. The Manchester newspapermen, who had enjoyed an annual holiday since 1891, argued that they should now have two weeks, but the most the employers would offer them was an extra two days by 'grace and favour'.

Many employers' organisations made approaches to the unions for changes which they hoped might lead to higher productivity. It had been common ground among the reconstructionists, and among the political parties in the 1918 election, that an increase in output per head would be necessary after the war, to allow Britain to regain her former trading position in the world, and to provide the better life which all agreed could and should be enjoyed by the British people. Many trade union leaders shared this view. In August 1919 Brownlie wrote a letter to Bowerman in which he argued that moral and economic chaos would prevail in Europe, unless supplies could be increased, and that rising prices were the consequence of low output. He wanted the Parliamentary Committee 'to disseminate accurate and reliable information' and to arouse the nation 'to the urgent importance of increasing the supplies of the vital necessaries of life'. He also made a statement to Congress in September, which was repudiated by the other delegates from his union, whose executive he had not consulted. In February 1920 many newspapers carried half-page advertisements which urged their readers to '1. Produce more. 2. Earn more. 3. Get more' and included messages from Clynes, Hodge, Brace and Thomas as well as Brownlie, along with their photographs. In the same month the Ministry of Labour asked the Parliamentary Committee to appoint representatives to a committee to consider 'the best means of securing the greatest possible production'. Stuart-Bunning and Purcell were appointed.

However, trade union negotiators showed considerable suspicion of specific proposals from employers for increasing output. In April 1919 the engineering unions had signed their first national agreement on piecework, which stipulated that piece prices should be sufficient to allow a worker 'of average ability to earn at least $33\frac{1}{3}\%$ over present time rates (excluding war bonus)'. The employers were also anxious to raise productivity through a general agreement on what was now called 'payment by results', but had been known as the premium bonus system in the engineering industry before the war. As things stood the unions left arrangements on payment by results to their districts, many of whom were hostile to its use. In April 1918 the Engineers' Glasgow organiser reported in their journal that some firms were working the system, but in others 'they have ceased owing to the attitude of the District Committees'. He added: 'It would be well if we were to try and get some control over payment by results. . . . Either that, or refuse to recognise it and exclude men working on it.' His advice was not taken. When the engineering employers approached the craft unions early in 1920 for a national agreement, the latter first replied that they were unable to recommend a general adoption of payment by results; next, that there was no objection to its introduction so long as it was done with the consent of the workers concerned and their district committees; and, finally, that they would take a ballot. Their members voted three to one against. The general unions would have been ready to sign an agreement, 'with proper safeguards', but the craft unions had settled the issue for them. The employers also made approaches to individual unions, especially to the predominantly timeworking unions, whose members continued to complain that their earnings were falling behind those of the pieceworkers. In 1920 the employers offered the Pattern-makers a lead of 40p a week over the fitter's rate, provided that they would agree to payment by results. Despite a survey which showed that about a third of the members were 'not limiting their earnings to simple time rates', a conference recommended rejection and a ballot overwhelmingly confirmed their view; although another ballot rejected a proposal that members working piecework or paid by results should be excluded. 'Our attitude as a society towards the bonus question has been hypocritical and pusillanimous to an extent which happily has hitherto been unknown in our annals.'[23]

The two industries whose productivity caused particular concern were coalmining and building. In the first half of 1919 output per man in the mines was less than 90 per cent of the prewar figure, and fell to three-quarters in 1920, as the labour force rose. Among the explanations put forward for this trend were concentration on production at the expense of development during the war, and the need for returning ex-servicemen to recover their skills; but it was also widely supposed that many faceworkers 'were working on the minimum wage, which, together with the war wage and flat rate advance . . . allowed of a considerable daily wage being obtained without recourse to piece-work'.

[23] Mosses, pp. 301–7.

In 1920, 'it was argued by mining experts that decrease in output follows automatically every advance in wages'.[24] When the Miners put in a further wage claim in the summer of 1920, the government responded with a proposal for a national bonus for all wage-earners in the industry provided the monthly tonnage exceeded a given figure.

There are no statistics to provide a reliable comparison between building output before and after the war, but by common consent the decline in productivity had been substantial, and this was confirmed by the rapid increase which began in 1921 and continued for several years. In December 1919 the employers proposed an agreement on payment by results, which made little progress. In their *Monthly Journal* of February 1920 the Amalgamated Carpenters and Joiners issued strict instructions to their members, which district and branch officers were told to accept 'as final':

All kinds of bonuses, whether termed 'Timekeeping Bonus', 'Merit Bonus', or sums of money paid at the end of the week in addition to the hourly wages earned, are all departures from the hourly method of payment and therefore must be considered systems of payment by results. Our branches and district committees must deal with members who accept any kind of bonus in accordance with rule.

Towards the end of 1920 the Ministry of Health proposed dilution schemes which would enable the employers to increase the numbers of skilled building workers through a shortened period of training for non-apprenticed ex-servicemen. The unions replied that the shortage of men for housebuilding—only a seventh of the labour force were so engaged—was due to the government's failure to restrain 'luxury' building, and that since the employers had not fully taken up the numbers of apprentices to which their existing agreements entitled them, there was no case for dilution. They also expressed fears of unemployment. In December, with unemployment generally rising fast, Dr Macnamara, the Minister of Labour, tried to persuade a conference of the operatives' federation that the government's proposals involved no serious danger of unemployment for building workers; but, in addition to the payment of £5 into union funds for each dilutee, which the government had offered, the unions wanted guarantees of employment. Eventually, the government went ahead by agreement with the employers' federation only. The target was fifty thousand dilutees, but no more than a few hundred were taken on by employers for training. In June the employers' federation reported that 'the depression in our trade . . . has militated against the rapid development of the scheme'. It

[24] Redmayne, pp. 223, 236.

is probable that fear of union retaliation was also a factor in the reluctance of employers to accept trainees.

Industrial Unrest and Its Causes

The record of collective bargaining in 1919–20 reveals an unparalleled development in both the machinery of industrial relations and the scope and nature of collective agreements. Before the war collective bargaining had directly affected only a minority of manual workers, and very few white collar employees; for many of those affected, negotiations had been entirely on a local basis, and, for most of the remainder, agreements on pay and conditions were negotiated district by district, with appeal to a national body only when local negotiations failed. By 1920 the great majority of manual workers were covered by national arrangements for dealing between unions and employers. In most instances where these arrangements could not be settled by voluntary means, statutory wage-fixing bodies had been set up. Salaried workers lagged behind, but substantial advances had been made even for them, especially in public employment. Agreements on pay and conditions were now mainly national in their coverage, setting standard rules on hours of work, overtime, and the like, and making national adjustments to pay, although in many instances the basic rates to which these adjustments applied varied from district to district.

Although they were foreshadowed by wartime changes, and helped on by government pressure and legislation, and although there were many instances of reluctance to change, of lipservice to fashionable ideas, and of backsliding, the embodiment of these developments in what was intended to be permanent form in 1919–20 shows a remarkable readiness for change, among both trade unionists and employers. Nevertheless, they were accompanied by a high level of industrial conflict. The first three postwar years surpassed the record of the Great Unrest for strikes and lockouts. In numbers of recorded stoppages, 1919 fell a little short of the record established in 1913, but 1920 exceeded it. In numbers of working days lost, 1920 fell behind 1893 and 1912; 1919 surpassed 1893 but fell short of 1912; and the figure for 1921 was more than double that for 1912.

Years of extremely high demand for labour such as 1919 and 1920 might, in any event, have been expected to bring a heavy crop of strikes, especially when accompanied by a relaxation of wartime controls and pressures, and a rapid conversion from wartime to peacetime production; but the majority of the large strikes of 1919 arose directly out of the reconstruction of industrial relations, being due either to the application of the shorter working week, or to the switch from district to national agreements on pay and hours of work.

Employers generally admitted the inevitability of a shorter working week in the circumstances of 1919. This was true even in the cotton industry which provided the major strike on this issue. In January 1919 the United Textile Factory Workers Association put in a claim on behalf of all the cotton unions for a reduction from $55\frac{1}{2}$ to 44 hours in their working week, which they asserted would require an increase of 50 per cent on 'standard' rates, or 25 per cent on current earnings, to avoid a reduction in take-home pay. The employers offered $49\frac{1}{2}$ hours with no compensation for loss of earnings, and then 48 hours with an increase of 15 per cent on 'standard'. The unions countered with $46\frac{1}{2}$ hours and 30 per cent on 'standard', and when this was refused, their members voted by 267,650 to 6,347 for a strike. On 23 June the stoppage began. The government had not intervened while the Lancashire bargaining rituals had been in progress, and they did not seem to be unduly concerned when the strike began, but the Cotton Reconstruction Board stepped in with the suggestion of 48 hours and an increase of 30 per cent on 'standard', which the employers accepted. The council of the operatives' federation decided to return to work while conducting a ballot on these terms, but then a hitch occurred. They had forgotten to make sure that the individual unions would accept their decision, and the aristocratic Spinners decided to keep the dispute going for a few more days, until their injured dignity was assuaged. It was the first time that all the cotton unions had struck together, and, with 450,000 employees away from work for eighteen days, the total loss of working days was about eight million, the biggest strike of the year.

Other strikes arose out of the application of agreements for a shorter working week. The Miners had taken up the issue of surfacemen's working hours before the end of the war, and by threats of direct action had persuaded the government to agree to a forty-nine-hour week at the end of November 1918. In January 1919 150,000 Yorkshire Miners stopped work for thirteen days in connection with the consequential adjustment to meal breaks; and 12,000 Fifeshire Miners struck over the changes in starting times. In February eight thousand London underground and Southern Railway train drivers struck when their managers refused to include a meal break in their newly-negotiated eight-hour day. In April fifteen thousand Mersey dockers struck over stopping and starting times. The most important strikes over implementation, however, arose over the payment of pieceworkers.

Besides instituting the one-break system, to which many traditionally-minded workers objected, the engineering agreement on a forty-seven-hour working week made no provision for adjusting pieceworkers' earnings, although, on 10 January 1919, the employers' federation circulated a letter to their constituents, telling them that adjustments should be made where it was impossible for the men 'to increase their output so as to nullify the effect of the reduction'. Textile machinery manufacturers, traditionally niggardly in setting piecework prices, were particularly affected, and the federation specifically sanctioned adjustments by them. Workers paid by premium bonus were not affected since the alteration in hourly rates automatically increased the value of 'time saved' as working hours were reduced. On 6 January forty thousand Tyneside engineering workers had already come out on unofficial strike against the one-break system, and for compensation for loss of piecework earnings; for good measure, they added that they also wanted a forty-four-hour week. Some of them went back at the end of the first week, but others stayed out, some of them into March, and the total loss of working days may not have been far off a million. The agreement, in April, that piecework prices should normally yield a third above basic time rates helped to alleviate the pieceworkers' grievances on Tyneside and elsewhere.

There was worse trouble in coalmining. On 20 March the Sankey Commission issued three interim reports, dealing with the Miners' claims on wages and working hours. Six members supported the Miners' demand for a 30 per cent advance and a statutory six-hour working day; three proposed an increase of 7.5p a day and a reduction in working hours from eight to seven a day; and the chairman along with the remaining three members proposed a seven-hour working day with the possibility of a further reduction to six hours later, and re-commended an advance of 10p a day. On the same day Bonar Law announced that the government would accept the third of these reports. The Miners having accepted this offer by nine votes to one, wages were increased forthwith and a Coal Mines Bill to amend the Eight Hours Act was passed in August.

Time rates were altered to yield the same earnings in seven hours as previously in eight, quite apart from the 10p a day increase. It was also agreed that piece rates should be adjusted to take account of the reduction in working hours, but the government fixed an overall limit of 10 per cent, subsequently raised to 11.1 per cent, to the increase in piece rates. By itself this might have been acceptable since no adjustment at all was needed in Durham and Northumberland, with their long-established seven-hour working day or less for faceworkers, but the government limited increases elsewhere to 12.5 per cent. This could have been the consequence of a simple mathematical error. At first sight it appears that since the reduction in hours was $\frac{1}{8} = 12.5$ per cent, the appropriate compensatory increase in pay should also be 12.5 per cent. However, that is not the case. If working hours fall from 8 to 7, earnings in each hour must be increased by $\frac{1}{7}$ ($= 14.3$ per cent) to maintain the previous level of earnings. The Yorkshire owners had in fact already offered an adjustment of 14.3 per cent which the Coal Controller now disallowed. The reaction of the Yorkshire Miners was wholly predictable. They came out on strike on 16 July—150,000 of them—and three days later brought out the safety men as well.

The fog of percentages obscuring the real issues became thicker. On 15 July the Miners' annual conference had decided to continue negotiations on the basis of a 14.3 per cent increase in piece rates on a daily basis. Districts such as Yorkshire which already worked a 'short Saturday' would therefore receive compensation at that rate for a reduction of five instead of six hours in the week, which was calculated to be 12.2 per cent. The districts mainly affected were Yorkshire, where the employers had already conceded 14.3 per cent, Lancashire, whose leaders had been told that their owners were ready to follow Yorkshire, and Kent. These three districts voted against the proposal, but once it had been accepted, the federation proceeded to negotiate, and on 25 July the government granted a maximum of 14.2 per cent on a daily basis. From this point onwards the Yorkshire Miners were represented as being on strike for the difference between 14.2 per cent and 14.3 per cent.

There were further problems. An eleven-day fortnight was a common alternative to the short Saturday, and in these instances the reduction in working hours was eleven a fortnight, not five a week, so that a percentage increase in piecework prices of 13.1 per cent was claimed instead of 12.2; but the Coal Controller did not admit the justice of this point until January 1920. Moreover, within the eight-hour day only $7\frac{1}{4}$ hours, on the average, had been spent at the face. Travelling to the face took as long as before, so that average time spent at the face—earning time—fell to $6\frac{1}{4}$ hours, and full compensation required an increase in piece rates of 16 per cent. In those pits—and there were such pits— where only $6\frac{1}{2}$ hours in an eight-hour shift had previously been spent at the face, full compensation for the loss of earnings due to the introduction of the seven-hour working day would have meant an increase of 18 per cent in piece rates.

Many miners in Lancashire, Nottingham, and Derby had struck at the same time as the Yorkshire Miners, but they were back within the week. In South Yorkshire the strike was called off on 14 August, and West Yorkshire went back on 21 August. Even then the negotiations continued. In November Walsh reported to the Lancashire Miners' monthly conference that the 'Coal Control Department is still in a state of confusion'; and in February 1920 he told them that a settlement had still not been reached with people 'who did not possess one single atom of information'. The Yorkshire strike had cost nearly four million working days.

Strikes over the reduction of the working week could be expected to diminish in number and disappear as workers became accustomed to the new arrangements. The other major cause of industrial unrest in 1919–20, the conflict between trade union districts, or branches, and their national headquarters, arising from the widespread shift from local to national bargaining, promised to be a more lasting element in postwar industrial relations.

After the armistice, the Clyde Workers Committee decided on a campaign for thirty hours, but then threw in their lot with the district committees of the Engineers and of the Federation of Engineering and Shipbuilding Trades who had voted for forty hours, as had the Glasgow Trades Council. On 18 January 1919 a conference of shop stewards and union officials decided to strike for this objective. They set up a committee with Emmanuel Shinwell, chairman of the Trades Council, in the chair and Gallacher as strike organiser. A manifesto claimed that the committee represented 'the official and unofficial sections of the industrial movement', and the Scottish Trades Union Congress added its blessing. The date of the strike was fixed for 27 January.

A number of other industries were affected by the strike, besides engineering and shipbuilding, so that it took on something of the character of a general strike on the Clyde, and there were indications that it might spread to the rest of Scotland. The Scottish Horse and Motormen's Association, whose secretary, Hugh Lyon, was a member of the committee, were pursuing claims for a shorter working week with the various groups of road transport employers in Glasgow, and joined in the strike. A few days later the Lanarkshire Miners stopped work unofficially in sympathy with the Glasgow strikers. The strike also spread to Forth.

Shinwell persuaded the Provost of Glasgow to intervene with the government, and a deputation was arranged to meet him at midday on 31 January to learn their reply. A crowd, estimated at thirty thousand, gathered in St. George's Square to see what would happen. Rioting broke out while the deputation was inside the City Chambers. The police cleared the square with a good deal of brutality. Although their part had been to try to control the crowd, Gallacher, Kirkwood, and Shinwell were arrested, and troops, including tank units, were moved to the Clyde. Lyon, who had already signed an agreement for forty-eight hours with the Scottish Co-operative Wages Board, went on to sign similar agreements with the railway companies, the Corporation and the local contractors' associations. His men returned to work, and he offered to resign from the strike committee and the Parliamentary Committee of the Scottish Congress, but was persuaded to stay on.

On 25 January a similar strike had started in Belfast, where the objective was forty-four hours.

Twenty-six unions were represented on the General Strike Committee. . . . Employees of the municipal transport and electricity services joined the strike. All factories, except those able to generate their own power, were closed. . . . No ship could move into or out of the harbour . . . without permission of the strike committee. Only hospitals were granted exemption from the electricity fade-out.[25]

In both Glasgow and Belfast, however, the majority of strikers were from the local engineering and shipbuilding unions, and their aim was to secure a further reduction in the working week beyond the forty-seven hours recently agreed by their national leaders and confirmed by a ballot. Their employers demanded that the unions should take immediate steps to see that the agreement was observed; and the unions accepted that it was their duty to do so. The Engineers' executive issued instructions for an immediate return to work, to allow negotiations to secure 'redress of any grievances arising out of the introduction of the 47 hours';[26] suspended their district committees in Belfast and Glasgow; and removed the district secretaries from office. They took similar disciplinary measures in London where their district committee had asked members 'to back the demand for a 40-hour week by such means as they shall decide', and on 31 January had joined with other London engineering unions in a meeting which decided to try to extend the strike throughout the country. However, the Londoners failed to spread the strike, and on 11 February the Glasgow strikers went back to work. The Belfast men followed on the 19th.

Another unofficial district strike arose from the claim of London shiprepair workers for a pay increase of 75p a week in addition to the 25p which had been awarded nationally by the Interim Court of Arbitration in December 1919. The claim was first put forward by the Allied Trades for the Thames and rejected by the employers as in breach of their national agreement. The River Thames Shop Stewards Committee then called an unofficial strike whose leader, a young boilermaker called Harry Pollitt, was in the anomalous position of secretary of the London district of the Boilermakers (not a full-time post) and paid organiser of the shop stewards committee. The strike began on 17 January and was called off in March without gaining any concessions. Altogether the strikes on the Clyde, at Belfast, and on the Thames accounted for the loss of over two million working days.

The new system of national bargaining had not only curbed district

---

[25] David Mitchell, p. 758.
[26] *Monthly Journal and Report*, February 1919.

autonomy. It had also diminished the freedom of individual unions to act on their own. The Ironfounders believed that they had a double grievance over their rates of pay. Prior to the war they had in many areas established a differential above the rates of most other engineering craftsmen which had been eroded by wartime flat-rate increases, and, as a predominantly timeworking trade, they believed that their earnings had fallen behind those of most other engineering trades. During 1919 an agitation for a special national increase for foundryworkers gathered force, after the rejection of general pay claims in March and July by the Interim Arbitration Court. The Ironfounders had been encouraged to believe they had the right to negotiate separately from the other engineering unions. During the spring they had been having separate discussions with the Engineering Employers Federation on their programme for postwar conditions, which included the replacement of individual piecework, where it existed, by the 'fellowship principle' (group piecework); the right to operate 'all Machines and improved methods of production'; and standardisation of basic wages. When the employers terminated these discussions in July, the executive substituted a demand for an immediate increase of 75p a week all round. In August they put this claim to the employers. Allan Smith told them that it was 'entirely out of order', so, along with the Coremakers, they decided to give a month's notice to withdraw from the four-monthly review agreement. Shackleton, from the Ministry of Labour, tried to persuade them that, as the reviews were four-monthly, a period of four months' notice was appropriate, but they brushed that aside and came out on 20 September, now joined by the Iron and Steel Metal Dressers Trade Society as well.

The Ironfounders' honorary president, Arthur Henderson, arranged a conference with the engineering employers in October at which he presented the unions' case. The employers were prepared to adjourn the matter, without prejudice, until after the next four-monthly review, which was due in November, provided the men would go back to work. This offer was rejected. Funds began to run short in November. The Associated Ironmoulders of Scotland voted by a small majority to join the strike, but they changed their minds when they learned of the general 25p increase awarded at the four-monthly review. On 21 November the employers wrote to tell the foundry unions that the only question at issue was that 'during the currency of an award, your members have thought fit to go on strike'. In December, the Parliamentary Committee, which had been 'watching with deep concern', intervened to secure a settlement in a local dispute over four men at West Bromwich which the employers insisted must precede further negotiations, and the unions proceeded to ballot on the employers' offer—that the strikers should go back and receive the 25p which had been awarded to the other unions. The vote was two to one against, but two weeks later the leaders announced that all funds were exhausted, and recommended resumption. Another ballot accepted the recommendation, and the strikers went back on the employers' terms on 31 January 1920. In all, the foundry dispute cost about six million working days.[27]

In 1920 the printing industry experienced trouble as a result of their national wages agreement. The newspapermen had already protested that the agreement had eroded their traditional differentials, and secured special pay increases. In May new wage claims were presented all round. The employers wanted to deal with them collectively through the Printing and Kindred Trades Federation, but the Typographical Association insisted on negotiating on their own. Then the matter was referred to the Joint Industrial Council, but the Typographical Association still insisted on their right to negotiate separately. Eventually, however, they decided in June to settle for the 50p a week that the other unions had accepted through the Printing and Kindred Trades Federation.

That was not the end of the matter. In July a joint committee of the Liverpool and Manchester branches began a campaign for an additional local bonus of 50p a week, and backed it with an embargo on overtime. The local employers threatened a lockout of all members of the union in the two cities. The executive instructed the branches to resume normal working, and undertook to support a special claim on behalf of their members if they would do so. In August the two branches called their members out on strike, confident that this step would force the newspaper proprietors to give in. Instead the employers threatened the Typographical Association with a general lockout; and the union instructed its members to go back.

The other printing unions were alarmed, and persuaded the Typographical Association to allow work from Liverpool and Manchester to be done by the union's members elsewhere. The Parliamentary Committee took a hand. On 13 September Poulton and Purcell attended a meeting with the strikers' joint committee and the union executive, at which both bodies were able to give full vent to their feelings. Eventually the two Parliamentary Committee representatives were able to arrange with the employers that, provided the men went back to

---

[27] In the *Yorkshire Factory Times* of 15 January the branch secretary at Cleckheaton thanked the 'public of Cleckheaton, and the people of the Spen Valley generally' for their support, saying that for eight weeks they had been able to pay out 'in addition to the strike pay', 45p for each moulder, 10p for a wife, 10p for each child, and 35p for apprentices. It seems unlikely that their colleagues in other parts of the country were all so well supported.

work, their case for special treatment would receive attention before the end of the month, and legal proceedings for breach of contract which had been started against more than 2,500 printers in Liverpool and Manchester would be dropped. No special concessions were made to the Liverpool and Manchester branches when the case was heard, but the negotiations led on to a further general increase of 25p a week in November.

These two causes of unrest—the reduction in working hours and conflicts over the right of individual districts or individual unions to seek improvements on national agreements on wages and hours— accounted for nearly all the major strikes of 1919. The pattern for 1920 was different. Apart from the printing dispute, and once the foundry strike was settled, no major strike was primarily concerned with these issues. There were several sizeable stoppages over claims for wage increases, and in the autumn, with rising unemployment, came two more over wage cuts. In September the Oldham Spinners struck because wartime payments for working without a full complement of labour had been withdrawn now that manning had been restored to prewar level; and in December shipyard joiners struck against the withdrawal of a special 60p increase which they had been granted earlier in the year. There was also a lockout of seven thousand electricians over the employment of a non-union foreman at Penistone in Yorkshire which threatened to stop the whole engineering industry.

The Electrical Trades Union had not cut much of a figure in the trade union world before 1911, when it began a period of rapid growth, primarily due to the expansion of the electrical trade, which took its membership from under two thousand in 1910 to 57,000 in 1920. Because of the rising demand for skilled electricians, the union could afford to recognise recruitment to the skilled grades from craftsmen's assistants as well as by apprenticeship, and in 1914 an auxiliary section was set up, mainly for assistant wiremen. Before the war the union's two main groups of members had been in electrical contracting and electrical engineering, but its membership in electricity supply then began to expand, and in 1918 the auxiliary section was opened to 'any person who is engaged as an electrical worker, or any person whose labour is incidental to the generation, maintenance, and supply of electrical energy'.

In 1914 the Electricians had their own dispute with the London electrical contractors, parallel to the building lockout, and the union began to show signs of syndicalist ideas and industrial militancy. During the war they began to invent for themselves the idea of an 'electrical industry' to fit their organisation into the theory of industrial unionism. In 1917 they were more heavily involved in the May strikes than any other union, apart from the Engineers. In his report for that month their Mersey district secretary, Walter Citrine, asserted with pride that the Leeds, Manchester, Mersey, and Sheffield districts had struck, presenting 'the spectacle of four of the largest districts in the Union acting jointly together', and the executive failed by only one vote to make the strike official. In February 1919 the executive appeared to be ready to call a national strike, including electricity supply, for a reduction in working hours beyond forty-eight hours a week; but thought better of it when the government issued an order under Defence Regulations to make such a strike illegal.

All the skilled engineering unions tried to retain members promoted to foremen, but, because of their 'industrial unionism', the Electricians were especially keen that such members should keep their cards; and their militancy led them to insist upon it. They won a strike on the issue at Aintree in 1918, and penalised another foreman for failing to join a strike in London in 1919. At Penistone the union demanded that a foreman who had left the union on his promotion should rejoin or lose his job. The Engineering Employers Federation voted nearly nine to one for a lockout. The other unions had no intention of backing the Electricians at the cost of being locked out themselves. The issue was debated at Congress, which was in session, and a Court of Inquiry was suggested. The Minister of Labour agreed, and the court began hearings on 14 September; but the union, realising that the court could not possibly find in their favour, called off the strike two days later, and the court was disbanded.

However, well over half the working days lost through strikes in 1920 were due to a single stoppage, that of the Miners in October which accounted for about 16.5 million out of the total of 26.5 million working days lost that year. This strike, along with the national railway strike of 1919 and the miners' lockout of 1921, is one of a series of strikes or threats of strikes which were mainly directed against the government, and in which resort to 'direct action' by the Triple Alliance or the whole trade union movement was always a risk, and sometimes an open threat.

'Direct Action'

During February 1919 the cabinet was driven close to panic by industrial unrest, especially during Lloyd George's absences in Paris for the peace conference. There were the Clyde, Tyne, and Belfast strikes. In London, besides the shiprepair strike, the underground and Southern railways were strikebound, the Electricians were threatening to cut off the supply of electricity, and the Railway Clerks had given notice of a national strike for recognition. The Miners Federation had rejected with scorn the government's offer of 5p a day and the consideration of their remaining demands by 'a strong representative committee'. They were now balloting on a strike which the Triple Alliance was pledged to support, for each of the three allies had undertaken to back their partners' postwar programmes. There was still considerable unrest in the armed forces. Their loyalty during strikes was in question, and the government's legal advisers expressed doubts concerning the legality of their use to control a strike.

The cabinet began to make preparations to cope with a major transport strike. On 4 February a Committee on Industrial Unrest was appointed, later to become the Supply and Transport Committee. They also set about appeasing the unions. On 19 February, having already taken soundings, they issued formal invitations to a National Industrial Conference of unions and employers' organisations to consider the causes of unrest, and what remedies they could propose; and by 26 February, when a Miners' conference met to consider what should be done in view of the six to one vote for a national strike, they had let the Miners' leaders know that, if the Miners would agree to the proposed inquiry, they would be allowed to 'nominate or approve' half the members.

Of whom were the cabinet so scared? It cannot have been the official leaders of the trade union movement, the seventeen members of the Parliamentary Committee elected in 1918. The most notable group among them were five 'patriots': Davis, Sexton, Thorne, Havelock Wilson and J. B. Williams, four of whom had been associated with the attempt to found a Trade Union Labour Party. None of the rest could be classed as politically on the left or industrially militant, with the possible exception of Hill, and even his views had been tempered by eleven years as secretary of the Boilermakers. Margaret Bondfield was notable as the first woman member, but not because her opinions differed widely from those of her colleagues. Thomas was a strong internationalist and an opponent of conscription, but politically he was more of a Lib–Lab than a socialist, and his skilful exploitation of threats of unofficial strikes went along with such a reluctance to call an official strike that it was almost impossible to imagine an industrial dispute in which he would voluntarily do so.

However, the Parliamentary Committee was not wholly representative of the movement nor even of its leadership. There were several outstanding leaders outside their ranks whose opinions were a good deal more radical than theirs, or were believed to be so. Most of these leaders were to be found in the unions affiliated to the Triple Alliance.

In 1918 Ashton at last retired from his post as the Miners' secretary, and the annual conference decided, against considerable opposition, that their president and secretary should henceforth be full-time employees of the federation residing in London. Despite his reluctance to live in London, Smillie allowed his name to go forward for the presidency, and the result was a foregone conclusion. After taking office he found that 'family difficulties' prevented him moving to London. For the post of secretary, South Wales nominated Frank Hodges. As every other major district except Scotland also put forward their candidate, the size of the Welsh vote took Hodges ahead on the first ballot and he stayed in front as successive rivals were eliminated.

Both were heroes of the left, and both disappointed their admirers, but for different reasons. Smillie, 'well-read, . . . the mildest and most humorous of men, . . . quietly spoken, but ruthlessly logical',[28] was a convinced and consistent socialist whose opposition to the war and refusal of ministerial office had endeared him to the left; but his record of industrial moderation was there for all who chose to remember his handling of the national coal strike in 1912. Hodges was as blatant a careerist as the British trade union movement has produced. He had risen to fame as the spokesman of the South Wales syndicalists at national conferences; and their influence helped to secure for him the Welsh nomination for his new post. Once he was elected, however, his career no longer needed their support.

By 1919 Concemore Cramp, known as 'Charlie', had emerged as second only to Thomas in the National Union of Railwaymen. He also was a careerist, but, unlike Hodges, his ambitions were confined within the trade union movement. He had been elected as a syndicalist to the executive of the Railway Servants in 1911, and won his spurs by championing the Central Labour College and other such causes. Under the three-year rule he would have retired in 1914, but in 1913 his colleagues accepted his plea that the National Union of Railwaymen was 'an entirely new union' which could not be bound by what had happened in its constituents, and he was elected to the new executive for another spell of three years. When he was again due to retire in 1917 he stood for and won the presidency, also for three years. Before this term had expired, the executive proposed and carried through conference a resolution to divide the chief office into two, a political secretaryship, which Thomas was to hold, and an industrial secretaryship, to which Cramp was elected. He had differed from most of his former Plebs League colleagues by supporting the war, and before it ended he was taking a lead in condemning unofficial strikes and approving the Whitley report. For whatever reason, however, his presidential address to his union's conference in 1919 showed him veering back towards militancy. He argued that workers should not heed those who said they must wait

[28] Lawson, pp. 70-1.

to secure a Labour majority in the House of Commons before they could achieve their goals: 'the centre of gravity is passing from the House of Commons to the headquarters of the great Trade Unions'.

Robert Williams, a former official of a small South Wales dockers' union, the National Amalgamated Labour Union, had been elected the first and only full-time secretary of the Transport Workers Federation in 1912. He was now the most leftwing of all senior trade union officials. However, power within the federation was firmly in the hands of the leaders of the individual unions, among them Sexton, Havelock Wilson and Thorne; and Stanley Hirst, of the Amalgamated Tramwaymen, who, like them, was no leftwinger. Tillett was still unpredictable, but real power in his union lay with the assistant secretary, Bevin. A former member of the British Socialist Party and a critic of the war, who told the 1917 conference of the Transport Workers Federation that he 'largely agreed' with Robert Williams, he was nevertheless too much his own man to be easily classified. Massive both in figure and personality, he could be persuasive or aggressive in negotiations as occasion demanded. He was fascinated by industrial power and contemptuous of politicians, but far too concerned with building up the bargaining power of his union, and extending its boundaries, to risk what he had achieved, and hoped to achieve, by militant action—unless the odds on success were high.

Accordingly, even when account is taken of the Triple Alliance unions, there was no good reason for the cabinet to fear that British union leaders might start a revolution, or so reduce the country to chaos through industrial action as to make effective government impossible. They might well have to expect hard bargaining backed by strikes, but that is another matter. Of course, the fears of the cabinet may have been due to poor briefing. Hankey, their secretary, wrote in his diary for 23 September 1919, during railway negotiations, that Thomas 'has been losing ground to his deputy, Cramp, a sinister looking fellow reported to be a Bolshevist'.[29] Basil Thomson's reports may have led them to apprehend that moderate leaders might be swept aside by rank-and-file extremists; but they must have been very ill-informed indeed if they envisaged the feeble remnants of the shop stewards' movement taking over the trade unions.

Churchill, who had more experience of dealing with unions than most of his cabinet colleagues, expressed a different misgiving in February 1919:

The curse of trade unionism was that *there was not enough of it*, and it was not

---

[29] Roskill, p. 121.

highly enough developed to make its branch secretaries fall into line with the head office. With a powerful trade union, either peace or war could be made.[30]

It was indeed true that unions were having difficulty in keeping their branches and districts in line. But there was no need for the government to fear that local revolts like the Clyde and Belfast engineering strikes, or even the Yorkshire coal strike, would lead to revolution or chaos. In the end the authority of union leaders and national agreements was reasserted. A more serious risk was that a coalition of local leaders would, through representation in union executives and conferences, take control over national decision-making in the unions, and prevent the national leaders reaching compromises acceptable to employers and government—not because the local men were revolutionaries, or because they were less patriotic than their leaders, but because they had greater expectations than their national leaders of what could be achieved by threats of strikes or actual strikes in the conditions of 1919. This danger existed particularly within the Triple Alliance, most of all within the Miners Federation and the National Union of Railwaymen, for the leaders of the main Transport Workers Federation unions were generally able to carry their members with them.

The Miners' executive consisted almost entirely of full-time officers from the districts, although from time to time a lay member was elected. Some districts elected and re-elected the same officers year after year; others practised rotation. Either way, those elected paid close attention to the views of their districts. In some districts full-time officers predominated on the local executive, but matters of importance were referred to monthly meetings of branch delegates, often mandated by their branches. Major national issues were settled by national conferences, which met frequently, with district delegations usually voting en bloc, often on mandates from district delegate conferences; or by direct reference from the executive to district delegate conferences; or by national ballots. Consequently, through their own votes or those of their branch delegates, the members exerted a greater authority over national decisions than did the members of any other great union.

The Railwaymen's branches sent delegates to their district councils which had little constitutional authority. National conferences, from which full-time officers were excluded, met far less frequently than in the Miners Federation. Representatives were limited to three successive terms of one year, and most were replaced after one year. With a conference membership of sixty, six of the 1917 representatives were re-elected in 1918, and ten of the 1918 representatives in 1919. Conferences were therefore inexperienced and unpredictable. Thomas tried to have

---

[30] Quoted from war cabinet minutes by Middlemas, p. 143.

their terms extended to three years, but the 1918 conference turned the proposal down. As it was, conference normally provided a battleground for contests between the general secretary and president on the one hand, and the most experienced leftwing delegate on the other—in 1915, 1916, and again in 1919, this was W. J. Abraham of Sheffield, and in 1920 John Marchbank of Glasgow. Both were rewarded, as Cramp before them, with the presidency.

Members of the executive, elected to represent the various sections of railwaymen, had a term of three years, eight of the twenty-four standing down each year. They tried to exercise their wide powers without reference to conference, which strove to control and curb them. Meeting as frequently as two or three times a month, often for several days at a time, the executive members were more exposed to the influence of the national officers than was conference. Towards the end of his term a member might have in mind the consideration that only by election to a full-time post could he continue to play a major role in the union, and that the backing of the national officers would be a major electoral asset. On the other hand, in a period when militant sentiment was running strong in the union, as in 1919–20, it was likely to be reflected among the new members. Consequently Thomas and Cramp could have trouble in bringing the executive round to their way of thinking; but not so much trouble as with conference.

The National Industrial Conference met on 27 February 1919. Its constitution followed the wartime model in that the union representatives were not selected by the Parliamentary Committee but by their unions, which received individual invitations. Some union officials and employers came as representatives of the Joint Industrial Councils which had also been invited. The Minister of Labour, Robert Horne, was in the chair, and Lloyd George addressed the conference. The discussion was diffuse, but a suggestion from Allan Smith that a committee should be set up to consider 'the causes of the present unrest' and what to do about them was seized upon by Henderson who, as in wartime, led for the unions. He proposed more precise terms of reference, including 'Hours, Wages and General Conditions of Employment' and 'Unemployment and its Prevention'. Lloyd George combined the two resolutions into one which was carried 'by a very large majority' and a 'Provisional Committee' of thirty from each side was appointed. *The Times* acclaimed the conference as 'the beginning of a new epoch in the evolution of industrial and social life'.[31]

Whether the conference was a genuine attempt to promote better industrial relations, or merely a device to gain time, its utility was diminished when the Triple Alliance unions decided to withdraw,

[31] 28 February 1919.

apparently because the committee had not been charged with considering proposals for the nationalisation of coalmining and transport. But this decision did not bind the constituent unions of the Transport Workers Federation. Clynes, for example, was a member of the committee. The Engineers also withdrew.

The committee set to work with speed and reported at the beginning of April. Their recommendations included a statutory maximum for normal working hours of forty-eight a week; a commission to establish statutory minimum rates of pay 'of universal applicability'; and 'full and frank acceptance of the employers' organisations on the one hand and trade unions on the other as the recognised organisations to speak and act on behalf of their members'. Some recommendations were made on 'the prevention of unemployment' and 'the maintenance of unemployed workpeople', but 'a satisfactory investigation' would have involved 'a far-reaching inquiry'. A permanent joint National Industrial Conference was proposed to consider 'general questions affecting industrial relations' and how to deal with potential and actual industrial disputes.[32]

It is unlikely that the employers' representative would have agreed to the first two recommendations unless they had shared the government's belief that there was an urgent need to mollify the unions. They came to the conference unprepared and disunited. Noting 'the difficulties experienced by employers in appointing a temporary Committee properly representative of the various Employers' Organisations',[33] Allan Smith took advantage of the conference to initiate discussions about a permanent employers' confederation. Eventually the National Confederation of Employers Organisations was set up as an industrial relations counterpart of the Federation of British Industries.

Lloyd George sent a letter to the conference, when it met again on 4 April, promising that, if the proposals were approved, as they were, 'the Government will give them their immediate and sympathetic consideration'.[34] Although there were difficulties over the suggested exclusion of agricultural labourers, domestic servants, and seamen from the statutory forty-eight-hour working week, and the government proposed only to set up a Commission of Enquiry into the national minimum wage, bills on both topics were presented to the House of Commons in August, where Lloyd George called them 'the most important measures dealing with Labour problems which have ever been submitted to the judgment of this House';[35] but nothing more was done. The bills were

[32] *Report*, pp. 6–13.
[33] *A Circular Issued to Employers' Organisations*, 28 February 1919.
[34] *The Times*, 5 April 1919.
[35] *Hansard*, 18 August 1919, col. 1996.

not discussed that session; nor were they reintroduced next year, despite much prodding at question-time.

The Ministry of Labour advised that the application of the Trade Boards Act, industry by industry, would be more effective than an overall minimum wage as an instrument for improving the lot of the low-paid; and the proposed legislation on hours of work conflicted with the international convention on a forty-eight-hour working week adopted by a conference of the International Labour Organisation in Washington in November 1919. This body had been created by the Peace Treaty with strong support from Britain, and the British delegates at Washington—government, union, and employer representatives alike—had voted for the convention. The most important difference between the bill and the convention was that the latter did 'not give any recognition to overtime as a regular feature of industrial work',[36] whereas many British union members were hoping that the forty-eight-hour week would enable them to increase their overtime earnings.

There was no more than a perfunctory protest from the unions when the Provisional Committee wound itself up in 1921. Nearly all powerful unions had by then got their forty-eight-hour week, or better, and few of their members would have benefited from a general minimum wage at the level it was likely to be set.

On 26 February 1919, the day before the first meeting of the National Industrial Conference, the Miners' conference had reassembled to discover that their executive had been persuaded by Smillie and Hodges to recommend acceptance of the government's offer of an inquiry with half its members nominated or approved by the Miners. Smillie told the conference that

if we did not take part in it the general public of the country, and certainly the whole Press of the country, will say that the miners were afraid to go into their own case.

The proposal was attacked by speaker after speaker, both militant and moderate. Varley of Nottingham asked Smillie what the public would say when they found that the Miners were only 'prepared to accept the findings of a Commission if we can pack the jury'. Herbert Booth prophesied that the Commission would 'issue two reports'; and asked how could they strike after '50 per cent of that Commission have proven against us'. At the end of the session it seemed that the vote next day would go against the executive; but the leaders continued to exercise their persuasive powers after formal proceedings had ended, and they were not unaided. As a Lancashire district delegate reported back to his

[36] T. J. Macnamara, *Hansard*, 27 May 1921, col. 486.

monthly district conference on 8 March, 'the Prime Minister was in the same building . . . and it was decided to send a deputation to him'. Next day the vote was unanimously in favour of the executive's recommendation.

Smillie was passionately concerned that the mines should be nationalised. Like the other Miners' leaders, he thought this was essential if the national wage was to be maintained and consolidated; but he was equally concerned to better the lot of the miner by improvements in other ways: miners' housing, conditions in the pits including pithead baths, and safety provisions. Rapid progress in all these respects, he thought, depended on nationalisation. But how could parliament be persuaded into nationalisation? By a strike? It was highly doubtful whether the miners would strike for nationalisation, once they were satisfied with the offers on wages and hours; and, if they did, what would the public, the press, and parliament itself make of such a patent attempt at unconstitutional coercion? However, parliament might perhaps be moved by a Royal Commission's recommendation for nationalisation arrived at after examining the evidence of mismanagement of the mines by the coalowners. If so, it was necessary to make sure that the commission would do the job as he wanted it done; and that meant that he and his colleagues must have as large a share as possible in selecting the members.

To impress the Miners, the commission was constituted by Act of Parliament instead of the usual procedure by royal warrant. Of the twelve members besides Sankey, three represented the owners, Arthur Balfour and two employers from other industries were chosen by the government, and Smillie, Smith, and Hodges were joined by Leo Money, R. H. Tawney, and Sidney Webb, whose names had been agreed between the Miners and the government. The interim report on wages and hours was to be ready by 20 March. Thereafter the commission proceeded to investigate the case for nationalisation, the Miners having been encouraged by a passage in the interim report signed by the chairman and the three government nominees in which they wrote that, 'even upon the evidence already given, the present system of ownership and working in the coal industry stands condemned'.[37]

Meanwhile the railway negotiations had run into trouble. The issues at this stage were overtime, shift rates, and holidays, on which the unions thought the government's offers niggardly. On 20 March a special conference of the Railwaymen resolved to ask the Triple Alliance to back them in a national strike. First the alliance leaders went to see the relevant ministers led by Bonar Law. The offers were improved and the strike was called off.

[37] *Interim Report*, p. viii.

Although each partner in the alliance had undertaken to back the postwar programmes of the others, the extent of their commitment was unclear. At an emergency meeting of the Transport Workers Federation on 10 March, Clynes asked whether the federation had 'handed over our executive functions and our right to settle industrial questions . . . to . . . the Triple Alliance Executive'. Williams made three wordy attempts to give an answer, floundering worse each time, until Bevin explained that union sovereignty was retained, and the alliance came in only to back a union which had not got what it wanted. However, he then qualified his statement by saying if either of the other members of the alliance thought the union in dispute was being 'unreasonable', then 'the merits of the claim' might be considered; and the fog of confusion descended again.

The alliance partners were also caught up in an agitation over conscription. During the election Lloyd George had given a firm pledge that conscription would cease with the Peace Treaty. However, as the pace of demobilisation increased, the government began to fear that there would soon be no army left. Churchill introduced a bill to continue conscription for another year which became law in April. The situation was complicated by the continued presence of a British expeditionary force in Archangel and Murmansk, and Churchill's eagerness to assist the White Russian armies. He was, wrote Hankey in his diary, 'quite barmy in his enthusiasm for the anti-Bolshevists'.[38] It was inevitable that the left should detect government preparation for a full-scale war against the Communist government in Russia, and the cabinet added credibility to these suspicions by failing to veto Churchill's plans to link up with the White Russians.

A 'Hands off Russia' committee had already been set up, with Cramp as one of its vice-presidents. At the beginning of March the Railwaymen's executive asked the Parliamentary Committee and the Labour Party executive to call a national conference 'with a view to forcing the hands of the Government' over their plans for a 'permanent scheme of conscription'; and on 26 March the Miners resolved to 'take such steps in conjunction with the organised Labour movement, both political and industrial' as would compel the government to drop the bill and withdraw troops from Russia.

It was agreed that the matter would be discussed at a special conference of Labour organisations summoned for 3 April to discuss plans for a League of Nations. Smillie carried a resolution demanding the dropping of the Conscription Bill, withdrawal from Russia, the end of the blockade on Germany, and the release of conscientious objectors, adding that the Miners wanted a national conference to decide whether,

[38] Roskill, p. 115.

and in what form, industrial action should be taken. When the Parliamentary Committee met on 8 April, a majority of them were against holding a conference, but agreed to join with the Labour Party executive in a deputation to Bonar Law (Lloyd George being in Paris) to deal with the matters covered by Smillie's resolution. However, the two bodies could not agree on whether to 'demand' the withdrawal of conscription. The Parliamentary Committee did not want to go that far, while the party executive insisted upon it. In the end the Parliamentary Committee were left to see Bonar Law on their own, and they took their time about it, for the meeting did not take place until 22 May.

By this time they had another complaint to make. A confidential military circular asking commanding officers whether their men could be relied upon to act as strike breakers had been published by the *Daily Herald* on 13 May. The Parliamentary Committee did not consider Bonar Law's response to their demand for its withdrawal was satisfactory, and were not entirely happy with his answer on conscription, but he had assured them that the government had no intention of interfering with the Bolshevik government so long as they had the support of the Russian people, and promised that troops would be withdrawn as soon as possible. On 28 May they decided that the interview had been sufficiently reassuring to refuse the request for a conference to consider industrial action. An amendment proposing a conference 'at the earliest possible moment' was lost by seven votes to five, with four absentees.

The Labour Party conference in June were told by their executive that the question of a general strike was primarily a matter for the unions. Consequently, although a majority of the delegates favoured direct action, all they could do was to ask their executive to take the matter up again with the Parliamentary Committee. This was done, and on 22 July the committee reaffirmed their refusal to call a conference by six votes to four, this time with six absentees. The division within the Labour movement on direct action was reflected in the Parliamentary Committee, but it was not quite as sharp there as the voting figures suggest. On both occasions most of the absentees would have been likely to side with the majority, and at the meeting on 22 July the minority were careful to stipulate that if a conference were to show 'a large volume of opinion in favour of industrial action, a ballot vote of affiliated members is essential'.

Up to this point the leaders of the Triple Alliance had been asking the Parliamentary Committee to act. Now it was clear that, if anything was to be done, they must do it themselves. At their conference on 23 July they decided to consult their members, each partner according to their own constitution. Before that could be done, Churchill announced in the Commons that British troops would be out of Russia before winter, and that it was 'possible to look forward to the complete passing away of conscription'.[39] Having consulted their branches, the Railwaymen's executive proposed that the matter be dropped. The annual conference of the Transport Workers Federation in June had unanimously resolved not to commit themselves to a Triple Alliance strike without a ballot vote; and no ballot was put in hand. On 3 September the Miners decided to ballot, but this decision was reversed at another meeting of the alliance next day.

From start to finish, it was evident that there would be no general strike. The divisions within the trade unions were too great for that. These divisions were not over the objects which the direct actionists sought to achieve. Few trade unionists apart from Havelock Wilson wanted to keep conscription or to use British troops to support the White Russians. There were sharp differences over whether a general strike should ever be used for political purposes, or indeed for any purpose, but, as was to be demonstrated a year later, an issue with a sufficiently powerful appeal could melt these objections away. The crucial divergence was over the government's intentions. The direct actionists believed there was a serious risk that the government would make conscription permanent and go to war with Russia. The majority of the Parliamentary Committee wanted more evidence before they took action.

On 29 July the executive of the Police and Prison Officers Union called a national police strike. General Macready had been appointed Metropolitan Police Commissioner after the 1918 strike, and had manoeuvred the union into boycotting a representative board which he had established. The board carried on without them. In May further substantial improvements in pay and conditions were announced in anticipation of the Desborough report; and, three days before the union gave out that a large majority of their members had voted for a strike for recognition, Macready announced that strikers would be dismissed. In July the government introduced a bill to make it unlawful for policemen to join or remain in a trade union; and to establish a compulsory representative Police Federation. The union executive went ahead with the strike. In London just over a thousand out of a force of over 18,000 came out. Elsewhere the response was worse except in Liverpool where half the force failed to report for duty, and an orgy of pillaging and riots demonstrated the dangers of a police strike. All the strikers were dismissed.

On 18 August Lloyd George announced the government's decision on the final reports of the Sankey Commission, which had appeared

[39] *Hansard*, 29 July 1919, col. 2001.

in June. The Miners' scheme for nationalisation under joint control had been supported by their representatives and by Money, Tawney, and Webb. Five other members had reported unequivocally against nationalisation. Sir Arthur Duckham had recommended amalgamation of collieries into private district trusts under a measure of government control. Finally, the chairman favoured nationalisation, but proposed that the Miners should have only minority representation on the bodies appointed to run the industry. On 15 July a Miners' conference sought to patch together a majority report by indicating their willingness to support the chairman's recommendations.

Lloyd George told the House of Commons that the government would bring forward proposals on the lines of Duckham's recommendations. Sankey's proposals for nationalisation, he said, were based

entirely on the expectation that there will be increased harmony between employer and worker in the mines. But since Mr. Justice Sankey penned that report two or three things have happened which I think would have induced him to change his mind had he had them before his mind at the time. . . . What is the theory of those who say that nationalisation will produce harmony? It is the theory that, while they would ask the worker to strike against the employer who is making a profit, he will not strike against the State, which has only the common interest of all to look after. But then there was the Yorkshire strike. The Yorkshire strike was a direct strike against the Government.[40]

Immediately the air was thick with cries of broken promises, referring to Bonar Law's statement on 20 March that 'the Government . . . are prepared to adopt the Report in the spirit and in the letter' However, it was clear from the context that Law was referring to the interim report signed by Sankey and the three other independent members, and he also said that nationalisation 'must be decided by the Parliament which represents the community'.[41]

It was now possible to gauge the Miners' readiness to strike for nationalisation. On 3 September a further conference voted unanimously for an executive recommendation to reject both the government proposals and the use of industrial action 'at this stage'. They did not propose to strike themselves, nor to call on the Triple Alliance. Instead they turned to Congress which met a few days later and decided that the Parliamentary Committee should intercede with the Prime Minister and call a special Congress if his answer was unsatisfactory. On 9 October came Lloyd George's inevitable refusal to change his mind; in December a special Congress decided to launch a 'Mines for the Nation Campaign'

[40] *Hansard*, 18 August 1919, cols. 2003–4.
[41] Ibid., 20 March 1919, col. 2347.

to arouse public support, and to review the results after a further two months.

The annual meeting of Congress in September also debated the failure of the Parliamentary Committee to call a conference to consider action on the Conscription Bill and related issues. The reference back of the committee's report was carried; and a debate on a resolution declaring 'against the principle of industrial action on purely political matters' was closed when the 'previous question' was moved and carried.[42] Both votes, however, showed the unions were divided almost equally over the question of direct action. Hodges made the telling point that it was not so much the principle as the issue that mattered. If that

is big enough, if it is unsocial enough, if it is sufficiently in antagonism with the best interests of the working classes, I have no fear but that the working classes will say: 'We will use to the greatest capacity the power we feel we possess . . .'.[43]

It appears that the nationalisation of the mines was not such an issue.

Soon after Congress dispersed, trade union attention was diverted from the Miners to the Railwaymen. In August the footplate grades had settled for the standardisation of wages at the highest existing rate, giving a maximum of £4.50 for drivers. The Railwaymen asked for the same principle to be applied to other grades, but the government replied that they wished to restore prewar differentials in standard rates which could be done, nearly enough, by fixing the rates of the remaining grades on the basis of the average pay in each grade instead of the maximum, so that the standard rates of many railwaymen would be less than their current wages. The main justification for this proposal was its effect on other industries. In many of them, including engineering and coalmining, wages were also made up of prewar basic rates and wartime flat-rate additions. It was a reasonable expectation that if prices fell, as it was anticipated they would sooner or later, the wartime additions would be taken off by flat-rate reductions, leading to the restoration of prewar differentials. If the government gave a signal in its railway settlement for the consolidation of wartime additions into standard rates, this would mean the perpetuation of what many employers—and skilled workers—saw as distortions of the labour market.

On the government side the negotiations were handled by the Geddes brothers, Eric, now Minister of Transport, and Auckland, president of the Board of Trade. They were abrasive negotiators, and riled the union executive by presenting their proposals on 19 September, not as a basis for negotiation, but as a 'definitive offer'. On 23 September the

[42] Trades Union Congress, 1919, pp. 288–300.
[43] Ibid., p. 295.

executive decided unanimously to reject the offer, and strike unless better terms were forthcoming, 'as this offer would ultimately mean such a serious reduction to many of our members as would not allow them to maintain a decent standard of life'. Strike instructions went out for midnight on the 26th.

A further conference was arranged for the 25th, at which Lloyd George was to be present, in order to see if a new offer could be made. The course of the negotiations was reviewed for the benefit of the Prime Minister, and the Railwaymen agreed to meet again the next day, assuring the other side that they were ready to cancel the strike notices immediately 'if the answer of the Cabinet is such that would warrant that step'. Next day Lloyd George set out the position:

The fixing of the standard is really only an attempt to establish a minimum below which wages will not in future drop . . . however much the cost of living diminishes. . . . In any event the issue does not arise until 31st December, as until then no man will receive less than his present aggregate earnings, and during that time there is time for negotiations which the Government are willing to continue. . . . In addition . . . there is no question of reducing the present total wage at 31st December if the cost of living should be the same as at present.[44]

At this point Thomas injected: 'This is something new', and Bonar Law said it was not new to him. The Prime Minister continued:

In dealing with any portion of the war wage which may remain when the standard rates come into operation, the Government undertake that such residue will not be reduced until the cost of living has fallen and remained for three months at not more than 110 per cent it is now 115 per cent; it was 125 when the [present] war wage . . . was fixed.[45]

There can be no question but that the Railwaymen's representatives fully understood what was on offer, for Thomas questioned the Prime Minister at some length on what he had said. Thomas next put forward cases of hardship which would arise under the government's proposal for standardisation, and Lloyd George assured him that the government was prepared to discuss them. The Railwaymen were then left alone to consider their answer. When Lloyd George and his colleagues returned, they were told that the strike was on. The Railwaymen now gave as their reason that 'the Government will not apply the principle which brought about the settlement for locomotive drivers and firemen'.

There was to be no reduction until the end of the year, and then only if the cost of living, which was currently rising again, had fallen below 110 and stayed there for three months; and meantime the government were

---

[44] Typescript report, MSS/127/NU/3, Modern Records Centre, University of Warwick.
[45] Ibid.

prepared to continue negotiations. Would it not have been reasonable to call off the strike and continue the talks? However, when analysing railway disputes it is always advisable to remember the sharp rivalry between the Railwaymen and the Locomotive Engineers and Firemen. From 1913 to 1918 the smaller union grew by 24 per cent and the larger by 53 per cent. At that time the latter had probably almost as many footplate staff in membership as the former. In 1918, however, the Locomotive Engineers and Firemen scored a victory by securing the promise of the eight-hour working day, and followed it up in 1919 with the principle of pay standardisation at the highest rate. In that year their membership rose by 43 per cent compared with 17 per cent for the Railwaymen; and in 1920 they gained another 25 per cent whereas the Railwaymen lost 4 per cent. By that time the Locomotive Engineers and Firemen must have had a substantial majority of the footplate staff. The Railwaymen's executive gave as their reason for rejecting the offer that they had not been treated on the same basis as their rivals. In terms of inter-union competition it was a readily comprehensible response.

Thomas did not officially inform the Triple Alliance of the failure of the negotiations, explaining later that he had sought 'a settlement right up to the last moment, and when the break-down came it was too late to use the machinery of the Triple Alliance in any effective manner'.[46] It is also true that Thomas, who tried hard to avoid the strike, was desperately anxious for a quick settlement. He feared that sympathetic action by the alliance would exacerbate and prolong the dispute, and lose public sympathy. Instead he called in the Labour Research Department which organised a well-designed and large-scale publicity campaign. Both they and the government placed full-page advertisements in the daily papers. The situation was much more favourable to the union side than in the Yorkshire Miners' strike. Then the press had suggested that the miners were striking over 0.1 per cent whereas they actually had substantial grievances. Now, although the Railwaymen were guaranteed against any reduction in wages for some months, and their pay would then come down only if prices fell, the 'definitive' offer on standard rates was made to appear as a wage cut imposed by the government; and has gone down in history as that.

Although Thomas had not called in the Triple Alliance, the trade union movement came to the aid of the Railwaymen. The Locomotive Engineers and Firemen struck in sympathy. They could afford to be generous. At Bevin's suggestion, the executive of the Transport Workers Federation invited the Parliamentary Committee, the Labour Party executive, and several major unions to a meeting on 1 October, which sent a deputation led by Henderson to see Lloyd George. Over

[46] Transport Workers Federation, Annual Conference, 1920.

the next few days the deputation, now called the 'Mediation Committee', kept talks going. On 4 October they told Lloyd George that it
would soon 'be impossible to avert a widespread extension of the strike
with all its consequences'.[47] On the other hand the government's
arrangements for road transport were working effectively, and it was
evident that the country was much less vulnerable to a railway strike
than it had been in 1911.

Lloyd George and Thomas kept in touch, and on 5 October Thomas
was able to bring a new offer to his executive which they accepted. The
terms were not very different from those they had rejected on
26 September. The guarantee of no reduction in pay was extended to
30 September 1920; and no adult railwayman was to receive less than
£2.55 a week so long as the cost of living index stood at 110 or above.
Otherwise negotiations on the standard rates were to be resumed on the
principles proposed by the government.

In November the form of future negotiations was settled. There was
to be a joint board of five representatives from the companies and five
from the unions; and issues on which they could not agree were to be
decided by another body of thirteen, including representatives of the
public and an independent chairman. In January 1920 came the government's revised offer on wages. The standard rates were now called
'B' rates, and the remainder of the war wage became the 'A' rates, which
were to fluctuate with changes in the cost of living index. The executive
had taken upon themselves to accept the government's offer which
terminated the strike, but these terms had to be presented to a special
conference, which voted by 54 votes to 2 for higher standard rates and
rejected the principle of indexation on the ground that it would tie
railwaymen to a given standard of living. They also objected to the
exclusion of the Irish railways from the settlement; to the absence of an
offer for railway shopmen; and to the failure to back-date the offer to
August when the footplatemen had settled. Further negotiations led to
the inclusion of the Irish railways, a promise of negotiations for
shopmen, and an offer of a lump sum of £1 for each railwayman in lieu
of back pay, which the government said would have been impossible to
calculate precisely. At a further special conference on 15 January,
Thomas drew on all his powers of persuasion to win a vote by 29–27 for
the terms 'under protest'. In later years railwaymen were to regard it as
the best settlement ever made on their behalf.

The government, apparently, still feared a general strike over coal
nationalisation. 'The Supply and Transport Committee of the Cabinet,
meeting on January 15, 1920, was more alarmed than at any time in its
history'.[48] They could hardly have been more wrong. The rail strike

[47] Bagwell. p. 398. [48] Armitage, p. 137.

had put the Triple Alliance into disarray. The 'Mines for the Nation' campaign was a flop. The Miners met in conference on 10 March to decide what to propose to the further special Congress which was due on 18 March to review progress. On a block vote by districts it was agreed to ask for 'a general Trade Union strike in the event of the Government continuing to refuse to nationalise the mines'. Had the decision been by ballot vote, under the federation's rules for calling a strike, the majority of three to two would have been insufficient to warrant a stoppage. Congress voted by 3,732,000 to 1,015,000 for 'intensive political propaganda in preparation for a General Election'.[49] There were very few unions in the minority apart from the Miners.

It seemed as though direct action was dead. Then, suddenly, at the beginning of August 1920 the whole movement appeared to forget its differences and hesitations for a few days in a united demand, backed by the threat of a general strike, that the government should not wage war on Russia. In the autumn of 1919 the Red Army had destroyed the remaining White armies in Russia; but in the spring of 1920, with financial assistance and materials supplied by Britain and France, the Poles swept into the Ukraine, capturing Kiev on 12 June. At the beginning of May, dockers in London had sought, and received, Bevin's backing for refusing to load the *Jolly George* with munitions for Poland. On 13 July a special meeting of Congress, called to discuss the government's policy of repression in Ireland, had voted for withdrawal of British troops from Ireland, and 'the cessation of production of munitions of war destined to be used against Ireland and Russia, and, in case the Government refuses these demands, . . . a general down-tools policy', each union to hold its own ballot.[50] However, the Red Army had now begun to roll the Poles back across their frontier, and was soon advancing on Warsaw. Negotiations for an armistice failed, and on 3 August the British government informed the Russians that their obligations to the League of Nations would oblige them to come to Poland's aid. On 6 August *The Times* warned that 'we stand on the edge of a crisis fraught with possibilities only less tragic than those that lowered over us in the first week of August six years ago'.

Next day a manifesto appeared over the signature of sixteen Labour leaders, including Henderson and Clynes, warning the government that they 'would not co-operate in a war as allies of Poland'. On Sunday, 8 August, demonstrations were held throughout the country. On 9 August a joint meeting of the party executive, the Parliamentary Committee, and the parliamentary party threatened that 'the whole industrial power of the organised workers will be used to defeat this war', and advised

[49] Trades Union Congress, 1920, p. 88.
[50] Ibid., p. 116.

union executives 'to instruct their members to "down tools" on instructions of the National Conference' which they were proposing to convene.[51] Hitherto every proposal for direct action had involved the unions concerned taking the decision to call a strike according to their own rules, a procedure so cumbersome that it would make a general strike almost impossible. Now a conference was to instruct union executives to bring their members out without regard to their rules. The unions responded—not only the Miners, Railwaymen, Engineers, and Dockers, but also the General Workers, whose executive agreed on 12 August 'to industrial resistance against the Government in the event of it declaring war with Russia'.

The joint meeting also set up a Council of Action with five representatives from each of the three organisations, who co-opted four more including Bevin and Smillie. Within hours, local councils of action were being set up all over the country. When the national council saw Lloyd George, Bevin acted as spokesman, bluntly stating their objections to every kind of aid or support for the Poles. The Prime Minister was diplomatic in his reply, and next day assured the House of Commons that no 'allied troops' were being sent to Poland. 'We have made that clear to Poland, and it is essential we should make it clear to this country.'[52] There was, therefore, nothing for the special conference on 13 August to do, except approve of what had been done. The tension eased, the Polish armies, reorganised by General Weygand, began to drive the Russians back, and in October an armistice was signed. In Britain the councils of action, both national and local, had so enjoyed their brief days of glory that they refused to disband themselves for some months—to the embarrassment of the Parliamentary Committee and the Labour Party which had called them into existence, but providing ample material for Thomson's alarmist reports to the cabinet.

Whether there really was a danger of war or not has never been established. What is clear is that, for the first time in their history, British trade unions were ready for a general strike, and the Parliamentary Committee were ready to take responsibility for it. The reason certainly was not a swing to the left. Politically most of the leftwing factions were involved in complex negotiations, under pressure from Moscow, to unite in a British Communist Party. Industrially, the number of strikes had fallen off sharply since the first half of the year, and the trade union movement had not seemed so quiescent since the armistice, or even earlier. What had been tapped was the movement's widely-shared and strongly-held sentiment in favour of peace, which owed as much to the Lib–Labs as to the socialists. It had been muted in 1914,

[51] Ibid., p. 117.
[52] Hansard, 10 August 1920, col. 263.

but only after war had been declared and the country appeared to be in danger. To enter upon a war by an act of aggression against a country which, whatever the merits of its regime, was offering no direct threat to Britain, was as repugnant to Clynes, Henderson, and Thomas as it was to Smillie and Robert Williams; and, with memories of 1914–18 fresh in their minds, war-weary trade union members, and the public, felt the same. For once union leaders 'took the initiative on a political issue instead of applying the brake and were sure of the support of the rank and file'.[53] Thomas told Congress next month that they had 'definitely challenged the constitution', but 'dangerous as was our remedy—and it was dangerous—it was justified by the result'.[54] Clynes was more ingenious. Speaking to the conference of the Federation of General Workers on 19 August, he said:

Labour is justified in using its industrial strength on the side of Peace when no political remedy can avail. . . . Now, in my judgment, that is not challenging the constitution, but it is requiring our Government to conform to the constitution. The constitution now includes provision for a League of Nations to settle international differences. If a few Ministers refused to use that League, the workers, without any danger to their country, are justified in refusing to take part in war-like measures of any kind whatever.

By the end of August the attention of the movement reverted to the Miners who had been engaged in a prolonged controversy with the government over wages and prices. The Miners accused the government of blaming them for increases in the price of coal which, they said, served to increase the profits of the coalowners, which were then creamed off by the government. They argued that prices should be brought down in order to reduce the cost of living—even after the price of household coal was cut by 50p a ton in December 1919. They threatened that they would have to claim another wage increase if there were no price cuts. The claim went in during March and was settled in April for an advance of 20 per cent on earnings, with a guarantee of a minimum increase of 10p a shift to every adult miner. In May the government withdrew the 50p price reduction to household consumers and added 21p a ton to the price of all coal sold in Britain. Exported coal was sold at the famine prices which still prevailed at that time. The Miners understood from the official figures that the government surplus from the coal industry was running at £66 million a year. Smillie, for whom nationalisation was still the overriding objective, feared that the government was aiming to increase prices until every colliery was making a profit, so that the industry could be decontrolled painlessly—

[53] Bullock, p. 142.
[54] Trades Union Congress, 1920, p. 62.

until prices fell. That would put the Miners' national wage agreement at risk, and destroy whatever chance there might be of nationalisation. On 10 June he told a Miners' conference:

We must put in a claim for an advance in wages—a substantial advance in wages—or we must force the Government to take off the 14s 2d [71p] a ton on coal; either the one or the other. Either one of these cuts fundamentally into the Government's policy.

In July they asked for both the price cut and the wage increase, although Lancashire and South Wales voted for a straight wage claim. When the government refused both, the men voted by well over two to one for a strike, although the vote in Yorkshire, whose leaders disagreed with Smillie's policy, was only marginally in favour. With the aid of the Labour Research Department and the Triple Alliance, the federation proceeded to organise a publicity campaign, hoping that their 'indivisible demand' for a wage increase and a price reduction would win popular support—even though the wage demand was the second within a few months. However, the response from the press was strongly hostile, even before the official returns for the second quarter of the year showed that the surplus was now running at £33 million a year, far less than would be needed to meet the 'indivisible demand' in full. The Miners doubted the figures, but could not prove that they were wrong. They therefore dropped the claim for a price reduction, asking instead for an inquiry into coal prices; and submitted a demand for a wage increase only, of 10p a day. The government indicated that they were willing to consider a wage increase if it was linked to an increase in coal output; and they were ready to go to arbitration, which the Miners refused. The strike was called for 25 September. Three days earlier the *Manchester Guardian* had 'no hesitation in declaring our belief that responsibility for any disastrous consequences will rest on the shoulders of the miners'.

Lloyd George had been conducting a daily exchange of letters with Smillie. He made a point of contrasting the Miners' rejection of arbitration with the Dockers' acceptance of a court of inquiry earlier in the year. The Triple Alliance was meeting almost every day, and both the Transport Workers and the Railwaymen were impressed by the offer of arbitration. On 22 September Thomas told the Miners that 'if . . . it is going to be a Triple Alliance fight it immediately comes out of the hands of the Miners' Federation'. Next day a special conference of the Railwaymen voted 28–27 against striking in support of the Miners, and soon afterwards the Transport Workers Federation reported that they 'could not join in general strike action'.[55]

[55] Transport Workers Federation, *Special Report on the Mining Crisis.*

Whether or not a strike would win a wage increase, Smillie knew it would do the cause of nationalisation nothing but harm. Again and again he pleaded with the Miners' conference, which was in almost daily session, for a ballot on taking their case to a tribunal, arguing both the effect on public opinion and the need to maintain the unity of the federation. Once this was broken, he said on 23 September,

it would take years to build up again, as a matter of fact it has taken the lives of men in this room during the last 25 years to knit together this great Federation, and on a mere wages question, we ought not, I think, to risk breaking it down.

He did not lack support among the leaders—Straker and Spencer, Doonan of Scotland, Hogg of Northumberland, and Hough of Yorkshire. Even Twist of Lancashire, not given to shrinking from conflict, said that, if 'we tremble at the thought of using [our] power', it would be better to go to arbitration. Nevertheless all that Smillie could achieve was further delay to carry on negotiations with the government. Their only concession was a reduction in the 'datum line' of national output at which a bonus would be paid, from a rate of 242 million tons a year to 240 million. (For 1920 as a whole output was 230 million tons.) This offer was referred to the men, notices being once more postponed. They rejected it by well over three to one, and, when conference met again on 14 October, even Smillie admitted that there was 'nothing for it' but to allow the notices to run out on 16 October. He went on to announce his resignation, saying: 'You will have enough to face without carrying about with you a Jonah in the shape of your President'; but, after delegate upon delegate had appealed to him, he agreed to stay in office.

The strike began on 16 October. The government rushed through an Emergency Powers Act which gave them considerable powers to commandeer resources, to run emergency services, and to take proceedings against anyone who hindered them, with the proviso that the right to strike remained intact. How far legislation was needed to authorise these powers only a lawyer can say, but the Act showed that the government meant business. It seemed as though there was to be a battle of attrition when the Railwaymen suddenly reversed their decision. Their conference delegates had asked to be recalled if there was no settlement. Reluctantly the executive invited them to a joint session on 20 October, but the delegates soon tired of that, and met separately next day when, led by Marchbank, they resolved that, if the Miners' claim was not met, they would be 'compelled to take the necessary steps to instruct our members to . . . cease work'. On hearing this the Parliamentary Committee summoned a special Congress for the 27th. Negotiations were hastily resumed, and a provisional agreement reached on the 28th. The datum line was fixed at an annual rate of output of 234 million tons, which was to bring an increase of 2.5p a day; each additional 4 million tons was to yield another 2.5p; and until 31 December 10p, the figure the Miners had asked for, would be guaranteed. Thereafter the figure was to be revised each month according to the previous month's output. The whole scheme was to remain in force only so long as it took the Miners and the owners to agree on a permanent system of regulating pay. The men rejected these terms by a very narrow majority, far below the two-thirds required to call or continue a Miners' strike, but indicating a widespread dislike of tying pay to output.

It was a Pyrrhic victory for the Miners. Up to Christmas 10p a day was paid. In January the amount was 17.5p, in February 7.5p, and that was all. To gain this fleeting advantage, most districts had paid out most of their reserves in strike pay; the Triple Alliance had been gravely weakened; much public sympathy was forfeited; the government had been convinced that the Miners were unreasonable men; and valuable time, which might have been employed in negotiating a permanent pay system, had been frittered away. With coal prices falling fast at home and abroad by the end of the year, the prospects for agreement in such negotiations now were poor, and they became a good deal worse shortly after they started by the government's announcement on 22 February that the industry was to be decontrolled at the end of March. The surplus which the government had reaped from control had already turned into a mounting deficit. The owners wanted the government to cut wages before decontrolling the mines, but accepted the decision once they were assured that their standard profits were guaranteed to the end of March. The Miners protested vigorously, but to no effect. Negotiations on the new wage system became desperately earnest.

It was common ground that the 'datum line' should go, and that wages should vary with profits. From the owners' point of view this arrangement was a substitute for the former selling-price sliding scale agreements which had ensured that falling prices would automatically bring lower wage-costs; and the Miners Federation, committed to a profits pool in order to sustain national wage adjustment, could hardly object to a proposal which would ensure that there were profits to pool. Standard wages were to be the first charge on the industry after other costs had been met, followed by standard profits, with any surplus divided between wages and profits. Thereafter the proposals diverged. The Miners wanted the relationship between wages and profits to be 10:1. The owners wanted a ratio of 100:17 for the standards, and 3:1 for the surplus. The owners' standard wage was to be 1914 district wages, plus changes to district standards since then, together with the adjustments granted when working hours were reduced from eight to seven. The Miners' standard included the percentage additions granted during and since the war, with the profits pool to pay for them. The flat rate national additions, now 25p a shift, were also included in the Miners' proposals, presumably as another charge on the pool, but the executive were prepared to bargain over this element in their scheme.

The owners steadfastly refused to maintain the pool. As always with the onset of depression, export prices for coal were falling faster than domestic prices, so that the pool would have entailed heavy subsidies to the exporting districts, especially to South Wales which had suffered the most drastic decline in productivity. The government also refused to have anything to do with the pool which, in the absence of agreement by the owners, would require legislation. Horne, now president of the Board of Trade, wrote to the Miners on 15 March to say that 'it would not only be contrary to the principles upon which we believe the commercial success of this country to be based, but it would be disastrous to the coal industry itself'.

Horne had replaced the Geddes brothers as Lloyd George's industrial adviser. Although he had been a successful and generally acceptable Minister of Labour, he had little sympathy with the Miners' case. According to Smillie, 'it was a virtual waste of time and words, as far as he was concerned, to attempt to negotiate at all'.[56] There had also been important changes in the Miners Federation. Following his victory in a parliamentary by-election, Barker had resigned from the executive at the beginning of the year. He was succeeded by Arthur Cook, as militant in his opinions as Ablett, but as emotional and warm as Ablett was hard and bitter. Of greater moment was the resignation of Smillie, whose policies were in ruins. He may by now have been reflecting that, since the fiasco of the final Sankey report, his time would have been better spent negotiating with the owners over a permanent pay settlement and with the government over their proposals for the future of the industry than in scheming for nationalisation.

The vice-president, Herbert Smith, had therefore to take over in the middle of a crisis. He was no match for Smillie either in intelligence or charm, being a stubborn, dour, and in many respects ignorant Yorkshireman, but he had one outstanding qualification for the post— he understood miners. 'He was the most perfect expression of the pitman that ever came to leadership. . . . Miners knew that he was bone of their bone, flesh of their flesh, and mentally living with them.'[57]

By the time the delegates met on 17 March to consider Horne's letter, the owners' proposed district rates had been posted in the pits to take effect on 31 March. According to the owners, they varied from slight

[56] Smillie, p. 278. [57] Lawson, pp. 85–6.

advances on current wages for some pieceworkers in Yorkshire to cuts of 30 per cent in Durham and 40 per cent in South Wales. With no comfort from the government, and coal stocks mounting fast, the Miners' executive proposed next day that the pool should be temporarily abandoned, and they should be empowered to make a settlement 'on a district basis'. Hodges put their reasons bluntly to the delegates.

Why is it these districts have to have such a big reduction? Because their productivity per person employed has gone down and down and down. . . . If we strike, what are we striking for? We are striking for a subsidy. . . . Do you think you can get a subsidy out of the Government by means of a strike? . . . You know you cannot.

The vote was two to one for the executive. The next stage was a vote of the district councils. They were being asked without warning to drop the national settlement of wages which had been the federation's greatest achievement so far. It was only natural that most of them should agree with Ablett's reply to Hodges:

We are the biggest union in this country—perhaps in the world—today, and the only one capable of fighting. We have used every other means of defence, and we say that these things are of such importance and contain such fundamental principles that every man with the spirit of Trade Unionism in him will attempt to resist.

The executive was supported by Yorkshire, many of whose miners were not threatened with an immediate pay cut, by Leicestershire and Derbyshire, where the cuts would be small, by Northumberland, and by such specialist groups as the enginemen, the cokemen and the Cleveland iron ore miners. The rest insisted on the national pool, and their decision was accepted.

On 30 March the Miners' executive sought the aid of the Triple Alliance. The previous autumn Bevin had been convinced that it was 'a paper alliance',[58] and no action had been taken over the memorandum on revising its constitution which the Transport Workers Federation had commissioned Williams to write.[59] Nevertheless a conference of affiliated unions on 5 April resolved to give the Miners 'all the assistance in our power', and three days later the Railwaymen's conference voted unanimously to strike in support of the Miners, provided the transport workers struck 'jointly and simultaneously' with them. The two organisations put in strike notices for 13 April. On 8 April the government called out reservists and appealed to 'loyal citizens' to join a new 'Defence Force'.

[58] Bullock, p. 152.
[59] Transport Workers Federation, *Special Report on the Mining Crisis.*

Another decision of the Miners' executive on 30 March, by ten votes to eight, was to bring out the safety men. Once the strike began, mass pickets prevented any safety work in many of the pits. This issue was seized on by the government and the press, which made a great outcry over the plight of the pit ponies, although the union had in fact made arrangements for them to be brought to the surface. Now their partners in the alliance persuaded the Miners to issue instructions that the owners and the government should be allowed to take measures to secure the safety of the pits by using managerial staff for the job. Thereupon the government agreed to reopen negotiations, but no major concession was offered on either side at conferences on 11 and 12 April. On the 13th the Triple Alliance unions therefore renewed their strike notices, which had been postponed for the discussions, fixing the time for 10 p.m. on 15 April. Enthusiasm ran high. The Locomotive Engineers and Firemen issued strike notices; the Electricians offered help; a joint meeting of the Parliamentary Committee, the party executive, and the parliamentary party pledged support.

However, despite the Miners' insistence that their allies had no right to take part in negotiations until they were on strike, the leaders of the Transport Workers and the Railwaymen saw Lloyd George on the 14th. He assured them that he was willing to negotiate on wages, but not to give way on the pool. According to Hodges's report to the Miners' conference on 22 April, their allies were already unhappy about the pool, and, when they met the Miners' executive after leaving Lloyd George, they 'brought out a sheaf of resolutions from the branches protesting against the Executive of their organisation leading them into a strike without first having a ballot on the issue'.

Later that evening Hodges spoke to Members of Parliament at the House of Commons. According to the Press Association report, he said, in answer to a question, that 'we are prepared to consider wages, provided that they are not to be regarded as permanently on a district basis, but only of a temporary character'. Lloyd George seized on these words, and next morning the Miners' executive had a letter from the Prime Minister saying that, if they were prepared to discuss a temporary settlement on a district basis, he would meet them that morning.

It was a favourable moment to reopen negotiations, for, 'worried about the public sympathy which the miners had aroused by publishing the size of the wage cuts', a deputation from the Federation of British Industries had proposed to Lloyd George a temporary arrangement to pool both profits and wages in order to subsidise wages in the worst-hit districts.[60] However, without consulting their allies, the Miners' executive decided by nine votes to eight to reject the invitation. Hodges

[60] Armitage, pp. 150–52.

offered his resignation but was persuaded to withdraw it. In the House of Commons at noon, according to the *Daily Mail* next day, 'the general tone of the Labour members was one of cheery optimism. . . . Then, like a thunderclap, came the utterly unexpected announcement that the miners . . . had decided . . . that the Government's invitation must be declined.'

The Miners' allies were meeting along with the executive of the Locomotive Engineers and Firemen in Unity House, the Railwaymen's headquarters, and, on hearing the news, all their hesitations rose to the top of their minds: the patchy response of their members; the high level of unemployment; the dangers of blacklegging; the fact that mining strikes become more effective as stocks run down whereas transport strikes have their maximum effect on the first day before alternative arrangements are made; and the risk that the Miners would continue to go their own way without listening to their allies. Telegrams poured in from the branches asking for instructions. As the afternoon wore on they had to take a decision. A resolution to try to see the Miners again was lost by 28 votes to 12. Then only five votes, all of them cast by railwaymen, were recorded against a proposal to call off the strike. A press communiqué stated: 'A partial and hopelessly incomplete stoppage would have weakened the power of the three organisations without contributing any material assistance to the Miners.' The Triple Alliance was dead.

Who was to blame? The myth of Black Friday made the union leaders who failed to strike into the villains of the piece; but this was grossly unfair. The Miners chose to make the profits pool into the central issue. The public did not understand the pool; the owners and the government had rejected it; Smith, Hodges, and a majority of the Miners' executive had proposed that it should be dropped, and they had been supported by a two-to-one vote at a Miners' conference. The Miners were already expecting a great deal of their allies in asking them to bring their members out on strike for the pool. Now their allies were expected to proceed with the strike, although the Miners had rejected a renewed offer of negotiations which the threat of a Triple Alliance strike had helped to bring about. Circumstances did not favour a strike. From December 1920 to March 1921 the percentage of insured workers unemployed had risen from 7.9 to 15.4; and at least some of the transport unions could not rely on their members. The road haulage unions had shown their weakness already in 1920, when unemployment figures were only starting to rise; and Hirst, now secretary of the United Vehicle Workers into which the Tramwaymen and Licensed Vehicle Workers had merged, told his annual conference later in the year that, in order not to prejudice the outcome, he had not once mentioned 'information I had in regard to the weakness of certain sections of our members'; but they must have influenced his vote. Nevertheless, as Citrine wrote long afterwards:

The refusal of the other unions in the Alliance to back the Miners by a strike caused tremendous indignation among those trade unionists who, like myself, had at that time no first-hand knowledge of the affair.[61]

Citrine was by then assistant general secretary of his union and therefore in a much better position to know what was going on than most trade unionists were. If he accepted the myth of Black Friday, it is not surprising that it became the firm belief of most of the movement.

After more than two years of experimentation with direct action, British trade unionists had learned no conclusive lessons. At Congress in 1919, shortly after the attempt to employ direct action over conscription had ended in farcical disarray, there had been considerable support for the view that it should not be used for purely political purposes. Next year Congress decided not to employ it over coal nationalisation—a political issue. In 1921 the Miners weakened their case against wage cuts by insisting on the pool, which would have required legislation. However, the aim of the Council of Action was purely political, and the council provided the one instance in which direct action appeared to have been a success. It seemed to confirm Hodges's opinion that success was most likely over that issue about which trade union members felt most strongly—and also on which they might expect to win most public support. If so, there was no general or Triple Alliance strike during these years because there was no issue of this kind, apart from the danger of war with Russia over Poland, although, without the pool, the Miners' dispute in 1921 might have provided another.

Bevin and Williams had come to the conclusion that the crucial factor was the machinery for conducting direct action, and that the machinery of the Triple Alliance had been shown to be inadequate. However, in August 1920, when there had been no machinery to co-ordinate strike action by the whole movement, an impromptu Council of Action was successfully improvised to do the job.

Trade Unions at a Peak of Growth

Trade union membership continued to grow over the first two postwar years, from 6.46 million at the end of 1918 to 8.25 million at the end of 1920. Since unemployment had then been rising for some months, it is possible that an even higher total may have been reached earlier in 1920. This expansion was more evenly distributed over the whole trade union movement than wartime growth; but disproportionately large contri-

[61] Citrine, p. 131.

butions were made by agriculture, still benefiting from the Corn Production Act; by road transport following the introduction of national negotiations in 1917; and by national and local government after civil servants had at last been granted the right to bargain, and National Joint Councils had been established in local government. Exceptional growth was also recorded in distribution, and in banking and finance, which should probably be regarded as a protest against the drastic squeeze of white collar incomes during the war. The largest single contribution to postwar expansion, however, came from the building unions, whose membership increased by 80 per cent over the two years. Within that increase there was an even more startling advance among building labourers. From 51,000 in 1918 the combined membership of the four major unions of building labourers[62] soared to 169,000 in 1920; and the general unions also had a considerable, and almost certainly rising, membership in construction. In 1920 trade union membership among building workers reached a peak unequalled before or since. Some of this expansion was probably due to the further development of collective bargaining in the industry; but more to an insatiable demand for labour in an industry which had been denuded by war.

By contrast the four major general unions, which had expanded so rapidly from 1910 to 1918, now grew at a slightly slower pace than the movement as a whole; but their overall figures hid a massive turnover in membership. Their wartime expansion had been predominantly in munitions. Now they lost the great majority of that membership, and needed heavy recruitment elsewhere merely to avoid decline.

Ten years' growth since 1910 had radically changed the composition of the trade union movement. In 1910 there was only one 'labourers' union' in the list of the 'top ten' unions—the Gasworkers, in bottom place. In 1920 there were five such unions, the Workers Union in second place, the General Workers (formerly Gasworkers) in fourth place, and the National Amalgamated Union of Labour, the London Dockers, and the Agricultural Workers in the seventh, eighth, and ninth places. Taking a broader view, in 1910 all the general, transport, and agricultural unions, with less than one-third of a million members between them, constituted 12 per cent of total trade union membership; and in 1920, with about 2.75 million members, they provided nearly a third of the total. By contrast coal and cotton, with 1.07 million members in 1910 and 1.73 million in 1920, had fallen from almost two-fifths of the total to just over one-fifth. By 1920 the relative decline of

---

[62] The National Association of Builders Labourers, the United Order of General Labourers, the National Builders Labourers and Constructional Workers Society, and the Altogether Builders Labourers and Constructional Workers Society (which had been founded in 1920 and claimed 58,000 members at the end of the year).

the Miners had slightly reduced the share of the 'top ten' to below 44 per cent of the total, although the share of the other nine unions had risen to 32 per cent compared with 22 per cent in 1910.

Overall trade union density rose from less than 16 per cent in 1910 to over 48 per cent in 1920. In 1910 only coal (71.4 per cent) and posts and telecommunications (53.5 per cent) exceeded 50 per cent. In 1920 fourteen industries exceeded 50 per cent and four of them—coal, docks, printing and publishing, and posts and telecommunications—were over 90 per cent. Construction had sustained the most impressive rate of growth over the period as a whole, rising from 16 per cent to 88 per cent.

Density among white collar workers had risen only slightly faster than among manual workers, but among women workers it had risen from 6 per cent to 25 per cent, and the proportion of women in total trade union membership was 16 per cent compared with 10 per cent in 1910, having reached a peak of 18 per cent in 1918. In 1910 cotton had accounted for more than half of women trade unionists; and education and national and local government for more than half the rest. After the war women trade unionists were more widely distributed, with cotton's share down to 22 per cent.

Interest in union amalgamations, encouraged by the 1917 Act, grew into a fever once the war was over. Amalgamation discussions were in progress during 1919 and 1920 in engineering, shipbuilding, paper and printing, building, steel, clothing, cotton, distribution, the civil service, and the Post Office, as well as many smaller industries and services; and there were also discussions among general and transport unions covering scores of industries and services. Some unions were engaged in concurrent talks with a number of other unions. During those two years the General Workers discussed amalgamation proposals with the Agricultural Workers, the Asylum Workers, the Birmingham Gasworkers, the Doublers and Kindred Trades, the Dry Dock Workers, the Enginemen and Cranemen, the Federation of Government Workers, the Federation of Women Workers, the London Dockers, the Municipal Employees, the National Amalgamated Union of Labour, the North Wales Quarrymen, the Poor Law Officers, the Prudential Agents, and the Workers Union.

Most of the proposed amalgamations fell through; many were bound to do so since they clashed with other proposals for mergers; but many were successful. The Engineers joined with the Steam Engine Makers, the Machine Workers, the Toolmakers, and six other engineering unions to form the Amalgamated Engineering Union. The foundry unions declined to take part because they were already involved in talks which united the Ironfounders, the Iron Moulders of Scotland, and the Coremakers in the National Union of Foundry Workers. Among carpenters and joiners, the Amalgamated Society (which had already absorbed the Cabinet Makers) joined forces with the General Union to form the Amalgamated Society of Woodworkers. The Plasterers withdrew from negotiations for a single union for the 'trowel' trades, but the Operative Bricklayers, the Manchester Bricklayers, and the Stone-masons remained to form the Amalgamated Union of Building Trade Workers. Bitter competition between the Printing and Paper Workers and the Bookbinders and Machine Rulers over the organisation of women workers was ended by their amalgamation into the National Union of Printing, Bookbinding, Machine Ruling, and Paper Workers. In clothing the Tailors and Tailoresses maintained their independence, but the Garment Workers absorbed a batch of smaller unions, including the Scottish Tailors, to become the Tailors and Garment Workers Union.

Outside the craft trades, the Amalgamated Society of Steel and Iron Workers, based in Scotland, the Tin and Sheet Millmen, the Wire Drawers, and the Tube Workers joined the Iron and Steel Trades Confederation. In distribution the Co-operative Employees merged with the Warehousemen and General Workers to form the National Union of Distributive and Allied Workers. The Postmen's Federation, the Postal and Telegraph Clerks, and the Fawcett Association joined together with six smaller unions to form the Union of Post Office Workers. Of the mergers affecting the administrative departments of the civil service the most important was the formation of the Civil Service Clerical Association.

Among the failures, the Amalgamated Union of Shipbuilding, Engineering, and Constructional Workers was intended to unite the Boilermakers, the Shipwrights, and the Associated Blacksmiths. In 1920 cards were issued and a temporary executive formed. Then disagree-ments about the structure of the permanent executive hindered further progress, and an alternative scheme for a wider federation was overwhelmed by the depression. The cotton unions floated a proposal for amalgamation, and replaced it by another for converting the United Textile Factory Workers Association into a federation explicitly for industrial as well as political purposes. Both failed.

Overshadowing all these amalgamations, both projected and achieved, were the various schemes under discussion among the general and transport unions, one of which affected more than a million members. The first to be tested was the revived scheme for a merger between the General Workers and the London Dockers. When the votes were counted at the end of 1919 both unions showed large majorities in favour, but the poll among the Dockers fell short of the legal requirement of 50 per cent. There were charges 'that Bevin had not been in favour of the scheme and by refusing to put his energy and influence behind it had killed it. Bevin indignantly denied the accusation but there was almost certainly some truth in it.'[63] He would not have been the chief officer of the amalgamated union.

Neither union showed much dismay at the failure, for each was already discussing an alternative scheme. Bevin was negotiating with all those unions in the Transport Workers Federation which had a predominant interest in transport, except the Sailors and Firemen who rejected his approach. The General Workers were brought into talks with the three partners who had formed the federal National Amalgamated Workers Union and were now planning a 'full amalgamation'.

Bevin's scheme went ahead the more rapidly. Early in 1920 the merger between the Amalgamated Tramwaymen and the Licensed Vehicle Workers had produced, in the United Vehicle Workers, a union which rivalled the London Dockers as the largest transport union outside the railways. Nevertheless, they fell in with his plans. The major road haulage union, the National Union of Vehicle Workers, which had up to now rejected the approaches of the road passenger transport unions, was persuaded to join in this wider scheme, as were the Liverpool Dockers and a number of smaller unions. Administratively the new union was to be a complete amalgamation, but separate trade groups with their own officers and committees were to handle industrial business, subject to a national executive (including both regional and trade group representatives) with final control over finance, policy, and strikes. Such a dual system of administration already existed in the Printing, Bookbinding, and Paper Workers and in the National Union of Clerks, but Bevin's scheme was on a far larger scale than theirs. Among its attractions were the trade group secretaryships and national trade group committees, which could be used to persuade the secretaries and executives of interested unions that, if they joined, they would continue to hold positions of wide-ranging authority within the new organisation.

Negotiations were finalised in December 1920, and voting began early in 1921. By March the London Dockers, the United Vehicle Workers, and six smaller unions had satisfied the legal requirements, but the National Union of Vehicle Workers, the Liverpool Dockers, the Scottish Dockers, the Stevedores and one or two smaller unions had failed to do so. They were persuaded either to keep the ballot open or to try again, and in the end only the Stevedores failed to ratify. The new union came into existence on 1 January 1922. It would have been a remarkable accomplishment at any time, but to carry it through in a year of severe depression was proof of Bevin's unique skill, personal

[63] Bullock, p. 155.

authority, and perseverance. Elections held early in 1922 confirmed Bevin as secretary and Gosling as president. Two major personalities excluded from the top posts were Tillett and Williams. Tillett had never had great administrative ability or liking for hard work. He was a less attractive figurehead than Gosling, and an impossible choice for the post of secretary. Williams would have made a better job of it, but he could not rival Bevin, and was politically unacceptable. Tillett was therefore made secretary of a new political and international department at head office, and Williams remained secretary of a federation dominated by a single union. Inevitably Bevin's handling of these manoeuvres left considerable ill-feeling.

Progress to full amalgamation within the National Amalgamated Workers Union was hindered by continued differences between the National Amalgamated Union of Labour and the Workers Union. The executive of the former, traditional in their methods, with elected officers closely under their control, were deeply suspicious of the go-ahead methods of the latter's appointed officials, who, they believed, 'acted on the principle that the members should have no say in the affairs of the Amalgamation, and the only use they had for them was to pay contributions and to provide the funds for other people to dispose of'.[64] They were therefore pleased to be able to introduce into the discussions the General Workers, whose methods were closer to their own, whose membership was almost as large as that of the Workers Union, and whose leaders had a higher standing in the movement. Nevertheless progress was slow, and meanwhile the General Workers absorbed several smaller unions, including the Federation of Women Workers and the Birmingham Gasworkers, which took their membership ahead of that of the Workers Union.

This spate of mergers made only modest progress towards rationalising the structure of the trade union movement. In engineering, the foundries, and building, the outcome was the absorption of a number, but by no means all, of the smaller craft unions into the major craft unions. The National Union of Printing, Bookbinding, Machine Ruling, and Paper Workers brought some of the crafts and most of the less-skilled workers in the printing and paper industries into a single union, which nevertheless left most of the crafts and many of the less-skilled workers outside. By joining with the Warehouse and General Workers, the Co-operative Employees had extended their domain out from the co-operative retail societies and the factories of the Co-operative Wholesale Society into private distribution and a range of private manufacturing industries, especially foodstuffs, clothing, chemicals, and rubber. The Iron and Steel Trades Confederation, and the

[64] National Amalgamated Union of Labour executive, 29 July 1919.

Union of Post Office Workers, were both designed to a more rational plan than the unions they replaced, but even they fell substantially short of the ideal of industrial unionism, for the Blastfurnacemen, and considerable bodies of engineering and building craftsmen and general workers employed in the steel industry still retained their separate unions; and the Post Office Engineering Union and several smaller organisations of Post Office employees also kept their independence.

At that time the Transport and General Workers might have been counted as a major contribution to a more orderly structure for British trade unionism; but their 'general workers' trade group gave them a stake in half the industries and services in the country, and was eventually to expand until it overshadowed all the transport trade groups put together.

The Trades Union Congress was also a target for the reformers. It was the belief of the *ad hoc* Mediation Committee formed in the 1919 railway strike that their own existence demonstrated the inadequacy of the authority of the Parliamentary Committee. Shortly after the strike had been settled, on 8 October, they sent a deputation to the Parliamentary Committee to propose that its powers should be extended 'to enable it to become the central co-ordinating body of all future Trade Union activities'. A Co-ordination Committee of six representatives from the Parliamentary Committee, four from the Mediation Committee, and five from the trade union side of the National Industrial Conference's Provisional Committee was set up to formulate proposals. All the members of the new committee were trade union leaders except G. D. H. Cole, who came as one of the representatives of the Provisional Committee. Much of the task of drafting fell to him.

There were five problems: to find a more satisfactory method of electing the executive body of Congress; to persuade the unions to equip it with greater powers; to provide it with staff commensurate with those powers; to improve co-ordination with the Labour Party; and to find the money to pay for the changes.

The need for a new electoral system at Congress became acute in 1919 when both the Miners' candidates for the Parliamentary Committee were defeated. In 1920 Smillie demanded the enforcement of the rule prohibiting the 'canvassing and bartering of votes'. In the previous year, he said, 'a few days before the election you could have had a list of the new members of the Parliamentary Committee. . . . It was known that the Miners would not be represented.'[65] A committee set up to investigate Smillie's complaint reported to Congress in 1921 that there had been a 'tremendous development in the vicious principle of bartering and bargaining which has grown up in recent years', especially

[65] Trades Union Congress, 1920, p. 248.

with the development of powerful federations; but to enforce the rule would have entailed disqualifying half the affiliated unions for three years.[66] The remedy proposed in Cole's draft was a new scheme of seventeen industrial groups with another group for women. There were to be thirty-two seats to allow from one to four representatives to a group, according to the membership represented. Nomination for seats within each group was to be restricted to the unions within it, but election was to be by Congress at large.

The new executive body thus elected was to be called a General Council. Its functions included the resolution of inter-union disputes; relations with trade union and labour movements abroad; and the duty to

keep a watch on all industrial movements, and, where possible, [to] co-ordinate industrial action. It shall promote common action by the Trade Union movement on general questions, such as wages and hours of labour, and any matter of general concern that may arise between . . . employers and Trade Unions or between the Trade Union movement and the Government, and shall have power to assist any union which is attacked on any vital question of Trade Union principle.

However, when Gosling, the chairman of the Co-ordination Committee, introduced the proposals to Congress in 1920, he referred to 'misgiving among some unions as to whether this would interfere with their freedom or affect their autonomy'. He therefore proposed a qualifying clause, approved by the Parliamentary Committee, making the new powers 'subject to the necessary safeguards to secure the complete autonomy of the unions and federations affiliated to Congress'; and secured its passage by 4,858,000 votes to 1,767,000.[67] The demand for the proviso came particularly from the Miners.

The affiliation fee was more than trebled, to yield about £25,000 a year, but detailed proposals on staffing had to wait until the scheme came into operation at the 1921 Congress, and the new General Council took over. Congress then approved the creation of a National Joint Council of Labour consisting of representatives from the General Council, the Labour Party executive, and the parliamentary party, over which the chairman of the General Council was to preside; and departments for research, international affairs, publicity, and legal matters jointly financed and jointly controlled by the General Council and the party executive. The Women's Trade Union League was to become the Women's Department of Congress, and to work closely with a new Trade Boards Department. The Co-ordination Committee had also wanted to give the General Council a full-time chairman, but the

[66] Ibid., 1921, p. 108.   [67] Ibid., 1920, p. 316.

proposal aroused so much opposition from the floor of Congress that it was withdrawn. The chairmanship remained a part-time post, rotating annually.

The General Council, therefore, began its existence in the knowledge that the unions wanted a single central trade union authority, but had refused to grant it power to interfere with the autonomy of individual unions. Since most of the fields of activity prescribed for the council—inter-union disputes, relations with unions abroad, co-ordination of action in industrial disputes, and matters of general concern between unions and employers or the government—were areas in which the old Parliamentary Committee had operated, at least on some occasions, the extent to which the General Council would be able to prove itself a more effective body was far from evident. All that could be said with reasonable confidence was that it would not face competition from rival centres, especially now that the Triple Alliance had disappeared and the General Federation was no longer in the running.

There was a continued centralisation of authority within individual unions, mainly caused by the expansion of national collective bargaining, and the refusal of many employers' organisations to grant concessions to union branches and districts beyond the terms of national agreements; but also due to alterations in union constitutions. Most of the main building unions had now switched from local executives to more authoritative bodies representing the whole membership of the union, and the Plumbers' executive was a full-time body. With amalgamation, the Engineers had recast their rule-book to group the districts into twenty-six divisions, each with its own divisional organiser, and two representatives on a 'National Committee' which replaced the delegate meeting and was the equivalent of the representative conferences in other unions. The new body met annually and had authority to revise the rules and to make policy.

After the strikes on the Clyde and the Thames at the beginning of 1919, there were few signs of unofficial shop steward organisations at work. One reason for the decline of the wartime shop stewards' movement was that its strength lay in the munitions factories. Many national factories were closed down, and, in the changeover to peacetime production elsewhere, many jobs were inevitably lost. It was easy for managers to arrange for those of prominent shop stewards to be among them. Where the stewards had been at odds with the local union officials there was little likelihood of complaint from them; indeed they might even give positive assistance by suggesting names. 'In the aftermath of the forty hours strike on the Clyde it proved impossible, in many cases, to re-establish organisation inside the factories.'[68] One of the govern-

---

[68] Hinton, p. 321.

ment factories at Slough was retained until April 1920 as a transport repair depot for the government. A strong and militant stewards' organisation developed there under the leadership of Dingley from Coventry and Wal Hannington; but once the factory closed, the stewards departed, Hannington to become, before long, the leader of the unemployed movement.

The two great issues which gave rise to the wartime movement were dilution and conscription. They disappeared with the restoration of prewar practices and the end of conscription. Furthermore the wartime movement was primarily, and on occasion almost exclusively, a movement of the Engineers, and two postwar changes affected the position of stewards within that union. The first was the union's adherence to the engineering shop stewards agreement, and the second was the new rule which instituted quarterly meetings of shop stewards within each district which once a year elected representatives to the district committee. Shop stewards now had a recognised position both in the negotiating procedure and in the government of the union.

The militants in the union scored a rather pathetic victory in the autumn of 1919 when Tom Mann was elected general secretary in place of Young, who had resigned following his election to parliament. Mann had only eighteen months to serve before retirement. A testimonial of £800 had already been collected by the Transport Workers Federation to set him up in a poultry farm in Kent. He was still full of vigour, but the post was traditionally an administrative job, and administration was not his strength. Policy remained firmly in the hands of Brownlie and the majority of the executive who shared Brownlie's views. There was little for Mann to do, other than proclaim his opinions in the section of the union journal allotted to him.

8

The Postwar Depression

The Impact of the Depression

THE economic collapse of 1921 was without recorded parallel in Britain. By the middle of the year industrial production was almost 20 per cent below the level reached twelve months earlier. Over the same period unemployment had risen from 2.7 per cent to 17.9 per cent of the insured population. Wholesale prices were down by over a third, and still falling rapidly. Retail prices followed behind. They had continued to increase up to November 1920, but then fell by 24 per cent over the next twelve months and continued downwards after other economic indicators had begun to turn. In such circumstances wages had to come down, and the negotiation and implementation of successive pay cuts provided a major test for the new system of industrial relations, which had been created over the previous few years in sharply contrasting circumstances.

The coalition government tried to minimise their responsibilities by abandoning economic controls. Disengagement from responsibility for the railways had been carried through in a measured and orderly fashion; but the mines were handed back to the coalowners in a panic. Equally panic-stricken was the repeal of the Agriculture Act 1920 which, to give some security to farmers and to farmworkers, had laid down that four years' notice must be given of a suspension of its provisions. Now, with prices tumbling and the prospect of heavy calls on the Exchequer to meet the price guarantees, the government gave two months' notice of their intention to repeal the Act, which was accomplished in August—before the harvest. In September agricultural wage-fixing machinery was replaced by county conciliation committees, without independent members. If these committees were set up, and that depended on the parties; and if they reached agreement, which was entirely a matter for them; then the rates they agreed would, if approved by the minister, be enforceable in the courts. In 1912 Lloyd George had launched a 'land campaign' to publicise what he saw as the next stage of radical reform by the Liberal Party. One of its main aims had been fair wages for farmworkers. Now his government took away from them the Agricultural Wages Board which had for the first time given them some hope of achieving that aim, and put in its place a contemptible sham.

The government was under strong pressure from an anti-waste campaign which had the support of the Rothermere press, and of Horatio Bottomley. Anti-waste candidates won four seats in by-elections in 1919–21, causing the coalition grave embarrassment. The budgets for 1920 and 1921 had both been severely deflationary, but apparently not sufficiently so for the electors, and in August Eric Geddes, who had recently left the government, was appointed chairman of a committee to recommend further economies for the budget of 1922. In April 1921 Addison was transferred from the Ministry of Health to be a minister without portfolio, and subsequently dropped from the government as a sacrificial victim to the anti-waste campaign; and the housing subsidies were first limited, and then terminated in 1922.

Nevertheless, there were some directions in which the government dared not economise. Although the Unemployment Insurance Act of 1920 had established unemployment benefit for the great majority of manual workers in time for the depression, its detailed provisions did not meet the circumstances of 1921. Benefits were not enough to live on, and were restricted to fifteen weeks in any one year. There were no allowances for dependants. The scheme had been intended to tide workers over relatively short periods of unemployment, but in 1921 the likelihood of an unemployed man or woman finding another job was low. Many of the unemployed were ex-servicemen, and the newly-founded Communist Party was now concentrating its attention on organising the unemployed. Once more the confidential security reports reaching the cabinet had opportune material to feed their fears of revolution. Arguments of both humanity and of prudence, therefore, drove them to amend the scheme. In March 1921 entitlement was extended to many, especially ex-servicemen, who had not qualified under the 1920 Act; rates of benefit were raised from 75p a week for men and 60p for women to £1 for men and 80p for women, and the limitation on payments in any one year was substantially relaxed. At the end of June the original rates of benefit were restored, but with falling prices they were worth a good deal more than they had been in March. On the other hand the limitation on payments in any year was further relaxed. At the discretion of the minister an additional period of 22 weeks of 'uncovenanted' benefit could be paid. Finally, in November, the third amending Act within a year provided an allowance of 25p a week for a dependent wife, and 5p a week for each dependent child. Contributions were raised three times during the year, but they did not come near to matching the demands on the Unemployment Fund, and a Treasury advance of £10 million was sanctioned and subsequently raised to £20 million. The depression also added greatly to the demands on the Poor Law Guardians to assist those who were not covered or were inadequately covered by unemployment insurance, and their expenditure and borrowing rose steeply through 1921. During the ten years of full employment, the harsh 'less eligibility' principle of Poor Law administration had been considerably relaxed, and more humanitarian treatment of those in need added to the cost of the Poor Law.

Unable to avoid these responsibilities, the government sought to shed others wherever they could. They recognised that they themselves had to achieve economies in the administration of national government. Elsewhere it was for local authorities and private employers to achieve the economies needed to put their undertakings back on their feet.

This approach complemented the attitude of organised employers. Already, on 21 July 1920, Peter Rylands, president of the Federation of British Industries, had told its Grand Council that he

had come to the conclusion that the time had arrived for industry to settle its domestic difficulties for itself without reference to the Government. He thought that the policy of the Government should be similar to that of the Federation in connection with labour matters [that is, to regard them as domestic to each industry and service]. It might be exceedingly dangerous if there should be any revolt against the Government, and it was therefore a measure of safety that the different industries themselves should undertake to deal with their own workpeople.

Over the next two or three years British trade unionists persisted in the belief that employers were engaged in putting into practice a carefully co-ordinated plan to attack their wages and conditions. In 1922 the General Council reported to Congress:

From the evidence submitted to us there appears to be no doubt about the existence of a widespread and carefully organised conspiracy to secure—
(a) *Unreasonable reductions in wages.*
(b) *A drastic extension of the normal working week.*[1]

It was widely assumed that the Federation of British Industries was at the centre of the plot, although the federation specifically excluded industrial relations from their functions, and the responsibility for securing 'the fullest co-operation of all Employers' interests in dealing with questions arising out of relations between Employers and their workpeople' belonged to the National Confederation of Employers Organisations. The negotiations over the formation of the confederation had been protracted, but by the beginning of 1922 it could be said to be functioning effectively.

Belatedly, on 30 January 1923, the *Daily Herald* acknowledged the injustice that had been done to the Federation of British Industries.

---

[1] Trades Union Congress, 1922, p. 135.

Who plots, plans and organises these attacks? The Federation of British Industries issued a statement last week, denying categorically any part in them.

The FBI was, strictly speaking, quite correct in its denial. . . . The attack has been planned and organised by another organisation which hides behind the FBI, known as the National Confederation of Employers Organisations.

In fact the two federal bodies maintained distantly formal relations, and this attribution of responsibility for the supposed plot was almost as absurd as the other—not because the employers did not want wage reductions. They did want them, but they did not use the confederation as an agency to co-ordinate their efforts to achieve them. The main purposes of the confederation under its constitution were legal and parliamentary; representing British employers at the International Labour Organisation; and records and statistics.

The confederation also had its own constitutional limitation forbidding it to do anything

which would constitute an interference with any member of the Confederation in the conduct or management by that member of its own affairs, or which is inconsistent with the retention by all members of the Confederation of their complete individual autonomy and independence of action.

In 1924, when the unions were again seeking wage advances, the flour milling employers asked for information about the 'present policy of the Confederation with regard to securing a measure of unanimity among organised employers when faced by widespread demands for increased wages'. The response from the General Purposes Committee on 21 May was such that the millers hastily explained that all they wanted was some information about what was happening elsewhere.

Thus the government proposed to leave the responsibility for handling the industrial relations consequences of the depression to the parties, and on their side the central employers' organisations regarded it as the business of their constituents, each acting on its own. What about the unions? Black Friday had dealt a heavy blow to those who believed that co-operation across industrial boundaries could provide more effective protection of the industrial interests of trade union members than separate and autonomous negotiations. Nevertheless another attempt was made to assist the locked-out miners. Shortly after Black Friday, imported coal began to come into British ports on a considerable scale. Following sporadic local refusals by railwaymen and dockers to handle such 'tainted' coal, on 22 April the executives of the Railwaymen and the Transport Workers Federation placed an embargo on imported coal, and on British coal except for domestic use. However, some of the federation's constituents were unenthusiastic. The Sailors and Firemen would have nothing to do with the embargo. The London Dockers therefore decided, according to the report of the federation executive for 1921, that 'until such time as there is unanimity and co-operation between those carrying coal and those handling it, we cannot accept any responsibility for the instructions being carried out'. Where the embargo was enforced, the employers promptly retaliated. When Glasgow dockers were dismissed for refusing to unload coal, the Scottish Dockers struck the whole port; but blacklegs were brought in to shift the cargoes. Railwaymen who refused orders were suspended. On 13 May the union leaders met to tighten the embargo and to seek assistance from Continental unions to keep coal out of Britain, but to no effect. On 31 May the embargo was called off, and local arrangements were made for reinstatement of those who had been suspended or dismissed. The Glasgow strike was settled on that basis.

Even so the idea of action across industrial boundaries did not die. At the beginning of 1922 the General Council circulated unions with proposals for 'Joint Defence for the Preservation of Trade Union Standards' through increased powers for the council to intervene in industrial disputes, and the creation of a defence fund.[2] The majority of unions were in favour of the principle, but against the fund. In September Congress rejected specific proposals for increasing the council's authority, and they were defeated again the following year. Although there was considerable sentiment within the unions in favour of the notion of 'joint defence' of some sort, their practice was in harmony with that of the government and the employers. They negotiated pay cuts industry by industry with no central co-ordination.

With each industry left to its own devices, the incidence of cuts was bound to vary widely. Throughout the nineteenth century economic fluctuations had been far more pronounced in industries which exported a considerable proportion of their output, or were heavily involved in the production of investment goods, than in industries and services providing for domestic consumption. In 1921 the depth of the decline in the major exporting industries was accentuated by special features of the situation. During the postwar boom British exporters had profited considerably from the devastation of much of Europe during the war. As the boom began to falter, European industries were getting back into production. The peace settlement had placed a heavy obligation of reparations on Germany, and their exports of coal, steel, and engineering products to meet it inevitably cut into the demand for British goods. In addition the wartime reduction in exports from Europe to the rest of the world had encouraged the development of new industries outside

---

[2] Trades Union Congress, 1922, pp. 157–9.

Europe, including textile industries in India and China which competed with exports from Lancashire.

Some British industries had been expanded during the war, and had therefore to find new markets at home or abroad if they were to maintain their increased productive capacity. Among them were engineering and shipbuilding, chemicals, agriculture, and papermaking—for the war had interrupted the normal supplies of newsprint.

It was, therefore, evident that some industries would have to face larger reductions in wages than others; but no one knew how much the reductions would be in either the more or the less fortunate industries, nor how to find out except by trial and error. In most prewar depressions the normal wage reduction or advance had been 5 per cent or thereabouts, with an occasional 10 per cent. In a depression the Miners would usually have to concede a 5 per cent reduction, with a second to follow as often as not, and maybe, in some districts, a third. Shipbuilding employees could expect much the same. The cotton unions would be unlucky to have to concede more than one such cut, as would the Engineers, although their experience differed from one district to another. Printing workers might hope to avoid any reduction at all except in an unusually severe depression. Building workers were affected by the incidence of their industry's own leisurely cycle. If the bottom of their own cycle coincided with a general economic depression they could expect severe cuts.

There had also been scope for argument over whether any particular proposal for a cut could be successfully resisted. Sometimes resistance was successful, if only because the stoppage cleared the market at a time when the upturn was not far distant; often it was not. However, the rules of the game had been familiar to everyone concerned, and it was possible to make tolerable guesses at the risks which resistance involved. Now the risks were incalculable. The scale of the depression was outside the experience of all concerned. Trade unions were being asked to concede 10 per cent, 15 per cent, even 20 per cent at once. If they resisted, the prospects of their industry might continue to worsen while the dispute lasted, making defeat certain. On the other hand, British unions had reached a peak of strength only a few months before. They could not be expected to accept reductions on this scale without putting up a fight.

Pay Reductions

There were, however, some industries with clear guidance as to the size of their pay reductions. These were industries with agreements relating wage adjustments to price movements. Outstanding among them was the iron and steel industry, where the pay of most workers was adjusted according to the selling price of iron and steel, which now fell catastrophically. Nevertheless, so far as the main union, the Iron and Steel Trades Confederation, was concerned, the agreement was honoured without serious protests or stoppages. The union was governed by the higher-paid workers on tonnage rates. With increasing size of furnaces, these rates had, over the years, brought them handsome returns, and they were well aware that wide fluctuation in steel prices over the trade cycle required complementary adjustments in costs, including wages. They were therefore willing to accept the heavy reductions in pay which the sliding scale brought in depression, knowing from experience that returning prosperity would bring generous compensation.

Other workers in the industry, however, had not the same traditional attachment to this method of wage regulation. Labourers and ancillary workers had in the past been paid on time rates. During the war they had received bonuses on much the same basis as other munitions workers. By 1919 it was evident that the sliding scale was yielding greater advances over prewar rates than were the wartime bonuses. Consequently these workers agitated to be transferred to the sliding scale. Although the immediate effect was an increase in wage costs, the employers agreed. The confederation signed an agreement, on behalf of their time-rated members, that their wages should henceforth be adjusted in relation to selling prices. Since the confederation had been tardy in organising lower-paid workers, many of them were members of the General Workers and the National Amalgamated Union of Labour, and a second agreement granting the same terms was signed by these unions. However, by 1922, the fall in steel prices to approximately 40 per cent over prewar brought the real wages of the lower-paid workers well below the level of 1914. The general unions began to agitate against their agreement. They said it had been forced on them because the confederation had already signed before the issue had even been discussed with them; and workers began to drift from the confederation to the general unions.

One of the most important groups of ancillary workers was the bricklayers who lined and relined the furnaces. Traditionally they had been paid the district rate of bricklayers in the building industry, but they too transferred to the sliding scale after the war. By 1922 their pay was far below the rates of the still relatively prosperous building industry. Their district committees began an agitation to revert to building rates, but the steel employers, who had now amalgamated their several associations into an Iron and Steel Trades Employers Association, would have none of it. There were strikes, first in Lancashire, and then a prolonged stoppage in the North East, where the district secretary of the Building Trade Workers had been told by the chairman of the new employers' association: 'If you go back on that agreement and call your men out we will see the grass growing on our works before we have any dealings with you again.'[3] As it happened, the works were able to carry on, and the stoppage was eventually brought to an end by the intervention of Pugh, who persuaded the steel employers to meet the national officials of the Building Trade Workers to sign a national agreement in January 1923, which cut out the district officials. The bricklayers were to negotiate through a procedure similar to those of the steel unions and to continue to follow the sliding scales; but their pay was now to fluctuate with output as well.

The experience of industries with cost-of-living sliding scale agreements was very different from that of steel. Although the details of the agreements—the exact relationship of wages to the price index, the frequency of adjustments, the size of the steps by which adjustments were made—varied widely from one agreement to the next, all of them shared one feature: the percentage change in pay was less than the percentage change in prices. During the postwar boom this had been a cause of complaint by the unions. In 1920 the railway unions had secured a further increase in their rates outside the sliding scale in acknowledgement of this feature of their agreement. However, the agreements began to work to the advantage of the unions as soon as prices began to drop. With every fall in prices the real income of their members rose—so long as they remained in full-time employment. The higher-paid railwaymen enjoyed a further advantage. Because of the principle upon which their standard (B) rates had been settled, a smaller proportion of their earnings came from the A rates subject to the sliding scale than was the case with the lower-paid. As prices slid down through the depression, the higher grades came to rest on their B rates after which the agreement provided for no further automatic reductions. Thus, by the end of 1923, drivers had exhausted their A rates, with their earnings well over double those of 1914 although the cost of living stood at about 75 per cent over 1914.

Higher-paid civil servants, including Post Office employees, enjoyed a similar advantage, for their pay was also divided into a basic rate and a bonus, with the sliding scale applying only to the bonus, and the bonus representing a smaller proportion of the pay of senior civil servants. As prices fell all civil servants were better off, and the highest-paid gained most. In July 1921 the Chancellor announced a 'supercut' in the bonus for all officers with salaries over £500 a year. His action raised such an uproar that no similar attack was made on the pay of the great majority of civil servants who received less than £500 a year.

Other unions had signed sliding scale agreements relating pay to the

[3] Pugh, p. 341.

cost of living after prices had begun to fall. In the autumn of 1920 a
strike for a pay increase had threatened in the tramway industry, and
when the Minister of Labour intervened with a court of inquiry, the
United Vehicle Workers asked Bevin who, as their annual report noted,
'had made his name as the Dockers' KC during the Dockers' Inquiry',
to present their case, although he was an official of another union and
had no experience of their industry. Additional staff was recruited to
collect material and assist Bevin prepare the case; but by the beginning
of 1921, when the inquiry took place, Bevin did well to persuade the
court to recommend that wages should be stabilised for a period at their
current level. Three months later the employers were back asking for a
sliding scale agreement, and the union had to agree, taking comfort from
the considerable fall in prices which had taken place before the scale
began to operate, and from the maintenance of the guaranteed week;
although that was subsequently reduced to thirty-two hours a week for
new entrants. In 1922 the employers asked for an additional cut of 60p a
week, which was eventually whittled down to 20p. At the end of 1923
the average of drivers' rates in fifty-two large towns was 90 per cent over
1914 and conductors' rates had more than doubled, with the cost of
living up about 75 per cent.

At the end of 1921 London busmen were persuaded by the leaders of
the new Transport and General Workers Union to agree to a proposal
that their wages should be stabilised at their existing high level until
April 1922, on condition that a sliding scale should operate thereafter.
There was considerable opposition even to this modest concession, and
the union had to agree that in future the London busmen should have
wide discretion to settle their own affairs through a London Bus
Committee elected by the members and endowed with special powers
and responsibilities—an arrangement known as the Anderton's Hotel
Agreement. At the beginning of 1923 the companies asked for an
additional pay cut. The men rejected the proposal and every compromise that the negotiators put before them. On 24 February ten thousand
busmen gave Bevin a rowdy reception at a meeting in the Albert Hall,
although he had come to tell them that the companies had withdrawn
their proposals.

Gasworkers signed their cost of living agreement in October 1921
after conceding reductions of 30–35p earlier in the year. Next year their
unions persuaded the employers to revise the agreement in the men's
favour and in June 1923 to forgo reductions then due under the scale.

Thus, although they served as guides to the amount of wage
reductions which were due, sliding scale agreements did not necessarily
determine the course of wage movements. In industries and services
which were little affected by the depression, unions were in some

instances able to avoid the full application of their scales; and elsewhere employers were able to insist on further cuts beyond those indicated by the scales. The agreement in the building industry specifically recognised that the cost of living was not to be the only regulator of pay by empowering the negotiators to take account also of the state of trade and other relevant circumstances. During 1921 the industry's fortunes had been sustained by the rapid increase in housebuilding under the Addison scheme, but in 1922 the scheme was running down. Building began to feel the full effect of the depression. The employers were able to persuade the unions to accept an additional cut beyond the scale in April and another in June.

In 1923 the employers sought a third additional reduction, comparing building craft rates with the much lower pay of shipbuilding joiners, and emphasising that the latter worked a forty-seven-hour week, whereas the building craftsmen worked forty-four hours a week with $41\frac{1}{2}$ hours in December and January. Their proposal was rejected by four to one in a union ballot. The employers posted notices which included a forty-seven-hour week in the summer along with the pay cuts. At this stage a lockout seeemed inevitable, but Ramsay MacDonald arranged a meeting between the parties at which they agreed to arbitration. The first award dealt with wages, cutting the proposed pay reductions in half and abolishing the 'state of trade' clause. The second increased the working week to $46\frac{1}{2}$ hours with 44 hours in winter, except that any district could opt by agreement to work forty-four hours a week throughout the year. The outcome of these various adjustments was that most craftsmen's rates were about 70 per cent above 1914, just below the change in the cost of living, but painters and labourers were better off with rates about 90 per cent over 1914.

The wool employers also sought wage reductions outside the terms of their sliding scale agreement. In June 1921, after long negotiations, the unions conceded cuts of between 5 and 10 per cent according to grade; and a year later they accepted further cuts outside the agreement amounting to 5 per cent or less, in return for a promise of stabilisation for six months. Ben Turner described the second agreement in the *Yorkshire Factory Times* of 1 June 1922 as 'a very decent one under the present gloomy conditions of trade, and under the present conditions also of trade organisation'. The upshot was that through the three depression years the fall of wages in the industry about kept pace with the decline in retail prices.

For exporting industries with no sliding scale to guide them, the outcome of the Miners' lockout in 1921 was likely to provide a strong indication of what they might expect. On 28 April the government made another effort to secure a settlement by offering a £10 million subsidy to cushion the decline in wages over the next four months, provided that a 'durable settlement' was concluded with no national pool. At a Miners' conference on the same day only Northumberland voted for acceptance. The proposal did 'not concede the fundamental principles for which we stand'.

The lockout now became a fight to the finish, to be settled, if not by actual starvation, by the expenditure of all personal resources, the exhaustion of every source of credit, and the hunger of wives and children. The datum line strike had eaten heavily into union reserves. Nottingham, the richest district, was able to pay full strike pay to 23 April, half pay to 28 May, and in June issued coupons at 6 per cent interest which were accepted by local tradesmen. Derby, which came next to Nottingham in wealth, issued its last strike pay on 5 May when it was already heavily in debt. By selling all its securities, Lancashire, a poor district, paid one and a quarter week's strike pay. The union offices were then mortgaged to pay another 25p a head. Durham borrowed £130,000 to make one payment of £1 a head. Everywhere, full-time officials went without their salaries for the duration of the dispute.

Appeals by the Parliamentary Committee, the Labour Party, the *Daily Herald*, and other bodies brought in over £180,000 which would have provided 20p per miner, but was used to relieve the worst cases of distress. Co-operative societies and shopkeepers extended credit to such an extent that many of them had not been fully repaid by 1926. A number of young miners were called up as reservists or volunteered for the defence force created for the emergency. It was a warm spring and summer, and other young miners went camping and lived off the land. Although the union tried to prevent 'outcropping' coal as a form of blacklegging, it was 'an extremely profitable business at a time when coal was being sold at famine prices'.[4] In Nottingham Joseph Birkin, a checkweighman, organised outcropping on a considerable scale. In Durham George Harvey, another checkweighman and a militant leftwinger of national reputation, 'organised teams of men to griddle and shovel the pit-heaps for coal. . . . Lorries were hired and the coal was sold to hospitals and factories. . . . The money went to Harvey's soup kitchen.'[5] Mardy lodge in South Wales charged time-and-a-half for caring for pit ponies and $12\frac{1}{2}$p an hour for building a wall to prevent the mountain encroaching on some houses.

Above all, however, the stoppage was sustained by public funds. 'The coal dispute of 1912 added temporarily about 50,000 persons to the number . . . then in receipt of poor relief, that of 1921 added some 650,000.' In twenty-six selected Poor Law Unions in mining areas the numbers on relief per thousand of the population rose from about

---

[4] Griffin, p. 88.   [5] Douglass, p. 284.

twenty in the first three months of 1921 to eighty in April, nearly a hundred in May, and over 110 by the beginning of July.[6] The law permitted the Poor Law Guardians to provide relief for strikers' families, but not for strikers so long as they were fit for work. The actual standards applied by the guardians varied widely. Many gave relief in the form of loans, most of it never repaid. Where there were Labour majorities the rules were liberally interpreted, and even where there were not the guardians might be subject to persuasion. At Mansfield a mass meeting of miners at the beginning of July sent a deputation to the local guardians which 'succeeded in getting 12s 6d [62½p] for a wife and child as 2s 6d [12½p] for each additional child'.[7] Previously 'miners and their families would starve rather than submit to such an indignity' as to accept poor relief. 'But we insisted in the new circumstances that it should be a point of honour to demand support from a society which was denying us the right to a living wage.'[8]

On 27 May Lloyd George told the union's leaders that he had 'never seen a great strike in which less pressure was brought to bear upon a Government to settle', but nevertheless renewed his offer of a subsidy. When the districts rejected his proposals, Lloyd George said that the offer of a subsidy would remain open for a fortnight only. The executive therefore met the owners, who were prepared to make concessions: the standard was to be 20 per cent above 1914 standards; and district boards were to fix minimum levels of pay to protect the lower-paid. The subsidy would allow the initial reduction to be limited to 10p a shift. Signs of a rift were visible when these terms were discussed at a Miners' conference on 10 June. Durham and Lancashire, both with much to gain from a national pool, wanted the conference to recommend rejection, but Herbert Smith warned them 'to let the men of Yorkshire make their own policy', or 'you will regret the day'. No recommendation went out from the conference, but the offer was rejected by five to two. No major district voted for it, but the majority was less than two to one in Yorkshire and most Midlands districts.

On 18 June the executive appealed to other unions facing wage cuts to meet with them to discuss 'national action with the miners to secure their mutual demands'. When the replies proved discouraging, the executive decided to go back to the government and the owners. According to a report which the executive subsequently prepared for the annual conference:

Each member was asked separately in the presence of colleagues as to the prospect of securing the pool, and with one exception it was declared that there

[6] Ministry of Health, *Annual Report*, 1926–7, p. 116; 1921–2, pp. 154–5, Appendix XII and XIII.
[7] *The Worker*, 9 July 1921.   [8] Horner, p. 57.

was no prospect of winning the principle of the National Pool by a continuance
of the stoppage.

The government renewed their offer of a subsidy, and the owners raised
the Miners' share of the surplus, if any, from 75 to 83 per cent. To avoid
delay and the risk of rejection this offer was not put to a ballot, but to the
district councils, with a strong recommendation to accept. The results
were announced on 1 July; among major districts only Lancashire was
against; the agreement was signed.

After the settlement came the recriminations. The Lancashire
Miners' council censured Ashton and McGurk for making public their
opinion that the pool should be dropped; and then refused to accept
their resignations, demanding the resignation of the national officials
and the national executive instead. Smith gave his reply at the national
conference in August:

The truth is that the officials of the Federation were too loyal, too loyal to so-
called majority rule, too loyal to their colleagues, swallowing their convictions
and better judgment. . . . It is infinitely preferable to do an undemocratic thing
in the interests of your people than to allow empty, high sounding formulas to
intensify the horror and misery of the people's life.

It was a mark of the miners' respect for Smith that, after this blunt
defence and his equally blunt refusal to live in London, he was
nevertheless elected later in the year to the presidency of the federation
which he had held on an acting basis since Smillie's resignation. The
executive's report on their conduct of the strike was unanimously
approved. The dispute had shown that in the conditions of 1921 the
might of the Miners Federation—the biggest union in the world—had
been overrated. As George Hicks, himself still reputedly a man of the
left, wrote in the Building Trade Workers' *Monthly Report* for July
1921:

Many of us believed that a lengthy stoppage in the mines would result in
industrial chaos too awful to contemplate. Yet this has not happened and the
life of the country does not seem to have been so terribly affected after all. It
means that one of our most cherished theories has had a very severe shock.

The agreement provided for a gradual reduction in wages up to the
end of September. By then only £7 million of the subsidy had been
spent, but the government refused to allow the balance to be used for
further graduation in the worst hit areas. These were the districts
producing for export and industrial consumption; the market for
household coal had held up remarkably well, assisted by the shortage

due to the lockout. Average earnings in January 1922, based on the November 1921 assessment, were 70p a shift in Yorkshire and the Midlands (the 'Eastern' District), but 51p in Scotland, 46p in Durham, and 48½p in South Wales, which had been the highest-paid district before the lockout. Prices continued to fall, however, and district after district came to rest on its minimum wage. By January 1923 average earnings were down to 52½p in the Eastern District, whereas the figure for Durham had fallen by only a fraction of a penny over the year. Average earnings for the whole industry fell by almost a half between the last quarter of 1920 and the last quarter of 1922.[9]

However, the agreement had some compensations. Although the minimum had been fixed at 20 per cent above so-called 1914 standards, these standards had been increased by adjustments over the years, so that, overall, the average increase over 1914 was 43 per cent. Moreover the minimum was a first charge on the industry, even in collieries running at a loss. In the summer of 1922 average real wages in the mines were about a quarter below the level of the last three months of 1920; but a year later, with retail prices still falling and coal prices beginning to rise, they were only 9 per cent behind. There had also been a remarkable recovery in the export trade due to the American coal strike of 1922 and the occupation of the Ruhr in 1923, so that the rate of unemployment in the coalmines was one of the lowest in the country.

Some district owners' associations took advantage of the Miners' defeat to seek alterations in local agreements and customs. In Nottingham and Derby the Miners had secured agreements shortly after the war for coal to be filled by shovels instead of forks, so that small coal would not fall through, and all coal cut would count for payment. The owners now proposed to revert to forks. No agreement was reached and the outcome depended on union strength, pit by pit. Similarly, although the unions in those two districts refused to agree to the reintroduction of the butty system, it began to reappear in a number of pits. Nationally the Miners asked for the system of joint committees contained in the 1920 Act to be applied, for, now that the issue of district wage settlement had been decided by the new agreement, their original objection to this machinery no longer applied. However, it was the owners' turn to object, and Part II of the Act was allowed to lapse.

Cotton prices were falling almost as fast as coal prices in 1921, and short-time working had started in the autumn of 1920. For most of the winter the American spinning section was running at half-time and the Egyptian section at thirty-six hours a week. The wage agreement of May 1920 ran for twelve months, so that it was not until May 1921 that the employers in all sections gave notice of a reduction of 95 per cent on

[9] *Nineteenth Abstract of Labour Statistics*, p. 113.

standard, or 30 per cent on current earnings. Negotiations reduced this to 80 per cent on standard, with the unions offering 50 per cent. The employers would not budge further, and refused arbitration. Thereupon the Spinners, the Cardroom Operatives and the Weavers all voted for a stoppage, and on 6 June almost four hundred thousand workers were locked out; but there was no great principle at stake as there was in the mining lockout, and negotiations continued throughout the stoppage. On 14 June a provisional agreement fixed on a reduction of 60 per cent on standard, with a further 10 per cent to follow a year later. The initial response of the Spinners and Weavers to hold out for better terms delayed the return to work until 24 June, without achieving any further concession.

Cotton prices continued downwards, and in April 1922 the unions agreed to a further reduction of 40 per cent on standard with another 10 per cent to follow in October. By the end of the year, therefore, the overall reduction in pay for a full week was about 40 per cent, less than the average reduction in coalmining, but short-time working continued for long periods in cotton, whereas the pits worked an average of more than five shifts a week in both 1922 and 1923.

The third major stoppage of 1921 was the lockout of shipyard joiners which had begun in December 1920 over the withdrawal of the extra payment of 60p a week they had secured earlier that year. The Woodworkers imposed a substantial levy to finance the conflict, and hoped to defeat the employers by transferring men to the building industry which was still expanding. However, with the prospects in shipbuilding worsening rapidly, the employers were under little pressure to give way, and in August the reduction was accepted, to be applied in three stages.

Meanwhile an agonisingly prolonged process of engineering and shipbuilding pay cuts had begun. First shipbuilding and then engineering accepted relatively modest reductions of 30p a week for timeworkers and 15 per cent for pieceworkers. In the autumn of 1921 the employers in both industries proposed the withdrawal of the wartime advances of $12\frac{1}{2}$ per cent on earnings for timeworkers and $7\frac{1}{2}$ per cent for pieceworkers. In shipbuilding, the unions negotiated through the Federation of Engineering and Shipbuilding Trades, but matters were more complicated in engineering. The Workers Union, with little interest in shipbuilding but its major section of membership in engineering, was not affiliated to the federation. The general unions therefore negotiated through the Federation of General Workers. The two largest craft unions, the Engineers and the Foundryworkers, attended in their own right, and not as affiliates of the federation, which therefore represented only the smaller craft unions in these negotiations.

Nevertheless the unions generally agreed to a 'pooled' vote when a ballot was taken, and on this occasion, faced with a common demand, the unions in both industries conducted a single ballot. There was a small overall majority for acceptance, but the Engineers and Boilermakers had voted the other way, and some of their leaders put the blame for the reduction on the general unions, whose vote was more than two to one for acceptance. Bell, of the National Amalgamated Union of Labour, remarked to his executive on 13 October that, on the contrary, they had 'saved the skilled unions from disaster' and blamed some of the craft representatives for obstructing negotiations.

During 1921 employment in shipbuilding had been sustained by the completion of orders received during the boom years, but by the first quarter of 1922 tonnage under construction had fallen to 2.6 million compared with 3.7 million in the first quarter of 1921, and by the last quarter of 1922 it was down to 1.6 million. The employers were back for another reduction early in 1922 and, after some weeks of talks, gave notice of a further breathtaking cut of 82.5p a week, an average of about 25 per cent on current rates, in two stages. A delegate conference of the federation instructed their members to stop work on 29 March when the cut was due to apply; but the employers were under no pressure to compromise, and on 25 April the union leaders agreed to recommend that the cut should apply in three stages. The ballot gave a small majority for rejection, but the leaders decided that the federation's rules required a majority of two-thirds to call or continue a stoppage. The members were instructed to resume work on 8 May. However, the Boilermakers had voted by almost two to one for rejection, and their branches in Barrow, London and the Mersey refused to go back to work for some days, to the dismay of the other unions who were not allowed to return without them. Their executive decided to take a ballot on withdrawing from the federation.

Meanwhile the engineering unions had been engaged in an exhausting lockout over managerial rights. As soon as their members were back at work in June, the employers proposed that the 82.5p reduction should apply to them, but with somewhat more favourable staging. The pooled voting was 70,900–43,937 for rejection, but the union leaders announced:

Your representatives, having regard to the recent lock-out, the large number of workpeople unemployed, the relative state of the respective organisations, and realising their responsibilities, have decided that they cannot in the circumstances recommend effect being given to the ballot vote, and therefore advise members to continue at work.[10]

---

[10] Amalgamated Engineering Union, *Monthly Journal*, August 1922.

Finally, at the end of 1922, with shipbuilding prospects still worsening while other industries were beginning to recover, a further reduction of 50p a week was accepted by the shipbuilding unions, including the Boilermakers, who had voted in favour of remaining in the federation.

Seamen's wages had not increased since the end of the war except to consolidate a £3 a month war-risk bonus of 1918 into the standard wage. In the autumn of 1920 their unions were discussing a comprehensive claim covering pay, hours of work, conditions, and safety at sea, and the employment of Asiatic labour. They could hardly have chosen a worse moment, for the index of freight rates, which had stood at 123 in January, was down to 84 in September and 58 in December. Early in 1921 the owners asked for a reduction of £4.50 a month, which was whittled down to £2.50 and put to a ballot. Havelock Wilson had no doubt that the cut should be accepted. He told his conference that year that 'when the Great War finished, if the leaders of the Trade Unions had been wise, we should . . . have endeavoured to make a compromise with the Employers of Labour for Industrial Peace'. As for unemployment, 'there is only one remedy . . . and that is mutual confidence between one class and another'. So worried was he that the ballot might reject the cut that he conducted a postal survey of his members' wives in the Liverpool area, where the opposition was strongest, and reported to his executive on 2 May that the returns so far were 601–13 for acceptance. The members also voted for acceptance, but the Cooks and Stewards, whose leader, Cotter, accused Wilson of negotiating the cut behind his back, voted by six to one for rejection, and were locked out on 6 May. The stoppage became effective only as vessels came into port, and the Sailors and Firemen, who already had a number of cooks and stewards in membership, did their best to provide catering staff for ships due to sail. On 3 June the Cooks and Stewards decided to accept the cut and return to work where they could.

There followed a grisly inter-union conflict, and an unequal internal conflict within Wilson's union. Since 1911 the British Seafarers Union, a breakaway organisation, had held sway in Southampton. The Cooks and Stewards now amalgamated with them to form the Amalgamated Marine Workers Union. This at last allowed the Seafarers' principal spokesmen, Shinwell, to attend the Trades Union Congress, for no one challenged the *bona fides* of the Cooks and Stewards except Wilson. He joined with the employers to exclude the new union from the Maritime Board, which instituted a form, known as PC5, requiring the signature of an officer of a union affiliated to the Board as a prerequisite of employment on ships whose owners were members of the Shipping Federation or the Liverpool Shipowners Association. Initially this requirement was not easily enforced in areas where the Marine Workers were strong, but in the majority of ports in which the Sailors and Firemen were unchallenged it could be used effectively both against the Seafarers, and against dissidents within their own union. The latter had formed vigilance committees in Liverpool and elsewhere to challenge Wilson's policies. He replied with accusations of Communist influence and a series of expulsions. The Transport Workers Federation took the Marine Workers' side. Wilson withdrew from the federation along with the Hull seamen's union, which shortly afterwards amalgamated with his union.

In March 1922 Wilson accepted a reduction of £1.50 a month in two stages. On 11 January he had told his executive that some Glasgow companies had already introduced cuts, and 'on a number of smaller boats he had found that the members were accepting a reduction in wages'. In April 1923, with the index of freight rates down to 24, he accepted a further reduction of £1 a month which was referred neither to a ballot nor to the executive. On 19 April he told the executive that there had been no time to call them together, but he had put the proposal to a meeting 'of the whole of the Officials of the Union, and they by a unanimous vote had accepted the settlement and recorded a hearty vote of confidence in the President'. He had decided to recommend acceptance only because he 'had himself for months personally enquired into the state of every shipping company throughout the land'.

Freight rates are the governing factor in the pay of the docker as well as of the seaman, and, although Bevin was a union leader of a very different mould from Wilson, he sought to persuade his members that there had to be pay cuts in the docks, where he acted as national trade group secretary as well as general secretary of the new union. In August 1921 the dockers accepted a reduction of 15p a day, followed by 5p a day in March 1922. During the summer of 1922 the employers asked for another 10p. Prolonged negotiations won substantial concessions: 5p was to go in October, but the second 5p was postponed to June 1923, and was to take effect only if the cost of living index fell by a further ten points below the level of September 1922. These terms were accepted by branch votes. On the employers' side, Lawrence Holt, a leading Liverpool employer, delivered a slashing attack on high labour costs and led the Liverpool employers out of the National Association of Port Employers. They gave notice to terminate the national agreement so far as Liverpool was concerned, and then thought better of it.

By June 1923 the cost of living index had fallen just ten points since September 1922, and the reduction went into force on 2 July. On the same day there were strikes of dockers in Hull, Grimsby, Bristol and Cardiff. 'The strike subsequently extended to London, Manchester, Liverpool, Birkenhead, Barry and Avonmouth, but at some of the ports, including London, the dispute was only partial, and at Liverpool it affected only a small minority of the dock workers.'[11] About forty thousand dockers, roughly half the labour force, were out at the peak of the stoppage.

Bevin responded firmly. The National Docks Group Committee decided the agreement must be honoured. At the first conference of the new union on 9 July he trounced the strikers' spokesmen by 136 votes to 18. The return to work started shortly afterwards and by the end of the month only eighteen thousand Londoners remained out, still refusing to give a hearing to their officials. They went back on 20 August.

The union journal sought a culprit. The first candidate was the Workers Union, one of whose officials had taken part in the strike at Hull. The next was the Communists. But the union's leading Communist, Fred Thompson, the secretary of the London docks section, 'ostensibly . . . remained loyal to the Union',[12] and after the strike the journal noted that the Communists 'now are appealing to the men to stick to the Union'. The guilt was therefore attributed to the Stevedores who encouraged several thousand London dockers and lightermen to join with them in setting up the National Amalgamated Stevedores, Lightermen, Watermen, and Dockers Union (the 'blue' union), which was excluded from the Joint Industrial Council for the Port Transport Industry, and from Congress. In 1927 the lightermen left this new organisation and reconstituted their pre-1922 Watermen, Lightermen, Tugmen, and Bargemen's Union.

Bevin had been unlucky. Had the index fallen by one point less, there would have been no cut and no strike. As it was, the cut had been applied, and the union had suffered considerable disruption in London. Bevin lacked Havelock Wilson's aids to union discipline; but he would not have wanted them.

By March 1923 sixty-three county agricultural conciliation committees had been set up, but 'there were effective agreements in only sixteen cases, and by the end of the year the number had fallen to four'.[13] The Norfolk branches of the Agricultural Workers had sustained a hard jolt in 1922 when Sam Peel, a lay official of the union, persuaded his colleagues on the local conciliation committee to accept a wage reduction from £1.80 to £1.50 a week which had been rejected both by the members and the union executive. Shortly afterwards he left to set up a rival union. By the end of the year a further reduction to £1.25 had been negotiated, and, early in 1923, the Norfolk farmers proposed that the working week should be increased from fifty hours to fifty-four, at an hourly rate which would yield a marginally lower weekly wage than

---

[11] *Ministry of Labour Gazette*, July 1923.
[12] Bullock, p. 217.   [13] Groves, p. 172.

before and carry the risk that 'wet time' would bring a loss of earnings. When these terms were rejected, the farmers gave notice to twenty thousand farmworkers which ran out early in March. Initially only four or five thousand came out, but the numbers rose to eight thousand after Bonar Law, who was now Prime Minister, had refused to intervene and attempts at conciliation had failed. On 17 April Ramsay MacDonald took a hand. Surprised by the men's resistance, the farmers were prepared to make concessions, and agreement was reached to maintain the rate of £1.25 for a fifty-hour working week, provided the first four hours of overtime were paid at ordinary time rates. It was a remarkable victory for a disastrously enfeebled union, but, despite the collection of considerable sums for the strikers, 'amost two years' worth of the total membership's subscriptions had been paid out in strike pay',[14] and the farmers interpreted the 'no victimisation' clause of the agreement to mean that they must not replace strikers by other workers, not that they must take all the strikers back. In June over a thousand strikers were still out of work, and some had been evicted from their tied cottages.

Naturally enough most of the major stoppages over wage cuts during these three years were in industries which suffered unusually severe cuts; but not all of them. The wage reductions in the printing industry were as modest as any, but the Typographical Association struck for nearly a month in 1922. Apart from the London newspapers, there were now three main printing wage agreements in England and Wales—the London agreement, the Typographical agreement, and a third agreement covering the other provincial unions. All the unions belonged to the Joint Industrial Council, however, and in 1921 the Master Printers used its machinery to negotiate a reduction. In the end the provincial unions, including the Typographical Association, settled for cuts amounting to 37½p in two stages, but the London Compositors would accept only a single reduction of 25p. The periodical firms constituted the weak link among the London employers, for they had almost as much to lose from a stoppage as the newspaper proprietors, who negotiated separately.

Next year most of the provincial unions accepted a cut of 62½p a week, but the Typographical Association and the Londoners rejected it. Shackleton proposed arbitration. The London Compositors refused, but the Typographical Association was tempted to submit their case to the Industrial Court, once they realised its awards were not legally binding. Before the court they made it clear that the award would have to be submitted to a ballot. The court awarded the 62½p reduction in three stages; the ballot rejected it by nearly two to one; and the employers posted notices for 21 July. The Minister of Labour told the

---

[14] Newby, p. 225.

House of Commons that although the court's award was not binding, 'if the purpose of the Act is not to be stultified, the decision of the Court must be final'.[15] The Newcastle magistrates were of the opinion that the award was binding and on 11 August granted damages of £1.25 a head with costs against 97 strikers for breach of contract.[16] The stoppage revealed considerable indiscipline among both union members and employers. On 15 August the union executive was told that 10,235 members were on strike, 2,731 were working on the terms of the award, and no less than 5,933 were still at work at the old rate of pay. Substantial levies were imposed on those at work, but even so the union was running into financial difficulties by this time. Next day they met the Master Printers to arrange a further spreading of the cuts in four stages over the next nine months with stabilisation thereafter until the end of 1923, in return for a firm undertaking from the executive to recommend an immediate return to work. The London societies settled later for cuts of 30p for compositors and 20p for machine operators.

Despite the pledge of reinstatement

several hundred members lost their jobs. Many firms became non-union and 'open houses'. Many members refused to pay the strike levy and the heavy fines which the EC imposed on those who had 'ratted', and there was a loss of several hundred in membership.[17]

The Printing and Kindred Trades Federation censured the Typographical Association for breach of federation rules, and for putting members of other unions out of work; and refused federation strike benefit. Nevertheless the printing workers had fared reasonably well. By the end of 1923 the rates of craftsmen in the provinces were down by about 22 per cent on 1920 and in London by considerably less. Thus their real wages had improved, as had their position relative to most other wage-earners.

The quarrel between the craft unions and the Railwaymen in the railway workshops was still unresolved. There were now three issues in dispute. Firstly, the Railwaymen wanted uniform national rates, whereas the craft unions preferred district rates. Secondly, there was the question of general wage adjustments: should they follow engineering or railway agreements? Finally, there was a difference over negotiating machinery. The Railwaymen wanted machinery similar to that for other railway employees, but the craft societies would not agree.

In August 1921 the shopmen conceded a reduction of 30p a week in line with the engineering industry, but the questions of principle were

[15] *Hansard*, 26 July 1922, col. 441.
[16] *Ministry of Labour Gazette*, August 1922.
[17] Musson, pp. 400–1.

referred to the Industrial Court which, after considerable delays, issued its award, No. 728, in July 1922. Instead of district rates or uniform national rates, the shops were graded into five groups, each with its set of rates for the various classes of worker. Most of the new rates were not far below the old, and no employee was to suffer an initial reduction of more than 10p a week. Future adjustments were to be settled by negotiations in which the railway service should be regarded 'as an industry in itself', so that there was no need 'to follow the rates of wages agreed on or recognised by employers and workers in other industries employing similar classes of labour'. The court left it to the parties to set up the machinery for conducting future negotiations. Despite the initial cuts, the award was to the advantage of the shopmen. By 1924 their average earnings were £3.18 compared with £2.65 in the engineering industry outside.

Strong trade union organisation was by no means a prerequisite of avoiding heavy wage cuts. In 1919 union organisation in the chocolate and confectionery industry had been considered too weak to support a full Joint Industrial Council, but by the time of the 1924 earnings census it stood in sixth place for male workers' weekly earnings with an average of £3.21, compared with a national average of £2.87½. In road haulage the unions had not been able to sustain their new system of national bargaining even in the boom year of 1920, but the rates of carters fell by only about 20 per cent over the next three years. The Joint Industrial Council for the heavy chemicals industry barely survived the depression. In April 1921 the employers imposed reductions of 40p to 80p a week, so the annual conference of the Federation of General Workers was told, 'without any agreement . . . and only out of courtesy had the matter been brought before their Council at all'. When further cuts were imposed in the autumn, Bevin wrote to the federation executive meeting of 27 October, saying that his 'attitude has always been to stand by the national form of organisation but in this trade it appears to be so weak that we cannot effectively resist'. However, when the employers' association decided on a further reduction for shift workers in the summer of 1923, many firms, especially in South Wales, paid no attention; and in the 1924 earnings census the average for male workers in chemicals was £2.99, more than 10p above the national average.

The explanation for these wage movements must be found in the economic circumstances of the industries concerned. Heavy chemicals suffered severely from the immediate impact of the slump, but, as a growth industry, its recovery was equally rapid. Road haulage, like the railways and road passenger transport, had not shared in the deep depression of sea and port transport, which was due to the decline in international trade. Demand for foodstuffs held up remarkably well throughout the depression, as did demand for other consumer products.

Wage rates of the footwear industry fell by less than 20 per cent. Nearly all the other sections of the clothing industry were now covered by Trade Boards. 'Between 1914 and 1922 the real wage rates' fixed by Trade Boards 'for females increased 20 per cent, while those for males increased 12 per cent.'[18] Since wage rates generally had moved roughly in step with the cost of living, there had therefore been a substantial improvement in both living standards and relative wages of workers covered by Trade Boards.

Employers in Trade Board industries protested vehemently that they were being forced by the law to pay uncompetitive wages. There were two main complaints: that the boards fixed wages too high; and that the machinery worked so slowly that it took many months to obtain even such reductions as were granted. The government appointed a committee under Viscount Cave to hear their complaints, and the defence was organised by the new Trade Boards Advisory Committee of Congress. However, the boards were not the main reason for the unaccustomed prosperity of the workers in these industries. That was due to the relative buoyancy of consumer industries. Distribution shared their experience. On 7 January 1922 the *Shop Assistant* commented that 'the Distribution Trades probably are the last to feel the full effects of a trade depression and the first to recover'.

Generally speaking, white collar employees seem to have done better than most manual workers. By 1922 local authorities had realised that the Local Government Officers could rely on the Industrial Court to enforce the payment of civil service bonuses in local government, and henceforth refused to refer disputes to the court. 'For this reason arbitration proved of little value to the association after 1922',[19] but by then the worst of the depression was over. The most favourably treated major group of employees in the country was undoubtedly the teachers. Their standard scales had been agreed at the end of 1920 to come into force by stages over the next few years. The consequence was that, despite the depression and a 40 per cent drop in retail prices, the average salary of teachers rose substantially over the years 1920 to 1923, from £271 to £346 a year for men, and from £200 to £270 for women. In 1920 the average male teacher's salary was about 10 per cent higher than the average fitter's rate; by 1923 it was 150 per cent higher. This development did not go unchallenged. The Geddes report proposed a 5 per cent cut in teachers' salaries and the transfer of their recent non-contributory pension scheme to a contributory basis. The government introduced a School Teachers (Superannuation) Bill to give effect to the

[18] Sells, p. 278.   [19] Spoor, p. 94.

second recommendation, despite accusations of broken promises; and later in 1922 the union reluctantly but wisely agreed to a 5 per cent reduction through the Burnham Committee. The average male teacher's salary declined to £335 in 1925. Even so his real salary was 80 per cent higher than in 1920.

Table 2 sets out changes in average money income of wage earners in

TABLE 2

Average money incomes of full-time wage earners by industrial groups, 1920–23

Industrial Group	Money income[a] 1923 (1920 = 100)	Real income[a] 1923 (1920 = 100)	Union density[b] percentage 1920	Unemployment[c] percentage July 1923
Iron and Steel	55	78	73[d]	21
Shipbuilding	55	80	73[d]	44
Mining and Quarrying	59	83	92	3
Cotton	62	89	79	22
General Engineering ⎫				21
Electrical Engineering ⎬	65	94	73[d]	7
Motor Vehicles ⎭				10
Construction	66	94	88	12
Agriculture	68	97	38	_[e]
Wool	70	101	58	10
Local Government	75	106	65	6
Furniture	75	107	36	8
Gas ⎫			68 ⎫	
Water ⎬	77	109	10 ⎬	7
Electricity ⎭			45 ⎭	
Distribution	81	117	18	6
Railways ⎫			74	6
Road Passenger Transport			⎫	3
Road Haulage ⎬			⎬ 79	17
Docks and Inland Waterways	82	118	⎭ 96	28
Sea Transport			100	_[f]
Post Office ⎭			77	_[e]
Printing	87	124	91	6

Notes:

[a] The figures for money and real incomes are derived from Mitchell and Deane, *Abstract of British Historical Statistics*, 'Wages and the Standard of Living', table 4, which is in turn derived from Chapman and Knight, *Wages and Salaries in the UK 1920–38*.

[b] Union density figures are derived from Bain and Price by relating 1920 union membership figures to 1921 census date.

[c] Unemployment figures are from Department of Employment, *British Labour Statistics*, table 164.

[d] Union density figures for these industries are the figure for the Metal, Engineering, and Shipbuilding group.

[e] At that time this industry was not covered by unemployment insurance.

[f] No separate entry is given for this industry in the relevant table.

full-time employment for most major industries or industrial groups from 1920 to 1923. It also shows union density in 1920, to give a rough indication of bargaining strength at the onset of the depression, and unemployment percentages in July 1923 to represent the economic impact of the depression. Since the definition of each industry or group varies from one column to the next, the figures are not strictly comparable, but the general picture which they present is nevertheless broadly reliable. There was a wide range of changes in money incomes from 1920 to 1923. For instance, since retail prices fell by about 30 per cent over the period, real wages in the wool industry were stable, whereas in printing they rose by almost a quarter, and in iron and steel they fell by more than a fifth. Union density figures show that these shifts cannot be explained by union bargaining strength. The industries with high union density include those which gained most and those which lost most. Finally, there is a fairly close inverse correlation between movements in incomes and the incidence of unemployment. In engineering and transport this relationship is obscured because incomes are averaged over several industries. However, the weighted average unemployment percentage of the three engineering industries is approximately 18 per cent; and in transport and communications the number of employees in railways, road passenger transport and the Post Office outnumbered those in the remaining industries, so that the overall unemployment percentage must have been relatively low. The relationship therefore appears to hold for these two groups as well. The only unemployment percentage which is markedly out of line is mining and quarrying, and that is due to the coal industry's extremely untypical export situation in 1923 caused by the occupation of the Ruhr.

The Engineering Lockout

Each January the *Ministry of Labour Gazette* included a short summary of the strike statistics for the previous year. During 1921 'nearly one-half of the disputes' had arisen 'out of proposed reductions of wages', and for 1922 the proportion ascribed to this cause was 'about one-half'; but by 1923 a change was visible. 'Refusal to accept proposed reductions continued to be the most frequently occurring cause of disputes, although the proportion of such disputes was much smaller than in 1922.' Stoppages for this reason bulked even larger in the figures for working days lost through disputes. The three major disputes over pay reductions in 1921—the coal lockout, the cotton lockout, and the lockout of shipyard joiners—alone accounted for almost 95 per cent of the nearly 86 million days lost that year.

In all three years the next 'most frequently occurring' cause was 'questions respecting the employment of particular classes or persons', although in 1923 second place was shared with 'questions of Trade Union principle'—largely the closed shop. Questions respecting employment were often manning issues, and it is not surprising that manning and other issues affecting efficiency should be matters of contention in depression years when many employers were desperately anxious to cut costs in order to stay in business. One or two of these disputes developed into major and intractable conflicts. From 23 February to 18 April 1923 twenty-nine thousand jute workers were locked out over a dispute concerning the number of spinning 'frames' per spinner in one of the mills. The lockout was renewed in the first week of June and then called off again leaving the original dispute still unresolved. However, by far the most important dispute concerning the efficient organisation of work during the period was the engineering lockout of 1922.

The origins of the dispute go back to the months after the armistice when trade unionists feared that the rundown of munitions production and demobilisation would bring heavy unemployment. Many unions instituted bans on overtime as a means of minimising the risk. Among the Engineers, bans were imposed by the district committees, including London, Manchester, and Glasgow where the union's organiser noted in their journal for June 1919 that the employers' association had protested strongly 'against having to apply for permission for our members to work overtime on emergency work'. Many of the bans continued after unemployment had almost disappeared. In June 1920 the journal noted that 'many Lancashire districts have practically abolished overtime'. Their district committees undertook to consider written applications from employers for overtime to be worked, but, as the employers' view was that it was for them to decide when overtime was necessary, they did not apply.

In September 1920 the Engineers signed their own national agreement on overtime and nightshift, apart from the other engineering unions. It established standard rates of pay for these forms of work; stated that 'systematic overtime is deprecated as a method of production'; and provided that 'when overtime is necessary . . . no union workman shall be required to work more than 30 hours overtime in any four weeks'; but failed to resolve the issue of the embargoes. In December their head office issued a circular advising district committees that the relevant 'paragraph implies that it is considered necessary by both parties', and that in making their decisions they should have regard to 'whether such overtime will tend to absorb members who are unemployed'. The engineering employers reacted sharply to this interpretation. On 17 February 1921 their executive board resolved to post notices dispensing with the services of members of the union who refused to work overtime, and, if need be, of all members of the union.

Before they could act on this decision their sense of grievance was increased by a strike in Bolton where the Engineers, on the instructions of their district committee and with the approval of their executive, were insisting that the practice of employing apprentices on payment by results should be discontinued. The employers' executive board resolved, if necessary, to propose a general lockout on this issue as well, and subsequently widened their demand into a general insistence on the rights of management so as to encompass three manning disputes which were shortly to be considered at central conference. Thus armed, their negotiators met the union representatives at the end of April to learn that the latter had been forbidden by their union conference to modify their interpretation of the overtime agreement. Nevertheless the employers were in no hurry to impose a lockout. Negotiations continued until November when a memorandum was provisionally agreed at 3.30 a.m. on 18 November, after '$16\frac{1}{2}$ hours continuous negotiation'. Management instructions were to be observed 'pending any question in connection therewith' being discussed through the procedure, and 'the employers have the right to decide when overtime is necessary'. The union could raise objections to any instance of overtime working through the procedure, but, 'meantime, the overtime required shall be proceeded with'.[20] In order to widen the responsibility for what they knew would be an unpopular decision, the union executive had called the national and divisional organisers into conference, and they jointly recommended acceptance of the memorandum, giving as their reasons the continued industrial stagnation; their ninety thousand unemployed members—almost a quarter of the total; and the consequent financial strain on the union, which had already paid out over £2 million in unemployment benefit that year.

Even these arguments did not convince the members, who rejected the memorandum by a vote of 50,240 to 35,525. Unless they were willing to admit defeat, the employers had to go ahead with the lockout. Notices were posted, and operated on 11 March 1922 after last-minute attempts to reach a settlement had failed. The meeting of the executive board which resolved to go ahead with the lockout also decided to ask the other engineering unions 'to declare their policy on the principle involved', and to lock their members out as well if they did not accept it.

This 'astounding act of aggression on the part of the employers'[21] took the other unions by surprise. Since they were not parties to the Engineers' overtime and nightshift agreement, they were not asked to

[20] Amalgamated Engineering Union, *Monthly Journal*, December 1921.
[21] Clynes, *Hansard*, 20 March 1922, col. 73.

accept the employers' interpretation of that agreement; but they were asked to sign the remaining clauses concerning the observation of management instructions pending reference to procedure. The pooled vote was 164,759 to 49,503 for rejection. The employers allowed time for further negotiations. In a series of conferences ending early on the morning of Good Friday, the employers offered to give prior notice of 'material' changes, and to allow disputes over what was material to be referred to central conference, but this was not enough to persuade the union leaders to recommend acceptance 'at the moment'—and the employers terminated the discussions. Notices were posted to operate on 2 May.

At the end of 1921 the employers' federation had conducted a survey of their local associations, asking them about restrictions on output imposed by unions within their districts; what modifications were wanted in 'the working conditions at present obtaining in respect of members of the AEU'; and whether their members wanted to terminate any of the current agreements with the unions. Having consulted their members, eight of the twenty-four associations which replied to the first question said there were no restrictions, or they had no knowledge of any, and most of the remainder gave no definite evidence of restriction or mentioned only the action of a single union such as the Pattern-makers' overtime ban. Fourteen of the replies to the second question mentioned dissatisfaction with the Engineers' overtime agreement, but five wanted no alteration to it. Several associations specifically asked for the termination of the agreement in answer to the third question, although they did so for a variety of reasons, among them that the rates fixed for the payment of overtime and nightshift were too high. Most of the replies gave no clear indication of a strong desire for a confrontation over either overtime or other issues.

Nevertheless the engineering employers voted by massive majorities to lock the Engineers out and to extend the lockout to the other unions; and throughout the country no more than thirty-seven firms were expelled from the federation for failing to post lockout notices. Only in Birmingham, where engineering employers had never suffered the craft restrictions imposed in older engineering centres, were there signs of dissent.[22]

According to Citrine, 'the man who was thought by the unions to be the instigator of the lock-out was . . . Sir Allan Smith'.[23] Smith had achieved a firm command over the Engineering Employers Federation,

---

[22] On 3 March 1922 *The Times* reported that Birmingham engineering employers were protesting at the 'autocratic attitude' of their federation, and proposing to hold local discussions with the Engineers.

[23] Citrine, p. 70.

especially remarkable for a man who had never been an engineering
employer. Within six years of leaving his solicitor's practice in Glasgow
to become secretary of the federation he had been appointed permanent
chairman of its executive board. 'Everywhere, whatever the issue, Smith
became the Federation spokesman and leader.'[24] An autocrat by nature,
he dominated the head office and committees of the federation. Early in
1922 he toured the local associations to report on negotiations with the
Engineers, and thus had an opportunity to appeal to their loyalty. The
correspondence with local associations and individual firms about the
dispute gives further evidence of his tight control. Few of them were
willing to make a move in any direction without obtaining prior
approval from him.

The history of conflict over 'managerial rights' in the engineering
industry provided him with persuasive reasons for challenging the
unions in 1922. After their victory in the great lockout of 1897–8 the
employers had imposed terms which, they believed, established their
rights beyond question; but by 1914 it was clear that the threat to
managerial control had not been overcome, and the employers did not
feel strong enough to prevent the Engineers terminating the 1898
agreement. During the war the employers had suffered further
humiliation over dilution and other workshop issues. The postwar boom
had not been the time for them to re-establish their position. Smith had
chosen to temporise both in the engineering industry, and as leader of
the employers' side of the National Industrial Conference. If managerial
rights were ever to be placed on a firm footing, the depression provided
the opportunity.

Smith also had a second reason for challenging the unions. He had an
obsessive fear of political interference in industrial relations, and he
perceived sinister political forces at work within the unions. He was
convinced that there was no real quarrel between the ordinary workers
and their employers, and he knew that it was possible for him to reach
agreement with the Engineers' leaders. He concluded, and persuaded
his colleagues to accept, that 'the difficulty . . . is one in which political
issues have been the motive and in which outside, and even international, policy has been the real cause of the present unfortunate state
of affairs'.[25] J. C. Gould, an engineering employer, put the point more
simply when he referred in a speech in the House of Commons to 'the
wild men who are assuming control of the unions'.[26]

Influential employers shared Smith's views. William Weir, who had
served as director of munitions in Scotland in 1915, ended the war as

[24] Wigham, p. 111.
[25] Extract from a letter from Smith to the Engineers quoted in *The Times*, 26 April 1922.
[26] *Hansard*, 20 March 1922, col. 95.

Secretary of State for Air. Throughout the interwar years he played a considerable role in both the Federation of British Industries and the Confederation of Employers Associations. He agreed with Smith as to the essential loyalty of ordinary workers. In 1915 he had believed that 'the men would have loyally done whatever the country required of them, if the position had been clearly put to them, as they would have done as soldiers'.[27] In 1919 his firm proposed to construct a mechanised foundry in which the operators would need no more than six weeks' training, and sought the agreement of the Associated Ironmoulders, among whom militant influence was strong at that time, to a new grade of 'machine moulders'; but at a meeting with the union leaders 'each of the firm's proposals was closely questioned, and the scheme as a whole was received with unyielding hostility and suspicion'. It had to be abandoned. 'Weir was extremely angry.'[28] Weir's half-brother and colleague, J. R. Richmond, was in close contact with Smith during the lockout.

Nevertheless there was little hard evidence of Communist or extremist influence. On 21 May 1921 the *Worker* had admitted that 'unofficial organisation was at its lowest possible point'. At the beginning of the lockout a 'Council of Action' in Barrow tried to promote a national rank and file conference, and on 4 April an invitation from the Engineers' Sheffield district committee brought together representatives of ten other districts, twenty-four lockout committees and two other unions;[29] but shortly afterwards the executive removed twelve members of the Sheffield committee from office, and little more was heard of such unofficial activities. Nor did the powers of shop stewards figure to any extent in the dispute, although one or two local associations had mentioned objections to the shop steward agreement in their replies to the federation's survey.

The issue was the traditional rights claimed by craftsmen to control their own jobs, and, among the Engineers, the powers claimed by the district committees to regulate working practices. The Woodworkers' *Monthly Report* for May 1922 quoted an exchange in the negotiations between Smith and Hutchinson of the Engineers' executive in which Smith said that no federated firm would put a labourer on a fitter's job—'unless there was justification for it', and Hutchinson replied: 'That is just the position. You are asking for such an amount of liberty that is really to much.' There is no need to introduce sinister political influences to account for union opposition to managerial freedom of that kind.

The extension of the lockout to the other unions seems to have been

---

[27] *Glasgow Herald*, 21 May 1915, quoted in Hinton, p. 142.
[28] Reader, pp. 113–14.   [29] *Worker*, 22 April 1922.

sprung on the governing committees of the federation as soon as they decided to lock the Engineers out. Up to that point Smith had been patiently negotiating with the Engineers. Had agreement been reached, he might well have opened negotiations with the other unions on the general issue of managerial rights. Once the decision to lock out had been taken, however, the case for immediate extension to the other unions became compelling. The main issue did not affect the Engineers alone. As the federation's survey made clear, engineering firms were almost as likely to quote restrictions by the Boilermakers, the Foundry Workers, or the Patternmakers as those imposed by the Engineers. Moreover, in 1898 most of the other unions had not been parties either to the managerial rights clauses or to the procedure. Now they were all within the procedure; and the prospect of the industry's major union committeed to accept managerial instructions before making objections through procedure, while the others could flout them so long as the procedure had not decided against them, might have appeared to engineering employers to be even worse than the current situation. Finally, if the Engineers were locked out, little work would be done in most engineering firms. Unless the other unions agreed to the employers' terms forthwith, it would be an economy to lock them out at the same time. The decision to extend the lockout was harsh, even unwarranted, but, given Smith's objectives, strategically sound. It was particularly unwarranted so far as the general unions were concerned, for they had no part in most of the practices to which the employers were objecting. But then, the employers might have replied, these unions had very little reason to reject the employers' terms.

The extension of the lockout made it impossible for the government to maintain its stance of non-intervention, and Sir William Mackenzie was appointed a one-man court of inquiry. He heard evidence from 3 to 6 May, and issued his report on 10 May. On overtime he found for the employers. 'The question of necessity in regard to overtime is related to the requirements of the work to be done and the business in hand, and as to this necessity the Management alone are in a position to judge.' As to other issues, the urgency to decide varied, and 'opportunities for prior consultation . . . should be fully utilised'. When a contested direction was acted upon, it should be 'merely as a temporary measure and pending discussion under the ordinary procedure'. As to the risk of skilled men being replaced, 'no fear need be entertained that . . . in the industry as a whole, skill and good workmanship will become super-abundant. . . . An agreement to the principle of making such arrangements as shall provide avenues of employment' for displaced men 'ought not to be difficult'.[30]

[30] *Report*, pp. 18–21.

The conflict became another battle of attrition. In April the Engineers rejected their executive's proposals for a 25p a week levy on members still at work, and on 27 May all benefits were suspended except to sick and superannuated members. Some of the other unions were in even worse financial trouble. The Poor Law Guardians had therefore to sustain the stoppage. In June 1922 the number of Poor Law Unions giving relief to more than one in ten of their population stood at thirty, compared with twenty-one in April and twelve in the following September. They included such engineering centres as Barrow, Birmingham, Coventry, Dartford, Derby, Greenwich, Lincoln, Newcastle, Sheffield, Walsall, and West Bromwich.[31] The employers' federation advised its local associations to keep careful watch on the scales of relief applied by the guardians.

Negotiations were reopened. Where changes would 'result in one class of workpeople being replaced by another' the employers offered to grant a right to consultation within the workplace. The Engineers rejected this concession as making little difference, but the other unions decided to ballot, and on 22 May the executive of the Federation of General Workers decided to 'strongly request' their affiliates to recommend acceptance. The result of the pooled vote was more than two to one for acceptance, but the Boilermakers and Foundry Workers had announced that they would not be bound by the pooled vote, and, as both of them had adverse majorities, they stayed out. Meanwhile the Engineers' executive conducted another ballot which showed two to one in favour of accepting these terms along with the overtime clause, and their members went back on 13 June. The Foundry Workers capitulated at the same time, and a week later the Boilermakers decided that honour was satisfied.

Following the return to work, there does not seem to have been any major difficulty with the Engineers over the overtime clause, but the other unions were not bound by it. Boilermakers still refused to work overtime without instructions from their union, and a series of complaints about the Woodworkers led to a request from the management committee of the federation for their executive to instruct their district committees to cease making difficulties. The Woodworkers replied that they knew of no difficulties, but subsequently agreed to investigate if they were given specific details. The federation decided on 6 June 1923 that 'the matter should not be pursued further at this stage'. Engineering employers may have begun to wonder whether their victory had been so complete as they had supposed.

The Boilermakers' capacity to sustain large-scale conflict had not yet been exhausted. There had been discussions about a national overtime

[31] Min.stry of Health, *Annual Report*, 1922–3, pp. 84–5.

and nightshift agreement in the shipyards off and on since 1907, and the issue was taken up in earnest again in 1922. The Boilermakers withdrew from the negotiations. The Federation of Engineering and Shipbuilding Trades went on to sign an agreement which was ratified by ballot, in which the Boilermakers did not participate, in March 1923. The Shipwrights and Woodworkers also refused to vote, but accepted the agreement once it was ratified. The Boilermakers, however, stood out, and gave notice to withdraw from the federation. Their Tyne branches struck on 30 April and ten thousand of their members were locked out of federated yards.

The Boilermakers had two substantial objections to the agreement. The first was that their existing district agreements gave them more favourable terms. The second was that the new proposals were unjust in principle. Most of the other shipyard trades were paid by time, and their unions had agreed with the employers that compensation for overtime and nightshift should be on the basis of equal monetary payments for timeworkers and pieceworkers, not equal percentage payments. On the assumption that pieceworkers earned twice as much as timeworkers, the agreement fixed 25 per cent of average hourly piecework earnings as the appropriate additional compensation where timeworkers received time-and-a-half, and 50 per cent where timeworkers received double time. The Boilermakers insisted that the assumption was incorrect. Their earnings were no more than 50 per cent above those of timeworkers. These objections, however, were not made clear to the public. *The Times* asserted on 28 April that the Boilermakers were prejudicing 'the principle of collective bargaining . . . which is a very precious heritage for the trade unionist. . . . Their real quarrel, if any, is not with the employers, but with their associated unions.' The Ministry of Labour refused to set up a court of inquiry.

Nevertheless the Boilermakers, convinced of the justice of their case, stayed out until November by selling their remaining investments left over from better times, borrowing from their superannuation fund and their members, raising a levy from members still at work, and running up a heavy overdraft. Federated shipyards were brought to a halt, and by September thirty thousand other shipyard workers were out of work because of the stoppage. Meanwhile an upturn in orders put pressure on the employers. The Boilermakers finally returned for further talks, and disputed points were referred to the Industrial Court. Where the original agreement had granted 25 per cent above average piecework earnings the court awarded one-third, and two-thirds in place of 50 per cent.

The strains imposed on the unions by national collective bargaining were visible in many of the major conflicts of the depression years. The

Boilermakers had been asserting their right to reject an agreement accepted by the other shipbuilding unions. Similar issues were involved in the lockout of the Typographical Association and in the stoppage of the Cooks and Stewards. The Engineers' lockout arose out of their refusal to allow their national leaders to sign away the rights of district committees to control overtime and regulate working practices in the plant. Moreover, the strains of national bargaining were also felt among employers. The Liverpool shipping employers had resigned from the Port Employers Association, and there were vigorous assertions of local independence among building employers.

Before 1921 painters had been paid less than other building craftsmen almost everywhere, but now the national agreement specified a single standard rate for all craftsmen. Many building employers thought the differential should be restored. In 1923 the Eastern Counties employers withdrew from the federation in order to impose it. On 1 March ten thousand building workers from all the trades in East Anglia struck in defence of the uniform craft rate. By 17 April this unexpected solidarity with the painters forced the employers to abandon their proposal, and in June they applied to reaffiliate to the federation. A further victory for national bargaining appeared to be in prospect next month when the Liverpool employers applied for readmission, and were told that they would be accepted, provided that they gave notice to terminate their local agreement and apply the national terms. However, these successes were for the time being offset by notice from the Northern Counties employers and the London Master Builders to withdraw from the federation; and a request from the Southern Counties Federation to revert to regional settlements. Fortunately for the stability of collective bargaining in the building industry, nothing came of these proposed defections.

The Effects on the Unions

'The year 1921 has not been a year at all, it has been a nightmare' were the words with which Duncan introduced the annual report of the Workers Union for that year. So it was for his union, which lost almost exactly half it members, and fell from second to fifth largest union. It was bad enough for the trade union movement as a whole, which lost a fifth of its membership. The drain continued over the next two years and by the end of 1923 the overall loss was a third. No concise set of figures can fully demonstrate the varying fortunes of different sections of the movement over those years, but Table 3 gives some indication by setting out the change in membership of twenty-two major unions. The dividing line indicates the unions which did better or worse than average.

TABLE 3
Trade union membership, 1920–23

Trade union	1923 Membership as a percentage of 1920
Teachers	96
Typographical Association	95
Boot and Shoe Operatives	85
Boilermakers	84
Post Office Workers	84
Cardroom Operatives	84
Woodworkers	83
Railwaymen	78
Miners Federation	77
Weavers	76
Transport and General Workers[a]	76
Iron and Steel Trades Confederation	64
Sailors and Firemen	57
Engineers	55
Textile Workers[a]	53
Tailors and Garment Workers	52
General Workers	46
Distributive and Allied Workers	42
Shop Assistants	39
Agricultural Workers	37
National Amalgamated Union of Labour	35
Workers Union	28

Note:
 [a] In these instances comparison is with the total membership of the constituent unions in 1920.

The table suggests that two different factors must be brought into play to account for the varying fortunes of the unions over those years. The first is the economic performance of the industries in which they operated, as measured in the size of wage reductions and the incidence of unemployment. Unions which suffered little in those respects might be expected to retain their members better than other unions. In the top half of the table, the Boot and Shoe Operatives, the Post Office Workers, the Railwaymen, the Teachers, and the Typographical Association clearly fall into that category; and in the bottom half, the Engineers, the Iron and Steel Trades Confederation, and the Sailors and Firemen suffered larger cuts and heavier unemployment than most other unions. So probably did the Workers Union with their concentration in the engineering industry, and certainly the National Amalgamated Union of Labour with most of their members in engineering, shipbuilding, steel, and coalmining. However, in the top half of the table, the Boilermakers, the Miners, and the cotton unions suffered severely from wage cuts, and the Boilermakers and cotton unions from unemployment as well, whereas the Tailors and Garment Workers, the Distributive and Allied Workers, and the Shop Assistants, in the bottom half, suffered less than most in these respects.

There is, therefore, need for an additional explanatory factor, which can be met by the strength of union organisation at the beginning of the depression, measured not merely by trade union density in 1920 but also by the length of time that the union had sustained a relatively high density, and had therefore been able to develop traditions of loyalty among its members. This factor can help to account for the position of the Boilermakers near the top of the table despite their unfavourable economic circumstances, and probably affects all the unions in the top half of the table, except for the Transport and General Workers. It can also help to account for the Textile Workers, the Distributive and Allied Workers, the Shop Assistants, the Agricultural Workers, and the three major general unions being in the bottom half. In all these latter unions, except for the Agricultural Workers, and perhaps the Textile Workers, the loss of membership was augmented by a high rate of labour turnover. The one union whose rate of decline seems inconsistent with the strength of its traditions is the Engineers. Perhaps the 1922 lockout provides the explanation.

Another factor which might be expected to influence growth and decline in trade unions is the extension and contraction of collective bargaining. However, although many individual employers left their associations and ceased to deal with trade unions, and although several local associations, for example in retail distribution, terminated their agreements with the unions, and there were several reversions from national to district bargaining, there was only one instance of a major union suffering a disastrous curtailment of its bargaining rights. When the Agricultural Wages Board was abolished and the conciliation committees proved worthless, the Agricultural Workers lost their chief means of influencing their members' pay and conditions. Nevertheless their loss of members was not markedly different from that of several major unions which retained most of their bargaining rights.

Several attacks on collective bargaining had been repulsed. The Geddes Committee had recommended that the Civil Service Arbitration Board should be abolished. Since its cost was negligible, the intention must have been to facilitate reductions in the pay of civil servants. The unions began an agitation for the restoration of the board. By February 1923 over four hundred Members of Parliament had indicated their support, and in March Baldwin, the Prime Minister, promised to reconsider the matter. Two months later his government accepted the principle of arbitration and a joint committee of the National Whitley Council was asked to report on its application.

The Cave Committee appointed to review the work of the Trade Boards criticised the powers of the boards under the 1918 Act, and recommended that, in future, the boards should revert to their original function of preventing 'sweating'. The absence of effective machinery for collective bargaining was to justify the establishment of a board only when accompanied by 'unduly low wages'; and the main task of a board should be to fix 'a minimum time-rate . . . with reference to the lowest grade of ordinary workers in the trade' and 'a piecework basis time-rate'. Piece rates (except for homeworkers) and higher rates for skilled workers should be settled only by agreement between the two sides.[32] Action on most of these recommendations was a matter for parliament, and although a bill was introduced in 1923, it had not received its second reading when Baldwin went to the country in November. The main outcome was that no new boards were set up for another ten years. The Grocery Trade Boards which, although appointed, had not yet had any of their proposals on wages approved, were now disbanded.

Since no national council of employer and union representatives had been established to hear appeals from the co-operative societies' joint district boards, unresolved disputes were sent to the Joint Committee of Trade Unionists and Co-operators, whose trade union members were drawn from the General Council. During 1922 cases flooded in, and the committee protested 'against the action of certain societies (notably the CWS and the Plymouth Society) in imposing reductions of wages either without prior consultation with the unions, or immediately after failure to reach a settlement by negotiation'.[33] The Co-operative Wholesale Society insisted that it must be allowed to follow the wage reductions settled by the various Joint Industrial Councils and Trade Boards in the industries in which it operated. In April 1923 a reduction agreed by the Sugar Confectionery and Food Preserving Trade Board was imposed, without negotiation, on employees at the co-operative factories in Pelaw and Silvertown. They struck, and after three months the Distributive and Allied Workers brought out six thousand more co-operative employees to force the issue.

The General Council could not deny that the Co-operative Wholesale Society should have regard to the wages paid by its competitors, but equally they could not allow the society to adjust wages without negotiation. Nor could they admit that Trade Board rates ranked as 'negotiated' rates. They therefore issued a verdict of extreme obscurity from which it emerged that, although the society must pay above Trade Board rates, it could apply to variations in those rates; but the unions had 'the right to discuss or negotiate on any question arising out of such

[32] *Report*, pp. 45–6.
[33] Trades Union Congress, 1922, p. 248.

variation', with reference to the Joint Committee of Trade Unionists and Co-operators where no agreement was reached.[34] The dispute at Pelaw and Silvertown was settled by arbitration in favour of the society; but the principle of collective bargaining had been preserved.

There was at least one advance in collective bargaining. In 1923 a dispute between an engineering firm and the Draughtsmen led to discussions with the Engineering Employers Federation. The federation, which had already granted recognition to the Clerical and Administrative Workers Union in 1920, now negotiated a procedure for dealing with disputes with the Draughtsmen on much the same lines as that for manual workers. Pay, however, was left to firm-by-firm negotiations in which the union tried to achieve target figures which they had drawn up. According to their returns the average salary for those aged 25–30 was £4.25 in 1923, and £5 for those over thirty. These figures compared very favourably with the average fitter's rate of £2.82½.

The impact of the depression on unions which had just established their own unemployment benefit schemes under the 1920 Act was disastrous. By March 1921 the General Workers were spending £10,000 a week out of their own funds on unemployment benefit alone—more than their weekly income. By April the figure was up to £15,000. A strict limit of benefit to eight weeks, with a levy on members at work, did little to stem the drain. In September an emergency conference met to put an end to the scheme and the union had therefore to cease to be an agent for administering state benefite. The London Dockers and the National Amalgamated Union of Labour were also driven to abandon their schemes. The Workers Union managed to maintain their scheme, at the cost of a deficit of £140,000 in 1921. Many of the skilled unions were able to weather the storm. Some of them had large reserves, and most paid benefits well above the minimum prescribed by the Act so that they could cut them without becoming ineligible to administer state benefit. Even so, the Engineers had to suspend payment at the beginning of their lockout, and the Foundry Workers followed a few weeks later.[35] At the beginning of 1921 the number of 'associations' administering the Act was 241, almost all of them unions, with a membership of over four million. By June 1923 the figures were 141 associations with about one million members.[36]

---

[34] Ibid., 1923, pp. 203–16.

[35] In 1921 the income of registered unions from their members was £11.3 million, including levies as well as normal contributions. Their expenditure on unemployment benefit from their own funds was £7.3 million and dispute benefit cost £3.4 million. To cover other benefits and running costs £4.9 million was drawn from their reserves. (*Nineteenth Abstract of Labour Statistics*, pp. 178–9.)

[36] Tillyard and Ball, p. 59.

Falling income forced unions into administrative economies. One of the hardest hit, the National Amalgamated Union of Labour, instituted the first of a series of reductions in salaries for its full-time officers in December 1921, and followed it up, in January 1922, with cuts in the numbers and salaries of office staffs and full-time branch secretaries, and in the size of delegations to all manner of bodies, including Joint Industrial Councils, Congress and the Labour Party. Further economies, salary reductions, and redundancies followed, although some of the latter were deferred in the hope that amalgamation might enable some jobs to be saved. The Workers Union, which suffered an even greater loss of membership, managed with fewer redundancies and smaller cuts in salaries.[37]

Although often accused of being bad employers, the unions generally treated their officers well, in spite of economic pressures. The available evidence[38] suggests that the ratio of officers to members rose sharply between 1921 and 1927, more than doubling in some unions, so that the overall scale of redundancies must have been relatively small; and their salaries were not ungenerous. With average earnings of adult male manual workers about £150 a year in 1923, the basic rate of the main grade of officials in the Workers Union was £278.20, and the salary range fixed for the General and Municipal Workers Union, which came into existence by amalgamation in 1924, was £234 to £312, although women organisers were paid only £208.

This was the first major amalgamation since the Transport and General Workers came into existence. It was approved towards the end of 1923 and became effective in July 1924. Once the General Workers had entered into negotiation with the three partners in the National Amalgamated Workers Union, differences between the General Workers and the Workers Union pushed the former quarrels between the Workers Union and the National Amalgamated Union of Labour into the background; and because the General Workers had now comfortably surpassed the Workers Union in membership, they generally had their way. Breakdown came over the arrangement for the ballot. The Workers Union pulled out, leaving the other three unions (the third was the Municipal Employees) to iron out the remaining problems at a conference which finalised the rules of the new organisation. The almost bankrupt National Amalgamated Union of Labour was not able to extract many concessions. With greater resources the Municipal Employees were able to insist on a municipal section at head office under the control of their own men. Otherwise, the constitution was that of the General Workers. Power was concentrated

---

[37] Hyman, p. 133.
[38] Clegg, Killick and Adams, p. 40.

in the hands of the district secretaries, with seats on the governing body of the union by virtue of their office. This, together with the tenure of the secretaryship and presidency of the union by the ageing Thorne and Clynes, robbed it of any chance of matching the dynamism of the Transport and General Workers, with its steamlined industrial structure and Bevin as its secretary.

With the formation of the Transport and General Workers and the General and Municipal Workers, the Transport Workers Federation and the General Workers Federation lost their *raison d'être*. Williams tried to give the former a further lease of life by bringing in the railway unions, but the negotiations failed. Both federations were wound up.

Under the new constitution of Congress a General Council took office in September 1921 in place of the Parliamentary Committee. With thirty-two members instead of the Parliamentary Committee's seventeen, the council was bound to include much new blood. In particular the left was strengthened. Already in 1919 John Hill had been joined by A. A. Purcell, an officer of the Furniture Trades Association, and Alonso Swales, a member of the Engineers' executive. Now the newcomers included George Hicks, secretary of the Building Trade Workers, who still sedulously fostered his reputation as a militant; John Bromley, secretary of the Locomotive Engineers and Firemen, who had won fame for his aggressive conduct of the campaign for an eight-hour day for footplate staff; and Ben Turner, president of the Textile Workers and a humanitarian sympathiser with leftwing causes. Back, after an absence of twenty-six years, Tillett no longer counted for much.

The major object of the reform had been to give greater authority to the central representative body of the British trade union movement. In 1921 Congress had refused to match these expectations with formal powers, and in 1922 they turned down the council's request for authority to enable them to organise a 'joint defence of trade union standards'. Nevertheless the council made the most of such powers as they had, if only to ensure that they were kept informed of what was going on, by asking union leaders involved in major disputes to report personally to them. In the engineering lockout this was done through the National Joint Council which offered its services as a mediation committee, and helped to persuade the engineering employers to extend the notices given to the unions, other than the Engineers, in order to allow further negotiations. On 28 March 1923 the General Council appointed sub-committees to meet the Agricultural Workers and the Federation of Building Trades Operatives (whose dispute was ultimately settled by arbitration) 'to deal, on behalf of the General Council, with any contingency which may arise'; and, in the Boilermakers' lockout of the same year, three members were deputed to enquire into the difficulties between that union and the Federation of Engineering and Shipbuilding Trades. Not much was achieved, but at least the council established that they had a part to play in all major disputes.

Less success attended the council's nation-wide recruiting campaign in 1923 under the slogan 'Back to the Unions'. Recruitment remained the prerogative of the individual unions, for, after all, no one can be recruited direct to the trade union movement, and the campaign led to one of the bitterest debates ever heard at Congress. Ellen Wilkinson of the Distributive and Allied Workers complained that there was no answer to the question: 'Which union?'. Havelock Wilson and Shinwell exchanged personal abuse. Bevin reprimanded them for their references to the dock strike, and proceeded to address unfriendly remarks to the Workers Union, whose spokesman replied in kind. Smillie's comment was that the debate had 'undone any little good that might have been done' by the campaign.[39]

[39] Trades Union Congress, 1923, pp. 264–73.

9

The First Labour Government

The Unions and the Labour Party, 1918–23

LIBERAL disunity and the decline of the coalition government afforded time for the Labour Party to carry through the organisational reforms hurriedly inaugurated in 1917–18. Thus 'by 1924 there were only three constituencies in Great Britain in which no sort of Local Labour Party was in existence'.[1] In the same year there were 113 full-time agents employed directly by the party, and thirty-six full-time 'supplementary agents', most of them employed by the Miners. In 1920 a complete scheme of 'regionalisation' was introduced, with Scotland, Wales, and London as separate regions. The regional organisers took over most of the work of supervising the constituencies. Within the constituencies, however, the nature of party organisation had not changed very much. Despite the decline of the socialist societies, relatively few divisional parties had a large individual membership, although the women's sections grew rapidly. 'The primary bases of most new constituencies, as of the old, were the trade-union branches, on to which an individual members' section may or may not have been tacked'.[2]

The increase in the party's strength therefore mainly reflected the growth of the unions. Trade union membership affiliated to the party had risen from 1.57 million in 1914 (a figure still somewhat affected by the Osborne judgment) to a peak of 4.32 million in 1920. At 3.16 million in 1924 it was still double the 1914 figure, and the number of full-time trade union officers and part-time branch officials willing and able to give time to the party during elections, and to sit on local committees and local authorities, had increased even faster, providing a key factor in Labour's progress.

The results of this development were more clearly visible in the local government elections of 1919 than they had been in the general election of 1918. In 1919 Labour took control of a number of London boroughs and urban authorities in other parts of the country. Taking one year with another, the area under their control continued to expand.

In the industrial areas of the country a number of social processes and forces were throwing into local prominence a vast army of Labour politicians now

---

[1] Cole, *A History of the Labour Party*, p. 140.   [2] McKibbin, p. 139.

ready to take over the politics of their . . . communities. We should never make
the mistake of taking the parliamentary Labour party as the start and finish of
the Labour movement.[3]

Elections to the Boards of Poor Law Guardians were also important,
because of the wide autonomy granted to the guardians in the
administration of poor relief. In 1921 Labour-controlled boards vied
with each other in providing relatively generous treatment for the
unemployed, although a number of others also joined in the competition. The West Derby union, for example, covering Liverpool and
Bootle, which had no Labour members, paid 'relief to a maximum of 41*s*
[£2.05] per week, half as much again as a worker could receive from
unemployment insurance'.[4] However, it was the Labour guardians in
Poplar, led by George Lansbury, who achieved fame in May 1921
because they refused to levy rates for the common London services, in
the hope of forcing the government to sustain their relief scales by
higher payments from the Metropolitan Common Poor Law Fund, and
were sent to prison for it; and they and their Labour colleagues
elsewhere claimed credit for the publication by the coalition government
early in 1922 of the 'Mond scale', which fixed a maximum relief
payment of £2.70 for a family of eight with a fuel allowance on top, and
led to a 'vast expansion in the cost of pauperism'.[5]

By comparison the achievements of the party's parliamentary
representatives were meagre. Without most of their best-known figures
the parliamentary party were not an impressive group, and most of the
trade union officers, who made up over four-fifths of their number, had
especially pressing industrial commitments during the immediate
postwar years. In their report to the annual conference in 1919, the
parliamentary party felt obliged to defend their record of attendance as
'as good as if not better than that of Members of other Parties'.
However, greater talents and more assiduous attendance would probably not have added much to their achievements. The pressures which
persuaded the prewar Liberal governments to listen to the Labour Party
had comparatively little influence on the postwar coalition. Even if they
had been able to get a more sympathetic hearing from the government,
the parliamentary party might not have had much influence on
legislation, for there was a further problem. As they reported to the 1921
party conference, the House of Commons was

deaf to argument and reason. . . . Time after time the Government has brought
forward Bills which are vitally necessary in any scheme of reconstruction, and it
has either had to withdraw them altogether or emasculate them to satisfy its
own supporters in the House.[6]

---

[3] Stead, pp. 207–8.   [4] Gilbert, *British Social Policy*, p. 213.
[5] Ibid., p. 217.   [6] Labour Party, 1921, p. 80.

The main service of the parliamentary party during these years was to advertise the party's growing strength in the country. Victory in fourteen by-elections between 1918 and 1922 was no mean record, and brought the party's total to seventy-five seats. Among them was Henderson, returned for Widnes in August 1919. Given his record and standing, he might have been expected to assume the leadership, but he saw as his main task the completion of party reorganisation, and rarely appeared in the House. He left the burden at Westminster first to Adamson, and then, from 1921, to Clynes, who made a better job of it.

The election which followed the break-up of the coalition in 1922 brought the party 142 seats—ahead of the combined total of 116 for the Asquith and the Lloyd George Liberals. It also showed that if reorganisation had not yet brought radical change in the constituencies, it was having a marked effect in the higher levels of the party. In 1918 fifty out of sixty-one Labour Members had been sponsored by trade unions. Now the proportion was down to eighty-eight out of 142, with no less than thirty-one sponsored by the Independent Labour Party, and nineteen by divisional parties. The Miners had forty-one Members, followed by the Engineers with seven, and the Transport and General Workers with five. Although some of these figures are a little misleading—Gosling, for example, was returned as a Divisional Labour Party representative—they indicate a considerable swing within the parliamentary party. Although Henderson was defeated again, and did not return to the House until January 1923, the two most prominent prewar leaders, MacDonald and Snowden, were back along with Jowett and Lansbury. In addition there were Labour Members of a new type— middle-class men with a background in social work or the Fabian Society, like Clement Attlee and Sidney Webb, or fugitives from the prewar Liberal Party, like Charles Trevelyan. There was also a change in the leadership. The support of the Independent Labour Party, and especially of its vigorous and radical group of Clydesiders, enabled MacDonald to defeat Clynes by 61 votes to 56 when the new parliamentary party met. A good many trade unionists criticised the decision and, even more, the way it was handled; but Clynes, although an outstanding speaker with a good record as Food Controller in 1918, was not the man to lead a Labour government.

The changed composition of the parliamentary party was to some extent matched in the national party organisation. The proportion of representatives of local Labour Parties at the party conference was increasing. New men who were neither trade union nominees nor identified with the Independent Labour Party were beginning to appear on the party executive, the first being Herbert Morrison, secretary of the London Labour Party. There had also been changes at head office. In

1918 a number of advisory committees had been introduced to provide information and ideas on the main areas of policy. They were to be co-ordinated by a secretary, originally Cole and later Arthur Greenwood. In 1920 they were linked more closely with the parliamentary party, and next year attached to the new joint department of research and information established to serve both the party and Congress. 'The extent to which Labour had mobilised support from the intellectuals, either in the civil service or outside it, can be seen from the list of luminaries who accepted with apparent enthusiasm the invitation to sit on the committees.'[7]

Even more important was a growing division between the job of Member of Parliament and that of trade union leader. Before the war, many senior officers of major unions had also been Members of Parliament: Pickard, Edwards and Mabon, all officers of the Miners Federation; and Shackleton, Barnes, Bell, Thomas, and Thorne. Already, by 1914, their number was diminishing. By 1923 the president and secretary of the Miners Federation were debarred from sitting in parliament. Hodges, it is true, won a seat at the general election of that year, but, much to his surprise and chagrin, the Miners insisted that he should cease to be secretary of the federation. Thomas was still a leading member of the parliamentary party, but the chief office of the Railwaymen was now divided. He was political secretary, with Cramp as industrial secretary. The Distributive and Allied Workers had adopted the same device. Neither president nor secretary of the Engineers was in the House, nor was Bevin. Among the major unions only the General Workers and the Workers Union were now led by parliamentarians. After the retirement of Bowerman as secretary of Congress, the General Council, on 28 February 1923, raised the salary of the post from £600 to £750 on condition that his successor, Bramley, 'shall devote his whole time to the work of the General Council'. Before 1906 the only satisfactory way for the unions to make their voice heard in parliament had been to send their leaders there. Now the Labour Party provided alternative spokesmen, and the growing demands of their industrial work made it impossible for union leaders to do both jobs adequately. More and more the position of trade union Member of Parliament became a form of superannuation.

Following the 1922 election, the parliamentary performance of the Labour Party improved considerably. The party now had an ample supply of talent to cover every debate. Since both sections of the Liberal Party might be expected to vote with them on many issues of reform, a good showing was usually ensured, and the chance of a snap defeat of the government was a possibility. The annual conference in 1923 was,

[7] McKibbin, p. 215.

rather optimistically, informed that 'the Party, as the Official Opposition, has done its work with efficiency and spirit, and has established itself as it has never done before. By general recognition it is the alternative Government.'[8] During the session it launched an attack on the government's social service proposals, bringing forward a series of bills and motions on old age pensions, widows' pensions, a national minimum wage and similar topics, on some of which the government's majority was dangerously small. A private member's motion on the grievances over pay of ex-servicemen who had originally entered the civil service on a temporary basis was carried against the government by 145 to 138, with the upshot that a select committee reported in favour of a higher starting rate. The parliamentary party was delighted, and so were the civil service unions.

In May 1923 Thomas introduced a private member's bill on workmen's compensation, embodying a series of reforms recommended in 1920 by a departmental committee chaired by Holman Gregory. Up to this point the government had taken no action on the report. They now carried a bill including most of the proposals, but omitting compulsion upon employers to insure against the risk of compensation, which would have safeguarded employees of bankrupt undertakings.

One issue on which the party's record may have won them electoral support was pacifism, broadly interpreted, for the mood of the 1918 Khaki election had long been forgotten. The party had consistently attacked the peace treaty and its provisions on reparations. The parliamentary party argued the need for revision 'to give Germany a chance to return to a position of ecomomic and social stability, and also in order to encourage a spirit of reconciliation'.[9] The Council of Action in 1920 had demonstrated that the unions and the party were united in their eagerness to preserve peace. In 1922 the General Council intervened in the Chanak crisis, when Lloyd George seemed about to go to war with Turkey. Without waiting for the Labour Party, on 21 September they asked to see the Prime Minister to urge that the dispute be settled by the League of Nations, and that there should be 'no more war'. On this occasion the Conservative Party agreed with them, and at last brought Lloyd George down; but the election of MacDonald as party leader, and the return of Snowden and other prominent pacifists to parliament, had already confirmed the Labour Party's claim to be the party of peace.

The Communists and the Left

Over the winter of 1920–21, local committees of unemployed workers came into existence in London and a number of other cities. In April

[8] Labour Party, 1923, p. 115.   [9] Ibid., 1920, p. 50.

1921 many of them joined together to form the National Unemployed Workers Committee Movement. Apart from those unions which paid unemployment benefit, the trade unions had little to offer their unemployed members. Most unions allowed them to keep their names on the books in return for a nominal subscription, so that they could be 'in benefit' as soon as they started work; but they could do little to occupy the time of the unemployed, or to assuage their sense of grievance. The unemployed workers' committees, by contrast, offered meetings, marches, deputations to the guardians, and lobbying to secure immediate objectives: higher rates of relief from the guardians, improved unemployment benefit, and funds for relief works from the government. The General Council, the Labour Party executive, and the parliamentary party held two national conferences on unemployment early in 1921, but found they had to ward off a demand for a national one-day strike in support of action on unemployment.

The unemployed movement therefore fell into the hands of the recently-founded Communist Party, which had come into existence in January 1921, after prolonged negotiations in which six groups had taken part: the British Socialist Party, the Communist Unity Group of the Socialist Labour Party, the Shop Stewards and Workers Committee Movement, a section of the National Guilds League, the South Wales Socialist Society, and the Workers Socialist Federation. All of them had been influenced by syndicalist and industrial unionist doctrines; and, although they were all anxious to claim the title 'Communist' and brotherhood with the Bolsheviks, most of them were not at all keen to accept the need for parliamentary action and affiliation to the Labour Party, on which the Russians insisted. It needed a great deal of persuasion, and a substantial injection of funds from Moscow, to bring the united party into existence. Among its members was a considerable number of unemployed shop stewards who were available to help with the establishment of unemployed workers' committees, and, when the national movement was formed, one of their number, Hannington, was chosen as its national organiser and soon became its outstanding leader.

So effective were Hannington and his colleagues as leaders of the unemployed that Congress agreed to suspend business in September 1921 in order to listen to them. Affiliation to Congress was refused, on the grounds that it would duplicate affiliation of the unemployed through their own unions; but on 20 October 1922 the General Council made a grant of £10 to the movement; sent a deputation to the Prime Minister to seek the recall of parliament to deal with unemployment; and set up an organising committee to work with the movement in arranging demonstrations of the unemployed. In January 1923 a joint advisory committee of three representatives from the General Council and three unemployed was set up and subsequently approved an 'unemployed workers' charter'.

Otherwise the Communists had little success in their dealings with the unions before 1924. Many of the prominent leaders of the shop stewards' movement had become full-time politicians, including MacManus, the party chairman, Tom Bell, Gallacher, Peet and Murphy. A number of trade union officers who had originally joined the party, such as Purcell, Ellen Wilkinson and Cook, found, like most other 'foundation' members, that they had not bargained for the kind of discipline to which they were subject, and withdrew. Robert Williams was expelled soon after Black Friday. The exodus continued until the party had effectively cut itself off from positions of influence in almost every union. A rare exception was Pollitt of the Boilermakers who, although not a full-time officer, could rely on election to his union's delegations to Congress and the party conference.

The party also lost support through violent demonstrations against union leaders. In April 1921 a group of busmen took possession of the head office of the United Vehicle Workers as a protest against a wage cut and Black Friday. Documents were stolen, including the expenses sheets of some of the full-time officers, and circulated among the members. In July 1921 some two hundred unemployed Engineers forced their way into their head office saying, according to the union's journal for August, that they were 'representatives of the "Rank and File" and Internationalists, and had come for the purpose of ejecting the Executive Council and taking control of the affairs of the Union'. They were removed by the police.

In December 1920 Murphy had returned from a visit to Moscow, well supplied with funds, to establish a 'British Bureau' of the Red International of Labour Unions, which had been set up in Moscow to complement the Communist International .With what was left of the Shop Steward and Workers' Committee Movement as a nucleus, the bureau undertook to persuade British unions to transfer their allegiance to the Red International. By the summer they claimed to have won the support of hundreds of trade union branches, and a few Trades Councils and district committees, but the only significant convert was the South Wales Miners Federation, and when the Welshmen proposed to the Miners' annual conference in 1922 that the national federation should affiliate to Moscow they could find no other district to support them.

In 1922 Moscow switched to 'united front' tactics, and the British party followed them. One consequence was that the party leaders disowned Philip Hodge, an officer of the Fife Miners' union, who led a breakaway in 1923 on the grounds that the union's leaders were hopelessly reactionary. Hodge himself was not a Communist, but the local Communists had at first supported him. Another was that Moscow began to press for the party to organise a Minority Movement of militants within the unions. A series of conferences in the coalfields led up to the formation of a Miners Minority Movement in January 1924.

Meanwhile the party had been pursuing its application for affiliation to the Labour Party. The first attempt had been made in August 1920 before unification had been fully achieved, and rejected on the grounds that the Communist Party's objects did not accord with 'the constitution, principles and programme of the Labour Party'.[10] Subsequent applications received similar answers. Nevertheless, Communists were still entitled to join the Labour Party as individual members, to be elected to its annual conference and to secure nomination as Labour candidates for local and parliamentary elections. In 1922 a Communist who had also been nominated by the local Labour Party won Motherwell. Another Communist was elected as an endorsed Labour candidate for Battersea North both in 1922 and 1924. However, the discovery that the endorsed Labour candidate at a by-election in Kelvingrove was the full-time organiser of the Communist Party in Glasgow helped to pave the way for the decisions of the Labour Party conference in October 1924, when affiliation was finally and conclusively rejected; Communists were debarred from standing as Labour candidates; and, by a narrow margin, Communists were made ineligible for individual membership, though they could still appear as union delegates.

The Communist Party attracted attention out of all proportion to its membership, which in 1923 was about three thousand. The Independent Labour Party, claiming ten times as many members, also felt the attraction of the Russian revolution and the 'workers' state' now established in Russia and spent much of their energy in the immediate postwar years, first in pursuing the possibility of affiliation to the Communist International; and then, when it became clear that the Russian requirements were totally at variance with the libertarian traditions of the party, in advocating a single, united, international socialist organisation. To this end they joined with several of the smaller Continental socialist parties in the Vienna Union, or 'Two-and-a-half' International—halfway between the Second (Socialist) International and the Third (Communist) International. However, in 1922, when the intransigence of the two major international oganisations had put an end to this enterprise, Clifford Allen, first as treasurer and then as chairman, pointed the party in a new direction. Setting out to make it the source of socialist ideas and plans for the Labour movement and for a future

[10] Ibid., 1921, p. 19.

Labour government, and to attract young men and women who were in search of progressive political ideas, he used his Quaker connections to collect substantial sums of money; moved the head office from back street rooms to an imposing building; employed new staff; created publicity and research departments, and transformed the party paper, the *Labour Leader*, into the *New Leader* with H. N. Brailsford as its editor and a considerably enlarged circulation.

Under Lansbury's control the *Daily Herald* continued to reflect his enthusiasm for almost every leftwing cause, now including almost uncritical admiration for the Russian revolution. However, even with a circulation of 300,000 copies he could not make the paper pay, and was obliged to ask the party and the unions for assistance. Continuing losses forced him to hand it over to them in March 1922. They showed no enthusiasm for this expensive gift, but it was the only daily Labour paper, and in the end Henderson proposed and the General Council agreed on an annual levy of nearly 1p a member from the unions, on condition that Lansbury ceased to be managing director. Congress ratified the deal in September. Although there were to be further crises over both finance and editorial policy during the next three years, the *Herald* was now under trade union control, which became tighter as the years went by.

The Central Labour College never fully recovered from its wartime closure, and was finally compelled to shut down in 1929, but from the start of the postwar period it was eclipsed by the Labour College movement which assured its future by entering into arangements to provide trade unions with their own education schemes, the first being for the Building Trade Workers in 1922. The Workers Educational Association was already in the field, having arranged to provide an educational scheme for the Iron and Steel Trades Confederation in 1920, and extended it to other unions through a Workers Educational Trade Union Committee which had the support of G. D. H. Cole, now on the staff of the London University extramural department. At one time it seemed that the General Council was going to take over both bodies, along with the Central College and Ruskin College too, in an all-embracing scheme of trade union education, but the scheme was rejected by Congress in 1926. Thereafter, the General Council continued to give support to both the National Council of Labour Colleges and the Workers Educational Trade Union Committee. Their example set a pattern for several major unions, including the Transport and General Workers and the General and Municipal Workers. The consequence was that Labour College commitment to Marxist education had to be muted to suit their trade union paymasters.

Most members of the National Guilds League were enthusiastic supporters of the Russian revolution, but a minority thought there was a world of difference between workers' control and the dictatorship of the proletariat. In Britain the league's doctrine was put to a practical test by the setting up of working guilds in the building industry. Two building guilds were established in 1920: one in London where Malcom Sparkes, a building employer, was the leading figure; and another in Manchester by S. G. Hobson, a member of the Guilds League, and Richard Coppock, an officer of the Building Trade Workers. Their objects were to tender for local authority housing under the Addison scheme; to make provision for continuous pay regardless of the weather; and to give the workers ultimate control of the organisations for which they worked. The National Federation of Building Trades Operatives provided much of the capital; many building workers invested their savings; the shortage of building labour made it virtually certain that the guilds would receive all the contracts they could fulfil; and the guilds 'had a huge success with the workers. . . . The Building Guilds attracted both through their practical idealism and because they offered unusual conditions of employment.'[11] However, their management was defective, and things were made worse after the forced amalgamation of the London and Manchester guilds in 1921 by the antipathy between the humanitarian Sparkes and the dishonest and autocratic Hobson. The depression added to their difficulties, and the Ministry of Health began to disallow the provision for continuous payment in their contracts. Final dissolution, with substantial costs to building workers in lost savings and unpaid wages, was delayed until 1923, but before the end of 1921 it was manifest that things were going wrong. The rifts in the National Guilds League widened. The substantial group of Communists stayed on while most of their opponents left; and the league was wound up in 1923.

Immediately after the war the league's offshoot, the Labour Research Department, had hopes of becoming the research centre for the whole Labour movement; but the joint departments of the Labour Party and the General Council put an end to that possibility. In 1921 the acceptance of an annual subsidy from the Russian trade delegation in Britain led to the resignation of most of the non-Communists, except for Cole who was finally driven out in 1924. However, 'the trade unions found so much use' for the Labour Research Department 'that it survived all the attempts by the central direction of the labour movement to outlaw it as Communist-tainted. But it had no further concern with workers' control.'[12]

Thus the process whereby British socialists were forced to choose between loyalty to the leaders of the Labour Party and support for the

[11] Matthews, p. 313.   [12] Margaret Cole, p. 283.

Communist Party was already well advanced by the end of 1923. It necessarily emphasised the importance of the tiny Communist Party.

However, a hardening of attitudes to the Communist Party did not prevent the Labour Party and the unions from proposing that the new regime in Russia should be recognised, and trade between Britain and Russia encouraged. Originally the case for trade was the need of the Russians for food and for equipment to rebuild their industries; but from the beginning of 1921 onwards the argument was put primarily in terms of a reduction in British unemployment. Each year resolutions at Congress and the party conference urged the benefits of trade with Russia. The need was 'for revising the Versailles Treaty and opening up trade with Russia, for only by a general resumption of European trade can the present state of unemployment be remedied'.[13]

In their attitude to Russia, the leaders of the British Labour movement differed from most of their socialist colleagues in France, Germany, and the other European countries where the Communists had split the Labour movement in two. The Continental socialists saw their domestic Communists and the Russian government as two parts of a single, hostile organisation; but most leaders of the British Labour movement distinguished between what they saw as the foolish, tiresome and contemptible British Communist Party and the Russian government whose attempt at social revolution deserved some sympathy.

The First Labour Government

Despite prewar divisions over tariff reform, the Conservative remedy for unemployment was now protection. In addition to retaining some wartime duties, they had experimented with the Dyestuffs (Import Regulation) Act 1920, the Safeguarding of Industries Act 1921, which was used to protect a few key industries from dumping, and the German Reparation Act of 1921, which imposed tariffs on imports from Germany to ensure that they contributed to the discharge of Germany's obligations under the Versailles Treaty. In the autumn of 1923 Baldwin, who had replaced the ailing Bonar Law as Prime Minister earlier in the year, uncharacteristically decided that it was time for bold measures and dissolved parliament on the issue of protection. It was a challenge the Labour movement was happy to accept, for their record on free trade was as good as that of the Liberals.

The election was held in December 1923. The distribution of votes between the parties was only marginally different from that of 1922. The Conservative share stayed at 5.5 million; Labour was up from 4.2 to 4.4 million; and the reluctantly-reunited Liberals got 4.3 millions in place of their combined total of 4.2 million in 1922. However, the swing was

[13] Trades Union Congress, 1922, p. 399.

enough to destroy the Conservative majority in the House. They now had 258 seats, compared with 191 for Labour, and 159 for the Liberals. There was much speculation as to what Asquith would do when parliament reassembled. Would he seek to avoid the dangerous experiment of a Labour government? Would he try to manoeuvre himself into office? In fact he did the obvious thing and joined with Labour to defeat Baldwin's tariff policy. The king sent for MacDonald.

Within the Labour Party the election carried a little further the change in composition which had been so marked in 1922. The major gains were made in the London area, with Herbert Morrison among the new Members. Trade union sponsored Members rose, less than proportionately, from eighty-eight to 102. The Miners, two seats up, had lost a little ground in comparison with the other unions. The Transport and General Workers were second with seven; the General Workers third with five; and the Engineers were down from seven to four. The Independent Labour Party showed a modest improvement to thirty-nine seats, but the divisional parties had doubled their share to thirty-eight seats. The remaining twelve seats were split between the Co-operative Party, the Fabian Society and the reconstituted Social Democratic Federation, survivor of innumerable splits.

There was plenty of time between the election results and the meeting of parliament on 15 January 1924 for MacDonald to decide what to do if he was sent for by the king. A coalition with the Liberals was easily rejected. Both the Labour Party executive and the General Council were as strongly opposed to that as was MacDonald. To refuse office would be to put Asquith in and relegate the Labour Party to its prewar status. It therefore had to be a minority Labour government. There was more room for argument over whether to court quick defeat with a bold programme, or to hold on to office in order to pass such measures of reform as the Liberals would support; but first a cabinet had to be chosen. MacDonald's senior colleagues left the choice to him, although they were not entirely happy when he retired to Lossiemouth to brood over his selection without further reference to them. He solved the difficulty of the Foreign Office by taking it himself, in addition to the premiership. Snowden was Chancellor of the Exchequer. Two other members of the cabinet were sponsored by the Independent Labour Party—Wheatley and Jowett, both on the left. Seven trade unionists—counting Henderson,[14] who insisted on the Home Office after MacDonald had tried to leave him out as party secretary—included Clynes as Lord Privy Seal and deputy leader of the House, Thomas as Colonial Secretary, Tom Shaw as Minister of Labour, and three miners.

[14] Henderson had again been a casualty in the election, but was returned at a by-election early in 1924.

Smillie refused office for the second time. There were four members sponsored by their local parties: Webb at the Board of Trade and three ex-Liberals, Buxton, Trevelyan, and Wedgwood. The remaining five places were filled by peers: two ex-Liberals, Haldane and Olivier, two Conservatives, Chelmsford and Parmoor, and MacDonald's friend General Thomson, ennobled for the purpose. There was some talk that more trade unionists should have been chosen, but, judging by results, seven were quite enough. By and large they were not the most successful members of the new administration.

Given their short term of office and dependence on Liberal votes, the government achieved a creditable record of social legislation. Trevelyan, at the Board of Education, increased the grants to schools starved of money as a result of the Geddes report, and set up the Hadow Committee to devise means of providing secondary education for all.

Shaw, at the Ministry of Labour, was responsible for two Unemployment Insurance Acts. The first abolished the gap of three weeks between periods of benefit, during which the unemployed had to resort to the Poor Law Guardians. The second combined a number of administrative improvements with a substantial increase in benefits— from 75p to 90p a week for men, from 60p to 75p for women, and from 5p to 10p for dependent children. Uncovenanted benefit became 'extended' benefit, payable as of right and not at the minister's discretion, although the Conservatives restored his discretion the following year. The entitlement of workers rendered idle by industrial disputes had long been a matter of contention. In the 1919–20 foundry strike the labourers put out of work complained that they were denied benefit, although the dispute had nothing to do with them. A new clause allowed benefit if the worker could prove that he was not supporting the dispute and had no direct interest in it. In addition, benefit was payable if he could show that the employer had broken an agreement.

As a safeguard, now that extended benefit had become a right, the applicant for benefit was required to prove that he or she was 'genuinely seeking work, but unable to obtain suitable employment'. First introduced in connection with donation benefit, this condition now became a feature of unemployment insurance. It attracted little attention at this stage, but was destined to notoriety. Finally, the Liberals embarrassed Shaw by forcing him to restore the initial waiting period, which had been increased to six days in 1921, back to three days—at considerable cost to the Exchequer.

The Conservative bill to attenuate the powers of the Trade Boards was dropped. The Grocery Trade Boards were set in motion once more, but minimum rates had not been approved by the time the government fell, and the Conservatives disbanded them again. Inquiries were instituted into the case for boards in catering, drapery, and meat distribution; but next year the Conservatives, as was to be expected, decided that they were not needed. The government gave support to a private member's bill for the regulation of the working hours of shop assistants which would have brought substantial improvements; but it fell by the wayside. Shaw also promised to introduce a bill to ratify the International Labour Organisation's 'Washington Convention' recommending a general limitation of the working week to forty-eight hours; but there were still problems about overtime and no bill had emerged when the government fell.

Buxton, the Minister for Agriculture, brought in a bill to reconstitute the agricultural wage machinery set up by the Corn Production Act. The Liberals, however, took away the power of the central board to fix rates. It was to intervene only where a county committee was unable to agree on a rate, and otherwise to confirm the rates proposed by the counties. However, in contrast to the current situation, in which the county committees had almost ceased to function, the Act ensured that a county rate would be fixed, and enforced. The consequence of limiting the powers of the central board was that county rates tended to move further apart, but, nevertheless, wages rose everywhere. Overall, the 'average rate of wages of ordinary male labourers' increased from £1.40 a week in December 1924 to £1.57 a year later.

Pride of place among the government's domestic achievements is generally given to Wheatley's Housing Act. Neville Chamberlain, Minister of Health in Baldwin's government, had already begun to make a name for himself as a social reformer with an Act which had remedied a major defect of the Addison scheme—its failure to give an incentive to economy on the part of local authorities. He offered them a fixed subsidy of £6 a year for a twenty-year period for each house which met his specifications; so that the lower the building costs, the less the charge on the rates. The subsidy was available to private builders, and local authorities had to satisfy the minister that it would be better for them to build the houses than to leave it to private enterprise. The majority of houses built under the scheme were therefore for sale, and beyond the means of most manual workers; and the scheme was to run for only two years. Wheatley now extended the period of Chamberlain's scheme, and added one of his own. Its subsidies were £9 for forty years in urban areas, and £12.50 in rural parishes; and in certain circumstances they could be increased. They were available to private builders only if they built to let at the rents charged by local authorities for similar houses, so that private builders were effectively confined to the Chamberlain subsidy.

To assist in securing the co-operation of the building industry, Wheatley set up a committee representing the building unions and employers, chaired by an employer, W. H. Nicholls, to advise him on the whole range of problems he had to face. They reported on 10 April, analysing the causes of the housing shortage; recommending a fifteen-year programme to deal with it; surveying the supply of building materials; and diagnosing a shortage of skilled labour. Permitted apprentice ratios, which varied between one apprentice to four craftsmen to 1:7 according to trade, would have allowed a considerably larger number of apprentices than were currently employed. The committee suggested local joint committees to stimulate recruitment up to the number allowed; the application of the limits district by district instead of firm by firm; relaxation of the limit in any trade not up to strength; a ratio of 1:3 on contracts under the new housing scheme; extension of the age of entry to apprenticeship from sixteen to twenty; and 'special consideration . . . to applicants who have had previous experience of the trade (e.g. building trade labourer)'.[15]

Wheatley claimed that he had solved the problem of the labour shortage; and historians have generally agreed with him. In fact, however, nothing happened. Every few weeks thereafter he was badgered by questions in the House asking him what was being done to implement the report.[16] Then, three days before the government fell, he informed the House that arrangements for applying the proposals of the report 'are progressing rapidly but have not been completed'.[17] Finally, in March 1926, Neville Chamberlain's parliamentary secretary, Kingsley Wood, announced that the unions had agreed a 'ratio of one apprentice to every three craftsmen . . . in the case of contracts for working class cottages built by Local Authorities'.[18] By this time, however, the labour shortage was rapidly disappearing, except for plasterers.

Wheatley's apparent success over this and some other issues was due to his skill in handling the House—'a new star in House of Commons dialectic, logical and humorous, with first-rate delivery'.[19] However, even he could not avoid trouble over rent restriction. Labour back-benchers were anxious to protect unemployed tenants from eviction for non-payment of rent. The difficulty was to protect the tenant without giving him a continuing right to live rent-free at the landlord's expense. A private member's bill was too strong for the government. Wheatley intervened with his own bill; but that also met heavy opposition, and had to be dropped.

[15] *Report*, pp. 15–16.
[16] For example, *Hansard*, 18 June 1924, col. 2115; 30 July 1924, col. 2045.
[17] Ibid., 5 October 1924, col. 502.
[18] Ibid., 2 March 1926, col. 1245.
[19] *Beatrice Webb's Diaries*, Vol. II, p. 11.

For seven months' work by a minority government this was a creditable record. Some issues had not been dealt with, but MacDonald assured the General Council that a bill to abolish the means test for old age pensioners was on its way and 'the question of pensions for mothers was purely a matter of arranging the finance'.[20] There was little point in introducing measures for nationalisation, and when the Miners did so on their own account, the bill was roundly defeated on the second reading. However, a Labour government might have been expected to take measures to provide work for the unemployed, and not much had been done. The Housing Act would increase employment in building. Cuts in taxation in Snowden's budget—on which he was widely congratulated—might be expected to increase employment by raising consumption. On the other hand, the repeal of the wartime McKenna duties on various imported goods, including cars, may have put some engineering workers out of a job, even if it demonstrated Labour's commitment to free trade. The fall in the unemployment rate from 10.6 per cent in December 1923 to 9.3 per cent by June 1924 was hardly more than the normal seasonal adjustment, and the figure was back to 10.6 per cent in September.

On 26 June a deputation from the General Council met the cabinet's unemployment policy committee. The ministers believed that a new approach to relief works was needed because existing schemes did little for the skilled trades. They wanted schemes which would pay and 'have their reactions upon other trades' as well. Besides housing, they quoted proposals for electrification, afforestation, road improvement, and the Severn Barrage scheme. 'The Deputation could rest assured that the schemes which were in contemplation would soon begin to fructify.' For the rest, unemployment was 'confined largely' to engineering, shipbuilding and cotton, which were especially dependent on exports. The government were eager to conclude their trade negotiations with Russia.[21] Thus, at least in the short run, further reduction in unemployment depended on MacDonald's foreign policy.

At the beginning of 1924 the French army still occupied the Ruhr. MacDonald arranged an international conference in London in July, at which the French agreed to evacuate the Ruhr in return for the acceptance of a new scheme of reparations which had been prepared by a committee of experts chaired by the American General Dawes. They proposed a reduced level of payment, which was to rise gradually from a modest threshold, and an international loan to help stabilise the Germany currency and get the German economy going again. There was also need to modify the harsh provisions of the Versailles Treaty for

[20] Trades Union Congress, 1924, p. 115.
[21] Ibid., pp. 162–3.

sanctions against German default. By universal consent MacDonald's handling of the negotiations was adroit and gracious; but the agreement was bound to increase unemployment in Britain. Not only would it put German coalminers back to work; in addition they would have to undercut British miners in order to expand exports to meet the renewed obligation to pay reparations.

If foreign policy was to alleviate unemployment, it had therefore to be by means of trade with Russia. The Soviet government had been recognised on 1 February, and negotiations on a treaty, begun in April, led to agreement in August, but only after a group of leftwing Members of Parliament had intervened to overcome a deadlock. Even then, most of the important decisions were deferred. A commercial treaty arranged for trading facilities, but a general treaty left a settlement for British bondholders and shareholders for further negotiation; and only when it was agreed would the British government recommend that parliament should guarantee the loan which was required to give substance to the commercial treaty. As soon as the texts of the two treaties were published, they were attacked in the press and by both Conservatives and Liberals. Parliament, however, had now adjourned for the summer recess. Before it reassembled the 'Campbell case' had reached the headlines.

J. R. Campbell, editor of the Communist *Workers' Weekly*, had been arrested and charged with incitement to mutiny for an article urging soldiers not to shoot their fellow workers in either the class war or a military war. It turned out that he was a wounded war-hero; Labour Members protested, especially the Clydesiders who knew Campbell; Hastings, the Attorney General, withdrew proceedings; and when parliament reassembled the Conservatives asked for a debate. MacDonald made a disastrous statement to the House; and then decided to take the Liberal proposal for an inquiry by a select committee, for which the Conservatives had decided to vote, as an issue of confidence. The government fell. Their days had already been numbered by Asquith's announcement that the Liberals would oppose the Russian treaties.

Industrial Disputes

When the government took office on 22 January, the railways had already been crippled for two days by a strike of the Locomotive Engineers and Firemen. Whereas most other grades were still experiencing reductions in pay through the cost of living scale, many of the footplate staff had reached their guaranteed standard rates some time ago. The companies now thought it was time the footplate staff made a contribution to lower railway costs by a number of alterations in their conditions. Their proposals went to the National Wages Board which narrowed them down to the substitution of 150 miles as the point at which mileage rates should be paid to footplate staff in place of the current 120 miles; and a lower rate for shunting than on main line work. Along with the other trade union members of the board, the representatives of the Locomotive Engineers and Firemen assented to these decisions, but their union conference decided to ballot and the vote rejected the award—which was not binding—by a large majority. Their members ceased work at midnight on 19 January. The Railwaymen's footplate members were instructed to stay at work but not to accept jobs assigned to their colleagues in the rival union. Some services were therefore maintained.

On 14 January the General Council interviewed the leaders of all three unions and appointed an emergency committee who tried their hand at conciliation. Their proposals were rejected, but on 29 January a compromise was reached. The change in mileage payments was to be introduced gradually, and drivers with a minimum period of main line working were to get the full rate when employed on shunting. The Railwaymen asserted that these concessions could have been obtained without a stoppage. Relations between the two unions were further embittered. The Locomotive Engineers and Firemen provided funds for disaffected signalmen to set up a Union of Railway Signalmen.

By the time the railway strike was over it was already clear that there would soon be a dock strike. Bevin was determined to re-establish his union's position in the docks, and moved swiftly. In November he encouraged the dockers to back a claim for an increase of 10p a day and a guaranteed week. The claim went in on 15 December, and was refused on 16 January. On 29 January a conference of dockers' representatives voted to give notice of a strike for 16 February. Shaw's intervention, as Minister of Labour, led to an offer of 5p a day with reference of the balance to arbitration, and of a sub-committee of the National Joint Council for Dock Labour to consider the guaranteed week. By comparison with recent settlements elsewhere the offer was generous, but its acceptance would not have provided a sufficiently resounding victory to serve Bevin's purpose, and he allowed it to be rejected. The strike began, isolating the dissident union of Stevedores, Lightermen, Watermen, and Dockers who stayed at work. On 18 February the minister announced a court of inquiry, and on the 19th Bevin reported to the London members of the General Council. He asked them not to mediate since that 'would encourage the Employers to hang on', but instead to 'say that the Dockers were right'; which they did. A provisional agreement was reached on 20 February at a meeting chaired by Shaw, and ratified by a delegate conference the next day. The employers had made a firm offer that the second 5p a day should be paid from the beginning of June and, on Bevin's insistence, the Liverpool employers were forced to ratify the agreement although they had withdrawn from the national employers' organisation two years earlier. The court of inquiry adjourned *sine die*.

MacDonald was rattled. On 4 February he had told Hugh Dalton that, if strikes went on, they would 'knock us out', and might prevent a trade revival. He spoke of the possibility of a national government to deal with them, and asserted: 'Men never want to strike, unless they are instigated by their leaders. The dockers can't get an advance at the present time.'[22] There was, however, worse to come.

Bevin's next target was the London tramway undertakings. In June 1923 the largest private undertaking in London had sought a pay reduction because its earnings were being drained by the competition of an increasing number of so-called 'pirate' buses (that is, outside the London Traffic Combine of which the company was a member). However, the claim was allowed to lapse, possibly because the Conservative government was preparing a draft bill to give the Minister of Transport powers to regulate London traffic with the aim of curbing such competition. In December, without any evidence that the fortunes of the company had improved, the union asked for an all-round increase of 40p a week for London tramwaymen in both private and public employment, although they were already the highest paid tramwaymen in the country. The claim was rejected both by the Metropolitan District Joint Council and the National Joint Council, the district council having decided that 'the only way out of the present deadlock is by united action on the part of the men and employers to secure Government regulation'.[23] In February the union executive granted the tramwaymen's request for a strike, which was called for 13 March, and approved the decision of the busmen to stop work in sympathy on the same day. Shaw obtained a postponement during which there were offers of from 10p to 25p a week from some of the local authority undertakings, but none from the private companies in the Traffic Combine.

On 20 March 16,000 tramwaymen and 23,000 busmen went on strike, and next day a court of inquiry was appointed. In his evidence the chairman of the Traffic Combine, Lord Ashfield, paid little attention to the wage dispute, but concentrated on the need for unification of London's passenger transport undertakings. On 24 March the court

[22] Dalton, p. 148.
[23] *Report* of the Court of Inquiry, p. 6.

issued an interim report saying that 'the merits of the claim' had not been 'seriously questioned' during the hearings; and that:

The present crisis has, in the main, arisen through the Tramway Undertakings in the Metropolitan Area being unable to earn sufficient to meet the claim. This has been brought about by the severe competition of the omnibuses in the absence of any co-ordinating control, by the heavy expenditure on renewals and upkeep of the permanent way at present high costs, and by the discharge of the statutory obligations for the maintenance of the surface of the highways. . . . A definite undertaking by the Government to introduce and press forward legislation placing the passenger traffic of the Metropolitan Area under some co-ordinating control affords, in our view, a basis, and the only one at present suggested, for reopening negotiations between the parties.[24]

At last the government took the hint. The bill was brought out of storage and given its first reading on 25 March. At once all the private undertakings and all but three of the local authority undertakings, offered 25p a week with reference of the balance to arbitration. Bevin and Ashfield both seemed to have got what they wanted, but Bevin decided that the offer was still not enough. The strike went on, and on 26 March the executive of the Locomotive Engineers and Firemen instructed their members on the underground to stop work in sympathy at midnight on 28 March, and the other two railway unions pledged support.

It is unlikely that Bevin would have failed to get the tramwaymen back to work at this stage if he had chosen to do so. The offer was not quite so much as he had got for the dockers, but it was nevertheless attractive, far more than most workers could hope to get in 1924, and sufficient to take the London tramwaymen into the ranks of the highest-paid manual workers. He probably decided that there was more to come, and determined to get it. If so, he proved right. At that stage of his life he had little liking for politicians, and was unlikely to be deterred by the embarrassment he was causing them. Indeed, he was always a bully, and may have taken pleasure in the prospect. Despite his eminence as a trade union leader, he was not yet wholly accepted as a member of the 'club' by other leaders; and in any case he took his own decisions. He was therefore unlikely to be held back by their disapproval.

MacDonald was understandably angry. His government had done everything it could for Bevin. Now they must look after themselves. Under Baldwin, responsibility for the Supply and Transport Committee had rested with Davidson as Chancellor of the Duchy of Lancaster. With the help of a civil servant, John Anderson, he had begun to refurbish the machinery and handed it over to Wedgwood when

---

[24] *Interim Report*, p. 5.

Labour came into office. Now Wedgwood was told to prepare for action. MacDonald announced that major services must be maintained and a proclamation of emergency under the 1920 Act was made ready for the king's signature. On 27 March the General Council and the party executive jointly deplored the government's intention to use the Act, and made the remarkable proposal that the government should take over the trams and pay the tramwaymen what they had asked for until the dispute was finally resolved. Negotiations continued, and at 10 p.m. on 28 March it was agreed that drivers and conductors were to get an increase of 30p a week, with 20p for the depot staff. The underground strike was called off, and the tramwaymen, having voted by more than two to one to accept, went back with the busmen on 1 April.

The London tramway strike posed, even more sharply than the rail and dock strikes, a question which the Labour movement had not attempted to answer before a Labour government came to power: what place was there for strikes under a Labour government? Before the war Snowden had argued that strikes could do little to improve the lot of the worker at any time. Probably most socialists had assumed that, whatever the case under capitalism, there would be no need for strikes under a socialist government. Now strikes were not only taking place under a Labour government, but in Snowden's view had 'caused the Government great anxiety, and diverted its attention in a large measure from the work of preparing its legislative measures'.[25] Hobson wrote in the *New Leader* of 4 April that 'trades must not press for a larger share for their particular members at the expense of the Community of Labour'. Bevin replied in his union's *Record* for April that 'what is described as a separatist policy is the seizing of an opportunity'. A co-ordinated policy would be agreed in time, but, he asked, were unions to hold back meanwhile 'on the plea that it is not politically expedient that those trades which can should attempt to force from the employers a larger share of the wealth they create?'

The General Council were uneasy. On 9 April Bevin came to their meeting to ask them to agree a policy with the government on intervention in industrial disputes. 'It was not fair that any one union should be put in the position of having to withdraw a strike because the government were embarrassed.' He then left, for the council had already decided that there should be no discussion with him. They agreed to write to the Prime Minister offering to discuss 'the whole question if he desires'. Fortunately for them all, there was no equally vexatious strike to follow, and the government were able to claim the credit for the settlement of the next dispute.

[25] Snowden, Vol. II, p. 635.

In January the Miners gave three months' notice to terminate the 1921 agreement. Shinwell, the Minister for Mines, joined in the discussions over a new settlement. The owners were reluctant to make any offer, foreseeing the consequences on their finances of a French withdrawal from the Ruhr. According to his autobiography, Shinwell bluffed them, by threats of unspecified 'drastic measures',[26] into a complex set of proposals which they put to the Miners on 27 March. Several changes in the method of 'ascertaining' the proceeds were suggested with the object of assuring the miners of the impeccability of the process; the minimum percentage on standard was to be increased from 20 per cent to $32\frac{1}{2}$ per cent along with a number of adjustments to the methods of protecting the earnings of the lowest-paid; and standard profits were to be cut from 17 per cent to 15 per cent of standard wages, with an increase in the proportion of the surplus which went to wages from 83 per cent to 87 per cent.

A ballot vote went marginally against acceptance, and the executive asked the government for an inquiry. A court of inquiry was set up under the chairmanship of Lord Buckmaster. They ducked the issue. Having reviewed the submissions, they found some points justified, some unsubstantiated, and others upon which they could not pronounce. They suggested that negotiations be resumed. Further talks brought an increase from $32\frac{1}{2}$ per cent above standard to $33\frac{1}{3}$ per cent, and from 87 per cent of the surplus to 88 per cent. The executive did not put this to a ballot, but accepted it on the basis of a conference vote on 29 May. The effect varied from district to district, and many pieceworkers did not benefit at all. In the third quarter of 1923, overall wage earnings a shift were 53p; in the same period in 1924, with the new agreement in force, they rose to 54p; but in 1925 the figure was down to 52p.

While the coalmining negotiations were in progress there occurred the third shipbuilding lockout in three years. There were two disputes. Nationally the unions were seeking the restoration of the latest wage cut, of 50p a week; and in Southampton the shiprepair workers alleged that they were paid less than elsewhere and wanted an additional increase. In February the Engineers in the Southampton yards came out on official strike, and were soon joined by the other trades, except the Boiler-makers. The Southampton employers offered $12\frac{1}{2}$p a week, which was rejected. The Shipbuilding Employers Federation refused to negotiate on the national claim until the Southampton men went back, and posted national lockout notices applying to all members of those unions taking part in the Southampton strike. The date, after several postponements, was fixed for 11 April. The Shipwrights saved themselves by expelling

[26] Shinwell, p. 93.

their Southampton members, and the other unions ordered their Southampton members back, but most of them stayed out. On 11 April twenty thousand shipyard workers were locked out.

The chairman and secretary of Congress, Purcell and Bramley, went to Southampton to talk to the strike committee. They persuaded the strikers to agree to go back to work in return for an immediate conference 'for the purpose of securing uniformity between the Southampton and London rates'. The employers and union executives agreed to the conference, and the lockout was called off. The conference submitted both the national and the Southampton disputes to a board of arbitration chaired by Sir William MacKenzie which awarded a general increase of 35p a week in two instalments, with Southampton shiprepair workers receiving an additional 15p.

The improvement in trade during the second half of 1923 had brought an upturn in prices which gave building workers a small advance under their sliding scale agreement in February 1924. The unions wanted more. In June they settled for a similar advance outside the scale with stabilisation until the end of 1925, and a joint committee to inquire into the problem of 'wet time'. However, there was still the question of Liverpool.

The employers insisted that Liverpool must conform to the national agreement. Following the reaffiliation of Liverpool to the national employers' federation, the unions nationally had agreed to a staged application of the terms of the national agreement there; but locally several of the unions had refused to accept this arrangement. Now a joint committee of the National Wages and Conditions Council visited Liverpool to secure compliance. Some of the local unions undertook to recommend the agreement to their members, but the Building Trade Workers and the Plasterers were obdurate. They struck, followed by the other trades. The national unions took the view that they had done all they could. They made no mention of Liverpool in their ballot, which approved the new national agreement. The employers, on the other hand, felt, as one of their representatives put it at their meeting of 17 June, that 'they were not going to leave Liverpool in the lurch'; and, in the words of another, that 'if they lost Liverpool they lost the lot. . . . If they were not careful there would be such a process of civil war within the Federation as would result in . . . disintegration.' After a misunderstanding with the union leaders, who believed that agreement had been reached, they announced a lockout for 5 July. Shaw persuaded them to postpone it for a week to give a court of inquiry time to find a solution, but the unions instructed their members to refuse to work after 5 July, except on the terms of the new agreement. The General Council issued a press statement condemning the action of the employers; lent the building unions £10,000; and issued an appeal to other unions for further help.

Buckmaster, who was appointed to chair this inquiry as well, was more positive this time. He and his colleagues accepted the employers' contention that Liverpool was the main issue in dispute and that its settlement was 'the only means by which the dispute can be brought to a speedy end and goodwill restored'.[27] Their report appeared on 15 July, but the two sides seemed in no hurry to renew negotiations. Many employers were paying the additional rate in order to keep their men at work, and elsewhere many men were content to remain at work at the old rate. It was only in January 1925 that the *Labour Gazette* ventured an estimate of the number of strikers, of 'about 100,000', which was less than a third of the trade unionists in the building industry, and some of the strikers must have been non-unionists. On 28 July the minister brought the two sides together. On 6 August there was another meeting, including representatives from Liverpool, which set up a sub-committee to draft terms. Their draft extended the dates for the national stabilisation of wage rates and postponed the commencement of the application of national rates to Liverpool to 1 February 1926. Work was resumed on 25 August.

Within the unions there was considerable bitterness against the Liverpool men. The Woodworkers' *Monthly Report* for September attributed the dispute to the attempt of the Liverpool men 'to enforce a purely local settlement. During seven weeks about 30 per cent of our members have been walking about at a cost to our society of over £200,000 and at an average loss of wages . . . of at least £14 a member.' But for Liverpool, 'the terms which our members voted upon and accepted last June would have been operating, and there would have been no dispute'.

In August a strike of Bevin's members in Covent Garden market caused far more embarrassment for him than for the government. After several weeks it was called off on the employers' terms, and 400 men failed to secure reinstatement. A subsequent inquiry within the union disclosed that the local officer had misled the executive by exaggerating the chance of success and failing to inform them of an attractive offer from the employers in the belief that he could get even more.

After three years of union defeat and retreat, the recovery in trade during the second half of 1923 was bound to bring a crop of wage claims and disputes. Bevin had given notice of it in June of that year when he secured the backing of his executive 'to take the first available opportunity to submit demands for an increase in wages and to select

27 *Report*, p. 21.

the most favourable section of the Union for that purpose to turn the tide'. The strikes in the docks and London transport had been the outcome of that considered policy. It might be said that the government had been unlucky to take office at this point, although the trade recovery helped them in other ways. However, the volume of unrest in 1924 was relatively modest. The number of recorded strikes, at 710, was slightly up on 1923, but the number of working days lost, at 8.4 million, was the lowest since 1918. The government's problem was that in 1924 the unions were in most instances the aggressors.

The Aftermath

The opportunity presented by the Russian treaties and the Campbell case for a 'red scare' in the election of October 1924 was exploited by the publication of the 'Zinoviev letter'. It purported to be addressed by the senior officials of the Communist International to the central committee of the British Communist Party, and set out instructions for preparing an insurrection in Britain by developing support among the armed forces. It was a forgery, but it was widely seen as authentic. The Foreign Office mishandled it, and MacDonald failed to give a clear lead on it. Labour candidates were left at a loss in dealing with what became at once a central issue in the election.

The poll was higher than in 1923, and Labour's share had increased; but the Liberals had collapsed. Their vote had fallen from 4.3 million to 2.9 million and their seats from 159 to 40. The outcome was that the Conservatives increased their vote from 5.5 million to 8.0 million, and their seats from 258 to 419, whereas Labour, despite an increase in votes from 4.4 million to 5.5 million, dropped from 191 seats to 151. The Conservatives were therefore back in office with a handsome majority. Within the Parliamentary Labour Party, the proportion sponsored by the Independent Labour Party and divisional parties had fallen slightly. Frank Hodges, who had hoped for a place in the cabinet but had to be content with the post of Civil Lord of the Admiralty, lost his seat and was out of a job. The Miners rescued him by getting him appointed secretary of the International Miners Federation.

Bevin proposed to the party conference in 1925 that it was 'inadvisable that the Labour Party should again accept office whilst having a minority of Members in the House of Commons'.[28] It was a silly proposition, as MacDonald was able to show, for it could do nothing but harm to the party to announce that in such circumstances they would be prepared to leave the country without a government; and the votes were against Bevin by five to one.

[28] Labour Party, 1925, p. 244.

More discerning were the leaders of the Independent Labour Party who concluded that the government had lacked plans, especially to deal with unemployment and low pay. They had already set up their own commissions to work on various aspects of policy. The reports were ready in 1926, when they were collected together as a programme for *Socialism in our Time*, with the 'living wage' as the first objective. By that time Allen had been ousted from the chairmanship by one of the Clydesiders, James Maxton, behind whom stood Wheatley, who, unlike most of his cabinet colleagues, had come to the conclusion that the lesson to be drawn was that Labour must move to the left. Between them they drove, first Snowden, and then MacDonald out of the Independent Labour Party.

When *Socialism in our Time* was presented to the Labour Party conference, MacDonald and his colleagues were able to dispose of the notion that they needed it, or any other carefully prepared programme. They were, on the whole, satisfied with what they had done, and looked forward with some confidence to the next time. They believed they now knew how to handle Whitehall, and would be able to cope with the problems that would then face them—unless they were hampered by inappropriate and doctrinaire programmes. MacDonald told the 1925 Labour Party conference that

they had to indicate their position in such a way that the nation would know their standpoint and frame of mind; not in the sense that the nation wanted a programme, because it did not. . . . In the minds of the Executive it would be the supreme achievement . . . if the wit of man, the mind of man, and the literary skill of man could, just in four or five clear, binding statements of principle, convince them all, and convince the nation, that men who believe in those three or four fundamental declarations would never require to be asked what their programme was.[29]

Most trade union leaders would probably have agreed with Smethurst, the Engineers' secretary, when he wrote in his union's journal of November 1924 that, although 'they had their little fads and failings', the 'members of the Labour Government individually and collectively gave excellent service'; and that 'when Labour representatives again take up the reins of Government—as they most assuredly will—the experience gained in 1924 will not be lost sight of'. Many of them would also have agreed with him when he went on to say:

Possibly we shall have a Conservative Government for the next four or five years, and venture to suggest that the only reforms obtained will be those which are forced by our industrial organisations.

[29] Ibid., pp. 218–19.

This was a prospect which the unions faced with some confidence. By 1924 most of their leaders had risen to their positions during the decade 1911–20 when trade union membership and power had increased from year to year; when employers and governments had listened attentively to trade union demands; and when strikes, or threats of strikes, had more often than not forced concessions. That was the environment in which they had learned their trade. The years 1921–3 had been a disastrous interlude due to the economic slump, the worst on record; but in 1924 economic recovery had begun to restore trade union membership and power. The unions no longer needed to fight—and often to lose—defensive battles. They had been able to go over to the offensive, and to win an encouraging series of wage advances. It was reasonable in the light of prewar experience to assume the recovery would continue for several years yet; that there were more wage increases to be had; and that the incoming Conservative government would have to pay more attention to the unions than had Lloyd George's coalition in its last two years, or the governments of Bonar Law and Baldwin in 1922–3.

Further changes within the General Council had added to the strength of the left. According to Walsh's report to the Lancashire Miners' annual conference in 1924, MacDonald told his first cabinet meeting of 'his desire that those of us who were directly connected with Trade Unions should, during our period of office, cease to have any positions of control in such organisations'. The General Council agreed. Gosling, Thomas and Margaret Bondfield, the chairman, resigned their seats. Purcell succeeded to the chair and was followed next year by Swales. Hicks took over from Thomas as chairman of the council's international committee where his influence was increased by Purcell's succession to the chair of the International Federation of Trade Unions in Bondfield's place. Finally, Bramley, who had succeeded Bowerman as secretary in 1923, was another man on the left.

One of the Russian delegates who came to negotiate with MacDonald was Tomsky, chairman of the All-Russian Central Committee of Trade Unions. He established friendly relations with the General Council's new leaders, who gave a dinner to the Russian delegation and promised to help them during the negotiations. In June, Purcell and Bramley persuaded the triennial conference of the International Federation of Trade Unions not to rule out the possibility of an agreement with the Russian trade unions to form a united international organisation.

Returning confidence within the British trade unions had at last enabled the Communist Party to launch the Minority Movement for which the Russians had been pressing. Following the formation of the Miners Minority Movement in January the inaugural conference of the

National Minority Movement in August decided that its aims should include:

a wage increase of £1 a week, with a minimum wage of £4; a 44-hour week, and no overtime; Workshop and Factory Committees with members guaranteed against victimisation; Workers' Control of Industry; a stronger TUC, with control over the Labour Party; industrial unionism; the affiliation of the National Unemployed Workers' Committee Movement and the trades councils to the TUC; and the repudiation of the Dawes plan.[30]

The Minority Movement claimed substantial successes at Congress which met at Hull in the following month. Tomsky, attending as a fraternal delegate, made 'an effective speech, combining salty good humour, clear-headed logic, and firm resolution. It got a splendid reception.'[31] There was unanimous support for an 'Industrial Workers' Charter' which summed up a number of resolutions passed in the preceding years on nationalisation, wages, unemployment, housing, education, industrial injuries, and pensions; and included a statutory minimum 'for each industry and occupation' and a statutory 44-hour working week.[32]

There was also a notable step towards the Minority Movement's objective of 'a stronger TUC'. By 3,608,000 votes to 259,000 the General Council was granted the wider powers to intervene in industrial disputes which previous Congresses had denied them. Henceforth the council was authorised to take action in a dispute which could not be contained within the industry in which it arose. Initially the council was limited to giving advice, but, where the union or unions concerned accepted the council's advice, and

the policy of the employers enforces a stoppage . . . the Council shall forthwith take steps to organise on behalf of the union or unions concerned all such moral and material support as the circumstances of the dispute may appear to justify.[33]

Cook, who seconded the resolution, acknowledged that 'even the miners, with their big forces in this Congress, have realised that the time has passed when they can fight alone'.[34] However, although Hicks, the mover, wanted the financial resources of the movement to be pooled behind 'any section of workers' who 'are finding their conditions of life challenged',[35] there was no mention of a levy in the resolution.

The success of the resolution indicated that the left had been converted to the policy of the right, for previous sponsors of similar

---

[30] Roderick Martin, pp. 37–8.　　　　　　[31] Calhoun, pp. 85–6.
[32] Trades Union Congress, 1924, p. 351.　　[33] Ibid., p. 347.
[34] Ibid., p. 349.　　　　　　　　　　　　[35] Ibid., p. 348.

resolutions had included Clynes and Pugh, who had been attacked by the left for wishing to subject militant unions to the restraint of a central authority. However, the overwhelming majority in its favour also owed much to the sensible use which the General Council had made of their existing powers, and to the mood of confidence within the unions.

The experience of a Labour government had the effect of distancing the unions from the Labour Party in more ways than one. This may have been to some extent the consequence of trade union disappointment with the government, for example with their failure to consult the General Council over the composition of the Balfour Committee on Industry and Trade, which led to the council's refusal to take part in its work; but it was due in greater measure to the division in functions between the party and the unions which the experience of a Labour government was bound to emphasise. In March 1925 the General Council refused to join with the party in an investigation of tariff policy which they felt was an 'industrial matter' to be left to them. In July 1925 they decided to hold their own conference on unemployment, inviting party leaders to attend but not to speak. In September, Congress approved a proposal that the General Council should acquire a building of their own, and dismantle the joint departments in favour of separate departments directly under the control of the council.

There had been some trouble over the joint departments in 1923 and 1924 when the heads of two of them, Greenwood and W. W. Henderson (Arthur's son), had been elected to parliament. The General Council had wanted to replace them, but had been persuaded by the party to allow them to stay on. In May 1925 the new assistant secretary of Congress, Walter Citrine, produced a report on the work of the joint departments, criticising their 'excessive cost, lack of staff control, salary anomalies and parliamentarians-cum-staff members'.[36] Bramley now told Congress that its functions were 'too big, too various, and too distinctly Trade Union to make it possible for them to be developed as one-half of joint departments'.[37] W. J. Brown added that

even with a complete Labour majority in the House and with a Labour government that was stable and secure, there would be a difference in point of view between that Government on the one hand and the Trade Unions on the other.[38]

Within the House the Miners' Members had for some years met together to discuss their industry's problems. In June 1923 the Engineers' journal reported that their Members had formed a group to

[36] Ross M. Martin, p. 190.
[37] Trades Union Congress, 1925, p. 359.
[38] Ibid., pp. 363–4.

handle 'problems that only skilled engineers can effectively deal with'; and, in his union's *Record* for April 1924, Sexton announced that the Transport and General Workers' Members 'together with Tillett and the Secretary of our Legal and Parliamentary Department, study the Order Paper every day, and meet weekly to discuss and deal with all matters affecting our members'. Now a Trade Union Group was formed of all these 'whose candidatures were promoted and financed by Trade Unions'. On 27 January 1926 the General Council approved a proposal that their officials should have periodic meetings with this group.

10

The General Strike

EXPECTATIONS of continuing economic recovery in 1925 were disappointed. Throughout the year the level of unemployment was slightly higher than in 1924. Retail prices fell a little, and the downward trend in wholesale prices was unmistakable. It was not a favourable environment for continuing the trade union offensive of 1924. The wage rate index remained almost stationary throughout the year; and the first nine months of Baldwin's administration was a period of industrial peace such as had not been seen for some years. Less than 1.5 million working days were lost from the beginning of October 1924 to the end of June 1925.

Baldwin presented himself to the country as a peacemaker. Some of his followers promoted a bill to substitute a requirement for 'contracting-in' in place of 'contracting-out' in the rules governing trade union political funds. He intervened in the debate to move that 'a measure of such far-reaching importance should not be introduced as a Private Member's Bill'. He told his party that their electoral victory had been won by 'creating an impression throughout the country that we stood for stable government and for peace in the country between all classes of the community'; and asked them to say:

We have our majority: we believe in the justice of this Bill which has been brought in to-day but we are going to withdraw our hand, and we are not going to push our political advantage home at a moment like this. . . . We, at any rate, are not going to fire the first shot.[1]

His amendment was carried, the mover of the bill himself voting for it.

There were of course some disputes. A strike of London bookbinders in March arose out of another conflict between national and local bargaining. Some London bookbinding members of the Printing, Bookbinding, and Paper Workers came within the national agreement, but others worked under a local agreement with the London Master Printers, who had recently conceded additional rates on new and faster machines. Their colleagues wanted similar rates, but they could be obtained only by amending the national agreement. Some of them

---

[1] *Hansard*, 6 March 1925, col. 840.

struck to expedite negotiations. The London Master Binders replied with a lockout of five thousand London bookbinders, and in retaliation the union brought out all its London members, including those employed by the London Master Printers. The Joint Industrial Council now intervened, and an agreement was reached on 27 March. Higher rates were conceded on the new machines, and henceforth national agreements were to apply to the whole of the binding trade.

In the same month the Lancashire co-operative societies locked out ten thousand employees in a dispute which arose out of claims for a national target scale of wages, which the Distributive and Allied Workers backed up by presenting strike notices to selected societies. Negotiations were renewed at the beginning of April, and led on to the issue of negotiating machinery. In 1924 the union had refused to submit any further disputes to the Joint Committee of Trade Unionists and Co-operators until they were granted equal representation with the co-operative societies on the committee. Eventually, in 1926, the committee was replaced by a National Conciliation Board of six chosen by each side, with an independent chairman. However, the Co-operative Wholesale Society refused to come within the board's jurisdiction.

These relatively minor stoppages did not seriously disturb the industrial peace which Baldwin was anxious to foster. Graver problems threatened in the export industries, where a decline in prices brought threats of wage reductions. The worst-hit was coalmining which was now feeling the full effect of renewed German competition. Unemployment in the mines rose sharply. The court of inquiry appointed in July reported that 'the number of collieries producing at a loss rose in April to over 64 per cent, and in May to 67 per cent. The amount of coal raised by such collieries in May reached 60 per cent.'[2] These figures may have been worse than expected, but both sides had been aware that the Dawes plan would create grave difficulties for their industry, and in December 1924 they set up a joint committee to investigate its problems. It was no secret that the owners were looking for further reductions in wage costs, but there was time to discuss how this might be accomplished and whether there were alternative remedies, for the current agreement did not run out until the end of July.

Although the worst-hit, coalmining was not the only industry in trouble. In July 1924, following the dock strike, rising freight rates brought the seamen an increase in pay of £1 a month. Now freight rates were falling again, and the owners asked for a reduction. As before, Havelock Wilson took his decision to accept a cut of £1 after consulting only his full-time officials. At the executive meeting on 21 July, shortly before the cut was to be applied, he explained that the head office

[2] *Report*, p. 10.

officials had authority to negotiate agreements, and if the members of the executive were not satisfied they could ask the union conference to dismiss him and his colleagues. Clearly the executive were in no mood for that. Instead they congratulated their leaders on the 'splendid manner in which they negotiated', and resolved that there was 'no possible alternative' to a reduction.

In 1924 the General Council had tried to promote an amalgamation between the Sailors and Firemen and the Amalgamated Marine Workers. Wilson was agreeable, provided that it was understood that his union would not take over Shinwell and three of his colleagues along with the Marine Workers' other officials. This condition split the Marine Workers. Some decided to strike against the cut from 12 August 1925, but some former officials of the Cooks' and Stewards' union, led by Cotter, transferred to Wilson's union, which subsequently became the National Union of Seamen. They were eventually followed, according to Wilson, by about four thousand of their members. The strikes were supported by the Transport Section of the Minority Movement, whose organiser was George Hardy. Although an Englishman, Hardy had played a leading role in the Industrial Workers of the World in North America during the war, and subsequently joined the Communist Party. Contacts through international Communist organisations enabled Hardy to help the Marine Workers to bring British seamen out on strike in ports in the United States, South Africa, Australia, and New Zealand by means of liberal but empty promises of financial aid. Wilson had considerable grounds for condemning the strike as a Communist plot. He told his executive on 29 October that: 'Intimidation had been rampant throughout the strike, and had resulted in a good many men being thrown out of employment.' They agreed to assist the families of such men, and eventually spent over £5,000 under this heading. But the strike was over by this time. The Marine Workers had called it off on 12 October. By the end of the following year their union had ceased to exist.

The largest stoppage of the year took place in the wool industry, where the percentage of unemployed rose from 5.8 in June 1924 to 19.7 a year later. The employers proposed a pay reduction, but the unions would not have it. The dispute affected the Northern Counties district of the Wool Textile Joint Industrial Council, which covered 80 per cent of the industry's labour force, but excluded the Welsh and West of England districts. On 25 July 150,000 workers were locked out. The General Council intervened with the proposal of a 'court of investigation' which found favour with both sides, and eventually work was resumed on 17 August at the old rate of wages to allow the court to set to work. About three million working days had been lost.

Two members of the court were chosen by the employers and two by the union, with Sir Harold Morris appointed chairman by the Minister of Labour. In contrast to the general practice of courts of inquiry, the proceedings were held in private, and the parties bound themselves to accept the findings. The report, which was not presented until 11 November, found general agreement that there was a depression in the industry, but a difference as to whether it was temporary or not. The court held that

> further experience was necessary before any definite conclusions can be arrived at as to the developments of foreign competition in Europe and the Far East. In our view the evidence before us is insufficient to justify a general reduction in wages.[3]

They recommended that wages should be stabilised until 1 January 1927. By December unemployment in the industry was down to 8.8 per cent, indicating that the resistance of the unions and the caution of the court had both been justified.

For three decades or more thereafter the accepted explanation for the difficulties of exporting industries in 1925 and the next few years was Britain's return to the gold standard in May 1925 at prewar parity with the dollar. The decision had been announced in April by Churchill, who had been Baldwin's surprising choice as Chancellor of the Exchequer. However, Churchill was carrying out the recommendation of one of the wartime reconstruction committees, the Cunliffe Committee on Currency and Foreign Exchanges, which had also been the accepted objective of every subsequent Chancellor, including Snowden. By the spring of 1925 their successive efforts had brought the pound very close to prewar parity with the dollar, and Churchill took this opportunity to restore the gold standard. Afterwards it became evident that the pound had been overvalued. The relationship with the dollar which had been reached in April 1925 could not be sustained without strain. Exporting industries would therefore have to reduce their prices if they were to maintain their sales in overseas markets. A common estimate of the degree of overvaluation was 10 per cent.

In recent years this account of the difficulties of British exporting industries in the second half of the twenties has fallen into disrepute. Almost certainly the pound was overvalued, but not necessarily by so much as 10 per cent; and the effects of overvaluation have been exaggerated. Exports rose faster than output over the years 1926–9. It is unlikely that a reduction of 10 per cent in the rate of exchange 'would have done much to boost the exports of the old staple trades since these were checked by a series of adverse factors including unfavourable long-

---

[3] *Ministry of Labour Gazette*, December 1925, p. 422.

run changes in demand'.[4] Above all it is unlikely that the return to gold had more than a marginal effect on the fortunes of the coalmining industry which was already in desperate trouble by the beginning of 1925. The adverse conditions which the industry's joint committee were currently examining had been present since 1921. During the intervening years they had been obscured by the American coal strike and the occupation of the Ruhr.

Red Friday

In May 1925 the joint committee moved on from reviewing the available information on the condition of coalmining to consider causes and remedies. They were unable to agree on either. The owners attributed the depressed state of the industry to the high cost of production of coal, which in their view was largely due to the seven-hour day imposed on them by the Act of 1919. They estimated that reversion to the eight-hour day would yield a 12 per cent increase in production enabling them to reduce prices and to limit the extent of wage reductions. The Miners issued a statement attributing the industry's plight to the Dawes plan, and the low level of consumption at home and abroad. The first could be put right only by political action, and the second needed 'a general policy of the world working-class' to provide a remedy.[5] Otherwise they questioned the owners' statistics, arguing that multi-product firms which owned collieries might be doctoring their accounts to show a loss on their coalmining activities; and suggested that a great deal could be done to improve efficiency. Before there could be any question of a worsening of miners' conditions, the owners must improve the organisation of production, distribution, and administration.

Reorganisation was to be a major issue in discussions of the coal industry over the next twelve months; and the views of the Miners and owners on what it could achieve were far apart. Of course improvements were possible, but how much? and how soon? Although the annual output of coal per man/year had still not reached the level of 1913, by 1923 there had been an improvement of 25 per cent from the low point of 1920. The failure to match prewar performance may have been partly due to the seven-hour day, but productivity had been falling for nearly fifty years due to deeper mines and narrower seams. Even to maintain its output per man, the coal industry had constantly to improve its methods of extracting coal.

The most readily available means to achieve this was the mechanisation of coal cutting and underground haulage. Throughout the interwar years there was a continual increase in machinery. By 1925 about 20 per cent of coal was mechanically cut—more than twice the

<hr/>

[4] Aldcroft, p. 251.   [5] Arnot, *The Miners*, p. 361.

proportion of 1913; and the number of conveyors in use had increased fivefold. No doubt the pace of change could be stepped up, but many coal faces were not geologically suitable for mechanical cutting with the machinery then available, especially in South Wales and Durham. Otherwise the main form of reorganising production which could contribute to efficiency would have been the sinking of new pits or the reconstruction of old pits to a better design, and either of them took years to complete. It was ten years after nationalisation in 1947 before the National Coal Board's determined and co-ordinated efforts to reorganise the coal industry began to yield substantial improvements in productivity.

With the wisdom of hindsight, it is therefore possible to see that the Miners, and many other people at that time, greatly exaggerated the contribution that the reorganisation of production could make, at least in the short term, to resolving the industry's economic problems. The Miners' demand—'not a penny off the pay, not a minute on the day'— could therefore only have been met by a government subsidy over a number of years, unless some means could be found of raising the price of coal. This might have been achieved by agreements to limit output and fix prices, such as were tried later in the twenties and given legislative backing by the second Labour government. However, the British coal industry was a major exporter. Arrangements of this kind could not raise prices in export markets because of foreign competition. Either coal exports would have to be subsidised, or there would be heavy unemployment.

At the end of June the joint committee broke up, and the owners gave notice to terminate the 1924 agreement on 31 July. For the future they proposed that, apart from low-paid daywagemen, whose case was to be dealt with district by district, there was to be no addition to the standard rates of 1914, except through the division of any district surplus at a ratio of 87:13 between wages and profits. The Miners refused to discuss these proposals. According to their calculations they would reduce pay by amounts varying between 6 and 23 per cent according to district, and transfer 'all the economic ills of the industry to the already overburdened shoulders of the mine-workers'.[6] There was no division of opinion among the Miners' leaders as there had been in 1921. Then the issues had been clouded by the demand for the national pool; now the federation was engaged in a straightforward resistance to wage cuts, as many of the leaders had wished it to be in 1921. It is likely that Herbert Smith foresaw ultimate defeat, but he knew that the Miners would not accept defeat until their capacity to resist had been destroyed.

---

[6] Ibid., p. 365.

On 13 July a court of inquiry was appointed. The Miners declined to take part 'in proceedings which . . . are so obviously designed to justify the present attack upon the mine workers' standard of living'.[7] Instead they turned to the General Council which appointed a Special Industrial Committee to organise support. The committee proposed 'that in the first stages at least the fight should be limited to the production and the distribution of coal'. They called the transport unions together. The Sailors and Firemen excused themselves on the ground that they could not arrange a meeting of their executive at such short notice, but the others attended and assented to an embargo on handling coal, with the condition that other unions should provide financial support for members of the transport unions who might be dismissed for refusing to obey orders. No arrangement had been made to meet this condition by 30 July, when instructions went out from the special committee, the leaders of the three railway unions, and the Transport and General Workers. A conference of trade union executives, which met that day to give 'unanimous and enthusiastic approval' to what the General Council had done, left it to the council 'to review the financial position and to bring forward a definite scheme'.[8]

Meanwhile the court of inquiry had reported on 28 July. After six months of discussion within the joint committee, and at a time when a national embargo on coal seemed to be only three days away, the two sides were advised to take 'common counsel together' to find a way of averting the worst consequences of their situation. The court found that the Miners were 'justified in claiming that any Wages Agreement which they can be asked to accept should provide for a minimum wage', but 'what that minimum should be is a matter for negotiation between the parties'.[9]

On 27 July Baldwin had met the special committee at their request. On the 29th he told the Miners' executive that the owners were willing to accept the principle of a minimum, but the executive was unimpressed, since the owners were apparently still proposing large but unspecified wage cuts. Later that day the special committee suggested to him that a government subsidy could avert the crisis. Next day, along with Churchill, he drafted proposals for such a subsidy, but did not reveal them. Instead he told the Miners that the government were prepared to establish

an authoritative inquiry to ty to get to the bottom of the economic difficulties of the industry . . . with a view to putting the industry as quickly as possible into a more healthy condition in which it can afford a better level of wages.[10]

---

[7] Ibid., p. 370.   [8] Trades Union Congress, 1925, pp. 176–80.
[9] *Report*, pp. 18, 20.   [10] Trades Union Congress, 1925, p. 181.

With the approval of the special committee, the Miners replied that they would not oppose such an inquiry, provided that they were satisfied with the terms of reference and that their existing wages and working hours were meanwhile maintained. Later that evening the cabinet agreed to a subsidy until next spring to allow time for the inquiry. In the end its cost turned out to be £27 million instead of the estimated £10 million. The Miners undertook to co-operate fully with the inquiry. On the 31st the owners suspended their notices, and the special committee called off the embargo. The unions were jubilant, christening the day 'Red Friday'. The *Daily Mail* on 3 August found it 'difficult to express in words the indignation and consternation with which the public has received the Government's capitulation to the extreme socialists'.

Apart from the Sailors and Firemen, there appears to have been no hesitation on the part of the unions. There was no sign of a division between left and right. The composition of the special committee was fairly balanced. It included Citrine, acting secretary of Congress in the absence of Bramley, who was ill; Hayday of the General and Municipal Workers, Marchbank of the Railwaymen, Poulton of the Boot and Shoe Operatives and Walkden of the Railway Clerks representing moderate opinion; Bromley, Hicks and Swales of the left; and Tillett. The question as to whether or not the proposed embargo was an unconstitutional challenge to the government was not seriously discussed at their meetings or at the conference of executives.

The attitude of the unions may have been influenced by negotiations which were then in progress to establish an enlarged and revised version of the Triple Alliance, which was to be called the Industrial Alliance. At the Miners' annual conference in 1924, a resolution proposing an alliance with the Railwaymen, the Transport Workers Federation, and 'any other union where it is practicable' was remitted to the executive, who, in January 1925, instructed Cook to arrange a meeting with the executives of relevant unions as soon as possible. The arrangements took time, and it was not until 4 June that the Miners, the three railway unions, the Transport and General Workers, the not yet defunct Transport Workers Federation, the Engineers, the Boilermakers, and the Federation of Engineering and Shipbuilding Trades met and agreed that a sub-committee of six should draft a scheme.

Their decision was influenced by a fear of widespread wage reductions. Besides the proposals of the mineowners, the shipowners, and the employers in the wool industry, the railway companies had replied to a wage claim with a proposal for wage reductions and the Engineering Employers had answered a similar claim with a demand for an extension of the working week to fifty hours, and worsened overtime and nightshift conditions. Union fears were reinforced by the persistent myth of a plot organised by the Federation of British Industries which, according to Citrine, was still 'regarded as a most sinister organisation, always working behind the scenes in some conspiratorial way to dictate the policy of the employers'.[11]

The leading figure on the committee of six was Bevin. He was convinced that the failure of the Triple Alliance had been due to the lack of firm and clear constitutional commitments from its constituent unions. He therefore saw the appointment of the committee as an opportunity to devise an organisation which would be free from those defects. In some respects his draft was similar to the new Congress rule on industrial disputes adopted the year before; but it was precise and explicit on several points where the Congress rule was vague. Forms of assistance were graded into negotiations, financial support, partial sympathetic action, sympathetic action by stages, and complete sympathetic action. Once assistance had been approved, the conduct of the dispute was to be in the hands of the executive. Above all, membership of the alliance obliged unions, 'notwithstanding anything in their agreements or constitutions to the contrary, to act as directed by the General Conference'.

Bevin's energy and enthusiasm turned what would otherwise have been a forlorn endeavour into a project which was taken seriously by the movement for at least a few months. According to the *Monthly Circular* of the Labour Research Department for July:

The June meeting had been sufficiently cool to the Miners' proposals; but the atmosphere had largely altered in six weeks. The July meeting heard a complete statement by Mr. Ernest Bevin, who had acted as Secretary to the Sub-Committee; and they unanimously accepted the draft constitution for consideration by the unions concerned.

There was no time for the constitution to be approved before Red Friday, but the enthusiasm shown at this meeting helped to create the mood of confidence in which the unions accepted the special committee's proposal for a coal embargo.

Within the government there was a division of opinion. According to the report given by the secretary of the cabinet, Hankey, to the king,

Many members of the Cabinet think that the struggle is inevitable and must come sooner or later—the PM does not share this view. The majority of the Cabinet regard the present moment as badly chosen for the fight though conditions would be more favourable nine months hence.[12]

The majority for postponement emerged only in the final stage of the negotiations. The prompt and virtually unanimous approval of the

---

[11] Citrine, p. 87.   [12] Middlemas and Barnes, p. 387.

unions for the coal embargo must have caused members of the cabinet to hesitate. Their offer of an authoritative inquiry demonstrated that they were not entirely certain of the merits of the coalowners' case, or at least that they did not believe that the public were convinced of the necessity for a drastic worsening of the miners' conditions. Once the need for such an inquiry was admitted, the justification for an immediate imposition of the owners' terms lost its force. Why should the Miners accept such terms until they were shown to be inevitable? But only a government subsidy could prevent their imposition.

Both at the time and subsequently, Baldwin and some of his colleagues gave the inadequacy of their preparations to deal with a general strike as a major reason for the subsidy. Over the previous two years the Supply and Transport Committee had created a skeleton regional and divisional organisation, with food officers and transport officers designated, and road haulage committees established. What had not been done was to build stocks of food and to make detailed arrangements with road hauliers for the use of their vehicles and drivers. However, there was bound to be a great deal of improvisation at the beginning of an unprecedented emergency such as a general strike. Food shortages would not become serious until some days had passed, during which further arrangements could be made. Hankey did not share the 'opinion that in July the preparations were not yet far enough advanced to meet a national emergency'.[13]

Autumn and Winter, 1925–6

The meeting of Congress at Scarborough in September has been called 'the high-water mark of' a 'movement to the left'.[14] Certainly the delegates exulted in the victory of Red Friday. The Minority Movement were present in some strength, and encouraged by what they saw as their success since Congress last met. They had been particularly active in South Wales, where they showed their strength in the election of Hodges' successor. They chose Arthur Cook rather than Ablett as their candidate. Cook carried South Wales; and then defeated the candidates from the other districts in the process of elimination as Hodges had done before him.

The Minority Movement was also in the forefront of the campaign to rebuild the membership of the South Wales Miners Federation, which had not succeeded in winning the loyalty of their members to the same extent as other districts, such as Durham. It was established that no-one worked in the Durham pits unless he was a union member, and the changing fortunes of the industry made almost no difference to membership figures. In South Wales, union membership responded

[13] Roskill, p. 411.   [14] Mowat, p. 288.

sharply to economic circumstances. From 198,000 in 1920 their membership fell to 87,000 in 1922. The traditional method of rebuilding the union was to organise recruitment campaigns, district by district. Where a campaign had been sufficiently successful, union members refused to work with the remaining non-unionists, and, where necessary, struck to enforce their decision. There were several strikes over non-unionism in 1923, when the South Wales federation set out to recover its strength; and in 1925, when the issue was taken up again, no less than three strikes over non-unionism in South Wales in May alone were classified among the month's 'principal disputes' by the *Ministry of Labour Gazette*.

In July 1925 a dispute over local customs broke out in the anthracite area. Because of the growing demand for anthracite, the area of West Wales around Ammanford, where it was mined, was more prosperous than the rest of the coalfield. Customs, such as the 'stint', which limited output, and the seniority rule, which protected the miner against victimisation, had generally been respected. In 1924 two combines were formed to amalgamate the collieries, and the managers of these new companies proved less indulgent. A miner was dismissed from one of the United Anthracite collieries for refusing an instruction which conflicted with the custom relating to transfers. The colliery stopped work. Others followed. Mass marches through the valleys stopped nearly all the pits in the district by the middle of July. By early August 'the town of Ammanford and some surrounding villages were under the virtual control of the Combine strike committee'. Towards the end of the strike, the miners formed their own 'defence corps'. A settlement was made on their behalf by the South Wales executive on 24 August. 'Wages and other terms and conditions prevailing at the several collieries before the stoppage' were to continue.[15] After the strike 198 miners were prosecuted, of whom 58 were sentenced to prison. The Miners levied themselves to support the families of those who were gaoled, and the Labour Party executive contributed £500. Communists enthused over the strike, seeing it as a dress rehearsal for the revolution, and a branch of the Minority Movement was established in the area.

The Minority Movement was also encouraged by the progress towards agreement with the Russian trade unions. A delegation from the General Council had visited Russia at the end of 1924. Besides Bramley, the members included, among others, Bromley, Purcell, Herbert Smith, and Tillett. They submitted a warmly favourable report on the Soviet system, and committed themselves to recommend that the International Federation of Trade Unions should hold 'a free and unconditional immediate conference' with the Russians. They also proposed that the

[15] Francis, pp. 20, 21.

General Council should seek power to 'act jointly with the Russians for unity'.

The response of the international federation was cautious, but did not close the door to negotiations. The General Council reacted more positively. In April 1925 they met the Russians to establish an Anglo-Russian Joint Advisory Council with the aim of promoting international unity, and also of extending 'joint contacts . . . for the purpose of developing the closest possible mutual aid between the two countries'.[16] Tomsky, again attending as a fraternal delegate, was given his usual appreciative reception by Congress in 1925. A Minority Movement resolution urging the General Council to 'do everything in their power towards securing world-wide unity of the Trade Union Movement through an all-inclusive International Federation of Trade Unions' was passed by acclamation after a perfunctory debate.[17]

Other resolutions promoted by the Minority Movement were passed declaring 'complete opposition to Imperialism',[18] proclaiming 'the overthrow of capitalism' as a trade union objective, and pledging Congress 'to develop and strengthen workshop organisation'.[19] They committed Congress to no specific action, and were accepted after superficial debates. Most trade union leaders did not yet see the movement as a serious danger, and had not organised themselves to counter its influence.

Far more significant was the debate on a further extension of the powers of the General Council in industrial disputes. The Vehicle Builders proposed that the council be authorised to exact levies, and 'to call for a stoppage of work, by an affiliated organisation, or part thereof, in order to assist a union defending a vital trade union principle'.[20] Individual unions were to amend their rules to comply with those provisions. If carried, the resolution would have given Congress much the same powers as Bevin was proposing for the Industrial Alliance. Among leaders of the major unions, only Cook spoke in support. Red Friday, he said, had proved the need for these powers, since the embargo would have relied on 'the goodwill of the railwaymen, the dockers, and the other people'.[21] However, other speakers were able to argue that the lesson of Red Friday's success was that powers of this kind were unnecessary, since in practice the council was able to act; and Bevin, Clynes, and Thomas all said they must have time to consult their unions. The matter was referred to the General Council for report to a special conference.

There were significant changes in the membership of the new

[16] Trades Union Congress, 1925, pp. 296–301. [17] Ibid., p. 485.
[18] Ibid., p. 553.   [19] Ibid., p. 437.
[20] Ibid., p. 380.   [21] Ibid., p. 384.

General Council. Pugh replaced Swales as chairman. Although a 'great mountain of a man' and 'the left's most impressive orator',[22] Swales had proved the most incompetent president of Congress of the twentieth century so far. On half a dozen occasions the debates at the 1925 Congress ran out of control, and he was for ever calling on the Standing Orders Committee to get him out of trouble. Thomas and Bondfield were back on the General Council. Bevin had at last allowed his name to go forward as one of the Transport and General Workers' nominees, and he was, of course, elected. Pugh now became chairman of the special committee, and Thomas replaced Marchbank as a member. Bramley, who had come back from sick leave to attend his last Congress, died a few weeks later. Citrine was acting secretary again, now with the almost certain prospect of being confirmed as secretary the following year. His reputation as an administrator, originally due to his reorganisation of the Electricians' finances before he joined the staff of Congress, had been reinforced by his report on the work of the joint departments; but as a newcomer, he did not yet wield the authority he was to acquire in later years.

The special committee decided against asking for an extension of the powers of the General Council in industrial disputes, asserting in a circular to affiliated unions that 'any effort in the way of active support to a union in dispute would be far more likely to be successful if coming spontaneously from the union or unions whose assistance is required'.[23] They did not think a levy would be acceptable. In January 1926 Citrine presented a memorandum dealing with the situation which might face them once the inquiry had reported and the subsidy had come to an end. He was anxious that the unions should agitate for a continuance of the subsidy after the end of April, in order to allow time to carry out whatever reforms the inquiry might propose; but the committee preferred to wait to see what those reforms were to be, and left open the question as to what form of action the council should organise in support of the Miners if the report failed to lead to a settlement. The Co-operative Union approached the committee to ask for guarantees for loans or goods supplied by co-operative societies to strikers and their families if there was a stoppage. They pointed to the miners' outstanding debts to the co-operatives from 1921. The committee decided that they could not bind the unions. The question whether they should co-operate with the government in the maintenance of essential services was raised, but not answered. The only clear and positive decision taken by the committee was made as a consequence of the

[22] Calhoun, p. 38.
[23] Trades Union Congress, 1926, p. 92.

Miners' request for a renewed statement of support. They asserted that the movement

would stand firmly and unitedly against any attempt further to degrade the standard of life in the coalfields. There is to be no reduction of wages, no increase in working hours, and no interference with the principle of national agreements. This is the position of the trade union movement today.

However, the statement was made with some reluctance. Bromley, as well as Thomas, expressed doubts. The committee were only 'agreeing to defend those principles so far as they could, and it would not debar the miners from making concessions in the course of negotiations'.[24]

Both then and after the strike, the Communist Party and the Minority Movement raised an outcry against the failure of the General Council to prepare. What they chiefly wanted, however, was 'a policy of rank and file mobilisation involving the reinforcement of Trades Councils, together with the creation of local Councils of Action and workers' defence corps'.[25] Not surprisingly, the committee would have nothing to do with such proposals. They believed that both the mobilisation of the rank and file and the organisation of industrial action could, if need arose, be adequately handled by improvisation after they had seen the report and knew the response of the government and the owners. Events proved them right. When the day came, the rank and file responded even more loyally than they had hoped, and, although there were some muddles over the last-minute strike instructions, mostly over which groups of workers should be out, they had no discernible effect on the outcome.

Over the winter the Communist Party and the Minority Movement were in some disarray. After a raid on party headquarters, the government decided to prosecute twelve leading members for seditious libel. In November five of them were sentenced to a year in prison and the remainder to six months; but this was not the main reason for their helplessness. Their ability to win the support of union branches and Trades Councils, and to steer resolutions through conferences, was of little value to them now. So far as the trade unions were concerned, the course of events would be decided by the special committee and the General Council. The Communist Party and Minority Movement could not object to that, for they had been foremost in demanding greater powers for the General Council; but they had no influence on either the council or the committee. Moreover they wanted a strike; the General Council wanted a settlement.

The government were also waiting for the inquiry to report; but they

---

[24] Quoted by Phillips, *The General Strike*, p. 89.
[25] Ibid., p. 84.

had no hesitation over making preparations. After all, inadequate preparation was their excuse for granting the subsidy, and they needed to complete arrangements already planned and partly executed. Local personnel were recruited, funds were allocated for stockpiling, detailed arrangements were made with the road haulage industry. Their one hesitation was over the recruitment of volunteers; and their problem was solved by the creation of the Organisation for the Maintenance of Supplies by a group of former senior officers and civil servants. Joynson-Hicks, the Home Secretary, welcomed this new body, whose function was to prepare lists of volunteers and to provide training. It was suggested that they should concentrate on the recruitment of road haulage drivers, and that their lists of volunteers should be handed over as soon as an emergency was proclaimed. However, they were short of funds and 'largely confined to the south of England'.[26] Probably not a great deal was achieved that could not have been left to last-minute improvisation in the second half of April 1926.

The inquiry had been entrusted to a Royal Commission of four members. The chairman was a former Liberal minister, Sir Herbert Samuel. His colleagues were Sir Herbert Lawrence, once a general and now a banker; Kenneth Lee, a cotton employer; and the economist, Sir William Beveridge. Collection of evidence took until the middle of January. The report, a best-seller of three hundred pages, appeared on 10 March.

The industry's prospects had deteriorated further since July 1925. Excluding the subsidy, 73 per cent of coal mined in the last quarter of that year was produced at a loss.[27] The cause did not lie in 'political unrest or restriction of output among miners' or in 'inefficiency in the day to day management of the mines'. Nevertheless, the owners' view that 'little can be done to improve the organisation of the industry' was rejected. Although nationalisation of the mines was not the means to accomplish them, 'large changes' were possible.[28]

In planning their report, the commissioners might have decided to give the country a clear and accurate review of the industry's problems, even if it showed that there was no easy solution, or they might have decided to recommend the solution on which the parties were most likely to reach agreement, even if it meant some distortion of the evidence. In fact they did neither. They fudged the evidence and upset the Miners, the owners, and the government with their recommendations. They diagnosed a failure to exploit economies of scale, and a lack of co-ordination between the collieries and the other elements in what they saw as potentially 'a great industrial complex, which will comprise also electricity, smokeless fuel, gas, oil, chemical products, blast

[26] Ibid., p. 27.   [27] *Report*, p. 22.   [28] Ibid., pp. 232–3.

furnaces and possibly other activities'.[29] To the extent that the commissioners' findings on the advantages of size related to pits rather than companies, they had, as the Mining Association pointed out, misled themselves by their emphasis on the efficiency of the large, new Yorkshire pits. In fact 'it was in Scotland where mines were smallest that figures of output per man were amongst the highest in Britain', because of the rapid pace of mechanisation there.[30] In any event they offered no calculations of the benefits that would acrrue from colliery amalgamation or from closer co-operation with related industries. It is not surprising that the owners informed the government that these proposals could have '"no appreciable effect on the economic condition of the industry", their benefits being "largely illusory"'.[31].

The report also proposed the immediate nationalisation of royalties. This might have had an effect on efficiency in the long run if it had led to a redistribution of existing leases, which does not appear to have been the commission's intention; but it offended the government, more on grounds of cost than of principle.

It was admitted that these proposals could not have an immediate effect. If costs continued near their current levels when the subsidy ended—and the commissioners were opposed to renewal—many miners 'to be numbered probably by hundreds of thousands' would be unemployed; prices would rise at those collieries which stayed open, pushing up the cost of living; and the depression in coal-using industries would be intensified. The extension of working hours proposed by the owners would not help since it would increase unemployment. Only a wage cut could provide the reduction in costs needed to prevent the impending disaster.[32] The report made no serious attempt to estimate how big a cut was required; but it considered that the owners' proposals were based on too pessimistic an estimate of future prices; and suggested that 10 per cent off the national wage bill might be nearly enough, although there would have to be variations between districts.[33]

The commissioners did not think that such a reduction in pay need bring excessive hardship. The wages of the lowest paid should be safeguarded. The miners habitually compared their real wages with those of 1914, but 1914 had been an exceptional year and a different result could be had by making the comparison with the years 1909–13. As it was, the pay of labourers in the industry was considerably above that of engineering and shipbuilding labourers. They calculated the average pay of pieceworking coal-getters at £3.80, and then, ignoring the difference between piecework and timework, compared this figure

[29] Ibid., p. 66.　　　　　　　　[30] Buxton, p. 481.
[31] Phillips, *The General Strike*, p. 81.
[32] *Report*, pp. 226–31.　　　　[33] Ibid., p. 294.

with weekly time rates of £2.82½ for a fitter and £2.78 for a shipwright.[34]

To improve industrial relations, the report proposed joint pit committees; the extension of payment by results to workers not already on piecework; profit-sharing schemes; improvement in housing, and the universal provision of pithead baths; a system of family allowances for miners; and, 'when more prosperous times return', the introduction of holidays with pay.[35] By themselves, most of these recommendations would probably have won the approval of the Miners, but they were hardly likely to gain their acceptance for the report as a whole.

Before announcing their response to the report, the two sides waited to hear from the government, who took a fortnight to study the findings and then pushed the responsibility for decision back to the two sides. Despite hesitations over, and indeed opposition to, some of its proposals, on 24 March they told the two sides that they would

be prepared to undertake such measures as may be required of the State to give the recommendations effect, provided that those engaged in the industry—with whom the decision primarily rests—agree to accept the Report and to carry on the industry on the basis of its recommendations.[36]

In addition, a continuation of the subsidy, at a tapering but unspecified rate, would be made available if a settlement was reached. The owners had already given the government their views in a confidential memorandum which found little merit in the proposals for reorganisation, and insisted that no solution could be found without lengthening the hours of work. When they met the Miners on 31 March, the owners interpreted the report's recommendations to mean a return to district agreements. The response of the Miners was decided at their conference on 9 April which reasserted their determination to maintain a national agreement on wages, and their rejection of lower wages and a longer working day. However, the special committee had been unwilling to commit themselves to this resolution when it was shown to them on the previous day. They felt that they would prejudice negotiations by doing so.

Negotiations

There matters stood for another two weeks. The government waited for the parties to negotiate, and the parties waited for the government to intervene. The government kept in touch, but, despite a plea from the special committee on 14 April, took no positive action. Notices posted in the pits announced the new rates settled by the district employers' associations. The average reductions ranged from 9 per cent in

[34] Ibid., pp. 156–7.   [35] Ibid., p. 185.   [36] Phillips, *The General Strike*, p. 81.

Yorkshire to 28 per cent in Durham. On 22 April the two sides met again, but made no progress. Later that day, Smith again told the special committee that the Miners would accept no reductions. He admitted the consequence of their intransigence would be to 'put upwards of 200,000 men out of work. They realised that. . . . They were determined that if the country wanted coal, it had to give the men who got it a respectable living.'[37] Pugh and Thomas 'agreed that the owners' terms were impossible', but they persuaded Smith that they should see Baldwin again to urge him to intervene.

Baldwin called the parties together next day. Nothing was achieved. On Sunday, 25 April, Pugh was invited to Chequers to talk with Baldwin, and suggested that the discussion should concentrate more on reorganisation and less on wages. After seeing the special committee again on Monday, Baldwin tried this approach on the parties. Nothing came of it. He then attempted to persuade the owners to concede a national minimum at the current rate if the Miners would agree to the eight-hour day. The furthest the owners would go was a national minimum of 20 per cent above standard (in place of the $33\frac{1}{3}$ per cent agreed in April 1924). Baldwin wrote to the Miners on Friday, the 30th, putting this proposal on the owners' behalf.

This was the day that notices were due to run out. On 23 April the special committee had decided that the risk of a lockout in a week's time justified them in calling a conference of trade union executives for the 29th. On that day the delegates were informed of the course of negotiations so far, and asked to authorise continued negotiations by the special committee. When they met the government, Smith 'was prepared to deal with the Report from page one to the end', which the special committee took to mean that he was willing to discuss wage adjustments in the context of the other recommendations of the commission.[38] Next day there was little for the delegates to do except to authorise the Miners to refuse the owners' terms transmitted through Baldwin. On Saturday, 1 May, the Miners, already locked out, were asked to place the conduct of the dispute in the hands of the General Council. Smith replied that 'they understood the position was that all negotiations would now be carried on through the General Council, but that they, the Miners' Federation, would be consulted'.[39] The conference then assembled and the delegates were asked to

place their powers in the hands of the General Council and carry out the instructions of the General Council from time to time, both regarding the conduct of the dispute and financial assistance.

[37] Lovell, 'The TUC Special Industrial Committee', p. 50.
[38] Trades Union Congress, *Mining Dispute National Strike*, p. 8.
[39] Ibid., p. 9.

The majority was 3,653,527 to 49,911. The Seamen announced their intention of holding a ballot.

A policy statement, *The Mining Situation*, prepared jointly with the Miners and approved by the General Council, had been presented to the conference. Arguing that 'the wages and working conditions of mine workers are already so depressed as to render it imperative to seek remedies other than a further degradation in their standards of life', the document emphasised reorganisation as the solution to the industry's problem, and foresaw the need for pit closures.

On Tuesday, 27 April, the General Council had appointed a Ways and Means Committee to prepare plans for industrial action which were approved next day, and distributed to the delegates on the Friday. Their scheme was far more ambitious than the embargo proposed the previous July. Then the transport unions had not been entirely happy about being placed in the front line by themselves, and they were now reluctant to serve in the same position. Consequently the plan proposed a strike, not an embargo, encompassing printing, iron and steel, heavy chemicals, and parts of the building industry, as well as transport. The unions in these industries were to be a first wave and, if necessary, a second wave, consisting mainly of the engineering and shipbuilding unions, was to follow later. These plans were put to the conference; and then, with further details supplied by the Powers and Orders Committee, which replaced the Ways and Means Committee on 1 May, they were circulated to union offices. Thus prepared, the delegates left to organise what the General Council insisted was not a general strike, since not all industries were to be stopped, but a 'national' strike.

Even now negotiations were not at an end. On 1 May the Miners' executive dispersed to the coalfields, but the special committee, now renamed the Negotiating Committee, and members of the cabinet met that evening, and appointed a sub-committee of Pugh, Swales, Thomas and Citrine, and Baldwin, Birkenhead, Steel-Maitland (the Minister of Labour) and Horace Wilson (the ministry's permanent secretary) to try to find a way out. A provisional formula was drafted:

The Prime Minister has satisfied himself as a result of the conversations he has had with representatives of the Trades Union Congress, that if negotiations are continued (it being understood that the notices cease to be operative) the representatives of the Trades Union Congress are confident that a settlement can be reached on the lines of the Report within a fortnight.[40]

This formula was reported to the cabinet and the General Council on the morning of Sunday, 2 May. Accounts of subsequent events differ

[40] Jones, p. 26.

widely. Some of them indicate that a settlement was very close, or that one side or the other was ready to settle only to be thwarted by the intransigence of the other. The evidence now available, however, makes it certain that agreement was never within reach, although many of the members of the General Council and some of the cabinet were anxious to avoid a strike.

Neither side of the sub-committee was happy with the formula. The Negotiating Committee were evasive as to whether it committed the Miners to wage reductions. The cabinet representatives understood that it did, but feared that it was too vague. After Cook had told them that he did not believe his colleagues would accept the formula, the General Council decided they could not endorse it without the agreement of the Miners' executive, whose members were summoned back to London. At Downing Street, according to Tom Jones, the ministers who had not been members of the sub-committee were 'aghast at the formula' which they 'felt . . . would be read by the whole country as a capitulation on the part of the Government'. They were further dismayed when they heard, apparently for the first time, that strike notices had gone out for midnight on the Monday. Tempers were not improved by the long wait for the Miners' executive to reassemble, during which the cabinet drafted an ultimatum, to be used by Baldwin at his discretion. It stipulated acceptance of 'such interim adjustments of wages and hours of work as will make it economically possible to carry on the industry' during reorganisation.[41]

Soon after 9 p.m. the General Council arrived in Downing Street to apologise for the delay and resume talks. The sub-committee discussed a new formula drafted by Birkenhead with a clear commitment to a concession 'either in the matter of hours or wages' and an alternative, suggested by Thomas, acknowledging that negotiations 'may involve some reduction in wages'. There was no agreement.[42] At 11.15 the Miners arrived at Downing Street and met the General Council. After some discussion, it was agreed that formulas should be set aside. Instead they should try to draft an agreement. They began to discuss a proposal from Bevin for a national board of Miners, owners and independent representatives responsible for carrying through reorganisation as well as arbitrating on wages.

Meanwhile the cabinet had heard, about midnight, that members of the Operative Printers and Assistants had objected to setting up the *Daily Mail*'s editorial for Monday on the grounds that it was provocative. This, along with the strike instructions, was treated by the cabinet as evidence that hostilities had already begun. At 1.15 a.m. the

[41] Ibid., pp. 28–30.
[42] Phillips, *The General Strike*, pp. 122–3.

four trade union members of the sub-committee were summoned to receive Baldwin's ultimatum. They reported to the General Council who sent Pugh and Citrine back to say that they had no responsibility for the *Daily Mail* incident; but the cabinet had dispersed and Baldwin had gone to bed. The trade unionists returned to Eccleston Square to draft their formal reply to the Prime Minister. Next day an attempt was made to renew negotiations on the basis of the Bevin scheme, but nothing was achieved.

The Strike

Over the winter the trade union movement had been holdings its fire, waiting for the General Council to act. Most of the working days lost through strikes from September 1925 to April 1926 were in coalmining. Many of them arose out of the failure of the government subsidy to give the Miners adequate protection against attempts by the owners to tamper with wages and conditions pit by pit. Things got so bad in Durham that the Durham Miners held a strike ballot in November, but the majority was insufficient to authorise a stoppage.

The General Council were confirmed as the sole central trade union authority by the collapse of the plans for the Industrial Alliance. The culmination of the alliance's brief career was the conference in July 1925 which gave provisional approval to draft rules. A few days later, Red Friday destroyed the reason for creating the alliance, by demonstrating that the General Council could organise successful sympathetic action in an emergency, despite the limitations and ambiguity of their powers. Rifts appeared at a further conference. The Railwaymen wanted it to be a condition of membership that the unions in each industry should 'prepare schemes for fusion' or at least 'a unified policy', and withdrew when this condition was rejected.[43] On 12 February 1926 the Miners' executive had before them a letter from their solicitors pointing out that the alliance would impose on them obligations which were in conflict with their own rules. In the same month the Federation of Engineering and Shipbuilding Trades, about to sign a new procedure agreement with the Shipbuilding Employers, rejected the alliance because they could not expect the employers to confirm the agreement while they themselves were preparing to enter into an undertaking to break it.

By general agreement, the response to the strike on Tuesday, 4 May, was excellent. The major weakness was road haulage, where a majority of the workers were unorganised. Nevertheless 'a mounting flood of inquiries, protests, reports, demands for clearer instructions, requests for rulings, problems no one had thought of, poured into Eccleston

[43] Labour Research Department, *Monthly Bulletin*, November 1925.

Square and soon threatened to engulf the General Council'.[44] Inevitably problems of interpretation arose over the instruction to stop work on 'luxury and commercial building', but otherwise to exempt housing. The militant Electricians were determined to come out, especially in London, and a plan was devised to deny power to industrial establishments, but to exempt power to hospitals and lighting everywhere. This arrangement, however, relied on the co-operation of the customers. Industrial consumers in Stepney were told by the borough electricity committee, whose chairman was Attlee, that they 'would have their fuses pulled, and would be without light also'[45] if they used power. The issue of permits for the use of vehicles to transport food also led to a great deal of confusion, and even abuse. Hugh Lyon, secretary of the Scottish Horse and Motormen's Association, was, according to one of the clerks in his office, 'in his element. There was a stream of employers, sometimes a queue waiting. Hughie sat there smoking a cigar; sometimes he would not give a permit. It depended on whether he thought the employer would be co-operative in future.' He also regarded whisky as a 'staple food stuff'.[46]

Originally the General Council had appointed committees for food and essential services, public services, publicity, and general services, in addition to those for negotiation and powers and orders. On Wednesday, 5 May, at Bevin's instigation, the Powers and Orders Committee was renamed the Strike Organisation Committee and given overall responsibility for running the strike, with subordinate committees of the transport unions and those in electricity supply. This central control diminished confusion, although problems continued to arise. Local transport committees were appointed to co-ordinate the issue of permits, but there were differences between the road transport unions and the railway unions, the latter being more restrictive, and instructions came from London to withhold all permits. Subsequently delivery of bread and milk by co-operative societies was exempted.

The original strike orders had instructed Trades Councils to assist in carrying out the council's directives in conjunction with the local officers of unions on strike; and made them responsible for 'organising the Trade Unionists in dispute in the most effective manner for the preservation of peace and order'.[47] Wider scope than this was opposed by union leaders, and by 'Bevin in particular, . . . on the grounds that unions would not hand over their functions to Trades Councils'.[48] The councils accepted their orders with enthusiasm and exceeded them liberally by appointing 'councils of action', or 'emergency committees',

[44] Bullock, p. 318.   [45] Jenkins, p. 113.   [46] Tuckett, p. 181.
[47] Arnot, *The General Strike*, p. 162.   [48] Citrine, pp. 177–8.

or strike committees to take over the running of the strike within their areas. These bodies met

once or twice every day and covered almost every conceivable aspect of the strike. There were Publicity and Entertainment Committees, committees to handle permits and picketing, distress, food, sport and transport. Their effectiveness varied from district to district, but the overall picture is one of triumph over local and sectional difficulties.[49]

Parallel improvisation provided excitement for government volunteers, who included not only those on the lists of the Organisation for the Maintenance of Supplies, but tens of thousands more who volunteered once the government's regional organisation had taken over. They included

old and middle-aged men who felt that the strike was a threat to the Constitution; undergraduates who joined in mostly from sheer exuberance; employees of various firms, men and women, who thought that they should support the Government, or were pressed into doing so; and a heterogeneous collection of old and young, including unemployed men and women and some union blacklegs.[50]

They were employed mainly in the docks and road haulage; in power stations, where the senior staff and naval ratings provided the nucleus of a trained labour force; and in road passenger transport and the railways. Few railwaymen were prepared to blackleg, and enthusiasm and brawn proved ineffective substitutes for skill and experience. By the end of the strike no main line company had as much as 20 per cent of its passenger services running, and, apart from the Great Western, there were hardly any goods services at all. Even on the Great Western the figure was only 8 per cent.[51] The difficulties of volunteers on the trams and the buses were increased by mass pickets in working class areas, and, after a day or two, few of the vehicles in use had much glass in their windows.

Nevertheless there were no riots to compare with Tonypandy in 1910. Many 'specials' enjoyed the same nine days of carefree excitement as did other volunteers, although there were plenty of disturbances and clashes. Trams and other vehicles were overturned in Glasgow and elsewhere. Many working-class areas of London and the North had incidents to report and hundreds of prosecutions and sentences followed. The Emergency Powers Act conferred wide powers to arrest for actions which might cause sedition or disaffection, and to search premises for evidence, which were used predominantly against Communists.

---

[49] Symons, p. 146.   [50] Ibid., p. 71.   [51] Ibid., pp. 95–6.

The government's plans for the road haulage industry worked with few hitches and 'appeared afterwards to be the most vital if not the most spectacular aspect of the success of the emergency administration'.[52] However, road haulage could not deliver the goods unless it had access to the ports. Volunteer labour was moved into the large provincial docks in the first days of the strike, and cargoes were loaded on to the lorries, 'sometimes under police protection, but with only occasional obstruction'.[53] In London the government faced sterner opposition. Refrigerated stores were supplied with electric power by submarines, but it was only on Friday, 7 May, that civilian volunteers came down river into the docks. Next day an armed convoy of over a hundred lorries with loads of flour and sugar drove through the East End and on to the depot established in Hyde Park.

The government had arranged to use the facilities of the British Broadcasting Company in the event of an emergency, and detailed plans were made just before the strike. The company was to broadcast officially approved news bulletins throughout the day, and to relay all government announcements. With the printing industry on strike it seemed that the government was to have a monopoly of the media, but, at the suggestion of the printing unions, the General Council arranged to publish a daily paper, the *British Worker*, at the office of the *Daily Herald*. The first issue appeared on 5 May, and on the same day Churchill succeeded in bringing out the *British Gazette*. For content the *Worker* had the best of the contest, but by the end of the strike its circulation, hampered by distribution difficulties and the requisitioning of most of its newsprint by the government, was about 700,000 copies whereas that of the *Gazette* was over two million.

The General Council has often been criticised for closing down the newspapers by calling out the printing workers. The argument is that, to succeed, the general strike required

active sympathy among a considerable section of the middle classes. This can only be attained if the Government is obviously aggressive, the leaders of Labour notoriously pacific, and the object of the strike such that the middle class prefer a settlement to the dangers of a lengthy stoppage.[54]

Only a free press, the argument goes, could have led the middle class in this direction, especially with the government in control of broadcasting.

There were signs that middle class opinion was not solid. Lloyd George appealed for a negotiated settlement in the Commons, as did Haldane in the Lords. Randall Davidson, Archbishop of Canterbury,

---

[52] Phillips, *The General Strike*, p. 156.
[53] Ibid., pp. 158–9.   [54] Kingsley Martin, p. 95.

and other leaders of the Church of England and the nonconformist churches agreed an appeal for a resumption of negotiations based on an extension of the subsidy, withdrawal of notices, and cancellation of the general strike. At first he was given permission to broadcast the appeal on 7 May, but then it was postponed to 11 May, the day on which the General Council decided to call off the strike. Had the government been hesitating, such an appeal, followed by evidence of widespread support in the country, might have persuaded them to reopen talks with the General Council; but those were not the circumstances. From start to finish the government showed no inclination to budge from their demand for unconditional surrender, and by 7 May they were confident that their plans for dealing with the strike were working satisfactorily. It may be true that, had they appeared, 'even the most hostile papers might have felt it good business to give the strikers' case prominence'.[55] If so, it was a mistake to call the printing workers out; but not necessarily so great a mistake as to make much difference to the outcome.

The General Council had other worries besides publicity. The strike had to be financed. On 6 May a telegram from the Russian unions' Central Council notified them of a donation of £26,247 which arrived next day. To avoid misinterpretation, they decided to return it. A further Russian cheque, and another from the International Federation of Trade Unions, were held up under emergency regulations. Had there been no political or legal complications, the General Council could have done with the money. An appeal on 4 May to unions so far not involved in the strike brought little response, and another, to individual union members still at work to send 5 per cent of their earnings to their union head offices, probably did no better.

The Iron and Steel Trades Confederation paid no strike benefit at all. The Engineers, whose members working on maintenance in 'first wave' industries had been called out, could pay only reduced benefits; and the Printing, Bookbinding, and Paper Workers were similarly placed. The Iron and Steel Trades Confederation, the Printing, Bookbinding, and Paper Workers, the Boilermakers, the Electricians, the Locomotive Engineers, the Transport and General Workers, and the Typographical Association all appealed to the General Council for help either during or immediately after the strike. The Railwaymen had spent almost half their assets of £2 million by the end of the strike. Strikes could, of course, and did, last for many weeks without strike pay because the strikers' families could turn to the Poor Law. However, it was one thing for strikers to rely on the Poor Law rather than accept wage cuts and worsened conditions for themselves, but it was a different matter to

[55] Ibid., p. 89.

expect them to stay out without strike pay in sympathy with other workers, when their own pay and conditions were not directly threatened.

The General Council also had to consider the legal status of their actions. On 6 May Sir John Simon told the House of Commons that, since the strikers had come out without giving due notice, they had broken their contracts, and were liable for damages. So much was not in doubt, but he went on to say that: 'Every Trade Union leader who has advised and promoted that course of action is liable in damages to the utmost farthing of his personal possessions.'[56] Such a leader was not protected by section three of the Trade Disputes Act, which removed liability for inducement to breach a contract of employment when it was 'in contemplation or furtherance of a trade dispute', because a general strike was not, as he alleged in a further speech to the House on the 11th, a trade dispute within the meaning of the Act. On the same day Mr Justice Astbury delivered judgment in a case brought by the Seamen against some of their officers. The union had not struck pending the outcome of their ballot, which later was said to have gone against a strike. Some members, however, had come out unofficially. Wilson instituted proceedings for an injunction to prevent branch officers paying them strike benefit. Astbury decided in his favour because, by paying benefit, the officers would be breaking the union rules; but he added, in passing, that the strike was illegal. However, Sir Henry Slesser, an expert in trade union law, asserted that it was not;[57] and the General Council did not know that the cabinet had authorised the introduction of a bill to allow restraint of union funds, and to prohibit the expulsion of members who refused to take part in a sympathetic strike 'calculated to intimidate or coerce the Government or the community'.[58] Thus, although there were rumours 'that the government intended to arrest the members of the General Council and of the local strike committees, to impound strike funds and to call up the army reserves',[59] the council do not appear to have been unduly alarmed; and the government decided not to proceed with the bill.

It was not until 12 May that the reports of the General Council's Intelligence Committee indicated the beginning of a drift back to work, but some members of the General Council were concerned that the strike might get out of hand locally. Charles Dukes's allegation that

every day the strike proceeded the control and the authority of that dispute was passing out of the hands of responsible Executives into the hands of men who

---

[56] *Hansard*, 6 May 1926, col. 585.

[57] His opinion received support next year in an article in the *Yale Law Review* by A. L. Goodhart which argued cogently that the general strike had been a trade dispute.

[58] Phillips, *The General Strike*, p. 165.   [59] Mowat, p. 323.

had no authority, no control, no responsibility, and was wrecking the movement from one end to the other[60]

was a justification after the event for calling off the strike, but not necessarily without some significance as an indication of fears in the mind of union leaders at the time.

Together with the government's manifest determination to hold out and the success of their emergency transport system, shortage of funds and the risk of a drift back to work provided the General Council with persuasive reasons for discussing the terms on which the strike might be called off. The opportunity arose when Sir Herbert Samuel arrived back from holiday in Italy on 6 May. He was soon in touch with Thomas, and a series of discussions between Samuel and the Negotiating Committee was set in motion. At first Smith and Cook wanted to come, but then decided that 'they didn't want to be in on conversations but only on definite negotiations'.[61] The government made clear to Samuel that he had no authority to negotiate on their behalf, and he told the Negotiating Committee so. However, they believed that the publication of whatever terms they could agree would put the onus on the government to respond one way or the other. By the evening of 8 May a draft was given to the General Council which included district wage reductions under a degree of national control for a provisional period of a year. Next day the proposals were shown to the Miners' executive who rejected them. On 10 May another 'formula' was ready which left the negotiation of a new agreement on wages until after reorganisation had been agreed. That evening the General Council met the Miners, who refused to accept the formula unless it was amended to exclude wage reductions, on the ground that reorganisation would render them unnecessary.

Next day the Negotiating Committee met Samuel to compose a final memorandum on the basis of the formula. That evening the General Council met the Miners' executive again. The Miners were now told that the council were considering calling off the strike. They still refused to accept the proposed terms, and left after they had prepared a written repudiation. After wrestling with their problem for some time, the council arranged to go to Downing Street at noon the next day, 12 May, to call off the strike; but orders already issued for the 'second wave' of strikers to come out on 12 May were not rescinded, and they struck.

According to Bevin, he and other members of the council who were not members of the Negotiating Committee had been led to believe that the government would accept the Samuel memorandum and that

[60] Trades Union Congress, *National Strike Special Conference*, p. 58.
[61] Citrine, p. 186.

lockout notices would be withdrawn,[62] but it is difficult to believe that they were not aware of what was going on. The Negotiating Committee was a convenient body to which to transfer their feelings of guilt towards the Miners which were not wholly assuaged by their belief that they were justified in what they were doing.

At Downing Street the leaders asked Baldwin to announce that there should be no victimisation, but he would make no promises, though in the Commons that afternoon and in a broadcast in the evening he asked that there should be no malice or vindictiveness. The original strike instructions had provided that there was to be no general resumption of work until all the strikers were assured that they were returning on their former terms of employment; but the announcement of the return to work made no reference to this condition, nor did it make clear that the miners were still locked out. There was consequently a good deal of confusion. Many strikers assumed that they had won, and there were victory celebrations in some areas that evening. It was not until the morning of Thursday, 13 May, that most of them were aware of what had happened. Then it seemed to them, including many of the local leaders, that they had been betrayed. From their point of view the strike was solid and successful. They had no means of knowing the reasons which had induced the General Council to call it off. Confusion and anger were increased by an announcement from the council on the evening of 12 May that they had 'sufficient assurances . . . as to the lines upon which a settlement could be reached to justify them in terminating the General Strike'.[63]

Few employers' associations proposed to alter the wages or working hours of returning strikers. They were more anxious to refuse blanket commitments to reinstatement, to insist on retaining workers taken on during the strike, and to obtain admissions from the unions that they had broken their agreements. In addition some employers insisted on individual re-applications for jobs or offered to re-engage clerical and supervisory workers only if they renounced their unions, or accepted inferior posts, or agreed to a loss of pension rights. A few refused to take any strikers back, or insisted that all strikers should resign from their unions. On 13 May the General Council received

reports . . . from many parts of the country that some employers are attempting to enforce humiliating terms. . . . Telegrams have therefore been sent to affiliated Unions declaring that it is imperative that agreements, understandings, and conditions existing prior to the dispute should be maintained.[64]

[62] Bullock, p. 330.
[63] Arnot, *The General Strike*, p. 216.
[64] Ibid., p. 235.

That evening Baldwin made a statement to the House of Commons:

I will not countenance any attack on the part of any employers to use this present occasion for trying in any way to get reductions in wages below those in force before the strike or any increase of hours. . . . It would be impossible, in our highly organized and highly developed system of industry, to carry on unless you had organisations which could speak for and bind the parties on both sides.[65]

On Friday, 14 May, a railway settlement for a return to work provided for taking back all employees except 'persons who have been guilty of violence and intimidation'. The unions acknowledged that the companies were not thereby surrendering their right to bring actions for damages, admitted their guilt for the 'wrongful act' of calling a strike in breach of their agreement, and undertook in future not to strike without first using the agreed procedure. A number of senior staff who had joined the strike were demoted to junior posts although they retained their former salaries. A week later, due to the reduction in traffic caused by the continued coal stoppage, a supplementary agreement suspended the guaranteed week except for employees who had not struck.

Bevin secured agreements on roughly similar lines in the docks and London Transport, but his officers were still trying to get their members back to work in some provincial passenger transport undertakings in the autumn. On 21 October the employers agreed that the Tramways Joint Industrial Council should resume its functions in return for admissions and promises on much the same lines, with an additional undertaking not to require white collar staff to belong to the unions, or to claim that the council should regulate their pay and conditions. Even so, reinstatement remained a matter for individual authorities, although one of the major undertakings concerned, Hull City Council, agreed to full reinstatement from 1 November.

It is less easy to trace the consequences of the strike in road haulage, which was poorly organised and without national negotiating machinery. In August the union's *Record* reported that agreements were 'practically where they were before the dispute', but there was some victimisation, and 'a certain stiffening of attitude towards us on the other side'. Discipline was harsher and 'cases of insubordination will be more difficult for us to handle'. Newspaper proprietors were incensed by what they regarded as an abrogation of their freedom to publish the news. Several Scottish employers refused to reinstate employees unless they resigned from their unions; and the *Manchester Guardian* set up a house union with a non-contributory pension scheme as an incentive to its employees to avoid strikes. House unions were also established by the

---

[65] *Hansard*, 13 May 1926, cols. 1048, 1050.

papermaking firm of Dickinson, and several other printing and paper companies.

The reports of the Engineers' district organisers for May were full of the difficulties, as the Dundee organiser put it, of 'endeavouring to get men reinstated on the strength of Baldwin's pledge'. In the Midlands and the South few difficulties were encountered with local employers' associations, but there had been dismissals in non-federated firms. In June two Dundee foundries were still refusing to take their shop stewards back, and many men were still out of work in Hull. At Woolwich Arsenal 'some thousands of men' were taken back as new entrants, thus losing entitlement to sick pay and other privileges. Only after appeals to the War Office and questions in the House was unconditional re-engagement offered to them.[66]

The Miners' Lockout

On 14 May Baldwin made a further attempt to persuade the Miners and the coalowners to resume negotiations by proposing legislative and administrative measures for the reorganisation of the industry; and offering a further subsidy of £3 million provided the Miners accepted an immediate wage cut leading on to district wage settlements, with a national board to frame general principles and to decide disputed issues, if need be by chairman's decision. Legislation on hours of work was offered if the parties wanted it. Both sides rejected the proposals. Baldwin announced that the offer of a subsidy would remain open until the end of the month; but the government also renewed the proclamation of emergency, and rationed coal. The industry settled down to a long struggle.

The Miners' reserves together with the funds raised on their behalf at home and overseas amounted to about £3 million. Of this the Russians contributed over £1 million. They transferred the money rejected by the General Council to the Miners and augmented it with further contributions. Three million pounds was roughly equivalent to the coalmining wage bill for one week. When such credit as co-operatives and local tradesmen would allow was exhausted, there were local charities and soup kitchens. Outcropping of coal by miners for their own use and for sale was widespread, and the union could not control it. Once more, however, the main support of the strikers was the Poor Law. The 1921 lockout had added 650,000 persons to the numbers in receipt of relief; in 1926 the increase was 1,200,000.[67] One reason for the increase was the practice adopted by many unions of relieving single

---

[66] Amalgamated Engineering Union, *Monthly Journal*, June, July 1926.
[67] Ministry of Health, *Annual Report*, 1926–1927, p. 116.

strikers, contrary to the Merthyr Tydfil judgment. The Ministry of Health tried to control the situation by issuing a circular to remind the guardians of the judgment, and suggesting a scale of 60p for a wife and 20p for a child up to a maximum of £1.60 a week. The ministry's main sanction was that guardians required its approval to raise loans; and if the banks refused a loan they had to apply direct to the ministry for help.

By the end of the year the total increase in borrowing authorisations was nearly £6 million. A number of boards in mining areas had started with more generous scales but 'by mid-June the official scale was generally accepted'.[68] In July the Boards of Guardians (Default) Act gave the Minister of Health additional powers, which were used to replace the guardians at Chester-le-Street and Bedwellty. By the end of the lockout, twenty-seven unions had 'declined to grant outdoor relief generally to the families of men engaged in the dispute'. Few of the rejected applicants accepted the offer of the workhouse instead. Throughout the stoppage, school meals were 'of the utmost value in dealing with the situation. . . . There is abundant evidence that the health of the children . . . actually improved in many areas during the dispute.'[69]

Beatrice Webb, whose husband was now Member of Parliament for Seaham Harbour, described the mining community in that part of the Durham coalfield in October 1926.

The surface facts show no exceptional distress: indeed the pit villages look clean and prosperous and the inhabitants healthy (death rate unusually low). Various people told us that the men and the boys had benefited by the rest, sun, and open air and abstinence from alcohol and tobacco. . . . And the women freed from coal dust and enjoying regular hours; whilst the children, through the ample supply of first-class food . . . were certainly improved in health and happiness. The one want was clothing and boots. . . . From the early hours of the morning until late at night there was a continual rumbling of hand-barrows past our hotel at Roker; and on the roads there were always long lines of push cycles going to and fro with bulging bags of slack and coal to miners' homes, or peddling the stuff to other workers. . . . As I looked at the gathering of 400 wives and daughters, in their best dresses, and prettily decorated tea tables, with piles of cake and bread-and-butter, it might have been a gathering of prosperous lower middle-class women. . . . They were in a jolly talkative state of mind; they were enjoying their lives.

The men and boys were more silent and sullen; some of the elder men were anxious and wistful.[70]

[68] Ryan, p. 367.
[69] Ministry of Health, *Annual Report*, 1926–1927, p. 122.
[70] *Beatrice Webb's Diaries*, Vol. II, p. 123.

Seaham cannot, of course, be taken as representative of all mining areas. Life was generally harsher where Labour was not in control of the local authorities and the guardians. In Nottingham 'local Boards of Guardians were unsympathetic'.[71] Most of the twenty-seven unions which refused to give outdoor relief generally to miners' families were in the Midlands coalfields. Some unions there cut relief below the ministry scale. In July Lichfield voted to stop all relief to miners' dependants; but that was going too far. The ministry instructed them to withdraw their resolution. Nevertheless, most accounts of life in the mining communities during the lockout emphasise the advantages of open-air life during that long hot summer and autumn—cricket matches and other sports events; collecting blackberries and mushrooms, fishing and poaching; entertainments, rallies, and band competitions; community life, community kitchens, and common meals, sometimes served outdoors.

If the men and boys were less cheerful than the wives and daughters at Seaham in October 1926 the reason may have been their concern about the progress of the lockout, for things were not going well. The rifts within the Miners Federation, which had been fairly well concealed in 1921, were exposed in 1926. As in 1921, the cuts in wages posted at the beginning of the lockout were harsh in the exporting districts—South Wales, Scotland, Durham and Northumberland—and in the dying Lancashire coalfield, but modest in Yorkshire and the smaller Midlands districts. Derby and Nottingham were in a special position, for there the owners had 'decided not to issue notices but to continue working on existing contracts'.[72] These two districts were therefore not locked out, but rather engaged in a sympathetic strike on behalf of the other districts of the federation. Inevitably, therefore, the inclination to settle was greater in Yorkshire and the Midlands than elsewhere, and especially strong in Nottingham and Derby. Moreover, the 1926 stoppage lasted almost seven months, nearly twice as long as the 1921 lockout, and the strains showed more and more clearly as the months passed.

There was also a political division. The strength of the Minority Movement among the miners had increased during the previous two years, and growth accelerated during 1926. The miners, fighting on, appeared to have been deserted by everyone else except the Communist Party. The other unions and the Labour Party leadership were manifestly in favour of a settlement. Even the support of the Independent Labour Party was muted. The Communist Party, however, gave them unstinting support and throve on it. The membership of the party rose from six thousand in April to nearly eleven thousand in

[71] A. R. and C. P. Griffin, p. 135.
[72] J. E. Williams, p. 696.

October—a peak not reached again until well into the thirties. The circulation of the *Workers' Weekly* was up from 60,000 in January to 80,000 in October. The strength of the Minority Movement was concentrated in the lower-paid districts, especially in South Wales, Scotland, and Lancashire, and weakest in the Midlands, thus reinforcing the economic pressures for and against a settlement.

There were also divisions among the majority of the leaders who had little sympathy with the Minority Movement. Most of them realised that their cause was lost long before the final settlement; but some took the view that they must carry on until the majority of their members recognised it too, whereas others thought it was their duty to promote a settlement in order to put an end to the hardships suffered by miners and their families. Both groups could invoke the hallowed argument of the unity of the federation. The diehards argued that to maintain unity, the weaker districts must hang on until the more determined districts were ready to settle; the rest believed that the diehards must appreciate that pressure on those districts which were not threatened by heavy wage cuts would destroy unity unless the federation as a whole agreed to end the lockout. This division existed right at the top of the federation. Cook, whose speaking tours through the coalfields cheered the Minority Movement and rallied the waverers, was nevertheless so eager for a settlement that he was involved in dubious negotiations which were subsequently investigated by a sub-committee of the Miners' executive who found that he had been at fault.[73] By contrast, the stubborn and dour Smith was determined to wait. He had no intention of allowing the Minority Movement to create another myth of betrayal by their leaders of a loyal rank and file who had victory in their grasp.

Soon after the end of the general strike, the Miners approached the transport unions for an embargo on the movement of coal. The railway unions replied that they had carried out their obligations by taking part in the general strike and were 'now engaged in a tremendous fight for the re-employment of all our members'.[74] Bevin also turned them down. He feared that the employers would dismiss dockers who refused to handle coal and the unions would then be faced with the choice between leaving them out of work or calling an all-out strike. The Miners also appealed to the International Miners Federation to prevent coal being exported to Britain, and were given little help by its secretary, Hodges.

In June the government introduced a new Coal Mines Bill to extend the statutory maximum daily hours underground from seven hours to eight. Their information was that the miners would prefer a longer

[73] Griffin, pp. 240–5.
[74] Arnot, *The Miners*, p. 466.

working day to a lower wage, and they believed that the bill, which became law on 8 July, would hasten a settlement. They were wrong. It brought the Miners' executive and the General Council together again, to make a joint protest. There were a number of attempts at private conciliation, the most notable from a group of churchmen headed by the Archbishop of Canterbury. Their proposals were mainly a rehash of the Royal Commission recommendations, but also provided for statutory enforcement of reorganisation and a four-month renewal of the subsidy, during which a new agreement was to be negotiated, with arbitration as a last resort. With Cook's support, these proposals were accepted by the Miners' executive. The Minority Movement opposed them. A conference on 30 July decided to refer them to a district vote. The outcome was a marginal majority against them.

On 19 August the Miners' executive met the Mining Association again, but this was their last meeting. The district employers' associations had rescinded the Mining Association's authority to negotiate on their behalf. Henceforth the only agreements were to be district agreements. On 2 September still another Miners' conference heard that nearly 37,000 men were back at work, almost all of them in the Midlands, and empowered the executive to make a new approach to the government. Next day, Cook wrote offering to negotiate 'a new national agreement with a view to a reduction in labour costs to meet the immediate necessities of the industry'. Churchill, in charge while Baldwin was abroad on holiday, took up the task of conciliation with as much enthusiasm as the editing of the *British Gazette*; but the owners would not consider a national agreement, and Baldwin sent messages advising caution. On his return, the government proposed a national arbitration tribunal to confirm or modify district settlements; but this was rejected by both sides.

On 29 September another Miners' conference heard that 80,000 men—about 6 per cent of the labour force—were back to work. The Mines Department's figures were a good deal higher. Something had to be done. South Wales put before the next conference on 7 October the proposals of the Minority Movement: to revert to the demand for no reduction in wages or increase in working hours; to withdraw the safety men; to place an embargo on imported coal; to ban outcropping; to ask a special meeting of Congress for financial support; and to intensify propaganda. Their resolution was put to a district vote and carried by rather less than a two-thirds majority.

The results were meagre. Intensified picketing brought a temporary drop in the number of men at work, and a rise in the number of miners arrested and sentenced. Calling out the safety men had little effect. The colliery enginemen's unions had left the Miners Federation after the

1921 lockout. Shirkie, their spokesman, explained their grievances to a meeting of the London members of the General Council on 11 July 1922. The Miners, he said, had allowed safety work to be done by 'military and naval men and any other persons . . . but the Executive would not authorise their own men to do the work'. As a result, 'Enginemen were idle today and officials or some of the underground workers who had taken the Enginemen's jobs during the strike were doing the work, where work was to be had'. The meeting decided that, deplorable though secession was, the enginemen's unions were now entitled to separate affiliation to Congress except in South Wales, where they had 'sunk their identity' in the South Wales Miners Federation. Consequently in 1926 Shirkie was able to call the Miners' decision 'a gigantic piece of bluff. . . . They have no power whatever to call out safety men.'[75] On 2 November the transport unions again refused to impose an embargo on the movement of coal. Next day a conference of union executives agreed to a levy on behalf of the Miners—but it was to be voluntary.

Meanwhile the unity of the federation had been openly breached. At the beginning of October a return to work was under discussion at the Digby and New London collieries in Nottingham. The men appealed to the secretary of the Nottingham Miners, George Spencer, to take over the negotiations to try to ensure that everyone got their jobs back. He agreed to try, and succeeded. For this he was excluded from the Miners' conference on 8 October. The Nottingham Miners' council suspended him. On 20 November he and some of his colleagues met the Nottinghamshire owners to negotiate a county settlement under which the faceworkers earning 64p a shift before the lockout would initially get 83p a shift; and went on to form the Nottinghamshire and District Miners Industrial Union. In South Wales it was none other than Ablett who signed an agreement at the Plymouth collieries in Merthyr on 13 November to save the jobs of the miners there. For this he was suspended by the South Wales Miners Federation, but subsequently reinstated. He had, of course, no thought of setting up a rival union.[76]

The unsatisfactory results of the policy of intensifying the strike led the Miners' conference on 5 November to send the executive back to the government, who told them the 'general principles' on which the district owners' associations were now prepared to conclude district settlements. Over the next few days the executive could extract no concessions on hours of work or on national negotiations. Despite a recommendation from the executive to accept these terms, they were rejected by a majority of three to two in a district vote. Durham, Lancashire,

[75] *The Times*, 9 October 1926.
[76] Francis and Smith, p. 237.

Northumberland, Scotland and South Wales all voted against acceptance. On 19 November the conference met again to learn that, according to the Mines Department, 366,000 miners, nearly a third of the labour force, were back at work.

In the Midlands districts the proportion at work was about three-quarters; in Lancashire close to a half; in Scotland a third; and nearly a quarter in Yorkshire; but only one in seven in South Wales. Lancashire proposed that they should fight on, but won no support. A proposal to ballot was also rejected, Carter of Nottingham pointing out that he had only four thousand members still on strike and eligible to vote. Before the vote could be taken, he said, 'there will be districts practically as bad as we are at the present time'. Eventually the South Wales delegates carried a resolution instructing the districts to negotiate their own agreements, subject to certain 'general principles', and report back to a further conference before signature. A final conference met on 26 November to hear the reports. The owners in Nottingham and the three tiny coalfields of Bristol and Somerset, Kent, and Leicester had refused to meet union representatives. Other districts were allowed to go ahead whether or not their draft agreements conformed to the executive's general principles. By the end of the month work had been resumed everywhere, with or without agreements.

For most miners, the immediate consequences were not so harsh as they might have feared. The main reduction in labour costs came from an increase in working hours, but the eight-hour shift underground which had now been sanctioned by law was by no means universal. Yorkshire, Nottingham, and Derby had settled for seven hours and a half, and so had the faceworkers in Durham and Northumberland. For surface workers the increase in most districts was half an hour a shift, making forty-nine hours a week. Because of the increase in the price of coal due to the stoppage, earnings per man/shift overall were 53p in the first quarter of 1927, just above the average for the year 1925. District earnings ranged from 66p a shift in Nottingham and Derby to $43\frac{1}{2}$p in Northumberland. However, several of the more prosperous districts had arranged for a relatively generous initial minimum percentage addition to standard which was to fall month by month. By the first quarter of 1928 average earnings a shift were down to 47p overall, with Nottingham and Derby at 52p and Northumberland at $40\frac{1}{2}$p.

The extension of working hours was followed by a considerable increase in output per shift. Between 1925 and 1927, annual output per head in coalmining rose by 12 per cent, and by 1929 there had been a further rise of 5 per cent. The increase in working hours is not, however, the only explanation for this improvement. Many unproductive pits were closed, and the tonnage cut by machines increased by a half between 1925 and 1929, while the number of conveyors doubled. Since the demand for coal did not rise significantly, the consequence was a level of unemployment far above the national average, at well over 20 per cent in 1928.

Inquest and Aftermath

Soon after the end of the general strike, the General Council and the Miners agreed to refrain from airing their differences over its conduct in public. A pamphlet by Cook, *The Nine Days*, containing a strongly-worded attack on the General Council, was withdrawn from publication; and the conference of trade union executives arranged for 25 June to review the council's discharge of their responsibilities was postponed. When it was finally held on 20 and 21 January 1927, it proved a disappointment for the council's critics. After all the recriminations and charges of bad faith had been heard, the difference amounted to this: the General Council insisted that the Miners had handed over the conduct of the dispute to them, and the Miners had therefore forfeited any claim to further support from the rest of the movement once they had rejected the Samuel memorandum; whereas the Miners declared that the memorandum was useless because it was not backed by the government. Less attention was paid to the central issue: whether or not at the end of the first week of the strike the time had arrived for the General Council to call off the general strike on the best available pretext. The Miners found few supporters, and the majority in favour of the council was not far off three to one.

Few wanted to argue that the general strike should not have been called. Bevin had already given his opinion in his union's *Record* for May–July 1926: 'We could have saved our money—but would have lost our soul.' For the future, there were those who said with Cramp: 'Never again',[77] and those who agreed with Ben Turner:

I hope never again, but if a great moral issue arises in this Kingdom where injustice is going to be done as was going to be done, or was tried to be done, to the miners, I hope a similar effort will be made by the great Trades Union Movement.[78]

However, both sides agreed on the choice of a scapegoat. Cramp told the conference that he did not blame the General Council for calling off the strike but 'our people who for years made it impossible for the General Council to resist the general strike'.[79] His audience knew whom he had in mind: the Minority Movement and the Communist Party. At the

[77] Trades Union Congress, *National Strike Special Conference*, pp. 56–7.
[78] Ibid., p. 59.
[79] Ibid., p. 57.

Railwaymen's conference in July 1926, Thomas had replied to attacks on his part in the strike by producing a Communist document instructing delegates how to vote on the resolutions on the agenda. Similar instructions were exposed at Congress that year, and at the Miners' annual conference in 1927. Early in 1927, the General and Municipal Workers' executive broke the movement's organisation in their London district by suspending branches and disqualifying members of the movement from office. It was ruled that no Communist Party or Minority Movement member could hold any official position in the union, and the rule was promptly and vigorously applied by the Lancashire district secretary, Dukes.

In 1924 the General Council had taken control of the Trades Councils. A National Federation of Trades Councils had been formed at a meeting in Birmingham in 1922. Its conference next year showed signs of Communist influence. Palme Dutt of the Labour Research Department had organised it, and Pollitt was in the chair. The General Council decided to move in. In 1924 they agreed with representatives of thirty-five major Trades Councils to set up a joint consultative committee of six a side, and established that the councils should be the local agents of Congress. The federation was therefore abandoned, and Trades Council conferences were henceforth held under the auspices of the General Council. Model rules introduced by the council in 1926 established that the affiliation of Trades Councils to the Minority Movement was inconsistent with the policy of Congress; and in 1927 this decision was enforced on those councils which had retained their affiliations with the movement. In May 1927 the Communist majority was ousted from the executive of the London Trades Council. The General Council's actions were approved by an overwhelming majority at Congress in September, including the Miners. Smith vented his feelings with an attack on

the abuse and . . . the obstruction that the minority movement is out for and has been carrying on all this time. I see no difference between the Minority Movement and Communism: they get their orders from Moscow in each case.[80]

The one significant achievement of the left on the General Council had been the Anglo-Russian Joint Advisory Committee through which they 'had gotten [the] TUC so hopelessly tangled up with the Russians that by the time anyone realised how constricting a net it could be, it seemed impossible to disentangle'.[81] However, the International Federation of Trade Unions continued to insist that the Russians must make a formal application to join the federation before unity negotiations could begin,

[80] Trades Union Congress, 1927, p. 320.
[81] Calhoun, p. 202.

and that the Russians refused to do. The general strike caused rifts between the Russians and the British. The Russians vehemently criticised its conduct and the General Council refused to accept their money. The General Council protested against the refusal of a visa to Tomsky to attend Congress in September 1926, but it did not follow that they wished to see him there.

Trade union membership in Britain fell by a little over 10 per cent between the end of 1925 and the end of 1927. The total loss was 570,000, and since the loss of the Miners and the groups mainly concerned in the general strike—railways, road transport, docks, printing, metals and engineering, and construction—was 483,000, it seems reasonable to attribute it mainly to the effects of the general strike and the miners' lockout. The Miners lost most (26 per cent), followed by the railway unions (22 per cent).

In 1925 the unions had feared a general attack by the employers on their wages and conditions. The aftermath of the general strike might have given the employers a convenient opportunity to carry through such an attack; but it did not happen. No considerable group of workers, apart from the miners, suffered an extension of agreed working hours, either in 1926 or 1927. The major reduction in wages outside coalmining in 1926 was in railways, due to adjustments under their cost-of-living sliding scale. In 1927 coalmining wages fell again as district minimum percentage additions were reduced under the agreements signed at the end of the lockout. Otherwise there were further reductions arising from cost of living scales in the railways and in several other industries, and in steel from their selling price scales, but these were offset by an increase of 20p a week for engineering timeworkers. Without the changes in miners' pay, the overall index of wage rates would have remained almost stable through 1926 and 1927.

Stability in wages was due to general economic stability. The employers did not attack because they did not have to attack. Apart from the effect of the miners' lockout in the summer and autumn of 1926, the unemployment index was steady in that year, and in 1927 it fell from 12 per cent in January to under 10 per cent in December. The 14 per cent fall in wholesale prices in 1925, which had led to threats of wage cuts, flattened out thereafter. Both wholesale and retail prices fell slowly through 1927 and 1928, the overall reduction being about 4 per cent in each index. Together with stable wages, falling retail prices increased the purchasing power of most British workers outside coalmining, while rising productivity prevented this trend from imposing any serious pressure on labour costs. These trends in wages and prices give further grounds for doubting that the return to the gold standard can have been the major cause of the coal industry's problems.

In July 1926 the cabinet returned at greater leisure to their proposal for a change in the law to penalise unions and union leaders for participation in a general strike. Various other proposals for amendments to existing labour law were dusted off and the employers' organisations were consulted. The Federation of British Industries and the Confederation of Employers Organisations again debated the boundaries of their respective responsibilities, and agreed that the confederation should deal with the matter, but after consulting with the federation. Their main proposals were for drastic amendments to the 1906 Act to curtail the protection of unions and union leaders from actions for damages or injunctions in industrial disputes, and to limit picketing. The cabinet's concern was to outlaw general strikes, and they 'discountenanced any alterations of the immunities granted in 1906 as politically inexpedient',[82] though they agreed to some modifications in the law on picketing. More effective pressure came from the Conservative backbenchers and constituency parties, who wanted legislation to injure the Labour Party by cutting back trade union expenditure on politics; and they had their way, despite the objection of Steel-Maitland to this partisan proposal. A bill was put together early in 1927, and became law in July.

The Trade Disputes and Trade Unions Act 1927, as it was called, declared a strike illegal if it

(i) has any object other than or in addition to the furtherance of a trade dispute within the trade or industry in which the strikers are engaged; and
(ii) is a strike designed or calculated to coerce the government, either directly or indirectly by inflicting hardship on the community.

Despite many confident assertions over the years that this section rendered sympathetic strikes illegal, it did so only if they fulfilled the requirement of the second sub-section. Illegal lockouts were defined in corresponding terms. The consequence was to remove the protection of existing legislation, including the 1906 Act, from disputes which fell within these definitions, and penalties were prescribed for declaring, instigating, and inciting others to take part in such stoppages; but it was not an offence merely to cease work. Those who refused to take part in such stoppages were protected from victimisation. No case was ever brought before a court under this part of the Act.

By defining 'intimidation' as causing 'reasonable apprehension of injury' to a person, or his family or his dependants, or 'of violence or damage to any person or property', section three raised fears that it had rendered useless the existing legal protection of picketing, since that did

---

[82] Phillips, *The General Strike*, p. 276.

not apply where intimidation was used. In fact it caused less trouble than might have been expected.

Section four revised the rules governing trade union political funds. Previously a union member who did not wish to contribute had to contract out; now contributions could be collected only from those who had contracted in. The effect was to make apathy work against the Labour Party instead of for it; but not necessarily to satisfy the Conservative desire to remove any danger of undue pressure to contribute. Where pressure had previously been effective to persuade union members not to contract out, as for example among Miners, pressure to contract in might be almost equally persuasive.

The fifth section prevented civil service unions from associating with unions outside the service, thus forcing them to withdraw from Congress and the Labour Party. However, it went on to make exceptions, one of which, strangely enough, had the effect of excluding the only civil servants who had participated on any scale in the general strike, namely those in government industrial establishments. The sixth section met the wishes of the National Confederation of Employers Organisations by forbidding local and other public authorities to require contractors to impose a closed shop on their employees. It also forbade such authorities to require their own employees to belong to a union, and made wilful breach of contract by their employees a criminal offence in certain circumstances.

The Labour Party and the General Council organised a national campaign against the bill while it was before parliament, drawing attention to what they saw as its defects; but they failed to arouse much enthusiasm and could not prevent its passage.

The general strike was the most important episode in the history of British trade unionism, and the inquest on it has continued to this day. Some points are established. There was no possibility of a settlement in the coal industry without outside intervention. The economic position of the industry was such that, without the subsidy, the coalowners had to secure a substantial cut in labour costs through wage reductions, or an extension of working hours, or both; and the Miners could not accept such a worsening of their position without resistance. Had their executive tried to settle on such terms before the lockout they would have been repudiated by a conference; and even if a majority of conference delegates had supported them, the terms would have had to be referred to a ballot which would have been overwhelmingly hostile, as would a vote by the district councils if the issue had been referred to them instead.

There is more room for argument over the inevitability of a general strike called by the General Council. The council was certainly anxious to settle, and tried hard to find a peace formula in their discussions with Baldwin and his colleagues over the weekend before the strike; but there was at no time any likelihood of agreement. The cabinet and their negotiators would not consider a settlement without a commitment to wage cuts, whereas the General Council were not prepared to accept wage cuts without the consent of the Miners' executive; and that could not be had. There were, of course, differences in approach within each side. Had it been agreed to refer the matter to Thomas and Baldwin for a final decision there might well have been no general strike; but it was not left to them, nor could it have been.

Even if some General Council members besides Thomas might have considered deserting the Miners, there were three considerations to deter them. The first was Red Friday: how could they persuade their members that the movement which had been able to save the Miners in July 1925 was not able to do so now? The second was their fear of a repetition of Black Friday. As Bevin put it in his union's *Record* for May–July 1926:

One had to face the psychological problem of one's own members with 'Black Friday' still looming in mind and the suspense and fear that something of the sort would happen again.

The same point was made by many other union leaders. The third was that the Miners gave the General Council no ready excuse for deserting them. On Black Friday the Miners had insisted on maintaining their demand for the national pool, which their own leaders were known to be anxious to drop and for which other union leaders, including their Triple Alliance partners, had little sympathy. On this occasion, by contrast, the Miners had relinquished authority to negotiate over their claims to the General Council, subject only to consultation.

There remains the government. It is almost inconceivable that they could have renewed the subsidy so as to allow further negotiations unless they had first been given a firm commitment to accept wage cuts. In addition to their own convictions on this point, they also had to consider their followers, especially those in parliament, many of whom had been unhappy over Red Friday, and would not have tolerated what they would have seen as an abject and wholly unnecessary surrender.

A number of historians have nevertheless maintained that the government could and should have averted the strike. Phillips, the author of the most authoritative account of the general strike, believes that the government could have achieved a settlement without 'a departure from cherished principle' although that 'may have required an intellectual capacity to grapple with complex industrial issues, an imagination to take the long rather than the short view, and the courage to meet ill-informed criticism'.[83] According to Bullock, the government should have taken 'action to provide the basis of agreement' instead of 'making agreement a precondition of Government action', thereby inviting 'one side or the other to exercise a veto'.[84]

For these opinions to be accepted, there must have been a solution to the economic problems of the industry which the government could have perceived by grappling with the issues, and imposed with at least the reluctant acquiescence of the Miners and the owners. Given the political circumstances, this solution had to enable the industry to pay its way with no more than a limited and temporary subsidy, and no worsening in wages and conditions beyond what the Miners could be persuaded to accept. The only proposals which purported to meet these conditions were those of the Samuel report. Although Baldwin and his colleagues disliked it, they were prepared to go along with it, provided it was accepted by both sides. The General Council were willing to accept it provided the Miners agreed, and the Miners at least did not refuse to discuss it. There seemed to be a possibility that some compromise could be put together provided the owners concurred; and there was even some sympathy for the report among the owners. Mond, who controlled one of the anthracite combines, was busy arguing the case for government loans to assist amalgamations, the closure of uneconomic pits, and co-operative selling along with international price agreements.

Mond, however, was a far from typical coalowner. His main experience had been in the expanding and profitable chemicals industry, where amalgamations had demonstrated their advantages, and international price agreements could be made between the big combines in the major producing countries; and anthracite differed from other types of coal in that it enjoyed an expanding demand. The great majority of coal-owners did not believe in the Samuel report's optimistic forecasts of the results of reorganisation. Both then and since, the coalowners have been condemned as pigheaded and smallminded. No doubt they were; but it does not prove they were wrong about the prospects for reorganisation. The commission's conclusions concerning the economies of large-scale colliery operations rested on a misreading of the evidence. They had not quantified the benefits of reorganisation; and they had not estimated how long it would take to carry through. In both respects their expectations were exaggerated.

The 'five counties' scheme[85] was soon to show that the price of coal on the home market could be forced up by limitation of output; but similar schemes introduced in Scotland and South Wales showed that

[83] Ibid., p. 133.
[84] Bullock, p. 294.
[85] See p. 483.

the exporting districts had little to gain in this way, and in any case the benefits in the five counties would not have gone far to fill the gap between the Miners' claim and the owners' offer in 1926. Only an open-ended subsidy could have permitted the owners to make an offer which the Miners might have accepted, and that had been rejected both by the report and by the government.

11

Industrial Relations in the Twenties

Collective Bargaining under Stable Conditions

INDUSTRIAL relations were unprecedentedly calm during 1927, 1928, and the first half of 1929. The number of recorded strikes and the number of working days lost through strikes fell to the lowest figures since systematic recording had begun nearly forty years earlier. Few people on either side of industry were looking for trouble, and they were helped to keep the peace by the stability of the economy.

Stability, however, did not begin in 1927. The economy as a whole had been nearly stable since the summer of 1923. Unemployment had not moved much above 12 per cent or much below 10 per cent, except during the coal lockout in 1926. In the first half of 1924 the index of wage rates had been pushed up by 3 per cent; from June 1924 to December 1926 it was almost stationary; and it then slid gently down towards the level of January 1924, which was almost reached by the end of 1929. Retail prices wavered around a slowly falling trend of about 1 per cent a year. Industrial relations had been disturbed by the opportunities for industrial action which the brief economic improvement during the second half of 1923 and the first half of 1924 offered to the unions, and by the special problems of the coalmining industry in 1925 and 1926.

It did not follow that wages were static. Most industries experienced wage adjustments upwards or downwards, and in some industries both; but many of these changes were the automatic consequence of the application of existing agreements. Where new rates of wages were negotiated, the discussions often went on for many months, even years, showing that neither side was anxious to precipitate a stoppage and that neither was under great pressure to produce results.

By January 1928 falling profits had brought every coalmining district down to the minimum rates prescribed by the profit-sharing agreements which had ended the lockout; and thereafter additional cuts were made in the North East. The Durham owners had already proposed a further reduction. Since organised resistance was impossible, the Durham Miners agreed to let the claim go to arbitration. The award reduced the earnings of faceworkers by about 6p a shift and cut the subsistence allowance of the lowest-paid adults by 1p a shift. Several collieries were struck unofficially when the award came into force on 1 March, and in others the owners subsequently served notices of dismissal to put an end to restriction of output which had cut the tonnage produced in at least one pit by more than half. Northumberland suffered similar cuts.

Seasonal fluctuations in prices brought wage adjustments under cost-of-living sliding scale agreements which now regulated the pay of some 2.5 million workers; and the scales began to work capriciously. The overall wage movement in the Yorkshire dyeing industry in the four years 1923–6 was from 78 per cent to 76 per cent over base rates, but meanwhile there were sixteen adjustments upwards or downwards in response to small fluctuations in the index. A movement of a few points in the index would bring wage adjustments in some industries but not in others because of differences in detailed arrangements. Some scales, including the Yorkshire dyeing agreement, prescribed quarterly adjustments; others, such as the civil service, had six-monthly reviews; whereas building and footwear held annual assessments. The usual criterion was the average level of the index figure over the previous three, six or twelve months compared with the preceding period, but there were differences in the minimum change in the index required for an adjustment in pay. A movement of five points triggered the civil service scale; building stipulated 6.25 points; and the footwear scale operated only outside the range of 50–70 per cent above the prewar base line. In these circumstances it became more and more common for employers to undertake for a period not to apply downward adjustments warranted by their scales, and such agreements cost them relatively little. Following a one-year period of stabilisation in 1923, the gas industry's negotiators agreed another in 1925 and renewed it every year until 1930; the Tramways Joint Industrial Council stabilised in 1924, and London busmen in 1926.

In 1928 Dukes, whose union—the General and Municipal Workers—was probably a party to as many sliding scale agreements as any other, proposed to Congress that sliding scale arrangements should be abolished, because 'the automatic adjustment of wages . . . seriously restricts freedom to secure advances in wages where an industry has the capacity and prosperity to meet fair and justifiable demands'. This may have been true of prosperous industries, but, with the abolition of sliding scales, railwaymen and civil servants would presumably have reverted to their standard rates, losing what was left of their cost of living bonuses. Cramp replied that Dukes's proposal was 'playing the employers' game so far as railwaymen were concerned', and it was voted down.[1]

[1] Trades Union Congress, 1928, pp. 486–7.

The railway companies experienced their most successful year of the decade in 1923. Thereafter receipts fell. In 1925 the companies asked for a pay cut in addition to sliding scale adjustments to put them back on their feet. The proposal went to the Railway Wages Board which found against a general reduction, but decided that new entrants should not be entitled to what was left of the cost of living bonus. They should receive only the standard rate. In 1928 the companies renewed their proposal for a temporary all-round pay reduction. Due mainly to increasing competition from road transport, the long-term trend in their financial results was still downward, despite a recovery from the heavy losses incurred during the general strike and the coal lockout, which had brought a restoration of the guaranteed week in 1927; despite the advantage of the fall in coal prices; and despite the benefits of rationalisation, which had brought total staff down from 736,000 in 1921 to 677,000 in 1928. In these circumstances the unions decided they should negotiate. They whittled down the proposals to a 2.5 per cent cut for every employee from directors downwards. After hearing their president extol the virtues of 'both sides putting their best into the industry without either side becoming sentimental or suspicious of the interests of the other, in order to improve and obtain the maximum results from the industry', the Railwaymen's delegates voted to accept; and the other two unions fell into line.

The railway workshops had at last acquired negotiating machinery acceptable to both the Railwaymen and the craft unions. In 1925 they had jointly resisted a wage reduction. Encouraged by this success, the unions proceeded to resolve their differences. By July 1926 they had accepted that each union should retain existing members, but henceforth follow agreed procedures on transfer and promotion. The vexed question of the recruitment of craftsmen by the Railwaymen was resolved by stipulating that non-union craftsmen should be approached 'to join a union catering for their occupation'. Next they agreed to conduct general negotiations jointly, leaving craft questions to be handled separately by the unions concerned. They met the companies to establish a Railway Shopmen's National Council for national negotiations, with elected line committees for issues concerning one company, and works and shop committees for local issues. The Railwaymen at first objected to the arbitration procedure for reference to the Industrial Court by consent of both sides, but in 1927 changed their minds. The new procedure was inaugurated. The craft unions were, therefore, understandably aggrieved to find that the Railwaymen had signed the 1928 agreement for a 2.5 per cent cut on behalf of the shopmen, subject to 'the assent of any other Trade Union concerned with the deduction'. According to the Engineers' journal for September

1928, the craft unions denounced this arrangement as 'unprecedented and without parallel in the annals of trade unionism', but, after meetings with the companies and the Railwaymen, which 'had a tendency to become acrimonious', they decided to accept. With weekly earnings averaging £3.48 in 1927, the shopmen would still be well in front of other engineering workers even after the cut had been applied.

The wool industry's 1925 agreement to stabilise wages ran out in 1927, but the employers made no proposals for reductions nationally, although there were one or two local wage cuts which the union decided it would be unwise to resist.

The cotton employers were seeking other means than wage cuts to promote the recovery of their industry. Early in 1923 a committee led by Macara proposed a prohibition on the sale of yarn below cost price, with a joint board of operatives and employers to regulate production and to protect operatives from undue hardship. Later in the year another committee set up by the Lord Mayor of Manchester made similar recommendations, but were forced to abandon them by opposition from the relatively prosperous Egyptian cotton spinning firms and the weaving employers.

In 1925 Macara's committee took advice on the legality of a proposal that minimum prices should be enforced by strikes. They were told such action would be within the law, but they had not consulted the unions. The *Cotton Factory Times* of 16 October ventured to doubt whether there could be a 'scheme of control which would meet in any substantial way the wishes of the workers'. Next year the committee were replaced by a more militant body, the Cotton Yarn Association, which, according to the *Cotton Factory Times* of 26 August 1927,

appears to be going to and fro with a big stick. We hear of threatenings of what may befall those firms who stand outside its scheme of salvation that put to shame the pressure which it is sometimes alleged the wicked trade unionist indulges in.

This new association set out to detach the spinning firms from their allegiance to the established federation. In this they achieved little success; but the *Cotton Factory Times* of 30 December attributed a proposal from the Master Spinners that there should be an extension of the working week and a reduction in pay to pressure from the new association.

The employers voted on the proposals in May 1928. Under the Master Spinners' rules, the votes of their members were weighted according to the number of spindles in use in each mill, and a majority of 80 per cent was required to sanction a lockout. In the American section the vote for posting notices was 66.68 per cent, but in the

Egyptian section only 28.39 per cent. The proposal was, therefore, dropped for the time being.

Wage changes in the steel industry resulted not only from their selling-price sliding scales, but also from a reform of the pay structure. In 1924 the Iron and Steel Trades Confederation had agreed to a temporary restoration of their Ways and Means agreement, which extended weekend working, in return for special bonuses for low-paid timeworkers. However, prices continued to fall and wages followed, including those of the low-paid. In 1926 their wages were stabilised, but the union wanted more than that. They forced the issue in 1927 by giving notice to terminate the Ways and Means agreement, unless tonnage rates were extended to those currently on time rates. This move reflected a shift of power within the union due to a change in production methods. At one time the melting shops had been manned by melters on tonnage rates and labourers on time rates, but now many of the ancillary workers, still paid time rates, were men operating charging machines, cranes, and other mechanical equipment, which demanded considerable skill. Promotion lines were established whereby labourers could rise to their positions; and their status and power within the union was recognised by a change in the structure of collective bargaining.

Traditionally negotiations had been conducted by branch delegates, and the 'branches were . . . dominated by the tonnage paid workers'. In the negotiations which now began, the employers insisted that there must be no reference back to the branches. The union gave plenary powers to its negotiators, but nevertheless called a meeting of branch delegates to get their acceptance to the principle of a reduction in the melters' earnings above a certain tonnage, if that would give a satisfactory agreement for the lower-paid. A series of settlements were signed over the winter of 1928–9. The Ways and Means agreement became permanent. There were increases in the base rates of all workers below 40p a shift, and tonnage rates were introduced for 'all grades of Workmen in occupations which directly influenced or controlled output'.[2] These changes were partly financed by a revision in the melters' tonnage rates. The lowest were increased, but most were reduced. The maximum reduction was 30 per cent and the average was 13 per cent. This was a considerable sacrifice on the part of the melters, but in 1925 the average earnings of first-hand melters had been £11.37, and the average for all melters £8.56,[3] compared with average earnings for male manual workers in all industries covered by the Ministry of Labour's 1924 inquiry of below £3, and the steel industry's average of £3.05.

[2] Wilkinson, pp. 124–5.
[3] Ibid., p. 119.

In the second half of the decade, the pay increase which affected the largest number of workers was in engineering, an industry which had suffered exceptional wage cuts and unemployment in the depression of 1921–3, but now began to show distinct signs of recovery. During 1927 the engineering labour force started to expand again as the growth of the motor vehicle, aircraft, and electrical engineering sections, situated mainly in the Midlands and the South East, began to outweigh the continued decline in locomotive building, marine engineering, textile machinery, and general engineering, concentrated in the North, Scotland and Northern Ireland.

In 1923 union district committees in the more prosperous areas began to submit claims for advances; but the employers' federation was determined that there should be no return to district bargaining over rates of pay and hours of work. Their local associations referred all the claims to central conference, where they were rejected. In 1924 the unions submitted a national application for an advance of £1 a week, which was also rejected. Next year the employers offered to discuss the possibility of increased pay, in return for concessions by the unions on working conditions. Initially the unions refused, but the Minister of Labour persuaded them to nominate members to a joint committee to investigate specific proposals. In return for an extension of the working week from forty-seven to fifty hours at current hourly rates, elimination of all restrictions on output, 'relaxation of the claim of any class of workpeople to an exclusive right to any operations or any particular job', and reductions in overtime and nightshift payments, they were offered a pay increase of 10p a week. These terms must have seemed harsh to every engineering worker, and especially so to the craftsmen who were being asked to sell their heritage for 10p a week. Nevertheless, the unions did not terminate the joint committee until January 1926, when they instructed the districts to put in their own claims. By April fifty-three district applications for an increase of £1 a week had been turned down, and the industry had been brought to the edge of another lockout.

In November 1925, with the approval of their district committee, the shop stewards at the London works of a printing machine manufacturer, R. Hoe, submitted a claim for the £1 advance to their employer, and supported it with an overtime ban. In January the seven hundred Engineers employed by the firm stopped work, adding to their pay claim a demand for a closed shop. They were joined by two hundred members of the Electricians, the Patternmakers, and the general unions. The employers' federation posted notices of a national lockout for 13 March. The union leaders ordered the strikers to return to work. Their instructions were rejected by the strike committee. The notices were postponed to allow the Engineers to summon a special conference which upheld the executive's decision. Even so the strike committee indulged in further cliff-hanging before giving in.

In April 1926 the employers' federation offered $12\frac{1}{2}$p a week for more modest concessions on conditions, but these were still too onerous for the unions. Finally a settlement was reached in 1927 for an increase of 10p a week for timeworkers only, with no changes in conditions, and ratified by two to one in a vote of union members. In 1928 the unions submitted a new national claim—this time for 40p a week—and instituted their own 'investigations with regard to the position in the various sections of the engineering industry' which may have been intended to lead on to sectional pay claims. Negotiations on the claim dragged on into 1930.

Discrimination in favour of timeworkers was justified by the rising earnings of pieceworkers. Average weekly earnings of male workers in federated firms rose from £3.03 in April 1924 to £3.20$\frac{1}{2}$ in March 1927—an increase of nearly 6 per cent. Since there were no general or district pay advances during that period, this increase was due to growth in pieceworkers' earnings, and to a rising proportion of pieceworkers. Workers paid by results earned substantially more than timeworkers, £3.63$\frac{1}{2}$ a week compared with £2.79 in 1927; and the proportion of workers paid by results, which had fallen in the aftermath of the war, was now rising again, from 38.4 per cent in 1923 to 49.6 per cent in 1927.[4]

The shipbuilding employers, like the engineering employers, had approached their unions with proposals for a joint investigation of their industry's problems in 1925. Unlike their colleagues in engineering, however, the shipbuilding unions refused to discuss changes in wages, and the talks concentrated on methods of production. An interim report, which appeared in the autumn, found that sub-division of labour in the British shipyards had hindered interchangeability, and suggested that greater flexibility could be introduced without 'infringing upon the broad principles of craftsmanship'. It also proposed that labour-saving machinery should be encouraged, and that both sides should co-operate in securing 'all such reductions in cost as can be obtained from the fullest use of machinery and methods conducive to economic output'.[5] However, no specific changes were agreed to further these objectives. The Shipwrights decided that 'all questions of interchangeability must

[4] Yates, pp. 117–24. The earnings of workers in federated firms, which were generally the larger firms, and accounted for about half the industry's labour force, were higher than those in the industry as a whole. The Ministry of Labour's figure for the average earnings of male engineering workers in 1928 was £2.80 a week.

[5] *Ministry of Labour Gazette*, November 1925.

be settled amongst the trades concerned as occasion arises',[6] and the other unions seem to have been of the same opinion.

The reluctance of the unions to discuss wages had been due to their fear that the employers might make proposals for further reductions. By 1928 there were sufficient signs of recovery for the unions themselves to raise the subject with a claim for an advance of 50p a week. Eventually a settlement was made for a 15p increase for shipbuilding workers, but not for shiprepair workers, who had up to this time enjoyed a 15p differential. The agreement therefore established standard national time rates.

There were no serious challenges to the principles of national bargaining in engineering. The district pay claims of 1926 had been concerted by union head offices, and were repulsed by the employers without difficulty, apart from the solitary instance of the Hoe dispute. So reconciled had the major craft unions become to the employers' insistence on one general pay agreement covering all manual workers that the Boilermakers, Engineers and Foundryworkers had consented to work together with the other engineering unions in an Engineering Joint Trades Movement which handled national pay negotiations. In 1929 the Patternmakers in Glasgow had the temerity to submit a district pay claim, and to support it with an overtime ban after it had been turned down at both local and central conferences. At this stage the Engineering Employers Federation had to concede that the ban was not in breach of procedure, but, on 31 October, their management board insisted that the Patternmakers were also party to 'an arrangement between the Federation and the various Trade Unions that wages questions should be dealt with on a national basis', which had been violated by the ban. They threatened to 'support' their members affected by the ban, and it was called off.

The shipbuilding employers were faced with more emphatic assertions of individual union autonomy, especially from the Boilermakers. Up to 1924 the unions had negotiated general issues through the Federation of Engineering and Shipbuilding Trades. In that year the Boilermakers left the federation as a result of their independent stand over the overtime and nightshift agreement. Shortly afterwards the other major craft unions—the Electricians, the Painters, the Patternmakers, the Shipwrights, and the Woodworkers—also withdrew, leaving the federation to a few minor craft unions and the general unions. It was this truncated body, dominated by the General and Municipal Workers, which negotiated the new procedure agreement of 1926. The dissident craft unions—except for the Boilermakers—then came together to form a Shipbuilding Trades Committee, which signed

[6] Dougan, p. 212.

a closely similar document in 1927. It was also put to the Boilermakers, who voted it down in two successive ballots. In 1929 the employers offered special concessions on piecework issues to tempt the Boiler-makers to think again. Two more ballots rejected their offer. The employers then gave notice that the agreement, together with the amendments on piecework, would be deemed to apply to the Boiler-makers from 1 November. Still another ballot was held. It returned an increased majority against the agreement. Nevertheless the unions continued to negotiate collectively over pay.

The most important conflict over craft and local autonomy took place in the building industry. In 1925 the Building Trade Workers and the Plasterers withdrew from the National Federation of Building Trades Operatives, and left the National Wages and Conditions Council in the following year. The motives of the Plasterers were not in doubt. Their craft was the most affected by the current labour shortage, and they believed they could force the employers to pay higher wages if they negotiated locally and on their own. The bricklayers, who formed the great majority of the Building Trade Workers' membership, may have been influenced by the same motive; but they gave as their reason the failure of the employers to negotiate an agreement to compensate them for 'wet time', an issue which concerned them more than most other trades since their work was mainly on the outside of buildings. Their general secretary, Hicks, may have believed that he could force the employers to make concessions on the issue if his union went ahead on their own. There were also suspicions that he was trying to construct some new alliance or merger of building unions in which he would be the dominant figure.

At first it seemed that the federation might break up, but the largest union, the Woodworkers, remained loyal. They had never allowed their districts the degree of autonomy enjoyed by the Bricklayers; their labour was not in short supply to the same extent as that of the Plasterers; and they attached a good deal of importance to the constitution of the National Joint Council for the Building Industry, which had been negotiated, through the federation, to replace the National Wages and Conditions Council. The employers delayed ratification when they found that the Building Trade Workers and Plasterers were withdraw-ing. However, the Painters had even stronger reasons than the Woodworkers for loyalty to the federation and the national agreements, which provided the main props for their members' claim to the same wage rate as other craftsmen. There had already been a good deal of erosion of this principle locally to show the Painters what to expect if the props were withdrawn. The smaller craft unions and the labourers' and general unions also remained within the federation. The employers therefore ratified the new constitution; and gave an undertaking that there would be no national negotiations with the dissident unions.

The first effect of their withdrawal was to undermine the arrangements for bringing Liverpool back within the scope of the national agreement. With the Building Trade Workers and Plasterers free to make their own terms in Liverpool, the employers there gave way, and once more withdrew from the employers' federation. In June 1926 they signed an agreement giving most Liverpool craftsmen 9p an hour, with a tool allowance in addition, compared with $8\frac{1}{2}$p in London and 8p in A-rated towns and cities. The Plasterers in Liverpool got $9\frac{1}{2}$p an hour, and the Painters a little less than the other trades. The Liverpool district secretary of the Building Trade Workers proudly announced in his union journal for June that 'we have been able to beat down the forces of the national body of employers'.

Towards the end of the year the Plasterers negotiated advances above the national craft rate for their members in Sheffield, Leeds, and Leicester. In the summer of 1927 a similar increase was granted in Birmingham, and was soon followed by another covering the whole of the North East, signed by the National Joint Council for the Plastering Industry. Plasterers were employed both by members of the National Federation of Building Trade Employers and by Master Plasterers, but hitherto the understanding had been that negotiations with the unions were to be left to the federation. The Master Plasterers decided that this obligation no longer applied, now that their employees were outside the national agreement, and entered into the business of pay negotiation on their own account, in order, they said, to bring the situation under control.

During the first half of 1928 several more local agreements for wage advances were authorised by the National Joint Council for the Plastering Industry. However, the labour shortage was coming to an end. In June the council reduced the rate for plasterers in the North East, and there was a further reduction in May 1929. At the beginning of 1929 the Birmingham Master Plasterers reverted to the rates authorised by the council for the building industry. Manchester followed suit; and, throughout the rest of 1929 and into 1930, the Plasterers in one town after another were brought back to the wage rates set out in the national agreement.

Meanwhile the Building Trade Workers had got no nearer payment for wet time on their own than previously through their federation. They had achieved nothing like the success of the Plasterers in local wage negotiations. Whatever ambitions Hicks had entertained for his own aggrandisement had not been fulfilled. At the end of 1927 his members balloted in favour of rejoining the federation and the National

Joint Council. Next year they were readmitted to both bodies. The system of national collective bargaining which had developed in Britain during and since the war had contained its greatest challenge from the unions so far.

Another challenge of a different kind found the building industry, both employers and operatives, united in their resistance. One solution proposed for the country's housing shortage was the construction of prefabricated steel houses for erection on site. It had the advantage of providing employment for the depressed engineering industry. Lord Weir was among those engineering employers who designed a steel house, and by 1925 his factory at Cardonald was ready to build 2,500 a year. Some of them had already been ordered by Glasgow City Corporation, where they were erected by engineering craftsmen and labourers, whose wage rates were substantially below those of the building trade. The building unions in Scotland threatened to strike unless their members were given the job of erecting the houses. Weir refused. In his view, both sides of the building industry were exploiting the housing shortage. The government set up a court of inquiry at which both unions and employers condemned Weir's methods, pointing out that they were already erecting other steel houses and were ready to erect Weir's houses, so long as the job was done under their agreed terms. In April 1925 the court reported in Weir's favour, but few local authorities were ready to defy the united opposition of the building industry upon which they were bound to rely for the bulk of their housing programmes. By the end of the year the Weir house was as good as dead.

Industrial Relations at the Workplace

The reports of organisers and letters from members published in the Engineers' journal in the early twenties provide evidence of the difficulty of sustaining shop steward organisation in the engineering industry at a time of heavy unemployment. 'We cannot expect our members to take up the position of shop stewards', wrote one member in September 1921, 'unless we can guarantee them at least the same measure of economic security as the average member possesses'. In January 1922 the Sheffield organiser reported 'much trouble at several firms in connection with the dismissals of shop stewards'. In August 1924 the Kingston district secretary explained that a steward was 'seldom, if ever, discharged for being a shop steward. . . . But a convenient slackness, a mild dissatisfaction with his output, petty irregularities in time-keeping, or casual conversation with other workmen' were used as pretexts.

The absence of shop stewards was used to prevent the remedying of grievances. The full-time officer was not officially entitled to intervene until 'failure to agree' had been recorded in the plant. In June 1923 the Portsmouth organiser reported that the local employers' association 'when it suits their purpose plead procedure must be carried out'; and in March 1924 the Sheffield organiser complained that he was not called in because 'when any man makes a complaint his services are no longer required'.

Nevertheless, since procedure provided for the appointment of shop stewards, it could be used to enforce their recognition. When the local employers' association at Bradford informed the management committee of their federation in June 1922 that the shop steward agreement was 'the cause of more unrest in the works than any other', and that several member firms refused to operate it, they were told that, where a recognised union informed a federated firm of the names of the shop stewards which it had appointed, 'there is no alternative for the employers but to recognise them as shop stewards'—although the agreement could be construed to require the consent of the employer before a works committee could be set up.

As employment improved the agreement was more frequently enforced. There were also members willing to take the job on. Writing of a meeting to elect a convener in October 1928, the Glasgow organiser said: 'After the experience I have had in trying to coax reluctant members to take up the duties of shop stewards, it was more than invigorating to find members willing to function.' There was even a case reported in April 1928 of a shop steward at Colchester who had been 'discharged under unpleasant circumstances, but we were able to secure his reinstatement'.

One of the shop steward's functions was to recruit members. In April 1928 the Glasgow organiser noted 'a more vigorous attitude to the non-unionist', adding cryptically that 'suggestions have been made at the recent shop stewards meeting which, if carried out, should certainly be of some assistance'. At a Southampton firm, the Plymouth organiser reported in March 1928, 'after several interviews with the management, discussions with the non-unionists, and meetings with our members inside and outside the docks, the non-unionists were "persuaded" to leave the firm's employ'. Where he could, the steward tried to protect his members' jobs. When a Glasgow firm contemplated the introduction of female labour, discussions led them in April 1928 to inform 'our convener of shop stewards that they had resolved to continue the employment of male labour on the operations'. In June 1929 the shop stewards at a Southall firm complained that 'the management was desirous of extending the method of one man working more than one machine', and asked their district committee to intervene.

The most common subjects of shop steward concern were piecework and payment by results. In a number of cases the men complained that they could not make reasonable earnings. In March 1928 an Acton firm was reported to have offered to look into such cases and the shop stewards gave the promise a month's trial. In other instances the employer wanted to reduce times or prices because he considered that earnings were too high. In May 1928 it was reported that the Manchester district committee had refused to ratify an agreement between a local firm and its works committee to deduct 'piecework balances earned . . . of more than 55 per cent' saying it was 'contrary to our Piecework Agreement for any man to give back to a firm any of the money he has already earned'; but a report from the Birmingham organiser in November 1929 said that a Wolverhampton firm had been allowed to cut rates because of long runs, and 'time and a half at least has been earned on the job'.

Although the formal position of the employers was that they were free to introduce piecework or payment by results when they chose, the federation thought it unwise to insist on this right. On 28 May 1925 the management board decided, on a complaint from a Scottish firm concerning the refusal of the Coppersmiths to accept payment by results, that 'no system of payment by results is likely to be a success unless a mutual arrangement is arrived at between the management and the men concerned'. The firm was advised to try persuasion.

The upward drift of piecework and bonus earnings left timeworking toolroom and maintenance workers further and further behind, and the 10p increase granted to timeworkers in 1927 was not enough to fill the gap. The Bolton and Bury district negotiated a special rate for maintenance men, but more commonly the redress of this grievance was left to workplace bargaining. In 1929 the toolroom workers in Coventry decided to aim for a special toolroom rate, but had to proceed firm by firm. Maintenance engineers in industries other than engineering might have to depend entirely on negotiations by shop stewards. In January 1928 a shop steward at a Maidstone newspaper office reported that he had obtained a 'full shop rate' of £5 a week, with new entrants on £4 for their first twelve months. Since these rates were respectively more than £2 and more than £1 above the skilled rate in the engineering industry, it is not surprising that the district committee accepted his report.

How did this situation compare with 1914? Since shop steward organisation had then been only in process of spreading from Scotland and the North to the Midlands and the South, it now had greater coverage. The extension of piecework and other forms of payment by results also helped to increase the numbers and widen the functions of stewards. The national agreement on shop stewards and their place in procedure could now be used, at least on some occasions, to secure recognition for shop stewards, and in some instances the union was able to protect them against victimisation. There was, however, no sign of the survival of a shop stewards' movement, and, apart from the Hoe dispute, no evidence of shop stewards seriously challenging, or even embarrassing, the leaders of the union.

No other union's records provide such ample material to assess the state of shop steward activity in these years; but some points can be established. In shipbuilding, shop stewards were on much the same footing as in engineering; chapels and chapel fathers were firmly rooted in the traditions of the printing industry; the building unions had their card stewards who were as often as not called shop stewards. Their primary job was to build and maintain union organisation on site, but, at least in some instances, they handled grievances as well. The Building Trade Workers made a small payment to their stewards, and their London and Birmingham districts set up shop stewards' councils. In addition shop stewards were to be found far beyond the boundaries of these traditional craft industries.

In Lancashire the General Workers organised their members as far as possible in a single branch for each town. Some of these branches ran to two or three thousand members or more, spread over a score or more of workplaces, and were run by full-time branch secretaries. The part played by their shop stewards was described by the Accrington branch secretary in the union's journal for March–April 1922. 'Their activities', he wrote,

range over a fairly wide field, conveying information from headquarters to the members, settling minor grievances which may arise in the particular place in which they work, enrolling immediately any new person who may be started in the shop, keeping defaulting members up to standard by having periodic reviews of cards, and keeping the [branch] office in touch with members' opinions on any question that may arise.

They meet once a month in their respective industries, the engineering section one week, clayworkers another. But in industries like gas, Corporation departments and other minor groups the stewards report frequently and receive information, if any, to convey to their respective bodies, without any set meeting.

There is also a chief steward at each works who first of all cultivates a discipline amongst the others, not—and this is important—imposing discipline upon them, but encouraging and assisting self-discipline. He attends to all matters that get beyond the power of the departmental stewards, and therefore this office necessitates the best possible man, he regularly having to meet the management upon important matters needing great tact, discretion, and some amount of courage.

The years of depression probably weakened these workplace organisations, but in 1925 Dukes, the Lancashire district secretary of what was
now the General and Municipal Workers, wrote in the journal for
November–December to emphasise the importance of 'making a big
effort to get the right type of shop steward. The importance of this
position cannot be over-estimated.'

In 1926 the directors of the Co-operative Wholesale Society agreed to
the appointment of shop stewards in their factories provided that there
was no waste of working time and the stewards did not interfere with the
duties of other workers.

Another form of workplace organisation, which might or might not
overlap, or even coincide, with shop steward organisation was the works
committee recommended by the Whitley Committee. The response to
their proposals varied widely from one industry to another.

The Cablemakers decided that they were optional, the Paint and Varnish JIC
put off consideration of the matter to another time and apparently never
returned to it. The Papermakers thought that the matter should be left to
decision at local level; the Tinplate Council that existing workshop organisation
was adequate while the Wool and Allied Trades after deliberating on the matter
for a time, never got round to taking any action.[7]

Other councils initially showed more interest, including cement,
flourmilling, pottery, electricity supply, gas, and tramways. Altogether,
according to a Ministry of Labour estimate in 1923, it was probable that
'considerably over 1,000 Works Committees have been formed'; but
three years later the Balfour Committee found that 'a considerable
number of Joint Committees established during and after the war have
ceased to function', and the total in the pottery industry had dropped
from a hundred to twenty-four.

The decline in the number of Works Committees would appear to have been
fairly rapid since 1920, and it is probably true to say that they have only
survived in establishments in which there is a very definite desire on the part of
both managements and workpeople to make the Committees a success.[8]

Many of these establishments were to be found in those large private
firms which were associated with the developing profession of personnel
management, or labour management as it was then called. The
profession had originated before the war among 'welfare workers' or
'social workers' employed in industry, many of them by Quaker firms;
and it had received strong encouragement from the Ministry of
Munitions during the war. The Quaker, Seebohm Rowntree, who called

[7] Charles, p. 160.
[8] Balfour Committee, p. 305.

the conference in 1913 which founded the Welfare Workers' Association (the predecessor of the present Institute of Personnel Management) and was put in charge of the welfare section of the Ministry of
Munitions, set up works committees in his York factories in the autumn
of 1916. Another Quaker firm, Cadbury, had set up works committees at
Bournville at the beginning of the century which were reconstituted
within the Whitley scheme. The third Quaker firm of chocolate
manufacturers, J. S. Fry of Bristol, established their committees in
1924.

These firms took trouble to maintain good relations with the unions.
At York, Rowntree agreed with the General Workers that shop stewards
could attend sectional meetings, and full-time officials were to be invited
to departmental meetings if required. Fry undertook to send the agenda
and minutes of the meetings to the unions, with 'full facilities made for
the attendance of D[istrict] C[ommittee] representatives. . . . Under
these arrangements', observed the Engineers' Bristol organiser in their
journal of February 1925, 'no member need permit any complaint to
become rusty'. Bournville managers committed themselves to the
desirability of trade union membership and to the principle that works
committees must not contravene 'trade union rules and customs . . .
without the written consent of the union concerned'.[9]

However, such methods of winning the goodwill of the unions were
not universally favoured by managers. The flourmilling employers took
the view that, although works committees were

valuable in the abstract, there is one great practical difficulty in operating them,
and that is the presence of the Trade Union official. The experience of the trade
is the Trade Union official tends to monopolise the business of the meeting,
and, as a consequence, the employer is not conferring with his own men, but is
providing a starting-off point where the official may originate some idea or
grievance which will ultimately find its way through to the National
Executive.[10]

Their opinion seems to have been shared by ICI, the amalgamation of
chemicals and explosives firms set up in 1927. Richard Lloyd Roberts, a
former official of the Ministry of Labour who had been labour manager
for Brunner Mond, was appointed head of a central labour department
in the new company, and it was proposed that a works council should be
set up in each plant. The General and Municipal Workers approached
the chairman, Mond, for an assurance that he would respect trade union
rights. Within weeks there was a contretemps over the right of a full-

---

[9] Cadbury Bros, Ltd, p. 3.
[10] Report of a committee of the Flour Milling Employers Federation quoted in the Transport
and General Workers *Record*, February 1927.

time official to visit a works. A few months later the unions took umbrage at the proposal for a 'staff grade' to which manual workers with five years' service could be promoted 'as a reward for good work and service'.[11] They saw it as a device to divide and rule. By the end of 1929 a Central Labour Advisory Council had been set up in ICI where union and company representatives could discuss 'such questions affecting the relations between the company and its operative employees as may be referred to it by the Board, and . . . suggestions that may be put forward . . . by the representatives of organised workers'.[12] Nevertheless, for decades thereafter a sharp distinction was drawn in ICI between the functions of works council representatives and those of shop stewards, where they existed.

However, the Whitley proposals for works committees had their greatest success in the Post Office and the railways. Senior managers were committed to set them up, and, although non-unionists were entitled to vote and to stand for election to the committees, the strength of the unions was sufficient to ensure that their candidates were almost invariably elected. In many instances the branch secretary was secretary of the staff side.

On 30 March 1921 the *Journal* of the Post Office Engineers noted that:

Whitleyism is becoming a most important factor in the working life of the staff of the Engineering Department of the Post Office. . . . The Whitley Committee should form a splendid training ground for Branch officers, since it gives them a unique opportunity of a more intimate acquaintance with Post Office machinery.

On 17 June 1922 the *Post* reported:

It is gratifying to know that in most cases branches of the UPW are well satisfied with the Whitley machinery, and it is satisfactory to know that the majority of Postmasters are anxious to work in the spirit of Whitleyism.

The initial experience of Local Departmental Committees on the railways was more disappointing. On 18 August 1922 the *Railway Review* reported that, on the Great Northern, 'officers have apparently been instructed that no matter be permitted on the agenda without headquarters' sanction'; and on 17 December 1926 that: 'Employers' representatives have little, if any, power to deal with most matters. In some cases where they come to an agreement it is vetoed by headquarters.' However, there were exceptions, as the editor had noted

[11] Amalgamated Engineering Union, *Monthly Journal*, August 1928.
[12] Ibid., December 1929.

when he published the results of a survey of branches on 26 May 1926. One Local Department Committee secretary replied that during the previous three years his committee had found it necessary to refer only two issues to their sectional council—the next stage in the procedure— and one of those was conceded. On 19 October 1928 a correspondent from Sheffield argued that, whereas sectional council members, dealing with regional issues, could not equal the knowledge of the senior railway managers whom they met in negotiation, Local Departmental Committee representatives, handling issues arising at their own place of work,

have in all cases an intimate and first-hand knowledge of all the material facts, at least equal to, and, in most cases, superior to the companies' officers. . . . Time and time again we have won case after case, when the Sectional Council has failed.

By this time, however, managerial attitudes were changing. The companies had decided to seek trade union co-operation in devising remedies for the railways' financial problems. On 28 September 1928 the editor wrote of 'a great change. . . . Matters hitherto regarded as somewhat sacred to the management have become subject to discussion'; and on 18 January 1929 that 'the whole aspect of local discussions has been altered as from purely arguments on the grievances of staff . . . to detailed examination of the possibilities of traffic. . . . Many of the items originate from the employees.'

The functions of the Post Office committees included local office arrangements, local revisions of duties, overtime, arrangements for annual leave, Christmas duties, and accommodation. The last issue became especially important when new offices or major alterations were planned. Staff representatives were given sketch plans and took part in discussions with the architects. In some instances sub-committees were appointed to review progress. Many of the same issues came up in the engineering committees—along with lodging allowances for the outside staff—except that the business of the committees in the engineering factories was dominated by piecework. On the railways the annual revision of rosters was, in many instances, the main business. For train crews the interlocking plans for thousands of separate duties involved weeks of detailed work and, with their consequences for overtime, weekend work, and mileage allowance, had a substantial effect upon earnings. The extent to which railwaymen had established control over rostering can be gauged from the rebuke administered to local representatives by the editor of the *Railway Review* on 28 September 1928 for rejecting company proposals on rosters 'without much thought and examination'. It was, he thought, 'up to them to argue their point of view, and if at all possible endeavour to come to an understanding'.

Promotion was one of the most important issues in both services, since jobs were organised in 'promotion lines', with progress from lower to higher status and pay in each line settled by seniority, subject to ability, and, in some instances, to technical qualifications as well. These arrangements applied even in the Post Office engineering department, where skilled workers were graded, and recruited from the unskilled grades as well as from 'youths in training'. Since judgements of ability gave considerable discretion to management to select 'blue-eyed boys', the staff side emphasised seniority. 'The absence of some agreed basis of the line of promotion amongst the majority of sections only tends to give certain people opportunities to retard an employee's progress', wrote the editor of the *Railway Review* on 2 March 1923. Early in 1929 there was an unofficial strike over proposals for filling a vacancy for a cartage foreman at Broad Street which was settled by reversing the decision to give the post to an outsider and recording that 'all vacancies consequent upon this promotion to be filled by Broad St. men in turn'.

In 1927 a new promotion procedure was introduced into the engineering department of the Post Office. In future the staff sides of the local committees were to be notified of vacancies. They would be entitled to nominate one or two of their members to give evidence to the promotion board; and to report any cases of alleged violation of the agreed principles of promotion to the staff side of the national council. They were also allowed to nominate a member to accompany an aggrieved employee who chose to make an oral appeal to the promotion board. On 6 May 1927 the editor of the Post Office Engineering Union's *Journal* expressed the hope that this agreement would reverse a falling off in the activity of the committees, which he detected from the failure of all but a few to report regularly. Two years later, on 3 May 1929, he noted with pleasure that 'most of the District Committees appear to be functioning satisfactorily'; but now a new item of business was at the top of the agenda. The Post Office was engaged in a drive for greater efficiency, and 'the present policy of the Department in regard to dismissals and economy methods gives the Committees ample scope for frequent meetings'.

The major setback to union organisation at the workplace was in coalmining, where there had been a tradition of workplace bargaining by branch officials and checkweighmen, and unofficial 'combine committees' had emerged in South Wales to deal with the amalgamated companies which had become a prominent feature of the industry there by 1914. The Nottingham Miners Association was no longer recognised by the owners, and although a few loyal checkweighmen were able to keep their positions, they were tolerated only so long as they kept their union activities strictly outside the pit. There were, of course, the branch officers and checkweighmen of the Spencer union, but it was dominated by 'butties', or subcontractors.

In most coalmining districts in which the butty system still operated at the end of the war—Derbyshire, Nottinghamshire and parts of Yorkshire—it had been officially terminated by agreement, but in Nottingham the butties had retained an organisation of their own, with links with the National Democratic and Labour Party. 'This organisation had the backing of some colliery owners and in the period of depression following the 1921 lockout it met with a large measure of success in re-establishing the butty system.'[13] It formed the basis of the Spencer union.

The Nottingham Miners Association was held together by its collectors.

Some of them stood on street corners to collect subscriptions; others went round from door to door. . . . Some . . . acted also as branch secretaries; and indeed, a few, where branches were not functioning, acted as Secretary, Delegate and Committee all rolled into one.[14]

In 1928 the General Council subsidised the pay of the collectors, and helped to finance a stoppage at the Welbeck colliery, where men had been dismissed for refusing to allow contributions to the Spencer union to be deducted from their pay, but their efforts to assist the union to regain recognition from the owners were of no avail. A minor victory in the same year was a successful application for fixing new statutory rates under the moribund 1912 Act. As the new statutory rates were almost all below those in the current agreement between the owners and the Spencer union, they had little or no effect on pay, but the decision gave official recognition to the union as far as the procedures of the Act were concerned. The 'chief service' rendered by the union was 'the relief of distress during unemployment', which absorbed most of their meagre funds, and helped the officials to keep their negotiating skills in trim by representing members 'very successfully' before the Courts of Referees who adjudicated on entitlement to unemployment benefit.[15]

At the end of 1926 the association's membership was ten thousand to Spencer's eighteen thousand; but by the end of 1929 they were in front with fourteen thousand to his 10,800. This was a considerable achievement, for Spencer 'certainly looked after the interests of his members', using the rival union 'as a bogeyman to frighten the owners, on occasion, into conceding claims which they had at first rejected'.[16]

The Derbyshire Miners Association shared some of these problems. Although they were still officially recognised by the owners' association,

---

[13] Griffin, p. 116.   [14] Ibid., p. 246.
[15] Ibid., p. 248.   [16] Ibid., pp. 251–2.

some companies dealt with Spencer. In many pits new checkweighmen had been elected by the first groups of miners to return to work, and subsequently 'became agents for the Spencer union in an attempt to safeguard their positions'.[17] In South Wales the membership of the federation fell from 136,000 in 1926 to 60,000 in 1928, when the South Wales Miners Industrial Union returned a figure of 7,635, making it by a fair margin the largest non-political union outside Nottingham. The new union was actively encouraged by the Ocean Coal Company, and found a capable leader in William Gregory.

More harm was done to the South Wales Miners, however, by changes in the attitude of those owners who continued to give them formal recognition. Outside the anthracite area, most of them refused to apply the seniority rule any longer, so that union activists were not protected from victimisation; and their association decided that its members should no longer countenance the custom of 'show cards' on colliery premises so essential to the maintenance of union membership in South Wales. The custom 'was now actively disrupted by the owners'.[18] In some areas this decision was challenged by the union, but that could only be done where the union was relatively strong, and not where the need to rebuild membership was most urgent. Union loyalties were weakened by the 'hatred and bitterness' of 'middle-aged men who had saved up' and 'had no possible hope now of recouping what they had spent in the strike'.[19] In these circumstances union organisation in the pits began to disintegrate, and the process was hastened by heavy unemployment. In Mardy, where the union branch had been the 'executive power of the village' during the general strike, there were 377 employed members and 1,366 unemployed in 1927, and next year the number of employed members fell to eight.[20]

Durham also had its 'non-political' union, which covered Northumberland as well and claimed almost four thousand members by the end of 1927; but the owners were fully committed to the Durham Miners Association whose membership stood at 138,000 compared with 156,000 two years earlier, and held up remarkably well thereafter despite rising unemployment. There was little enough that the union could do for its members in county negotiations. It could not fend off a cut in minimum and subsistence rates in 1928. Resistance was offered only in individual pits. Earnings within the pits were no longer protected by the 'county average' system which had been in force from 1872 to 1914. A joint committee had then been empowered to adjust piecework price lists in any colliery where piecework earnings diverged from the county average by more than 5 per cent. The system had been

[17] J. E. Williams, p. 738. [18] Francis and Smith, p. 117.
[19] Ibid., p. 78. [20] Ibid., pp. 163–4.

suspended during the war, and it had proved impossible to re-establish it afterwards. Colliery managers were therefore free to negotiate reductions in piecework price lists, for the county agreement guaranteed a uniform percentage addition to the colliery price lists, but not the lists themselves. In 1927 and 1928 notices were posted in a number of Durham collieries to enforce reductions in price lists. Some were accepted; others led to local strikes. In March 1928 three thousand Durham miners were fined $57\frac{1}{2}$p each with costs for stopping work in breach of their contracts in sympathy with colleagues in a neighbouring pit who were striking in protest against piece rate cuts. Next spring four thousand men at Dawdon Colliery achieved national fame by staying out over a similar issue for nearly four months. They returned to work on reasonably honourable terms of further negotiation with a commitment to arbitration if there was no settlement.[21]

Colliery organisations therefore retained a measure of strength in Durham. One reason for the continued loyalty of the miners to their union spokesmen in the pit was the practice of 'cavilling', which was the main instrument by which Durham miners exercised control over their jobs. This had started as a method of redistributing good and bad 'places' on the faces by lot each year when coal was worked in a series of relatively small 'bords' separated by 'pillars'. As 'long-wall' methods were introduced, it continued as a means of redistributing miners along the face and teams between faces. Teams were self-selecting and their 'cavil leaders' acted as shop stewards and negotiated on their behalf. The system gave powerful encouragement to group solidarity, and protection against victimisation. The militant Harvey, branch secretary at Wardley, drew up the cavilling rules for the Follonsby pit at the depth of the depression, in 1931; and also introduced a rota system which increased the total number of men working at each individual place to eight.

Two of them spent a fortnight on the dole, while the other six were kept at work. Wages were divided amongst all eight so that those on the dole were kept up to an equal wage. . . . This was such an effective system that collieries all over the country wrote to Wardley for details of it.[22]

In other coalfields the continuing shift to long-wall mining weakened the cohesion of the faceworkers. Higher output at the face reduced the proportion of faceworkers to haulage and surface workers. At the same time the faceworkers were reorganised into grades, each one performing one of the tasks which had previously made up the collier's job. Except where the men were able to insist on the 'all-throw-in' method of payment, each grade had its own payment system, further undermining

[21] Garside, pp. 243, 249.   [22] Douglass, p. 250.

solidarity. The number of supervisors and the intensity of supervision were increased, overturning the tradition that colliers worked on their own and chose their own pace. In some instances payment by the yard replaced payment by the ton, rendering checkweighing unnecessary. In Scotland, where long-wall mining had been introduced more rapidly than elsewhere, this change in the method of measuring output was employed in at least one instance to get rid of militant check-weighmen.[23]

Inside the Unions

Continuing pressure towards centralisation in trade union government, arising from the extension and strengthening of national bargaining, was reinforced by further constitutional changes within some of the unions. Government was already highly centralised in the Post Office Workers and the Railwaymen. Bevin concentrated authority within the Transport and General Workers by means of the trade groups. These were given much greater weight than the other intermediary level between the executive and the branches—the regions; and national trade group secretaries operated in London under Bevin's eyes. In 1924 the Woodworkers decided to move their head office from Manchester to London and replace their former part-time executive of seven members by five full-timers.

Although the depression forced many unions into staff redundancies, the number of full-time officers did not fall in step with the membership. The Workers Union fell from nearly half a million members in 1920 to a hundred thousand in 1929, but the reduction in the number of officers was from 160 to a hundred. In 1933 the Engineers had one officer for six thousand members compared with one for twelve thousand in 1921. Over the same period the number of members per officer fell from 33,000 to 18,000 among the Railwaymen; from 4,800 to 2,600 in the Iron and Steel Trades Confederation; and from 6,200 to 4,200 among the Railway Clerks.[24] Overall the item for 'working expenses'—mainly the salaries and expenses of officials and clerical staff—rose from 24 per cent of the income of registered trade unions in 1911–14 to 37 per cent in 1927–33. Generally speaking, an increase in the number of full-time officers adds to the capacity of the executive to exercise control over union members; and this tendency was reinforced by a trend towards the appointment rather than election of full-time officers.

The allegiance of an elected officer is divided between the members who choose him and the executive which is ultimately responsible for his work. Appointment and promotion by the executive strengthens the second tie at the expense of the former. Before 1914 the overwhelming

[23] Macintyre, pp. 68–9. [24] Clegg, Killick and Adams, p. 40.

majority of full-time officers were elected either periodically or to hold office subject to satisfactory performance. The Workers Union, however, appointed its officers except for the secretary and president. The Transport and General Workers adopted the same rule, and in 1924 Bevin abolished the elected office of president, previously held by Gosling. In 1926 the General and Municipal Workers adopted a procedure whereby, apart from senior posts, officers were, in the first instance, appointed as temporary organisers for two years. Thereafter they had to stand in an election in which any qualified member of the union could put up against them. From that day to this no appointed officer has lost such an election. Appointment was also the general rule in the white collar unions which were contributing an increasing proportion of the movement's total membership. In the largest union which prescribed periodic election for full-time officers—the Engineers—the rule was left in abeyance for eight years after 1920 to allow the amalgamation to settle down.

Full-time officers, and executive members, were affected by the changing pace of trade union work. In 1919–20 they had to cope with an unusually heavy workload. New bargaining procedures were being designed for most major industries; national agreements on wages, hours of work, and a variety of conditions were being negotiated and approved; almost every union was engaged in discussing a number of projected schemes of amalgamation; and the number of industrial disputes was running at a record level. For a year or two thereafter the demands on their time continued at a high level, with frequent negotiations over cuts in pay or worsening of conditions, and a series of massive lockouts; but after that the pace slackened off. The job of most full-time officers became more comfortable, especially as salary cuts in most unions had not matched the decline in retail prices. According to a union officer who was then an office-boy in a large regional office of one of the general unions, office work, visits, and meetings were regularly completed by lunch-time. Afterwards the playing-cards came out.

During the hectic postwar years, meetings of executives, sub-committees, negotiating bodies, Joint Industrial Councils, union conferences, and other union business had occupied most, or perhaps all, the time of executive members, even in those unions in which their posts were not full-time. In most major unions they rarely if ever worked at their nominal jobs during that period and drew a daily allowance from the union which almost invariably exceeded the pay they would otherwise have earned. Now the pressure of union business was much reduced, and did not prevent them going back to their jobs for a substantial part of the year—unless, of course, the duties of the executive could be supplemented and spread out sufficiently to avoid that. In the Workers Union the executive fixed their allowances in addition to fares at

£2 for each day spent on union business or in travelling to and from meetings. In the same period, the Executive also increased considerably its own volume of work; by 1925 some members were therefore drawing on average £7 a week in expenses—far more than the rank and file membership could hope to earn.[25]

The executive of the Railwaymen and the Locomotive Engineers and Firemen also stretched their business until they became virtually full-timers for their period of office. In January 1922 the general secretary of the latter union complained of the cost of having the executive in 'continuous session' and of excessive hotel and other expenses, and pointed out that the London members charged for loss of wages for six days a week, although the executive met only from Tuesday to Friday. In the matter of fees even the General Council of Congress did not set the best of examples. They were paid fees for attending meetings of the council and its committees, and for time spent travelling to meetings. On 18 December 1929 it was proposed that, for meetings which finished before 2 p.m. or started after lunch, London members should be entitled to half a day's fee instead of a day's fee, and outside members should be entitled to fees for only two days instead of three. 'Next business' was carried by sixteen votes to nine.

Especially at a time of heavy unemployment, clerical posts in union offices provided convenient jobs for the sons and daughters, or other relatives, of senior full-time officials. It was also the custom in the General and Municipal Workers to allow bright young clerical workers in their offices to compete for posts as union officers. Hence there emerged a number of dynasties—the Eccles and Dukes-Cooper families in Lancashire, the Williamsons and Basnetts in Liverpool, the Haydays in Nottingham, the Wrights in London. Theirs was the outstanding instance of nepotism, but it was not unique. The secretary of the South Wales Miners was Tom Richards. His step-brother was assistant secretary. Two of Tom's children and one of his step-brother's were on the staff, and a son-in-law worked at the union's convalescent home.

These various methods of making the lives of executive members, full-time officers, and their families more comfortable did not have a direct effect on the process of centralisation; but they emphasised the distinction between trade union bureaucrats and members. Equally the process of centralisation did not necessarily enhance the authority of the chief officers of unions at the expense of their executives, or vice versa. The authority of both was enhanced and the relationship between them

[25] Hyman, p. 138.

was influenced by other factors, especially personality. Bevin, Thomas, Smillie, Herbert Smith, and Hicks rarely failed to sway their executives. Chief officers had the advantage of superior information, and many of them could draw another advantage from close relations with leading employers. Thomas and Cramp knew the railway directors well. Brownlie got on well with Allan Smith of the Engineering Employers Federation, and among the employers with whom Bevin had close contact was Ashfield of the London Transport Combine. In the General and Municipal Workers, Thorne and Clynes formed an oligarchy along with the district secretaries—a rather decrepit oligarchy, for by 1929 Thorne was seventy-two and Clynes was sixty; and both assistant secretaries and seven of the twelve district secretaries were either in their sixties or seventies. Almost all major unions had introduced superannuation schemes by the early thirties, but the General and Municipal Workers did not fix an age for compulsory retirement until 1936.

Both chief officers and executives strengthened their positions by a successful onslaught on their most persistent antagonists and critics—the Minority Movement. Following the general strike, the movement developed 'a more self-conscious approach to organisation, and a more systematic attempt to secure the election of sympathetic union officials'.[26] By organising the vote in individual unions, the movement was able to send sizeable groups of supporters to Congress in 1926 and 1927, but from 1926 onwards the example of the General Council and the General and Municipal Workers in taking disciplinary action against the movement was followed by other unions, including the Boilermakers, the Distributive and Allied Workers, the Engineers, the Iron and Steel Trades Confederation, the Miners, and the Shop Assistants. Before this hardening of attitudes had had time to take full effect, the Communists completed the rout of their own movement by following Moscow into a 'class against class' policy which entailed condemnation of social democrats as traitors to the working class, 'independent leadership' from the Communist Party, and, where possible, independent unions. The most experienced trade unionists in the party, including Pollitt and Horner, were reluctant to apply the policy, but the Communist International saw that it was forced through a conference of the British party at the end of 1929, and, even before that, conflicts among the Scottish Miners and London clothing workers had led to Communist-controlled breakaways.

By the end of 1926 two Communists held office as president and secretary of the Lanark Miners, although their opponents still held a majority on the executive. During the lockout the split between the Fife

26 Roderick Martin, p. 82.

Miners and Hodges' reform union had been healed, and the election for the executive of the reunited union gave the left 'about half' the seats.[27] Next the election to the Scottish Miners' executive produced a majority for the left which the old executive kept out of office by postponing their 1927 conference at which the new executive was due to take over. Later in 1927 the Fife Miners dismissed their rightwing secretary, Adamson, who left with his followers to form a second Fife miners' union in 1928. His union was recognised as the official representative of the Fife miners by the Scottish Miners Federation and by the national Miners Federation, on the ground that his action had been justified by subversive activities. There were now two unions in Fife, and the situation was little better in Lanark where there were two executives, the one taking legal action against the other. The leftwing groups in the two counties therefore formed the United Mineworkers of Scotland with William Allan as secretary. In 1929 the new union claimed ten thousand members. One effect of the split was that some owners began treating both the Scottish unions with contempt, overriding their customs and traditions.

A number of prominent leftwing miners, including Cook and two members of the national executive, signed a protest against the resolution of the Miners' annual conference in 1928 which had condemned the actions of the Communists and the Minority Movement 'particularly in Scotland'. At a meeting of the executive on 12 October, Cook and his two executive colleagues were forced to retract pending an inquiry; and Cook signed the report of the inquiry which roundly condemned the Minority Movement, thus finally breaking his connection with it.

The clothing breakaway had its origin in an unofficial strike of five hundred women at the London firm of Rego which began in October 1928 to enforce a closed shop. After a settlement was reached at the end of the year, the Garment Workers' executive in Leeds decided that their London organiser, Sam Elsbury, a Communist, had disregarded their instructions during the course of the strike. He was dismissed in March 1929, and, with the support of the union's traditionally independent-minded London district, he followed the Communist Party's instructions to form a breakaway, the United Clothing Workers. The new union began life with a majority of the Garment Workers' membership in London and signs of support from the provinces, but within a few weeks Elsbury was forced into another strike at the firm of Polikoff, which decided to recognise the Garment Workers. The courts found the strikers had broken their contracts, and the Communist Party failed to deliver the money which they had promised to find for strike pay. The

[27] Macfarlane, p. 264.

strike was broken, and with it the union, which nevertheless dragged on a feeble existence even after Elsbury had been hounded out by the Communist Party.

Unabashed, the Communists set about establishing Trades Councils independent of the General Council's control. Their most successful endeavour was the London Industrial Council which began life with the survivors from six disaffiliated borough Trades Councils, some district representatives from the Engineers and the Furniture Trades, and delegates from the United Clothing Workers. Its existence was brief and feeble.

The three groups which chafed most vigorously against the centralised government of the Transport and General Workers were the London dockers, the London busmen, and the Glasgow dockers. There was evidence of Communist influence among the first two of them. In May 1925 Bevin complained to his executive that the National Joint Council for the docks

has benefitted London more than any other [port]; nearly every case referred to the Council from London has been settled in favour of the workpeople, and yet, while the provinces adhere to the Council and utilise its machinery to the fullest possible extent before considering the question of strike action, requests are made to take immediate strike action in connection with almost every problem arising in the Port of London.

The problem in the London docks, however, was created as much or more by the disaffection of the full-time officers as by unrest among the members. In October 1926 one of the officers was dismissed. With Bevin absent abroad, the Communist London docks secretary, Thompson, the dismissed officer, and four of their colleagues seceded, along with some members of the London docks committee, and set up a rival union in the belief that they had the support of 'not less than 75 per cent of the Dockers in the Up-Town area'; but they were mistaken, and their new union failed ignominiously.[28]

Towards the end of 1929 the London busmen sought permission to strike to enforce a closed shop. The executive refused, but Bevin undertook to discuss the issue with Ashfield. This was not enough for the busmen, some of whose branches began to pass strike resolutions. On 20 November the executive came 'to the conclusion that there is a deliberate attempt on the part of certain members to wreck the union'.

The Glasgow dockers had been persuaded into the amalgamation only with great difficulty, and could not be made to abandon their own rules and practices. They went to court to establish their right to continue annual elections for their full-time officers, and refused to

---

[28] Transport and General Workers executive, 19–21 October, 2 November, 1926.

apply the union's rules on entrance fees and admission to membership. Successive Glasgow docks committees were disbanded, and eventually in 1932 the Glasgow dockers seceded to set up the Scottish Transport and General Workers Union.

The Communists suffered a doctrinal defeat through the rejection by Congress of industrial unionism, a dogma which they shared with most other leftwing groups and many trade unionists who were not on the left. Intellectually, industrial unionism had held the stage in the British trade union movement for twenty years. It was a simple and appealing doctrine. But its devotees failed to examine why the majority of British trade unionists remained within trade unions of a different pattern and showed little inclination towards structural reform on industrial lines, no matter how long the devotees preached at them; just as their opponents failed to develop intellectually respectable arguments to expose the doctrinaire weaknesses of the case for industrial unionism. Debates on the issue at Congress in the early twenties were conducted at the level of knockabout comedy with the opponents of industrial unionism taunting its supporters with the alternative revolutionary doctrine of the 'one big union', and drawing attention to the effect which industrial unionism would have on the structure of their own unions by quoting: 'Hail Caesar, those who are about to die salute thee'. At the end of one of these debates, at Hull in 1924, Congress resolved by a vote of five to three to ask the General Council to draw up 'a scheme for organisation by industry'; and 'a scheme which may secure unity of action, without the definite merging of existing unions, by a scientific linking up of same to present a united front'.[29] The task was given to the new assistant secretary, Walter Citrine.

Despite the inelegance of its language, his report was notable for its serious attempt to analyse union structure. Citrine began by pointing to the competition for members, demarcation disputes, and failure to co-ordinate policy which were the outcome of existing structure. He then distinguished no less than five types of union structure. Craft unionism, he said, could not 'possibly comply with the terms of the Hull resolution'. Industrial unionism was little better. It was 'attainable only when the industry has reached a certain stage of development'; and 'there is the fact that beyond a few industries the grouping of the unions is such as to make industrial unionism difficult of realisation without the splitting up of existing unions'. Occupational unionism, by which he meant equating the boundaries of trade unionism with the boundaries of a group of employing organisations, as the Railwaymen had tried to do, was 'far more likely to aggravate the existing differences' than to promote unity. Class or general unionism, which he equated with the

[29] Trades Union Congress, 1924, pp. 439–45.

theory of the 'one big union', was left to 'be borne in mind as the direction in which future efforts ... should be made'. 'Federal unionism' was therefore left as the only remedy immediately available to satisfy the second part of the Hull resolution. Since 'it would be suicidal to try to impose any theoretical conception of unionism', federation 'would be much more likely to secure the united front which is the first essential of the Hull resolution' than would other forms of organisation.[30]

The delegates to the 1925 Congress were baffled. 'While ... quite prepared to pay a compliment to the literary abilities of Mr Citrine', said a spokesman for the Engineers,

he had to express dissatisfaction with the result. For instance, he went on page after page, introducing theses on different matters, and in the long run delegates were confused, and their confusion was made worse confounded by the General Council not giving any lead whatsoever.[31]

However, the council knew what they were doing. They interpreted the narrow defeat of both a resolution in favour of the one big union and an amendment rejecting it as approval of Citrine's report. Thereafter the organisation committee circulated an extensive questionnaire to affiliated unions. The replies were analysed in reports to Congress in 1926 and 1927, the second giving a lucid account of the obstacles to trade union amalgamations, and substituting 'joint working arrangements' for federal unionism as the short-run objective.[32] A final account of the committee's work was submitted in 1929. No progress towards joint working arrangements had been made in eleven of the seventeen industrial groups into which affiliated unions were divided for electoral purposes. Discussions were currently in progress on amalgamation or joint working arrangements, or both, in five others. The one definite achievement was a federation of some, but not all, of the unions in the glass trades.[33] This rate of progress was criticised by the Engineers at Congress in 1928, but the General Council could not see what else they could usefully do. When Citrine wrote to the Engineers in November to ask for proposals 'of a practical nature', he received no reply.[34] Henceforth British unions would have to learn to live with their existing structure.

Practical lessons in how this was to be done were already being given by the General Council's disputes committee which exercised the wide powers given to the council in 1921 to settle inter-union disputes. The number of cases referred to the committee rose to a peak of twenty-eight in 1923–4, and in 1924 'certain main principles' were laid down 'which,

---

[30] Ibid., 1925, pp. 226–36.   [31] Ibid., p. 422.   [32] Ibid., 1927, pp. 109–10.
[33] Ibid., 1929, pp. 101–7.   [34] Ibid., pp. 110–11.

if followed, would reduce the number of disputes'. Members of another union should not be accepted without investigation, nor allowed to escape financial obligations by transfer; and 'under no circumstances' was a member to be accepted from a union engaged in an industrial dispute.[35] By 1927 the annual total of inter-union disputes before the committee was down to seven, due to observance of the principles 'and to the adoption by the majority of unions of the proposal for a model form of application'.[36]

Up to that time trade union members had been allowed to transfer, provided the principles were observed and there was no improper influence. However, in 1927 the Distributive and Allied Workers carried a resolution through Congress which directed the General Council to refuse 'the affiliation of any Trade Union which is composed of members who have broken away from an existing union'.[37] They had in mind the Tobacco Workers who had resigned from Congress rather than return several branches which had seceded to them from the Distributive and Allied Workers. Two years later, with the United Clothing Workers in mind, the Tailors and Garment Workers persuaded Congress to direct the General Council 'to refuse to accept the affiliation of any breakaway membership'.[38] This instruction was interpreted by the disputes committee as debarring all transfers of union members without the consent of the union which they wished to leave. 'Since then, whether workers secede to form a separate union or to join another TUC union, whether they are "poached" or act on their own initiative, their actions are automatically condemned.'[39] The consequence was to maintain existing union boundaries wherever they had been drawn.

As case-law hardened, unions could predict the result of an appeal to the committee, and they more frequently settled out of court. In 1927 the committee ruled that no dispute should be heard until after the unions concerned had made an effort to settle it themselves; and unions were encouraged to make inter-union arrangements for the purpose, such as the joint standing committee of the Transport and General Workers and the General and Municipal Workers, set up in 1925 to regulate recruitment and deal with recognition of cards and transfer arrangements. Dealings between unions were often more flexible than the decisions of the disputes committee of Congress. An experienced union officer might be prepared to let a few disgruntled members take their discontent to another union.

These developments could not, of course, eliminate inter-union conflict. In the late twenties the railway companies decided that the best way to meet the competition of road transport was to go into road

[35] Ibid., 1924, p. 157.   [36] Ibid., 1927, p. 83.   [37] Ibid., p. 436.
[38] Ibid., 1929, p. 312.   [39] Lerner, p. 71.

transport themselves. Because their legal power to do so was questionable, they secured the passage of private bills which had the warm support of the railway unions, but were opposed by the Transport and General Workers. After a brief battle of acquisitions, the companies reached an understanding with the largest road passenger transport undertakings on joint control of bus companies. Agreement between the unions was not reached so easily. The Railwaymen followed their established principle that they were entitled to recruit any employee of the railway companies. Since provincial busmen were not so solidly organised as tramwaymen and London busmen, the Railwaymen's organisers were able to establish a footing, most successfully in the West and South Wales. Complaining loudly, Bevin also stepped up his organising activities, and by the end of 1930 his union's road passenger transport group passed a hundred thousand members for the first time.

The General Council could not prevent competition between established unions and the new non-political miners' unions or the Communist-inspired breakaways of Scottish miners and London clothing workers, since these latter unions were not affiliated to Congress; nor could they prevent Havelock Wilson from giving a £10,000 interest-free loan to the non-political unions, since he was ready to accept expulsion for what he had done. A complaint against him was upheld by the disputes committee in October 1927. The General Council recommended expulsion, and Congress gave its unanimous approval in the following year.

Wilson's audacity had been encouraged by the demise of the Marine Workers. In 1926 one of the former officers of the Marine Workers who had come over with Cotter brought proceedings against his old union on the grounds that the ballot of the Cooks and Stewards to join in the amalgamation which formed the Marine Workers had been fraudulent. The court granted an injunction restraining the Marine Workers from touching the property and funds of the Cooks and Stewards. Since there was no way of separating the property and funds brought into the amalgamation by the Cooks and Stewards from those contributed by the Seafarers, the Marine Workers could no longer operate and ceased to exist.[40] Under the compulsion of the PC5,[41] Wilson's membership rose from 54,000 at the end of 1925 to 73,000 a year later. Wilson told his executive on 7 July 1927 that, although he was due to retire in 1928, 'he thought the feeling would be at the next AGM that he do not retire'.

With the disappearance of the Marine Workers, the expulsion of the Seamen from Congress left no *bona fide* trade union for a seaman of principle to join. Bevin was reluctantly persuaded to fill the gap by setting up a marine section. His reluctance was justified in June 1929

[40] Mogridge, pp. 405–6. [41] See page 328.

when some members of the section declined to pay contributions to the Seamen as well. The employers refused to sign them on. Dockers came out in sympathy in ports all around the country. The London port employers complained to Bevin that his men were in breach of procedure, and demanded that he should provide substitutes. He got the men back to work. However, an easier solution to the problem was at hand. Wilson had died in April 1929. His successor, W. R. Spence, terminated the Seamen's association with the non-political unions, and applied for reaffiliation to Congress. His application was accepted, and Bevin wound up his marine section.

A lasting legacy of this quarrel was a new rule of Congress, on the 'conduct of affiliated organisations', approved in 1928. The General Council was empowered to investigate the conduct of any affiliate 'on the grounds that the activities of such organisation are detrimental to the interests of the Trade Union Movement or to the declared principles and policy of Congress'; and to suspend it, if that seemed appropriate. The next meeting of Congress was to extend the suspension, terminate it, or expel.

A new section opened by another union ultimately achieved a substantial success. After havering since 1892, the Engineers in 1926 introduced two new sections for 'industrial members', with lower contributions than other members and limited benefits, intended for semi-skilled and unskilled male engineering workers. The immediate impact was small. By the end of 1928 the section had less than eight thousand members; but since relatively few semi-skilled and unskilled engineering workers were in any union at this time, the Engineers would be free to recruit them when prosperity returned, with little risk of complaints to the disputes committee.

This opening of their ranks was a belated response by the Engineers to the rapid increase in the proportion of semi-skilled employees in engineering. The returns of the Engineering Employers Federation show that between 1914 and 1926 the proportion of their employees classified as skilled fell from 60 per cent to 40 per cent, whereas the proportion classified as semi-skilled rose from 20 per cent to 45 per cent; and a national survey of apprenticeship showed the proportion of skilled workers who acquired their skill through an ill-defined 'learnership', involving 'a less exacting degree of responsibility of the employer in the matter of imparting instruction' than apprenticeship, and no 'understanding, explicit or implicit, that the boy shall be employed throughout the whole of the recognised period',[42] was higher in engineering than in other craft industries. In engineering 25.1 per cent of trainees were learners, compared with 18.1 per cent in building, 11.9 per cent in

[42] Ministry of Labour, *Report on Apprenticeship and Training*, Vol. VII, p. 8.

printing and allied trades, and 0.9 per cent in shipbuilding. Learners were heavily concentrated in grinding and polishing and in machining, at 48.6 and 62.3 per cent of trainees respectively[43]—both trades being within the province of the Engineers. The influence of the newer branches of engineering is shown by the 51.2 per cent of trainees who were learners in motor engineering compared with 0.7 per cent in marine engineering.[44]

After the formation of the General and Municipal Workers in 1924 the only substantial amalgamations of the decade were further accessions to the Transport and General Workers. In 1926 the National Union of Enginemen, Firemen, Mechanics, and Electrical Workers brought in 20,000 members, and demonstrated the attractions of the Transport and General Workers' structure by becoming a separate trade group—the 'Power Group'—and retaining their own title and separate affiliation to Congress. In 1929 they were followed by the Workers Union.

After the disasters of the depression years the membership and finances of the Workers Union had begun to pick up in 1924 and 1925, but the general strike brought renewed losses, which became worse after a controversy over the expenses of members of the executive was aired at a conference in 1926, and broke in the national press next year. The executive members were forced to resign, but the most prominent of them, Neil Maclean, a Member of Parliament, launched a fierce attack on the shortcomings of Beard and Duncan, and took his case to the courts. By 1927 amalgamation with another union was 'an urgent necessity if bankruptcy was to be avoided'.[45] The leaders approached Bevin. A scheme of amalgamation was drawn up in 1928, approved by ballot early in 1929, and put into force in August. In the first instance the Workers Union became a single trade group of the Transport and General Workers. Subsequently they were distributed between the existing general workers' group and two new trade groups, one for metals, engineering, and chemicals, and the other for agriculture. Duncan retired, but Beard stayed on as a trade group secretary, and continued to hold his seat on the General Council until 1935.

Although the Workers Union brought Bevin considerable financial liabilities along with its 90,000 members, Bevin did not see it primarily as a near-bankrupt organisation. 'I made up my mind', he wrote in his union's journal for March 1932, 'that never would we pay too much attention to money when asking other organisations to join us. The goodwill of workers who had held together through all the difficulties of

---

[43] Ibid., pp. 29–30.   [44] Ibid., Vol. VI, pp. 11–13.
[45] Hyman, p. 160.

the economic depression was of far greater value than money.' He therefore offered generous financial terms, allowing the agricultural workers to retain a lower rate of contribution than the rest of the union, and guaranteeing the Workers Union friendly benefits until the end of 1930 after which they were continued as an option for an additional subscription. Over the next few years far fewer full-time officers of the Workers Union lost their jobs than would have had to go if there had been no amalgamation.

It was a wise investment. From the days of its greatness the Workers Union retained the right to organise in thousands of plants in engineering and other manufacturing industries. Thus Bevin acquired assets which were in due course to make his union the biggest in the country, and to change its character. Up to 1929 it had been an organisation of road transport workers and dockers with subsidiary interests elsewhere; it was ultimately to become the most wide-ranging general union of all, with its largest group of members in the engineering industry.

A New Philosophy

In the second half of the nineteenth century, most trade union leaders had held that their organisations could look after the interests of their members without outside help. By acting in unison their members could raise standards of pay and conditions of work in their trades to a level which would provide them with a reasonable livelihood and security, supplemented by the benefits which their union could provide out of the subscriptions which their wages enabled them to afford. Strikes might be necessary, from time to time, to remind employers of the need to have regard to union claims, but theirs was not a doctrine of class warfare. Wise employers would see the advantage of trade unionism. The unions made few demands of politicians beyond demanding freedom to go about their business, without special restraints and obstacles imposed by law.

This creed fell into disrepute because it was too narrow. It might suit skilled and highly-paid workers in a thriving industry at a time of economic prosperity, but had little to offer the less-skilled and low-paid; it did not answer the needs of skilled occupations threatened by technological change; and it offered no solution for the problem of economic depression. New doctrines emerged with claims to overcome these shortcomings. The socialists argued that a new order could be constructed by dispossessing the employers through political action, whether revolutionary or parliamentary, in which planned collective control would look after the needs of everyone, and permit the undesirable effects of economic progress and economic fluctuations to be avoided. Meanwhile trade unions might be able to achieve something, but working men and women should not put their hopes and efforts primarily into industrial action. The syndicalists, on the other hand, taught the folly of trusting politicans of whatever persuasion. The new order of planned collective control should indeed be the aim of trade unionists, but they had in their trade unions the means of achieving it. Properly organised, industrial action could force employers and governments not only to yield concessions in pay and conditions of work, but to yield to organised workers the power to change society.

Neither doctrine gained a large body of adherents in Britain, but British trade unionists, being empiricists, nevertheless listened to what their adherents had to say. The defects of their former philosophy having been revealed, they were willing to try out at least some of these new ideas to see how far they worked. Piecemeal experiment converted them to the welfare state. Political action could guarantee a minimum standard of life to all members of society, through a network of benefits and services instituted by parliament. However, promises to provide effective remedies for economic depression and declining industries through political action had still to be made good.

Industrial action had not resolved any of the three problems which had defeated nineteenth century trade unionism, but it had extracted impressive concessions from parliament before the war, and from coalition governments during and after the war. For a time, therefore, many trade unionists were prepared to envisage that more could be achieved, especially if such action could be co-ordinated through a Triple Alliance, an Industrial Alliance, or Congress itself. However, in 1926 the general strike and the miners' lockout demonstrated that the limits of industrial action were narrower than many trade unionists had supposed. By 1927 there was good reason to seek a new philosophy.

Citrine set himself to provide it, proceeding cautiously, and mainly through the mouths and pens of others. A theoretical exposition did not appear until 1934 when Milne-Bailey's *Trade Unions and the State* was published. Milne-Bailey was head of the research and economic department of Congress and close to Citrine, although, as he acknowledged in his introduction, he had drawn heavily on Harold Laski, the Labour Party's major political theorist of the interwar years. A popular exposition was available earlier in Tillett's presidential address to Congress in 1929. Having progressed from new unionism to compulsory arbitration, and on through syndicalism and wartime chauvinism to elder statesmanship, Tillett was as always a useful pointer to the direction in which the trade union wind was blowing. Introduced by Hicks as 'the Peter Pan' of the movement, Tillett told the delegates that they represented a mighty movement dealing week by week, day by day, hour by hour, with the host of problems that face us. Our tremendous organisation engages in so many activities and performs such diverse functions as to be almost impossible of enumeration. The services of union agents and officers, of the shop steward and the branch secretary, the energetic and sturdy characters who defend principles and enforce the observance of agreements, who negotiate and bargain and organise, quietly and efficiently carrying on the work of the unions from day to day, are contributing every day to human welfare and defending at all times the claims of the workers to live and breathe in freedom. . . .

To-day the unions are an integral part of the organisation of industry. They hold an unchallenged position as representatives of the workers in all negotiations affecting conditions of employment. The whole range of collective bargaining is wider now, taking account of economic questions which in former years the employers jealously insisted upon excluding from the purview of the unions. There is nothing in the organisation and direction of industry that can now be regarded as the exclusive concern of the employer. . . . Our unions now negotiate as equals, with the power of the organised masses behind them.

He looked forward to co-operation between Congress and the central employers' organisations, and, beyond that, to a State Economic Council. In France, he said, an Economic Council had 'proved an amazing success',[46] and had contributed to the low level of unemployment there.

Citrine himself had expounded 'The Next Step in Industrial Relations' in a *Manchester Guardian Supplement* for 30 November 1927. The unions, he said, were ready for active participation

in a concerted effort to raise industry to its highest efficiency by developing the most scientific methods of production, eliminating waste and harmful restrictions, removing causes of friction and avoidable conflict, and promoting the largest possible output so as to provide a rising standard of life and continuously improving conditions of employment.

In addition to discussions over the distribution of the proceeds of industry, and provision for security of employment in the face of rationalisation,

a wide field of fruitful negotiation . . . lies in the application of . . . the results of research into industrial fatigue, the physical and psychological conditions under which work is carried on and the proper planning and layout of work. . . . Inevitably consideration must be given to the allegation that production is restricted by 'ca'canny' methods, demarcation and trade union rules and customs. . . . Profit-sharing and co-partnership . . . may be worthy of exploitation as another field wherein the functions of trade unions can be extended.

[46] Trades Union Congress, 1929, pp. 62–3, 66.

To accomplish these things there was need for a National Industrial Council, composed of the General Council and representatives from the Confederation of Employers Organisations, with separate joint councils for each industry.

Trade unions, therefore, were able to protect the liberties and advance the economic interests of their members within existing capitalist society, or would be able to do so provided that the scope of collective bargaining was extended to its full potential, and adequate means of consultation between industrial organisations and the government were established. Citrine therefore rejected the socialist and syndicalist philosophies, and was also ready to trample on the prejudices of the traditional trade unionist in defining the boundaries of collective bargaining.

The instrument chosen to begin the practical application of his ideas was Hicks, the former syndicalist. His turn to deliver the presidential address to Congress came in 1927, two months before Citrine's article appeared. Having told his audience that he was dealing with 'the toilsome and difficult period through which we are passing' which was 'a transitional period'—socialism might come later—Hicks asserted that

much fuller use can be made . . . of the machinery for joint consultation and negotiation between employers and employed. . . . It is more than doubtful whether we have seen the fullest possible development of machinery for joint consultation in particular industries. And practically nothing has been done to establish effective machinery of joint conference between the representative organisations entitled to speak for industry as a whole.[47]

The Mond–Turner Talks

Hicks's speech was a challenge to the employers' organisations which they could not easily ignore. At the beginning of 1927, new year messages from the king, Baldwin, and MacDonald had emphasised the need for a new spirit in industrial relations. They were supported by Cramp, Henderson, Pugh, and Thomas. Bevin told a union dinner that, 'if there is a new conception of the objects of industry, then there can be created in this country . . . conditions which will minimise strikes and probably make them non-existent for 25 years'.[48] Discussion of this new conception was postponed by the controversy over the Trade Disputes and Trade Unions Bill, but by September the subject was in the air again.

Nevertheless the official response was discouraging. On 18 October the council of the Confederation of Employers Organisations issued a press statement welcoming Hicks's sentiments, but suggested that

[47] Ibid., 1927, pp. 66–7.
[48] Transport and General Workers *Record*, January 1927.

practical results could be most readily achieved in individual industries. It was from a group of prominent employers acting as individuals and led by Mond that the General Council received an invitation on 23 November, which explained that 'no single existing organisation of employers . . . can take the initiative in inviting discussions to cover the entire field of industrial reorganisation'.[49] Including those who added their signatures after the original letter had been sent, there were in Mond's group eight peers and eighteen knights out of a total of forty. Banking, chemicals, coal, cotton, distribution, electricity, engineering, flourmilling, gas, motor-vehicles, printing, railways, rubber, shipbuilding, shipping, steel, and wool were all represented; and, including Mond himself, there were no less than four directors of ICI. There was the current president of the Confederation of Employers Organisations, Lord Weir, soon to be succeeded by another member of the group, Sir David Milne-Watson; Gilbert Vile was president of the Associated Chambers of Commerce; there were several ex-presidents and vice-presidents of the Federation of British Industries, and numerous office-holders in employers' organisations in individual industries. Ashfield, Courtauld, Milne-Watson, and Mond all had considerable reputations as innovators in industrial relations and personnel management.

The Times on 20 October had reported Citrine as saying that the 'acid test of the sincerity of the employers would be the answer they made collectively, and not as individuals'; but confronted with this list of names, and faced with the prospect of meeting them or no one, the General Council accepted the invitation. A meeting took place on 12 January 1928. Mond assured them that, although he and his colleagues could not impose any principles which might be agreed 'on employers generally, they could use their influence to get them adopted all round'; and that no topic, 'managerial or otherwise', would be ruled out.[50] At this stage only Cook, who had been elected to the General Council in September 1927, dissociated himself from his colleagues, and on 24 January 1928 the council voted by eighteen to six to carry on the discussions. A sub-committee was set up for that purpose. Subsequently Hicks, never a reliable ally, moved to discontinue the talks at a meeting of the council on 26 June, which accepted the sub-committee's interim report. Seconded by Cook, the resolution was defeated by fifteen votes to six, and on 4 July a full meeting of the joint conference adopted a series of final reports.

These began by approving the practice of collective bargaining based on strong organisation on both sides of industry, stating bluntly that 'full recognition should be given to . . . bona fide Trade Unions'.

---

[49] Trades Union Congress, 1928, p. 220.
[50] Ibid., pp. 212–14.

Victimisation was condemned, and appeals machinery was proposed as the remedy. Rationalisation was approved, with safeguards 'to ensure that the interests of workers do not suffer'. Experimental variations in trade union rules and practices, under proper safeguards, were suggested. The deflationary consequences of the gold standard were forcefully condemned, and a 'full inquiry into the best form of credit policy for this country' was proposed. Finally, in order to overcome the limitations imposed by the different spheres of interest of the Confederation of Employers Organisations and the Federation of British Industries, it was proposed that a permanent National Industrial Council be set up with the General Council on one side and representatives in equal numbers from the two central employers' organisations on the other. Its main functions were to be 'continuous investigation into industrial problems' and the provision of conciliation boards to deal with disputes not settled within the industry concerned.[51]

The next stage was to seek the approval of Congress and the two employers' organisations. Within the unions the opposition of the Minority Movement was reinforced by the appearance on 21 June of a document which became known as the Cook–Maxton manifesto. Its authors complained that the Labour movement was being diverted from the 'unceasing war against capitalism' into a 'new conception that Socialism and Capitalism should sink their differences'.[52] Their campaign ran into trouble at once. Cook was acting without the approval of the Miners Federation, and Maxton had not consulted the Independent Labour Party of which he was chairman. Maxton's colleagues sympathised with his aims but thought that the party should have conducted the campaign. After an unhappy start in Glasgow, the series of meetings they had arranged fizzled out, despite support from Hicks. Among the unions, the most substantial opponents of the talks were the Engineers, who proposed to Congress in September that they should be suspended on the grounds that the General Council had exceeded their authority by accepting Mond's invitation. The debate was one of the longest in the history of Congress but, because of the legalistic issue on which the Engineers had chosen to make their challenge, not one of the most interesting. The General Council carried the day by nearly four votes to one.

Mond and his colleagues were less successful. Both he and Weir, who respectively presented the reports to the federation and the confederation, showed in their speeches that the main obstacle to be overcome was the suspicion among their colleagues of the political affiliations of

---

[51] Ibid., pp. 225–30.
[52] *The Times*, 21 June 1928.

the unions. On 11 July Mond told the federation that the talks 'meant the abandonment of class war and communist political trade unionism', and Weir explained to the confederation that, although Congress 'have been political in the past, now they show themselves determined to be industrial'. The federation declared itself 'whole-heartedly at one with the conference in its prime objects' and set up a sub-committee to prepare a detailed reply. In October the sub-committee reported that it was impossible for them to accept the proposals 'in their present form' because of the exclusion of labour matters from the federation's functions. Since a blank refusal would shock public opinion, the best course might be to discuss with the General Council some alternative form of consultative machinery which would not violate the federation's constitution. The response of the confederation was even more discouraging. Gregorson of the steel employers was 'glad to think that Lord Weir believes the leopard has changed its spots', but he did 'not think so'. Their decision was to refer the proposals to their constituent organisations without comment.

These bodies took their time to reply. On 9 November a *Times* editorial complained of the delay, and on the 27th another made adverse comparison between the secret sessions of the employers and the General Council's submission of its case in public 'to a testing debate in which the critics were overwhelmed'; but the confederation's sub-committee was not able to report the final tally until 28 January 1929. Seven affiliates with 6 per cent of the voting strength of the confederation were in favour of the National Industrial Council; four affiliates with 17 per cent of the votes accepted it with reservations; nineteen organisations with 62 per cent of the votes rejected the National Industrial Council but were willing to meet the General Council to see whether something could be achieved; and five (including the Engineering Employers) with 14 per cent of the votes were against even this. The overwhelming opposition expressed in the replies to the Mond–Turner recommendations on conciliation boards, trade union recognition, and victimisation made clear that organised employers generally rejected the spirit of the talks, and were unwilling to grant much scope or authority to a National Industrial Council, even if one were to be set up. Because the Engineering Employers Federation was the founder and doyen of the confederation, and because of the prestige and influence of Allan Smith, their reply on 30 November, which bore the marks of Smith's thought and style, carried special weight. Congress, it said, was trying to recover its influence and authority after defeat in the general strike, but it was still 'bound by the policy of the Labour Party' which was 'the alteration of the present social order and the abolition of capital. . . . There is as little justification for discussion with a political Trades Union Congress as with a political Conservative, Liberal or even Communist Party.'

On 13 February a joint letter from the federation and the confederation explained to the General Council that 'each organisation within its own province has reached the conclusion that it cannot accept the Report' but proposed a meeting to consider consultations 'upon matters of common interest to British industry'.[53] Even this modest step, said Cuthbert Laws of the Shipping Federation to the confederation's general purpose committee on 8 February, was taken 'not in the interests of the Mond–Turner Report, but in the interests of the unity of employers'. The meeting, on 23 April, led to agreement by the end of the year that consultations could be held between the General Council and the confederation on any matter within the latter's scope at the request of either party; and between the General Council and the federation on similar terms, 'it being understood that these discussions will not invade the provinces or trespass upon the functions of the individual constituents of the TUC, Confederation, or FBI'. The scheme was ratified by Congress in September 1930. Some consultations followed in which the federation showed more readiness to co-operate than did the confederation, but after 1932 the procedure fell into disuse.

Meanwhile the Mond–Turner talks had continued in order to report on unemployment. The remedies proposed included a development fund, colonial development, more liberal trade facilities, export credits, augmented pensions for those retiring at sixty-five, 'serious consideration' for raising the school-leaving age, and, above all, 'the substitution of modern plant and techniques for existing machinery and methods'—in consultation with the unions and with 'measures . . . for safeguarding workers displaced by rationalisation'.[54] However, the Mond–Turner spirit was in a fatal decline. If Smith had suffered a technical defeat in the battle over consultation machinery, he had won an overwhelming victory in the war over the introduction of 'a new conception' into industrial relations.

On the employers' side the conflict was between the impressive array of chairmen and directors of major companies assembled by Mond and the senior officers of the employers' associations and federations led by Smith.[55] Not all of the major companies in Mond's group were federated, and among the remainder were others who did not conform

[53] Trades Union Congress, 1929, pp. 203–4.

[54] Ibid., pp. 188–202.

[55] These senior officers were not, however, unanimous. L. H. Green, secretary of the flour millers, was reported by the *Daily Herald* (23 April 1928) as saying: 'The employers' associations were organised on the narrow basis of repelling trade union aggression, but things altered so quickly that this was no longer the kind of mentality that was needed.'

to the practices and attitudes of their associations, like ICI itself which was to withdraw from the Chemical and Allied Employers Federation in 1936. Mond's firms were mostly expanding and profitable, had weathered the depression without much difficulty, and could afford to take a long view. Several of them had little experience of the attitudes and practices of hard-line craft and other skilled unions at district level. When the members of Mond's group met trade unionists, they were usually general secretaries and other national officials. Some members of the group did not represent the opinions of their own managers. In May 1928 the Transport and General Workers, who were trying to organise workers at Courtauld's Coventry factory, sought the company's assistance. To Sam Courtauld's embarrassment, Harry Johnson, the joint managing director, wired from the United States:

Am not agreeable to any step being taken in the direction of encouraging active union propaganda. . . . Your telegram reads to me an admission that extremists are by threats going to be permitted to rule. You had better acquaint Chairman with my views.[56]

Mond's firms were not representative of the great majority of federated firms, which, although not small—then as now most firms with less than a hundred employees were not federated—were middle-sized, in the 100–5,000 bracket. Most of them had experienced a hard time during the depression, and were still primarily interested in producing acceptable results over the next year or two. Their managers were ready to deal with the unions; otherwise the firms would not have been federated. But they looked to their association to keep their labour costs down, to protect them from attempts by the unions to widen the scope of union influence, and to assist their firms if they ran into a dispute. They had no desire for a 'new conception' of industrial relations.

The senior officials of their associations and federations understood and sympathised with these opinions. They also had experienced difficulty during and after the war in limiting the demands of the unions. They got on well enough with the national officials of the unions, but they believed that the real power lay in the union branches and the district committees, often under the influence of Communists, the Minority Movement or other extremists. Their experience was that the national union leaders could not be relied on to control their local militants, at least not without strong pressure from employers' organisations. As a result of the depression, a series of lockouts and the general strike, they were now experiencing less trouble from the unions than at any time in their lives. In such circumstances, it seemed close to madness to offer partnership in industry to the unions along with

[56] Coleman, pp. 437–8.

generous terms of recognition, protection from victimisation and redundancy, and other concessions; and a new system of conciliation boards to deal with unresolved disputes would only give the unions a chance to appeal against the decisions of employers' associations and federations to men who might not appreciate the reason for rejecting the unions' claims. The experience of courts of inquiry was that most of them recommended additional concessions by the employers.

The structure of the Federation of British Industries differed from that of the Confederation of Employers Organisations. Most of the employers' organisations affiliated to the federation dealt with commercial issues only, so that their officers lacked knowledge of labour matters; and individual firms, whether federated or not, were entitled to affiliate in their own right. Many large firms did so. Consequently the federation was more ready to listen to Mond than were the employers' organisations dealing with labour matters, which were the sole constituents of the confederation. But for the constitutional exclusion of labour matters from the functions of the federation, Mond might have been able to win its support. With the confederation he had little chance.

However, Smith's position was not impregnable. In 1934 he was persuaded to resign, ostensibly on grounds of health, but mainly because his 'domineering behaviour and conduct of affairs was causing increasing resentment' within the Engineering Employers Federation.[57] Mond might have been able to carry the majority of federated employers with him if he had been able to offer them some solid advantage. Had the late twenties been a period of acute labour shortage, British employers might have welcomed a general agreement on rationalisation to allow them to redeploy their labour force in return for compensation to any workers who lost their jobs. As it was, most of them could shed their labour without much trouble. Had it been a period of frequent aggressive strikes, they might have seen advantage in a central disputes procedure which harnessed the authority of the General Council and the confederation to keeping the peace. As it was, the peace was being kept as never before.

On the trade union side it seems plausible to attribute the majorities which approved the Mond–Turner reports to the anxiety of trade unionists at all levels, after the general strike and the coal lockout, to avoid further large-scale industrial conflict; and to their consequent willingness to accept negotiations which might be expected to help preserve the peace. It does not seem likely that rank and file trade union members had been converted to Citrine's new philosophy, which was élitist. Nineteenth century trade unionism had relied on the solidarity of the members to regulate industrial relations. Citrine, by contrast,

57 Wigham, p. 137.

emphasised negotiations and the skills of the negotiator. Converts were therefore to be found primarily among full-time officers and executive members. Consequently support for Mond–Turner was probably assisted by the additional authority conferred on trade union leaders by national collective bargaining, the centralisation of power in the unions, and the advance of bureaucratisation.

12

The Second Labour Government

The Unions and the Labour Party, 1925–9

BALDWIN'S second government had a creditable record of political and social reform. Women at last got the vote in parliamentary elections on the same terms as men. When Labour had proposed this reform early in 1925 he had rejected it, on the ground that such a measure would have to be followed by an early election; but by 1928, with an election already in the offing, that argument had lost its force, and universal suffrage was introduced. Social reform was mainly the work of Neville Chamberlain at the Ministry of Health. In 1925 he introduced a measure which provided that old age pensions should henceforth be financed by contributions from employees, their employers, and the state on the same basis as health and unemployment insurance; and that the contributions should also cover pensions for widows and orphans. His Local Government Act 1929 finally satisfied the ambition of the Webbs, by putting an end to the Poor Law. The Poor Law Guardians were abolished with their separate rating powers, and their functions transferred to Public Assistance Committees of the local authorities.

Labour opposed both measures. The party would have preferred non-contributory pensions, and they refused to support the Local Government Bill because it

perpetuates the evils of the Poor Law system and extends the vicious practice of unrepresentative persons being nominated to membership of elected bodies, makes no provision for the prevention of destitution, fails to make unemployment a national responsibility, and will not appreciably relieve the financial position of necessitous areas.[1]

However, provision for widows and orphans filled what all parties agreed was a major gap in the system of social security, and the Local Government Act was an important administrative reform which prepared the way for transferring the burden of relief to the national government, and for unifying the local authority maternity and child health services with the hospitals previously run by the Poor Law Guardians. The relatively minor amendments which Labour attempted to make to both statutes after they formed a government, suggested that they might well

[1] *Hansard*, 26 November 1928, col. 107.

have taken a different attitude to the bills if there had been any chance that their opposition could have defeated them.

The Conservatives also tried their hand at reform of unemployment insurance. In 1925 they restored the waiting period to a week, and reduced unemployment insurance contributions so as to offset some of the new contributions now required for pensions. They also appointed the Blanesburgh Committee to review the whole system. The committee accepted the principle of insurance, and set themselves the task of making it a reality by putting an end to the payment of 'extended' benefit after the normal entitlement had been exhausted. To make this acceptable, they had to protract entitlement to insurance, leaving only a small core of long-term unemployed to be relieved by the guardians. They therefore proposed that the limitation to one week's benefit for six weeks' contributions, and to twenty-six weeks' benefit in all, should be replaced by the requirement of thirty contributions paid in the last two years. Because of the detailed administrative arrangements this meant that, in the extreme case, benefit could be paid continuously for seventy-eight weeks.

The original check on the 'scrounger' had been the limited period of entitlement to benefit under the 1911 Act. Once the unemployed man or woman had exhausted their entitlement, they had to find and hold a job in order to qualify for benefit again. In 1924 the additional check of the 'genuinely seeking work' clause had been included in the insurance scheme. Now for a period of up to seventy-eight weeks it was to be the only check, and the committee proposed to emphasise it by, among other things, instituting frequent review of claims. Even so their scheme would cover the cost of the proposed benefits only at an average rate of 6 per cent unemployment, which would have been an acceptable estimate before 1914, but proved to be hopelessly optimistic for the whole of the interwar period after 1920.

Nevertheless the Unemployment Insurance Act 1927 closely followed the main recommendations of the report, except for the inclusion of a 'transitional' benefit which was 'extended' benefit under another name. It was open to claimants who had paid eight or more contributions in the previous two years, or not less than thirty contributions overall, and restricted to a period of twelve months from the date the Act came into force; but there was no good reason to suppose that parliament would have the courage at the end of the year to do what they had failed to do when the Act was passed; and, in fact, the insurance principle was then flouted once more by a twelve months' extension. Finally, the 1927 Act removed the entitlement of strikers to benefit where the employer had broken an agreement, because of the difficulty of determining whether an agreement had been broken, and by whom.

There was an uproar in the Labour movement when the Blanesburgh report appeared. Three of its representatives had sat on the committee and signed the report, the most prominent of them being Margaret Bondfield, parliamentary secretary to the Ministry of Labour in 1924 and a member of the General Council. She stood her ground. Many of the recommendations, she said,

I regarded as extremely imperfect. But the main principle of the Report was so valuable as to outweigh in my view those disadvantages, and by signing it I had brought much nearer the possibility that the improvements might be embodied in legislation.[2]

In their evidence to the committee the General Council and the party executive had proposed a non-contributory scheme as their ultimate aim, and for the time being a halving of contributions and an increase in benefits, but it is doubtful whether many of the parliamentary leaders thought these were viable proposals. By 1929 the unions were also seeking the abolition of the 'genuinely seeking work' test. Local trade union officers, who handled cases before the referees, had been forced to recognise that many claimants were being required to demonstrate that they had sought long and diligently for work which was not to be found, and the test 'was a futile and sometimes brutal ritual'.[3] Within parliament—apart from the Clydesiders—opposition to the test was most widespread among the trade union group.

The government had to admit complete failure over its proposals for factory legislation. When Henderson had indicated his intention of introducing a bill in 1924 there had been general agreement that legislation was necessary, both because there had been no general revision since 1901, and because the provisions on hours of work—which still prescribed a maximum of sixty hours for women—were hopelessly out of date. The Conservatives therefore brought in a bill on much the same lines as Henderson's draft, only to find they had stepped onto a minefield. The provisions extending to workshops the more stringent requirements applied to factories, and considerably enlarging the powers of factory inspectors, were savagely criticised by employers' organisations, and attacked in the *Daily Express* on 2 September 1926 as 'Prussianisation'; whereas the attempt to conciliate employers by accompanying the statutory maximum of 48 hours a week for women with a relaxation of overtime provisions evoked a storm of protest from women. No accommodation was reached, and after the bill had been withdrawn in three successive sessions due to 'pressure of business', Baldwin had to admit failure over a measure 'on which I personally have

---

[2] Bondfield, p. 271.   [3] Deacon, p. 61.

been very keen for the last two or three years'.[4] Attempts to make progress towards the ratification of the Washington Convention also came to nothing.

There was room for criticism of the government's general economic policy. Churchill's budgets did not show a high standard of professional competence; little was being done for the most depressed industries; and not much to stimulate the economy as a whole, apart from the complete derating of agriculture and the reduction of the rate burden on industry and the railways by 75 per cent in the Local Government Act 1929— with the compensatory introduction of 'block' grants from the Exchequer to the local authorities. However, the economy remained stable and the Labour Party seemed to tire of attacking the government's economic management. They were more at home when they used their parliamentary time to debate motions on such topics as municipal banks and socialism. As the parliamentary party reported in 1928, while the Conservatives had been using their 'unshakable majority' to benefit their 'political friends', Labour had been 'attempting to show the country, both in home and in foreign affairs, upon what lines we should govern, what aims we should place before us, and how we should do our work'.[5]

In this respect, however, the main task was being carried on outside parliament in the preparation of a new party programme. MacDonald persuaded the party executive that it was time to replace *Labour and the New Social Order*, and work began in 1927. MacDonald's main concern was to confine the new document to a general statement of principles, leaving their application to future Labour governments. The new programme, *Labour and the Nation*, drafted by R. H. Tawney, achieved MacDonald's purpose and was adopted by the 1928 conference; although that did not dispose of all specific proposals. Three in particular continued to be subjects of debate.

One was birth control, which the Independent Labour Party and many women's groups regarded as essential for removing one of the chief causes of poverty. The issue was the provision of advice by local authority maternity centres, which was currently banned by the Ministry of Health. Labour had to pay the price of replacing the Liberals as the recipient of the political support of the Catholic church, by refusing to commit themselves to family planning. The Catholic church also intervened over the second issue, the party's proposals for education. These included raising the school leaving age to fifteen, both on educational grounds and to reduce unemployment, but that would involve additional expenditure by the schools, on both running costs

[4] *Hansard*, 6 November 1928, col. 34.
[5] Labour Party, 1928, p. 84.

and buildings. The bishops wanted to revise the settlement of 1902 so as to allow denominational schools to receive larger grants to help cover the cost.

The third issue was family allowances, which arose out of the Independent Labour Party's proposals for the 'living wage'; but on this issue the opposition came from the trade unions, many of which took the view that family allowances would be used to reduce wages because the employer would need to pay only enough to support a man without children. In 1927 a joint committee of the General Council and the party executive had been set up to consider proposals on the living wage. A majority of the committee was in favour of family allowances, but the General Council proposed to consult their affiliated unions, and finally came down against them in May 1930.

The controversies over the living wage policy indicated a growing rift between the Independent Labour Party and the majority of the Labour Party, which was further widened by changes in personnel. Allen resigned from the National Advisory Committee in 1925; Brailsford ceased to be editor of the *New Leader* in 1926; in 1927 the party decided not to nominate MacDonald as Treasurer of the Labour Party, although he was nevertheless re-elected; and a number of Members of Parliament changed their sponsorship from the Independent Labour Party to local Labour Parties.

Meanwhile, the controversy within the movement over Russia lost its force. Meetings of the Anglo-Russian Joint Advisory Committee had continued through the miners' lockout and on into 1927, mainly to give the Russians an opportunity to voice their criticisms of the British unions, and the British a chance to demand that the Russians withdraw their accusations. In 1927 Congress decided to wind it up, and a police raid on 'Arcos', the Soviet trading agency in London, was followed by the government's decision to break off relations with Russia. The General Council and the party protested, and the party undertook to restore relations if they regained office; but the whole subject was charged with much less emotion and importance than in 1924–6. In dealing with domestic Communists, the 1928 party conference matched the General Council's moves to curb Communist activity in the unions by a series of restrictions on members of parties ineligible for affiliation to the Labour Party, such as excluding them from party platforms and from serving as delegates to party meetings—even if elected by their unions.

The Labour movement, as a whole, strove to minimise the adverse consequences on the party of the 1927 Trade Disputes and Trade Unions Act. Civil service unions were required to obtain a certificate to show that they had complied with the Act, but this did not prevent their officers and members attending meetings of bodies to which the civil service unions were no longer permitted to affiliate, so long as they did so in their personal capacity or as fraternal delegates. Many unions made special efforts to persuade their members to 'opt into' their political funds. But there was no way of preventing a heavy decline in the party's income. Between 1927 and 1928 the number of trade unionists affiliated to the party fell by a third. Even so, the 1929 party conference would not agree to increase affiliation fees, although they accepted the need for a special levy. An immediate victim of the Act was the *Daily Herald*. The party felt obliged to terminate its contribution; and, soon afterwards, falling trade union membership led to a reduction in the subsidy from the General Council. Bevin searched for an alternative source of support. In August 1929 the council entered into a joint venture with Odhams Press, a highly successful publishing company which so far lacked a daily paper. Henceforth the *Herald* was run by five directors from Odhams and four from the General Council, but only the latter could vote on the political and industrial policy of the paper.

Labour and the Nation was too long a document to serve as an election programme. A shorter statement was approved by the party executive for this purpose. It concentrated on proposals for reducing unemployment, listing development schemes for housing, road-building, electrification, land reclamation, and afforestation, and promising that special assistance should be given to depressed industries. In this field, however, the party had been outclassed by the Liberals. Lloyd George gathered a highly talented group of experts to devise a better-argued case for a more ambitious set of proposals, and spent generously from the funds which he had inherited from the coalition to advertise his programme, *We Can Conquer Unemployment*.

The General Council also put out an election manifesto, which Labour politicians had cause to remember during the next two years. It did not begin with proposals for creating new jobs. They came after 'the position of the unemployed workers' which

under the present Conservative Government . . . has become definitely worse. Rigorous administration of unemployment insurance has deprived many thousands of benefits they have paid for, and has driven them to seek Poor Law relief. Decent, hard-working men and women, who care deeply for their homes and the welfare of their children, have been humiliated when they applied for what is sneeringly called 'the dole'. In despair they turned to the Guardians for help, and found their way to adequate relief barred by the harsh and unsympathetic policy of the Conservatives.[6]

If any one issue carried more weight than others in the 1929 election, it

---

[6] Trades Union Congress, 1929, p. 252.

was unemployment. The Conservatives, who had failed during nearly five years in office to effect a significant improvement, suffered a sharp decline in their share of the votes. Labour, who claimed that they could do better and would have done so in 1924 had their term of office not been so short, considerably improved their share, winning 8.4 million votes to the Conservatives' 8.7 million, and became the largest party in the House of Commons with 288 seats to 260 for the Conservatives. The Liberals, whose programme on unemployment probably seemed to most people to be on much the same lines as Labour's, no longer had any serious chance of winning enough seats to put it into practice. They had 5.3 million votes, but only fifty-nine seats. Nevertheless they held the balance of power.

Within the Parliamentary Labour Party there had been a radical change. The 115 trade union sponsored Members took second place to the 128 sponsored by local Labour parties. The Independent Labour Party came a poor third with thirty-six Members, and there were nine from the Co-operative Party. The decline in the proportion of trade union Members, for the first time less than half the parliamentary party, was not due to a failure on the part of trade union candidates. With 115 victories among 136 candidates, they had done remarkably well. It was due to the failure of the unions to increase their stake in the party in proportion to the party's ability to win seats.

Their caution may have been partly due to the effect of the 1927 Act, although with nearly five years since the last election, three of them before the 1927 Act took effect, their political funds were reasonably buoyant; but it was also due to a decline in the commitment of the unions to the Labour Party, visible in the rising number of unions which debarred their chief officers from standing for parliament; in the increasing authority and independence of the General Council; in the withdrawal of the council from the joint departments; in trade union emphasis on achieving their aims by non-parliamentary means, first through industrial action on Red Friday and in the general strike, and next through the Mond–Turner talks; and in Citrine's new philosophy of trade unionism. Among union sponsored Members, the Miners stayed put with forty-one seats, the Transport and General Workers and the Workers Union (whose amalgamation was not yet completed) had thirteen between them, the Railwaymen eight, the Railway Clerks seven, and the General and Municipal Workers and the Woodworkers six apiece.

The Government

Baldwin resigned without waiting for parliament to reassemble, and the king had no choice but to send for MacDonald. Twelve of the twenty members of his first cabinet were among the nineteen he selected in 1929, seven of them in the same posts. Snowden went back to the Exchequer. MacDonald surrendered the Foreign Office to Henderson, although he would have preferred to have Thomas, and to make Henderson responsible for tackling unemployment. That responsibility therefore went to Thomas with the office of Lord Privy Seal. Clynes went to the Home Office. As in 1924 there were four peers. Two of them, Parmoor and Thomson, had served in 1924 and held the same offices as before. Sidney Webb, as Lord Passfield, was at the Colonial Office; and Sankey was Lord Chancellor. The number of trade union sponsored Members in the cabinet fell from seven to six. Two miners had lost their places, although one of them, Hartshorn, was recalled in 1930, and there was one newcomer, Margaret Bondfield, as Minister of Labour and Britain's first woman cabinet minister. There was no representative of the leading group within the Independent Labour Party. The only men of the left were Trevelyan, once more at Education, and Lansbury as Minister of Works. Greenwood took Wheatley's place as Minister of Health, but perhaps the most notable of the newcomers was William Graham, the only man in the party whose grasp of economics approached that of Snowden. He was given the Board of Trade. Outside the cabinet were Oswald Mosley, Chancellor of the Duchy of Lancaster, and Morrison, Minister of Transport. Lansbury and Mosley, along with Tom Johnston, parliamentary undersecretary at the Scottish Office, were detailed to assist Thomas with his task of reducing unemployment.

As in 1924, the government's main successes were in foreign affairs, but this time it was not a one-man show. MacDonald dealt personally with the revision of the five-power naval agreement in 1922 between the United States, Britain, Japan, France, and Italy; and with persuading Gandhi to the Round Table Conference after he had launched an impressive campaign of civil disobedience in support of self-government. Others, however, also took a hand, including Snowden. A further revision of German reparations had been proposed by a committee of experts, with German obligations scaled down, mainly at the expense of the British. Snowden would have none of it, expressing his criticisms of the Continental powers freely and loudly. To the surprise of the other powers his stand proved immensely popular in Britain, not least with the Labour Party and the trade unions. Snowden, commented the Transport and General Workers' *Record* for July 1929, had 'proved to the people of Great Britain that their interests are far safer in Labour's hands than in of those of its predecessors, and the whole of the nation has rallied to his support'. A further revision was made to meet Snowden's objections, mainly at the expense of the Germans.

Meanwhile Henderson had persuaded the French to withdraw their troops from the Rhineland in return for the new arrangement on reparations. He dismissed Britain's High Commissioner in Egypt, Lord Lloyd, whose hard-line attitude was obstructing negotiations for a new treaty more acceptable to nationalist opinion. A firm believer in 'procedure' at home and abroad, and the dominant figure at the League of Nations, he first committed Britain, with minor reservations, to accept the arbitration of the International Court in justiciable disputes, carrying all the dominions with him; and then, in 1930, announced to the League of Nations assembly that, subject to discussion at the Imperial Conference, Britain would sign the General Act on Arbitration, Conciliation, and Judicial Settlement. All the dominions except South Africa supported him. Disarmament talks proved more troublesome, but, by January 1931, Henderson won agreement to a conference to be held in February 1932, at which he was asked to take the chair. Meanwhile diplomatic relations had been resumed with Russia, but the issue of Russian debts still obstructed progress towards a commercial treaty.

In foreign and Commonwealth affairs, the government had considerable scope to act without reference to parliament, and when the support of parliament was needed the Conservative and Liberal Parties were nearly always willing to give it. In domestic affairs, the consent of parliament was more frequently required, and more frequently refused; in several instances the government was faced with revolts among its own supporters to add to its problems with the other parties. The first measure of social reform was a bill to extend Chamberlain's widows', orphans', and old age pensions to several categories whom he had excluded. This was allowed through. The Education Bill, whose main objective was to raise the school leaving age to fifteen, ran into trouble with the Catholics. The government were not unsympathetic to the need of denominational schools for additional financial assistance, but negotiation with the churches had produced no solution by the time the bill was introduced. At the report stage a group of Labour Catholics moved an amendment to defer the operation of the Act until the matter was settled. No less than thirty-six Labour Members voted for the amendment, which was carried. Then the Lords rejected the bill in February 1931. All MacDonald could do was to announce the government's intention of carrying it under the Parliament Act. Trevelyan resigned in disgust not only at the loss of his bill, but also with the government's general performance.

As their difficulties multiplied in 1930, the government discussed with Lloyd George some form of co-operation with the Liberals which would allow them to carry more of their domestic measures through the House. The bait was a reform of the electoral system, not as the Liberals wanted, by proportional representation, but by the alternative vote which they believed would be less damaging to Labour. A bill was introduced in February 1931, but soon ran into wrecking amendments, and the opposition of the Lords. Lloyd George maintained his preference for Labour compared with the Conservatives, but many of his colleagues, and notably Sir John Simon, were ready to attack the government wherever they could.

Friction with the Liberals over electoral reform came at a bad moment. The trade unions had been promised the repeal of the Trade Disputes and Trade Unions Act. Since there was no Conservative support for this, the co-operation of the Liberals was essential, but they would not accept total repeal. The bill therefore provided that the provisions on picketing, on contracting in, on the disabilities of civil servants, and on local and public authorities and their employees were to go; but a distinction was to be made between sympathetic strikes, which were to have the same status as other industrial disputes, and general strikes, which were to be illegal. The General Council, who had appointed a sub-committee to work with the government on drafting, gave their consent to this compromise. However, under Simon's influence, Liberal amendments concerning illegal strikes which appeared to go even further than the 1927 Act were moved at the committee stage. On 25 February 1931 the General Council decided to regard the acceptance of these amendments as 'a declaration of war on the Trade Union Movement', and the bill was dropped.

The government had no more success than their predecessors with factory legislation and the ratification of the Washington Convention. Despite the urging of the General Council, parliamentary time could not be found for a Factory Bill. Bondfield introduced an Hours of Employment Bill early in 1930 and struggled hard to find a formula that the Railwaymen would accept. Cramp reported to his conference in June that, following several meetings with the minister, a revised bill would allow 32 hours' overtime in any 28 days. Sunday duty would count against the 32 hours, and, if that did not give enough latitude for weekend work and overtime during the week, the minister was to have power to extend the limit. It is hardly conceivable that this arrangement would have been found consistent with the Washington Convention, but the issue was not put to the test, for in 1931 this bill also fell victim to the 'pressure of business'. Bevin had the last word at Congress in 1932. He blamed neither Conservatives nor Labour, he said, for failure to ratify the convention. 'The people who made the Washington

Convention impossible of ratification were certain sections of our own Trade Union Movement who would not fall into line.'[7]

Some of the government's measures related to individual industries. By now it was apparent that, although the large volume of housebuilding under the Chamberlain and Wheatley schemes had substantially reduced the demand for housing among the middle class and the better-off section of the working class, it had done little for those members of the working class who could afford neither to buy nor to pay council house rents. To meet their need, Greenwood introduced a Housing Bill to encourage slum clearance, which was passed. However, most local authorities preferred to rely on the Wheatley subsidies which ensured them a better class of tenant, and little use was made of the Act until 1933 when the Ministry of Health began to badger them to submit programmes of slum clearance.

As a result of the arguments over the incursion of the railway companies into road transport, Baldwin had appointed a Royal Commission on Transport which produced its second report, on road passenger transport, in 1929. Morrison's Road Traffic Act 1930 closely followed its recommendations, which in turn were largely derived from the evidence of the Transport and General Workers. Traffic commissioners took over responsibility for licensing public service vehicles in thirteen traffic areas into which the country was divided, with the power to regulate services and fares. The objects were to discourage competition at the expense of the service, and to maintain safety standards. Drivers and conductors also required licences. Their hours on duty were limited by the Act, and a fair wages clause was included to protect their pay.

Morrison then turned his attention to the regulation of London transport. Neither Ashfield nor Bevin had been satisfied with the results of the 1924 Act; and Morrison had always criticised the London and Home Counties Traffic Advisory Committee which it created as an insufficiently representative body. Now he had the opportunity to devise a scheme on which Ashfield, Bevin and he himself could agree. All the London passenger transport undertakings, bus, tram, and underground, private companies and local authority undertakings, were to be brought into a single publicly-owned undertaking. Ashfield was satisfied, but Bevin disliked Morrison's proposal for a controlling board chosen entirely on merit. He wanted trade union representatives on the board. The bill had its second reading in March 1931, shortly after Morrison had been invited to join the cabinet, but the final stages had not been completed when the government fell.

In June 1930 Buxton resigned because of ill health, and was

[7] Trades Union Congress, 1932, p. 418.

succeeded as Minister of Agriculture by his parliamentary secretary, Christopher Addison, now a Labour Member of Parliament. Addison, who had lost none of his capacity for hard work, set about a major programme of reform. Besides an Agricultural Land Utilisation Act, he was responsible for the Agricultural Marketing Act 1931 which provided for the producers of specified products to regulate marketing by elected boards. Imports from abroad were to be relied on to prevent the boards exploiting the consumer. Eventually it was to become a major instrument for the regulation of British agriculture, but, by the beginning of 1933, only a Hops Marketing Board had been established.

The 'five counties' scheme established by the coalowners in Yorkshire, Lancashire, and the Midlands for control of output and prices had by 1930 'for two years restricted output and subsidised export sales with some success'.[8] The owners generally believed that a similar scheme could be extended throughout the industry, provided that it had statutory support. The government's main concern was to honour their pledge to restore the underground miner's working day to seven hours. There appeared to be room for compromise, and over the winter of 1929–30 a committee of ministers chaired by William Graham negotiated with the Miners and the owners. The Miners wanted a National Wages Board as well, but the owners insisted on district settlements, and refused to consider a seven-hour working day without loss of pay. The government admitted that the industry was in no state to withstand such an addition to labour costs at that time, and persuaded the Miners to accept seven and a half hours as an interim arrangement.

The Miners agreed with extreme reluctance. Seven and a half hours was already the limit underground in Yorkshire and most of the Midlands districts, and for faceworkers in Durham and Northumberland. At the Miners' conference on 7 November 1929 to discuss the government's proposal, Yorkshire wanted it referred to the districts, their spokesman saying that for conference to decide such an issue before it had been discussed in the districts was 'without precedent'. Herbert Smith insisted that conference had the right to decide, telling Yorkshire that if they took part in the decision, they would be bound by the majority. The Yorkshire delegates took the hint, and walked out. Smith followed them, after the conference had voted for the executive to review the matter and make a recommendation. On 20 November conference reassembled to receive Smith's resignation as president of the federation, and to accept the executive recommendation to approve seven and a half hours. This time Yorkshire stayed to record their adverse vote.

After much drafting and redrafting, the bill was published in

[8] Court, p. 17.

December. It included the seven-and-a-half-hour working day; district marketing and output quota schemes; a levy to finance export subsidies; and a National Industrial Board—despite the owners' objections. Since the owners had not accepted even the seven and a half hours, the Conservatives voted against the bill. The Liberals argued, with some justice, that the marketing and quota scheme was a means to keep inefficient pits in production; and that there was no incentive or sanction to promote amalgamations which, following Duckham in 1919 and Samuel in 1926, they believed to be the instrument to regenerate the industry. At the second reading enough Liberals and Conservatives abstained to let the bill through, and the Liberals pressed amendments for compulsory amalgamation in committee. Graham accepted them. Henceforth the bill included a Part I whose effect would be to keep inefficient collieries in business, and a Part II which was intended to rationalise them out of existence.

There were still the Lords to reckon with. At the instigation of the owners they carried an amendment permitting what was called the 'spreadover'. Previously the bill had limited working hours to forty-five a week. Now the owners were allowed to spread the permitted hours over a fortnight to make a total of ninety hours, and to work eight hours on any day. Consequently, because of the existing arrangements for a 'short Saturday', they need lose no time at all in Scotland, and no more than an hour a week in Lancashire. The Miners were outraged, and a compromise was reached to allow the spreadover to be worked in any district, but only with the approval of the Miners Federation and the Mining Association. On 11 August 1930 the federation reluctantly agreed to accept this compromise rather than abandon the bill, but on 28 November decided not to give their approval to spreadovers. On 3 December MacDonald begged them to change their minds. He alleged that two hundred thousand miners were already working spreadovers, which would become illegal under the Act unless variations were allowed. Prosecution was out of the question, so that the government would have to take power to sanction the spreadover if the Miners did not give way. Eventually they did so by 271 votes to 265 at a conference on 30 December.

However, this was not the end of legislation on miners' hours of work. The Act had amended, but not superseded, the 1926 measure which had introduced the eight-hour working day for a period of five years and was due to expire in July 1931. Unless something was done to prevent it, the statutory limit would then revert to seven hours. MacDonald therefore introduced a bill to continue the provisions of the 1930 Act on hours for another twelve months, which received the support of both the Conservatives and the Liberals. Because of complaints of wage cuts in some districts following the reduction in the working week, the Act provided that wage rates should not be further reduced after it came into force. A year later, in the absence of agreement between the parties on any other course, the 1930 provisions on hours of work were made permanent, but the provisions on wages were dropped.

The Labour Party had promised to help two other depressed industries—cotton, and iron and steel. To find out how this was to be done the government set up committees of inquiry. Graham, the original chairman of the cotton committee, was later replaced by Clynes, who had begun his working life as a little piecer. In July 1930 the committee reported that the main means by which Lancashire could 'keep her trade and her wage standard' was 'by reducing costs and improving methods'. In spinning, the switch from mule-spinning to ring-spinning should be speeded up and 'high-draft' machinery should be more extensively used. In weaving, the traditional Lancashire power loom ought to be replaced by the automatic loom.

These looms do not, as a rule, give a greater output per loom, but each weaver can mind a very much larger number than in the case of the ordinary power loom, and thus an important saving in wage costs is possible, concurrently with an improvement in the remuneration of the individual weaver.[9]

There were difficulties with both proposals. Although the ring could produce yarn more cheaply than the mule, the latter could still spin high-quality yarn to a standard which no ring-spindle could match; and Lancashire's high-quality yarn was under less competitive pressure than the coarser end of the trade. With the heavy decline in exports over the first half of 1930 it appeared doubtful whether many coarse-spinning firms in Lancashire had much of a future whether they re-equipped or not. The economic advantage of the automatic loom was not in doubt, so long as the weaver received a wage for tending ten or a dozen automatics which was not much higher than for tending the traditional complement of four Lancashire looms; and automatics had been slowly coming into use in Lancashire since before the war. The Weavers made no attempt to hinder their introduction, or to place narrowly restrictive limits on the complement of automatic looms to a weaver. Equally, they made no attempt to negotiate a uniform piece-price list for their operation. Instead they negotiated rates, mill by mill, which they believed would give their members a satisfactory share of the additional proceeds. Re-equipment was, however, expensive; and, as the Lancashire power looms were well-nigh indestructible, the employers were not forced to replace them as a result of wear and tear. Experiments were already in

[9] *Report*, pp. 11, 18.

progress to test an alternative method of cost-reduction—a redeployment of labour which would allow each weaver to tend six or eight Lancashire looms instead of four.

The iron and steel committee, chaired by Sankey, reported in August 1930. The government decided against publication, but the recommendations eventually appeared in a German newspaper. The committee had apparently proposed that the industry should be reorganised into integrated regional units, and that protection should be considered only if these units were unable to compete with foreign imports. There was no reference to compensation for workers who might be displaced in the process of integration. The Iron and Steel Trades Confederation prepared an alternative scheme for reorganisation under a central board on which the unions would be represented, with a levy and an import tax to finance unemployment and redundancy payments; and an Imports and Exports Board to negotiate with foreign producers, empowered to 'regulate, restrict or prohibit imports' and, if need be, fix prices on the home market. One union at least had abandoned free trade.[10]

Neither report led to action by the government. The fourth of the great depressed industries of the interwar years, shipbuilding, received some indirect help from the Bankers Industrial Development Company set up in April 1930. This new company, supported by most of the major banks and financial institutions, was the result of discussions between Thomas and Montagu Norman, Governor of the Bank of England, about the availability of finance for projects of rationalisation. It did not propose to put money directly into such projects, but to vet them and guarantee the investors against loss. Later in the year the company helped to establish another, National Shipbuilders' Security, which had the support of nearly all the shipbuilding firms for its scheme of buying and scrapping redundant or obsolete shipyards, with the aid of a levy on sales.

Bondfield did not reconstitute the Grocery Trade Boards. Instead she launched the government's main endeavour on behalf of the low-paid in the catering trades. An inquiry begun under the previous Labour government had demonstrated low wages and an almost total lack of collective bargaining in these trades, but, when the report appeared, the Conservative government took no action. In October 1929 Bondfield set up another inquiry, which again drew attention to low pay and lack of organisation on both sides, and also showed that many catering workers were required to be on duty for more than sixty-six hours a week with insufficient provision for rest periods. In August 1930 she issued a draft

[10] Pugh, pp. 456–8.

order to extend the Trade Boards Act to cover 'all work performed in or in connection with a catering establishment'.

Naturally there were objections from the employers. Sir Arthur Colefax, who was appointed to inquire into them, decided that the area to which the minister proposed to apply the Act was far too wide to constitute a 'specified trade' as required by the Act. The employers took the matter to the courts, and secured a judgment which supported Colefax's decision: Bondfield appealed, and won her case. The employers then appealed to the House of Lords, but the government fell before the case was heard. Her successor had no intention of proceeding with a board for catering, and the case was dropped.

Even if their approach was selective and piecemeal, the Labour government had tried much harder than Baldwin and his colleagues to assist British industry, and within the space of two years they had achieved at least as much as the Conservatives had in five; but, by the time the government fell, the effect on employment had been negligible. Several of the schemes had still to be put into operation, and the others had had little time to produce results.

Pay Cuts and Industrial Disputes

The first Labour government had taken office during an economic recovery which encouraged the unions to submit claims for wage increases and back them with a series of aggressive strikes. The depression which soon overtook the second Labour government encouraged employers to submit demands for reductions in pay and cost-saving alterations in conditions which were in several instances backed by lockouts, or threats of lockouts. Moreover, just as the union offensive of 1924 was petering out even before the government's brief tenure of office came to an end, so in 1929–31 most employers failed to press their apparent advantage home. In some industries pay cuts were averted, and in most of the remainder they were kept well below the fall in retail prices, so that the real earnings of workers in full-time employment rose. There were also several serious and costly industrial stoppages, but nothing on the scale of those in the previous depression of 1921–3.

The fortunes of the cotton industry were flagging some months before the depression affected most other industries, and at the end of June 1929 the Federation of Master Cotton Spinners Associations proposed a reduction in piece rates which would amount to a cut of nearly 13 per cent in earnings. A ballot of their members showed a very different mood from the year before, when the proposal for a lockout had been decisively rejected. On this occasion over 94 per cent of the votes were in favour. The weaving employers gave notice of a reduction by the same amount. The mood of the operatives was shown by their rejection of the terms by majorities of twenty to one or more. The new government sent the permanent secretary of the Ministry of Labour, Horace Wilson, to promote a settlement; and the meetings which he chaired elicited some willingness to compromise. The employers were prepared to modify their demands if they could achieve a quick settlement. The unions were prepared to accept arbitration. However, neither side would move further, and on 29 July the bulk of the industry closed down, locking out 350,000 workers.

On 6 August MacDonald appealed to the two sides to settle, offering them his assistance; on 11 August he saw the employers' leaders in Edinburgh; and on 15 August it was announced that the parties had agreed to arbitration. Pending the award, the mills were to reopen on the previous terms on 19 August, after a stoppage of three weeks. A special Board of Arbitration was appointed, with Sir Digby Swift as chairman. The award was announced on 22 August. The board found that 'the cotton industry in Lancashire was in a very distressed state'. Although 'not at all convinced that a reduction in wages is the only remedy for the present state of affairs', they felt that 'something must immediately be done to alleviate the present position', and awarded, 'as an immediate easement', a reduction of half the amount the employers had asked.[11] The speed with which they had reached their conclusion did not make a good impression in Lancashire. On 30 August the *Cotton Factory Times* expressed surprise that

the court could have so speedily digested the voluminous evidence placed before it and arrived at a deliberate and considered opinion thereon. In view of the award and all the circumstances arbitration is hardly likely to be popular for some time amongst either employers or operatives.

Since the spinning employers, especially those associated with the Yarn Spinners Association, had been agitating for wage cuts for some time, the Spinners and the Cardroom Operatives felt they had not done too badly; but the weaving employers had associated themselves with the demand only just before the notices went up, and the Weavers felt a good deal of resentment. There were protests from all their district associations, and in the autumn their union decided to try to recover all they had lost and more, by submitting a claim for an advance of 13 per cent on earnings. As the industry's affairs were then going from bad to worse, the claim did not make much progress.

Meanwhile there were more local conflicts in the woollen industry, such as had been occurring off and on since the existing agreement ran out in 1927. In May and June strikes against reductions in Bradford and

[11] *Ministry of Labour Gazette*, September 1929.

the Calder Valley forced most of the mills to reopen on the old terms. The employers decided that they might have more success with an application for a general reduction throughout the West Riding. In July they asked for a cut of 16 per cent. By October the unions were prepared for some reduction and the employers were ready to moderate their demands, but they could not reach an agreed figure, and at the end of the year a crop of disputes over local pay cuts helped to persuade Bondfield to appoint a court of inquiry consisting of H. P. Macmillan (now Lord Macmillan) alone.

The parties now returned to their original position, the employers proposing cuts averaging about 16 per cent, and the unions arguing for the maintenance of current rates. According to Macmillan's report, the unions believed that there was room for cutting costs elsewhere, especially by conducting operations on a larger scale, and that the loss of exports was mainly in markets in Australia and Japan, 'which, as a result of the tariff policies of these countries, we should never recover'. However, Macmillan was impressed by two of the employers' arguments. The first was that the decline in British exports had been accompanied by a rise in the exports of the main Continental producers, with whom the British industry might be expected to be able to compete on even terms; and the second was that the industry was 'bleeding to death' because it was paying wages out of capital. With the consent of the parties, he conducted his own investigation into a sample of firms which led him to 'conclude that the employers' case is proved'. He also tended towards the employers' view that there was little room for economies in other directions. A reduction in wages was therefore 'imperative'.[12] He recommended that it should be a little over 9 per cent for timeworkers and a little less for pieceworkers, with further alterations according to subsequent changes in the cost of living index.

His report, published in February 1930, was not open to the criticism of superficiality which had been made against the arbitrators in the cotton dispute. The union ballot, nevertheless, showed a majority of more than three to one against his recommendations, and on 26 March a mass meeting of employers at Bradford decided to enforce them. Notices were posted on 31 March to run out on 12 April. In order to exploit the differences known to exist among the employers, the unions proposed modified pay cuts of between 5 and 6 per cent, and authorised settlements on that basis. The stoppage was therefore never universal and its coverage shrank as individual employers settled on the unions' terms, and workers in badly organised areas straggled back to work on the employers' terms. At the end of May a union ballot of those still out gave the required two-thirds majority for continuing the stoppage. To

[12] *Report*, pp. 23–5.

provide some way out of the impasse, the union executives agreed to sanction mill or local agreements so long as their terms were more favourable than those recommended by Macmillan. Many settlements followed. According to the Ministry of Labour the numbers locked out were seventy thousand at the end of April, forty thousand by the end of May, and three thousand at the end of June. The major union, the Textile Workers, were still paying strike pay in July, and at the end of that month three hundred overlookers in Huddersfield were still not back at work. Their union refused to sign agreements for reductions of more than 5.8 per cent.

The outcome was the disintegration of the Northern Counties agreement, and the dissolution of the Joint Industrial Council. Since the agreement had covered 80 per cent or more of the workers employed in the wool industry, it can be regarded as a national agreement. The lockout therefore put an end to national bargaining in one of Britain's major industries for a number of years to come; and it was the only instance in which national bargaining was abandoned by the unions. However, groups of employers had been breaking away from the agreement ever since 1927, and by 1930 they showed so much disunity that the unions could secure better terms for most of their members by local settlements than by a national agreement.

Before the wool dispute was finished it was clear that another storm was brewing in Lancashire over the employers' attempts to increase the number of looms to a weaver. Although continued small improvements in the Lancashire loom had gradually reduced the weaver's workload, the union had insisted on a complement of four looms to a weaver for standard cloth since the end of the nineteenth century, and had hitherto contained attempts by employers in Burnley and Nelson to increase the number. However, at the end of the twenties the employers at Burnley tried again, arguing that they were not proposing to increase the workload, but to allow the weaver to concentrate on the most skilled part of the job—mending breakages—by transferring the work of fetching, carrying, and cleaning to labourers, so that the weaver could handle more looms without additional effort. The Weavers agreed to an experiment, and from March 1929 certain Burnley employers were allowed to run 4 per cent of their looms at a ratio of eight looms to a weaver. The weavers concerned were to be paid a time rate of £2.50—reduced to £2.34 by the arbitration award in September. This wage was more than a weaver on four looms could achieve, but a good deal less than the joint earnings of two weavers tending four looms each at the piece rates prescribed by the uniform list.

The experiment was unpopular, not necessarily with the small number of weavers working the new system, but with their colleagues who feared that many of them would lose their jobs if it were to be extended. The Communist Party, which had a small following in Burnley, began an agitation against it. At the end of March 1930 the Burnley Weavers' Committee issued a strong recommendation against renewing the experiment, saying that there was no guarantee that its extension would 'enable us to recoup an appreciable volume of our lost trade'.[13] Instead, the outcome would be the 'displacement of a large number of weavers, many of whom would never again obtain employment in the cotton trade'. The current rapid increase in unemployment in Lancashire added force to their argument, and their members supported them by a vote of almost twenty to one. The executive of the Weavers Amalgamation gave notice to terminate the experiment at the end of the year.

However, in June the employers' association applied for a renewal of eight-loom working in Burnley, and its extension to other districts. The Weavers were willing to talk, but nothing was agreed. In December the employers gave notice that they proposed to introduce eight-loom working where they chose, although for the first three months it was to be applied to no more than 10 per cent of the looms in any mill. The new secretary of the Weavers, Andrew Naesmith, announced:

The employers claim the right to introduce this system, and equally the operatives claim the right to refuse to work under it if it is unsatisfactory to them. As a matter of fact it is unsatisfactory to them, and they refuse to work it.[14]

Eight of the ten Burnley mills working the eight-loom system were struck on 5 January 1931, and on the 10th the Burnley employers began a general lockout, which was soon extended to the other weaving centres. The Weavers' executive asked for powers to negotiate on the 'more looms' issue, but were turned down by a vote of two to one. Nevertheless, they sent a deputation to London to meet MacDonald along with representatives of the employers, and returned with proposals which they put before their General Council. The council flatly refused to let them go forward to the members.

As it turned out, their intransigence was well-judged. The divisions among the employers were deeper than those in their own ranks. Most employers had no wish for their employees to work more than four looms to a weaver. A number of them were currently operating on a complement of three looms in order to keep their employees in jobs; and the advantages of the new system differed according to the quality of the cloth. Weaving fine counts of yarn, which was Lancashire's most

---

[13] *Cotton Factory Times*, 4 April 1930.
[14] Ibid., 2 January 1931.

saleable product, was less suited to the 'more looms' system than weaving coarse counts, and was less subject to competition from foreign manufacturers. According to the *Cotton Factory Times* of 20 February

Most of the manufacturers who had closed their sheds were losing money and trade for the sake of something which would have brought no advantage to them had the cause been won.

There had been an attempt to gain wider support by adding to the employers' demands a proposal for a further pay reduction—'making the stakes worthwhile, so to speak'—but 'wise statesmanship . . . was finally brought into play on the employers' side'; and the lockout was called off on 13 February. The *Cotton Factory Times* attributed this decision primarily to John Grey of Burnley, the employers' new president.

Thereafter tempers cooled, despite one or two local disputes at Burnley and Nelson over the introduction of eight-loom working in individual mills, and in August the Weavers' executive was authorised to accept a request from the employers for renewed negotiations on the terms on which an eight-loom system might be introduced. The employers' proposal was for a special piece rate list with a guaranteed minimum of the average earnings on four looms; the provision of mechanical attachment to looms where that was necessary; the employment of ancillary labour to allow the weavers to concentrate entirely on weaving; and the slowing down of the looms. Negotiations started just after the Labour government fell.

The 'more looms' dispute had been enlivened by more than one leftwing group. After the executive had been to see MacDonald, an unofficial deputation from Lancashire led by Zeph Hutchinson, secretary of the Bacup Weavers, went to London to impress upon the cabinet that Naesmith and his colleagues had no authority to negotiate. All they achieved was a meeting with Greenwood, in his capacity as a Lancashire Member of Parliament, and another with Maxton and other members of the Independent Labour Party's parliamentary group to formulate a resolution seeking a 'fundamental reorganisation' of the cotton industry with compensation for those who lost their jobs. Naesmith repudiated the deputation, and so did the Minority Movement, which had set up a 'rank and file' committee to organise mass picketing in Burnley and some rowdy lobbying in Manchester at delegate meetings of the Weavers. In their view the deputation consisted of ' "left" phrasemongers . . . playing the part of a smoke-screen, behind which the betrayal of the workers was being arranged'.[15]

There was no stoppage of work over a second round of pay cuts in the

[15] Ibid., 27 February 1931.

wool industry in August 1931. Since there was now no national machinery for negotiation, the employers announced the cuts, and took objection to the ballot by which the unions proposed to find out whether their members wished to resist or not. 'In some cases', reported Shaw, the union secretary, 'the ballot papers were actually collected by the managers and not returned'. Only one-third of the papers reached the union, giving 17,503 votes for a stoppage and 12,323 for acceptance. 'The vote', said Shaw, 'clearly indicated that there is no resisting power on the part of the operatives.'[16]

Overall, the three national textile stoppages in 1929–31, two in cotton and one in wool, accounted for thirteen million out of a total of 19.7 million working days lost through industrial disputes in Britain over those three years. The main contribution to the total from outside textiles came from coalmining, where working days lost through disputes had fallen in 1927–30 to a lower total than in any other four-year period since reliable statistics had become available; but the figure for 1931 was almost three million, mainly due to the introduction of the seven-and-a-half-hour working day with the spreadover.

With the Act due to come into force on 1 January 1931, strikes or lockouts threatened in every coalfield except those already working the seven-and-a-half-hour day. Almost all the districts concerned appealed to the National Industrial Board, which the government had set up despite the refusal of the Mining Association to participate. Independent coalowners and non-federated employers from other industries had been found to sit with representatives of the Miners, Congress, and the Co-operative Union. A dispute could be referred to the board by either side without the consent of the other, but the awards were not binding.

The board strove to find compromises. Their proposal for South Wales was that current rates should continue to be paid for a working week of forty-five hours made up of 7 hours 40 minutes on weekdays and 6 hours 40 minutes on Saturdays (or 7 hours 36 minutes on weekdays and 7 hours on Saturdays), thus avoiding the spreadover by marginally exceeding the seven-and-a-half-hour day. In other districts they awarded reductions less than those the owners had proposed. In Scotland they recommended a resumption of negotiations.

The Scots struck at the beginning of January, but at the end of the week they agreed to return, on the basis of a temporary spreadover. In South Wales the owners had stayed away from the board's hearings, and ignored the award. The Welsh Miners struck. On 15 January the Lancashire representatives on the national executive proposed a conference to consider a national strike in support of the Welshmen, as 'it is not fair to let them fight alone', but it was left to the officials to call a

[16] *The Times*, 6 August 1931.

conference if circumstances warranted it, and meantime the other districts were asked to send money to South Wales. On 17 January the men went back to work without a spreadover at current rates, pending a decision by the chairman of the South Wales Conciliation Board on the rates to apply from 1 March. He awarded cuts in both standard and subsistence rates. The Minority Movement had wanted to continue the strike after 17 January. Arthur Horner had advised against it and forfeited his post as secretary of the movement, which now called a strike for 1 March. It was a fiasco.

On 19 March a national Miners' conference voted to terminate spreadovers, but allowed the Scots to wait until their agreement ran out at the end of June. In July 30,000 Scottish miners struck for three weeks until an agreement was reached to terminate the spreadover in return for a pay cut. Faced with a pay reduction awarded by the National Industrial Board when their spreadover was terminated, the Cumberland Miners came out on official strike on 24 June and stayed out until the middle of August, securing some modifications in the cuts for the lower-paid.

The National Industrial Board had issued awards also for Bristol, North Staffordshire, and Warwickshire. 'In general', said the Miners' executive in their report for 1931, the board's decisions were 'favourable to our people', but the owners had ignored them in most cases. Nevertheless, they believed the board had performed 'a useful service. . . . Certain districts of owners have acknowledged the Board and implemented its findings.' They praised the courage of the owners who had accepted seats on the board.

Railway finances improved in 1929. The railway unions applied for a restoration of the 2.5 per cent cut which they had accepted in 1928. In October the companies agreed that it should cease in May 1930 and that they should make no further reductions in pay for at least six months thereafter. The decision was ill-timed. By the end of 1930 the companies were seeking economies in all directions, and in December they submitted proposals for a general reduction of 30p a week.

The unions were in no mood to agree. Co-operation had lost its attraction for them. Addressing the Railwaymen's annual conference in July 1930, their president said that

a large number of our members have by some curious and erratic reasoning conceived the idea that co-operation meant on the part of the managerial side a change of heart from the mercenary to the humane. The answer of the companies . . . is that, if under the guise of economy we can extract one copper from your earnings, then . . . the law of capitalism entitles us to do so without remonstrance on your part.

A counterclaim went in to increase the existing £2 minimum wage to £3. Both claims went to the National Wages Board early in 1931, and the findings were announced in March. The pay of all conciliation grades was to be cut by 2.5 per cent provided this did not reduce any adult male employee's weekly wage below £2; and there was to be an additional cut of 2.5 per cent on the amount by which each man's wage exceeded £2 a week. Salaries were also to be cut by 2.5 per cent, and by an additional 2.5 per cent on the excess over £100 a year. The average reduction was rather less than 4 per cent. The award was to apply for a year, after which each side could ask for a revision. Separate negotiations on the Railway Shopmen's National Council led to a general reduction of a little more than 4 per cent there, in return for a promise by the companies to maintain full-time working for as long as possible.

The cost-of-living sliding scale in the building industry brought a general reduction in February 1930, and another a year later. The employers in the footwear industry insisted on the application of their sliding scale agreement, which brought reductions of about 4 per cent. In March 1931, after months of negotiation to find means to reduce labour costs, the union agreed that the 25 per cent minimum by which piecework earnings were to exceed time rates should become a maximum also; although loopholes were allowed for 'exceptional skill or length of training', and there is little evidence that the employers made much use of the opportunity given them to reduce piece rates. In both gas and electricity supply, the employers proposed to terminate their stabilisation agreements in order to apply cuts due under their sliding scales, but the unions managed to stave off action until well into 1931, and then settle for cuts only in the hardest hit regions.

At the beginning of 1930 the engineering unions were still pursuing the wage claim which they had submitted the year before. On 26 February the employers offered them a joint investigation into 'working conditions, cost of production etc., in competitive countries', but the unions approached the government instead for a departmental inquiry on the lines of those in progress in the cotton and steel industries. After deputations from the employers had seen, first MacDonald, and then Bondfield, this suggestion was turned down, and the unions were advised by the Ministry of Labour to reopen negotiations with the employers. Meanwhile, a sub-committee of the employers' federation had been at work for some months to devise a package of proposals to put to the unions. In October 1930 their report was considered by the management board, and referred to a vote of the members to determine priorities.

The most popular proposals, in order of preference, were: a cut in shift and overtime rates, an extension of the working week from forty-seven to forty-eight hours, and a reduction in the minimum percentage specified for piecework earnings. A wage reduction came next, with the views of the members 'divisible into three categories of almost equal weight': those for, those against, and those who believed that 'while a reduction is warranted it may not be possible of attainment at the moment'. Changes in demarcation rules, manning practices, the closed shop, apprenticeship, and restrictions on the employment of women all secured less support than a wage reduction. At their meeting on 20 November 1930 the management board therefore decided to go ahead with the first three proposals, to reserve the question of a wage cut, and to drop the remainder.

Discussions with the unions opened in January 1931, and proceeded slowly until May when the unions withdrew. The employers posted notices imposing the changes in overtime and shift rates and in the piecework minimum, but not the forty-eight hour working week. The negotiators had already told the unions that this item would be dropped if the others were accepted. In addition they proposed another vote on wage cuts, informing their members that wage adjustments were 'liable to be of a more or less transitory character' whereas modifications in conditions were 'likely to be of a more abiding character'. Eighty-two per cent of the votes were against a general wage reduction, and 69 per cent against a withdrawal of the additional 10p granted to timeworkers in 1928. Notices were posted on 4 June to operate five weeks later. Thus time was allowed for further talks, and on 17 June the unions asked for negotiations to be reopened; three days later a joint recommendation had been agreed; and after three more days the union representatives were back to announce that the recommendation had been accepted by their executives without reference to a ballot. The first two hours of overtime each day were to be paid at the rate of time-and-a-quarter, instead of time-and-a-half; nightshift rates were to be time-and-a-sixth, instead of time-and-a-third; and the minimum percentage over basic rates specified for piecework earnings was to be 25 per cent, instead of $33\frac{1}{3}$ per cent. At the next meeting of the management board, one of the members observed that 'the element of goodwill which had been evidenced by the Trade Unions in the recent negotiations and which had been of material assistance to the parties in reaching a joint recommendation' would be prejudiced if the employers were now to raise the question of a wage cut; and his colleagues agreed with him.

A general wage reduction was also avoided in shipbuilding, although there were some cuts. The shipbuilding employers proposed that pieceworkers should lose 35p a week, and that timeworkers paid more than the new uniform national rates should henceforth receive the uniform rates, except that none of them was to suffer a cut of more than 12.5p a week. When the employers threatened to enforce these alterations in August 1931, the unions advised their members to remain at work 'under protest'. There was little hope of successful resistance. More than half the industry's labour force was unemployed, and, in the spring, London Boilermakers employed on shiprepair had struck for seven weeks without success in protest against a cut in their local additional rates.

Although indexes of wage rates do not take account of alterations in working conditions such as had been applied in engineering, or of pay cuts beyond the agreements which were no doubt enforced in many non-federated firms, the Ministry of Labour index nevertheless provides a guide to the extent of pay cuts settled by collective bargaining. From June 1929 to June 1931 the index fell by just under 2 per cent, while the cost of living index fell by over 9 per cent. Despite the depression, most employees covered by collective agreements who were working full-time were distinctly better off just before the fall of the Labour government than they had been two years earlier.

Unemployment

Meanwhile unemployment figures were mounting, despite the government's efforts to assist depressed industries. The alternative was to stimulate the economy as a whole. A lowering of interest rates would have reduced costs to British industry and therefore promoted expansion. Devaluation would have reduced British prices to importers overseas, and therefore created employment by increasing the volume of exports. Bilateral trade agreements with other countries, or multilateral agreements with groups of countries, would have stimulated exports to those countries. A general tariff on imports would have increased the competitiveness of British goods in the home market and led to an expansion of employment in firms producing for domestic consumption.

There were, however, serious objections to all these devices. Snowden and the Treasury were convinced of the merits of the gold standard. In cabinet and in party discussions Snowden was logical, masterful, convincing, and, if need be, vitriolic. He was both admired and feared. It would have taken a well-organised and determined revolt to shift him. Devaluation was therefore ruled out, and manipulation of interest rates to promote industrial expansion was also excluded, for maintenance of the gold standard required interest rates to rise and fall according to the flow of gold in and out of the country. However, the Mond–Turner talks had recommended an inquiry into the best form of credit policy, and the Macmillan Committee on Finance and Industry was appointed in November 1929, with Bevin and Keynes among its members. It was instructed

to enquire into banking, finance and credit, paying regard to the factors both internal and international which govern their operation, and to make recommendations calculated to enable these agencies to promote the development of commerce and the employment of labour.

This move, welcomed by the General Council, had the merit of deferring action at least until after the committee had reported.

Snowden was as devoted to free trade as he was to the gold standard. Tariffs could not, therefore, be used as a major instrument of economic policy. Trade agreements were unlikely to give preferential treatment to British exports unless Britain offered special terms to the countries concerned, and that could not easily be done except by imposing restrictions on trade with the rest of the world by means of tariffs or quotas. Consequently this device was also disqualified.

There remained one other remedy for unemployment, which had formed part of Labour's policy since before the war, and had been included in every Labour programme since then. Snowden was committed to it along with his colleagues, and could not veto it. This remedy was public works. Employment could be provided directly by starting new projects or expanding existing projects. Thus, the main burden of fulfilling the government's pledge to reduce unemployment fell on public works.

Even here there were difficulties, both theoretical and practical. There was confusion among economists as to whether public works could be expected to cure depression. Although the crude 'Treasury view', that additional government expenditure would merely divert resources from the private sector, had few eminent academics among its supporters, most of them had not yet been converted to the Keynesian view that, at less than full employment, the additional incomes generated by new government expenditure would lead on both to further economic expansion as they were spent, and to additional savings to pay for the original expenditure. Indeed that view was only in the process of formulation. Consequently the maxims derived from the Treasury view—for example that public works must be paid for by taxes, not borrowing, and that their direct economic justification must be rigorously examined—continued to serve as persuasive guides to action.

The practical difficulties lay in the procedures for generating, progressing, approving, and financing projects. A proposal for a new road, town hall, or swimming pool needed months of planning by architects and civil engineers before there was a scheme available for the consideration of the government departments or agencies whose approval was necessary. At any time there might be some plans in local authority pigeon-holes ready to be dusted off, but not enough for a major national expansion. When the relevant committee or department had given its approval, the Treasury had to sanction the expenditure. Government grants met only part of the cost of approved projects, varying with the rate of unemployment in the area concerned, or, in more prosperous areas, with the willingness of the local authority to import labour from depressed areas. Many local authorities considered the amount of the grants they might expect to receive to be insufficient to enable them to proceed with projects they would otherwise have put forward, and the worst-hit took the view that nothing short of 100 per cent grants would permit them to go ahead. Once a scheme had been approved, it was necessary in most instances to acquire land, often from several owners, involving considerable administrative work, and in some instances the passage of a private bill through parliament. Even though some of these procedures did not apply to projects which came under the direct control of central government, such as trunk roads, no government, however enthusiastic and determined, could, given existing administrative practices, make a major contribution to reducing unemployment by means of public works in much less than two years.

Although Labour's election manifesto spoke of the first Labour government's 'schemes of a comprehensive and far-reaching character which it had already begun to put into effect'[17] and which could presumably be taken up again now, it soon became clear that there were no schemes. It was Thomas's job, along with his assistants, to produce them. He made a trip to Canada in August 1929, returning full of stories of increased orders for British products, which turned out to amount to very little. On 4 November he reported to the House on the results of this visit, and on other projects including a bridge over the Zambesi. However, Thomas and his assistants had no power to take any action concerning these or any other projects which might occur to them, and the most solid contribution to increasing employment was a road programme to cost £37.5 million spread over five years which Snowden had approved in July. Even so 'by February 1930 less than four thousand men altogether were employed on road schemes, and most of them were on schemes taken over from the Conservatives'.[18]

By the end of 1929 Thomas and his assistants were aware that nothing very much was likely to be done to increase employment for some time to come. Thomas found refuge in the bottle, to which he was already no stranger, and his assistants decided that they must draft their own proposals which would have to be more far-reaching than any plans

[17] Labour Party, 1929, p. 304.   [18] Skidelsky, p. 107.

considered so far, if they were to be of use. The task was given to Mosley who went to work with a will. His proposals were unquestionably radical. The aim of recovering our former position in overseas trade was to be abandoned as unrealistic. Free trade should be set aside in favour of import controls in order to expand the home market as rapidly as possible. Meanwhile, unemployment was to be tackled by increased expenditure on public works (a £200 million programme over three years was suggested), by a pensions plan to encourage retirement, and by raising the school-leaving age. Procedural obstacles were to be tackled by an executive committee of ministers with the Prime Minister in the chair, backed by a powerful secretariat of senior civil servants, and given wide powers to act. This executive committee was to be supported by sub-committees on specialised aspects of the work, and a development bank to finance the projects. Mosley attacked the Treasury view and argued that the money could be found.

Believing that Thomas would pigeon-hole his scheme, Mosley submitted it direct to MacDonald, who referred it to the cabinet in February 1930. Its reception was chilly. Thomas made play with Mosley's alleged failure to consult him. It was referred to a cabinet committee and the examination of the Treasury, whose comments were predictably damning. Final rejection came in May. Mosley decided to fight on, without the support of Lansbury or Johnston. He resigned, defended his memorandum in the House of Commons, and pushed the issue to a vote at a meeting of the parliamentary party which went overwhelmingly against him.

Mosley had grossly overplayed his hand, Such radical proposals had invited rejection by the cabinet, but he made little effort to win alternative support in the party or in the unions. He was suspect as a member of the landed gentry, extremely rich, clever, and arrogant. In addition, he moved too soon. At the time he was writing his memorandum, unemployment had begun to rise again, and rise sharply. By the middle of 1930 there were three-quarters of a million more unemployed than in June 1929. This frightening trend helps to explain the narrow victory of the Labour Party executive on a conference resolution in October which instructed them 'to go fully into the proposals of the Memorandum and to issue an early and comprehensive report'.[19] Mosley made an effective speech, winning 1,046,000 votes to 1,251,000, and was triumphantly re-elected to the executive. The vote enabled many local parties and even trade unions to express their concern—although no trade union leader supported the resolution. In December Mosley drafted a new manifesto in collaboration with Aneurin Bevan, W. J. Brown, and John Strachey. In all it was signed by

[19] Labour Party, 1930, p. 200.

seventeen Members of Parliament. But Mosley was no longer interested in the Labour Party. Only four of the seventeen followed him when he founded a New Party in February 1931, and one of them, Strachey, quickly drew back as Mosley's fascist traits became more evident.

In June 1930 MacDonald had put an end to Thomas's misery by dividing the Colonial Office and appointing him Secretary for the Dominions. Vernon Hartshorn became Lord Privy Seal, but MacDonald himself assumed special responsibility for unemployment with Hartshorn as his assistant. He had already, in February, set up an Economic Advisory Council of fifteen members including Bevin, Citrine, Cole, Keynes, and Tawney and several employers. It was to them that he looked for ideas. Since agreed advice could hardly be expected from such a body, a committee of five economists with Keynes as chairman was asked to advise him on what could be done. They reported in October. They were agreed that unemployment benefit should be restricted so as to increase the flexibility of labour; they wanted a big public works programme; and a majority favoured a general tariff.

In some respects they were pushing at an open door. The government were already edging their way towards a reform of unemployment insurance. Although there was little likelihood of public works stemming the rapidly rising tide of unemployment, the numbers employed in this way were rising to a more respectable total—schemes employing 64,000 were in operation by July 1930; a Public Works Facilities Bill was passed in August to expedite procedures; the proportion of costs borne by central government had been stepped up; and Morrison had persuaded Snowden to increase the trunk road programme. Tariffs, however, were a different matter; if MacDonald might be willing to listen to the case for them, Snowden's opposition was still decisive. Meanwhile, the unemployed total continued to rise, by another three-quarters of a million between mid-1930 and mid-1931.

Even then the unions did not condemn the government's record. In September 1930 Congress resolved, without opposition, that 'the present Government has not a majority over the combined opposition parties, and is consequently prevented from operating effective Socialist measures for the only solution of unemployment'. The president, Beard, complained that

manifestations of disunity within the Party, at a time when unity is most needed, are dispiriting to the mass of men and women who, at the last general election, gave up rest, time and money they could ill afford out of their sparse earnings to place the Labour Party in office . . . I stand by the captain—by James Ramsay MacDonald.[20]

[20] Trades Union Congress, 1930, pp. 69, 287.

The unions might have been expected to use their great power within the party to force the government into more energetic action over unemployment. No issue was of greater importance to them; as the fall of the government was to demonstrate, they were not slavishly loyal to their political leaders, but they did nothing, or next to nothing. To take decisive action, the union leaders and members would have had to believe that something could be done to increase employment in the circumstances of 1930. As it was, most of them appeared to accept the depression as a natural disaster, an 'economic blizzard' which they must wait to blow itself out. The minority felt something more ought to be done, but they had to define what that something was before they launched a campaign to persuade the government to do it.

The unions might have been ready to accept a proposal from the government for a general tariff, but they were far from ready to take the lead. In its report to Congress in 1930 the economic committee of the General Council argued that the unions should be ready to consider tariffs in appropriate circumstances. The free traders moved the reference back to their report, and were defeated by no more than 1,878,000 votes to 1,401,000. As for the gold standard and devaluation, they were mysteries better left to experts.

If anyone within the unions was qualified to give a lead on what was to be done, it was Bevin, who was a member of both the Economic Advisory Council and the Macmillan Committee, and manifestly trying to discover a remedy for unemployment; but he had not found it. Presenting the report of the economic committee to Congress in 1930, he said that the committee's aim was

to put before the Labour Government . . . a proposal for a definite economic organisation within what is called the British Empire. This organisation will be an investigating organisation. . . . Tariffs are only the froth; they are merely the kind of thing that lazy minds jump to. We have taken a different way. We have gone to the foundation.[21]

A month later he told the Labour Party conference:

They had had a glut created, which had reduced the wholesale price level in the world and had brought about the present situation, mainly because the consuming power of the world was in no relation at all to the remarkable scientific genius in the world of production. He did not believe that in one or two years, or in ten years, they were going to solve that problem [but] . . . they (the State) must accept responsibility, and from that basis build, year by year, finance and other things that would follow in its train.[22]

[21] Ibid., pp. 259, 261.
[22] Labour Party, 1930, p. 198.

Lacking clear guidance from their own leaders, the unions were nevertheless unwilling to listen to outsiders who were anxious to tell them what to do. Mosley had no appeal for them; and the Independent Labour Party were well on their way into the wilderness. In 1930 their conference limited their parliamentary group to those who pledged themselves to support Independent Labour Party policy, such as *Socialism in our Time*, even where it was unacceptable to the Labour Party; and incidents of indiscipline in the Commons became more frequent. If maintained, such a course was bound to lead to a split, and Henderson and Maxton strove to find a compromise. They failed, and in 1932 the Independent Labour Party disaffiliated from the Labour Party.

Most accounts of the second Labour government were written during the twenty-five years of full employment after the Second World War when it seemed that unemployment had been conquered, and that, with the aid of Keynes's *General Theory*, economists knew how it had been done and how, if need be, it could be done again. It followed that there had been a remedy for unemployment in 1930–31, and the government was to be condemned for not discovering it, or at least for not trying harder, for if they had done so they might have stumbled upon it, as Rooosevelt later appeared to have done with his New Deal. Accordingly, the unions were at fault for not pressing the government harder. Admittedly the government had not a majority in the House, but since the Liberal programme had included many of the proposals which the government might have tried, especially large-scale public works, this was not an excuse for inaction. However, writing in the nineteen-eighties, when it is only too evident that there is no reliable remedy for unemployment, a more cautious attitude is in order. Perhaps there was as much to be said for trying to ride out the storm as for trying this new course or that. The evidence of the New Deal is inconclusive. Roosevelt came to power just as economic recovery began throughout the world. He could hardly avoid showing results, but they were not better, probably a little worse, than the achievements of the far less bold and innovative government then in power in Britain.

The unions had no hesitation in pressing the government hard on those issues which they understood. They knew from experience about the 'genuinely seeking work' test, and they were determined that it should go. Bondfield, who was preparing a bill to fulfil Labour's election pledges, referred the test to a committee which accepted the General Council's proposal, known as the 'Hayday formula', under which a claimant would be disqualified if he refused the offer of a suitable job; but they also wanted to provide for the situation where a claimant knew of a suitable job, even though it had not been offered to him, and had failed to make reasonable efforts to obtain it. The bill, which made some increases in benefit but did not honour the party's pledge to raise the rate for adults over twenty-one, followed the report of the committee closely. If a claimant 'could be reasonably expected to know' that a suitable job was available, he was to be disqualified unless

he shows that he has taken all such steps as (having regard to the means usually taken for such a purpose and to the extent to which such employment was available) he could reasonably be expected to take for the purpose of obtaining such employment.

To the unions this was taking away with one hand what had been given with the other, and they were not prepared to accept it. However, they did not wish their parliamentary representatives to join in the flamboyant public opposition of Maxton and his colleagues. Instead Thorne, the trade union group's senior member, wrote to MacDonald on their behalf to say that he understood that the cabinet would not allow Bondfield to accept the Hayday formula, or a reduction in the waiting period, and went on

For the sake of approximately £4,000,000 per annum the Cabinet is making it most difficult for us, and I am firmly convinced that even now at the eleventh hour if the Cabinet could see its way clear to accept these two propositions, we should be able to kill the opposition which has been going on for some days in the House by John Wheatley, Kirkwood and Co. What we have seen and heard pains us all I am sure. We, at any rate, are anxious to support the Government in every way, but on the foregoing two points we feel strongly.[23]

A few days later Bondfield announced that she was accepting the Hayday formula.

As the unemployment figures rose and successive appeals were made to parliament to extend the limit of the unemployment insurance fund's borrowing powers, the system of unemployment insurance was subjected to increasingly strident attacks on several grounds. Firstly, there was the cost. Snowden balanced his budget in April 1930 by an increase in income and other taxes, but far larger increases would be necessary if he were to do the same in 1931. One alternative was a cut in the rates of benefit, which could be justified by the fall in retail prices since the rates were last altered. Another was to limit entitlement to transitional benefit. The Blanesburgh Committee had sought to abolish this 'uncovenanted' benefit, but the numbers receiving it were now increasing at an alarming rate as the period of unemployment lengthened with the intensity of the depression. Thirdly, the 'anomalies' of the system could be curtailed. Many thousands of married women

[23] Quoted by Skidelsky, p. 129.

who had no intention of returning to work, it was alleged, were drawing benefit. Seasonal workers who had no intention of working at other times were, nevertheless, able to claim benefit. The system allowed workers on short-time to draw benefit for days off work even if their earnings for days at work in the same week exceeded the weekly rate of unemployment benefit. Workers and their employers were, it was said, arranging patterns of work to maximise total weekly income which prevented rationalisation of the labour force to reduce costs.

In the summer of 1930 a committee of the Economic Advisory Council, chaired by Cole, reported in favour of radical reforms of the system. All-party discussions, set in motion by Bondfield, reached agreement on substantial changes, but they were too harsh for the cabinet, who chose instead to appoint a Royal Commission. On 9 December 1930 MacDonald announced that Judge Holman Gregory was to be the chairman, and there were to be no representatives of either the unions or the employers' organisations. This had not been the original intention, but Bondfield had been maladroit in consulting the General Council, who believed that the offer to discuss the terms of reference was made only after the cabinet had decided on terms which were objectionable to the unions. They therefore refused to discuss them or to nominate members. On 17 December the council instructed Citrine to send the Prime Minister 'a very strong protest' on the manner of setting up the Royal Commission, and on the terms of reference.

The General Council's proposals to the commission were that rates of benefit should be increased to £1 for both men and women, with 50p for a wife or other dependent adult, and 25p for each child, paid for by an 'unemployment levy' on all incomes, and that the unions should take over the administration of the scheme on behalf of their members. The interim majority report of the commission, published on 4 June 1931, was on very different lines. Although a self-supporting scheme was not possible in current conditions, borrowing should be limited by raising contributions, cutting benefits, and restricting receipt of benefit to twenty-six weeks in any one year; and a means test should be introduced for applicants for transitional benefit. The conditions under which married women and casual, seasonal, and short-time workers were entitled to benefit should be tightened. On 12 June a letter from Hayday, who was in Geneva, was read to the General Council. He did not think that 'any Government would dare to implement' these findings. If the government tried to do so, 'he was certain that there would be a revolt in the minds of the people, and anything might happen'.

Whether or not they dared to act on the report, the government did not do so at this stage. Snowden had balanced his budget in April by 'raiding' various funds in the manner of Churchill, and his colleagues now decided to deal only with the 'anomalies', leaving over the proposals on contributions, benefits, and qualification period. Their excuse was that they could not make up their minds on these issues until they had seen the final report. A bill to give the minister power to vary the conditions, amount, and period of benefit for casual, seasonal, and short-time workers and for married women went forward with the reluctant acquiescence of the unions and the full-blooded opposition of Mosley and the Independent Labour Party, who forced thirty-three divisions in one all-night sitting on 15 July.

The General Council's suggestion that rates of benefit should be increased is perhaps to be seen as a bargaining counter in a situation in which demands for cuts were being made by employers, politicians, and economists; but the unemployment levy was a serious proposal. The system was not an insurance scheme. The suggestions regularly put forward to make it look more like an insurance scheme were designed to transfer a larger share of the costs to workers and employers, to cut benefits, and to worsen the conditions of those receiving benefit or to transfer them to poor relief. There was no moral justification for singling out the latter group for punitive treatment. Unemployment was a national problem, and it was reasonable that the nation should take the responsibility for resolving it, and meeting the cost through taxation in proportion to income.

It was of course quite out of the question that the government would accept these proposals. Nevertheless, once MacDonald's shiftiness and Bondfield's tactlessness had convinced the General Council that the government intended to worsen the conditions of the unemployed, it was sensible on their part to put forward proposals which they could whole-heartedly support, to refuse to take part in discussing the details of schemes which seemed to them to be wrong in principle, and to reserve their considerable political influence to block the adverse changes in benefits and conditions which they rightly expected the Royal Commission to recommend.

Meanwhile financial crisis was spreading from one European country to another, and a run on the Bank of England led to dangerously large losses of gold and foreign currency, forcing the Bank to borrow from France and the United States. On 31 July came the report of the Economy Committee, set up by MacDonald in response to pressure from the opposition parties to advise on 'all possible reductions in National Expenditure', with Sir George May as chairman and Pugh among the members. By including the normal sinking fund provision of £55 million and the £50 million borrowed by the unemployment insurance fund, the committee estimated the budget deficit for 1931–2 as £120 million. To balance the budget the majority report proposed tax increases and a saving of £97 million, of which £67 million was to come from increases in unemployment insurance contributions, limiting benefit to 26 weeks in a year, tightening conditions, extending the scheme to the self-employed, and introducing a means test for transitional benefit. A further £17 million was to come from pay cuts for teachers, the armed services, and the police. Pugh and another member signed a minority report rejecting most of the economies, and proposing that the deficit should be met almost entirely by higher taxes. Henceforth it was assumed, both at home and abroad, that the deficit reported by May was the cause of the run on the pound, although this was in fact due to the instability of the Central European financial system; and that the remedy was a package of expenditure cuts such as May had recommended.

The Fall of the Government

On 30 July the cabinet appointed their own economy committee of MacDonald, Snowden, Henderson, Thomas, and Graham to make proposals for dealing with the crisis. The first meeting was arranged for 25 August when the members would have had time to take a holiday. MacDonald went off to Lossiemouth. The drain on gold continued. Snowden urged a meeting of the committee as soon as possible. MacDonald arrived back in London on the 11th to meet representatives of the major banks along with Snowden. When the economy committee met the next day, Snowden told them that the Treasury had revised the May Committee's estimate of the prospective budget deficit from £120 million to £170 million; and proposed that it should be covered by increased taxation and cuts in expenditure in roughly equal amounts. The committee met several times in the next few days, reporting to the cabinet on the 19th. The cabinet then wrestled with the proposed economies until they took their final decision on the 23rd.

If the long-run objective was to put the nation's finances in order, in the short term they had to stop the loss of gold by regaining foreign confidence; and, as the pressure on gold increased, the immediate need became a foreign loan to tide Britain over. The money would have to come primarily from New York, whose bankers would need to be satisfied that the British government was creditworthy. They, like their colleagues elsewhere, believed that the government's failing was extravagance, especially in their provision for the unemployed. Consequently, they not only wanted to see a balanced budget, but were particularly concerned that there should be savings at the expense of the unemployed.

The members of the economy committee and the cabinet accepted the need to balance the budget, but most of them were reluctant to do it at the expense of those whom they thought they had a special duty to help. They found tax increases easier to stomach. But more taxes and fewer cuts would not win confidence abroad. The other possible remedies for the loss of gold were devaluation and tariffs. The first was not given much consideration, but tariffs were discussed at length by both the committee and the cabinet. A substantial majority of the cabinet were prepared to consider a tariff of some sort, but in the end the matter was dropped.

Snowden's main proposals in relation to the unemployed were: a 20 per cent cut in benefits, an increase in contributions, and a transfer of £20 million of the cost of transitional benefit to the local authorities. Together with several smaller items they would reduce central government expenditure by £67 million. The economy committee rejected the cut in benefits, and the cabinet rejected the transfer of transitional benefit.

Whatever they proposed would require support from the opposition in parliament—preferably official support from both opposition parties, so that the nation would be seen to be united. On the morning of 20 August, MacDonald saw the opposition leaders, except for Baldwin who was abroad and Lloyd George who was ill. They told him that the proposed tax increases were far too high, and the economies were ridiculously inadequate. Only by restoring the economies at the expense of the unemployed could the cabinet produce a package acceptable to parliament. That afternoon the economy committee met the Labour Party executive and the General Council to inform them of their decisions. The executive decided to leave the matter in the hands of their members in the cabinet. The General Council went away to consider their position.

None of them wished to accept the cuts. They went through them item by item. First they rejected any worsening in the lot of the unemployed; and then, one by one, a series of proposals for public sector pay cuts. Finally they decided against economies in the road construction programme. As alternatives they suggested a tax on fixed interest securities and suspension of the sinking fund. They also discussed tariffs, but decided that issue would have to be referred to Congress, due to meet at the beginning of September. A deputation of Bevin, Citrine, Hayday, Pugh, and Walkden was sent to report to the economy committee. Citrine presented the council's decisions, and Bevin undertook most of the arguing with Snowden. At the end MacDonald said that the General Council had given the government no help, and

Thomas asked Citrine what he would do in their desperate situation. Citrine denied that the situation was desperate. 'There are enormous resources in this country.'[24]

The cabinet heard of the General Council's response when they met next morning. All accounts agree that its effect was considerable, encouraging Henderson and others to maintain their opposition to cuts in unemployment benefit. MacDonald appealed for economies sufficient to restore confidence, but his colleagues would not go beyond what they had already agreed. The total was £56 million. Next day he tried to persuade them to accept a further £20 million derived mainly from a 10 per cent cut in unemployment benefit, on condition that the opposition parties would accept it. They reluctantly allowed him to approach the opposition leaders, without commitment. The opposition leaders were equally cagey. They wanted to know what the New York bankers thought. Their reply arrived during another cabinet meeting on the evening of Sunday, 23 August. They wanted to know the opinion of the Bank of England and the City, and said that much would depend on the response of public opinion to the government's programme.

In this uncertainty, MacDonald made a last appeal, and then put the revised list of economies to the vote. It was carried by twelve votes against nine, the minority being Adamson, Addison, Alexander, Clynes, Graham, Greenwood, Henderson, Johnston, and Lansbury. Three trade union ministers, Bondfield, Shaw and Thomas, voted with the majority. It was generally agreed that the cabinet could not carry on, and that MacDonald should inform the king of their resignation and ask him to meet all three party leaders next morning.

The formation of a national government had already been discussed on several occasions in the cabinet, and in MacDonald's meetings with the other party leaders. After the cabinet meeting the latter arrived to persuade MacDonald to agree to that course, but he waited for the meeting with the king. Next day he came back from Buckingham Palace to tell his former colleagues that he had consented to stay on as prime minister of a small national government, which it emerged later was to consist of ten ministers. Snowden, Sankey, and Thomas stayed in their old posts. Baldwin was Lord President; Samuel was at the Home Office; Chamberlain at the Ministry of Health; Lord Reading at the Foreign Office; Hoare at the India Office; and Cunliffe-Lister at the Board of Trade.

On 26 August a joint meeting of the General Council, the Labour Party executive and the consultative committee of the Parliamentary

[24] *General Council Minutes*, 20–21 August 1931.

Labour Party[25] repudiated all responsibility for the new government which was

a Government of persons acting without authority from the people. . . . Britain whose social standards and services have greatly contributed to the raising of standards of life throughout the world is now, under pressure from international and national financial interests, to take the lead in a process of worldwide degradation.[26]

When parliament reassembled on 8 September the government won a vote of confidence by 309 votes to 249. Twelve Labour Members voted for the government, and there were a few abstentions. It was no national government, but a Conservative–Liberal coalition with four Labour ministers.

The part played by the General Council in the fall of the government was criticised then, and has been criticised since, as 'dictation' to the government. Formally, of course,

they were asked by the Prime Minister to express their views and told him that they believed the proposals which he and his Chancellor put before them represented the wrong policy to follow and that they could not support them. They were fully entitled to hold this view and express it to the Cabinet when called upon to do so.[27]

However, it is also true that their answer was decisive. MacDonald and Snowden could no longer hope to put together a package of economies which would have the support of their own party and of the opposition parties. The members of the General Council were also the leaders of the major unions. They controlled the votes at the party conference; they provided the bulk of the party funds; many of the members of the party executive were subordinate officers of their unions; and the unions also sponsored and financed the candidatures of two-fifths of the Labour Members of Parliament, who were organised in a trade union group which maintained close touch with the General Council. So long as the General Council were expressing views which had the support of the executives and conferences of their unions—and subsequent events were to show that was the case—then they were telling the cabinet that the party would not support the cuts which had been put to them. That might be described as dictation.

There remains the question whether the General Council's action was justified. Although the immediate case for the cuts was that they would enable Britain to raise loans abroad, their main justification had to be the

[25] With Labour in office, a consultative committee had replaced the executive committee of the Parliamentary Labour Party.

[26] Trades Union Congress, 1931, pp. 519–20.

[27] Bullock, p. 489.

contribution they would make to the recovery of the British economy. Most businessmen, economists, and Conservatives took the view that cuts in unemployment benefit and a tightening of the conditions of its receipt would assist recovery. The alleged consequence would be a lightening of the burden on industry, and an opportunity for employers to cut wages which should reduce costs, boost sales, and create new jobs. Snowden may by now have accepted these arguments, but the Labour Party certainly did not, and there is no evidence that a majority of the cabinet had been converted to them. By rejecting all the alternatives—tariffs, devaluation, suspending the gold standard, and a heavy increase in taxes—the cabinet had got themselves into a dilemma in which they had to choose between resignation and drastic economies at the expense of the unemployed; but it did not follow that they believed that the economies would cure the depression. Certainly the General Council did not. Citrine told Congress two weeks later:

We were not only opposed to the details, and some of the details of the reductions mentioned to us seemed terribly severe, but we felt we must oppose the whole thing. For years we had been operating on the principle that the policy which has been followed since 1925 in this country, of contraction, contraction, contraction, deflation, deflation, deflation, must lead us all, if carried to its logical conclusion, to economic disaster.[28]

[28] Trades Union Congress, 1931, pp. 81–2.

13

The Turn of the Tide

The National Government

SNOWDEN introduced the new government's budget on 10 September. The deficit estimated for a full year was still £170 million. The proposals for increased taxation were much the same as those of the Labour government. The main item was an increase in the standard rate of income tax, but there were also changes in allowances and surtax, and increased duties on beer, tobacco, and petrol. The economies were also very similar to the final proposals on which the Labour government had failed to agree. Those at the expense of the unemployed actually came to a smaller total than had been proposed by the Labour cabinet's economy committee on 19 August; but they included a cut of 10 per cent in the standard rate of benefit, and a means test for transitional benefit. The chief innovation was a reduction of nearly £20 million in the amount put aside for the sinking fund which Snowden had not allowed Labour to touch. Within a fortnight Snowden had abandoned another of his orthodox principles. Although the formation of the new government had been enough to secure substantial loans from abroad, even before the budget was introduced, the drain on gold continued, and became worse after the news of a mutiny of the navy at Invergordon against pay cuts. On 21 September the gold standard was abandoned. The pound fell from 4.86 dollars to 3.40 dollars by the end of the year, but there were no disastrous consequences. Retail prices rose by 2 per cent.

Already the Conservatives were arguing for an election which would allow the government to adopt their chosen remedy for unemployment—tariffs. MacDonald's feeble resistance was easily overcome. Snowden and the Liberals showed a little more fight. They had to agree to an election, but not to tariffs. Instead the government was to ask for a 'doctor's mandate'—for a free hand to investigate every proposed remedy, including tariffs, and to apply those which appeared to promise good results. Parliament was dissolved on 7 October, and the election was held on 27 October.

The election confirmed the Labour movement's breach with MacDonald and those he had taken with him. At first many Labour Party members believed that the split was a temporary difference which might be healed when the crisis was over. The opinion of the *Cotton Factory Times* on 28 August was that

MacDonald and Snowden . . . are the same men they were a month or a year ago, and though they are to be opposed by the whole Labour machine, we think nobody will question their sterling purpose, high courage and patriotism. At the moment rash judgments are particularly to be deprecated. The perspective of today's doings will be clearer in twelve months' time.

However, many bitter words were spoken on both sides in the election campaign, especially by Snowden; and even if they might have been forgiven, the electoral damage done to the party could not. The Liberals lost most votes. Split into three groups, two of them supporting the government and the third, consisting of Lloyd George and his family, in opposition, they received in all 2.3 million votes, compared with 5.3 million for the united party in 1929; but because of the free run given to selected government supporters by the Conservatives, the number of Liberal seats increased from fifty-nine to seventy-two, including four Lloyd Georgeites. The Conservative vote increased from 8.7 million to 12.0 million, giving them a record total of 473 seats and absolute control of the new House of Commons. Labour's vote was down from 8.4 to 6.6 million. This in itself was bad enough, but the coalition of their opponents increased the number of their straight fights to 361, and many of the third and fourth candidates who intervened in the remaining contests were nonentities of one sort or another— Communists, candidates for Mosley's New Party and independents. This factor, along with the increased Conservative vote, reduced Labour to forty-six seats. In terms of representation in the House of Commons, Labour was back to 1910. Another six seats went to the Independent Labour Party. Their rift with the Labour Party had not been healed, so they fought without its endorsement. Thirteen coalition Labour candidates were returned with Conservative support. Exactly half the successful Labour candidates were sponsored by the Miners Federation; nine more by other trade unions; thirteen by local Labour Parties; and one by the Co-operative Party. Two of the successful Independent Labour Party candidates were sponsored by trade unions.

The cabinet was reconstructed. There were now twenty members instead of ten, with a majority of Conservatives. Snowden went to the Lords as Lord Privy Seal. One of their first actions was to push through the Abnormal Importations Bill, to empower the Board of Trade to impose duties of up to a hundred per cent on manufactured goods being 'dumped' in this country. The new powers were quickly and liberally used. The Horticultural Products (Emergency Duties) Act gave the

Ministry of Agriculture similar powers in relation to fruit, vegetables, and flowers. These measures were accepted by the free traders in the cabinet. Permanent legislation for a general tariff was more of a problem, but an 'agreement to differ' allowed them to remain in the cabinet and oppose the legislation, while the Conservative majority saw it through. The Import Duties Bill, introduced in February 1931, provided for a general 10 per cent tariff with exceptions for a short list of exempted goods, and for imports from the empire—pending an Imperial Economic Conference to be held in the summer. The Treasury could impose additional duties on the recommendation of an Import Duties Advisory Committee. A number of agreements were signed at the Imperial Conference whereby Britain and the dominions gave preference to each others' exports, in many instances by further increasing the duties on imports from elsewhere; and the free traders at last resigned from the cabinet. In April 1932 the Import Duties Advisory Committee recommended further increases in duties on manufactured and semi-finished goods, which were adopted. The duties on iron and steel imports were made conditional on a reorganisation of the industry which came in 1934 with a cartel—the British Iron and Steel Federation. In 1933 an Agricultural Marketing Act allowed the Board of Trade to fix quotas on agricultural products from abroad. These quotas were employed to buttress marketing boards set up under Addison's 1931 Act, which the new government used vigorously from 1933 onwards. Wheat production benefited from a guaranteed minimum price and a duty on imported wheat.

Bank rate had been raised to 6 per cent in September 1931, but within a year it was down to 2 per cent. Other interest rates followed, and Chamberlain was able to convert over two billion pounds of war loan from 5 per cent to 3.5 per cent. The immediate effect was a substantial saving in government expenditure, but lower rates must also have encouraged investment once the recovery got under way. They also reduced the cost of housing, although this does not appear to have been the main factor in the housing boom of the thirties. Local authority housing was affected by subsidies more than by the cost of borrowing, and the Wheatley subsidy was terminated in 1933. Although slum clearance rose thereafter, it did not lead to local authority housebuilding on the same scale as before. The boom was in private housing, and it had begun in 1929. Among the influences at work were the falling price of building materials; the growth of the building societies; the falling size of families, which meant that even a static population would require more houses; and the growth in the number of potential owner-occupiers. White collar employment increased from 4.1 million in 1921 to 4.8 million in 1931. The number of private, unsubsidised houses built rose from 66,000 in 1928–9 to 149,000 in 1932–3, and continued sharply upwards.

The Agricultural Marketing Act was not the only Labour measure employed by the national government in their attempt to promote recovery. The application of the Coal Mines Act of 1930 went ahead. The system of output quotas and export subsidies helped to stabilise, and even in some instances raise, prices, but the effect was not as great as had been hoped. Some of the potential benefit had already been reaped by the 'five counties' scheme which had applied output quotas and export subsidies in the coalfields where they could have most effect; and the working of the Act revealed defects which required modifications. The results of Part II of the Act, intended to promote rationalisation, were frankly disappointing. In the face of the hostility of the owners, the Coal Mines Reorganisation Commission found their powers insufficient.

The London Passenger Transport Bill was not allowed to fall with the Labour government. It was Ashfield's scheme as well as Morrison's. After an interval it was brought forward again with some amendments, the most notable of which concerned the appointment of the board. This was taken out of the hands of the minister, and invested in six appointing trustees—the holders of such office as the chairman of the London County Council, the chairman of the London clearing banks and the president of the Institute of Chartered Accountants. This extraordinary arrangement does not seem to have made much difference to the membership of the board. After the bill became law in 1933, Ashfield was appointed chairman, and John Cliff, assistant secretary of the Transport and General Workers, became a part-time member with special executive responsibilities for staff matters to make up a full-time job. The strong antipathy between Bevin and Cliff had prevented the effective use of Cliff's abilities within the union, and Bevin was now able to appoint a second-in-command to his taste—Arthur Deakin.

No immediate action followed the final report of the Royal Commission on Transport, but in 1932 the government organised a conference, chaired by Sir Arthur Salter, to make recommendations for the regulation of road haulage, which led to the Road and Rail Traffic Act 1933. In order to control the number of goods vehicles on the road, the Act introduced a licensing system akin to that provided for passenger vehicles by the 1930 Act. Limits were placed on the speed of vehicles and the time which drivers could spend at the wheel, and it was made a condition for A licensees (general carriers) and B licensees (who transported mainly their own goods, but wished to be allowed to carry for others as well) that they should pay 'fair wages'. The Transport and General Workers had not been entirely happy about the working of the fair wages clause in road passenger transport, because comparison was restricted to the 'district', which gave them no leverage to raise wages in a locality where wages were generally low or where there was only one employer. The 1933 Act directed the Industrial Court to have regard also to relevant national agreements. However, the fair wages clause did not apply to C licence holders, who carried their own goods only; and there was no restriction on the number of vehicles with C licences.

The government showed greater sympathy than Baldwin's administration of 1925–9 for the extension of the protection of Trade Boards to low-paid workers. The Labour government had instituted inquiries to discover whether there was a case for Trade Boards in the tiny fustian cutting industry and in the cutlery trade. The reports favoured the establishment of boards. In cutlery the larger, organised firms complained of undercutting by the unorganised employers. Boards were set up in both industries in 1933.

Parliament had always found the regulation of hours worked by shop assistants a highly contentious issue. Despite an almost continuous agitation by the Shop Assistants, a series of private members' bills, and several government proposals for legislation, by 1933 the main restrictions in force were still a maximum working week of 74 hours for young persons dating from 1886, and a weekly half-holiday for all shop assistants introduced in 1911. In addition, wartime provisions for the early closing of shops had been continued on an annual basis until 1928, when a requirement to close by 8 p.m.—except for one night a week at 9 p.m.—was made permanent, but with exemption for some types of shop.

In 1930 the House of Commons appointed a select committee to review the whole subject, and in particular the feasibility of a general limitation of working hours to 48 a week. Reporting in December 1931, the committee found that a working week of over sixty hours was 'quite common'.[1] They were unanimous in proposing that young persons should be limited to 48 hours, but split six to five in favour of extending the limit to adults. A bill was put together over the next two years to impose a 48-hour limit for young persons, and to make a number of requirements relating to rest periods and working conditions. Passed in 1934, it was at least a substantial improvement on previous legislation.

In 1933 the Weavers sought the assistance of parliament to check wage-cutting in the manufacturing section of the cotton trade. The proposal of statutory enforcement of collective agreements throughout the trade or industry to which they applied was no novelty. It had been put forward by the Industrial Council in 1913—provided both sides wanted it and were sufficiently representative; it had been imposed in the munitions industries during the war; and it was advocated after the

[1] *Ministry of Labour Gazette*, December 1931.

war as a means of supporting the agreements of Joint Industrial Councils. The Whitley Committee had mentioned it as a possibility, several councils asked for it, and an Association of Joint Industrial Councils, which 'seems not to have gained the confidence of the JICs as a whole',[2] agitated for its implementation. Congress rejected the proposal in 1923 and 1924 when it was equated, quite unjustly, to compulsory arbitration, but changed their minds in 1925. Meanwhile a bill was introduced in 1924 with the support of a number of trade union Members of Parliament, securing 236 votes to sixteen on its second reading; but it fell with the Labour government.

In 1930 the Association of Joint Industrial Councils came to an agreement with the Trades Union Congress on a Rates of Wages Bill. This would have applied to wage agreements only, but to all of them, not only those of Joint Industrial Councils; and was entrusted to Hayday. The government would not give it priority, and it failed to make much progress before the government fell. The association then approached the new Minister of Labour, Henry Betterton, who told them that he wanted to be satisfied that the principle of the bill had the approval of the employers' organisations. In 1933 the National Confederation of Employers Organisations decided they could not give their support.

Up to this point, however, there had not been much head of steam behind the proposal. Trade unionists were concentrated in federated firms, and although they might have gained an advantage from having their agreements enforced on other employers, many of them small employers operating near the margin, in most instances the maintenance of their agreements did not depend upon it. Now the continued depression in Lancashire was leading to widespread undercutting of the agreements in the manufacturing section. The average size of weaving firms was much less than that of spinning firms. They had smaller resources and were more difficult to control. Too impoverished to strike against every infringement of the agreement, the Weavers concluded that their only remedy was for parliament to make it illegal for an employer to pay less than the agreed rate. They approached the Minister of Labour. After establishing that the Cotton Spinners and Manufacturers Association was also in favour of the proposal, he promised sympathetic consideration. The Cotton Manufacturing (Temporary Provisions) Act was passed in 1934 to give the required powers.

Resisting Pay Cuts

The May Committee had proposed pay cuts for the public services financed wholly or largely by the Exchequer. These were justified by

[2] Charles, p. 205.

reference to the extent to which pay in these services had failed to follow the decline in retail prices over recent years, and by comparisons with pay in relevant outside employments. No special cuts were proposed for the non-industrial civil service because a reduction would soon fall due under the sliding scale agreement, 'and it is on this assumption that our recommendations are made'.[3] The rates paid to manual workers in the dockyards and ordnance factories were 10–20p a week above those in private industry and were to be reduced to the outside levels. The rates of the armed services had been cut in 1925, and the committee were willing to accept the current rates for other ranks, except that in the navy the 1925 cuts had not been applied to those already in the service but only to new recruits; and long-service men had since kept their old rates on re-engagement. That practice, said the committee, must cease. Except for a deduction of $2\frac{1}{2}$ per cent, the pay of police constables and sergeants was still 'at the level fixed in 1919'; the committee thought a $12\frac{1}{2}$ per cent cut would be appropriate.[4] For teachers, however, 20 per cent was 'the minimum reduction which should be made', and, even so, would leave elementary teachers 'with more than double their pre-war remuneration'.[5]

The government altered the May Committee proposals into a more acceptable package. There were to be cuts in the salaries of government ministers, members of parliament and judges, and those proposed for teachers and the police were modified, the reduction for teachers being put at 15 per cent; but those for the navy remained unaltered. The cut in the long-service able seaman's basic rate was therefore 25 per cent, although when account was taken of allowances, which were not altered, the figure became less than 14 per cent for an unmarried able seaman, and less than 11 per cent for his married colleague with children. Pensions were also to be reduced.

Naval ratings had a long history of organisation and clandestine agitation on pay and conditions through lower-deck death-benefit societies. The arrangements for informing the fleet were muddled, so that they heard the news over the radio after arrival at Invergordon. On 15 September 1931, after three days of lower deck discussions and meetings in the shore canteen, the crews of most ships failed to muster for duty, and thereafter avoided officers so far as possible in order to minimise the risk of a charge of disobeying a direct order. The Admiralty ordered a return to home ports, and on the evening of 16 September the navy put to sea again. Nevertheless, the government had had a nasty shock; and the navy was not alone in agitating against the cuts. Protest meetings of teachers were held all over the country, and on 15 September the Association of Education Committees wrote to the

[3] *Report*, p. 33.   [4] Ibid., pp. 44–5.   [5] Ibid., p. 51.

Prime Minister, the president of the Board of Education and all Members of Parliament to say that the cuts in teachers' salaries were unduly severe. Even the tightly-controlled Police Federation made the displeasure of its members evident.

No cuts had yet been made. The National Economy Bill, which provided the necessary powers, did not receive royal assent until 30 September. The government therefore had time to back down. On 21 September MacDonald told the Commons that the government had been examining the cuts in detail.

There are undoubtedly classes of persons who are unfairly affected, and the Government have, in view of all the circumstances, come to the conclusion that the simplest way of removing just grievances is to limit the reductions as regards teachers, police and the three Defence Services to not more than 10 per cent.[6]

Teachers' pay had increased since 1914 more than that of any other profession, and theirs was therefore the most vulnerable service to a government seeking economies. The education committees were well aware of this. In March 1931 they had given a year's notice to terminate their 1925 agreement with the teachers. The teachers' unions refused to discuss reductions and meetings of the Burnham Committees were suspended. However, the May Committee proposals horrified both sides, and the government, who had much to learn about the conduct of industrial relations, further alienated the education committees by their failure to consult them or make use of the Burnham Committees in formulating their proposals. The government made a clumsy attempt to remedy this omission. They wanted

to secure the maintenance, so far as is practicable, of the full machinery of the Burnham Committees. In addition to minor matters affecting the interpretation and application of the Government's decision, it would be open to the committees to submit for . . . consideration . . . proposals which, while securing to the Exchequer the same aggregate saving, would vary the relative share to be borne by individuals.[7]

The Burnham Committees were not impressed by this announcement. They refused to take any responsibility for the cuts, continuing instead to renew their 1925 agreement year by year until in the end the cuts were restored.

However, ministers were not incapable of learning. Anticipating 'panic economy decisions' relating to the services for which the local authorities were directly responsible, Levi Hill, the secretary of the

---

[6] *Hansard*, 21 September 1931, col. 1271.
[7] Ibid., col. 1285.

Local Government Officers, saw Chamberlain before the economies were announced. As a result of their interview, the Ministry of Health circular which recommended economies also warned that because of local variations there could be no 'hard and fast rule' and recommended that each authority should discuss the situation with its officers.

Only seven hundred out of more than two thousand authorities made salary cuts.[8] The ministry decided that more could be done, and set up two committees, one for England and Wales, and another for Scotland, to suggest further economies. Both committees reported in November 1932, suggesting further reductions in pay. After a deputation from the union had discussed the reports with officials at the ministry, a new circular rejected some of the proposals and informed the authorities that 'what is needed is not ill-considered and all-round reductions of salaries', but 'a cautious and fair examination of the work to be done and the remuneration reasonable for that work in present conditions'.[9] Discussions with the officers were again recommended, and the circular even suggested talks between the associations of local authorities and the union. Although nothing came of that proposal, there were few further pay reductions, and before long some authorities began to restore the cuts already made.

There was no need to caution the local authorities to hold discussions with the unions on their proposals for reductions in the pay of their manual employees, since there were established national negotiating procedures. Some of the provincial councils for the non-trading services negotiated reductions, and others did not. The average figure for labourers' rates, based on returns from twenty-eight large towns, fell by a little more than 3 per cent between 1930 and 1932. At the 1934 conference of the General and Municipal Workers, Dukes, who had recently taken over from Thorne as secretary, was able to announce that:

The panic demand of the National Government two years ago for drastic economies in the wages of municipal employees met with only half-hearted approval by the local authorities, and, in so far as cuts were made at all in those wages, there has now been practically complete restoration.

In January 1932 the Tramways Joint Industrial Council negotiated a 'temporary abatement' of wages. Unlike the councils in electricity and gas supply, the tramways council had so far maintained wage rates despite the depression, and even now the cut was only 3 per cent.

When the General Council's representatives met the Labour government on 20 August 1931, Citrine said that the proposed pay cuts in the public services 'would be the signal for a wage cutting campaign in trades and industries generally'. If such a signal was intended it was widely

---

[8] Spoor, pp. 113–15.   [9] Ibid., pp. 117–18.

disregarded. No further cuts were put to the engineering unions. There were some local cuts in shipbuilding where pay exceeded the standard national rate, but no suggestion of a reduction in the standard rates themselves. There were no further cuts on any scale in coalmining or in the wool industry. Further cuts were imposed under the building industry's cost-of-living sliding scale in 1932, and under the selling-price sliding scales in iron and steel, but these were not triggered by the government's economies. In March 1932 the printing employers proposed a 20 per cent reduction in pay, and radical changes in craft rules. When the Printing and Kindred Trades Federation rejected these and subsequent proposals, the employers put modified terms to the individual unions, which adopted delaying tactics. The employers were clearly not prepared for a general lockout, and in the spring of 1933 they let the matter drop. The printing unions had not conceded a wage reduction of any kind, nor adverse changes in conditions, throughout the whole period of the depression.

In Burnley more cotton manufacturing firms were adding to the number of looms tended by their weavers, in many instances with the consent of the weavers concerned, but without an agreement with the union. In February 1932 nineteen firms were struck, and by the end of the month thirteen of them had been forced to resume four-loom working. Meanwhile national negotiations on the issue had been renewed in an effort to reach a general agreement. A draft was ready early in March, but there was a strong feeling among the weavers against accepting an increase in the complement of looms at any price, because of its effect on employment, and the delegate meeting of the Weavers Amalgamation voted it down. The employers then asked for talks on wage reductions. The employers' chairman, Grey, explained that this move was not a reprisal for the failure of the 'more looms' negotiations. He had already told the unions that the firms which could not benefit from adopting higher loom complements would have to ask for a pay cut.

In prolonged negotiations the two sides began to narrow the distance between them. Deciding that they could wait no longer, some Burnley employers imposed cuts in June. The Burnley Weavers struck. There were more stoppages elsewhere, and the problem of reinstatement added a new and contentious issue for the negotiators to settle. On 16 August the employers generally gave a month's notice of a reduction of 13.7 per cent on earnings, but the unions replied with a week's notice of a strike which began on 29 August, when the forty-five thousand workers already on strike were joined by a hundred thousand more.

After a fortnight tempers began to cool. On 13 September the Ministry of Labour's conciliator, F. W. Leggett, brought the two sides together in a conference which appointed a sub-committee to deal with all the issues in dispute. Firstly, both sides accepted the need to restore a general wage agreement, and to create machinery to ensure that its terms would be observed. Then a reduction in wages was settled at 8.5 per cent on earnings. Next the employers undertook to recommend that their members should offer re-employment as soon as possible. A new procedure provided that unresolved disputes should, in future, be referred to a conciliation committee, consisting of an independent chairman and two other members from outside the cotton industry, one to be nominated by each side; and the 'more looms' issue was to be settled under this new procedure. This agreement, known as the Midlands agreement after the hotel in which it was negotiated, was signed on 27 September; and a 'more looms' agreement was negotiated with Leggett serving as independent chairman. Its object was to provide earnings of £2.05 for a weaver operating six looms as against an average of about £1.75 on four looms, and it included various guarantees against exceptionally low earnings.

However, by the end of December, when the 'more looms' agreement was ratified, there were already complaints that individual employers were failing to honour the Midlands agreement. Allegations of breaches came in increasing numbers during the early months of 1933. Mills were working at cut rates, exceeding the forty-eight hour week, and working more than four looms to a weaver outside the terms of the new agreement. It was these complaints that led to a request for statutory enforcement of the weaving section's agreements.

While the Weavers and their employers were moving from guerilla warfare to a pitched battle, in the spring and summer of 1932, little progress was being made in spinning negotiations, which had begun with a proposal from the employers for an extension of the working week without a compensating increase in pay, and, when this was rejected, moved on to pay cuts. Both unions refused to discuss them. The Master Spinners did not give notice of a reduction until August 1932, when they also proposed a figure of 13.7 per cent; and even so they waited for the weaving dispute to be settled. In October Leggett persuaded them to postpone their notices again, in order to allow talks under his chairmanship. He first obtained the withdrawal of the proposal for extending the working week. Then the employers agreed that the pay cut in spinning should be marginally smaller than in weaving, 7.7 per cent instead of 8.5 per cent. It seemed that open conflict had been avoided.

However, the Spinners' council rejected the draft agreement. Although the Cardroom executive had authority to settle, they decided to join the Spinners in a ballot. Meanwhile, any mill in which the cut was imposed on 31 October, when notices ran out, was to be struck. The employers enforced the notices, and 125,000 operatives stopped work. The Spinners voted by six to four for a strike, but the Cardroom vote was two to one for acceptance, and both unions decided to ratify. The final agreement provided for a new procedure on the same lines as that of the Midlands agreement.

The two stoppages in the cotton industry accounted for 5.3 million out of 6.5 million working days lost that year. There is no need to offer further explanation for the domination of the strike statistics of 1929–32 by cotton beyond saying that during those years it suffered heavier wage cuts than any other major industry except wool, and that the cuts were due to its position as Britain's leading exporter, selling a far higher proportion of its products abroad than any other major industry.

During the autumn of 1931 discussions in the docks on a reduction in pay and alterations in conditions and minimum rates ended in agreement on a cut of 4p a day, to operate from 4 January 1932. In London the independent Lightermen's union voted to reject the agreement, and struck along with lightermen and tugmen in the Transport and General Workers. After a month Bevin and his executive ordered a return to work of their members—who had not received official strike pay, as they were in breach of their agreement, but had been paid £1 a week from the union's London area benevolent fund—and the Lightermen followed them back. There was also an unofficial stoppage on the Mersey, and the long-awaited secession of the Glasgow dockers took place on 1 January 1932, although they remained at work.

Negotiations by the Seamen's leaders over a proposal for a pay cut of £1.50 a month were a little more open than dealings with the shipowners in Havelock Wilson's day. They told the executive on 16 January 1932 that,

having in view their responsibilities to the membership and the hopelessness of a strike at the present time owing to the depression in the industry, and thousands of men out of employment and willing to go to sea for whatever wages they could obtain,

they had offered a cut of 50p, next 62.5p and then 75p. The owners then came down to 90p, but would budge no further. The executive authorised a settlement.

In the autumn of 1932 the railway companies decided that railway wages must come down again, and proposed that a general reduction of 10 per cent should be substituted for the existing cuts ranging from 2.5 per cent to 5 per cent; and that the £2 minimum, below which no cuts were to apply, should be reduced to £1.90. The unions refused and the claim went to the National Wages Board, who were told by the companies that receipts were down by 9 per cent compared with the previous year, that the return on ordinary stock was below 1 per cent, and that the railways were starved of capital.

Between them the board's seventeen members produced no less than six verdicts. With relatively minor differences between them, the representatives nominated by the railway companies, the Federation of British Industries and the British Chambers of Commerce were generally favourable to the claim. The representatives of the railway unions, Congress, and the Co-operative Union were against further reductions. Special significance therefore attached to the chairman's report. He recommended that the existing cuts should be replaced by a general reduction of just over 4 per cent, with an equivalent proportion deducted from wages in excess of £2.50 a week and salaries over £125 a year. The minimum was to stay at £2 a week. The secretary of the Railway Managers' Committee wrote to the unions to say that, on reflection, the companies were prepared to accept the chairman's findings, but the unions replied, on 24 January 1933, that they could not 'accede to the companies' proposals', and the companies decided not to face the strike which must have followed an attempt to impose the chairman's recommendations. Instead they gave the required twelve months' notice to terminate their procedure agreement, hoping that within the year the unions would accept a new procedure which could be relied upon to produce less anarchic results.

At the beginning of 1932 the London Traffic Combine proposed that the cuts awarded on the railways in 1931 should be extended not only to underground railwaymen, whose wages usually followed those paid by the four main line companies, but also to London's road passenger transport employees. The tramwaymen held out until July, when the Metropolitan Tramways Joint Industrial Council settled for a cut of less than 2 per cent to apply to both Combine and local authority tramwaymen. At the same time a provisional agreement was reached for the busmen. Their pay was to be cut by a similar amount and their guaranteed week was to be suspended, to allow seasonal lay-offs as an alternative to redundancies. There was an uproar among the busmen when the terms were known. An unofficial body, soon known as the Busmen's Rank and File Committee, complained that the deal had been made without consulting the garage delegates. The central bus committee held a ballot which rejected both parts of the agreement. On 30 August an official conference of garage delegates voted by fifty-one to seven for a strike.

Bevin realised that he and his colleagues had misread the feelings of the men. He diverted the negotiations into a new area—cutting costs by increasing efficiency—and negotiated what became known as the 'speed' agreement. The proposals of the companies (for Tillings was a party to the negotiations as well as the Combine) were withdrawn, in return for an undertaking to introduce such higher speeds as might 'in their opinions be found safe and convenient'. The resultant economies, which resulted mainly from reduced overtime, since the higher speeds permitted a reduction in the maximum time on duty, were to be divided in the proportion of 60 per cent to the busmen and 40 per cent to the companies. This agreement was ratified by thirty-three votes to twenty-five at another conference of garage delegates on 19 September.

The rank and file committee nevertheless decided to remain in existence. They began to issue a lively journal, *Busman's Punch*. At the end of 1933 the proceeds of the speed agreement allowed the busmen to increase their annual holidays and add 5p a week to the driver's pay and 10p to that of the conductor; but their weekly earnings were still below those they had received before the agreement, due to the loss of overtime. Since the pay cuts for London tramwaymen had been conditional on the acceptance of similar cuts by the busmen, they were withdrawn.

TABLE 4

Average money incomes of full-time wage earners by industrial groups:[a] *1933 incomes as a percentage of 1929 incomes*

Wool	88
Cotton	90
Transport and Communication	93
Gas, Water, Electricity	93
Construction	94
Engineering	96
Local Government Service	97
Iron and Steel	98
Shipbuilding	98
Agriculture	98
Printing	100
Mining and Quarrying	101
Distribution	103

Note: [a] For sources see footnote to Table 2.

Table 4 shows changes in average money incomes in the major industries between 1929 and 1933 for those working full-time. The reductions in money wages were far smaller than those in the depression of 1920–23. Then the overall reduction had been 30 per cent. In 1929–33 it was 5 per cent. Since retail prices fell by about 15 per cent, there was an increase in real incomes of about 10 per cent for those in full-time employment, whereas the overall change in real full-time incomes from 1920 to 1923 was almost nil. The explanation for this remarkable contrast lies partly in the change in the terms of trade during the depression. The prices of raw materials and foodstuffs fell far faster and further than the prices of manufactured goods. As the leading importer of the former and one of the main exporters of the latter, Britain was bound to gain. The other main factor was the rapid increase in productivity in Britain. Throughout the interwar years Britain sustained an annual rate of increase in output per head approaching 2 per cent. In the years 1929–33 it was substantially higher. For the most part the firms which were closed, and the workers who were made redundant, were the less efficient, and their departure necessarily raised the average performance.

The pattern of pay changes revealed by Table 4 is not so easy to explain as that of 1920–3. For example, whereas it is no surprise to find the severest reductions in wages in cotton and wool, it is surprising that the two industries which secured advances in money incomes, and therefore the biggest gains in real income, were distribution and mining (although this applied only to miners working full-time, and in 1933 many of them were not). The reductions of 1931, following the introduction of the statutory seven-and-a-half-hour working day in coalmining, were small and confined to a minority of districts; otherwise coalminers remained on the minimum rates prescribed by their agreements. Overall the industry's wage ascertainments returned a fall of 1 per cent in earnings per man/shift, between 1929 and 1933, compared with the 1 per cent increase in money income shown in Table 4. The main factor affecting the pay of distributive workers must have been the continued expansion of their industry, outpacing all others.

Industrial Relations in the Depression

Trade union resistance played a part in limiting and avoiding wage cuts during the depression. There was, for example, no economic reason to explain why wages fell further in wool than in cotton. The cotton industry was the harder hit of the two. However, the cotton unions were far better organised and richer than the unions in wool, and put up a far more prolonged resistance to their employers' attempts to reduce wages and cut labour costs in other ways, a resistance which accounted for well over half the days lost in Britain through disputes from 1929 to 1932. The railway companies would probably have imposed the findings of the chairman of their National Wages Board in 1932, if they had not expected the consequence to be a national railway stoppage. The cuts proposed for London busmen would have gone through in the same year, if the busmen had not made it clear that they would strike unless they were withdrawn. The print unions refused to negotiate on pay cuts, and as a result they suffered none. But union resistance is not the whole story. Many employers seemed reluctant to ask for pay cuts.

Almost the only reductions proposed by the coalowners in this period were the consequences of increases in labour costs imposed by statute. The engineering employers voted against a straight pay cut. Admittedly they negotiated other changes which would reduce earnings, but the effect was relatively modest. Many employers' associations put off proposals for wage cuts until the autumn of 1931, after two years of depression, and others did not raise the question until 1932. Many local authorities rejected the government's recommendation for cuts in the pay of their employees, and the Association of Education Authorities were sharply critical of the amount by which the government cut teachers' pay. Many of the cuts which were finally imposed were modest—2, 3 and 4 per cent in a period in which the cost of living fell by 15 per cent. Surely the employers could have had more if they had insisted upon it?

For years they had repeated their complaints that wages were too high; that the high level of wages in the sheltered trades and services—such as building, rail and road transport, gas and electricity supply, and local and national government—were imposing unwarranted and damaging costs on manufacturing industry; and that a further intolerable burden was put on them by the cost of the social service benefits which were so high that they prevented reductions in industrial wages. Late in 1925 the Confederation of Employers Organisations had submitted a report to the Prime Minister on the causes and remedies of the current industrial depression, asserting that at the end of the war Britain had adopted

idealistic standards of life and working conditions and new standards of national and public expenditure which were entirely divorced from pre-war economic considerations, which could not be maintained once the cold blast of foreign competition reasserted itself, and which nevertheless this country has gone on endeavouring to maintain without having the productivity to enable it to do so.

They went on to quote a recent report of the Department of Overseas Trade to the effect that

The vital factor which differentiates English from German costs of production is labour. The German workman receives considerably less than the pay of his English colleague and often works a longer day; further, he works unremittingly except for the usual pauses, during the whole of this time, unhampered by any trade union restrictions as to the quantity of his output.

If these had been the ruling considerations in the thinking of British employers on the subject of wages in 1929–33, they would have tried harder to extract larger pay reductions from their employees, and the unions would not have had the strength to stop them—although there might well have been major conflicts outside as well as inside the textile trades, as there had been in 1921–2.

One important influence on the behaviour of employers in both depressions was the rate of decline in the demand for and the prices of their goods and services. Industrial output was down by almost 20 per cent in 1921 alone, although recovery began in 1922. Over the two years wholesale prices fell by half and retail prices by nearly a third. Consequently in 1921 and 1922 even employers who were currently making ends meet faced the prospect that they would soon need to cut their costs in order to stay in business. Between the formulation of a proposal for a wage reduction and the decision, the number of firms in favour would have increased. It would continue to increase while negotiations were going on. If the trade unions refused to give way, there was not much doubt that an overwhelming majority of employers would be in favour of posting notices. A rapidly falling price level favoured unity among employers over cuts in pay and cost-saving changes in working conditions.

Things were different in 1930–33. The decline in industrial production was little more than 10 per cent over four years. Wholesale prices fell by about a quarter from the 1929 level, and retail prices by about 15 per cent. Most firms in most industries were not facing disastrous losses, nor even the prospect of disastrous losses. The worst-hit firms might decide that they must have a reduction in pay in order to stay in business. Their colleagues, or enough of them, might agree that a reduction in labour costs would improve their prospects too, so that negotiations with the unions could begin. However, when the unions proved reluctant to make concessions, the employers would have to contemplate the possibility of a lockout. Those who were not hard-pressed and in no immediate danger of running at a considerable loss might have no strong incentive to vote in favour of a course which threatened them with heavy losses in the immediate future. The conditions of 1930–33 were unfavourable to unity among employers.

Examples of disunity abound. In their ballot on a wage cut reported on 20 November 1930, the engineering employers were divided three ways. About a third were in favour. Presumably these were the hard-pressed firms. About a third were against. It is reasonable to suppose that they were not under much pressure, or at least that they would find sufficient relief in the reduction in overtime and shift rates, and in the minimum piecework guarantee, which their federation thought there was a better prospect of obtaining. The remainder would have favoured a wage cut if they had not believed that 'it might not be possible of attainment at the moment'. It seems plausible to interpret this statement as indicating that they believed it could not be had without a lockout, and that their circumstances were such that, while a wage cut would be welcome to them, it was not so desperately needed as to make them ready to face the probable costs of a lockout.

In gas and electricity supply, the employers dropped their claims for general pay reductions, and settled for reductions in some regions, varying according to local conditions, and no cuts in others. Disunity had been most evident in the textile industries before the general depression began, with the American cotton spinning firms favouring pay cuts (although not by the required 80 per cent majority) and the Egyptian cotton spinners rejecting them; and in Yorkshire, with some local wool employers breaking away from the national agreement to impose reductions, whereas the majority continued to honour it. The disastrous fall in textile exports which began in 1929 brought greater unity, and lockouts. Even so most wool employers were ready to make local agreements with the unions for smaller pay reductions than their association was demanding; and the cotton manufacturing employers abandoned their lockout over the 'more looms' issue when it became clear that most of them had no direct interest in insisting on a union capitulation.

It is beyond the scope of this volume to attempt any detailed explanation of the contrast in movements of prices and output between the depression of the early twenties and that of the early thirties; but two points can be briefly noted. Government monetary policy and expenditure cuts were more severe in 1921–2 than in 1930–33; and the growth in cartels and price-fixing arrangements among manufacturers enabled them to limit price reductions more successfully in the second period than the first. Cotton and wool were exceptions in this respect because they were major exporters, and one of the few areas in which Britain's economic performance was worse in the early thirties than it had been ten years before was the export trade. Between 1929 and 1932 exports fell by almost 40 per cent, whereas in 1922 the volume of exports was almost back to the level of 1920.

Unemployment also was higher in the early thirties than ten years earlier, with substantially more unemployed throughout 1931–3 than in 1921, the worst year in the early twenties. However, if the comparison is made in terms of employment, instead of unemployment, the second depression was the less severe. Between 1920 and 1922 the numbers in employment fell by nearly 2.5 million, whereas the decline in employment from 1929 to 1933 was only a third of a million. The explanation for these apparently contradictory trends is that the total labour force employed and unemployed, fell in the earlier period by almost a million, whereas in the second period it rose by nearly 1.25 million. Among the influences at work in the first period was the withdrawal from the workforce of many women who had taken jobs during the war and of men and women who had postponed retirement. In the second period there was an increase both in population and in the proportion of the population of working age, due mainly to increased longevity. The British economy was therefore more successful in maintaining old jobs and creating new jobs in 1930–33 than in 1921–2. Had the working population been static over 1929–33, unemployment would have increased by less than 350,000; and if it had declined by the same amount as in 1920–22, unemployment in 1933 would have been more than half a million below the 1929 figure.[10]

The contrasts between the two depressions suggest that employers pay greater attention to their immediate economic conditions than to general arguments that wage rates are too high, or working hours too few, or restrictive practices too onerous; although they may sincerely believe that those arguments are well-founded. But there was more than assessment of direct economic advantage in the attitude of organised British employers to their dealings with the unions in the depression of the early thirties. There were also signs of concern to maintain good relations with the unions, which can be seen in the efforts which some groups of employers made to improve their negotiating procedures.

Both sections of the cotton industry revised their procedures after the stoppages of 1932. During negotiations in 1930–31, the building employers made a number of alterations in their procedure at the request of their unions. To the satisfaction of both sides, the Plasterers were brought back within the scope of the agreement. In 1932 they were forced to accept the standard building rate in London, and readmitted to the operatives' federation, so that there was no longer any obstacle to their inclusion in the national agreement. In 1933 the Co-operative Wholesale Society at last accepted a procedure to cover their employees.

There were also procedural improvements in the public sector. In 1932 the Post Office resolved a dispute which had prevented the department's National Whitley Council from operating since 1928. In 1927 secessions of counter clerks from the Civil Service Clerical Association, and of sorters and night telephonists from the Union of Post Office Workers, had led the official side to propose that the numbers on the staff side should be increased to allow a federation of the secessionist groups to be represented. When the two unions refused, the

---

[10] Figures of unemployment, employment, and the total labour force are taken from Feinstein, table 57.

Post Office suspended the council and the local Whitley committees. Business had to be conducted by direct dealings and *ad hoc* arrangements. In 1931 the unions asked for the Whitley machinery to be reconstituted as it had been in 1927. The official side thought that the numbers of the secessionists made that impossible, but they were willing to establish a new council which excluded sorters, counter clerks, telegraphists, and night telephonists. As for local Whitley committees, these could resume business except in London, where the secessionists were concentrated. Direct dealings with the several unions would have to continue there.

The Post Office Engineers also had trouble with secessions among the skilled inside staff, but they managed to avoid adverse consequences for their Whitley machinery by altering their constitution to allow the internal staff to constitute a separate section within the union, with its own officers, conference, and executive representatives; and then negotiating an amalgamation with the secessionists. This success was assisted by the remarkable achievement of their secretary, Charles Smith, and his colleagues in negotiating a pay increase of about 4 per cent at the beginning of 1930 in settlement of a claim which had first been put forward in 1924; and by pressure on the secessionists from the Post Office.

A development which cannot have been wrung from employers by union power was compensation for redundancy for manual workers. In June 1930 the Joint Industrial Council for the gas industry provided that workers dismissed as a result of schemes of rationalisation were to receive in compensation a payment of one or two weeks' pay, according to age, for each year of service. In 1933 the flourmilling employers put up a fund of £20,000 which was to be used by their secretary in consultation with trade union officials to pay compensation to the victims of rationalisation schemes.

Workplace relations were inevitably quiet during the depression. One reason for this was given by the Glasgow organiser of the Engineers, in the June 1931 issue of their journal: 'Whilst the local situation is peaceful, it is a peace of death, due to the active elements being removed from the workshops.' In the issue for March 1931 he had already noted that the dismissal of shop stewards and conveners who had 'rendered excellent service for years past' had made it 'extremely difficult, if not impossible . . . to maintain the established conditions of the district'.

However, his complaints were not echoed from other parts of the country; and a number of instances of shop steward activity were reported. At a Millwall firm the question of reductions in piecework prices was taken up through procedure, and at the same time a shop steward was elected (November 1930); a meeting was arranged by the union to secure the election of shop stewards at a Newcastle firm, so as to avoid every issue going to the district office (June 1932); after the election of shop stewards in each section of the toolroom at Lucas in Birmingham, it was hoped that conditions in the toolroom would improve (June 1932); the refusal of a manager in Halifax to recognise shop stewards was taken through procedure, and the stewards were recognised (June 1933); at a Bristol firm the shop stewards and the management set up 'negotiating machinery to deal with payment by results problems' (June 1933). On 27 October 1932 the management board of the employers' federation discussed the issue of victimisation of shop stewards as a result of complaints by the Patternmakers. Federation policy, 'often declared to the unions', was that 'everything possible would be done to prevent victimisation of shop stewards. . . . Owing to the human factor, however, it is impossible to eliminate entirely friction between individual foremen and shop stewards.' The board decided to circulate local associations with the suggestion that foremen should not have the final authority to dismiss shop stewards.

Although the suspension of Whitley machinery in the postal side of the Post Office interrupted the operation of the local Whitley committees there, it seems that the issues previously raised at those committees were then settled between local managers and branch officials. The district Whitley committees of the Post Office engineering department, and the local departmental committees on the railways, continued to function much as they had in the second half of the twenties. A much abbreviated list of the items discussed at Post Office engineering district Whitley committees in the period January–June 1933 includes: promotion, acting duties, staffing, rotas, redundancy, transfers, workloads, night duties, meal reliefs, premises, equipment of many kinds, protective clothing, and piecework in the factories. Towards the end of 1933 the constitution of these district committees was revised with the aim, among others, of ensuring that decisions should not be pigeon-holed, even if they concerned matters outside the competence of the committees to settle. Such decisions were not to be 'negatived' without reference to the departmental engineering council. If the council failed to agree, it was suggested that deadlock might be avoided by consultation between the chairmen of the two sides, or by reference to a sub-committee of those two officers along with the joint secretaries.

The most telling evidence that the depression had not entirely eroded union strength in the workplace was a series of workplace strikes resulting from the application of the Bedaux work study system, which set a time within which workers should be expected to complete a given task. This system had been brought to Britain from the United States shortly before the onset of the depression, and its practitioners rapidly secured contracts with British firms. It had an inherent defect, in that it presupposed a precise law which determined the optimum relationship of effort and rest required to complete each task. The validity of such a law has never been demonstrated. Two defects in its application arose from the unfamiliarity of its practitioners with British industrial relations: they failed to consult the unions; and they neglected to win the goodwill of the workers to whom the system was to be applied.

Given these omissions, it was to be expected that the Engineers' district committees and shop stewards would resist the introduction of the Bedaux system, as they did in several instances. More surprising was the response of the workers at Wolsey's Leicester hosiery factories, two-thirds of whom were women. After eighteen months of friction as the system was introduced department by department, one department struck in December 1931. The strike was made official. The firm posted notices, and a lockout of three thousand workers at all the Wolsey factories lasted until the middle of February 1932, when the workers went back under terms negotiated at a conference chaired by the Lord Mayor of Leicester. The Bedaux system was radically altered and simplified, with guaranteed levels of earnings. Workers from each factory were to choose one of their number to be trained in Bedaux methods. Works councils were to be established, and the role of the union was assured. The dispute cost the union nearly £25,000. The other hosiery unions levied themselves to help the Leicester union, and contributions were also received from unions outside.

ICI introduced Bedaux at a number of their works. In 1933 the General and Municipal Workers' members working at the ICI limestone quarries in Derbyshire secured the withdrawal of the system to allow a reversion to straight tonnage rates. 'Workmen with a sense of freedom and manliness resent the implications of the Bedaux system', commented their *Journal* in September. In April 1933 a thousand of their members began a six-week strike against the system at the Venesta plywood works in London. The strike was settled by an agreement that its application should be under the control of a joint committee. A few weeks later both general unions were involved in another six-week strike at the Smethwick works of Hope and Son, where there had been few union members before the strike began. The return to work took place after the firm had agreed that joint committees were to investigate complaints, and meanwhile the system was not to be extended to new departments. On 25 May the chairman of the engineering employers' management board told his colleagues that the firm had committed a number of indiscretions, and 'altogether failed to appreciate the psychology of the situation'.

By this time the trade union movement as a whole was taking an interest. The General Council and the Scottish Trades Union Congress undertook a joint investigation, enquiring into the experiences of affiliated unions and consulting the Bedaux company and the National Institute of Industrial Psychology. Their equivocal findings were that, while trade unions were opposed to every 'method of payment by results involving the timing of operations, . . . Bedaux is capable of being applied in a manner, and with modifications, that may make it less harmful than many other systems'. In any event, 'the fullest consultation with the Trade Unions concerned' was 'essential'.[11]

The experience of the Bedaux system shows that, in the depths of the depression, British workers, both men and women, from a range of industries, in some instances poorly organised, were capable of putting up a spirited resistance to the introduction of a system of organising work and payment whose assumptions and methods of application violated their traditions and neglected their interests; and that in many instances their resistance forced the withdrawal of the system, or its subjection to control through collective agreements.

The Unions

Trade union membership declined from 4.80 million in 1929 to 4.35 million in 1933, and density fell from 26.0 to 22.9 per cent, but both rates of loss were much lower than those between 1920 and 1923. The contrast is perhaps to be explained by comparing the composition of trade union membership in 1920 with that of 1929. The 1920 figure included millions of relatively new members; by comparison most of the 1929 members were seasoned campaigners.

The decline between 1929 and 1933 was by no means universal. One major union, the Local Government Officers, grew by almost 50 per cent during the period. No other union could match this rate of increase, but several others were up by more than 10 per cent, including the Civil Service Clerical Association, the Distributive and Allied Workers, the Shop Assistants, and the Teachers. The Typographical Association showed a modest rate of growth; and so did the Electricians, the Railway Clerks, and the Post Office Engineers. All these unions operated in areas of expanding employment, and most were white collar unions. Indeed there was an increase in the overall membership of white collar unions.

Most of the heavy losses were in industries where the labour force was static or declining: metals and engineering, cotton, and other textiles all lost over 20 per cent, coalmining 10 per cent, and sea transport no less than 35 per cent. The outstanding exception was construction, where the loss was 15 per cent despite a 19 per cent increase in the labour force. This deviation can be at least partly explained by the rise in private

[11] Trades Union Congress, *Bedaux*, p. 16.

housebuilding, in which union membership was relatively low, and the associated shift in building from the North to the Midlands and the South, where the building unions were traditionally weak.

In sharp contrast to the experience of the general unions in 1921–2 the Transport and General Workers and the General and Municipal Workers did not experience a dramatically faster rate of decline than other unions. Their losses were respectively 11 per cent and 17 per cent. Each of them had by now a strong base in expanding industries. Even after amalgamation with the Workers Union, the largest section of the Transport and General Workers was road passenger transport, which provided more than a quarter of their membership; and about half the General and Municipal Workers were in local government service and gas, water, and electricity supply.

Most unions faced fewer financial problems than in the postwar depression and in the months after the general strike, although many of those which provided unemployment and superannuation benefits were forced into economies. In 1929 the Boilermakers cut their sickness benefit and restricted superannuation benefit to those with at least forty years' membership. In 1931 the Engineers ceased to exempt those on benefit from paying contributions. However, the proportion of trade unionists who received unemployment benefit from their unions was far less than in 1921, and among major unions only those in textiles had to make substantial payments of strike benefit. Moreover, there was no repetition of the disastrous loss of income experienced in 1921–2 due to the loss of nearly 2.7 million members. Overall the unions returned a modest surplus for the period.

It was not to be expected that such a period would bring radical alterations in trade union structure. The rules and machinery which had been developed to protect existing union boundaries during the twenties continued to operate, apparently effectively, and there was only one significant amalgamation. In 1932 the Tailors and Tailoresses at last joined forces with the Tailors and Garment Workers to form the National Union of Tailors and Garment Workers.

The circumstances of the depression reinforced the centralisation of power within the unions. The only serious defection from national collective bargaining was the wool industry, and that was not a consequence of a revolt of local groups within the union, but of a decision by the union leaders that they were most likely to minimise wage reductions by exploiting disunity among the employers.

In several instances trade union leaders chose to ratify decisions without putting the issue to a vote of the members. The most notable instances were the acceptance of the seven-and-a-half-hour working day by the Miners in place of the seven-hour working day which the government had promised them, and the endorsement of the 1931 agreement on working conditions in the engineering industry by the union executives, including that of the Engineers. In both instances there were rumblings, but no revolt. However, there were other occasions where union leaders were refused authority to negotiate, as in the 'more looms' lockout in Lancashire at the beginning of 1931, or had their provisional agreements rejected by their members, as in the dispute in cotton spinning in the autumn of 1932 and the London busmen's negotiations a few weeks earlier. Union leaders still risked repudiation if they flouted their members' wishes.

Until 1932 the Communists and the Minority Movement continued to reinforce the authority of union leaders by the folly of their attacks upon them. They continued their support for the United Mineworkers of Scotland and the United Clothing Workers. They sought to make capital out of most of the major strikes of the period, including the wool dispute of 1930, the 'more looms' dispute in cotton, the mining disputes over the spreadover, and many of the Bedaux disputes. In pursuit of their 'class against class' policy, they sent their agents to establish local councils of action, or mill committees, or 'rank and file' strike committees, separate from the unions. In most instances their agents went away at the end of the dispute with little more support than they had in the beginning. In 1931 several prominent Engineers, including Jack Tanner, who had recently been elected London organiser, published a demand for the repudiation of the engineering settlement and the creation of committees of action 'to prepare for rank-and-file resistance'. The executive suspended them, and subsequently expelled all except Tanner who recanted and thus broke with the Minority Movement, setting his feet on the path which was to take him to the presidency of the union seven years later. At the beginning of 1932 came a final act of folly. Under the direction of the Red International, another attempt was made to establish an independent seamen's union, leading to 'a brief and ineffective strike'.[12]

By this time, however, the rise of the Nazis in Germany was pushing Moscow towards the imposition of another change in tactics on its satellites abroad. They began to advocate the 'united front from below' which in Britain meant a reversion to working as an opposition group within existing trade union organisations. The change came just in time for the British party to give its approval to, and of course claim the credit for, the busmen's rank and file movement in London. The Communists gained publicity from Bevin's attack on the busmen's movement at his 1933 conference. By the end of the year the busmen's movement held five of the six places on the Central Bus Committee and

[12] Hardy, p. 222.

its leading personality, Bert Papworth, had been elected to the union's executive. The Railwaymen's Minority Movement was renamed the Railwaymen's Vigilance Movement to recall the wartime vigilance committees, and achieved some success by working through 'the constitutional means offered by the railway unions, the Local Departmental Committees, Shop Committees, Sectional Councils instead of through ad hoc depot committees which tended to *rival* the established institutions',[13] and by claiming that their opposition had helped to avert the wage cuts recommended by the chairman of the National Wages Board.

There were a number of changes in union leadership. In 1930 Herbert Smith was succeeded as president of the Miners Federation by Tom Richards of South Wales. Richards died next year, to be followed by Ebby Edwards of Northumberland. Cook died the following year, and as the full-time presidency had ended with Smith, Edwards stood for the secretary's post, and won it. Peter Lee of Durham was elected president. By joining the national government, Thomas made his position as political secretary of the Railwaymen impossible. The executive instructed its parliamentary representatives to join the majority of the Labour Party in opposition, and Thomas resigned. At fifty-six, he was not yet entitled to his pension, and by a majority the executive decided not to set the rules aside to allow him to have it. He was allowed to appeal to a special conference, but the decision was upheld.[14] The office of political secretary was terminated and Cramp reigned alone, to be replaced on his retirement in 1933 by the assistant secretary, John Marchbank. Bondfield resumed her position as chief woman officer of the General and Municipal Workers as soon as the government fell, despite her disregard for the policies of her union and Congress while she was Minister of Labour. By the end of 1933 Dukes was in process of taking over from Thorne as secretary of the union. In 1930 Brownlie retired as president of the Engineers. W. H. Hutchinson, an executive member, was elected in his place, but dismissed within two years for alleged misbehaviour at a union meeting. His successor was another executive member, Jack Little. However, these and other changes in personnel made little difference to the policies of the unions.

The authority of the General Council had been built up by means of the powers granted them to intervene in industrial disputes, and through acceptance by Congress of the Mond–Turner talks and the subsequent dealings with the central employers' organisations. However, neither source of authority was of much direct significance now.

---

[13] Bagwell, p. 522.
[14] The delegates may have been influenced by the much larger pension to which he would be entitled as a cabinet minister.

From time to time the council still intervened in a dispute. In 1930 they tried to intercede with the wool employers, but were repulsed. In 1932 Congress unanimously pledged its support to the Weavers and authorised the council 'to organise all possible moral and financial assistance' on their behalf.[15] The sum of £58,000 was raised through local 'TUC cotton fund committees', but there was no suggestion that the council should consider organising industrial action in support of the Weavers, and the cotton disputes of that year were the last major stoppages in Britain for several years. Similarly the council issued a statement jointly with the Federation of British Industries before the Imperial conference in 1932, but that was the last time use was made of the consultative machinery which was the only concrete outcome of the Mond–Turner talks.

After 1929 these aspects of the council's work were overshadowed by dealings with governments, with the national government as much as the Labour government, or perhaps even more. These dealings depended on the willingness of the governments to intervene in areas of economic and social life of interest to the unions, or to give serious attention to union proposals for intervention. Both of them were more interventionist than Baldwin's 1924–9 administration, and both were willing to listen to the General Council, but the unions did not expect from the national government the sympathy which they considered to be due to them from a Labour government. They were therefore less aggrieved by rejection, and the better pleased by considerate attention. Moreover, the national government was the more interventionist. Labour met demands for help from the steel and cotton unions with inquiries. Their successors gave tariffs to steel and statutory enforcement of wage agreements to cotton weaving.

Meanwhile the council sought to increase their control over dealings between government and unions. Following the Blanesburgh report, Congress instructed the council to review arrangements for union representation on government bodies, and the council reported its conclusions in 1928. For appointments to administrative boards and international conferences they wanted the right to nominate. For other administrative and advisory bodies they proposed they should submit lists of names from which the minister should select, except where technical qualifications were concerned. In such cases they claimed the right to approve the minister's choice. Only where a specific industry was concerned should the government make a direct approach to individual unions.[16] Thereafter, so far as they could, the council saw that these guidelines were followed.

[15] Trades Union Congress, 1932, p. 242.
[16] Ibid., 1928, pp, 202–3.

Administrative changes increased the efficiency of the council's lobbying. In 1929 a standing economic committee was appointed, and soon became the council's main committee. By the end of 1930 the council's full-time staff had increased to about forty members. Committees and deputations were better briefed, and fewer committee meetings were needed.

The administrative developments of these years had more subtle consequences as well. The greater expertise of staff members facilitated informal consultation, especially on technical matters. Almost certainly, too, it enhanced their role in the initiation and formulation of policy as the TUC's policy concerns became wider and more complex. One indication of this is that the practice of including one or two staff members, other than Citrine, in some ministerial deputations dates from this time.[17]

In one new venture the council achieved no more than moderate success. This was the organisation of the unemployed. In 1927 they had finally terminated their uneasy relationship with the National Unemployed Workers Committee Movement, which was shortly afterwards renamed the National Unemployed Workers Movement. In 1928 the Trades Council Joint Consultative Committee proposed that other Trades Councils should experiment with organising the unemployed, on the lines of an unemployed association run by the Bristol Trades Council. At the time the majority of unions failed to support the proposal, either through indifference, or because they considered the organisation of their unemployed members to be their own affair, and the General Council took it no further. However, it was revived in 1932 and the council reported to Congress in September that fifty-eight associations had been formed with memberships of between fifty and a thousand. Next year they conducted a survey which showed that membership of the associations far outnumbered that of the Unemployed Workers Movement.[18] The movement, however, continued to exercise undisputed control over unemployed demonstrations. Hannington and his colleagues had continued to organise a series of 'hunger marches' on London, and another was planned for the autumn of 1932 to protest against the means test, and to publicise a demand for higher scales of relief. Before the marchers reached London, violent demonstrations in Birkenhead and Belfast were followed by an increase in relief scales there; and after their arrival in London the marchers were involved in a number of skirmishes with the police followed by the arrest of their leaders. The General Council's associations made no attempt to compete or co-operate. They were wound up in 1935.

[17] Ross M. Martin, p. 222.
[18] Trades Union Congress, 1933, p. 121.

The authority of the General Council within the Labour movement was emphasised by the reconstitution of the almost moribund National Joint Council in December 1931. Henceforth, the party executive and the parliamentary party were to be represented by their chairmen and two other members each, and the General Council by its chairman and no less than six other members. The formal functions of the National Joint Council were not radically altered, but the council went about them in a much more energetic manner than before, taking decisions on major issues of party policy and announcing them to the public—thus diminishing the authority of the leader and executive of the party.

After two years' deliberation, the executive reported to the party conference in 1933 their recommendations on the procedure to be followed when Labour was next asked to form a government. The National Joint Council was to 'meet and record its opinion as to the advisability or otherwise of taking office' before the parliamentary party took their decision; if the prospect was of a minority government, a special party conference was to be summoned with the National Joint Council in attendance; in selecting his ministers a Labour prime minister was to be assisted by three members of the parliamentary party and its secretary; he was also to be subject to majority decisions of the cabinet, and a dissolution was to require the assent of the parliamentary party as well.[19] It is doubtful, however, whether the General Council had any desire to take permanent control of the Labour Party. The disastrous results of the 1931 election forced them to appear as the overwhelmingly dominant partner in the alliance, but they looked forward to the day when another election might restore the balance.

Besides asserting their authority in their relations with affiliated unions, in the Labour movement as a whole, and in dealings between government and unions, the council played a significant part in a further reshaping of trade union philosophy after the fall of the Labour government. The ideas which had inspired union participation in the Mond–Turner talks were not abandoned, but they were modified. Collective dealings between unions and employers remained the central feature of trade union action, but the depression had shown how much the outcome of these dealings could depend on government action to create a favourable economic climate, and on government intervention in particular industries. Consequently the philosophy which had been enunciated by Citrine and in the speeches of Congress presidents at the end of the twenties had now to be reformulated to take greater account of the role of the government.

Two weeks after the national government took office, Pugh moved, and Bevin seconded, a resolution at Congress which welcomed 'the

[19] Labour Party, 1933, pp. 8–10.

present tendency towards a planned and regulated economy', and asserted that 'only by a comprehensive planning of our economic development and regulated trading relations can the needs of the present day be met'.[20] Despite leftwing protests that they were asking for 'planned capitalism' they carried Congress by four votes to one. A powerful plea for planned capitalism came from none other than Cook, who asked: 'Are we to wait until capitalism has been smothered and there is no work?' The Labour government's Coal Mines Act had, he said, eliminated

> competition between pit and pit and district and district. Every ton of coal produced in Great Britain is now regulated. . . . Then my colleagues agreed that we want an international agreement—under capitalism. . . . By our agitation we have even convinced the coalowners, and they are meeting in a fortnight's time to consider an international agreement to stop cut-throat competition abroad. And what have we done it for? So as to be able to give regular work and protection to the men I represent.[21]

This was also the justification for trade union support for the two Road Transport Acts, the London Passenger Transport Bill, agricultural marketing boards, and tariffs for the steel industry. The aim was the same as that of the Mond–Turner talks—profitable and expanding industries, in whose proceeds union members could share; but the method had changed. Since many private industries were unable to expand and to increase their profits on their own, the government must be persuaded to help them.

The use of tariffs as an instrument of planning was still a contentious issue, for there were even now many free traders in the unions. In 1932 the General Council submitted a report on fiscal policy in which they denied 'willingness to expose wages and working conditions to the blast of free competition', but considered that tariffs were

> so liable to become merely a disguised form of indirect taxation, and the administration of tariffs so frequently corrupted by sectional pressure, . . . that we should be inclined to say that this is a protective device we should adopt with great reluctance.[22]

As to the tariffs recently introduced, experience was too limited, they said, for them to express an opinion on the likely results. Even so the free traders supported the reference back of the report and secured nearly a third of the votes. But there was no pressing need for Congress to take a firm stand on the matter. The government were going to impose tariffs whatever Congress said.

---

[20] Trades Union Congress, 1931, p. 406.
[21] Ibid., pp. 423–4.   [22] Ibid., pp. 202–6.

Concern with the rehabilitation of capitalist industries did not necessarily diminish the long-term commitment of the unions to socialism. The General Council became involved, along with the Labour Party, in working out detailed plans for the nationalisation, or 'socialisation', of several industries.

One issue which was debated at great length, following Morrison's London Passenger Transport Bill, was the composition of the boards of nationalised undertakings: were trade unionists to sit on these boards, and if so, how many? and were they to be union representatives or appointed on the same basis as other members? Eventually in 1933 the General Council and the party executive issued a joint memorandum with an agreed formula for the boards to 'consist of competent and suitable persons' with the unions concerned having the right to nominate and to be consulted by the appointing minister. Congress was taken to have approved this formula when the delegates defeated a resolution proposed by Dukes, which asked for '50 per cent of the representation on Managerial Committees' to 'be accorded to workers' nominees'; with workers' control as the ultimate aim.[23] At the Labour Party conference a month later Dukes carried a resolution for direct trade union representation on the boards.

The debate was abandoned for a good many years in this inconclusive state. Nevertheless, the joint memorandum contained a clear and unchallenged statement on the function of trade unions in nationalised industries:

A considerable part of the activities of industrial managements at present is concerned with the settlement of wages, hours, and all the other working conditions that most nearly affect the worker day by day. These matters are at present adjusted by negotiation between employers and Trade Unions. In our view, this method must continue to apply in the case of socialised undertakings. . . . Trade union rights, including the right to strike, must be fully maintained.[24]

On this view, pluralism would apply under socialism as under capitalism, and the question as to whether trade union nominees or representatives would sit on the boards of nationalised industries became a relatively minor issue. Either way, the role of the unions would remain unchanged.

[23] Ibid., 1933, pp. 210, 370.   [24] Ibid., p. 210.

14

Trade Unions in 1933

Growth

THE years 1911–33 covered a cycle of growth and decline in British trade union membership which cannot be matched in the ninety-odd years since reliable figures have been collected. An upturn in membership had begun in 1910, and continued, with a pause in 1914 due to the outbreak of war, to a peak in 1920 of over three and a half times the 1909 figure. Density had risen from 14.2 per cent to 48.2 per cent. Thereafter there was an almost continuous decline, interrupted by brief and feeble recoveries in 1924 and 1929, to a low point in 1933 when membership was little above half of the 1920 figure and density had fallen to 22.9 per cent. Total membership was then almost exactly the same as in 1915, and density was below that of 1913. The record shows no remotely similar period of decline; and the pace of the only other long period of sustained growth, from 1933 to 1948, was much less rapid than that of 1909–20. In 1933–48 membership rather more than doubled, and density almost doubled to 45.0 per cent.

The main factor in any explanation of this unique cycle must be the fluctuation in the demand for labour. The prewar boom showed clear signs of breaking in 1914, but it was sustained by the war, with its voracious demand for manpower, and kept going for two years thereafter by the accumulated shortages of wartime. Then came thirteen years of unemployment, with two deep depressions separated by a weak recovery.

The structure of the trade union movement also changed. Between 1910 and 1933 the number of unions fell from 1,269 to 1,081, and the average size of union doubled to four thousand. There were proportionately more women and white collar members. Female membership grew by 159 per cent compared with a 56 per cent increase in male membership. White collar membership was up by 200 per cent compared with 46 per cent for manual membership. Part, but a relatively small part, of the explanation for these contrasting rates of growth was the increased proportion of women and white collar workers in the labour force. The main cause was a doubling or more of union density in both groups, compared with an overall increase of 43 per cent.

Another way of measuring these changes is to single out male manual trade unionists. They accounted for the bulk of total membership in both 1910 and 1933, but their share was declining—from 79 per cent in 1910 to 66 per cent in 1933. Part of this decline was due to the falling proportion of male manual workers in the total labour force, but by no means all of it. In addition, male manual density grew substantially less than overall density—from 22.5 per cent in 1910 to 28.4 per cent in 1933, or by 26 per cent, compared with the overall increase of 43 per cent.

Despite these structural changes, there had been only two alterations in the list of the ten largest unions since 1910. The Boilermakers and the Cardroom Operatives had been pushed out by the Transport and General Workers and the Distributive and Allied Workers. Moreover, most of the remaining eight had not shifted their positions much, if at all. The Miners were still at the top; the Railwaymen had risen from fourth to third; and the Engineers were down from third to fifth. The proportion of total trade union members accounted for by the top ten had risen only from 45 to 49 per cent.

However, this apparent stability hides important changes. All but three of the unions on the 1933 list had experienced substantial amalgamations since 1910, the exceptions being the Miners, the Teachers, and the Weavers; and the Engineers had now opened their ranks to all classes of male manual engineering workers. The Miners, who had provided over half the top ten membership in 1910, were down to less than a quarter. In 1910 the other nine unions in the list had accounted for 22 per cent of total trade union membership; now the figure was 37 per cent. In 1910 there had been only the one general union in the list, the Gasworkers, who had accounted for less than 3 per cent of the top ten membership. Now there were two, the Transport and General Workers (in second place) and the General and Municipal Workers (in fourth place), with 28 per cent of the top ten membership between them.

Another aspect of union structure can be indicated by listing the ten industries with the highest figures for trade union density in 1910, 1920, and 1933. The relatively high densities returned for shipping and the docks in 1910, before the beginning of the 'great unrest', are mainly due to the substantial membership of the merchant navy officers' associations at that time, and to the successes already achieved by the dockers' unions in the south end of the Liverpool docks, in the Bristol Channel ports, and among lightermen, stevedores, and other specialists in London. The exceedingly high densities achieved by these two industries in 1920 are the consequence of the control which their unions had gained over hiring, in shipping by agreement with the Shipping Federation, and in the docks by local agreement or custom. By 1933 the

TABLE 5
Top ten industries for trade union density, 1910–33

1910 Industry	Density per cent	1920 Industry	Density per cent	1933 Industry	Density per cent
Coalmining	(71.4)	Sea Transport	(100.0)	National Government	(84.0)
Posts and Telecoms	(53.4)	Port and Inland Water Transport	(96.4)	Port and Inland Water Transport	69.1
Cotton, Flax, and Man-Made Fibres	(49.1)	Coalmining	(92.4)	Posts and Telecoms	(63.5)
Printing and Publishing	(35.3)	Printing and Publishing	(91.4)	Railways	56.9
Sea Transport	(33.0)	Construction	(87.9)	Footwear	54.7
Local Government and Education	(32.7)	Road Transport	(78.9)	Coalmining	52.4
Port and Inland Water Transport	(31.5)	Cotton, Flax, and Man-Made Fibres	(78.5)	Local Government Education	(51.9)
Metals and Engineering	(24.0)	Posts and Telecoms	(76.6)	Cotton, Flax, and Man-Made Fibres	51.4
Footwear	(20.1)	Railways	(73.7)	Road Transport	47.3
National Government	(18.8)	Metals and Engineering	(73.2)	Sea Transport	43.2

Note on sources: These figures are derived from Bain and Price. Annual figures of the labour force in each industry are not available for 1910 and 1920, and densities are derived by relating figures of trade union membership for those years to labour force data from the censuses of 1911 and 1921. Figures of the labour force of most, but not all, industries are available for 1933. Otherwise census data for 1931 have been used. Density figures derived from census data are given in brackets.

Seamen's grip had been weakened, but the Transport and General Workers had held on fairly successfully in the docks.

The presence of National Government, the Post Office, and Local Government and Education in the 1910 list testifies to the considerable influence that the unions had already acquired in these services even without national recognition of their right to bargain collectively on behalf of their members.

Together these public and private services took five of the top ten places for union density in 1910, leaving only half the places for manufacturing, coalmining, and construction which are generally regarded as the nurseries of British trade unionism; although the five services accounted for only 343,000 union members compared with a total of 1.59 million for the other five industries in the list.

By 1933 service industries occupied seven of the top ten places. Railways and road transport had displaced printing, and metals and engineering. Moreover, the seven service industries now accounted for 1.45 million members compared with just under a million for the three other industries in the list. These figures indicate a substantial shift in the centre of gravity of British trade unionism due to a number of influences all working in the same direction.

Firstly, employment in manufacturing, coalmining, and construction expanded less rapidly between 1911 and 1931 than employment in the service industries, by 24 per cent compared with 56 per cent.

Secondly, 'density of unionisation is likely to be higher among larger rather than smaller groups of employees'.[1] Most of the service industries—national government, the Post Office, local government, education, railways, and road passenger transport—consisted entirely, or predominantly, of large-scale organisations. By contrast, small-scale organisation predominated in construction, and in clothing, and in a number of other manufacturing industries; and even in manufacturing industries with a relatively high concentration, such as engineering and chemicals, there was, nevertheless, a substantial fringe of small undertakings.

Thirdly, union membership is affected by the attitude of employers towards trade unions. In 1910 the Shipping Federation and the railway companies, except for the North Eastern, refused to recognise trade unions for any purpose, and toleration of unions in the civil service and the Post Office stopped short of recognition of the right to bargain. Such collective bargaining as existed in local government and education rested on the goodwill of individual authorities. By 1933 the right to bargain had been recognised on a national basis in all these services, except for the white collar employees of the local authorities.

Finally, from 1921 onwards most of Britain's major manufacturing industries, including cotton, wool, steel, engineering, and shipbuilding, had to face unprecedented overseas competition in addition to the impact of the depressions of 1921–2 and 1929–33. The consequences for their employees were heavy unemployment and relatively low pay. By contrast, all the public services and most of the private services experienced relatively low unemployment and relatively high pay, for which their trade unions, now in most instances the recognised organisations to bargain on behalf of their employees, could plausibly claim some of the credit.

Technological change might also be expected to influence union growth, especially in craft trades, but it does not seem to have had much effect during this period, except in engineering. The printing unions had established their control over linotype and monotype machinery before 1910, and they experienced no further comparable challenge until after the Second World War. Concrete and mechanical equipment continued to advance in the construction industry, but mainly in civil engineering where few craftsmen were employed and where, apart from

[1] Bain, p. 72.

the first two or three postwar years, trade unionism was weak. Most building operations continued to employ the traditional craft methods. The chief innovation in shipbuilding was electric and oxy-acetylene welding. The Shipbuilding Federation wanted to introduce a new grade of welder specially trained for the job. The unions, led by the Boilermakers, argued that their existing members could handle it. At the end of 1933 the two sides were squaring up for a battle, which was ultimately settled yard by yard, and 'the greater part of the welding work in the industry remained in the hands of members of the Boilermakers' Society'.[2]

In engineering, the techniques of mass production, which had been so extensively used in munitions work during the war, were widely applied in car manufacture and electrical engineering, where union membership was generally agreed to be lower than in those sections of the engineering industry in which craft methods of production continued in general use. However, the decline in union density was not the direct consequence of the new technology. Trade unionism appears to have collapsed in these sections of the industry during the postwar depression. Then, during the following years, mass-production techniques were applied in largely non-unionised undertakings. The continued decline in union density in engineering thereafter was the consequence of the expansion of these sections of the industry, combined with a further fall in employment in the older sections.

Collective Bargaining

From 1910 to 1920 the coverage of collective bargaining expanded roughly in step with union membership. During the prewar years dockers', carters', and seamen's unions achieved recognition in all major ports. The number of local authorities which dealt with the unions increased rapidly, and the Post Office, civil service, and railway unions crept nearer to full recognition. More private firms and associations recognised trade unions, most notably the Midlands Employers Association in 1913. From 1915 onwards the Ministry of Munitions and the Committee on Production promoted national wage bargaining in a number of industries, including chemicals, engineering, road transport, shipbuilding, and wool. Under government control, national wage increases were negotiated on the railways and in coalmining, and the Shipping Federation joined with the seamen's unions to establish the National Maritime Board. An Agricultural Wages Board was set up by legislation. The government appointed an arbitration board for its employees, to which the Post Office unions had access. After the war most of these and similar wartime innovations were converted into

[2] Mortimer, p. 231.

permanent institutions, many of them as Joint Industrial Councils following the Whitley recommendations. However, most of the industries in which collective bargaining had been firmly established before the war preferred to retain their traditional procedures, with adaptations to cope with national agreements on pay and conditions.

Thereafter the coverage of collective bargaining and trade union membership cease to move in step. There were several defections from collective bargaining as membership plummeted in 1921–2, but some of them, as in road haulage, were reversions from national to local agreements rather than the abandonment of collective bargaining. The Agricultural Wages Board was abolished in 1921, but county committees were restored in 1924. In 1926 coalmining reverted to local bargaining, and was followed by the wool industry in 1929. A large but unknown number of employers withdrew from their associations between 1920 and 1933, and thus divested themselves of the obligation of observing the relevant collective agreements. However, by 1933 the overall coverage of agreements was still very much greater than in 1910, or even in 1914.

In 1910 the Labour Department estimated that the number of workers whose conditions of labour were 'specifically regulated' under 'Collective Agreements of a general trade or district character' was 2.4 million.[3] The department interpreted this formula to include the decisions of the railway company conciliation schemes, but otherwise agreements covering single firms were excluded, and so were public sector agreements with local authorities. Consequently the coverage of collective bargaining at that time must have been somewhere near three million workers. There is no official estimate for 1933, but a rough assessment can be made. Total employment in national government, the Post Office, local government, education, and the health services was about 1.5 million; and the number covered by agreements must have been more than a million. The employers' associations affiliated to the National Confederation of Employers Organisations claimed to represent firms employing about seven million workers.[4] This number includes their white collar employees, few of whom came within the scope of collective bargaining, so that the coverage of agreements signed by their associations should probably be put at six million or less.[5] Allowing for the agreements of a few employers' organisations outside the confederation, and those of the co-operative societies and some non-federated firms, the overall total might be as high as eight million. This

    [3] *Report on Collective Agreements*, p. iii.   [4] J. H. Richardson, p. 83.

    [5] This assumes the proportion of about 13 per cent of white collar to total employment in manufacturing industry in 1935 (Bain, p. 16) holds good for the other sectors covered by the confederation. In mining and construction it would have been less.

figure includes some of the two million workers covered by Trade Boards and County Agricultural Wages Committees. If they were all to be included the overall total might rise to nearly nine million—and, since some of the smaller employers' organisations affiliated to the confederation dealt with the unions only through these statutory boards, the total covered by voluntary agreements might be not much more than seven million.

Between 1910 and 1933, therefore, the coverage of collective bargaining may have increased as much as threefold, while trade union membership rose by only two-thirds. The disparity between these two rates of growth is mainly due to developments among employers, both public and private. In 1910 formal collective bargaining in the public sector was confined to a minority of local authorities. By 1933 it was the acknowledged practice of the great majority of national and local authorities. National employers' associations had emerged in many private industries and services where none, or only local associations, had existed in 1910; and most of them entered into national bargaining arrangements with the relevant trade unions, which they maintained even when union membership declined in the years of unemployment.

Besides emphasising the national level of negotiations and recommending statutory procedures where voluntary bargaining could not be sustained, the Whitley Committee sanctioned a form of bargaining within the plant. Previously the recognised function of the plant in collective bargaining had been to apply agreements reached outside the plant, either nationally or for the district. It was now acknowledged that plant bargaining might supplement those agreements.

Of course there had been bargaining in the plant ever since unions came into existence—and before. External rules had been modified and supplemented in the process of application. Customs had grown up which workers in the plant would not allow to be altered without their consent, but hitherto their right to bargain had not been formally acknowledged. Now many national agreements obliged managers to deal with works committees, or shop stewards, or both.

However, there was an ambiguity about works committees except where they consisted of shop stewards, as they did in engineering. Elsewhere managers could regard them, not as vehicles for negotiation with representatives of the unions, but as meetings with representatives of their own employees to discuss the affairs of their own undertakings before taking decisions which would be the responsibility of management alone. Moreover, by 1933 the provisions of national agreements on the recognition of shop stewards and the establishment of works committees were widely disregarded.

Accordingly, just as national agreements in poorly organised industries were at that time more of a promise for the future than a source of current strength, so the full significance of the agreements on works committees and shop stewards was reserved for a later period of prosperity. It was not until the third quarter of the century that their implications were widely realised, although even in 1933 the discerning observer of industrial relations might have perceived signs of what was to come.

The spread of national agreements on pay and conditions affected the pattern of strikes. There had been industry-wide stoppages before 1911—for example, the 1897–8 engineering lockout, the Boilermakers' lockout of 1910, and several stoppages in the cotton industry where national agreements had been the practice for almost twenty years—but they were exceptions. More typical were the district strikes over wage reductions in engineering in 1902–3 and 1908 and the coalmining strikes in the North East over the application of the Eight Hours Act in 1910. After the war the situation was different. Excluding the general strike, there were four industry-wide stoppages in shipbuilding from 1919 to 1926, three in coalmining, two each in cotton and in railways, and one each in building, docks, engineering, foundries, printing, and wool.

The point can be illustrated most effectively by the proportion of total working days lost through strikes and lockouts which were industry-wide stoppages. In 1901–10 the figure had been about a quarter. In 1911–14 it rose to half, and in 1919–26 it was 80 per cent, even excluding the general strike. Thereafter the incidence of industry-wide stoppages declined, but nevertheless the series of such stoppages in the textile trades from 1929 to 1932 provided over 60 per cent of all the working days lost through industrial disputes in 1927–33.

Government

The changing pattern of strikes was associated with a centralisation of power within the unions. National bargaining narrowly circumscribed the power of district committees to call strikes, as was discovered in 1919 by the Engineers in Clydeside, Tyneside, and Belfast, and by the London shiprepair workers. Their disputes brought home the lesson that district strikes in breach of national agreements had little chance of success in the face of united opposition from the employers and union executives. District strikes could still succeed where district agreements survived, as in the London bookbinders strike in 1925, although it is significant that its settlement provided for the extension of the national agreement to cover the Londoners; but district strikes were no longer the typical form of large-scale stoppages as they had been before the war. The normal procedure was for major strikes to be called and conducted by union headquarters.

Both in 1910 and 1933 the majority of strikes were, as they always had been, plant strikes. Some of them received official backing, as did most of the Bedaux strikes. Others were condemned by the unions, and a few, such as the Hoe dispute, brought the threat of a lockout from the employers. Most, however, were brief affairs, ventilating a grievance which was quickly settled or dropped, and the question of official union sanction did not arise. Consequently it would be misguided to look for further evidence of increasing central control in the decreasing annual average of recorded stoppages from 1,019 in 1911–20 to 480 in 1921–33. The main influence at work was the changing demand for labour.

Amalgamations also concentrated union power, and the constitution of the Transport and General Workers was particularly centralised. All major unions now had national, not local, executives, and the trend to national delegate conferences continued. There had been a substantial shift from election of full-time officers by the members to appointment by the national executives—except for general secretaries and, where they existed, full-time presidents. The proportion of full-time officers to members had risen considerably.

These changes within the unions were matched by a concentration of power at the apex of the movement, assisted by the collapse of several federal bodies. The Federation of Engineering and Shipbuilding Trades had dwindled to a rump. Both the Transport Workers Federation and the Federation of General Workers had lost the reason for their existence with the formation of the two great general unions. Secession robbed the General Federation of Trade Unions of its claim to be a nationally representative body. The Triple Alliance had collapsed on the first occasion its strength was seriously tested, and the Industrial Alliance did not get beyond a draft constitution. The only significant new federation was the National Federation of Building Trades Operatives.

The beneficiary of this general decline in federal bodies was Congress. In 1921 a new constitution had replaced the Parliamentary Committee by a General Council with specific, if limited, powers to co-ordinate the industrial activities of the movement. These powers were subsequently enhanced to provide the basis for the conduct of the general strike and the Mond–Turner talks.

Between 1910 and 1933 several outstanding leaders had come and gone, including Cook, Smillie, Thomas and Robert Williams; but by 1933 the two most remarkable leaders that the British trade unions have produced, Bevin and Citrine, had established their ascendancy over the movement as a whole.

With Bevin's support, Citrine had developed a new trade union philosophy which nevertheless re-emphasised traditional union methods. Collective bargaining (which had replaced the term 'conciliation' in general use) was once again asserted as the chosen means to attain trade union objectives, in opposition to the doctrines of the socialists and syndicalists who taught that the overriding aim of the Labour movement was to create a society in which there would be no place for traditional trade union action. The novelty of the new philosophy lay in its emphasis on the scope for agreement with employers over the development and rationalisation of British industry to the benefit of both sides; in the notion that such agreements might be encouraged and guided by a joint national body representing Congress and the central employers' organisations; and in its emphasis upon protecting and advancing the rights of workers in their place of employment as well as improving their conditions of employment.

Citrine had also played a major part in laying to rest the controversy over industrial unionism which had obsessed the movement for many years. He emphasised that reconstruction of British unions on industrial lines was unacceptable because it would entail the dismemberment of most major unions; and diverted attention instead towards reducing the frictions arising from existing structures by means of improved arrangements for handling inter-union relations and disputes.

Finance

In 1933 trade union contributions took a smaller proportion of the average pay packet than they had in 1910. Compared with an increase of 90 per cent in wage rates, contributions were up 40 per cent. One reason for this relative decline in contributions was the increased proportion of trade unionists in general and white collar unions, most of which had relatively low rates of contribution and offered a narrower range of benefits. Another reason was the introduction of special sections with low contributions and limited benefits into some of the older unions, notably the Engineers.

Some items of expenditure varied widely from one period to another. In 1911–14 the cost of dispute benefit was unusually high. During 1915–18, with little unemployment and few official strikes, unions were able to save a third of their income. Both unemployment and dispute benefit ran at high levels in 1919–26, and reserves were run down at a rate of about 7 per cent of income a year.

On the other hand fluctuations in expenditure on friendly benefits were relatively small; and the proportion of income spent on these was almost the same in 1927–33 as it had been in 1911–14. Administrative costs rose fairly steadily throughout 1911–33, from about a quarter to over a third of income. Between 1911–14 and 1927–33 this increase was offset by the decline in the cost of strike benefit. The most remarkable feature of the comparison between these two periods is the modest rise in the cost of unemployment benefit, although the first period was one of unusual prosperity whereas unemployment remained at a high level throughout the second period, reaching unprecedented proportions in 1931–3. The unions would have been overwhelmed had not many of them terminated their unemployment benefits in 1921–2 to avoid bankruptcy. Disengagement continued slowly thereafter, and quickened again in 1930, either by abandoning schemes or by temporary suspension, so that union expenditure on unemployment benefit actually fell in 1932, despite the continued rise in the unemployment figures.

There were, therefore, two main reasons why the unions ended 1933 with reserves substantially higher than at the end of 1926, and higher than in 1929, despite the depression, and despite the continued increase in the proportion of their income spent on administration. They were the low level of expenditure on disputes and the curtailment of unemployment benefit.

Political Action

The most conspicuous development in politics for the unions since 1910 had been the continued rise of the Labour Party. Despite the freak result of the 1931 election, which gave the party only four more seats than they had had at the end of 1910, it was now, without question, one of the two major British parties. It had provided two minority Labour governments, and even in 1931 had secured almost a third of the votes. Since Labour and Conservative voters together accounted for about 86 per cent of the total votes cast, it was evident that the Labour Party provided the only prospect of replacing the current Conservative-dominated 'national' government.

Moreover, the position of the unions within the party was stronger than ever before. Their alliance with the Independent Labour Party, on which the party was founded, had rarely been easy. On the one hand the union leaders had sometimes been disconcerted by MacDonald's manoeuvres and vagaries; and, on the other, most of them had little time for the posturing of doctrinaire socialists. Now MacDonald had manoeuvred himself into leading what was, in all but name, a Conservative government, and the remnants of the Independent Labour Party had taken their doctrine into the uncontaminated air of the wilderness. The unions were in command of the party, and the constituency party nominees in parliament who would be likely to provide many of the members of a future Labour government could hardly fail to appreciate the need to work closely with them.

However, in 1933 another Labour government seemed a long way off. Meantime union members expected their leaders to secure benefits for them from whatever government was in power. The leaders therefore had to employ such pressure as they could muster to extract what concessions they could. Their leverage for this purpose had fluctuated widely since 1910.

At times they had been in a position to hold political threats over governments. From 1910 to 1914 the Liberal government was dependent on Labour votes unless it was sure of Irish support. During the war the unions were able to exact a price for participation in the Asquith and Lloyd George coalitions. After the war they had it in their power to bring down a Labour government whenever they chose. However, these weapons could easily be overrated. Before the war the unions had no intention of defeating Asquith's government in circumstances which would have risked an election followed by a Conservative victory. The most favourable opportunity to bargain in the wartime coalitions was when they were being put together. The unions did very well out of Lloyd George's cabinet-making, but thereafter the Labour ministers were prisoners. They would have had to be very adroit and lucky to find an issue on which a resignation would not have done more harm to the Labour Party than to their coalition partners. The power of the unions over a Labour government was also a double-edged weapon, as was demonstrated in the 1931 crisis. The General Council had refused the support which the government needed to carry through their package of cuts in government spending. The consequence, however, was not to modify the package in the direction desired by the unions. Instead the Labour government made way for a 'national' government which pushed through an almost identical package. No doubt the unions considered this outcome worthwhile because it avoided the disastrous effect on the morale and unity of the Labour Party which might have been expected to follow from the imposition of the cuts by a Labour government, but the demonstration of their power had brought little by way of material concessions.

Another means for the unions to extract concessions from a government was a strike, provided that it was so damaging, or potentially damaging, that the government would feel obliged to put pressure on the employers to settle; or, where the government themselves were in control of the industry or service concerned, to raise their offer. The railway strike of 1911 induced the government to push the companies further towards full trade union recognition, and to increase maximum railway charges to cover wage increases. The coal strike of 1912 elicited legislation to oblige the owners to pay the minimum wages they would not concede by agreement. The railway strike of 1919 and the coal strike of 1920, both in industries under government control, brought improved pay offers. In wartime the risk of a strike—or, more likely, of an outburst of unofficial strikes—was rarely absent from government dealings with the unions. Union leaders made liberal use of the argument that they needed an offer acceptable to their members so as to avert the unrest which both they and the government were anxious to avoid; and they were able to quote examples of the unhappy consequences of meagre or tardy concessions, such as the interruption of the supply of South Wales steam coal in 1915 and the engineering strikes of May 1917.

However, in time of peace the great majority of strikes did not threaten sufficient damage to elicit government action beyond the normal offer of their conciliation services. Even many national strikes fell into this category. In the early twenties the government allowed the foundry strike, the engineering lockout, and no less than three shipbuilding lockouts to run their course. The prospect of stocks of cotton and woollen goods being run down by a stoppage caused them no great alarm. Lloyd George and Baldwin sat out the coal lockouts of 1921 and 1926. Only a major transport strike was guaranteed to bring government intervention.

The unions could try to force an unwilling government to intervene by extending the scope of the stoppage. The Triple Alliance was specifically designed for that purpose, and the powers granted to the General Council in 1921 and 1924 could be used in the same way.

The Triple Alliance never achieved its objective of stopping the coal mines, the railways, and road, port, and sea transport together, each industry striking for its own objectives. On the two occasions when a proposal for a sympathetic strike came up for decision by the alliance, in the coal stoppages of 1920 and 1921, the Railwaymen and the transport unions backed down, although in the 1920 stoppage the Railwaymen changed their minds. In 1925 the threat of a coal embargo by the General Council caused the government to intervene in the coal dispute with the offer of a subsidy; but next year, when the subsidy was withdrawn, the general strike went down to defeat.

Both an alliance strike and a general strike were powerful weapons. However, to employ them in sympathy with other workers, union leaders had to persuade their members throughout whole industries to strike on behalf of others, with no prospect of anything but loss to themselves. To do so, they had to convince their members that the cause was just, and that there was a reasonable prospect of success. In 1920 the leaders of the Railwaymen and the transport unions decided that the

Miners had made that impossible by rejecting arbitration. Thereafter the Railwaymen's conference reversed their leaders' decision against a strike, but there is little evidence to show that the transport unions were anxious to repudiate their leaders. In 1921 the Miners' allies believed that the Miners had made a grave error in tactics by refusing to abandon the pool, and some of them also feared that the high level of unemployment would cause their members to disregard a strike call.

In 1925 there was no doubt that trade unionists generally believed that the wage cuts proposed by the coalowners were unjust, and very little doubt that the coal embargo would have been enforced if the deadline had been reached. As it was, the threat was enough. Next year, however, they were called on to honour their commitments. They did so most loyally, but thereby brought a new factor into play. Once begun, a major sympathetic strike, or a general strike, creates the conditions in which the government is able openly to mobilise the resources of the nation to defeat the strike. The odds against the unions are thereby sharply raised; and on this occasion they were defeated.

A third important factor in the political influence of the unions, besides their ability to hold political threats over governments and their capacity to call strikes to force government intervention, is the desire of a government to intervene in matters of particular interest to the unions, and especially to exercise control over the industries which employ their members.

Many leading members of the prewar Asquith administration were eager to maintain their party's reputation as the party of reform, and to avoid further erosion of the traditional Lib–Lab alliance with the unions. These motives played a large part in the National Insurance Act and the many concessions made to the unions in its drafting and passage, in the 'repeal' of the Osborne judgment (although it did not fully meet trade union wishes), and in their general readiness to listen to union leaders.

The inexorable wartime extension of particular controls from one industry to another, and the multiplication of general controls over the deployment of manpower, meant that successive wartime governments had to rely on the acceptance by workers of a mass of unusual and often unwelcome instructions and regulations. To win acceptance, the governments sought union co-operation in designing and operating controls, with the consequence that the political influence of the unions increased to an extent not matched again until 1940.

After the war the reconstruction programme, and the government's lively fears of industrial unrest, sustained the wartime influence of the unions, but decontrol diminished it. By 1921 reconstruction was halted, heavy unemployment had robbed industrial unrest of much of its capacity to terrify ministers, and the level of trade union political influence was lower than at any time since 1906.

Thereafter Baldwin's governments were reluctant to extend the scope of economic regulation—except by tariffs which the electorate would not allow them to use—and the minority Labour governments were unable to carry most of their proposals through parliament. Nevertheless there was an underlying trend in favour of intervention. The social services continued to expand. Governments extended subsidies for public and private housing, public works schemes, and road programmes; regulated road transport; and created the Electricity Commissioners and the Central Electricity Generating Board.

The 'national' government accelerated the trend, and were ready to consult with the unions over their proposals for intervention. For their part, the General Council increased their resources to make full use of the opportunities which government intervention offered them. The creation of the economic committee in 1929, the expansion of full-time specialist staff, and the detailed preparation and careful briefing on which Citrine insisted, enabled the General Council to deal with government departments on fairly equal terms. Moreover, with the growing complexity of government, and the ineffectiveness of the enfeebled parliamentary opposition after 1931, it was more and more in the departments that decisions were made. Close relations between specialist staff at Transport House and the responsible civil servants could be expected to achieve better results more economically than deputations and parliamentary debates.

Public Standing

The first volume of this history identified five developments between 1889 and 1910 which had increased the status of the unions in public esteem.[6] Previous sections of this chapter have already shown that four of them—the growth of political influence, the extension of recognition by employers, the substitution of written agreements for custom and practice, and government intervention in support of collective bargaining—continued after 1910.

The fifth development was in labour law. Between 1889 and 1910 'the privileges of trade unions had been extended by statute and made far more precise'.[7] The two main changes between 1910 and 1933 were the affirmation and regulation of the right of unions to take political action in the 1913 Act and the restrictions imposed on them by the 1927 Act. Since the former was of considerable practical value to the unions, whereas the visible impact of the latter (except for the substitution of

---

[6] Vol. I, pp. 483–5.   [7] Ibid., p. 484.

'contracting-in' for 'contracting-out') was slight, the balance of advantage, even here, might be judged to be in favour of the unions. Certainly it is remarkable that the 1927 Act, passed when the unions were at their most vulnerable, placed a relatively light curb on their activities.

The final verdict of the previous volume was that 'by 1910 the unions had become more closely integrated into the fabric of British society'.[8] They were even more closely integrated into that fabric by 1933. New ties developed as the numbers of trade unionists and the functions of their unions increased; as the development of collective bargaining brought more trade unionists, from general secretaries to shop stewards, into more frequent contact with employers and managers, both formally and informally; and as the scope of trade union political action widened to bring more ministers, Members of Parliament, civil servants, local councillors, and local government officers into contact with union representatives. Integration was all the smoother because the circumstances in which these contacts took place were generally regarded as legitimate, or became legitimised by repetition.

It is true that there were occasions which emphasised the differences between trade unionists and the rest of society, and brought the legitimacy of trade union action into question. Sectional strikes could provide such occasions, but even unpopular sectional strikes did not necessarily lead to condemnation of trade unionism in general. When *The Times* of 28 April 1923 criticised the Boilermakers for repudiating an agreement approved by the other shipbuilding unions, they called the Boilermakers' action 'a blow at trade unionism'. It would not be easy to find a more telling demonstration of the acceptance of trade unionism.

There were also a few occasions when a strike, or the threat of a strike, appeared to range unions generally—even the Labour movement as a whole—against the rest of society in a conflict which had something of the character of a class war. Three outstanding instances occurred in the postwar years: Black Friday, Red Friday, and the general strike. The Council of Action incident in 1920 does not rank with them because it did not come to a confrontation with the government, and it is not clear how other groups in society would have responded to such a confrontation. However, the three instances where there was a confrontation did not sever the ties which bound the unions within British society. After each of them the pull of these ties restored the unions to their normal role in industrial relations and their place in public esteem; although, since Red Friday left unresolved the problem of wages and hours of work in the coal industry, the smell of class warfare lingered in the air over the autumn and winter of 1925–6 and into the following spring.

[8] Ibid., p. 485.

One measure of public standing is the distribution of honours. When Citrine received a knighthood in 1935 he told Congress that

honours have been accepted by very important persons in our Movement, not only in the last few years, but ranging over many years. I have in my hand a list—it runs into about 12 pages of foolscap matter—of individuals in the Labour Movement, some of them occupying very important positions, others union officials in their localities, and others national officials of their unions.[9]

Wages and Welfare

The two main sources of information concerning the pay of manual workers are the figures of wage rates regularly collected and summarised by the Labour Department and its successor, the Ministry of Labour, and their periodic censuses of earnings which were conducted in 1886, 1906, 1924, 1931, 1935, 1938, and later at six-monthly intervals. Wage rates are generally the major factor determining earnings, but earnings are also affected by overtime and short-time, shiftworking, additional payments such as merit pay, and, for pieceworkers and workers paid by results, by changes in output. Thus weekly earnings commonly exceed weekly rates of pay, but can be less; and are a better guide to the welfare of wage-earners and their families than wage rates—although for that purpose both rates and earnings have to be adjusted to take account of changes in the cost of living. Normally, average earnings move in the same direction as the index of wage rates, but often not at the same speed. In times of prosperity, with rising output and plentiful overtime, earnings usually rise faster than rates. In depressions, with short-time working and falling output, earnings may be expected to fall faster than rates.

The results of the earnings censuses for this period are summarised by Bowley in *Wages and Income in the United Kingdom since 1860*. Given the dates at which the censuses were conducted it is impossible to derive precise measures of the change in earnings between 1910 and 1933. However, since 1906 and 1910 were both years of economic recovery, and 1931 and 1933 were both years of deep depression, the relationships between wage rates and earnings were probably much the same in 1906 as in 1910, and in 1931 as in 1933. Consequently, given that the wage index rose by 3 per cent between 1906 and 1910 and fell by 3 per cent between 1931 and 1933, it is possible to estimate earnings for 1910 and 1933 without risk of serious distortion.

Bowley gives the average earnings of adult male wage-earners as between £1.42½ and £1.47½ a week in 1906 and as £2.95 in 1931.[10] The

---

[9] Trades Union Congress, 1935, p. 429.
[10] Bowley, *Wages and Income*, pp. 49–50.

figure for 1910 may therefore be put at about £1.50 a week; and for 1933 at roughly £2.85. Cash earnings had risen by 90 per cent over the period. Since the cost of living records an increase of 46 per cent over the same period, average real earnings of male wage-earners were up by about 30 per cent.

The earnings censuses were too infrequent to give much guidance concerning the course through which this change was accomplished. However, the 1924 census shows that average earnings of adult males were then about £3.00. Between 1924 and 1933 the cost of living fell by 20 per cent. Real earnings, therefore, rose by about 19 per cent between 1924 and 1933. Since the wage index was almost static from 1924 to 1929 and then fell slowly to 1933, whereas the cost of living index fell throughout the period, slowly at first and more rapidly after 1929, it is possible to infer that the rise in real earnings continued fairly steadily over the period. The years 1911–24 present greater problems.

Wage rates lagged behind prices in the early years of the war, caught up again by 1919, and went ahead in 1920. Average earnings certainly rose faster than wage rates over these years, so that by 1920 wage-earners were substantially better off than in 1910, but it is impossible to put a figure on it. It is almost certain that earnings fell faster than wage rates in the subsequent depression, eroding some of the previous gains, but leaving average real earnings by 1924 roughly 10 per cent up on 1910.

In addition to the peak in real earnings reached in 1920, the low level of unemployment which persisted through most of the year, and the increased number of women who were still in employment compared with 1910, must have led to an increase in household earnings over and above whatever increase there was in adult male earnings. Another factor working in the same direction was a more rapid increase in the average earnings of women than of men, especially in wartime, with many women performing men's work. Here again there is no means of estimating the amount of the change. However, it had not entirely disappeared by 1931. In 1906 the average earnings of women and girls was 44 per cent of the average for men and boys. In 1931 the comparable figure was 48 per cent. There is no reason to suppose that the comparison between 1910 and 1933 would be substantially different.

Women did not gain a comparative advantage in every industry. During the war years and the postwar boom the cotton industry, which accounted for such a large proportion of women workers, had continued its practice of percentage adjustments to wages, so that women's earnings moved in step with those of men, except in so far as women were transferred to men's jobs. Between 1906 and 1931 there was even a small increase in the sex differential in the textile group of industries as a whole. More typical was the metals and engineering group of industries, where the average earnings of women and girls rose from 38 per cent of male earnings in 1906 to 48 per cent in 1931.

There are no overall figures of skill differentials in earnings, which must have been squeezed hard by the wartime practice in most industries of flat-rate increases, and some of the compression remained in 1933. The earnings censuses conducted by the Engineering Employers Federation show that the average earnings of labourers in engineering were 60 per cent of those of fitters in 1914 and $67\frac{1}{2}$ per cent in 1934.[11] This change is less than that of the differential in wage rates. In 1914 the average rate of engineering labourers was 59 per cent of the average rate of fitters and turners, and by 1933 it was 71 per cent, having reached 79 per cent in 1920. The building labourers' average rate was 67 per cent of the bricklayers' average rate in 1914, 87 per cent in 1920, and 75 per cent in 1933.[12]

An impression of changes in inter-industry differentials can be derived from figures given by Bowley (p. 51) for some major industrial groups, which reveal a surprisingly wide dispersion.

Table 6 shows that the exceptionally large increases in pay received by the metals group, chemicals, and coalmines during the war were more than reversed by the postwar squeeze on exporting industries. The remarkably small increase in miners' average earnings is due to widespread short-time working in 1931, as well as to the wage cuts which followed the lockouts of 1921 and 1926. Coalmining was the only group which suffered a decline in real earnings over the period.

TABLE 6

Changes in average earnings for men and boys by industrial group, 1906–31

Group	Cash Increase (per cent)
Paper and printing	164
Food, drink, tobacco	146
Miscellaneous (including transport and local government)	141
Gas, water, electricity	138
Clothing	121
Chemicals, coke, building materials	121
Textiles	110
Construction and furniture	109
Metals, engineering, shipbuilding	91
Coalmining	43

[11] Yates, pp. 124–6.
[12] The figures for engineering rates are averages for sixteen 'principal centres' of the industry and those for building are averages of 39 large towns (*Twentieth* and *Twenty-second Abstract of Labour Statistics*).

A great deal of information is available on movements in white collar pay in these years, much of it in Routh's *Occupation and Pay in Great Britain 1906–60*, but not in a form that can be easily summarised. The general experience of white collar employees was a sharp decline in both their relative and their real pay in the early war years; a marked recovery in 1919–20; another decline in pay, but not relative pay, in 1921–3; and, thereafter, a fair degree of stability in relative pay. However, some groups of white collar employees fared better than others. Among those whose pay rose substantially more than the average were teachers (especially women teachers), civil service clerical officers, and railway clerks. On the other hand, clerks employed in private business (other than banks and insurance) fared far worse than the average.

Pay is by no means the only aspect of the welfare of workers and their families which is subject to trade union influence. Nearly all employees gained a reduction in their working week between 1910 and 1933. For manual workers it was generally from between 51 and 56 hours to 47 or 48 hours, with building workers on 44 hours in winter, and some of them in summer as well; and dockers on 44 hours throughout the year.

Outside the realm of collective bargaining, a national insurance system had been created and extended by legislation. In 1910 non-contributory old age pensions at 70 had just been introduced. Now manual workers were insured against sickness and unemployment, with pensions for widows and orphans, and contributory old age pensions at 65. Originally intended to supplement savings, unemployment benefit was now fixed at a level considered sufficient to maintain an unemployed worker, with additional allowances for dependants, and the period over which benefits were payable had been greatly extended. The Poor Law had gone, and the grants available for the indigent were on a more generous scale than before. Provision for compensation for accidents at work and industrial diseases was substantially improved. Much local authority housing had been built to be let at subsidised rents, and town planning was bringing improvements to the environment.

The worker met part of the cost of these benefits through his national insurance contributions and payment of rates and taxes, but the insurance contributions of employers, and taxes and rates paid by other social groups, bore a good deal of the burden. In addition, there was the unquantifiable benefit of greater security.

It is not easy to identify and evaluate the extent of trade union responsibility for all these advances in welfare. The unions were not primarily responsible for the increase in productivity which was the main cause of rising real earnings between 1910 and 1933. It is true that trade unionism was relatively strong among those groups of white collar employees who enjoyed exceptionally large pay increases—teachers, civil service clerical officers, and railway clerks—but the strength of trade unionism among coalminers, cotton operatives, and metal and engineering workers did not prevent a relative decline in their pay. It is also true that the decline in skill and sex differentials was accompanied by the rise of the general unions, and an increase in the relative density of trade unionism among women workers; but it is not evident which was cause and which was effect. It is perhaps more plausible to attribute both the changed differentials and the increase in trade union organisation among less privileged workers to a wider shift in society, as a whole, towards greater egalitarianism and humanitarianism.

Similarly legislation on national insurance and other aspects of social welfare went alongside the rise of the Labour Party and an increase in the influence of trade unions on governments, but these developments also can be seen as aspects of the wider change in society as a whole. The only verdict which can be accepted with some confidence is that trade unionism in 1933 was a stronger and more influential element in society than it had been in 1910, and could, therefore, rightly claim a greater share in the credit for social change than would have been justified in 1910.

The Future

At the end of 1933 British trade unions could look to the future with some confidence. Although their membership had been falling almost continuously for thirteen years, it was still well ahead of the 1910 total, and membership density was also substantially higher than it had been then. Moreover, the current figure of membership was not swollen by large numbers of recent recruits, such as accounted for the peak total of 1920. It was a tried and loyal body of men and women who had come through four years of deep depression with remarkably few defections.

Trade union organisation was in fair shape. The incidence and intensity of the inter-union conflict had been diminished by agreements between unions, by improved machinery for handling inter-union disputes, and by the acceptance of a body of principles to regulate relations between unions. The authority of trade union leaders had been enhanced by constitutional change, and even more by the extension of national collective bargaining. Up to 1927 trade union leaders and executives had been harassed by opposition inspired, first by syndicalists and industrial unionists, and then by Communists and the Minority Movement, but the danger from these sources had been abated by the stupidity of Communist tactics dictated from Moscow and by a tightening of trade union rules.

At the centre of the movement, the authority of Congress and its executive body had been enhanced almost beyond recognition. Potential rivals to Congress had disappeared, and the powers of the General Council had been extended and put to the test. The council's warrant to determine the policy of the movement, subject to the vote of Congress, had been accepted with little more than formal opposition. The unquestioned leaders of the movement, Bevin and Citrine, had many years of service ahead before they were due to retire.

The new system of national collective bargaining had been tested by the two most severe economic depressions since the hungry forties of the last century. There had been a few defections, but the system as a whole had survived in remarkably good order. It could not have done so without firm support from employers' organisations, and their attachment to it had been demonstrated during the depression from which the country was just beginning to emerge. In the years 1919–26 it appeared that national bargaining had amplified the scale and volume of industrial conflict by making national strikes and lockouts more common than before, but the low level of strikes and strike losses (outside textiles) since 1926 showed that national bargaining was compatible with industrial peace.

The Labour government of 1929–31 had been a disappointment to the unions, but they had reasserted their authority over the Labour Party, which remained unquestionably the second party in the country in terms of electoral support, and they were engaged with the party in working out new policies more to their liking.

There was therefore good reason for British trade unionists to look to the future with confidence; but there were also dangers ahead. Firstly, with their reversion to united front tactics, the Communist Party were again attracting groups of trade unionists with grievances against their leaders. Secondly, the unions had not learned how to control the workplace organisations which had in wartime acquired the strength to fend for themselves. The challenge had withered after the end of the war and the onset of mass unemployment; but, in different circumstances, it might recur. Thirdly, and of far greater immediate importance, there was a new challenge to trade unionism from overseas. Fascism in Italy had seemed a remote Latin aberration, but the destruction of the German unions by the Nazis was a threat that could not be, and was not, ignored.

From April 1933 the issue became a major and continuing item on the agenda of General Council meetings. They interviewed the German ambassador, tried to promote a boycott of German goods, and prepared a statement on *Dictatorships and the Trade Union Movement* for Congress in September.[13] Presented by Citrine, the statement asserted that the movement's answer to 'this attempt to undermine democratic

[13] Trades Union Congress, 1933, pp. 425–35.

institutions' must be 'to reaffirm its adherence to the democratic spirit which has made its existence possible'. Leftwing criticism that the statement failed to distinguish between dictatorships of the right and of the left was forestalled by dissociating the General Council from those 'who deny that freedom can exist in a capitalist society', and by insisting that dictatorships of both left and right destroyed the safeguards of trade union independence. British union leaders had perceived the dangers of Nazism sooner than most of their compatriots.

Statistical Appendix

TABLE 7
General indicators

Year	Total union membership (000s)	Total union density (per cent)	Number of stoppages beginning in year	Total working days lost by all stoppages in progress during year (000s)	Cost of living (1914= 100)	Weekly wage rates (July 1914= 100)[a]	Percentage unemployed (yearly mean) among members of certain trade unions	among insured workers[b]
1911	3,129	19.0	872	10,155	97	95	3.0	
1912	3,394	20.6	834	40,890	100	98	3.2	
1913	4,107	24.8	1,459	9,804	102	99	2.1	3.6
1914	4,117	24.7	972	9,878	100	100	3.3	4.2
1915	4,335	25.9	672	2,953	123	110–115	1.1	1.2
1916	4,611	27.4	532	2,446	146	120–125	0.4	0.6
1917	5,452	32.3	730	5,647	176	155–160	0.7	0.7
1918	6,461	38.1	1,165	5,875	203	195–200	0.8	0.8
1919	7,837	46.0	1,352	34,969	215	215–220	2.4	—
1920	8,253	48.2	1,607	26,568	249	270–280	2.4	3.9
1921	6,512	37.9	763	85,872	226	231	14.8	16.9
1922	5,573	32.1	576	19,850	183	191	15.2	14.3
1923	5,382	30.7	628	10,672	174	188	11.3	11.7
1924	5,463	30.9	710	8,424	175	194	8.1	10.3
1925	5,430	30.4	603	7,952	176	196	10.5	11.3
1926	5,152	28.6	323	162,233	172	195	12.2	12.5
1927	4,860	26.8	308	1,174	167½	196		9.7
1928	4,753	25.9	302	1,388	166	194		10.8
1929	4,804	26.0	431	8,287	164	193		10.4
1930	4,783	25.7	422	4,399	158	191		16.1
1931	4,569	24.3	420	6,983	147½	189		21.3
1932	4,395	23.3	389	6,488	144	185		22.1
1933	4,350	22.9	357	1,072	140	183		19.9

Sources: Figures for union membership and density are from Bain and Price, table 2.2. Union density figures for individual industries are available only for Great Britain. For the sake of consistency, therefore, figures of trade union membership in this table, and throughout the volume, are given for Great Britain and not for the United Kingdom. In the years 1911–33 the figures of total union membership in Great Britain and the United Kingdom were never much more than one per cent apart.

With the exception mentioned below, all the remaining figures are from the Department of Employment and Productivity, *British Labour Statistics* (stoppages: table 197; cost of living: table 89; wage rates: tables 11, 12, 13; percentage unemployed: tables 159, 160). However, the official cost of living series begins in 1914. The figures for 1911–13 are therefore from a series (also based on 1914) in Bowley, *Wages and Income*, table VII.

The cost of living and wage rate figures relate to the United Kingdom; figures for stoppages relate to Great Britain and Northern Ireland throughout; figures for unemployment among trade union members are for the United Kingdom, and among insured workers for Great Britain and all Ireland up to and including 1921, and for Great Britain and Northern Ireland thereafter.

Notes: [a] Up to 1914 the wage rate index is the 'unweighted mean of indices representative of wage movements in building, coal mining, engineering, textile trades and agriculture' (*British Labour Statistics*, p. 52). From 1914 to 1920 it is the 'estimated average percentage increase in weekly full-time rates of wages compared with July 1914. . . . The information available is insufficient to provide an accurate basis for the calculation of index numbers' (ibid.). From 1921 onwards it gives 'an indication of the general movement in basic rates of wages or minimum entitlements' (ibid., p. 53).

[b] The coverage of statutory unemployment insurance under the 1911 Act was about 2.5 million. The 1916 Act (which came into operation in October 1916) increased the number to nearly four million; and the 1920 Act (which took effect in November 1920) increased it to about 11.75 million.

No figures are available for the percentage unemployed among insured workers for 1919 because of the out of work donation scheme (see p. 239).

TABLE 8

Total trade union membership compared with trade union affiliated membership of the Trades Union Congress and the Labour Party

Year	Total (000s)	Trades Union Congress (000s)	Labour Party (000s)
1911	3,129	1,662	1,502
1912	3,394	2,002	1,858
1913	4,107	2,232	—[a]
1914	4,117	—[b]	1,572
1915	4,335	2,682	2,054
1916	4,611	2,851	2,171
1917	5,452	3,082	2,415
1918	6,461	4,532	2,960
1919	7,837	5,284	3,464
1920	8,253	6,505	4,318
1921	6,512	6,418	3,974
1922	5,573	5,129	3,279
1923	5,382	4,369	3,120
1924	5,463	4,328	3,158
1925	5,430	4,351	3,338
1926	5,152	4,366	3,352
1927	4,860	4,164	3,239
1928	4,753	3,875	2,025
1929	4,804	3,673	2,044
1930	4,783	3,744	2,011
1931	4,569	3,719	2,024
1932	4,395	3,613	1,960
1933	4,350	3,368	1,899

Notes: [a] No affiliation figures were reported to the Labour Party conference 1913 because of the effects of the Osborne judgment.

[b] No Congress was held in 1914.

TABLE 9

Membership of the ten largest unions in 1910, 1920, and 1933

1910	(000s)	1920	(000s)	1933	(000s)
Miners Federation	597	Miners Federation	948	Miners Federation	501
Weavers	112	Workers Union	492	Transport and	
Engineers	100	Railwaymen	458	General Workers	371
Railway Servants	75	General Workers	439	Railwaymen	270
Teachers	69	Engineers	423	General and	
Boilermakers	49	Weavers	224	Municipal	
Cardroom		Agricultural		Workers	241
Operatives	45	Workers	181	Engineers	168
Am. Carpenters	43	Nat. Am. Union of		Teachers	153
Postmen	38	Labour	152	Distributive and	
Gasworkers	32	London Dockers	140	Allied Workers	128
		Am. Carpenters	125	Weavers	116
				Post Office	
				Workers	98
				Woodworkers	97
TOTAL	1,160		3,582		2,143

TABLE 10
*Expenditure of registered trade unions*ᵃ *as a proportion of income, by periods, 1911–33*

	1911–14	*1915–18*	*1919–26*	*1927–33*
Unemployment benefit[b]	13.4	3.0	22.2	18.0
Dispute benefit	20.3	2.7	22.3	3.1
Friendly benefits[c]	30.6	24.8	19.9	30.4
Expenditure from political funds	0.2	1.1	1.7	1.7
Administration[d]	28.9	32.8	41.6	40.8
Surplus or deficit	+6.4	+35.6	−7.7	+6.1
TOTAL	99.8	100	100	100.1

Notes: [a] No overall information on trade union income and expenditure is published. For most of the period covered by this volume, two official series applying to the bulk of trade union members are available, one for registered trade unions and the other for the 'hundred principal trade unions'. The latter series, however, ceased after 1932, and the former has therefore been used throughout, except on p. 16 where figures of income per member are given for groups of unions in 1910. This information is not available for registered trade unions in that year, and the figures therefore relate to the hundred principal trade unions.

The proportion of total trade union members covered by registered trade unions was 74.2 per cent in 1911; 84.0 per cent in 1920; and 76.9 per cent in 1933.

All the figures in the table have been derived from the relevant tables in the 18th and 22nd *Abstracts of Labour Statistics in the United Kingdom.*

[b] From 1913 onwards part of the income of the unions came from the Board of Trade (later the Ministry of Labour) to cover disbursement of state unemployment benefit by those unions which acted as agents for the government in this respect, and also the associated administrative costs. Since, in years of heavy unemployment, these payments constituted a large proportion of total union income (not far short of half in 1921), their inclusion would obscure the way in which unions spent their income from contributions, levies, and investments, and the extent to which expenditure under different headings varied from one period to another. They have, therefore, been excluded from income and deducted from total union expenditure on unemployment benefit. However, since the payments covered administrative costs as well as state benefit paid out, the consequence is that trade union expenditure on unemployment benefit is somewhat understated.

[c] This item includes, among other payments, sickness and accident benefit, funeral benefit, superannuation benefit, and grants to members.

[d] This item includes both 'management and other expenses' and 'grants to federations and other societies, etc.', on the assumption that these grants were primarily used to pay the administrative expenses of those federations and other societies.

Biographies

These biographies include leading trade unionists of the period who are mentioned in the text, and a small number of employers and civil servants who played a significant part in trade union affairs. Unless qualified on one of those two grounds, politicians are not included.

ABLETT, Noah (1883–1935). Miners' Agent, Merthyr, South Wales, 1918–35. Executive Committee, Miners Federation of Great Britain, 1921–6.

ADAMSON, William (1863–1936). Assistant Secretary, Fife Kinross and Clackmannan Miners Association, 1902–8; Secretary, 1908–27. Secretary, Fife Clackmannan and Kinross Miners Association, 1928–36. Executive Committee, Miners Federation of Great Britain, 1911–12, 1922–3. Executive Committee, Labour Party, 1923–4. MP, 1910–31. Secretary of State for Scotland, 1924, 1929–31.

APPLETON, William Archibald (1859–1940). Secretary, Lace Makers Trade Union, 1896–1907. Secretary, General Federation of Trade Unions, 1907–38.

ASHTON, Thomas (1844–1927). Secretary, Ashton and Oldham Miners Association, 1879–81. Secretary, Lancashire and Cheshire Miners Federation, 1881–1919. Secretary, Miners Federation of Great Britain, 1889–1919. Executive Committee, Labour Party, 1910–11.

ASKWITH, George Ranken (1861–1942). Assistant Secretary, Railway Branch of Board of Trade, 1907–9; Controller-General, Commercial, Labour, and Statistical Department, 1909–11. Chief Industrial Commissioner, 1911–19. Kt, 1911. Baron, 1919.

BARKER, George (1858–1936). Miners' Agent, Western Valley, South Wales, 1908–?. Executive Committee, Miners Federation of Great Britain, 1911–21. MP, 1921–9.

BEARD, John (1871–1950). Organiser, Workers Union, 1899–1913; President, 1913–29. Secretary, Agricultural Trade Group, Transport and General Workers Union, 1931–6. Parliamentary Committee, later General Council, Trades Union Congress, 1920–34; Chairman, 1929–30.

BELL, John Nicholas (d. 1922). Corresponding Secretary, National Amalgamated Union of Labour, 1890–98; Secretary, 1898–1922. General Council, Trades Union Congress, 1921–2. Executive Committee, Labour Party, 1903–9. MP, 1922.

BEVERIDGE, William Henry (1879–1963). Assistant Secretary, Board of Trade, 1913–16. Second Secretary, Ministry of Food, 1916–19; Permanent Secretary, 1919. Under Secretary, Ministry of Labour, 1940–44. Director, London School of Economics and Political Science, 1919–37. Vice-

Chancellor, London University, 1926–8. Master, University College, Oxford, 1937–44. MP, 1944–5. Kt, 1919. Baron, 1946.

BEVIN, Ernest (1881–1951). District and later National Organiser, Dock Wharf Riverside and General Workers Union, 1911–20; Assistant Secretary, 1920–21. Secretary, Transport and General Workers Union, 1922–46. General Council, Trades Union Congress, 1925–40; Chairman, 1936–7. MP, 1940–51. Minister of Labour, 1940–45. Foreign Secretary, 1945–51. Lord Privy Seal, 1951.

BONDFIELD, Margaret (1873–1953). Assistant Secretary, National Amalgamated Union of Shop Assistants, 1898–1908. Assistant Secretary, National Federation of Women Workers, 1915–21. Chief Woman Officer, National Union of General Workers, later National Union of General and Municipal Workers, 1921–38. Parliamentary Committee, later General Council, Trades Union Congress, 1917–24, 1925–9. MP, 1923–4, 1926–31. Parliamentary Secretary to Minister of Labour, 1924. Minister of Labour, 1929–31.

BOWERMAN, Charles William (1851–1947). Secretary, London Society of Compositors, 1892–1906. Parliamentary Committee, Trades Union Congress, 1897–1911; Chairman, 1900–1; Secretary, Parliamentary Committee, later General Council, Trades Union Congress, 1911–23. MP, 1906–31.

BRACE, William (1865–1947). Miners' Agent, Monmouthshire, 1890–1920. Vice-President, South Wales Miners Federation 1898–1911; President, 1911–20. Executive Committee, Miners Federation of Great Britain, 1900–11, 1912–15, 1919–20. MP, 1906–20. Parliamentary Secretary, Home Office, 1915–18. Chief Labour Adviser, Department of Mines, 1920–27.

BRAMLEY, Fred (1874–1925). Organising Secretary, National Amalgamated Furniture Trades Association, 1912–17. Parliamentary Committee, Trades Union Congress, 1916–17; Assistant Secretary, Parliamentary Committee, later General Council, Trades Union Congress, 1917–23; Secretary, 1923–5.

BROMLEY, John (1876–1945). Organiser, Associated Society of Locomotive Engineers and Firemen, 1910–14; Secretary, 1914–36. Executive Committee, Labour Party, 1920–21. General Council, Trades Union Congress, 1921–36; Chairman, 1931–2. MP, 1924–31.

BROWN, William John (1894–1960). Secretary, Assistant Clerks Association, 1920–22. Secretary, Civil Service Clerical Association, 1922–42; Parliamentary Secretary, 1942–7. MP, 1929–31, 1942–50.

BROWNLIE, James Thomas (1865–1938). Chairman, Executive Council, Amalgamated Society of Engineers, 1913–20. President, Amalgamated Engineering Union, 1920–30.

CITRINE, Walter (b. 1887). Secretary, Mersey District, Electrical Trades Union, 1914–20; Assistant Secretary, 1920–23. Assistant Secretary, Trades Union Congress, 1923–6; Secretary, 1926–46. National Coal Board, 1946–7. Chairman, Central Electricity Authority, 1947–57. Kt, 1935. Baron, 1946.

CLYNES, John Robert (1869–1949). Organiser, National Union of Gasworkers and General Labourers, 1891–6; Lancashire District Secretary, National Union of Gasworkers and General Labourers, later National Union of General

Workers, 1896–1917; Chairman, 1912–16; President, National Union of General Workers, later National Union of General and Municipal Workers, 1916–37. Executive Committee, Labour Party, 1904–39; Chairman, 1908–9. MP, 1906–31, 1935–45. Lord Privy Seal, 1924. Home Secretary, 1929–31.

COLE, George Douglas Howard (1889–1959). Research Adviser, Amalgamated Society of Engineers, 1915–18. Honorary Secretary, Labour Research Department, 1918–24. Reader in Economics, Oxford, 1925–44; Professor of Social and Political Theory, 1944–57.

COOK, Arthur James (1883–1931). Miners' Agent, Rhondda, South Wales, 1919–24. Executive Committee, Miners Federation of Great Britain, 1921–2; Secretary, 1924–31. Executive Committee, Labour Party, 1924–5. General Council, Trades Union Congress, 1927–31.

COPPOCK, Richard (1896–1971). Organiser, Operative Bricklayers Society, 1916–20. Secretary, National Federation of Building Trades Operatives, 1920–61. Chairman, London County Council, 1943–4. Kt, 1951.

CRAMP, Concemore Thomas Thwaites (1876–1933). President, National Union of Railwaymen, 1918–1919; Industrial Secretary, 1920–31; Secretary, 1931–3. Executive Committee, Labour Party, 1918–29; Chairman, 1924–5. General Council, Trades Union Congress, 1929–33.

DAVIS, W. J. (1848–1923). Secretary, National Society of Amalgamated Brassworkers, later National Society of Metal Mechanics, 1872–83, 1889–1920. Factory Inspector, 1883–9. Parliamentary Committee, Trades Union Congress, 1881–3, 1896–1902, 1903–20; Chairman, 1912–13.

DEAKIN, Arthur (1890–1955). Organiser, Dock Wharf Riverside and General Workers Union, 1919–21. Assistant District Secretary, Transport and General Workers Union, 1922–32; National Secretary, General Workers Trade Group, 1932–5; Assistant Secretary, 1935–45; Secretary, 1945–55. General Council, Trades Union Congress, 1940–55; Chairman, 1951–2.

DUKES, Charles (1881–1948). Full-time Branch Secretary, National Union of General Workers, 1911–15; Organiser, 1915–24. Leeds District Secretary, National Union of General and Municipal Workers, 1924–5; Lancashire District Secretary, 1925–34; Secretary, 1934–46. General Council, Trades Union Congress, 1934–46; Chairman, 1945–6. Baron, 1947.

DUNCAN, Charles (1865–1933). President, Workers Union, 1898–1900; Secretary, 1900–28. Executive Committee, Labour Party, 1920–22. MP, 1906–18, 1922–33.

EDWARDS, Ebenezer (1884–1961). Financial Secretary, Northumberland Miners, 1920–32. Executive Committee, Miners Federation of Great Britain, 1926–30; Vice-President, 1930–31; President, 1931–2; Secretary, Miners Federation of Great Britain, later National Union of Mineworkers, 1932–46. General Council, Trades Union Congress, 1931–46; Chairman, 1943–4. Chief Labour Relations Officer, National Coal Board, 1946–53. MP, 1929–31.

EDWARDS, Enoch (1852–1912). Secretary, North Staffordshire Miners Association, 1877–1912. President, Midland Miners Federation, 1886–1912.

Treasurer, Miners Federation of Great Britain, 1889–1904; President, 1904–12. MP, 1906–12.

GOSLING, Harry (1861–1930). Secretary, Amalgamated Society of Watermen and Lightermen, 1893–1921. President, Transport and General Workers Union, 1922–4. President, National Transport Workers Federation, 1910–24. Parliamentary Committee, later General Council, Trades Union Congress, 1908–23; Chairman, 1915–16. MP, 1923–30. Minister of Transport and Paymaster General, 1924.

GREENALL, Thomas (1857–1937). Miners' Agent, Lancashire and Cheshire Miners Federation, 1889–1930; President, 1908–29. Executive Committee, Miners Federation of Great Britain, 1915–16, 1922–3, 1924–5. MP, 1922–9.

HANNINGTON, Walter (1896–1966). National Organiser, National Unemployed Workers Committee Movement, later National Unemployed Workers Movement, 1921–39. National Organiser, Amalgamated Engineering Union, 1942–50; Assistant Divisional Organiser, 1951–61.

HARTSHORN, Vernon (1872–1931). Miners' Agent, Maesteg, South Wales, 1905–31. Executive Committee, Miners Federation of Great Britain, 1911–18, 1919–21, 1922–4. MP, 1910–31. Postmaster General, 1924. Lord Privy Seal, 1930–31.

HARVEY, William Edwin (1852–1914). Assistant Secretary, Derbyshire Miners Association, 1883–1906; Financial and Corresponding Secretary, 1906–13; Secretary, 1913–14. Executive Committee, Miners Federation of Great Britain, 1891–2, 1893–4, 1895–8, 1899–1903, 1904–5, 1906–7, 1908–9, 1910–11; Vice-President, 1912–14. MP, 1907–14.

HAYDAY, Arthur (1869–1956). Organiser, Gasworkers and General Labourers Union, 1900–8. Midland District Secretary, Gasworkers and General Labourers Union, later National Union of General Workers, later National Union of General and Municipal Workers, 1908–37. General Council, Trades Union Congress, 1922–37; Chairman, 1930–31. MP, 1918–31, 1935–45.

HENDERSON, Arthur (1863–1935). Organiser, Friendly Society of Ironfounders, 1892–1902; National Organiser, 1902–11; Parliamentary Representative, 1911–13; President, Friendly Society of Ironfounders, later National Union of Foundry Workers, 1913–35. Executive Committee, Labour Party, 1904–11; Secretary, 1911–35. MP, 1903–18, 1919–22, 1923, 1924–31, 1933–5. President of Board of Education, 1915–16. Paymaster General, 1916. Minister without Portfolio, 1916–17. Home Secretary, 1924. Foreign Secretary, 1929–31.

HICKS, George Ernest (1879–1954). National Organiser, Operative Bricklayers Society, 1912–19; Secretary, Operative Bricklayers Society, later Amalgamated Union of Building Trade Workers, 1919–40. General Council, Trades Union Congress, 1921–40; Chairman, 1926–7. MP, 1921–50. Parliamentary Secretary to Minister of Works, 1940–45.

HILL, John (1862–1945). District Delegate, United Society of Boilermakers and Iron and Steel Shipbuilders, 1901–9; Secretary, 1909–36. Parliamentary

Committee, later General Council, Trades Union Congress, 1909–36; Chairman, 1916–17.

HILL, Levi Clement (1883–1961). Secretary, National Association of Local Government Officers, 1909–43. Head of Sub-Department of Public and Social Administration, University of Exeter, 1946–56.

HIRST, Stanley (1876–1950). Secretary, Amalgamated Association of Tramwaymen and Vehicle Workers, later United Vehicle Workers, ?–1921. Financial Secretary, Transport and General Workers Union, 1922–41. Executive Committee, Labour Party, 1924–34; Chairman, 1930–31.

HODGE, John (1855–1937). Secretary, British Steel Smelters Amalgamated Association, 1886–1917. President, Iron and Steel Trades Confederation, 1917–31. Parliamentary Committee, Trades Union Congress, 1892–4, 1895–6. Executive Committee, Labour Party, 1900–15; Chairman, 1903–4. MP, 1906–23. Minister of Labour, 1916–17. Minister of Pensions, 1917–19.

HODGES, Frank (1887–1947). Miners' Agent, Garw, South Wales, 1912–18. Secretary, Miners Federation of Great Britain, 1918–24. Executive Committee, Labour Party, 1920–24. MP, 1923–4. Civil Lord, Admiralty, 1924. Central Electricity Board, 1927–47.

HORNER, Arthur Lewis (1894–1968). Miners' Agent, Anthracite Area, South Wales, 1934–6; President, South Wales Miners Federation, 1936–44. National Production Officer, National Union of Mineworkers, 1945–6; Secretary, 1946–59. Executive Committee, Miners Federation of Great Britain, 1927–8, 1936–44.

LARKIN, James (1876–1947). Organiser, National Union of Dock Labourers, 1906–8. Secretary, Irish Transport and General Workers Union, 1908–23 (in USA 1914–23). Secretary, Workers Union of Ireland, 1924–47.

LAWTHER, William (1889–1976). Miners' Agent, Durham Miners Association, 1933–9. Vice-President, Miners Federation of Great Britain, 1934–9; President, Miners Federation of Great Britain, later National Union of Mineworkers, 1939–54. Executive Committee, Labour Party, 1923–6. General Council, Trades Union Congress, 1935–53; Chairman, 1948–9. MP, 1929–31. Kt, 1949.

LEE, Peter (1864–1935). Miners' Agent, Durham Miners Association, 1919–30; Secretary, 1930–34. Vice-President, Miners Federation of Great Britain, 1931–2; President, 1932–4. General Council, Trades Union Congress, 1933–4.

MACARA, Charles (1845–1929). President, Federation of Master Cotton Spinners Associations, 1894–1914. President, Employers Parliamentary Association, 1912–16. Baronet, 1911.

MACARTHUR, Mary (1880–1921). Secretary, Women's Trade Union League, 1903–21. President, National Federation of Women Workers, 1906–8; Secretary, 1908–21. Executive Committee, Labour Party, 1919–21.

MCGURK, John (1874–1944). Miners' Agent, Lancashire and Cheshire Miners Federation, 1908–44; Vice-President, 1924–9; President, 1929–44. Executive Committee, Miners Federation of Great Britain, 1912–13, 1920–21, 1929–30,

1936–7, 1940–41, 1943–4. Executive Committee, Labour Party, 1917–19; Chairman, 1918–19.

MANN, Thomas (1856–1941). President, Dock Wharf Riverside and General Labourers Union, 1889–1900. Secretary, Amalgamated Society of Engineers, later Amalgamated Engineering Union, 1919–21. Secretary, Independent Labour Party, 1893–5.

MARCHBANK, John (1883–1946). President, National Union of Railwaymen, 1922–4; Assistant Secretary, 1925–33; Secretary, 1933–42. General Council, Trades Union Congress, 1924–5, 1933–43.

MILNE-BAILEY, Walter (d. 1935). Research Officer, Union of Post Office Workers, 1920–22. Research Assistant, Joint Research and Information Department of the Trades Union Congress and the Labour Party, 1922–6. Secretary, Research and Economic Department, Trades Union Congress, 1926–35.

MOND, Alfred Moritz (1868–1930). Director, later Managing Director, Brunner Mond and Co., 1895–1926. Chairman, ICI, Amalgamated Anthracite Collieries, 1926–30. MP, 1910–23, 1924–8. First Commissioner of Works, 1916–21. Minister of Health, 1921–2. Baronet, 1910. Baron, 1928.

MOSSES, William (1858–1943). Secretary, United Pattern Makers Association, 1884–1917. Secretary, Federation of Engineering and Shipbuilding Trades, 1890–1917. Parliamentary Committee, Trades Union Congress, 1907–11, 1913–17. Director, Labour Enlistment Complaints Section, Ministry of Munitions, 1917–18. Industrial Relations Department, Ministry of Labour, 1919–24.

MULLIN, William (1855–1920). Secretary, Amalgamated Association of Card Blowing and Ring Room Operatives, 1886–1920. Parliamentary Committee, Trades Union Congress, 1897–1903, 1908–13, 1915–16; Chairman, 1910–11.

NAESMITH, Andrew (1888–1961). Official, Oldham Weavers Association and later of Todmorden and District Weavers Association. Assistant Secretary, Amalgamated Weavers Association, 1925–8; Secretary, 1928–53. General Council, Trades Union Congress, 1945–53.

OGDEN, John William (d. 1930). Secretary, Heywood Weavers Association, 1891–1930. President, Amalgamated Weavers Association, 1911–30. Parliamentary Committee, later General Council, Trades Union Congress, 1911–30; Chairman, 1917–18.

O'GRADY, James (1861–1934). Organiser, Alliance Cabinet Makers, 1899–1902. National Organiser, National Amalgamated Furniture Trades Association, 1902–17. Secretary, National Federation of General Workers, 1917–24. President, Trades Union Congress, 1898. MP, 1906–24. Governor, Tasmania, 1924–30. Governor, Falkland Islands, 1931–4. Kt, 1924.

POULTON, Edward L. (1865–1937). Full-time Branch Secretary, National Union of Boot and Shoe Operatives, 1890–1908; Secretary, 1908–29. Parliamentary Committee, later General Council, Trades Union Congress, 1917–30; Chairman, 1920–21.

PUGH, Arthur (1870–1955). Local Secretary, British Steel Smelters Amalgamated Association, 1890–1906; Assistant Secretary, 1906–17. Secretary, Iron and Steel Trades Confederation, 1917–37. Parliamentary Committee, later General Council, Trades Union Congress, 1920–36; Chairman, 1925–6. Kt, 1935.

PURCELL, Albert Arthur William (1872–1935). Secretary, Amalgamated Society of French Polishers, 1898–1910. Organiser, National Amalgamated Furniture Trades Association, 1910–28. Full-time Secretary, Manchester and Salford Trades Council, 1929–35. Parliamentary Committee, later General Council, Trades Union Congress, 1919–28; Chairman, 1924. MP, 1923–4, 1925–9.

ROBERTS, George Henry (1869–1928). National Organiser, Typographical Association, 1904–6. Executive Committee, Labour Party, 1910–18; Chairman, 1912–13. MP, 1906–23. Lord Commissioner of Treasury, 1915–16. Parliamentary Secretary to Board of Trade, 1916–17. Minister of Labour, 1917–19. Food Controller, 1919–20.

SEDDON, James Andrew (1868–1939). President, National Amalgamated Union of Shop Assistants, 1902–19. Parliamentary Committee, Trades Union Congress, 1908–16; Chairman, 1913–15. MP, 1906–10, 1918–22.

SEXTON, James (1856–1938). Secretary, National Union of Dock Labourers, 1893–1921. National Supervisor, Docks Trade Group, Transport and General Workers Union, 1922–8. Parliamentary Committee, Trades Union Congress, 1900–6, 1907–8, 1909–21; Chairman, 1904–5. Executive Committee, Labour Party, 1902–4. MP, 1918–31. Kt, 1931.

SHACKLETON, David (1863–1938). Secretary, Darwen Weavers Association, 1894–1907. President, Amalgamated Weavers Association, 1906–10. Parliamentary Committee, Trades Union Congress, 1904–10; Chairman, 1907–9. Executive Committee, Labour Party, 1903–5. MP, 1902–10. Labour Adviser, Home Office, 1910–11. National Insurance Commissioner, 1911–16. Permanent Secretary, Ministry of Labour, 1916–21; Chief Labour Adviser, 1921–5. Kt, 1916.

SHAW, Thomas (1872–1938). Secretary, Colne Weavers Association, 1892–? Secretary, Northern Counties Textile Trades Federation, 1906–? Executive Committee, Labour Party, 1919–23. MP, 1918–31. Minister of Labour, 1924. Secretary of State for War, 1929–31.

SHINWELL, Emmanuel (b. 1884) Full-time Assistant Secretary, Glasgow Branch, National Sailors and Firemen's Union, 1911–12. Organiser, British Seafarers Union, later Amalgamated Marine Workers Union, 1912–27. Executive Committee, Labour Party, 1940–51; Chairman, 1947–8. MP, 1922–4, 1928–31, 1935–70. Parliamentary Secretary, Department of Mines, 1924, 1930–31. Financial Secretary to War Office, 1929–30. Minister of Fuel and Power, 1945–7. Secretary of State for War, 1947–50. Minister of Defence, 1950–51. Baron, 1970.

SMILLIE, Robert (1857–1940). President, Scottish Miners Federation, 1894–

1918, 1921–40. Vice-President, Miners Federation of Great Britain, 1908–11; President, 1912–21. Parliamentary Committee, Trades Union Congress, 1918–19; General Council, 1921–7. MP, 1923–9.

SMITH, Allan MacGregor (d. 1941). Secretary, Engineering Employers Federation, 1908–16; Chairman of the Board, 1916–34. MP, 1919–23. Kt, 1918.

SMITH, Herbert (1862–1938). Miners' Agent, Yorkshire Miners Association, 1902–6; Vice-President, 1904–6; President, 1906–38. Executive Committee, Miners Federation of Great Britain, 1911–16, 1934–7; Vice-President, 1917–22; President, 1922–9. Parliamentary Committee, Trades Union Congress, 1913–17; General Council, 1922–5, 1931–2.

SMITH, Walter R. (1873–1942). National Organiser, National Union of Boot and Shoe Operatives, 1916–35. President, National Agricultural Labourers and Rural Workers Union, later National Agricultural Workers Union, 1911–23. Executive Committee, Labour Party, 1923–4, 1927–34, Chairman, 1933–4. MP, 1918–22, 1923–31. Parliamentary Secretary to Ministry of Agriculture, 1924. Parliamentary Secretary to Board of Trade, 1929–31.

SPENCER, George Alfred (1872–1957). President, Nottinghamshire Miners Association, 1912–18; Secretary, 1918–26. Leading figure in Nottingham and District Miners Industrial Union, and President, National Federation of Industrial Unions, 1926–37. President, Nottingham and District Miners Fedcrated Union, 1937–45. MP, 1918–29.

STANTON, Charles Butt (1873–1946). Miners' Agent, Aberdare, South Wales, 1900–15. Executive Committee, Miners Federation of Great Britain, 1911–12. MP, 1915–22.

STEADMAN, William Charles (1851–1911). Secretary, Barge Builders Union, 1879–1908. Parliamentary Committee, Trades Union Congress, 1899–1905; Chairman, 1901–2; Secretary, 1905–11. MP, 1898–1900, 1906–10.

STRAKER, William (1855–1941). Corresponding Secretary, Northumberland Miners Association, 1905–13; Secretary, 1913–35. Executive Committee, Miners Federation of Great Britain, 1908–25.

STUART (later STUART-BUNNING), George Harold (1870–1949). Parliamentary Secretary, Postmen's Federation, 1903–11; Secretary, 1911–19. Secretary, Sub-Postmasters Federation, 1920–25. President, Civil Service Federation, 1920–25. Parliamentary Committee, Trades Union Congress, 1916–21; Chairman, 1918–19.

SWALES, Alonso Beaumont (1870–1952). Organiser, Amalgamated Society of Engineers, 1912–17; Executive Committee, Amalgamated Society of Engineers, later Amalgamated Engineering Union, 1917–35. Parliamentary Committee, later General Council, Trades Union Congress, 1919–35; Chairman, 1924–5.

TANNER, Frederick John Shirley (1889–1965). Organiser, Amalgamated Engineering Union, 1931–9; President, 1939–54. General Council, Trades Union Congress, 1943–54; Chairman, 1953–4.

THOMAS, James Henry (1874–1950). Organiser, Amalgamated Society of Railway Servants, 1906–10; Assistant Secretary, 1910–13. Assistant Secretary, National Union of Railwaymen, 1913–16; Secretary, 1916–19; Parliamentary Secretary, 1919–31. Parliamentary Committee, later General Council, Trades Union Congress, 1917–24, 1925–9; Chairman, 1919–20. MP, 1910–36. Colonial Secretary, 1924, 1935–6. Lord Privy Seal, 1929–30. Secretary of State for Dominion Affairs, 1930–35.

THORNE, William James (1857–1946). Secretary, National Union of Gasworkers and General Labourers, later National Union of General Workers, later National Union of General and Municipal Workers, 1889–1934. Parliamentary Committee, later General Council, Trades Union Congress, 1894–1934; Chairman, 1911–12. MP, 1906–45.

TILLETT, Benjamin (1860–1943). Secretary, Tea Operatives and General Labourers Union, later Dock Wharf Riverside and General Labourers Union, 1887–1921. Political Secretary, Transport and General Workers Union, 1922–30. Parliamentary Committee, Trades Union Congress, 1892–5; General Council, 1921–32; Chairman, 1928–9. Executive Committee, Labour Party, 1901–2. MP, 1917–24, 1929–31.

TURNER, Ben (1863–1942). Organiser, National Union of Textile Workers, 1889–1902. President, National Union of Textile Workers, later General Union of Textile Workers, 1902–33. General Council, Trades Union Congress, 1921–9; Chairman, 1927–8. Executive Committee, Labour Party, 1903–4, 1905–21, 1930–32; Chairman, 1911–12. MP, 1922–4, 1929–31. Parliamentary Secretary to Department of Mines, 1929–30. Kt, 1931.

WALKER, Robert Barrie. Clerical Officer, National Agricultural Labourers and Rural Workers Union, 1912–13. Secretary, National Agricultural Labourers and Rural Workers Union, later National Agricultural Workers Union, 1913–28. Parliamentary Committee, later General Council, Trades Union Congress, 1917–27; Chairman, 1921–2.

WALSH, Stephen (1859–1929). Secretary, Ashton and Haydock Miners Union, 1890–1901. Miners' Agent, later President, Lancashire and Cheshire Miners Federation, 1901–29. Executive Committee, Miners Federation of Great Britain, 1914–15, 1921–2; Vice-President, 1922–4. Executive Committee, Labour Party, 1912–13. MP, 1906–29. Parliamentary Secretary to Ministry of National Service, 1917. Parliamentary Secretary to Local Government Board, 1917–18. Secretary of State for War, 1924.

WEIR, William Douglas (1877–1959). Managing Director, G. & J. Weir, 1902–12; Chairman, 1912–53. Scottish Director of Munitions, 1915–16. Controller, Aeronautical Supplies, 1916–18. Director General of Aircraft Production, 1918. Secretary of State for Air, 1918. Director General of Explosives, 1939–41. Chairman, Tank Board, 1942. Kt, 1917. Baron, 1918. Viscount, 1938.

WILLIAMS, James Edwin (1857–1916). Assistant Secretary, Amalgamated Society of Railway Servants, 1903–10; Secretary, 1910–13. Secretary, National Union of Railwaymen, 1913–16. Parliamentary Committee, Trades Union Congress, 1910–16.

WILLIAMS, Joseph Bevir (1872–?). Secretary, Amalgamated Musicians Union, later Musicians Union, 1893–1924. Parliamentary Committee, later General Council, Trades Union Congress, 1907–11, 1912–13, 1917–25; Chairman, 1922–3.

WILLIAMS, Robert (1881–1936). President, National Amalgamated Labourers Union. ?–1912. Secretary, National Transport Workers Federation, 1912 25. Executive Committee, Labour Party, 1918–21, 1922–6; Chairman, 1925–6.

WILSON, Joseph Havelock (1858–1929). Secretary, National Amalgamated Sailors and Firemens Union, 1889–1903. President, National Amalgamated Sailors and Firemens Union, later National Union of Seamen, 1894–1929. Parliamentary Committee, Trades Union Congress, 1889–98, 1918–19. MP, 1892–5, 1918–22.

WINSTONE, James (1863–1921). Miners' Agent, Eastern Valleys District, South Wales, 1891–1921. Vice-President, South Wales Miners Federation, 1912–15; President, 1915–21.

YOUNG, Robert (1872–1957). Clerical Officer, Amalgamated Society of Engineers, 1906–8; Assistant Secretary, 1908–13; Secretary, 1913–18. MP, 1918–31, 1935–50. Deputy Speaker, 1924, 1929–31. Kt, 1931.

Bibliography

References to articles, books, and pamphlets cited in the text, in footnotes, and in the Statistical Appendix have been abbreviated. In most instances the names of the author or authors are given with a page reference. Where more than one work of a given author or authors has been cited, the relevant title (if possible abbreviated) has been added. The full bibliographical identification is given here.

A similar practice has been adopted with government publications. In addition there are lists of newspapers, periodicals, and trade union journals cited, and a note on the use that has been made of the records of trade unions, the Labour Party, and employers' organisations.

Articles, Books, and Pamphlets

Addison, Christopher, *Four and a Half Years: a personal diary from June 1914 to January 1919*, Vol. I (London: Hutchinson, 1934).

——, *Politics from Within 1911–1918: including some records of a great national effort*, Vols I & II (London: Herbert Jenkins, 1925).

Alcock, G. W., *Fifty Years of Railway Trade Unionism* (London: Co-operative Printing Society, 1922).

Aldcroft, D. H., *The Inter-War Economy: Britain 1919–1939* (London: Batsford, 1970).

Allen, G. C., *British Industries and their Organisation* (London: Longmans, 4th edn., 1959).

Allen, V. L., 'The National Union of Police and Prison Officers', *Economic History Review*, XI (1958), No. 1.

Armitage, Susan, *The Politics of Decontrol of Industry: Britain and the United States* (London: Weidenfeld and Nicolson, 1969).

Arnot, R. Page, *South Wales Miners: a history of the South Wales Miners Federation 1898–1914* (London: Allen and Unwin, 1967).

——, *The General Strike: its origin and history* (London: Labour Research Department, 1926).

——, *The Miners: years of struggle: a history of the Miners Federation of Great Britain (from 1910 onwards)* (London: Allen and Unwin, 1953).

Askwith, G. R., *Industrial Problems and Disputes* (London: John Murray, 1920).

Bagwell, P. S., *The Railwaymen: the history of the National Union of Railwaymen* (London: Allen and Unwin, 1963).

Bain, G. S., *The Growth of White-Collar Unionism* (Oxford: Clarendon Press, 1970).

——, and Farouk Elsheikh, *Union Growth and the Business Cycle: an econometric analysis* (Oxford: Blackwell, 1976).

Bain, G. S., and Robert Price, *Profiles of Union Growth: a comparative statistical portrait of eight countries* (Oxford: Blackwell, 1980).

Bealey, Frank, *The Post Office Engineering Union: the history of the Post Office Engineers 1870–1970* (London: Bachman and Turner, 1976).

Bean, R., 'Employers Associations in the Port of Liverpool, 1890–1914', *International Review of Social History*, XXI (1976), part 3.

Beveridge, W. H., *British Food Control* (London: Oxford University Press, 1928).

——, *Power and Influence* (London: Hodder and Stoughton, 1953).

Blaxland, Gregory, *J. H. Thomas: a life for unity* (London: Muller, 1964).

Bondfield, Margaret, *A Life's Work* (London: Hutchinson, 1948).

Bowley, A. L., *Prices and Wages in the United Kingdom, 1914–1920* (Oxford: Clarendon Press, 1921).

——, *Wages and Income in the United Kingdom Since 1860* (Cambridge: Cambridge University Press, 1937).

Bullock, Alan, *The Life and Times of Ernest Bevin*, Vol. I: *Trade union leader 1881–1940* (London: Heinemann, 1960).

Butler, David, and Jennie Freeman, *British Political Facts 1900–1960* (London: Macmillan, 1963).

Buxton, N. K., 'Entrepreneurial Efficiency in the British Coal Industry Between the Wars', *Economic History Review*, XXIII (1970), No. 3.

Cadbury Bros, Ltd, *A Works Council in Being: an account of the scheme in operation at Bournville Works* (Bournville Works, Publication Department, 1921).

Calhoun, D. F., *The United Front: the TUC and the Russians 1923–28* (Cambridge: Cambridge University Press, 1976).

Carr, J. C., and W. Taplin, *History of the British Steel Industry* (Oxford: Blackwell, 1962).

Carter, G. R., 'The Coal Strike in South Wales', *Economic Journal*, September 1915.

Ceadel, Martin, *Pacifism in Britain 1915–1945: the defining of a faith* (Oxford: Clarendon Press, 1980).

Chapman, A. L., and Rose Knight, *Wages and Salaries in the United Kingdom 1920–1938* (Cambridge: Cambridge University Press, 1953).

Charles, Roger, *The Development of Industrial Relations in Britain 1911–1939: studies in the evolution of collective bargaining at national and industry level* (London: Hutchinson, 1973).

Citrine, Walter, *Men and Work: the autobiography of Lord Citrine* (London: Hutchinson, 1964).

Clay, Henry, *The Problem of Industrial Relations: and other lectures* (London: Macmillan, 1929).

Clegg, H. A. *General Union in a Changing Society: a short history of the National Union of General and Municipal Workers 1889–1964* (Oxford: Blackwell, 1964).

——, A. J. Killick and Rex Adams, *Trade Union Officers: a study of full-time officers, branch secretaries and shop stewards in British trade unions* (Oxford: Blackwell, 1961).

Clyde Workers Committee, *To All Clyde Workers* (n.d.).

Cole, G. D. H., *A History of the Labour Party from 1914* (London: Routledge and Kegan Paul, 1948).

——, *Labour in the Coal-Mining Industry (1914–1921)* (Oxford: Clarendon Press, 1923).

——, *Labour in War Time* (London: Bell, 1915).

——, *Trade Unionism and Munitions* (Oxford: Clarendon Press, 1923).

——, *Workshop Organisation* (Oxford: Clarendon Press, 1923).

——, *The World of Labour* (London: Bell, revised edn., 1915).

——, and R. Page Arnot, *Trade Unionism on the Railways: its history and problems* (London: Allen and Unwin, 1917).

Cole, Margaret, 'Guild Socialism and the Labour Research Department' in Asa Briggs and John Saville (eds.), *Essays in Labour History 1886–1923* (London: Macmillan, 1971).

Coleman, Donald, *Courtaulds: an economic and social history*, Vol. II: *Rayon* (Oxford: Clarendon Press, 1969).

Court, W. H. B., *Coal* (London: HMSO and Longmans Green, 1951).

Cuthbert, N. H., *The Lace Makers Society: a study of trade unionism in the British lace industry 1760–1960* (Nottingham: Amalgamated Society of Operative Lace Makers and Auxiliary Workers, 1960).

Dalton, Hugh, *Call Back Yesterday: memoirs 1887–1931* (London: Muller, 1953).

Dangerfield, George, *The Strange Death of Liberal England 1910–1914* (London: Constable, 1935).

Deacon, Alan, *In Search of the Scrounger* (London: Bell, 1976).

Dobbs, S. P., *The Clothing Workers of Great Britain* (London: Routledge, 1928).

Dougan, David, *The Shipwrights: the history of the Shipconstructors and Shipwrights Association 1882–1963* (Newcastle-upon-Tyne: Frank Graham, 1975).

Douglass, Dave, 'The Durham Pitman' in Raphael Samuel (ed.), *Miners Quarrymen and Saltworkers* (London: Routledge and Kegan Paul, 1977).

Evans, E. W., *The Miners of South Wales* (Cardiff: University of Wales Press, 1961).

Fayle, C. E., *The War and the Shipping Industry* (Oxford: Clarendon Press, 1927).

Feinstein, C. H., *National Income, Expenditure and Output in the United Kingdom 1855–1965* (Cambridge: Cambridge University Press, 1972).

Fox, Alan, *A History of the National Union of Boot and Shoe Operatives* (Oxford: Blackwell, 1958).

Francis, Hywel, 'The Anthracite Strike and Disturbances of 1925', *Llafur*, May 1973.

——, and David Smith, *The Fed: a history of the South Wales Miners in the twentieth century* (London: Lawrence and Wishart, 1980).

Fusion of Forces: report of the fifth national rank and file conference, Newcastle-on-Tyne, 13–14 October, 1917.

Gallacher, William, *Revolt on the Clyde: an autobiography* (London: Lawrence and Wishart, 1936).

Garside, W. R., *The Durham Miners 1919–1960* (London: Allen and Unwin, 1971).

Gilbert, B. B., *The Evolution of National Insurance in Great Britain: the origins of the welfare state* (London: Michael Joseph, 1966).

——, *British Social Policy 1914–1939* (London: Batsford, 1970).

Goodhart, A. L., 'The Legality of the General Strike in England', *Yale Law Journal*, XXXVI (1926–7), No. 4.

Gosden, P. H. J. H., *The Evolution of a Profession: a study of the contribution of teachers' associations to the development of school teaching as a professional occupation* (Oxford: Blackwell, 1972).

Gregory, Roy, *The Miners and British Politics 1906–1914* (London: Oxford University Press, 1968).

Griffin, A. R., *The Miners of Nottinghamshire 1914–44* (London: Allen and Unwin, 1962).

——, and C. P. Griffin, 'The Non-Political Trade Union Movement' in Asa Briggs and John Saville (eds.), *Essays in Labour History 1918–1939* (London: Croom Helm, 1977).

Groves, Reg, *Sharpen the Sickle! the history of the farm workers union* (London: Porcupine Press, 1949).

Gurnham, Richard, *A History of the Trade Union Movement in the Hosiery and Knitwear Industry* (Leicester: NUHKW, 1976).

Halévy, Elie, *The Rule of Democracy 1905–1914* (London: Benn, revised edn., 1952).

Hardy, George, *These Stormy Years: memories of the fight for freedom in five continents* (London: Lawrence and Wishart, 1956).

Harris, José, *Unemployment and Politics: a study in English social policy 1886–1914* (Oxford: Clarendon Press, 1972).

——, *William Beveridge: a biography* (Oxford: Clarendon Press, 1977).

Harrison, Royden, 'The War Emergency Workers' National Committee, 1914–1920' in Asa Briggs and John Saville (eds.), *Essays in Labour History 1886–1923* (London: Macmillan, 1971).

Henderson, H. D., *The Cotton Control Board* (Oxford: Clarendon Press, 1922).

Higenbottam, S., *Our Society's History* (Manchester: Amalgamated Society of Woodworkers, 1939).

Hinton, James, *The First Shop Stewards Movement* (London: Allen and Unwin, 1973).

History of the Ministry of Munitions (Hassocks, Sussex: Harvester Press, 1976). (Microfilm reproduced with permission of the Controller of HMSO.)

Horner, Arthur, *Incorrigible Rebel* (London: MacGibbon and Kee, 1960).

Howe, Ellic, and Harold Waite, *The London Society of Compositors: a centenary history* (London: Cassell, 1948).

Hughes, Fred, *By Hand and Brain: the story of the Clerical and Administrative Workers Union* (London: Lawrence and Wishart, 1953).

Humphreys, B. V., *Clerical Unions in the Civil Service* (Oxford: Blackwell and Mott, 1958).

Hyman, Richard, *The Workers Union* (Oxford: Clarendon Press, 1971).

Jenkins, Roy, *Mr Attlee: an interim biography* (London: Heinemann, 1948).

Jevons, H. S., *The British Coal Trade* (London: Kegan Paul, Trench, Trubner, 1920).

Jones, Tom, *Whitehall Diary*, Vol. II: 1926–30 (London: Oxford University Press, 1969).

Kendall, Walter, *The Revolutionary Movement in Britain 1900–21: the origins of British Communism* (London: Weidenfeld and Nicolson, 1969).

Kirkaldy, A. W., *British Shipping: its history, organisation and importance* (London: Kegan Paul, Trench, Trubner, 1919).

Lawson, Jack, *The Man in the Cap: the life of Herbert Smith* (London: Methuen, 1941).

Leask, J., and P. Bellars, *Nor Shall the Sword Sleep* (n.d.).

Lerner, Shirley, *Breakaway Unions and the Small Trade Union* (London: Allen and Unwin, 1961).

Lloyd George, David, *War Memoirs*, Vol. I (London: Odhams, 1938).

Lockwood, David, *The Blackcoated Worker: a study in class consciousness* (London: Allen and Unwin, 1958).

Lovell, John, *Stevedores and Dockers: a study of trade unionism in the Port of London, 1870–1914* (London: Macmillan, 1969).

——, 'The TUC Special Industrial Committee: January–April 1926' in Asa Briggs and John Saville (eds.), *Essays in Labour History 1918–1939* (London: Croom Helm, 1977).

McCarthy, Charles, *Trade Unions in Ireland 1894–1960* (Dublin: Institute of Public Administration, 1977).

Macfarlane, L. J., *The British Communist Party: its origin and development until 1929* (London: MacGibbon and Kee, 1966).

Macintyre, Stuart, *Little Moscows: Communism and working-class militancy in inter-war Britain* (London: Croom Helm, 1980).

McKibbin, Ross, *The Evolution of the Labour Party 1910–1924* (London: Oxford University Press, 1974).

Marquand, David, *Ramsay MacDonald* (London: Cape, 1977).

Martin, Kingsley, *The British Public and the General Strike* (London: Woolf, 1926).

Martin, Roderick, *Communism and the British Trade Unions 1924–1933: a study of the National Minority Movement* (Oxford: Clarendon Press, 1969).

Martin, Ross M., *TUC: the growth of a pressure group 1868–1976* (Oxford: Clarendon Press, 1980).

Matthew, H. C. G., R. I. McKibbin and J. A. Kay, 'The Franchise Factor in the Rise of the Labour Party', *English Historical Review* (October 1976).

Matthews, Frank, 'The Building Guilds' in Asa Briggs and John Saville (eds.), *Essays in Labour History 1886–1923* (London: Macmillan, 1971).

Middlemas, Keith, *Politics and Industrial Society: the experience of the British system since 1911* (London: Deutsch, 1979).

——, and John Barnes, *Baldwin: a biography* (London: Weidenfeld and Nicolson, 1969).

Miliband, Ralph, *Parliamentary Socialism: a study in the politics of Labour* (London: Allen and Unwin, 1961).

Milne-Bailey, W., *Trade Unions and the State* (London: Allen and Unwin, 1934).

Minchinton, Walter, *The British Tinplate Industry: a history* (Oxford: Clarendon Press, 1957).

Mitchell, B. R., and Phyllis Deane, *Abstract of British Historical Statistics* (Cambridge: Cambridge University Press, 1962).

Mitchell, David, 'Ghost of a Chance: British revolutionaries in 1919', *History Today* (November 1970).

Mogridge, Basil, 'Militancy and Inter-union Rivalries in British Shipping 1911–1929', *International Review of Social History*, VI (1961), part 3.

More, Charles, *Skill and the English Working Class, 1870–1914* (London: Croom Helm, 1980).

Morgan, Kenneth, 'The New Liberalism and the Challenge of Labour: the Welsh experience 1885–1929' in Kenneth Brown (ed.), *Essays in Anti-Labour History: responses to the rise of Labour in Britain* (London: Macmillan, 1974).

Mortimer, J. E., *History of the Boilermakers Society*, Vol. 2: *1906–1932* (London: Allen and Unwin, 1982).

Mosses, William, *The History of the United Pattern Makers Association, 1872–1922* (London: The Association, 1922).

Mowat, C. L., *Britain Between the Wars 1918–1940* (London: Methuen, 1955).

Murphy, J. T., *Preparing for Power* (London: Pluto Press, 2nd edn., 1972).

——, *The Workers Committee: an outline of its principles and structure* (republished, London: Pluto Press, 1972).

Musson, A. E., *The Typographical Association: origins and history up to 1949* (London: Oxford University Press, 1954).

Newby, Howard, *The Deferential Worker: a study of farm workers in East Anglia* (London: Allen Lane, 1977).

Phelps Brown, E. H., *The Growth of British Industrial Relations: a study from the standpoint of 1906–14* (London: Macmillan, 1959).

Phillips, G. A., *The General Strike: the politics of industrial conflict* (London: Weidenfeld and Nicolson, 1976).

——, 'The Triple Alliance in 1914', *Economic History Review*, XXIV (1971), No. 1.

Pigou, A. C., *Aspects of British Economic History 1918–1925* (London: Macmillan, 1947).

Pollard, Sidney, *The Development of the British Economy 1914–1967* (London: Arnold, 2nd edn., 1969).

Postgate, Raymond, *The Life of George Lansbury* (London: Longmans Green, 1951).

Pratt, E. A., *British Railways and the Great War: organisation, efforts, difficulties and achievements*, Vol. II (London: Selwyn and Blount, 1921).

Pribićević, Branko, *The Shop Stewards Movement and Workers Control, 1910–1922* (Oxford: Blackwell, 1959).

Price, Richard, *Masters Unions and Men: work control in building and the rise of labour 1830–1914* (Cambridge: Cambridge University Press, 1980).

Pugh, Arthur, *Men of Steel: a chronicle of eighty-eight years of trade unionism in the British iron and steel industry* (London: The Iron and Steel Trades Confederation, 1951).

Reader, W. J., *Architect of Air Power: the life of the first Viscount Weir of Eastwood 1877–1959* (London: Collins, 1968).

Redmayne, R. A. S., *The British Coal-Mining Industry during the War* (Oxford: Clarendon Press, 1923).

Richardson, J. H., *Industrial Relations in Great Britain* (Geneva: International Labour Office, 2nd edn., 1938).

Richardson, William, *A Union of Many Trades: the history of USDAW* (Manchester: USDAW, 1979).

Roskill, Stephen, *Hankey Man of Secrets*, Vol. II: *1919–1931* (London: Collins, 1972).

Routh, Guy, *Occupation and Pay in Great Britain 1906–60* (Cambridge: Cambridge University Press, 1965).

Rowe, J. W. F., *Wages in the Coal Industry* (London: King, 1923).

——, *Wages in Practice and Theory* (London: Routledge and Kegan Paul, 1928).

Ryan, Patricia, 'The Poor Law in 1926', in Margaret Morris (ed.), *The General Strike* (Harmondsworth: Penguin Books, 1976).

Schwartz, Marvin, *The Union of Democratic Control in British Politics during the First World War* (Oxford: Clarendon Press, 1971).

Selley, Ernest, *Village Trade Unions in Two Centuries* (London: Allen and Unwin, 1919).

Sells, Dorothy, *The British Trade Board System* (London: King, 1923).

Sexton, James, *Sir James Sexton Agitator: the life of the dockers MP: an autobiography* (London: Faber, 1936).

Shepherd, E. C., *The Fixing of Wages in Government Employment* (London: Methuen, 1923).

Shinwell, Emanuel, *Conflict Without Malice* (London: Odhams, 1955).

Skidelsky, Robert, *Politicians and the Slump: the Labour government of 1929–1931* (London: Macmillan, 1967).

Smillie, Robert, *My Life for Labour* (London: Mills and Boon, 1924).

Snowden, Philip, *An autobiography*, Vols I & II (London: Nicholson and Watson, 1934).

Soldon, Norbert, *Women in British Trade Unions 1874–1976* (Dublin: Gill and Macmillan, 1978).

Spoor, Alec, *White-Collar Union: sixty years of NALGO* (London: Heinemann, 1967).

Stead, Peter, '1922 and All That', *The Historical Journal*, XVII (1974), No. 1.

Symons, Julian, *The General Strike: a historical portrait* (London: Cresset Press, 1957).

Tawney, R. H., *The Establishment of Minimum Rates in the Chain-Making Industry under the Trade Boards Act of 1909* (London: Bell, 1914).

——, *The Establishment of Minimum Rates in the Tailoring Industry under the Trade Boards Act of 1909* (London: Bell, 1915).

Taylor, A. J. P., *English History 1914–1945* (Oxford, Clarendon Press, 1965).

Thompson, Donna, *Professional Solidarity among the Teachers of England* (New York: Columbia University Press, 1927).

Tillyard, Frank, and Frank Ball, *Unemployment Insurance in Great Britain 1911–1948* (Leigh-on-Sea: Thames Publishing, 1949).

Tropp, Asher, *The School Teachers: the growth of the teaching profession in England and Wales from 1800 to the present day* (London: Heinemann, 1957).

Tuckett, Angela, *The Scottish Carter: the history of the Scottish Horse and Motormens Association 1898–1964* (London: Allen and Unwin, 1967).

Turner, H. A., *Trade Union Growth Structure and Policy: a comparative study of the cotton unions* (London: Allen and Unwin, 1962).

Walker, William, *Juteopolis: Dundee and its textile workers 1885–1923* (Edinburgh: Scottish Academic Press, 1979).

Webb, Beatrice, *Beatrice Webb's Diaries 1912–24* (1952), *1924–32* (1956), ed. Margaret Cole (London: Longmans).

Webb, Sidney, and Beatrice Webb, *The History of Trade Unionism 1666–1920* (London: Longmans, 1920).

——, and Beatrice Webb, *Industrial Democracy* (London: Longmans, 1920).

White, Joseph, *The Limits of Trade Union Militancy: the Lancashire textile workers 1910–1914* (Westport, Connecticut: Greenwood Press, 1978).

Wigham, Eric, *The Power to Manage: a history of the Engineering Employers Federation* (London: Macmillan, 1973).

Wilkinson, Frank, 'Collective Bargaining in the Steel Industry in the 1920s' in

Asa Briggs and John Saville (eds.), *Essays in Labour History 1918–1939* (London: Croom Helm, 1977).

Williams, J. E., *The Derbyshire Miners: a study in industrial and social history* (London: Allen and Unwin, 1962).

Williams, Richard, 'The First Year's Working of the Liverpool Docks Scheme' in *Liverpool Economic and Statistical Society Transactions* (1913–14).

Wright, Arnold, *Disturbed Dublin: the story of the great strike of 1913–14* (London: Longsmans Green, 1914).

Wrigley, C. J., *David Lloyd George and the Labour Movement: peace and war* (New York: Harvester, 1976).

Yates, M. L., *Wages and Labour Conditions in British Engineering* (London: MacDonald and Evans, 1937).

Government Publications

Balfour Committee. Board of Trade, Committee on Industry and Trade, 1924, *Survey of Industrial Relations*, 1926. Chairman: Sir Arthur Balfour.

Cave Committee. Ministry of Labour, Committee appointed to Inquire into the Working and Effects of the Trade Board Acts, 1921, *Report*, 1922 (Cmd 1645). Chairman: Viscount Cave.

Changes in Rates of Wages. Labour Department of the Board of Trade, *Report on Changes in Rates of Wages and Hours of Labour in the United Kingdom in 1911*, 1912 (Cd 6471).

——. *Report on Changes in Rates of Wages and Hours of Labour in the United Kingdom in 1912*, 1913 (Cd 7080).

Clynes Committee. Economic Advisory Council, Committee on the Present Conditions and Prospects of the Cotton Industry, 1929, *Report*, 1930 (Cmd 3651). Chairman: J. R. Clynes.

Coal Industry (Sankey) Commission. *Interim Report*, First Stage of the Inquiry, 1919 (Cmd 359); Volume II, *Report*, Second Stage of the Inquiry, 1919 (Cmd 360).

Coal Output and the War: national conference of representatives of the coal mining industry at the Central Hall, Westminster, 25th October, 1916 (London: Home Office, n.d.).

Collective Agreements. Board of Trade (Labour Department), *Report on Collective Agreements between Employers and Workpeople in the United Kingdom*, 1910 (Cd 5366).

Colliery Strike Disturbances in South Wales. Home Office, *Correspondence and Report*, 1911 (Cd 5568).

Commission of Enquiry into Industrial Unrest, *Summary of the Reports of the Commission by the Right Honourable G. N. Barnes, M.P.*, 1917 (Cd 8696).

Court of Inquiry Concerning the Dispute in the Building Industry, 1924, *Report*, 1924 (Cmd 2192). Chairman: Lord Buckmaster.

Court of Inquiry Concerning the Coal Mining Industry Dispute, 1925, *Report*, 1925 (Cmd 2478). Chairman: H. P. Macmillan.

Court of Inquiry Concerning the Engineering Trades Dispute, 1922, *Report*, 1922 (Cmd 1635). Chairman: Sir William Mackenzie.

Court of Inquiry Concerning the Stoppage of the London Tramway and Omnibus Services, 1924, *Interim Report*, 1924 (Cmd 2087); *Report*, 1924 (Cmd 2101). Chairman: Sir Arthur Colefax.

Court of Inquiry Concerning Transport Workers' Wages and Conditions of Employment of Dock Labour, *Report and Minutes of Evidence*, 1920 (Cmd 936). Chairman: Lord Shaw of Dunfermline.

Court of Inquiry Concerning the Matters in Dispute between the Parties to the Northern Counties Wool (and Allied) Textile Industrial Council, *Report*, 1930 (Cmd 3505). Chairman: Lord Macmillan.

Heath Committee. Application of the Whitley Report to the Administrative Departments of the Civil Service, Sub-Committee of the Inter-Departmental Committee on the Application of the Whitley Report to Government Establishments, *Report*, 1919 (Cmd 9). Chairman: Sir Thomas Heath.

Industrial Council, Inquiry into Industrial Agreements. *Report*, 1913 (Cd 6952); *Minutes of Evidence*, 1913 (Cd 6953). Chairman: Sir George Askwith.

Labour Statistics

    Department of Employment and Productivity, *British Labour Statistics: Historical Abstract 1886–1968*, 1970.

    Labour Department of the Board of Trade, *Fifteenth Abstract of the Labour Statistics of the United Kingdom*, 1912 (Cd 6228).

    Ministry of Labour, *Eighteenth Abstract of the Labour Statistics of the United Kingdom*, 1927 (Cmd 2740).

    ——, *Nineteenth Abstract of the Labour Statistics of the United Kingdom*, 1928 (Cmd 3140).

    ——, *Twentieth Abstract of the Labour Statistics of the United Kingdom*, 1931 (Cmd 3831).

    ——, *Twenth-second Abstract of the Labour Statistics of the United Kingdom*, 1937 (Cmd 5556).

Macmillan Committee. Committee on Finance and Industry, 1929, *Report*, 1931 (Cmd 3897). Chairman: Lord Macmillan.

May Committee. Committee on National Expenditure, 1931, *Report*, 1931 (Cmd 3920). Chairman: Sir George May.

Ministry of Health, *Annual Report 1921–1922*, 1922 (Cmd 1713).

——, *Annual Report 1922–1923*, 1923 (Cmd 1944).

——, *Annual Report 1926–1927*, 1927 (Cmd 2938).

Ministry of Labour, Apprenticeship and Training for Skilled Occupations in Great Britain and Northern Ireland, *Report of an Inquiry, 1925–26; VI: Engineering, Shipbuilding and Shiprepairing and Other Metal Industries*, 1928; *VII: General Report*, 1928.

National Industrial Conference, Provisional Joint Committee, *Report of a Meeting of April 4th 1919*, 1919 (Cmd 501). Chairman: Sir Allan Smith.

National Provisional Joint Committee, Application of the Whitley Report to the Administrative Departments of the Civil Service, *Report*, 1919 (Cmd 198). Chairman: Sir Malcolm Ramsay.

Nicholls Committee. Committee on the Building Industry, 1924, *Report*, 1924 (Cmd 2104). Chairman: W. H. Nicholls.

Royal Commission on the Civil Service, 1912, *Fourth Report*, 1914 (Cd 7338). Chairman: Lord MacDonnell.

Royal Commission on the Coal Industry, 1925, *Report*, 1926 (Cmd 2600). Chairman: Sir Herbert Samuel.

Samuel Commission—*see* Royal Commission on the Coal Industry.

Sankey Commission—*see* Coal Industry Commission.

Strikes and Lockouts. Labour Department of the Board of Trade, *Report on Strikes and Lock-outs and on Conciliation and Arbitration Boards in the United Kingdom in 1912*, 1914 (Cd 7089).

———. *Report on Strikes and Lock-outs and on Conciliation and Arbitration Boards in the United Kingdom in 1913*, 1914 (Cd 7658).

Whitley Committee. Reconstruction Committee, Sub-Committee on Relations between Employers and Employed, *Interim Report on Joint Standing Industrial Councils*, 1917 (Cd 8606). Chairman: J. H. Whitley.

———. Ministry of Reconstruction, Committee on Relations between Employers and Employed, *Supplementary Report on Works Committees*, 1918 (Cd 9001); *Second Report on Joint Standing Industrial Councils*, 1918 (Cd 9002). Chairman: J. H. Whitley.

Newspapers and Periodicals

Builder
Call
Cotton Factory Times
Daily Express
Daily Herald
Daily Mail
Durham Chronicle
Economic Journal
Economic Review
Glasgow Herald
Hansard
Industrial Syndicalist
Labour Gazette (*Board of Trade Labour Gazette* to December 1916; *Labour Gazette* from January 1917 to December 1921; thereafter *Ministry of Labour Gazette*)
Labour Leader

Labour Research Department Monthly Bulletin
Manchester Guardian
Ministry of Labour Gazette—see *Labour Gazette*
New Leader
Plebs
Solidarity
The Times
Worker
Workers Dreadnought
Yorkshire Factory Times

Trade Union Journals

Amalgamated Engineering Union *Monthly Journal and Report* to December
1921; *Monthly Journal* thereafter.
Amalgamated Society of Carpenters and Joiners *Monthly Report*
Amalgamated Society of Engineers *Monthly Report* to December 1912;
Monthly Journal and Report thereafter.
Amalgamated Society of Woodworkers *Monthly Report.*
Amalgamated Union of Building Trade Workers *Monthly Report.*
Amalgamated Union of Co-operative Employees. *The Co-operative Employee.*
Dock Wharf Riverside and General Workers Union *Dockers Record.*
London and Provincial Union of Licensed Vehicle Workers *Licensed Vehicle
Trade Record.*
National Amalgamated Union of Shop Assistants Warehousemen and Clerks
The Shop Assistant.
National Association of Operative Plasterers *Monthly Report.*
National Union of General Workers *Journal.*
National Union of Railwaymen *Railway Review.*
Operative Bricklayers Society *Trade Circular and General Reporter.*
Operative Stone Masons Society *Journal.*
Postmen's Federation *Postman's Gazette.*
Post Office Engineering Union *Journal.*
Transport and General Workers *Record.*
Union of Post Office Workers *The Post.*

The Records of Trade Unions, the Labour Party and Employers' Organisations

The main records of the Trades Union Congress, the Labour Party, and most
trade unions are the minutes and reports of their executive bodies, and the
minutes or verbatim reports of their delegate conferences. Such records are
quoted at many points in the text. In some instances, a footnote reference is
given, but more often the text itself indicates the union, the type of record, and
the date. Page references are not given, except to the volumes containing the
annual reports and conference reports of Congress and the Labour Party
(referred to as 'Trades Union Congress' and 'Labour Party' respectively,
followed by the relevant year). From time to time unions also issue special

reports, such as the Operative Stone Masons' *Report and Financial Statement of the Central Dispute Committee*, following the London building lockout of 1914. Three such reports of the Trades Union Congress which are not included in their annual volumes have been quoted in the text. They are:

Mining Dispute National Strike. Report of the General Council to the postponed conference of executives, which was to have been held on 25 June 1926; and Supplementary Report of the General Council to the conference of executives on 20 January 1927.
National Strike Special Conference. Verbatim report of the conference of executives on 20 January 1927.
Bedaux, 1933.

The records of four employers' organisations—the Engineering Employers Federation, the Federation of British Industries, the National Confederation of Employers Organisations, and the National Federation of Building Trade Employers—are also quoted in the text. References follow the same conventions as for trade union records.

Index

Ablett, Noah, biog. 572, 31, 44, 50 n., 298, 299, 392, 417
Abraham, W. J., 280
Abraham, William ('Mabon'), 31, 356
Adams, Harry, 69–70, 105–6
Adamson, William, biog. 572, 228, 238, 355, 453, 509
Addison, Christopher, 137 n., 157, 159–60, 172, 174, 181, 207, 232, 245, 313, 321, 483, 509
Admiralty, 94–5, 120, 139–40, 141, 152, 155, 170, 185, 518
Agricultural Labourers and Rural Workers, National Union of (later National Union of Agricultural Workers):
  collective bargaining, 89, 166, 330–1, 347
  finances, 331
  government, 89
  membership, 197, 303, 346, 347, 570
  strikes, 89, 330–1
Agricultural Wages Board, 166–7, 245, 312, 347, 366, 547, 548
Agricultural Wages (Regulation) Act (1924), 366
Agriculture, 317
  collective bargaining, 89, 166–7, 245, 312
  county conciliation committees, 312, 330, 347
  county wages committees, 336, 548, 549
  district wages committees, 166
  government control, 166–7, 245, 312
  marketing boards, 483, 514, 541
  pay, 89–90, 167, 330–1, 335, 366, 525
  price guarantees, 166, 245, 312
  protection, 514
  strikes, 89, 330–1
  tied cottages, 331
  trade union membership, 1
Agriculture Act (1920), 245, 312
Aircraft manufacture, 149–50, 159, 182–3, 184–5, 194, 432
Alexander, A. V., 509
Allan, William, 453
Allen, Clifford, 226, 360–1, 476
Ammanford strike (1925), 393
Anderson, John, 372
Anderson, W. C., 225
Angell, Norman, 224
Anglo-Russian Joint Advisory Council, 394, 420–1, 476
Anti-waste campaign (1921), 313

Appleton, W. A., biog. 572, 231
Apprenticeship, 3–4, 459–60; see also individual industries and unions
Arbitration, 22, 53, 57, 60, 127, 204, 239; see also Committee on Production; Interim Court of Arbitration; Industrial Court
Armaments Committees, 125–6
Armaments Output Committee, 125, 126
Armaments, supply of, 123–6, 134, 152, 160
Armed forces:
  dependants' allowances, 120, 149
  pay, 241, 518–19
  use of in strikes, 29, 38, 222, 270, 285, 299, 406
Ashfield, Lord, 371–2, 452, 454, 482, 515
Ashton, Thomas, biog. 572, 21, 31, 48, 276, 324
Askwith, George, 31, 34, 35, 40, 42, 56, 59, 62, 97, 98, 99, 116 n., 121, 122, 130, 145, 148, 185, 198, 203–4
Asquith, H. H., 38, 45–6, 49, 95, 98, 99, 128, 135, 144–5, 147, 153, 154, 156, 160, 209, 220, 232, 234, 364, 369, 554
Astbury judgment, 408
Astor, Lord, 226
Asylum Workers, National Union of, 304
Attlee, C. R., 355, 404

Bain, G. S., and Farouk Elsheikh, 196
Bakers and Confectioners Union, Amalgamated Operative, 109, 198
Baldwin, Stanley, 347, 348, 363, 383, 386, 389, 400, 401, 402–3, 410, 411, 412, 416, 424, 425, 464, 472, 474–5, 478, 482, 508, 509, 555
Balfour, A. J., 123, 283
Balfour Committee, 381, 441
Balfour of Burleigh, Lord, 131
Banbury, Frederick, 91
Bank of England, 506, 509
Bank Officers Guild, 261
Bankers Industrial Development Company, 486
Banks, 187, 261–2, 303
Barker, George, biog. 572, 23, 48, 49, 298
Barnes, George, 17, 20, 157, 162, 173, 188, 210, 213, 228–9, 235, 238, 356
Barrow engineering strike (1917), 169, 185
Beard, John, biog. 572, 58, 176, 460–1, 501
Belfast strike (1919), 271
Bell, J. N., biog. 572, 203, 327
Bell, Richard, 20, 356

Bell, Tom, 192, 359
Bell, Walter, 137–8
Bellamy, A., 116, 197
Belloc, Hilaire, 219
Betterton, Henry, 517
Bevan, Aneurin, 500
Beveridge, William, biog. 572–3, 95, 132, 137, 145 n., 397
Bevin, Ernest, biog. 573, 109, 145, 203, 205, 257–8, 278, 284, 290, 292, 293, 299, 302, 305–7, 320, 329–30, 333, 351, 352, 356, 370–3, 376, 377, 391, 394, 395, 402–3, 404, 409, 415, 419, 424, 449, 450, 452, 458–9, 460–1, 464, 477, 481–2, 498, 501, 502, 508, 515, 523, 524–5, 541, 551–2, 564
Birkenhead, Lord, *see* F. E. Smith
Birkin, Joseph, 322
Black Friday, 301–2, 315, 424, 558
Blacksmiths Society, Associated, 305
Blain, Hubert, 92
Blanesborough Committee, 473–4, 504, 538
Boards of Guardians (Default) Act (1926), 413
Boilermakers and Iron and Steel Shipbuilders, United Society of:
absenteeism, 80
apprenticeship, 80
collective bargaining, 18, 80–1, 327–8, 343–4, 434–5, 558
finances, 344, 407, 535
general strike, 407
government, 18, 19, 452
industrial policy, 434–5
membership, 3, 346, 347, 544, 570
relations with other unions, 256, 305, 327, 328, 344–5, 351–2, 390, 434
restrictive practices, 9, 342, 547
sponsored parliamentary candidates, 236
strikes, 10, 18, 327, 343–4, 344–5, 497, 550
trade cards, 159
Boilermakers' lockout (1910), 10
Boilermakers' lockout (1923), 343–4, 351–2
Bonar Law, Andrew, 126, 154, 160, 161, 207, 234, 283, 285, 287, 289, 331, 363
Bondfield, Margaret, biog. 573, 276, 379, 474, 479, 486–7, 489, 495, 504, 505, 509, 537
Bookbinders and Machine Rulers, National Union of, 305
Bookbinding, *see* paper and printing
Boot and Shoe Manufacturing Joint Industrial Council, 206
Boot and Shoe Operatives, National Union of, 85, 86, 87, 109, 148, 346
Booth, Alfred, 34, 36, 39
Bottomley, Horatio, 91, 313
Bowerman, C. W., biog. 573, 21, 63, 67, 111, 208, 210, 263, 356

Bowley, A. L., 149, 166, 257–8, 559–61
Bowman, Guy, 55 n., 106 n.
Brace, William, biog. 573, 30–1, 48, 110, 235, 263
Brailsford, H. N., 361, 476
Bramley, Fred, biog. 573, 210, 356, 375, 379, 381, 390, 393, 395
Bricklayers, Manchester Unity of Operative, 305
Bricklayers, Operative Society of, 65, 67, 68, 69–70, 81, 105–6, 107, 111, 142, 305
Brickmaking, 51, 88
Bristol Miners Association, 46, 418, 494
Bristol Trades Council, 539
British Broadcasting Company, 406
British Socialist Party, 136, 222–3, 226, 227, 228, 230, 235, 358
British Workers League, *see* National Democratic and Labour Party
Brockway, Fenner, 226
Bromley, John, biog. 573, 194, 197, 253, 351, 390, 393, 396
Broomfield, William, 84
Brown, W. J., biog. 573, 95 n., 381, 500
Brownlie, J. T., biog. 573, 132, 133, 134, 231, 263, 311, 452, 537
Buckmaster, Lord, 374, 376
Builder, The, 67
Builders Labourers and Constructional Workers Society, National, 303 n.
Builders Labourers and Constructional Workers Society, Altogether, 303 n.
Builders Labourers, National Association of, 303 n.
Builders Labourers Union, United, 88
Building guilds, 362
Building industry:
apprenticeship, 4, 265, 367, 459
closed shop, 65–8
collective bargaining, 7, 10, 18, 64–8, 81, 88, 143, 206, 259, 263, 303, 321, 345, 375–6, 436–7, 530
cyclical fluctuations, 18, 64, 317, 514
dilution, 265
hours of work, 255, 263, 321, 562
labourers, 69, 88, 186, 303, 561
pay, 142, 143, 146, 186, 259, 321, 335, 345, 375, 428, 436, 521, 525, 561
payment by results, 265
productivity, 265–6
relations between unions, 105–6, 107–8, 111, 304–5, 307
restrictive practices, 64–5, 437
shop stewards, 440
strikes, 26, 64–70, 345, 375–6, 550
subcontracting, 69
technology, 546–7

trade union membership, 2, 4, 303, 335, 376, 421, 534–5, 544–5
unemployment, 335
'wet time', 362, 375, 435, 436
Building Industry, National Conciliation Board for the, 65, 66, 67–8, 88, 143, 255
Building Industry, National Joint Council for the, 435–7
Building Industry, National Joint Industrial Council for the, 206
Building Industry, National Wages and Conditions Council for the, 255, 259, 263, 375, 435
Building lockout (1924), 375–6
Building Trade Employers, National Federation of, vii, 65, 67, 255, 265–6, 345, 375–6, 435–7
Building Trade Workers, Amalgamated Union of, 305, 318–19, 361, 435–7, 440
Building Trades Council, National Associated, 202
Building Trades Operatives, National Federation of, 202, 351, 362, 435–7, 551
Building Workers Industrial Union, 108, 111
Building Workers Union, 107–8
Bullock, Alan, 425
Burnham Committees, *see* education
Burns, John, 35, 98
Burt, Thomas, 13 n., 48
Busmen's Punch, 525
Busmen's Rank and File Committee, 524–5, 536–7
Buxton, Sydney, 33, 94, 98, 100, 482–3

Cabinet Makers, Amalgamated Union of, 305
Cadbury Brothers Ltd, 442
Call, The, 193, 226
Calthrop, Guy, 163
Cambrian strike (1910–11), 28–32, 43, 48, 50, 72, 73
Campbell, J. R., 369, 377
Capital levy, 233
Car manufacture, 58, 432, 460
Card Blowing and Ring Room Operatives, Amalgamated Association of, 3, 5, 6, 10, 16, 19, 41, 81, 127, 346, 487–8, 544, 570
Carmen's Trade Union, London, 56
Carpenters and Joiners, Amalgamated Society of:
  affiliation to Trade Union Congress, 113, 209
  'black labour', 159
  finances, 67
  government, 19, 68, 70
  membership, 3, 108, 570
  political action, 223
  relations with other unions, 107–8, 111, 113, 305

restrictive practices, 65
strikes, 68, 70
Carpenters and Joiners, General Union of, 305
Carter, W., 418
Catering Trade Boards, 486–7
Cathery, Edmund, 33
Cave Committee, 334, 348
Cement industry, 88, 203, 205, 248, 441
Chainmaking, 100–1, 200, 262
Chamberlain, Austen, 157, 248
Chamberlain, Neville, 170, 189, 366, 472, 509, 520
Chambers of Commerce, Associated, 465
Chanak crisis (1922), 357
Chandler, Francis, 113
Chelmsford, Lord, 365
Chemical and Allied Employers Association, 168, 469
Chemicals industry, 317, 425, 547, 561
  collective bargaining, 88, 168, 205, 333
  pay, 333
  relations between unions, 307
  trade union membership, 58
Chocolate and confectionery manufacture, 203, 205, 333
Churchill, Winston, 29, 38, 174, 181, 183, 184–5, 217–18, 239, 241, 278, 284, 285–6, 386, 389, 406, 416
Citrine, Walter, biog. 573, 235, 275, 302, 339, 381, 395, 401, 403, 455–6, 462–4, 465, 470–1, 501, 505, 508–9, 511, 520, 540, 551–2, 559, 564
Civil engineering, 546–7; *see also* building
Civil Service:
  arbitration, 186, 249, 347
  Boy Clerks Association, 95
  clerical officers, 562, 563
  Clerks Associations, 95
  collective bargaining, 8, 12, 93, 95–6, 186, 206–7, 248–9, 260–1, 347, 547
  employment, 548
  general strike, 412
  grading, 95–6
  hours of work, 151–2
  pay, 142, 151, 186, 260, 319, 428, 518
  recruitment, 95–6
  relations between unions, 305
  Trade Disputes and Trade Unions Act, 423, 476–7
  trade union membership, 303–4, 545–6
  See also Post Office
Civil Service Arbitration Board, 249, 347, 547
Civil Service Clerical Association, 305, 530–1, 534
Civil Service Federation, 142
Civil Service, National Whitley Council for the, 248–9, 260, 347

Clarke, Edward, 54

Clerks, National Union of (later National Union of Clerical and Administrative Workers), 198, 261, 306, 349

Cleveland Iron Ore Miners Association, 299

Cliff, John, 515

Closed shop, 41–3, 65–9, 423; *see also* individual industries and unions

Clothiers Operatives, Amalgamated Union of, 86, 87, 101, 200

Clothing industry:
  closed shop, 453
  collective bargaining, 86
  dilution, 154
  pay, 86, 101, 334, 561
  relations between unions, 200, 305
  strikes, 86, 453–4
  Trade Boards, 86, 101, 250
  trade union membership, 200

Clothing Workers, United, 453–4, 457, 536

Clyde strike (1915), 120–1

Clyde strike (1919), 270–1, 310

Clyde Workers Committee, 121, 135–8, 175, 179, 180, 181, 236, 270

Clynes, J. R., biog. 573–4, 62, 166, 171, 187, 203, 224, 234, 235, 238, 263, 284, 292, 294, 351, 355, 364, 381, 394, 452, 479, 485, 509

Clynes Committee, 485

Coal Board, National, 388

Coal Controller, 163, 185, 186, 209, 269

Coal embargo (1921), 315–16

Coal embargo (1925), 389, 391

Coal embargo attempted (1926), 415, 416–17

Coal Industry Act (1920), 247, 325

Coal Industry (Sankey) Commission, 246–7, 268, 282–3, 286–7

Coal lockout (1921), 275, 299–302, 321–5, 551, 555

Coal lockout (1926), 412–19, 555

Coal Mines Act (1930), 483–5, 493–4, 515, 541

Coal Mines Act (1931), 484–5

Coal Mines (Eight Hours) Act (1926), 415–16, 418

Coal Mines (Minimum Wage) Act (1912), 49–52, 70–1, 112, 221–2, 446

Coal Mines Regulation (Eight Hours) Act (1908), 10–11, 18–19, 28, 550

Coal Mines (Seven Hours) Act (1919), 268–9

Coal strike (1912), 43–52, 72, 554–5

Coal strike (1920), 295–7, 555

Coalmining:
  abnormal places, 30–1, 43–4, 46
  absenteeism, 156, 177, 299
  arbitration, 295, 296, 493–4
  'butty' system, 47 n., 325, 446
  checkweighmen, 11, 445–6, 449
  closed shop, 28, 198, 393

collective bargaining, 7, 30, 31, 43–6, 82, 128–30, 150–1, 212, 268–9, 294–6, 297–301, 323–4, 374, 384, 387–8, 417–19, 445–9, 493–4, 547–8

craftsmen, 2, 29, 129, 300, 416–17

daywagemen, 31, 44, 51, 388, 398

district agreements, 7, 325, 398, 412, 414

economics, 27, 48, 51, 52, 71, 72, 384, 397

employment, 26, 156, 163

faceworkers, 5, 10–11, 44, 45, 47, 51–2, 398–9, 418, 427, 448–9, 483

'five counties' scheme, 425–6, 483

government control, 151, 162, 163, 209, 247, 297

haulage workers, 5, 11

hours of work, 10–11, 18, 27, 52, 211, 267, 268, 387, 398, 412, 415–16, 418–19, 483–5, 493–4

minimum wage, 30–2, 43–7, 51–2, 70–1, 446

National Industrial Board, 485, 493–4

national wage agreements, 82, 163, 186, 212, 268–9, 297–8, 324–5, 374

nationalisation, 212, 233, 246, 283, 287, 291–2, 296, 298, 302, 368

'outcropping', 322, 412, 413

pay, 27, 46, 51–2, 70–1, 84, 128–30, 141, 142, 146, 150–1, 163, 177, 186, 264–5, 268–9, 294–9, 324–5, 335, 374, 388, 389, 398–9, 399–400, 402, 403, 414, 418, 421, 427–8, 447–8, 493–4, 521, 525, 526, 561

piecework, 7, 28, 32, 264, 268–9, 448–9

price control, 147, 163, 294–5

price-fixing, 425–6, 483

productivity, 26–7, 156, 163, 264–5, 296–7, 299, 387, 398

profits pool, 163, 212, 297–9, 300, 301, 302, 323–4, 388

'recoupment clause', 27, 45, 50, 52, 72

relations between unions, 29, 129, 198, 446–7

reorganisation of industry, 388, 397–9, 484

safety, 11, 29, 300, 416–17

'spreadover', 484, 493–4

strikes, 10–11, 24–31, 43–52, 70–1, 115, 128–30, 189, 269, 299–302, 321–5, 392–3, 403, 412–18, 446, 448, 493–4, 550, 555

supervisors, 8, 449

surface workers, 2, 49, 87, 163, 198, 267

technology, 27, 387–8, 418–19, 448–9

trade union membership, 1, 2, 303–4, 335, 534, 545–6

unemployment, 325, 335, 336, 384, 419, 446, 447

Coalmining Organisation Committee, 147, 177

Coalowners, 43–52, 247, 297–9, 386–90, 397, 400, 403, 541

Derbyshire, 325

Durham, 46, 427–8
Federated Area, 45, 46, 72
Lancashire and Cheshire, 269
Nottinghamshire, 325, 417, 445–6
Scottish, 72
South Wales, 27–8, 46, 72, 150, 493
Yorkshire, 70–1, 72, 269
see also Mining Association of Great Britain
Cole, G. D. H., biog. 574, 74, 109, 113, 308–9,
   356, 361, 362, 501, 505
Colefax, Arthur, 487
Collective agreements, enforcement of, 9, 10,
   54, 66–7, 99–100, 332, 516–17, 522
Collective bargaining, 6–8, 9–10, 21–2, 75–97,
   266, 344, 347–8, 463–4, 547–50
   coverage of, 347, 547–9
   district and regional, 7, 347, 432, 550
   national, 9–10, 21–2, 163, 167–8, 177–8,
   202–6, 211, 248–51, 253–62, 266, 271–4,
   344–5, 347, 427–37, 547–9, 550, 564
   workplace, 136–7, 178–9, 187–9, 204–5, 262,
   437–49, 531–4, 549–50
See also individual industries and unions
Colliery Enginemen's Federation, 416–17
'Coloured' labour, 155, 159
Committee on Production, 121, 122, 128, 142,
   143, 145, 148, 149, 151, 155, 166, 167–8,
   169, 184, 185, 203–4, 240, 255, 547
Communist International, 360, 377, 563
Communist Party, 293, 313, 329, 330, 340–1,
   358–63, 377, 385, 393, 396, 405, 414–15,
   419–20, 452–5, 476, 491, 513, 536–7, 563,
   564
Conciliation Act (1896), 12, 248
Connolly, James, 60
Conscientious objectors, 226–7, 284
Conscription, 119, 152–4, 156–9, 209, 226,
   284–6, 288, 311
   exemption from, 156–9, 169–74, 189–90
Conservative government's record (1924–9),
   472–5
Conservative Party, 126, 160, 161, 231, 233,
   234, 237, 238, 357, 363, 365–6, 369, 422,
   472–5, 478, 480, 484, 513
Cook, Arthur, biog. 574, 298, 359, 380, 390,
   392, 402, 409, 415, 416, 419, 453, 465, 466,
   537, 541, 551
Cook–Maxton Manifesto, 466
Cooks and Stewards, *see* Ships Stewards etc.
Co-operative Employees, Amalgamated Union
   of, 90, 108–9, 142, 197, 198–9, 262, 305
Co-operative National Conciliation Board, 384
Co-operative Party, 237, 364, 478, 513
Co-operative Societies:
   closed shop, 90
   collective bargaining, 90, 262, 348, 384, 530
   hours of work, 262, 270

pay, 90, 262, 348, 384
   relations between unions, 109, 197, 198–9,
   307
   strikes, 90–1, 198–9, 384
Co-operative Union, 262, 395
Co-operative Wholesale Society, 90, 108–9,
   199, 307, 348, 384, 441, 530
Co-ordination Committee (1919–20), 308–9
Coppersmiths, Braziers and Metal Workers,
   National Society of, 131–2, 439
Coppock, Richard, biog. 574, 362
Coremakers, Amalgamated Society of, 272, 304
Corn Production Act (1917), 166–7, 303, 366
Cornish clay strike (1913), 89
Cost of living, 120, 141–52, 173, 335–6, 421,
   525–6, 560, 568
Cost of living sliding scales, 259, 291, 319–21,
   428–9; *see also* individual industries
Cotter, J., 328, 385, 458
Cotton:
   'bad materials', 81
   'bad spinning', 81
   closed shop, 41–3
   collective bargaining, 7, 10, 19, 81, 267, 490–
   2, 521–3
   government control, 164–5, 194
   hours of work, 11, 267, 522
   looms per weaver, 8, 485–6, 490–2, 521–2
   pay, 5, 7, 42, 82, 127–8, 142, 146, 165, 186,
   267, 325–6, 335, 487–8, 490–2, 516, 521–
   2, 525, 526, 529
   piece-price lists, 7, 42, 83–4, 485
   political action by unions, 11, 12, 237
   price-fixing, 430
   productivity, 485–6
   promotion, 4–5
   relations between unions, 305
   short time, 325, 326
   strikes, 10, 26, 41–3, 81, 194, 267, 274, 326,
   487–8, 490–2, 493, 521–3, 550
   technology, 485–6, 491–2
   trade union membership, 196, 303–4, 335,
   534, 545–6
   unemployment, 335
   unemployment benefit, 165, 194
Cotton Control Board, 165, 194, 209
Cotton Factory Times, 146, 488, 492, 513
Cotton lockout (1929), 487–8, 493
Cotton ('more looms') lockout (1931), 491–3
Cotton Manufacturing (Temporary Provisions)
   Act (1934), 516, 522
Cotton Reconstruction Board, 267
Cotton Spinners and Manufacturers Associa-
   tion, 10, 41–3, 491
Cotton Spinners, Federation of Master, 41 n.,
   430, 487–8, 522, 529
Cotton strike (1919), 267

Cotton strikes (1932), 521–3
Cotton Yarn Spinners Association, 430, 488
Councils of Action (1920), 293, 302, 357, 558
Courtauld, Samuel, 469
Courts of Inquiry, 247–8, 386, 470
  Building Industry (1924), 375–6
  Coal Mining Industry (1924), 374
  Coal Mining Industry (1925), 384, 388–9
  Engineering Trades (1922), 342
  London Tramway and Omnibus Services (1924), 371–2
  Northern Counties Wool Textile Industry (1930), 489
  Tramways Industry (1921), 320
  Transport Workers (dockers) (1920), 257–8
Covent Garden strike (1924), 376
Coventry Engineering Joint Committee, 179, 181, 187–8, 191, 192
Coventry Workers Committee, 181, 192
Craft unions, 3–4, 16, 70, 75–84, 111, 139, 173, 192, 197–8, 332, 341, 429, 455
Cramp, C. T., biog. 574, 115 n., 277, 278, 280, 284, 356, 419, 428, 452, 464, 481, 537
Cranedrivers, 67
Crooks, Will, 222
Cumberland Miners Association, 113–14
Cummings, D. C., 97
Cunliffe Committee, 386
Cunliffe-Lister, Philip, 509

Daily Citizen, 74
Daily Herald, 57, 74, 113, 314–15, 322, 361, 477
Daily Mail, 402–3
Dalton, Hugh, 371
Dangerfield, George, 116
Davidson, J. C. C., 372
Davidson, Randall (Archbishop of Canterbury), 406–7, 416
Davis, W. J., biog. 574, 21, 230–1, 276
Dawes plan, 368–9, 384, 387
Deakin, Arthur, biog. 574, 515
De Leon, Daniel, 22
Demarcation, 8–9, 80, 122, 131–2
Demobilisation, 232, 233, 239, 240–1
'Derby scheme', 152–3
Derbyshire Miners Association, 47, 193, 215–16, 269, 299, 322, 414, 446–7
Desborough Committee, 195, 286
Devaluation, 497, 508, 512
Development Commission, 221
Devonport, Lord, 35, 56, 166, 204
Dictatorships and the Trade Union Movement, 564–5
Dilution commissioners, 136–7, 138, 188, 207
Dilution of labour:
  on munitions, 122, 131–41, 159, 207, 209,

242, 311, *see also* individual industries and Munitions Acts
  on private work, 157, 159–60, 169, 171, 173–4, 175, 242
Dingley, Tom, 172 n., 192 n., 311
Distribution:
  closed shop, 90
  collective bargaining, 90–1, 262, 348–9, 384, 530
  early closing, 91, 516
  hours of work, 91, 120, 262, 366, 516
  living-in, 91, 120
  pay, 90, 120, 142, 262, 334, 335, 525, 526
  relations between unions, 90, 108–9, 198–9, 305, 307
  strikes, 90–1, 198–9, 348
  Trade Boards, 250–1, 348, 365–6
  trade union membership, 303, 335
  unemployment, 335
Distributive and Allied Workers, National Union of:
  collective bargaining, 348, 384
  government, 356, 452
  membership, 346, 347, 534, 544, 570
  origins, 305
  political action, 356
  relations with other unions, 457
  strikes, 348, 384
District Railway, 7, 12
Dixon, A. H., 165
Dock Labour, National Joint Council for, 258, 370
Dock Labourers, National Union of (Liverpool Dockers):
  closed shop, 36
  collective bargaining, 36, 55, 104
  decasualisation, 104
  finances, 56
  industrial policy, 55
  Liverpool Dockers Battalion, 155
  membership, 2, 36
  relations with other unions, 109, 113, 306
  strikes, 34, 36, 39, 104, 267
Dock strike (1923), 329–30
Dock strike (1924), 370–1
Dock Wharf Riverside and General Labourers Union (London Dockers):
  closed shop, 35
  collective bargaining, 35, 36, 53–4
  'direct action', 292, 293
  finances, 349
  industrial policy, 151, 176
  membership, 56, 303, 570
  relations with other unions, 109–10, 198–9, 304, 305–6
  sponsored Members of Parliament, 237
  strikes, 35, 54–6

unemployment benefit, 244, 349
unofficial action, 36
Docks:
  closed shop, 35, 36
  collective bargaining, 35, 36, 53–5, 204, 206, 248, 257, 258, 329–30, 370–1
  decasualisation, 103 4, 258, 370
  general strike, 405, 406, 411
  hours of work, 155, 255, 267, 562
  pay, 35, 141, 146, 155, 186, 257–8, 329–30, 335, 370–1, 523
  productivity, 258
  relations between unions, 305–6, 330, 370, 523
  strikes, 26, 33–41, 53–6, 61, 104, 267, 329–30, 370–1, 459, 523, 550
  trade union membership, 2, 36, 56, 304, 335, 544–6
  Transport Workers Battalion, 156
  unemployment, 335
Domestic service, 1
Donation benefit, 239, 241, 365
Doonan, J., 296
Doublers and Kindred Trades, 304
Draughtsmen, Association of Engineering and Shipbuilding, 349
Dry Dock Workers, 304
Dublin lockout (1913–14), 60–4, 71, 73, 74, 112
Dublin Trades Council, 63
Duckham, Arthur, 287
Dukes, Charles, biog. 574, 408–9, 420, 428, 441, 520, 537, 542
Duncan, Charles, biog. 574, 132, 176, 226, 235, 345, 460
Durham Miners Association, 10–11, 18, 45, 47, 49, 193, 322, 323, 392, 403, 413–14, 427–8, 447–8
  'cavilling', 448
  county average, 447–8
Dutt, R. Palme, 420
Dyers, Bleachers and Finishers, Amalgamated Society of, 86
Dyers and Finishers, National Society of, 86

Economic Advisory Council, 501, 505
Economic trends and fluctuations, 312–13, 316–17, 379, 383, 384, 421, 427, 487, 528–9
Economy Committee of the Cabinet (1931), 507–8
Education:
  Board of, 12, 93, 95, 152, 186, 365, 518
  Burnham Committees, 250, 261, 335, 519
  collective bargaining, 7, 12, 92–3, 250, 261, 519
  Education Committees, 7, 92, 152, 518–19, 527

employment, 548
  pay, 92, 152, 186–7, 261, 334–5, 518–19, 562, 563
  pensions, 12, 334–5
  reform of, 233, 243
  relations between unions, 93
  school leaving age, 243, 475, 480
  strikes, 92–3, 187
  trade union membership, 1, 3, 93, 545–6, 570
Edwards, Ebby, biog. 574, 193, 537
Edwards, Enoch, biog. 574–5, 21, 44, 47, 215, 356
Egypt, 480
Eight-hour working day, 112
Elections, General:
  1906: 13
  1910 (January), 13
  1910 (December), 13
  1918: 234–8, 357
  1922: 355
  1923: 363–4
  1924: 377
  1929: 477–8
  1931: 512–13
Electoral truce, 224, 234
Electrical contracting, 184, 248
Electrical engineering, 432
Electrical Trades Union, 91, 172, 184, 274–5, 300, 404, 407, 432, 434, 534
Electricity Commissioners, 557
Electricity Generating Board, Central, 557
Electricity supply:
  collective bargaining, 91, 248, 249
  general strike, 404, 405, 406
  government regulation, 240, 557
  pay, 184, 335, 495, 525, 529, 561
  strikes, 275
  trade union membership, 335
  works committees, 441
Ellis, Thomas Ratcliffe, 62
Elsbury, Sam, 453–4
Embargo strike in the Midlands (1918), 191
Emergency Powers Act (1920), 296, 373, 405
Employers Advisory Council, 253
Employers' attitudes to:
  collective bargaining, 253, 266, 310, 469–70, 527–30
  dilution, 133–4, 141
  Mond–Turner talks, 467–70
  postwar reconstruction, 252–3, 281
Employers Confederation, British, vii
Employers Organisations, National Confederation of, 281, 314–15, 422, 423, 464–70, 517, 527, 548
Employment Department Clerks Association (later Ministry of Labour Staff Association), 95

Engineering Allied Trades Committees, 135, 178, 179, 189–90, 191, 192

Engineering and Shipbuilding Amalgamation Committee, 180–1

Engineering and Shipbuilding Trades, Federation of, 2, 20, 79, 108, 182, 189–90, 253, 270, 326, 344, 352, 390, 403, 434, 551

Engineering Employers Association, North West, 133–4

Engineering Employers Federation, vii, 78–80, 119, 121, 140, 147, 148, 167, 185, 188, 242, 253, 267–8, 272, 275, 337–43, 390, 432, 434, 438–9, 459, 467, 470, 495–6, 528–9, 532, 533

Engineering industry:
  apprenticeship, 4, 338, 459–60
  changing composition of, 432, 459
  closed shop, 9, 79–80, 432, 438, 496
  collective bargaining, 7, 8, 10, 17–18, 78–80, 83, 88, 151, 167, 178, 255, 256, 270–1, 326–8, 337–43, 345, 349, 432–3, 495–7, 532–3, 547
  dilution, 121–2, 131–41, 160, 242
  employment, 459
  general strike, 401, 409, 412
  hours of work, 79, 253, 254–5, 262, 267–8, 270–1, 337, 496
  less-skilled workers, 58–60, 88, 121, 132–5, 138–40, 151, 171, 183, 191, 242, 459, 561
  'machine question', 9, 78–9, 121, 338, 341
  managerial rights, 337–43
  overtime, 82–3, 253, 262, 337–43
  pay, 58–9, 82, 121, 141, 142, 143–4, 145–6, 148–9, 151, 167–8, 169, 182–4, 185, 255, 256, 272–3, 326–8, 335, 349, 421, 432–3, 495–7, 521, 525, 527, 561
  piecework, 8, 78, 82–3, 169, 182, 263–4, 267–8, 433, 439, 496, 531
  premium bonus (payment by results), 78–9, 264, 268, 439, 532
  relations between unions, 108, 304, 307, 308, 326, 434
  restrictive practices, 9, 78–80, 83, 121, 239, 241–2, 337–43, 432, 496
  shop stewards, 8, 9, 83, 121, 135, 179–81, 187–9, 253, 262, 311, 437–40, 531–2
  strikes, 17–18, 59–60, 120–1, 147, 168–74, 188–9, 191, 268, 270–1, 272–3, 338–43, 432–3, 533, 550
  technology, 58, 140, 242, 437, 547
  trade union membership, 335, 421, 534, 545–6
  unemployment, 335, 336, 338
  unemployment insurance, 101

Engineering Joint Trades Movement, 434

Engineering lockout (1897–8), 340

Engineering lockout (1922), 327, 338–43, 345, 347, 351

Engineering Union, Amalgamated:
  closed shop, 432–3, 438
  collective bargaining, 326–8, 337–43, 432–3, 437–40, 495–7
  finances, 338, 343, 349, 407, 535
  general strike, 407
  government, 310, 311, 449, 450, 452, 536
  industrial policy, 337–43
  membership, 304, 346, 347, 459, 544, 570
  Mond–Turner talks, 466
  origins, 304
  political action, 356, 381–2
  relations with other unions, 326, 390, 434, 454, 456
  restrictive practices, 337–43
  shop stewards, 311, 341, 437–40, 531–2
  sponsored Members of Parliament, 355, 364
  strikes, 338–43, 374, 432–3
  unemployment, 338, 349
  unofficial action, 341, 359, 432–3

Engineers, Amalgamated Society of:
  affiliation to Trades Union Congress, 210
  closed shop, 78–9
  collective bargaining, 17, 78–80, 83, 94, 256
  conscription, 157–8
  dilution, 125, 132, 134–7, 138–9, 160, 171, 175, 242
  'direct action', 293
  government, 17–18, 19, 103, 135–6, 169, 175–6, 178, 271
  industrial policy, 151, 264
  membership, 2, 3, 58, 196, 200, 570
  National Industrial Conference, 281
  overtime, 82–3
  political action, 223
  relations with other unions, 108, 189, 197, 199–200, 209, 210, 304
  restrictive practices, 9, 78–9, 241–2
  shop stewards, 9, 83, 158, 179, 262
  strikes, 17–18, 120–1, 168–74, 270–1
  trade cards, 158–9, 171–2
  unofficial action, 168–74, 176, 270–1

Enginemen, Firemen, Mechanics and Electrical Workers, National Union of, 460

Enginemen's Federation, 198

Export trades, interwar economic problems of, 386–7

Fabian Society, 74, 230, 364

Factory legislation, 11, 474–5, 481

Fair Wages Resolutions, 13, 94

Family allowances, 476

Family planning, 475

Fascism, 564

Fawcett Association, 93, 305

Federated (coalmining) Area, 7, 45, 198, 212
Federation of British Industry, 231, 252–3,
    281, 300, 314–15, 391, 422, 465–70, 538
Fenwick, Charles, 13
Fertilisers, *see* chemicals
Fife, Clackmannan and Kinross Miners Associa-
    tion, 453
Fife, Kinross and Clackmannan Miners Associa-
    tion, 193, 267, 359–60, 453
Finney, Sam, 215
Fisher, Admiral, 126
Fisher, H. A. L., 186, 250
Five-Power Naval Agreement (1922), 479
Flourmilling, 203, 248, 315, 441, 442, 531
Food and drink industry, 58, 88, 100, 307, 348,
    561
Food Controller, 162, 166, 187
Food, Ministry of, 166, 187
Food rationing, 162, 166, 187
Footwear industry:
    collective bargaining, 10, 85, 86, 206, 495
    dilution, 154
    hours of work, 85
    pay, 85, 86, 148, 428, 495
    piecework, 495
    Trade Board, 250
    trade union membership, 545
    unemployment insurance, 243
Foremen, 8, 274–5
Foundry strike (1919–20), 272–3, 550
Foundry Workers, National Union of, 304, 326,
    342, 343, 349, 434
Franchise, extension of, 220, 233, 236, 238, 472
Free trade, 363
Friendly societies, 102, 244
Fry, J. S. and Sons Ltd, 442
Furniture manufacture, 4, 85, 335
Furniture Trades Association, National Amal-
    gamated, 85, 454

Gallacher, William, 136–8, 180, 192 n., 270,
    359
Gandhi, Mahatma, 479
Garment Workers, United, 200, 305
Gas supply, 91, 203, 248, 249, 320, 335, 441,
    495, 525, 529, 531, 561
Gasworkers and General Labourers, National
    Union of (later National Union of General
    Workers):
    closed shop, 194
    collective bargaining, 19, 88, 91, 260, 318
    'direct action', 293
    finances, 349
    government, 16, 19, 440
    industrial policy, 151, 176
    membership, 3, 6, 58, 88, 91, 303, 346, 544,
        570
    political action, 176, 223, 356
    relations with other unions, 33, 109–10, 113,
        200, 304, 305, 306, 307, 350
    shop stewards, 83 n., 441, 442
    sponsored Members of Parliament, 237, 364
    sponsored parliamentary candidates, 235–6
    strikes, 63, 92, 169, 194
    unemployment benefit, 244, 349
Gasworkers, Brickmakers and General
    Labourers Union, Amalgamated (Bir-
    mingham), 235, 304, 307
Geddes, Auckland, 189, 288, 298
Geddes Committee, 313, 334, 347, 365
Geddes, Eric, 240, 246, 288, 298
General and Municipal Workers, National
    Union of, vii
    collective bargaining, 428, 434, 442–3, 520,
        533
    Communist Party, 420
    finances, 350
    government, 350–1, 420, 450, 451, 452
    industrial policy, 351
    membership, 535, 544
    nepotism, 451
    officers, 350, 451
    origins, 350–1
    relations with other unions, 434, 457
    shop stewards, 441
    sponsored Members of Parliament, 478
    strikes, 533
    trade union education, 361
General Council of the Trades Union
    Congress:
    attitude to dictatorships, 564–5
    'Back to the Unions' campaign, 352
    campaign against Trade Disputes and Trade
        Unions Bill, 423
    chairman, 309–10
    coal embargo (1925), 389
    co-ordination of trade union action, 309, 310,
        351–2, 462
    Daily Herald, 361, 477
    departments, 309, 356, 362, 381, 539, 557
    Economic Committee, 539, 557
    finances, 309, 380, 394–5, 451
    functions, 309–10, 537–41
    general strike, 396, 400–4, 407–10
    Intelligence Committee, 408
    inter-union disputes, 385, 417, 456–7, 458
    lobbying, 357, 358, 368, 373, 539, 557
    membership, 351, 379, 395, 451
    Mond–Turner talks, 464–70, 537–8, 540,
        551
    National Joint Council of Labour, 309, 351,
        540
    nationalisation, 542
    Negotiating Committee, 401–3, 409–10

General Council (*cont.*)
  origins, 308–10
  powers, 309–10, 351, 380, 391, 394, 395, 396, 400, 403, 510, 537–40, 551, 555, 563–4
  Powers and Orders Committee, 401, 404
  protection, 381, 508, 541
  Red Friday, 389–90
  relations with Russian unions, 393–4, 407, 420–1, 476
  relations with the Co-operative movement, 348–9
  relations with the first Labour government, 373, 379, 554
  relations with the Labour Party, 309, 364, 382, 476, 478, 510, 540, 564
  relations with the national government, 509–10, 538
  relations with the second Labour government, 498, 505, 508–9, 510–11, 520, 554
  representation on government bodies, 538
  Special Industrial Committee, 389, 395–6, 399, 400, 401
  Strike Organisation Committee, 404
  strikes, 309, 351–2, 370–1, 373, 375–6, 380, 385, 538
  trade union education, 361
  trade union law, 423, 481
  Trades Councils, 404, 420, 454, 539
  unemployment, 358–9, 368, 381, 539
  unemployment insurance, 477, 503, 505, 506, 508–9, 510–11
  Ways and Means Committee, 401
General Federation of Trade Unions, vii, 20, 123, 231
  conscription, 154
  finances, 20, 113
  functions, 20, 102, 113–14, 208–10, 551
  membership, 113, 209, 210
  relations with the Trades Union Congress, 20, 210, 310
  strikes, 52–3, 76, 113
General Labourers National Council (later National Federation of General Workers), 20, 109, 183, 202–3, 205, 242, 294, 326, 333, 343, 351, 551
General Labourers, United Order of, 88, 303 n.
General Railway Workers Union, 3, 38, 106–7
General strike, 555–6, 558
  attitude of the General Council, 395–6, 400, 408–9
  attitude of the government, 391, 402, 407, 409
  attitude of the Miners to reorganisation of the coal industry, 387, 399, 400
  British Gazette, 406, 416
  British Worker, 406
  causes of, 386–7

  Churchmen's proposals, 406–7
  coal subsidy, 389–90, 392, 395, 397, 403
  Conference of Trade Union Executives (29 April–1 May 1926), 400–1
  food permits, 404
  government conduct of, 405–6
  government preparations for, 392, 396–7
  inquest on, 419–20
  legality of, 408, 481
  negotiations between the government and the General Council, 401–3, 410
  relations between the Miners and the General Council, 395–6, 400, 402, 409–10
  reorganisation of the coal industry, 387–8, 397–9
  Russian donation, 407
  Samuel memorandum, 409, 419
  Special Trade Union Conference (20–1 January 1927), 419–20
  strike notices, 402
  termination, 409–11
  trade union finances, 407–8
  trade union preparations, 396, 401, 403–4
  trade union response, 400–1, 403–4, 408–9, 410
  unofficial action during, 408–9
  verdict on the coalowners, 425–6
  verdict on the General Council, 423–4
  verdict on the government, 424–5
  verdict on the Miners, 423
  victimisation, 410–12
General unions, 6, 83
  collective bargaining, 87, 88, 91, 202–3, 256
  industrial policies, 151, 176, 183, 205, 242
  membership, 2, 87, 88, 91, 196–7, 303
  relations with other unions, 109–10, 201–2, 326–7
  strikes, 183, 342, 432, 533
  trade card scheme, 170, 171
General Workers, National Federation of, *see* General Labourers National Council
General Workers, National Union of, *see* National Union of Gasworkers and General Labourers
George, David Lloyd, 12, 17, 38, 40, 49, 54, 98–9, 124–31, 137, 144, 152, 154 n., 157, 160, 161–6, 168, 173–4, 182, 185, 195, 196, 201, 209, 214, 219, 228, 232, 233, 234, 236–7, 238, 275, 280, 281, 283, 284, 285, 286–7, 289, 290–1, 293, 295, 298, 300, 312, 323, 357, 477, 481, 508, 513, 554, 555
German reparations, 357, 363, 368–9, 479–80
Gibb, George, 122
Gilmour, David, 193
Glasgow Trades Council, 270
Glassmaking, 51, 88
Gold standard, 386–7, 421, 466, 497, 512

Gosling, Harry, biog. 575, 21, 56, 63, 156, 174–5, 257, 307, 309, 355, 379, 450
Gould, J. C., 340
Government control of industry, 120, 127, 151, 162, 211–12, 240, 556–7
Government economic policy, 144, 251–2, 312–14, 475, 497–503, 506–11, 512–15, 529, 540
Government Employees, Conciliation and Arbitration Board for, 186
Government interventiion in industrial disputes, 45–6, 49, 54–5, 97–101, 121, 127–31, 137–8, 142–3, 150–1, 158, 171–4, 191, 194, 275–6, 289–91, 295–300, 321–2, 323–4, 342, 371–6, 389–90, 391–2, 399–400, 401–3, 405–7, 412, 416, 488; *see also* Labour Department; Labour, Ministry of; Munitions, Ministry of
Government policy on industrial relations, 98–100, 185, 275–6, 278–9, 314, 315, 383, 411
Government wartime wage controls, 144–6, 148, 182–6, 239, 294–9
Government Workers, Federation of, 304
Graham, William, 237, 479, 483–5, 507, 509
Great Western Railway, 96, 405
Greenall, Tom, biog. 575, 46, 48, 50
Greenwood, Arthur, 356, 381, 479, 482, 509
Gregorson, John, 467
Gregory, Holman, 357, 505
Gregory, William, 447
Grey, Edward, 98, 224
Grey, John, 492, 521
Grocery and Provisions Trade Boards, 251, 348, 365, 486
Guilds League, National, 358, 361–2

Hadow report, 365
Haldane, R. B. (later Lord), 94, 365
Hall, Frank, 50
Hallas, Eldred, 235, 237
Hancock, J. G., 216
Hankey, Maurice, 278, 284, 391, 392
Hannington, Walter, biog. 575, 311, 358, 539
Harcourt, Lewis, 147
Hardie, J. Keir, 14, 214, 221, 222, 224, 225, 237
Hardy, George, 385
Hargreaves strike (1916), 158
Hartshorn, Vernon, biog. 575, 48, 114, 479, 501
Harvey, George, 322, 448
Harvey, W. E., biog. 575, 31, 216
Haslam, James, 44, 215
Hastings, Patrick, 369
Hawarden Bridge strike (1910), 10, 85
Hayday, Arthur, biog. 575, 390, 505, 508, 517
Health, Ministry of, 232, 475, 520
Health services, 472, 548
Heath Committee, 248

Henderson, Arthur, biog. 575, 13, 38 n., 111, 112, 124, 126, 127, 132, 150, 158, 159, 161, 162, 187, 208, 210, 213–14, 217, 219, 224, 225, 228, 229, 232, 235, 236, 237, 272, 280, 290, 292, 294, 355, 364, 464, 474, 479, 480, 503, 507, 509
Henderson, W. W., 381
Hickens, Harry, 193
Hicks, George, biog. 575, 69, 105–6, 324, 351, 379, 380, 390, 435–6, 452, 462, 464, 465, 466
Hill, John, biog. 575–6, 18, 21, 80, 174, 211, 276, 351
Hill, Levi, biog. 576, 92, 519–20
Hirst, Stanley, biog. 576, 278, 301
HMSO, 76
Hoare, Samuel, 509
Hobhouse Committee, 93
Hobson, J. A., 373
Hobson, S. G., 362
Hodge, John, biog. 576, 108, 162, 167, 182, 201, 226, 231, 235, 263
Hodge, Philip, 359–60, 453
Hodges, Frank, biog. 576, 114, 277, 282, 283, 288, 299, 300–1, 302, 356, 377, 415
Hoe strike (1926), 432–3, 551
Hogg, William, 296
Holidays with pay, 263
Holmes, David, 20–1
Holt Committee, 94, 96, 97
Holt, Lawrence, 329
Home rule for Ireland, 24, 73, 221
Hope and Son Ltd., 533
Hopkins, 'Father', 55
Hopwood, Francis, 122
Horne, Robert, 280, 298
Horner, Arthur, biog. 576, 452, 494
Hosiery industry, 85, 533
Hosiery Union, Ilkeston and District, 85
Hosiery Union, Leicester and Leicestershire Amalgamated, 85
Hosiery Workers Union, Nottinghamshire and District, 85
Hours of work, reduction of, 211, 253–5, 267–71, 562
Hours of work, statutory limitation of, 11, 281–2, 474–5; *see also* Washington Convention
Howe strike (1910), 10
Hunger marches, 539
Hutchinson, W. H., 341, 537
Hutchinson, Zeph, 492
Hyndman, H. M., 193, 222, 226

ICI, 442–3, 465, 469, 533
Imperial Economic Conference (1931), 514
Import Duties Advisory Committee, 514
Independent, The, 61

Independent Labour Party, 14, 22, 48, 74, 136, 137, 222, 224, 225, 226, 227, 228, 230, 235, 237, 355, 360–1, 364, 377, 378, 466, 475–6, 478, 492, 503, 506, 513, 553
Industrial Alliance, 390–1, 394, 403, 551
Industrial conscription, 153, 154 n., 156
Industrial Council, 99–100, 516
Industrial Court, 247, 255, 256, 260, 331–2, 334, 344, 429, 516
Industrial Courts Act (1919), 247, 332
Industrial Syndicalist, 106
Industrial Syndicalist Education League, 23, 106
'Industrial truce' (1914), 118–19
Industrial unionism, 6, 23, 74, 110–11, 307–8, 455–6
Industrial Unrest, Commission of Inquiry into, 173–4, 205
Industrial Workers of the World, 385
Insurance Officers, Guild of, 261
Interim Court of Arbitration, 240, 247, 255, 272
Interim Industrial Reconstruction Committees, 248, 250
International Committee of Seafarers Unions, 33
International Federation of Trade Unions, 379, 393–4, 407, 420–1
International Labour Organisation, 282, 315
International Miners Federation, 377, 415
Inter-union disputes, *see* General Council of the Trades Union Congress; Parliamentary Committee of the Trades Union Congress; Trades Union Congress
Invergordon Mutiny (1931), 512, 518
Irish Transport and General Workers Union, 60–4
Irish Worker and People's Advocate, 61
Iron and steel, 51
   collective bargaining, 85–6, 86–7, 317–19, 431
   hours of work 86–7, 254
   labourers, 87, 152, 318
   pay, 120, 141, 146, 184, 254, 317–19, 335, 431, 521, 525
   productivity, 254
   promotion, 4, 8, 86, 139, 431
   rationalisation, 486
   relations between unions, 108, 200–1, 305, 308
   selling-price sliding scales, 120, 141, 146, 317–19, 521
   strikes, 10, 85, 318–19
   subcontracting, 10, 85
   technology, 431
   tonnage rates, 10, 182, 254, 318, 431
   trade union membership, 335

unemployment, 335
Ways and Means Agreement, 431
Iron and Steel Federation, British, 514
Iron and Steel Metal Dressers Trade Society, 272
Iron and Steel Trades Confederation:
   collective bargaining, 317–19, 431
   finances, 407
   general strike, 407
   government, 431, 452
   industrial policy, 486
   membership, 201, 346
   origins, 200–1
   relations with other unions, 305, 307–8
Iron and Steel Workers, Associated, 10, 85
Iron, Steel and Kindred Trades Association, British, *see* Iron and Steel Trades Confederation
Ironfounders, Friendly Society of, 159, 208, 272–3, 304
Ironmoulders of Scotland, Associated, 159, 183, 192, 272, 304, 341

Jevons, H. S., 51–2
Jewish Tailors, Machinists and Pressers, Amalgamated Union of, 101
Johnson, Harry, 469
Johnson, William, 216
Johnston, Tom, 479, 499–500, 509
Joint Board, 20, 62, 108, 109, 114, 118, 119–20, 197, 210, 218, 219
Joint Committee of Trade Unionists and Co-operators, 198, 349, 384
Joint Industrial Councils, 204–7, 208, 232, 248–50, 253, 260, 280, 348, 441, 517, 548
   Association of, 517
Jones, Jack, 235, 237
Jones, Jenkin, 21, 103
Jones, Tom, 402
Jowett, Fred, 220, 224, 355, 364
Joynson-Hicks, William, 397
Justice, 226
Jute and Flax Workers Union, Dundee and District, 52–3
Jute industry, 26, 52–3, 71, 250, 337
Jutland, battle of, 160

Kellaway, F. G., 170, 188
Kent Miners Association, 269, 418
Keynes, J. M., 498, 501
Keynesian economics, 498, 503
King George V, 126
Kirkwood, David, 135, 136–7, 235, 236, 270, 504
Kitchener, General, 123–4, 125, 154, 157

Knight, Robert, 20–1
Knox, Driver, 97

Labour and the Nation, 475, 477
Labour and the New Social Order, 232, 475
Labour College, Central, 23, 193, 277, 361
Labour Colleges, National Council of, 361
Labour Department of the Board of Trade, 2,
    151, 548
  intervention in industrial disputes, 31–5, 39,
    54, 59, 97–8
Labour Enlistment Complaints Committees,
    170
Labour Exchanges, 13, 95, 100, 103, 219–20
Labour Leader, 114, 217, 361
Labour, Ministry of, 162–3, 182, 185, 205, 206,
    232, 250–1, 275, 282, 401
  conciliation service, 247–8, 272, 331 2, 370,
    488, 495, 521–?
Labour, National Amalgamated Union of:
  collective bargaining, 88, 256, 318
  finances, 349, 350
  government, 307
  industrial policy, 151, 176
  membership, 58, 87, 88, 303, 346, 570
  officers, 350
  relations with other unions, 109, 113–14,
    198, 201–2, 256, 304, 307, 350
  shop stewards, 83 n.
  strikes, 169
  unemployment benefit, 244, 349
Labour, National Joint Council of, 309, 351,
    540
Labour Party, 13–14, 213–38, 353–7, 472–8,
    553–4
  attitude to conscription, 153–4
  attitude to Russia, 363
  attitude to war, 118, 357
  breach with the Independent Labour Party,
    503
  campaign against the Trade Disputes and
    Trade Unions Act, 423
  'Clause 4', 231–2
  constitution, 217, 229–30, 231–2
  'direct action', 285, 292–3, 300
  discipline, 213, 217, 220–1, 231, 360, 476
  electoral arrangement with the Liberal Party,
    13, 214–15, 234
  executive, 159, 161, 210, 226, 229, 234, 290,
    292–3, 300, 309, 358, 364, 393, 500, 508,
    509–10, 540
  finances, 217–19, 229–30, 422, 477, 478
  in local government, 353–4
  influence of Catholic church, 475–6, 480
  nationalisation, 231–2, 246, 542
  organisation, 14, 214–17, 229–30, 235, 353,
    355–6

  parliamentary party, 13, 14, 111–12, 153–4,
    161, 166, 213, 219–22, 224, 225, 226, 229,
    234, 237, 292–3, 300, 301, 309, 355–7, 358,
    364, 377, 475, 478, 500, 509–10, 540
  postwar reconstruction programme, 211,
    232–3
  relations with the Communist Party, 360,
    476
  relations with the Trades Union Congress,
    111–12, 208, 210, 230–1, 381, 540
  relations with trade unions, 356, 378, 553–4
  relations with wartime coalition govern-
    ments, 126, 161–2, 233–4
  strikes, 112, 290, 322, 373
  trade union affiliations, 14, 209, 223, 353,
    422–3, 477, 570
  wartime divisions in, 223–9, 230–2, 234
Labour Party Conferences:
  1912: 219
  1913: 221
  1917: 229
  1918 (January), 229–30, 234
  1918 (February), 229
  1918 (June), 232–3, 234
  1918 (November), 234
  1919: 285
  1925: 377, 378
  1930: 500, 502
  1933: 542
Labour Research Department, 290, 362, 420
Labour Union, National Amalgamated, 278
Lacemakers, Amalgamated Society of Opera-
    tive, 84, 87
Lanarkshire Miners County Union, 193, 270,
    452–3
Lancashire and Cheshire Miners Federation,
    46, 48, 49, 269, 322, 323, 324
Lancashire and Yorkshire Railway, 36
Lang and Sons Ltd, 132, 134, 137, 138
Lansbury, George, 74, 220–1, 354, 355, 361,
    479, 499–500, 509
Lansdowne, Marquis of, 233
Lapworth, Charles, 74
Larkin, James, biog. 576, 60–4, 73
Laski, Harold, 462
Laundries, 250
Lawrence, Herbert, 397
Laws, Cuthbert, 468
Lawther, William, biog. 576, 193
League of Nations, 284, 292, 357, 480
Lee, Kenneth, 397
Lee, Peter, biog. 576, 537
Leeds Convention (1917), 227
Leeds Corporation strike (1913), 92
Leicestershire Miners Association, 299, 418
Leslie, J. R., 235
Leverhulme, Lord, 211

Lewis, William, 27
Liberal Party, 13–14, 22, 89, 160, 161, 215–16, 234, 237, 238, 312, 355, 356, 365, 366, 369, 477, 478, 480–1, 484, 513, 556
Licensed Vehicle Workers Union, London and Provincial, 57, 155, 193, 203, 301, 306
Lightermen, *see* Watermen
Liquor restrictions, wartime, 126, 173
Little, Jack, 537
Liverpool Shipowners Association, 328, 329, 345
Liverpool transport strike (1911), 36, 39, 73
Liverpool Workers Committee, 192
'Living wage' policy, 378, 476
Lloyd, Lord, 480
Local authorities:
  administrative, professional, clerical and technical staff, 249–50, 519–20
  collective bargaining, 7, 91–2, 206, 249–50, 261, 334, 520, 547, 549
  employment, 548
  non-trading services, 249, 520
  pay, 92, 187, 261, 335, 519–20, 525, 527, 561
  Public Assistance Committees, 472
  Trade Disputes and Trade Unions Act, 423
  trade union membership, 91, 303–4, 335, 545–6
  unemployment, 335
Local authority associations, 249–50
Local Government Act (1929), 472, 475
Local Government Officers, National Association of, 92, 187, 249, 261, 334, 520, 534
Locomotive Engineers and Firemen, Associated Society of:
  collective bargaining, 143, 253–4, 370
  'direct action', 290, 300–1
  finances, 407
  general strike, 407
  government, 451
  membership, 3, 290
  promotion, 4, 5
  relations with other unions, 38, 106, 194–5, 197, 290–1, 300, 372–3
  strikes, 38, 194–5, 267, 290, 369–70
  unofficial action, 195
London and North Western Railway, 97
London Building Industry Federation, 66, 67
London building lockout (1914), 64–70, 73, 74, 110
London busmen, 57, 193, 320, 371–3, 454, 524–5, 526–7; *see also* road passenger transport
London cab strike (1913), 57, 72
London County Council, 91
London dock strike (1912), 53–6, 71, 74, 112, 222
London General Omnibus Company, 193
London Master Bookbinders Association, 384

London Master Builders Association, 66–9
London Master Printers Association, 76, 383–4
London Passenger Transport Bill, 482, 515, 541, 542
London printing strike (1911), 16, 74, 75–6
London Society of Compositors, 16, 75–6, 143, 154
London Society of Tailors and Tailoresses, 86, 200
London Trades Council, 420
London Traffic Combine, 371–3, 482, 524–5
London tram strike (1924), 371–3
London Workers Committee, 180–1
Long, Walter, 157
Lucas, Joseph, Ltd, 432
Lyon, Hugh, 270, 404

'Mabon', *see* William Abraham
Macara, Charles, biog. 576, 99, 430
Macarthur, Mary, biog. 576, 132
Macassey, Lynden, 131, 136, 137, 257
MacDonald, James Ramsay, 13–14, 40 n., 94, 111, 112, 213–14, 220, 224–5, 227, 228 n., 229, 237, 321, 331, 355, 357, 364–5, 368–9, 371–3, 377–9, 464, 475–6, 479–80, 484, 488, 491, 492, 495, 500, 501, 504, 507–9, 510, 512–13, 553
MacDonnell, Lord, 95
Macdougall, James, 193
McGurk, John, biog. 576–7, 324
Machine Workers Association, United, 171, 304
McKenna, Reginald, 56 n., 144
MacKenzie, William, 375
McLaine, William, 172
Maclay, Joseph, 163–4
Maclean, John, 135, 137, 138, 193
MacLean, Neil, 237, 460
Macmanus, Arthur, 137, 172 n., 179, 180, 359
Macmillan Committee, 497–8, 502
Macmillan, Lord, 489
Macready, General, 29, 286
Maintenance of Supplies, Organisation for the, 397, 405
Mainwaring, W. H., 28
Managerial prerogative, 78–80, 338–43
Manchester Guardian, 295
Manchester Joint Engineering Shop Stewards Committee, 171, 179
Manchester Workers Committee, 180
Mann, Tom, biog. 577, 23, 33, 36, 37, 55, 56, 74, 106 n., 141, 227, 311
Manpower (1914–18), 121–2, 152–60, 161, 163, 189; *see also* conscription; dilution of labour
Manpower Distribution Board, 157, 160, 163, 174

Marchbank, John, biog. 577, 280, 296, 390, 395, 537
Marine Workers Union, Amalgamated, 328–9, 385, 458
Martin, James, 216
Masterman, C. F. G., 98
Mawdsley, James, 20
Maxton, James, 378, 466, 492, 503, 504
May Committee, 506–7, 517–18
May, George, 506–7
May munitions strikes (1917), 168–74, 176, 180, 192, 555
Mediation Committee, 290–1, 308
Mellor, William, 74, 113
Mersey engineering strike (1917), 169
Middleton, J. S., 225
Midland Employers Federation, 59, 88, 143
Midland Miners Federation, 46, 47
Midland Railway, 97
Midlands strike (1913), 59–60, 71, 74, 199
Military Service Acts (1916–19), 153–4, 209, 226, 284–6
Mill and Factory Operatives Union, Dundee and District, 52–3
Milne-Bailey, W., biog. 577, 462
Milne-Watson, David, 465
Milner, Lord, 226
Miners Federation of Great Britain:
  absenteeism, 156
  anxiety to preserve unity, 48, 50, 296, 415
  collective bargaining, 18–19, 30–1, 43–6, 82, 212, 268–9, 295–302, 323–4, 374, 387, 399
  'direct action', 282, 284, 286, 293
  finances, 30–2, 45, 297, 322, 412
  government, 17, 18–19, 50, 116–17, 177, 279, 298, 418, 452, 453, 466, 535–6
  industrial policy, 44, 48, 49–50, 211, 212, 282–3, 483–4
  membership, 2, 196, 303–4, 346, 421, 446–7, 544, 570
  nationalisation, 212, 246, 247, 287–8, 291–2, 368
  political action, 11, 12, 13, 49 n., 99, 162, 215–16, 223, 231, 356, 359, 381, 484
  relations with other unions, 113–17, 197, 198, 308, 323, 390–1, 403
  relations with the Communist Party and the Minority Movement, 452–3
  sponsored Members of Parliament, 215–16, 237, 355, 364, 478, 513
  sponsored parliamentary candidates, 215–16, 236
  strikes, 30–2, 43–52, 72, 73, 275–6, 296–7, 299–302, 321–5, 400–10, 412–19, 493–4
  unofficial action, 192–3, 194
  wartime dealings with the government, 125, 127, 128, 129, 154, 186, 189, 190, 209

Miners Industrial Unions, 417, 446–7, 458
Miners' Next Step, 106
'Mines for the Nation' campaign, 287–8, 292
Mineworkers, National Union of, vii
Mineworkers of Scotland, United, 453, 536
Minimum wage, 221–2, 281–2; *see also* coal-mining; Trade Boards
Mining Association of Great Britain, 18, 43, 128, 398, 416, 484; *see also* coalowners
Mining Situation, The, 401
Mitchell, Isaac, 97, 136
Mond, Alfred, biog. 577, 425, 442, 465–70
Mond group of employers, 465
Monetary policy, 251, 386–7, 468, 497, 512, 514, 529
Money, Leo, 164, 283, 287
Montagu, Edwin, 157, 159, 232
Morel, E. D., 224
Morris, Harold, 386
Morrison, Herbert, 355, 364, 479, 482, 501
Mosley memorandum, 500
Mosley, Oswald, 479, 499–501, 503, 506, 513
Mosses, William, biog. 577, 21, 124, 208
Muir, John, 135, 137–8
Muir Mackenzie, Lord, 150
Mullin, William, biog. 577, 21
Municipal Employees Association, 91, 109, 197, 201–2, 304, 350
Munitions Acts (1915–18), 125, 127, 135–6, 140–1, 152
  ban on strikes and lockouts, 127, 128–31, 141, 239, 240
  compulsory arbitration, 127, *see also* Committee on Production
  dilution, 127, 131–41
  'embargoes', 191
  enforcement, 131, 136, 137–8, 141, 167, 171, 172–3, 199, 204
  'L' circulars, 132–3, 135–6, 141, 143–4, 175
  Leaving Certificates, 127, 130, 131, 136, 149, 156–7, 173–4, 181–2, 191
  opposition to, 133, 135, 141
  War Munitions Volunteers, 126–7, 134, 158–9, 191
  works rules, 130–1, 141
Munitions Committees, Local, 125–6
Munitions Labour Supply Committee, Central, 132–3, 208
Munitions, Ministry of, 126, 130–1, 132, 137, 146, 151, 152, 157, 158, 170, 171, 183, 185, 207, 227, 241, 441–2, 547
Munitions of War Committee, 126
Munitions Tribunals, 127, 130–1
Munro, Thomas, 136
Murphy, J. T., 158, 180, 181, 192, 359
Murphy, W. M., 61

Naesmith, Andrew, biog. 577, 491, 492
National Alliance of Employers and Employed,
    231, 252
National Democratic and Labour Party, 226,
    231, 235, 237, 446
National factories, 123, 134, 140, 240
National Industrial Conference (1919), 276,
    280–2, 308, 340
  Provisional Committee of, 280–2, 308
National Industrial Council (1927), 464,
    466–70
National Institute of Industrial Psychology,
    534
National insurance, 95, 101–5, 111, 114, 219–
    20, 221, 222, 472, 556, 562
National Maritime Board, 164, 328, 547
National Service, Department of, 163, 170, 189
National Shipbuilders Security Ltd, 486
National War Aims Committee, 227
Navvies, Bricklayers Labourers, and General
    Labourers Union, 88, 235
Nazis, 536, 564–5
New Leader, 361, 476
'New Unionism' of 1889: 15, 40, 58, 60
Newspaper Proprietors Association, 76
Nicholls Committee, 366–7
Nicholls, George, 89
No Conscription Fellowship, 226, 227
Norman, Montagu, 486
North Eastern Railway, 7, 12, 38, 97
North Staffordshire Miners Federation, 47,
    215, 494
Northumberland Miners Association, 10–11,
    46, 193, 299, 414, 428
Nottinghamshire Miners Association, 47, 193,
    216, 269, 322, 414, 417, 445–6

Odhams Press, 477
Ogden, John, biog. 577
O'Grady, James, biog. 577, 56, 203, 220–1
Olivier, Lord, 365
Onions, A., 48
Orbell, Harry, 56
Osborne judgment, 14, 114, 217–19, 353, 556,
    570
Overseas Trade, Department of, 527

Pacifism, 223, 224; *see also* No Conscription
    Fellowship
Paint manufacture, 203, 441
Painters and Decorators, National Amalga-
    mated Society of House and Ship, 64, 107,
    345, 434, 435
Paper and printing:
  apprenticeship, 77, 263, 459–60
  chapels, 84, 440

collective bargaining, 75–7, 206, 258–9, 262–
    3, 273, 331–2
  dilution, 154
  general strike, 402–3, 406–7, 411–12
  holidays with pay, 263
  hours of work, 20, 75–7, 259
  pay, 142, 143, 186, 258–9, 273–4, 317, 331–2,
    335, 336, 383–4, 521, 525, 527, 561
  relations between unions, 75, 199, 200, 307,
    331–2
  restrictive practices, 76–7, 262–3
  strikes, 75–7, 273–4, 331–2, 383–4, 550
  technology, 384, 546
  Trade Board, 100
  trade union membership, 200, 304, 335, 421,
    545–6
  unemployment, 335
Paper Mill Workers, National Union of, 200
Papworth, Bert, 537
Parker, Gilbert, 94
Parker, James, 234, 235
Parkhead, 135, 137
Parliament Act (1911), 219, 221
Parliamentary Committee of the Trades Union
    Congress:
  attitude to war, 118–19
  conscription, 154, 285
  'direct action', 285–6, 287–8, 292–3, 300
  eight-hour day, 112
  election manifesto, 234
  elections to, 230–1, 308–9
  endorsement of parliamentary candidates,
    234
  finances, 210
  functions, 62, 112–13, 310
  inter-union disputes, 20, 109, 198, 202
  lobbying, 13, 111, 147, 159, 167
  membership, 21, 276
  national output, 263
  powers, 308–10
  relations with the General Federation of
    Trade Unions, 208, 210
  relations with the Labour Party, 111–12,
    208, 210, 230–1
  secretary, 111, 208
  staff, 210
  strikes, 56, 62–4, 73–4, 112, 115, 118, 272,
    273–4, 290, 322
  trade union structure, 106, 107–8, 111
  wartime dealings with the government, 123,
    147, 154, 161–2, 201, 205, 208, 209–10,
    554
Parliamentary electorate, 236–7
Parmoor, Lord, 365, 479
Parsonage, J., 107
Patternmakers Association, United, 139, 264,
    339, 342, 432, 434, 532

Pay movements, 25, 46, 73, 120–1, 141–52, 182–7, 255–63, 316–36, 383, 421, 427, 497, 517–26, 559–62
 causes of, 142, 149, 260–1, 333–6, 421, 523, 526–9
Pay statistics, 46, 335–6, 525–6, 561, 568
Payment by results, 9, 149, 182–3; *see also* individual industries
Peel, Sam, 330
Peet, George, 172 n., 180, 181, 359
Penistone Electricians' strike (1919), 274–5
Pensions for mothers, 368
Pensions for widows and orphans, 472, 480, 562
Pensions, Ministry of, 162, 182
Pensions, old age, 13, 120, 147–8, 368, 472, 480, 562
Personnel management, 441–2
Peters, Arthur, 217
Petroff, Peter, 135
Phillips, Gordon, 424–5
Pickard, Ben, 20, 356
Picketing, 29, 37, 57, 61, 300, 405, 416, 422–3
Pickford, Lord Justice, 150–1
Piecework, *see* payment by results
Plasterers, National Association of Operative, 64, 66, 67, 68, 70, 305, 435–7, 530
Plastering Industry, National Joint Council for the, 436
Plebs League, 22–3, 28, 31, 49–50, 106
Plumbers Association, United Operative, 107, 111, 310
Pointer, William, 225
Pointsmens and Signalmens Society, United, 3, 38, 106
Police:
 pay, 195, 286, 518–19
 strikes, 195, 286
 use in strikes, 29, 89, 222, 270, 405
Police and Prison Officers, National Union of, 195, 286
Police Federation, 286, 518
Pollitt, Harry, 271, 359, 420, 452
Ponsonby, Arthur, 224
Poor Law, 49, 232, 233, 313–14, 407, 412–14, 562
Poor Law Guardians, 261, 313, 323, 343, 354, 412–14, 472
Poor Law Officers Association, National, 261, 304
Poor relief, 313–14, 322–3, 343, 354, 412–14, 472, 477, 562
Port and Transit Executive Committee, National, 156, 209
Port Employers, National Association of, 258, 329
Port of London Authority, 35, 36, 56, 204

Port Transport Industry, National Joint Council for the, 258, 330
Post Office:
 collective bargaining, 8, 94, 96, 206–7, 260–1, 530–1, 547
 discipline, 97
 employment, 107, 336
 hours of work, 151–2
 pay, 94, 142, 151, 260–1, 319, 531
 promotion, 445, 532
 relations between unions, 107, 304, 307–8
 trade union membership, 3, 305, 335, 545–6
 Whitley Committees, 443–5, 530–1, 532
Post Office Engineering and Stores Association (later Post Office Engineering Union), 93, 107, 260–1, 308, 443–5, 531, 532, 534
Post Office Workers, Union of, 260–1, 305, 308, 346, 443–5, 449, 530–1, 570
Postal and Telegraph Associations, National Joint Committee of, 93
Postal Clerks Association, United Kingdom, 93, 94, 305
Postal Telegraph Clerks Association, 93, 305
Postgate, R. W., 104
Postmen's Federation, 3, 6, 16, 19, 93–4, 96, 305, 570
Pottery industry, 51, 154, 206, 441
Pottery Industry, National Joint Council for the, 206
Poulton, E. L., biog. 577, 273, 390
Price control, 147, 161, 162, 187
Printers and Assistants, National Society of Operative, 88, 402
Printers, British Federation of Master, 76, 77, 258, 331–2, 521
Printers, Warehousemen and Cutters, National Amalgamated Society of, 88, 200
Printing and Kindred Trades Federation, 2, 75, 76, 259, 263, 273, 332, 521
Printing and Paper Workers, National Union of, 200, 305
Printing, Bookbinding, Machine Ruling, and Paper Workers, National Union of, 305, 306, 307, 383–4, 407
Productivity, 263, 421; *see also* individual industries
Protected Occupations, Schedule of, 170, 171, 189
Protection, 363–4, 368, 381, 497, 498, 501, 508, 512, 513–14, 541
Provisional Committee for the Amalgamation of Existing Unions, 105
Public works, 368, 477, 498–501, 557
Pugh, Arthur, biog. 578, 201, 254, 381, 395, 400, 401, 403, 464, 508, 540
Purcell, Albert, biog. 578, 263, 273, 351, 359, 375, 379, 393

Quarrying industry, 88, 248
Quarrymen's Union, North Wales, 304

Railway and Canal Traffic Act (1913), 39, 222
Railway Clerks Association, 3, 236, 261, 275, 449, 478, 534, 562, 563
Railway companies, 37–40, 212, 245–6, 390, 457–8, 523–4, 526, 546
Railway Executive Committee, 120, 124
Railway Review, 443–5
Railway Servants, Amalgamated Society of, 3, 5, 19, 37–41, 103, 105, 106–7, 111, 277, 570
Railway Servants (Hours of Labour) Act (1893), 11
Railway Shopmen's National Council, 429, 495
Railway Signalmen, Union of, 370
Railway strike (1911), 36–9, 71–2, 554
Railway strike (1919), 278, 289–91, 555
Railway strike (1924), 370
Railwaymen, National Union of:
    collective bargaining, 62, 143, 150, 177–8, 246, 253–4, 283, 288–91, 429–30, 443–5, 494–5, 523–4
    'direct action', 283, 284, 286, 293, 295, 296, 299, 300–1
    finances, 407
    general strike, 407
    government, 166, 143, 150, 177, 277, 279–80, 296, 449, 451, 537
    industrial policy, 205, 212, 429, 494
    membership, 106–7, 290, 346, 570
    origins, 106–7, 111
    political action, 223, 356, 458, 481
    relations with other unions, 114–17, 194–5, 197–8, 283, 290–1, 316, 370, 389, 390–1, 403, 429–30, 458
    relations with the Communist Party, 420
    sponsored Members of Parliament, 237, 478
    sponsored parliamentary candidates, 236
    strikes, 62, 115, 150, 177, 289–91, 370
    unofficial action, 143, 150, 194, 195, 537
    Vigilance Committees, 177, 192, 537
    wartime dealings with the government, 154, 155, 195, 209
    Washington Convention, 481
Railwaymen's Vigilance Movement, 537
Railways, 51
    amalgamation of companies, 245–6
    collective bargaining, 7, 38, 40, 116, 246, 288–91, 332–3, 370, 429–30, 443–5, 494–5, 523–4, 547
    dilution, 154–5
    discipline, 97, 246
    employment, 336
    general strike, 405, 411
    guaranteed week, 411, 429

holidays with pay, 263
    hours of work, 11, 194–5, 212, 253–4, 267, 481
    Local Departmental Committees, 443–5
    nationalisation, 245–6
    pay, 37, 39, 120, 141–2, 142–3, 150, 155, 186, 195, 212, 246, 288–91, 319, 332–3, 335, 369–70, 421, 428, 494–5, 523–4, 526
    promotion, 4, 5, 445
    relations between unions, 38, 106–7, 290, 370, 429–30
    rosters, 444
    strikes, 26, 38–41, 71, 72, 150, 194–5, 267, 289–91, 369–70, 550
    trade union membership, 335, 421
    trade union recognition, 7, 38–41, 72, 96, 212, 546, 547
    unemployment, 335
    workshops, 107, 197–8, 291, 332–3, 429–30, 495
Railways Act (1921), 246
Reading, Lord, 509
Reconstruction Committee, 204, 232
Reconstruction, Ministry of, 205, 232
Red Friday, 389–90, 394, 403, 424, 555–6, 558
Red International of Labour Unions, 359, 536
Redmayne, Robert, 247
Redundancy, 531
Rees, Noah, 28
Release of workers from the armed forces, 122, 134, 156
Rent control, 147, 367
Representation of the People Act (1918), 236, 238
Restoration of prewar practices, 122, 127, 212, 233, 239–40, 241–2
Restrictive practices, 121, 122, 123, 127, 337–43; *see also* individual industries and unions
Retrenchment Committee, 142, 144, 151
Rhineland, French occupation of, 480
Richards, Thomas, 48, 451, 537
Richardson, Guard, 97
Richardson, Tom, 47, 224
Richmond, John, 134, 341
Right to Work Bill, 22, 221
River Thames Shop Stewards Committee, 271
Road and Rail Traffic Act (1933), 515–16
Road haulage:
    collective bargaining, 203, 248, 260, 547, 548
    employment, 336
    general strike, 405, 406, 411
    hours of work, 270, 515
    pay, 203, 260, 335, 515
    regulation of, 515–16, 541, 557
    strikes, 33–41, 270

trade union membership, 301, 303, 335, 421, 545–6
unemployment, 335
Road passenger transport:
  closed shop, 454
  collective bargaining, 91, 248, 249, 320, 371–3, 524–5, 547
  dilution, 154–5
  employment, 336
  general strike, 405, 411
  guaranteed week, 320, 524
  hours of work, 11, 194–5, 212, 253–4, 267,
  pay, 155, 320, 335, 371–3, 428, 525, 526–7
  regulation of, 371–3, 515, 557
  relations between unions, 458
  strikes, 39, 57, 92, 193, 371–3
  trade union membership, 303, 335, 421, 458, 545–6
  unemployment, 335
Road Transport, National Joint Industrial Council for Commercial, 260
Roberts, G. H., biog. 578, 182, 226, 235
Roberts, Richard Lloyd, 442
Roosevelt, President, 503
Rothermere, Lord, 313
Routh, Guy, 562
Rowntree, Seebohm, 232, 244, 441–2
Royal Commission on Agriculture (1919), 245
Royal Commission on Labour (1891), 204
Royal (MacDonnell) Commission on the Civil Service (1912), 95–6
Royal (Samuel) Commission on the Coal Industry (1925), 389–90, 397–9, 416, 425
Royal (Harrel) Commission on the Railway Conciliation and Arbitration Scheme of 1907 (1911), 38, 39–40
Royal Commission on Transport (1928), 482, 515
Royal (Holman Gregory) Commission on Unemployment (1930), 505, 506
Rubber manufacture, 203, 205, 260, 307
Ruhr, French occupation of, 325, 368, 387
Runciman, Walter, 129, 144
Ruskin College, 22–3, 361
Russia, British intervention in, 284–6, 293–4, 302
Russian relations with Britain, 369, 377, 476
Russian revolution (1917), 227, 360
Russian trade unions, 379, 393–4, 412, 420–1, 476
Rylands, Peter, 314

Sailors and Firemen, National Union of (later National Union of Seamen):
  closed shop, 164, 328, 458–9
  collective bargaining, 34–5, 55, 141, 164, 328–9, 384–5, 523
  expulsion from Trades Union Congress, 458–9
  general strike, 401, 408
  government, 55, 328–9, 384–5, 458
  industrial policy, 55, 141, 164
  membership, 33, 196, 346, 458
  political action, 227
  Red Friday, 389, 390
  relations with other unions, 306, 316, 328–9, 385, 458–9
  sponsored parliamentary candidate, 235
  strikes, 33–41, 55, 64, 329, 385
  unofficial action, 164, 329, 385
  wartime dealings with the government, 164, 209
St Aldwyn, Lord, 150
Salter, Arthur, 515
Sankey Committee, 486
Sankey, Lord, 246, 283, 287, 479, 486, 509
Scottish Co-operative Wages Board, 270
Scottish Horse and Motormen's Association, 270, 404
Scottish Miners Federation, 7, 17, 46, 116–17, 118, 192–3, 414, 449, 452–3, 493–4
Scottish Trades Union Congress, 211, 270, 534
Scottish Transport and General Workers Union, 454–5, 523
Scottish Typographical Association, 75, 77
Scottish Union of Dock Labourers, 316
Seafarers Union, British, 328
Seamen, National Union of, *see* Sailors and Firemen, National Union of
Second International, 223
Seddon, J. A., biog. 578, 63, 226
Sexton, James, biog. 578, 55, 104, 155, 230–1, 276, 278, 382
Shackleton, David, biog. 578, 14, 20–1, 111, 162, 272, 356
Shaw, A., 493
Shaw, Lord, 257
Shaw, Tom, biog. 578, 364, 365, 370–1, 375, 509
Sheet Metal Workers, 159
Sheffield Engineering Joint Shop Stewards Committee, 158
Sheffield Workers Committee, 158, 180, 181
Sherwood, Will, 205
Shinwell, Emanuel, biog. 578, 328, 352, 374, 385
Shipbuilding:
  apprenticeship, 80, 460
  collective bargaining, 7, 9, 10, 18, 80–1, 168, 326–8, 343–5, 374–5, 434–5, 547, 558
  dilution, 122, 125, 139–40
  discharge notes, 80, 131
  hours of work, 79, 253, 343–5

Shipbuilding (*cont.*)
    interchangeability, 433–4
    labourers, 256
    pay, 7, 120, 121, 141, 256, 271, 317, 326–8, 335, 344, 374–5, 434–5, 496–7, 525, 561
    payment by results, 182
    piecework, 10, 80, 256, 344, 435, 496
    rationalisation, 386
    relations between unions, 305, 434, 558
    restrictive practices, 9, 121, 433
    shop stewards, 84
    strikes, 10, 131–2, 271, 327, 343–4, 374–5, 497, 550
    technology, 547
    trade union membership, 2, 335
    unemployment, 335
    unemployment insurance, 101
Shipbuilding Employers Federation, 7, 9, 121, 253, 256, 547
Shipbuilding, Engineering, and Constructional Workers, Amalgamated Union of, 305
Shipbuilding lockout (1922), 327
Shipbuilding lockout (1924), 374–5
Shipbuilding Trades Committee, 434
Shipping:
    Asiatic seamen, 155
    closed shop, 164, 328, 458–9
    collective bargaining, 34–5, 164, 328–9, 384–5
    employment, 155, 164
    freight rates, 34, 40, 328, 329, 384
    government control, 163–4
    pay, 120, 141, 155, 164, 328–9, 335, 384–5, 523
    relations between unions, 328–9, 385, 458–9
    strikes, 26, 33–41, 64, 164, 328, 385
    trade union membership, 335, 534, 544–6
    trade union recognition, 35, 164, 212, 546, 547
    wartime contracts, 155
Shipping Federation, 33, 34, 164, 212, 328, 544, 546, 547
Shipping, Ministry of, 163–4, 209
Ships Stewards, Cooks, Butchers, and Bakers, National Union of, 328, 345, 385, 458
Shipwrights Association, Ship Constructive and, 125, 131, 159, 182, 305, 344, 374–5, 433–4
Shirkie, R., 417
Shop Assistants Warehousemen and Clerks, National Amalgamated Union of:
    collective bargaining, 90, 142, 262
    government, 452
    industrial policy, 90, 120
    membership, 90, 105, 346, 347, 534
    relations with other unions, 108–9, 198
    strikes, 90

Shop Distributive and Allied Workers, Union of, vii
Shop stewards, 9, 83–4, 135, 178–81, 187–9, 310–11, 437–41, 531–3, 549, 564; *see also* individual industries and unions
Shop Stewards and Workers Committee Movement, 180–1, 189–90, 191–2, 193–4, 278, 310, 358
    National Administrative Council of, 180, 181, 191, 194
Silk industry, 84
Sime, John, 52–3
Simon, John, 130, 408, 481
Sinn Fein, 237
Skill differentials, 561, 563
Skinner, Herbert, 76
Smethurst, A. H., 378
Smillie, Robert, biog. 578–9, 21, 32 n., 45, 47–8, 50–1, 114, 156, 166, 193, 216, 224, 234, 277, 282–3, 284, 293, 294–5, 296, 298, 308, 352, 365, 452, 551
Smith, Allan, biog. 579, 132, 252, 254, 256, 272, 280, 281, 339–41, 467, 468, 470
Smith, Charles, 531
Smith, F. E. (Lord Birkenhead), 176, 401, 402
Smith, Herbert, biog. 579, 44, 46, 47, 48, 283, 298, 301, 323, 324, 388, 393, 400, 409, 415, 452, 483, 537
Smith, Walter, biog. 579, 89
Smuts, General, 189
Snowden, Philip, 95, 220–1, 222, 224, 225, 227, 355, 357, 368, 373, 378, 386, 479, 497–9, 501, 505–6, 507, 509, 510, 511, 512–13
Social Democratic Federation, 22, 364
Social Democratic Party, 22, 222
Socialism in Our Time, 378, 503
Socialist Labour Party, 22–3, 136, 180, 192, 358
Socialist National Defence Committee, *see* National Democratic and Labour Party
Somme offensive, 160
South Wales coal strike (1915), 128–30, 142, 177, 555
South Wales Miners Federation, 46, 277
    anthracite area, 393, 447
    closed shop, 28, 128–30, 198, 393, 447
    collective bargaining, 7, 28, 31–2, 128, 129–30, 150–1
    combine committees, 28, 445
    effect of coal lockout (1926), 447
    finances, 30, 32, 45, 49–50, 110
    government, 17, 48, 50, 106, 110
    industrial policy, 212
    membership, 392–3, 447
    nepotism, 451
    Red International of Labour Unions, 359
    relations with Miners Federation, 18–19, 30–2, 48, 72

relations with other unions, 29, 128, 417
seniority rule, 393, 447
strikes, 11, 28–32, 73, 128–30, 189, 393, 493–4
unofficial action, 47, 193
Unofficial Reform Committee, 106, 110, 193
South Wales Siemens Steel Association, 87
South Wales Socialist Society, 193, 358
Sparkes, Malcolm, 362
Spence, W. R., 459
Spencer, George, biog. 579, 212, 296, 417, 446–7
Spinners, Amalgamated Association of Operative Cotton, 4, 16, 19, 81, 127, 194, 267, 274, 488, 522–3
Spoor, Ben, 237
Stanley, Albert, 195, 253
Stanley, Lord, 12
Stanton, C. B., biog. 579, 28, 45, 48, 225, 226
Steadman, W. C., biog. 579, 111
Steam Engine Makers Association, 304
Steel and Iron Workers, Amalgamated Society of, 305
Steel-Maitland, Arthur, 401, 422
Steel Smelters Amalgamated Association, British, 4, 10, 85–6, 87, 108, 159, 201, 237
Stevedores Labour Protection League, 54, 56, 306
Stevedores, Lightermen, Watermen, and Dockers Union, National Amalgamated, 330, 370
Stockholm Conference, 228
Stonemasons, Friendly Society of Operative, 64–6, 68–9, 73, 107, 305
Strachey, John, 500–1
Straker, William, biog. 579, 44, 48, 296
Strike breaking, 29, 34, 61, 92, 316, 328, 405–6, 417–18
Strike funds, 56, 57, 59, 62–4, 74, 76, 273 n., 322, 407–8, 412–13, 538
Strike statistics, 11, 24–6, 84, 194, 266, 377, 383, 427, 493, 523, 550, 568
Strikes, 10–11, 17–19, 24–74, 75, 115, 194–5, 222, 266–302, 370–7, 487–94, 550–1
causes of, 24–5, 32, 40–1, 52, 57, 60–1, 71–4, 173–4, 266, 366–7, 564
costs of, 51, 324
impact on governments, 554–6
violence in, 29, 36–7, 61, 222, 270, 405
Stuart, G. H. (later Stuart-Bunning), biog. 579, 94, 263
Subcontracting, 9, 10, 47 n., 69
Submarine menace, German, 160, 163–4
Sub-Postmasters, Federation of, 93
Suffragettes, 24, 73, 220
Sugar refining, 205

Supply and Transport Committee, 276, 291, 372–3, 392
Surface Workers Federation, 198
Swales, Alonso, biog. 579, 351, 379, 390, 395, 401
Swift, Digby, 488
Syndicalism, 22–3, 25, 66, 69–70, 73, 81–2, 105–6, 109, 110, 111, 114–15, 130, 223, 462

Taff Vale case, 22
Tailors and Garment Workers, National Union of, 305, 346, 347, 453–4, 457
Tailors and Tailoresses, Amalgamated Society of, 86, 109, 198, 305
Tailors Society, Scottish National Operative, 305
Tanner, Jack, biog. 579, 181, 536
Tariffs, *see* protection
Tawney, R. H., 100–1, 283, 287, 475, 501
Taylor, A. J. P., 154, 218 n.
Teachers in Technical Institutions, National Union of, 93
Teachers, National Union of:
  collective bargaining, 5–6, 92–3, 152, 186, 334–5, 518
  industrial policy, 5–6
  membership, 1, 3, 346, 534, 544, 570
  political activity, 95, 152
  relations with other unions, 93
  strikes, 92–3, 152
  unofficial action, 187
Teachers, National Union of Women, 93
Telephone Company, National, 93, 107
Telephone Employees, Amalgamated Society of, 93, 107
Tevenan, Peter, 235
Textile bleaching, dyeing, and finishing, 86, 154, 428
Textile Factory Workers Association, United, 12, 194, 236, 237, 267, 305
Textile Trades, National Association of Unions in the, 166
Textile Workers, General Union of (later National Union of), 86, 165, 346, 347, 488–90, 492–3
Textiles, 51, 534, 561; *see also* cotton; hosiery industry; jute industry; textile bleaching, dyeing, and finishing; wool industry
Thomas, D. A. (Lord Rhondda), 27–8, 32 n., 166, 187
Thomas, J. H., biog. 580, 21, 40 n., 114, 143, 162, 194–5, 232, 263, 277, 280, 289–91, 294, 295, 356, 357, 364, 379, 394, 395, 396, 400, 401, 402, 409, 420, 424, 452, 464, 479, 486, 499–501, 507, 509, 537, 551
Thompson, Fred, 454

Thomson, Basil, 227–8, 278, 293
Thomson, Lord, 365, 479
Thorne, Will, biog. 580, 21, 99, 109, 153, 176, 220–1, 235, 278, 356, 452, 504
Tillett, Ben, biog. 580, 21, 22, 54, 74, 104, 110, 153, 219, 226, 231, 257, 278, 307, 351, 382, 390, 393, 462
Times, The, 344, 467
Tin and Sheet Millmen's Society, 305
Tinplate industry, 84, 206, 441
To All Clyde Workers, 135
Tobacco industry, 250
Tobacco Workers, National Union of Cigar Makers and, 457
Tomsky, M., 379–80, 394, 421
Toolmakers, Engineers and Machinists, Amalgamated Society of, 304
Trade, Board of, 11, 209; *see also* Labour Department of the Board of Trade
Trade Boards, 13, 100–1, 186, 204, 250–1, 262, 282, 334, 348, 365–6
Trade card scheme, 157–9, 169–73, 207
Trade Disputes Act (1906), 12, 22, 408, 422
Trade Disputes and Trade Unions Act (1927), 422–3, 464, 476–7, 478, 481, 557–8
Trade Union Act (1913), 217–19, 223, 557–8
Trade Union Acts (1871 and 1876), 12, 201
Trade Union (Amalgamation) Act (1917), 201
Trade Union Labour Party, 230–1
Trade Union Parliamentary Group, 382, 504, 510
Trade unions:
  administrative expenditure, 15, 553, 570
  amalgamations, 105–10, 197, 199–202, 304–8, 460–1, 551–2
  approved societies, 102–3, 105, 244
  attitude prior to general strike, 379
  attitude to Labour governments, 378, 501–3, 564
  attitude to law, 11, 22
  attitude to Mond–Turner talks, 466, 470–1
  attitude to the Labour Party, 356, 478
  attitude to war, 118–19, 293–4
  ballots, 19, 111, 535–6
  branches, 16, 19, 279
  centralisation of power in, 16–19, 68, 70, 73, 175–9, 207–8, 270–4, 279, 310, 449–52, 550–1, 563
  conferences, 19, 279, 551
  dispute benefit, 15–16, 552–3, 571
  districts, 16, 19, 110, 177–9, 279
  executives, 19, 70, 279, 310, 449, 450–2, 551
  federations, 20, 202, 551
  finances, 14–16, 349–50, 535, 552–3, 571
  friendly benefits, 14, 552–3, 571
  full-time officers, 19–20, 102, 110–11, 174–7, 178, 350, 449–52, 551

  legal status, 12–13, 422–3, 557–8
  local autonomy in, 175–9, 270–4
  membership, 1–3, 105, 195–6, 302–4, 345–7, 421, 534–5, 543–4, 563, 568, 570
  philosophy, 21–3, 461–4, 470–1, 478, 540–2, 552
  political action, 11–14, 22, 111, 356, 382, 383, 422–3, 478, 533–7
  political funds, 14, 217–19, 383, 422–3, 477, 478, 571
  public standing, 557–9
  recognition, 465
  responsibility for improvements in welfare, 563
  sponsored Members of Parliament, 237–8, 355, 364, 478, 510, 513
  sponsored paraliamentary candidates, 235–6, 478
  staffs, 103, 350, 451
  structure, 6, 23, 105–17, 455–7, 535, 543–4, 552, 563
  success as pressure groups, 554–6
  unemployed members, 358, 539
  unemployment benefit, 14, 101, 244, 349, 553, 571
Trades Councils, 14, 215–17, 229, 230, 235, 396, 404–5, 420, 454, 539
Trades Union Congress:
  Communists, 420, 452
  conferences of trade union executives, 389, 400–1, 417, 419–20
  conscription, 150, 288
  'direct action', 288, 292, 302
  enforcement of collective agreements, 517
  finances, 210, 309, 394
  functions, 13, 394
  Industrial Workers Charter, 380
  inter-union disputes, 108–9, 114, 456–7, 563
  powers, 551, 563
  protection, 502
  reconstruction, 308–10, 351
  relations with the Co-operative movement, 348–9
  relations with the General Federation of Trade Unions, 114
  relations with the Labour Party, 20, 114, 381
  relations with the second Labour government, 501
  strikes, 62–4, 73, 538
  trade union affiliations, 108–9, 209, 210, 458–9, 570
  trade union restructuring, 106, 198, 455–6
  unemployment, 358
  See also General Council of the Trades Union Congress; Paraliamentary Committee of the Trades Union Congress

Trades Union Congresses:
1906: 109
1910: 106
1911: 102, 106, 222
1913: 61, 89, 114
1913, special Congress (December), 63–4
1915: 153, 162, 209
1916: 162, 230
1916: special Congress (June), 147–8
1917: 174, 205
1918: 211, 230, 231, 232
1919: 263, 288, 302
1920: 294, 302, 308
1920: special Congress (March), 287, 292
1920: special Congress (July), 292
1921: 308–10, 351, 358
1922: 351, 363
1923: 352, 517
1924: 380, 455, 517
1925: 392, 395, 456
1926: 452
1927: 420, 452, 457, 464
1928: 428 456, 459, 466
1929: 462–3, 457
1930: 501, 502
1931: 511, 540–1
1932: 481–2, 538, 541
1933: 542, 564–5
1935: 559
Tramwaymen and Vehicle Workers, Amalgamated Association of, 91, 92, 155, 203, 301, 306
Tramways, *see* road passenger transport
Tramways National Joint Industrial Council, 371, 411, 428, 524
Transport and communications:
pay, 335, 525, 561
Select Committee on, 245
strikes, 33–41, 53–7, 60–4, 71–3, 74, 115, 301, 555
unemployment, 335
See also docks; railways; road haulage; road passenger transport; shipping
Transport and General Workers Union, vii
amalgamations, 460–1
closed shop, 454
collective bargaining, 320, 329–30, 524–5
finances, 407, 461
general strike, 407
government, 306, 320, 449, 450, 454–5, 461–2, 523, 551
industrial policy, 376–7, 454
industrial structure, 351
marine section, 458–9
membership, 308, 346, 347, 458, 460–1, 535, 544, 570
origins, 305–7

political action, 382, 458, 482
Red Friday, 389
relations with other unions, 330, 370, 390, 457, 458–9, 523
sponsored Members of Parliament, 355, 364, 478
strikes, 329–30, 370 3, 376–7, 523
trade groups: agricultural workers, 460; commercial road transport, 411; docks, 330, 370, 454, 455; general workers, 308, 460; metals, engineering and chemicals, 460; power, 460–1; road passenger transport, 320, 371–3, 411, 454, 459, 524–5
trade union education, 361
unofficial action, 329–30, 454–5, 459, 523, 524–5
Transport, Ministry of, 246
Transport Workers Federation, National, 146, 193, 311, 329
amalgamations, 109–10, 136
Black Friday, 300–1
coal embargo (1921), 315–16
collective bargaining, 35–6, 203, 205–6, 257
conscription, 154, 209–10
government, 278, 279, 284
Industrial Alliance, 390
Leeds Convention, 227
Mediation Committee, 290–1
origins, 20, 33
strikes, 35, 36, 53–6, 260
sympathetic action, 115
termination, 351, 551
Triple Alliance, 114–17, 286, 295, 299, 300–1
Treasury, 94, 123, 151
Treasury agreement, 126, 141
Treasury conference, 122–3, 124–5, 140, 208, 209
'Treasury view', 498, 500
Trevelyan, Charles, 224, 355, 479, 480
Triple Alliance, 159, 297, 390, 462, 555
Black Friday, 301–2
coal lockout (1921), 299–302
'direct action', 275, 276, 278, 279, 283–4, 285–6, 291–2, 295
dissolution, 301–2, 310, 551
government, 115–17, 210–11, 299, 391
National Industrial Conference, 280–1
origins, 114–16
railway strike (1919), 290–1
Tube Trade Society, Amalgamated, 305
Tupper, 'Captain', 37, 55
Turner, Ben, biog. 580, 165, 321, 351, 419
Tweedale and Smalley, 171, 173
Tyne engineering strike (1917), 168–9, 185
Typographical Association:
apprenticeship, 77

Typographical Association (*cont.*)
  collective bargaining, 76–7, 258–9, 273, 331–2
  dilution, 154
  finances, 302, 407
  general strike, 407
  government, 16, 273–4
  membership, 346, 534
  relations with other unions, 259, 273, 331–2, 345
  restrictive practices, 76–7
  strikes, 273–4, 331–2
Typographical Association, Scottish, 75, 77

Unemployed Workers Committee Movement, National (later National Unemployed Workers Movement), 311, 357–9, 539
Unemployment, 281, 529–30, 568
  at outbreak of war, 119–20
  in postwar years, 211, 241, 301, 312, 313–14, 337, 529–30
  in 1929–33 depression, 497, 501, 529–30
  remedies for, 368–9, 468, 477, 479, 497–503, 510–11
Unemployment insurance, 101–2, 243–4, 313, 349, 365, 473–4, 501, 503–6, 507–11, 512, 562
  'anomalies', 504–5, 506
  entitlement of strikers to, 365, 473
  extended benefit, 365, 473
  'genuinely seeking work' clause, 365, 473, 474, 503–4
  'Hayday formula', 503–4
  transitional benefit, 473
  uncovenanted benefit, 313, 365, 504
Union of Democratic Control. 224–5, 226, 230, 233, 237
United Socialist Council, 227

Varley, Frank, 282
Varley, Julia, 58
Vehicle Builders, National Union of, 394
Vehicle Workers, National Union of, 306
Vehicle Workers, United, 301–2, 306, 320, 359
Venesta Ltd, 533
Versailles treaty, 357, 363
Vienna Union, 360
Vile, Gilbert, 465

Wages (Temporary Regulation) Act (1919), 240, 241
Wake, Egerton, 229
Walkden, A. G., 390, 508
Walker, R. B., biog. 580, 89
Walsh, Stephen, biog. 580, 48, 157, 235, 269, 379
War aims, 233

War Emergency Workers National Committee, 118, 120, 147, 208, 210, 225–6
War Office, 94, 119, 123, 152, 156–7, 159, 170
War Output, National Advisory Committee on, 126, 145, 208
Ward, John, 235
Wardle, G. J., 229, 235
Warehousemen and General Workers, National Union of, 197, 199, 305
Warwickshire Miners Association, 216, 494
Washington Convention, 282, 366, 475, 481–2
Water supply, 91, 249, 335, 525, 561
Watermen and Lightermen, Amalgamated Society of, 54
Watermen, Lightermen, Tugmen, and Bargemen's Union, 330, 523
Watson, W. F., 172 n., 180, 181
We Can Conquer Unemployment, 477
Weavers, Amalgamated Association of:
  closed shop, 41–3, 72
  collective bargaining, 41–2, 267, 485–6, 490–2, 521–2
  government, 6, 16, 19, 491, 536
  industrial policy, 485–6
  membership, 2, 6, 43, 346, 570
  political action, 223, 517, 522
  relations with other unions, 305
  strikes, 41–3, 72, 267, 326, 487–8, 490–2, 521–2
  unofficial action, 42
Weavers Protection Society, Nelson and District, 43
Webb, Beatrice, 213, 214, 232
Webb, Sidney, 229, 232, 283, 287, 355, 365, 479
Webb, Sidney and Beatrice, 15, 104, 162, 472
Wedgwood, Josiah, 237, 365, 373
Weir, William (later Lord), biog. 580, 134, 137, 340–1, 437, 465, 466–7
Welsh Plate and Sheet Trade Joint Industrial Council, 206
West London Workers Committee, 181
White collar pay, 151–2, 186–7, 260–2, 303, 334–5, 562
White collar trade unions:
  collective bargaining, 260–2, 266, 518–19
  general strike, 410
  government, 450
  membership, 304, 450, 534, 543
  strikes, 261–2
  See also individual unions
Whitley Committee, 188, 204–7, 232, 239, 247, 441–3, 517, 548, 549
Wilkinson, Ellen, 352, 359
Williams, James E., biog. 580, 21, 97, 103, 105
Williams, John B., biog. 581, 230–1, 276
Williams, Richard, 104

Williams, Robert, biog. 581, 115, 146, 227, 257, 278, 284, 294, 299, 302, 307, 351, 359, 551
Williamson, Henry, 52–3
Wills, J. V., 69, 106
Wilson, Horace, 401
Wilson, J. Havelock, biog. 581, 33, 34, 55, 56, 114, 141, 164, 230–1, 235, 276, 278, 328–9, 330, 352, 385, 408, 458, 459, 523
Wilson, John, 13 n., 44, 47
Wilson, President, 233
Winstone, James, biog. 581, 23, 225
Wire Drawers of Great Britain, Amalgamated, 305
Wolsey Bedaux strike (1931–2), 533
Women in trade unions, 1, 197, 543
  clothing, 87, 200, 533
  cotton, 5–6, 304, 560
  education, 6, 93, 304, 562
  engineering, 199–200
  general unions, 197, 199–200, 307
  jute, 52
  national and local government, 304
  paper and printing, 77, 200, 305
  Trades Union Congress, 309
Women Workers, National Federation of, 197, 199–200, 304, 307
Women's franchise, 220–1, 236, 472
Women's pay, 132–3, 134–5, 138, 143–4, 151, 155, 167, 175, 560–1, 563
Women's Trade Union League, 199–200, 309
Wood, Kingsley, 367
Woodcutting Machinists, Amalgamated Society of, 182
Woodworkers, Amalgamated Society of:
  collective bargaining, 343, 344, 435
  finances, 376
  government, 435, 449
  industrial policy, 435
  membership, 346, 570
  origins, 305
  relations with other unions, 434, 435
  restrictive practices, 343
  sponsored Members of Parliament, 478
  strikes, 326, 341, 376
Wool industry:
  collective bargaining, 86, 165–6, 248, 385–6, 441, 489–90, 529, 547, 548
  dilution, 154
  government control, 165–6, 209
  hours of work, 165–6

pay, 142, 165–6, 321, 335, 336, 385–6, 430, 489–90, 492–3, 525, 526, 529
  relations between unions, 166
  strikes, 385–6, 488–9, 493, 550
  trade union membership, 86, 335
  unemployment, 335, 385, 386
Wool lockout (1925), 385–6
Wool lockout (1930), 488–9, 493
Wool Textile Joint Industrial Council, 248, 385, 490
Woolwich Arsenal, 96, 132, 412
Worker, The, 137, 341
Workers' Committee, The, 181
Workers Educational Trade Union Committee, 361
Workers Socialist Federation, 358
Workers Union:
  affiliation to Trades Union Congress, 201–2, 210
  collective bargaining, 58–60, 143, 207–8, 326
  finances, 201, 349, 350, 451, 460
  government, 176, 207–8, 449, 450, 451, 460
  industrial policy, 176
  membership, 58, 88, 89, 170, 303, 345, 346, 449, 460, 570
  officers, 176, 350, 451, 460
  political action, 356
  relations with other unions, 199–200, 201–2, 209, 304, 307, 326, 330, 350, 352, 460–1
  shop stewards, 83 n.
  sponsored Members of Parliament, 478
  strikes, 58–60, 88, 89
  unemployment benefit, 201, 244, 349
Workers Union, National Amalgamated, 201–2, 306, 307, 350
Workmen's Compensation Acts (1897–1923), 12, 357, 562
Works committees, 441–5, 547, 564; *see also* collective bargaining; Whitley Committee; individual industries

Yorkshire coal strike (1914), 71
Yorkshire coal strike (1919), 269, 287, 290
Yorkshire Factory Times, 187
Yorkshire Miners Association, 26, 46, 49, 70–1, 189, 267, 269, 323, 483
Young, Robert, biog. 581, 103, 311

'Zinoviev letter', 377